Physical Education and Psychological Well-Being

Physical Education and Psychological Well-Being

Editor: Bronson Christensen

Callisto Reference
www.callistoreference.com

Callisto Reference,
118-35 Queens Blvd., Suite 400,
Forest Hills, NY 11375, USA

Visit us on the World Wide Web at:
www.callistoreference.com

ISBN: 978-1-64116-758-1 (Hardback)

Cataloging-in-Publication Data

Physical education and psychological well-being / edited by Bronson Christensen.
p. cm.
Includes bibliographical references and index.
ISBN 978-1-64116-758-1
1. Physical education and training. 2. Satisfaction. 3. Motivation (Psychology).
4. Well-being. 5. Sports. I. Christensen, Bronson.
GV206 .P49 2023
796--dc23

Table of Contents

Preface

This book has been an outcome of determined endeavour from a group of educationists in the field. The primary objective was to involve a broad spectrum of professionals from diverse cultural background involved in the field for developing new researches. The book not only targets students but also scholars pursuing higher research for further enhancement of the theoretical and practical applications of the subject.

Physical education refers to an educational process which helps in developing specific understanding, knowledge and skills that encourage physical competence. It is useful to improve a sense of confidence among students. The common objective of physical education is to make students familiar with the basic elements of exercise that will help them in leading a healthy lifestyle. The adoption of physical activity in daily life also has an impact on the psychological well-being of people. It helps in lowering somatic anxiety levels, increasing concentration and improving the quality of sleep. Regular physical activities also help in managing and preventing non-communicable diseases including diabetes, heart disease, stroke and numerous cancers. This book aims to shed light on some of the unexplored impacts of physical education on psychological well-being. It will also provide interesting topics for research which interested readers can take up. This book, with its detailed analyses and data, will prove immensely beneficial to professionals and students involved in this area of study at various levels.

It was an honour to edit such a profound book and also a challenging task to compile and examine all the relevant data for accuracy and originality. I wish to acknowledge the efforts of the contributors for submitting such brilliant and diverse chapters in the field and for endlessly working for the completion of the book. Last, but not the least; I thank my family for being a constant source of support in all my research endeavours.

Editor

1

Influence of Organized vs. Non-Organized Physical Activity on School Adaptation Behavior

Adrian A. Mosoi[1], Jürgen Beckmann[2,3,4], Arash Mirifar[2], Guillaume Martinent[5] and Lorand Balint[6]*

[1] Department of Psychology, Education and Teacher Training, Faculty of Psychology and Education Sciences, Transilvania University of Braşov, Braşov, Romania, [2] Department of Sport and Health Sciences, Chair of Sport Psychology, Technical University of Munich, Munich, Germany, [3] Faculty of Health and Behavioural Sciences, School of Human Movement and Nutrition Sciences, University of Queensland, Brisbane, QLD, Australia, [4] Department of Physical Education and Sport Sciences (PESS), University of Limerick, Limerick, Ireland, [5] Laboratory of Vulnerabilities and Innovation in Sport, University of Claude Bernard Lyon 1 – University of Lyon, Lyon, France, [6] Department of Physical Education and Special Motricity, Faculty of Physical Education and Mountain Sports, Transilvania University of Braşov, Braşov, Romania

***Correspondence:**
Adrian A. Mosoi
adrian.mosoi@unitbv.ro

It is now well-established that physical activity has positive effects on both physical and mental health. However, the influence of organized physical activity (i.e., programs controlled and supervised by a trainer) on school adaptive behavior of adolescents with disabilities and/or behavioral disorders remains unclear. School behavior adaptation involves the ability to learn, conform to school norms and manage school activities without major behavior conflicts. A cross-sectional study was conducted to test the differences between organized physical activity and non-organized physical activity in an after school program. Eighty Romanian adolescents were recruited and allocated to three groups: (a) with disabilities [Ds; N = 17, M_{age} = 14.55 years (SD = 1.16), 12 males and 5 females], (b) with conduct disorders [CDs, N = 21, M_{age} = 14.52 years (SD = 1.11) 16 males and 5 females], and (c) participants who had not shown signs of conduct disorders or disabilities [as a control group; N = 42, M_{age} = 14.2 years (SD = 0.46) 20 males and 22 females]. Personality traits, school behavior, and sensorimotor coordination were assessed by using the Eysenck personality questionnaire—junior scale, school in-adaptability questionnaire scale, and Vienna Test System Sport (SMK—sensorimotor coordination test) respectively. Multivariate analysis of variance MANOVA (3 × 3) and discriminant analysis were used to examine differences between the psychological and sensorimotor coordination outcomes across three groups and three types of physical activity context: (a) organized physical activity, (b) non-organized physical activity, and (c) no physical activity. The findings indicate that not participating in an organized physical activity program results in a reduced level of physical mobility and consequently is associated with maladaptive social and psychological outcomes. Thus, we argued that attending in an organized physical activity program is more beneficial for participants with disabilities and/or behavior disorders, due to an increase in the probability of school integration and development of their motor skills. Clearly more research is needed in order to investigate these effects in neurophysiological levels.

Keywords: physical activity, disabilities, conduct disorders, school behavior, adolescents

INTRODUCTION

Adolescence has often been described as a period of turmoil during which: (a) young people are more at risk for emotional maladjustment, and (b) physical activity typically declines or is completely avoided (Skinner and Piek, 2001). Particularly among adolescents with either disabilities or conduct disorders, the aforementioned issues could be more prominent. Thus, it is assumed that being involved in an organized practice of physical activity during adolescence could prevent such maladjustments (Moore and Werch, 2005; Taliaferro et al., 2008). Participating in organized physical activity during adolescence at schools in after-school programs (in addition to the regular physical activity sessions included in the compulsory teaching program) has been shown to promote the development of psychological skills (Owen et al., 2014; Esteban-Cornejo et al., 2015; Hills et al., 2015; Timo et al., 2016), and improve school behavior (Rasberry et al., 2011; Beckmann and Elbe, 2015; Naylor et al., 2015), as well as motor function (Hands et al., 2009; McIntyre et al., 2015). In contrast, lack of physical activity (inactivity) has been associated with mental health risks (Delisle et al., 2010; Biddle and Asare, 2011; Elinder et al., 2011), and impairment of learning (Davis et al., 2011). Physical activities in an organized setting refer to the use of sports halls or fields with availability of appropriate equipment's for sports activities (team or individual) and physical activity lessons. In these types of activities, under the supervision of a trainer, facilities are adapted to meet a participant's demands. Participants, in this organized setting, usually are required to follow their trainer's guidance (Vella et al., 2016) to perform extracurricular activities (Rasberry et al., 2011) and the environment is usually competitive (Eime et al., 2013). However, this is not the case in non-organized activities, whereas the type of activities are indicated by lack of practical instructor training or lack of structured activities (Walters et al., 2009).

Although, the benefits of physical activity in school adjustment and academic performance are well documented for typically developing adolescents (Fox et al., 2010; Rasberry et al., 2011; Booth et al., 2014; Jewett et al., 2014), the effects of physical activity on adolescents with conduct disorders and adolescents with disabilities are less understood (Stathopoulou et al., 2006; Kasser and Lytle, 2013; Clow and Edmunds, 2014). By considering that the adolescents with the above-mentioned conditions are part of the regular school system, there is high demand for research in this area (Malone et al., 2012; Sachlin and Lexell, 2015).

The present study focuses on school adjustment comparing adolescent groups in terms of the variables included in the study such as personality traits: extraversion; neuroticism; and psychoticism (Rhodes and Smith, 2006), school behavior: rebelliousness and school neuroticism (Clinciu, 2014), and motor functions: sensorimotor coordination (Perkins and Noam, 2007). These variables were reported (Rhodes and Smith, 2006; Reiss, 2009; Poitras et al., 2016) by distinct groups of adolescents (i.e., adolescents with disabilities, adolescents with conduct disorders, typically developing adolescents).

Physical Activity Involvement Among Adolescents With Disabilities

In general, it has been shown that adolescents with physical disabilities are less involved in physical activities, particularly in school. For instance, McIntyre et al. (2015) reported that adolescents with decreased motor abilities tend to avoid participating in physical activities. The rate of participation in leisure activities of adolescents with disabilities is associated with several variables, such as the degree of coordination (e.g., sensorimotor coordination), communication capacity, cognitive functions, and poor rehabilitation outcomes (Henderson and Bryan, 1997). These variables are particularly important for social integration of adolescents with disabilities (Bult et al., 2011) given the fact that the level of social inclusion is dependent on community access rather than on the high number of friendships (Simplican et al., 2015).

Numerous studies have provided evidence that participation in leisure physical activities increases well-being and life satisfaction of adolescents with disabilities (Johnson, 2009; Yazicioglu et al., 2012). For example, Dahan-Oliel and Shikako-Thomas (2012) highlighted significant improvements not only in motor functions of adolescents with disabilities, but also regarding their perceived quality of life and friendships as a consequence of participating in an organized physical activity program during the school programs. Additionally, other researchers (e.g., Shapiro and Martin, 2014) have reported participation in physical activity fosters growth and development of friendships outside of these settings. Furthermore, Edwards (2015) pointed out that physical activity could allow consolidation of the abilities required for social co-existence and for increasing social cohesion.

Physical Activity Involvement Among Adolescents With Conduct Disorders

One disability that affects around 5% of adolescents worldwide is conduct disorder (Erskine et al., 2017). Conduct disorder is defined as a repetitive and persistent pattern of behavior in which the basic rights of others or major appropriate norms are violated, such as failure to conform to norms, or cruel and aggressive behavior (American Psychiatric Association [APA], 2013). Research has shown that conduct disorder can occur in childhood and adolescence, and adolescents with learning disabilities have an increased risk of developing associated conduct disorders (Sadock and Sadock, 2007; American Psychiatric Association [APA], 2013). According to Mahoney and Stattin (2000), participation in organized leisure activities (e.g., sports) was negatively associated with antisocial behavior compared with participation in unorganized leisure activities (e.g., recreation centers). However, the efficacy of social rehabilitation and reintegration through physical activity remains a challenge to develop sufficient empirical support, especially for disadvantaged groups (Archie et al., 2007; Desha et al., 2007). The shared nature of benefits in school sport participation has been demonstrated in several other studies. Alternatively, Jewell et al. (2015) highlighted that school sport participation during adolescence was significantly associated with higher self-rated mental health in young adulthood. For instance, Samek et al. (2015) found that adolescents involved in sports showed fewer conduct disorder symptoms than those not involved in sports. Furthermore, it was found that conflict behavior rates peak when adolescents with conduct disorders participate in unsupervised after school programs (Jewell et al., 2015). Therefore, this means that a careful management of physical activity or sports in an organized framework would be most beneficial for adolescents with conduct disorders improving their opportunities to adapt to school and social norms.

The Present Study

There are a number of potential reasons for analyzing the benefits of organized physical activity participation in adolescence regarding school integration (Marcus et al., 2000; Reiss, 2009; Biddle and Asare, 2011). To the best of our knowledge no previous studies have yet focused on the relationship between organized physical activity and personality traits, school behavior and sensorimotor coordination among different groups of adolescents (adolescents with disabilities, adolescents with conduct disorders, and adolescents who develop normally). Adolescents who develop normally have no physical or mental disabilities and are free from any diagnosed disorders, are also known as typically developing adolescents (Pan et al., 2015). Moreover, the research conducted on adolescents with disabilities and adolescents with conduct disorders regarding school integration are rather scarce. When considering the fact that there are no differences in the education system between those with and without disabilities, we therefore assumed no differentiation would be necessary between groups. In this study, all adolescents with disabilities or conduct disorders were diagnosed by trained physicians in public hospitals and were assessed by qualified school district personnel according to the guidelines of the Diagnostic and Statistical Manual of Mental Disorders, 5th edition (DSM-V; American Psychiatric Association [APA], 2013). Additionally, school behavior outcomes should be an important factor in the development of the adolescent regarding school integration, acknowledging whether the individual suffers from a disability or a disorder. Therefore, the present research aimed to fill this gap by evaluating the effectiveness of organized physical activity on school behavior, psychological, and sensorimotor coordination among different groups of adolescents: adolescents with physical disabilities (Ds), adolescents with conduct disorders (CDs), and participants who had not shown signs of conduct disorders or disabilities (as a control group; Cs). On the basis of the literature (Heaven et al., 2008; Johnson, 2009; Rockhill et al., 2009; Dahan-Oliel and Shikako-Thomas, 2012; Yazicioglu et al., 2012; Hoolis et al., 2014; Shapiro and Martin, 2014; Edwards, 2015) we hypothesized that: (a) the participants in Ds group will show significantly lower scores of sensorimotor coordination in comparison to other groups, and (b) the participants in Cs group will show higher levels of school behavior in comparison to other groups. We also hypothesized that adolescents participating in organized physical activity will report significantly lower scores of psychoticism, school neuroticism and rebelliousness in comparison to adolescents not taking part in physical activity.

MATERIALS AND METHODS

Participants

Originally 120 Romanian adolescents voluntarily participated, 80 of which completed all questionnaires and were therefore included in the present study (48 boys and 32 girls; M_{age} = 14.3 years, SD = 0.9): (a) Seventeen adolescents with physical disabilities (Ds) diagnosed with associated motor deficiencies. (b) Twenty-one adolescents with conduct disorders (CDs). (c) Forty-two participants who had not shown signs of conduct disorders or disabilities (as a control group; Cs). With approval and financial support from both the European Social Fund and the Romanian Government, a group of adolescents participated in our research study investigating the relevance of the qualitative level of psychological and motor components designed to improve school adaptation in this age group. Therefore, only adolescents with disabilities and conduct disorders, as well as typically developing adolescents were included in the study.

The participants of these three groups were distributed according to the involvement in physical activity after school programs, such as: (a) organized practice of physical activity (OPA)—their performance was controlled by the coach or instructor (controlled physical activity 3–4 times per week); (b) non-organized practice of physical activity (NOPA)—their performance was not controlled by the coach or an adult (unstructured physical activity 1–2 times per week); or (c) no physical activity (NPA)—they were not involved in any physical activity or do not participate in any form of organized sport or physical activity after the school program.

Instruments

To assess personality traits we used the Romanian validated version of Grigoriu-Şerbănescu (1984) the Junior Eysenck Personality Questionnaire—Junior EPQ (Eysenck and Eysenck, 1975), measuring extraversion (action orientated; enthusiastic; talkative; assertive), neuroticism (irritable, nervous, apprehensive), and psychoticism (hostile, aggressive, impersonal, foolhardy), which was developed for individuals ages 10–18 years old (81 items). Participants responded on a dichotomous scale (yes = 1, no = 0). Cronbach's alpha was used to determine the internal consistency reliability of the total score. were α = 0.28, α = 0.79, and α = 0.67 for extraversion, neuroticism and psychoticism, respectively. However, due the poor reliability, extraversion was not included in the data analysis. To further assess the internal reliability of the Junior EPQ scores, item analyses were conducted (DeVellis, 2003). To test each item, the following criteria were adopted: (a) a minimum item-total correlation coefficient of r = 0.40 and (b) a mean inter-item correlation value of 0.20–0.70 (DeVellis, 2003; Piedmont, 2014). With the scale, the overall value of the corrected item-total correlation was observed to be in the range of 0.23–0.50 for psychoticism and 0.27–0.51 for neuroticism, respectively.

After exclusion extraversion, all items of the psychoticism and neuroticism fulfilled these criteria, providing evidence for the reliability of these two scales.

The SIQ—School In-adaptability Questionnaire (Clinciu, 2014) is a Romanian questionnaire consisting of 67 items covering the dimensions of school neuroticism (43 items; e.g., scholar stress, failing, $\alpha = 0.90$) and rebelliousness (24 items; e.g., school indiscipline, antisocial behavior, $\alpha = 0.80$). Participants responded on a dichotomous scale (yes = 1, no = 0). Reliability was good in the present study with Cronbach's $\alpha = 0.83$ for school neuroticism and $\alpha = 0.75$ for rebelliousness, respectively. The value of the corrected item-total correlation with the scale overall was observed to be in the range of 0.23–0.60 for school neuroticism and 0.22–0.55 for rebelliousness, respectively. Moreover, all items of the SIQ fulfilled the aforementioned criteria (DeVellis, 2003; Piedmont, 2014), providing evidence for the reliability of these scales.

To assess sensorimotor coordination, we used SMK (short form S1), from Vienna Test Systems Sport of the research Institute of Transilvania University in Braşov. This test is a computerized task using a joystick and was applied to measure the motor control ability (Mosoi and Balint, 2015) by utilizing the feedback in real time of sensorimotor information from the movement currently being executed by the adolescents. With this test, the task was to use a synchronous joystick to maneuver a circular yellow segment that is drawn as a piece of pizza into a required position with a tip touching a bar upright in the upside "T" position. The circle segment, which is standing on its tip, has three types of movement, including tilting to left/right, horizontal movement to left/right and movement along the depth perspective with corresponding change in size randomly made in a three-dimensional space. All the participants were properly instructed on how to use the joysticks. Overall, the test takes 15 min, including 5 min of a practice phase and 10 min of evaluation. A total test score was obtained based on the calculation of the actual positioning time of the segment at the desired position (Schuhfried, 2013).

Procedure

The current study was approved by the Transilvania University of Braşov (POSDRU/159/1.5/S/134378). The school inspectorate of Braşov County and the principals of the participating adolescents' schools were approached by a research team at the beginning of the procedure. Participation of adolescents was voluntary. Written informed consent from adolescents and their parents was obtained prior to participation in the study. The inclusion and exclusion criteria of the study were as follows: (a) are in the first year of grammar school; (b) take part in school classes every day; (c) take part in school physical exercise lessons every week; (d) do not take any medication; (e) complete both sessions. The measurements were conducted in 2 consecutive weeks. During the first week, participants completed the psychological questionnaires and during the second week they participated in the sensorimotor coordination assessment. The clinical groups completed the questionnaires on 3 consecutive days. Due to reduced concentration skills, this group required more time for the test than the other groups. Additionally, the sensorimotor test was conducted in individual sessions which took place in a quiet room at school, while questionnaires measurements were taken in group sessions. The teachers, caregivers, and the parents were comprehensively informed about the research project and the conditions of the participation. During the assessments with principals' agreements, the adolescents completed the EPQ, SIQ, SMK, as well as the demographic questionnaire.

Sample

The participants were divided into three distinct groups. The first non-clinical group consisted of participants from conventional schools, which were defined as typically developing adolescents. The second group included adolescents with disabilities represented by the "Inclusive School." These two groups were divided according to the participation on physical activities in after school programs. Lastly, the third group consisted of adolescents with conduct disorder selected from "Adolescents Psychiatry Hospital." In the first two groups the differences were between specific participation in physical activities in after school programs, where typically developing adolescents were involved in different sports and adolescents with disabilities were involved in exercise therapy to improve especially their mobility. The third group, controlled in a hospital institution, included adolescents with conduct disorders that were involved only in unorganized physical activities, because after school programs are not offered. In Romanian schools, adolescents with disabilities and conduct disorders were included in the compulsory teaching programs. Those with disabilities were taking part in exercise therapy to increase their motor adaptability toward different tasks or to prevent injury risks. Adolescents with conduct disorder, on the other hand, were practicing physical exercise to prevent antisocial interaction (Romanian Law Education, 1/2011, art. 48–50). Both groups participated in the school's general physical education program 100% of the time. In order to be included in data analysis, participants needed to have met the five criteria, as well as completed both the individual and group sessions.

Data Analysis

A multivariate analysis of variance (MANOVA) was conducted to examine the main effects of adolescent groups (Ds, CDs, and control group) and physical activity groups (OPA, NOPA, NPA) on all the dependent variables (EPQ, SIQ, and SMK scores). With such a 3 × 3 MANOVA, we also explored the interaction effect of adolescent groups × physical activity groups. In the analyses, in case of significant multivariate effect ($p < 0.05$) *post-hoc* comparisons (Tukey's HSD) were conducted. Partial eta squared (η^2) provided an index of effect size (Ferguson, 2009). Finally, the MANOVA was complemented by discriminant function analyses (Field, 2013).

RESULTS

Descriptive Results

Information, regarding age, sex, parental educational background (primary school; grammar school; university), family structure (mono parental; intact family; divorce) and their current participation status in physical activity (no physical activities; non-physical activity; organized physical activity) was collected before starting the measurements. The Ds, CDs, and Cs were well matched on age and sex, but not on the family structure and parental educational backgrounds. Participants indicated the weekly frequency of organized physical activity (controlled physical activity 3–4 times per week) and non-organized physical activity after school programs (unstructured physical activity 1–2 times per week; not participate in any form of physical activity). The details of the participants included in this study are presented in **Table 1**.

Results of Comparison Groups

The results of the Box's M test ($p = 0.168$) were not significant and provided evidence for the assumption of equality of covariance matrices. Also, the tests of homogeneity of variance for all dependent variables were not significant (psychoticism, $p = 0.244$; neuroticism, $p = 0.066$; school neuroticism, $p = 0.084$; rebelliousness, $p = 0.653$; and sensorimotor coordination, $p = 0.094$). However, results of the MANOVA showed significant main effects for adolescents' groups [Wilk's Lambda, $\Lambda = 0.57$ $F(10, 138) = 4.44$, $p < 0.001$, partial $\eta^2 = 0.24$] and physical activity groups [$\Lambda = 0.73$, $F(10, 138) = 2.38$, $p < 0.012$, partial $\eta^2 = 0.15$] as well as a significant effect for the interaction of adolescents' groups × physical activity groups [$\Lambda = 0.76$ $F(10, 138) = 2.06$, $p < 0.032$, partial $\eta^2 = 0.13$]. Results of *post-hoc* comparisons, using Tukey's HSD, are presented in **Table 2**. Results of *post-hoc* comparisons adolescents' groups showed that: (a) CDs reported significantly higher scores of psychoticism, neuroticism, school neuroticism and rebelliousness than Cs; (b) CDs reported significantly higher scores of school neuroticism than Ds; (c) Cs reported significantly higher scores of sensorimotor coordination than Ds and CDs. The effect size found on adolescents groups was small, $\eta^2 = 0.18$ for rebelliousness (Cs < CDs) and $\eta^2 = 0.30$ for sensorimotor coordination (Ds; CDs < Cs).

Additionally main effects were obtained in the physical activity group showing that: (a) NOPA reported significantly higher scores of psychoticism and neuroticism than OPA, and (b) OPA reported significantly lower scores of school neuroticism and significant higher scores of sensorimotor coordination than Ds and CDs. The effect size found on physical activity groups was small, $\eta^2 = 0.16$ for sensorimotor coordination (NPA, NOPA < OPA).

Comparing the study variables in interaction of adolescents' groups × physical activity groups, a significant interaction effect emerged for psychoticism [$F(2, 73) = 5.05$, $p = 0.009$, partial $\eta^2 = 0.12$]. Adolescents with conduct disorder had a higher score compared with Ds and Cs groups. In these results adolescents with conduct disorders were compared only on the NOPA factor. Results showed that for the control group there is no significant difference between groups. In contrast, in the disability group there is a significant difference between NPA and NOPA. Indeed, adolescents from the NPA group had a higher score on psychoticism in comparison with the NOPA group. Another important aspect to consider is the OPA in relation to the variables included in analysis, where adolescents who are involved in OPA had less opportunities to develop maladaptive behaviors during their time at school. All the other variables included in the analysis show the differences between the groups, specifically the OPA. The main effects and interaction effect are presented in **Table 3**.

Results of Discriminant Function Analyses

For the three groups of adolescents, the discriminant analysis including psychoticism, neuroticism, school neuroticism, rebelliousness and sensorimotor coordination indicated two discriminant functions: F1 ($r_{can} = 50.$; Wilks $\lambda = 52.03$; $p < 0.001$), explaining 75.1% of the variance, canonical $R^2 = 0.38$, and F2 ($r_{can} = 0.82$; Wilks $\lambda = 14.59$; $p = 0.006$), explaining 24.9%, canonical $R^2 = 0.17$. Overall, 66.3% of the cases were correctly classified into the three groups of adolescents—47.1, 47.6, and

TABLE 1 | Descriptive statistics of the participants.

Group type		Ds ($N = 17$) *M (SD)*	CDs ($N = 21$) *M (SD)*	Cs ($N = 42$) *M (SD)*	Overall ($N = 80$)
Age (year)	Mean (SD)	14.55 (1.16)	14.52 (1.11)	14.2 (0.46)	14.36 (0.90)
Gender	Male	12	16	20	48
	Female	5	5	22	32
Family structure	Mono parental	3	3	13	19
	Intact family	12	7	31	50
	Divorce	–	11	–	11
Parental educational background	Primary school	4	6	4	14
	Grammar school	11	12	20	33
	University	2	3	18	23
No physical activities	Not participate in any form of physical activity	5	–	14	19
Non-organized physical activities	Unstructured physical activity 1–2 times per week	7	21	7	35
Organized physical activities	Controlled physical activity 3–4 times per week	5	–	21	26

Ds, Disabilities; CDs, Conduct disorder; Cs, control group.

83.3% for the Ds, CDs, and Cs, respectively. Sensorimotor coordination loaded highly on the first function (r = 0.86), whereas neuroticism (r = 0.70), rebelliousness (r = 0.57), school neuroticism (r = 0.48), and psychoticism (r = 0.46) loaded on the second function. As indicated in **Figure 1**, the discriminant function plot showed that the first function differentiated the Cs group from the CDs and Ds, whereas the second function differentiated the Ds from Cs and Cs from CDs group.

For the three groups of physical activity, the discriminant analyses including psychoticism, neuroticism, school neuroticism, rebelliousness and sensorimotor coordination also indicated two discriminant functions: F1 (r_{can} = 0.56; Wilks λ = 43.64; $p < 0.001$), explaining for 91.9% canonical R^2 = 0.39, and F2 (r_{can} = 0.94; Wilks λ = 4.61; p = 0.353) explaining 8.2% of the variance, canonical R^2 = 0.05. Altogether, 65% of the cases were correctly classified into the three groups of physical activity—26.3, 74.3, and 80.8% for the NPA, NOPA, and OPA. Sensorimotor coordination (r = 0.75), school neuroticism (r = −0.60), neuroticism (r = −0.36), and psychoticism (r = −0.35) loaded on the first functions, whereas rebelliousness (r = 0.84) highly loaded on the second function. As indicated in **Figure 2**, the discriminant function plot showed that in the first function the OPA group differentiated from the NOPA and NPA, whereas the second function differentiated the NPA from OPA, and OPA from NOPA group.

DISCUSSION

As mentioned in the literature review, although physical activity generally has been shown to have positive effects on physical and mental health, the influence of organized physical activity on school adaptive behavior of adolescents with disabilities and/or behavioral disorders remains unclear. Therefore the present research investigated the effects of organized physical activity on school behavior, psychological variables (personality factors), and sensorimotor coordination in different groups of adolescents. The three groups consisted of adolescents with disabilities, with conduct disorders, and individuals without diagnosed disabilities or conduct disorders as a control group. Increased knowledge of the role of physical activity in relation to these variables could potentially help teachers foster school integration among adolescents who suffer from Ds and CDs.

Organized Physical Activity on Personality Traits and School Behavior

The results of the study provided insight into the facilitating role of organized physical activity regarding adolescents' school adaptability. In particular, adolescents who practiced organized physical activity reported significantly lower scores of psychoticism and neuroticism than their counterparts who were not involved in organized physical activity. Moreover, adolescents who practiced organized physical activity reported significantly lower scores of school neuroticism in comparison to the adolescents who practiced non-organized physical activity or who did not practice physical activity at all. These results are consistent with previous research indicating, that school

TABLE 2 | The main effects of adolescent groups and physical activity groups on the study variables.

	Ds (N = 17) M (SD)	CDs (N = 21) M (SD)	Cs (N = 42) M (SD)	F	p	η^2	Tukey HSD[a]	NPA (N = 19) M (SD)	OPA (N = 26) M (SD)	NOPA (N = 35) M (SD)	F	p	η^2	Tukey HSD[a]
Psychoticism	5.29 (2.31)	6.57 (1.88)	4.86 (2.14)	3.03*	0.042	0.08	C < CD	5.74 (2.51)	4.5 (1.7)	5.89 (2.23)	2.52	0.087	0.06	OPA < NOPA
Neuroticism	9.47 (2.81)	12.67 (4.29)	10.14 (3.17)	2.86	0.064	0.07	C < CD	10.95 (2.95)	9.19 (2.65)	11.6 (4.22)	1.28	0.284	0.03	OPA < NOPA
School N	15.76 (7.44)	21.38 (9.45)	13.71 (8.97)	1.99	0.144	0.05	D, C < CD	18.79 (9.15)	10.23 (5.9)	19.14 (9.5)	2.03	0.138	0.05	OPA < NPA; NOPA
Rebelliousness	6.06 (2.56)	8.00 (2.32)	5.60 (2.67)	4.89*	0.011	0.18	C < CD	5.53 (2.65)	6.08 (2.57)	6.94 (2.80)	1.00	0.370	0.02	–
Sensorimotor C	1.52 (1.58)	2.76 (2.21)	5.14 (2.31)	15.6*	0.000	0.30	D, CD < C	2.94 (2.12)	5.73 (2.18)	2.71 (2.37)	7.16*	0.001	0.16	NPA, NOPA < OPA

*School N, School neuroticism; Sensorimotor C, Sensorimotor coordination; Ds, Disabilities; CDs, Conduct disorder; Cs, Control group; NPA, No physical activity; OPA, Organized physical activity; NOPA, Non-organized physical activity. All the Tukey's HSD post-hoc are significant at *p < 0.05.*

TABLE 3 | Comparison of the study variables across the three groups in interaction with physical activity.

		Ds M (SD)	CDs M (SD)	Cs M (SD)	*F*	*p*	η^2
Psychoticism	NPA	7.40 (2.07)	–	5.14 (2.44)			
	NOPA	3.71 (1.49)	6.57 (1.88)	6.00 (2.64)	5.05*	0.009	0.12
	OPA	5.40 (1.94)	–	4.29 (1.61)			
Neuroticism	NPA	9.80 (2.38)	–	11.36 (3.10)			
	NOPA	10.43 (3.59)	12.67 (4.29)	9.57 (4.03)	0.645	0.528	0.01
	OPA	7.80 (1.09)	–	9.52 (2.82)			
School N.	NPA	16.80 (7.36)	–	19.50 (9.85)			
	NOPA	15.29 (7.47)	21.38 (9.45)	16.29 (10.64)	1.33	0.270	0.03
	OPA	15.40 (9.04)	–	9.00 (4.35)			
Rebelliousness	NPA	6.60 (2.30)	–	5.14 (2.74)			
	NOPA	4.57 (2.63)	8.00 (2.32)	6.14 (2.91)	2.00	0.142	0.05
	OPA	7.60 (1.81)	–	5.71 (2.63)			
Sensorimotor C.	NPA	1.2 (1.78)	–	3.57 (1.91)			
	NOPA	0.57 (0.78)	2.76 (2.21)	4.71 (2.21)	0.763	0.470	0.02
	OPA	3.2 (0.83)	–	6.33 (1.95)			

*Ds, Disabilities; CDs, Conduct disorder; Cs, Control Group; NPA, No physical activity; OPA, Organized physical activity; NOPA, Non-organized physical activity; School N, School Neuroticism; Sensorimotor C, Sensorimotor Coordination. All the Tukey's HSD post hoc are significant at *$p < 0.05$.*

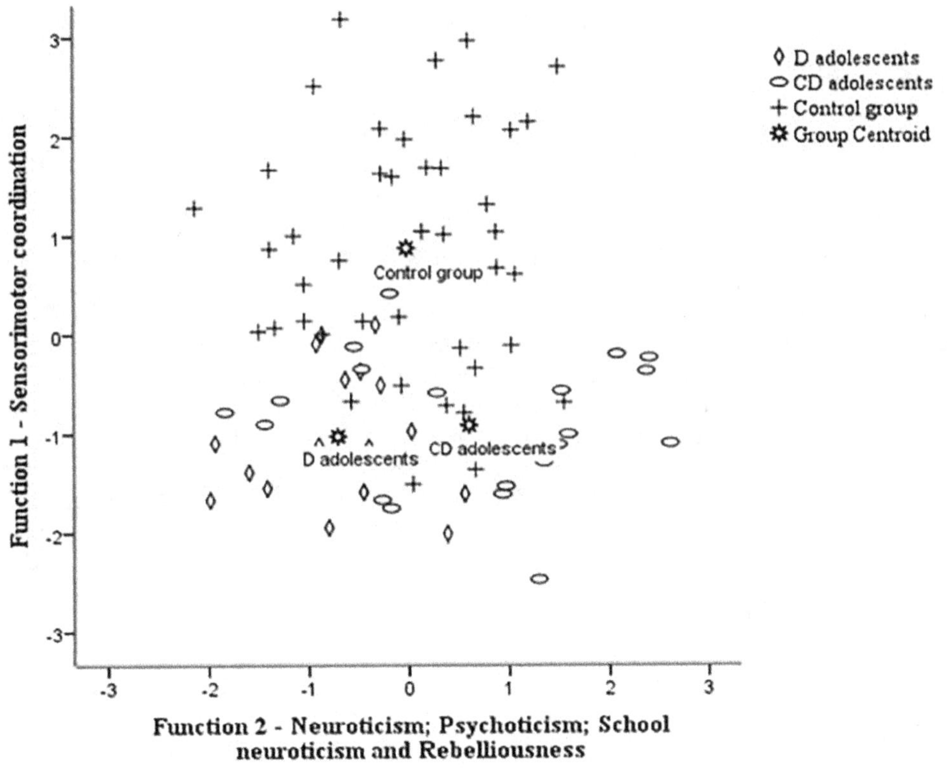

FIGURE 1 | Canonical discriminant function—distribution of adolescents groups based on significant scores of sensorimotor coordination in first function and neuroticism, psychoticism, school neuroticism, and rebelliousness in second function. Ds, disabilities; CDs, conduct disorders; Cs, control group.

neuroticism mainly occurs among adolescents who do not practice any physical activity in comparison with those who do practice organized physical activity (Berse et al., 2014). Taken as a whole, our results provided evidence for the positive relationship between organized physical activity and only a reduced level of maladaptive behavior (Carrasco et al., 2006; Rockhill et al., 2009; Esteban-Cornejo et al., 2015). Thus, the benefits of organized physical activity programs among adolescents should be further explored in the future through the prism of the remote effects of decreased recidivism (Rockhill et al., 2009). As expected, results of the present study also showed that adolescents with conduct disorder reported significantly higher levels of school

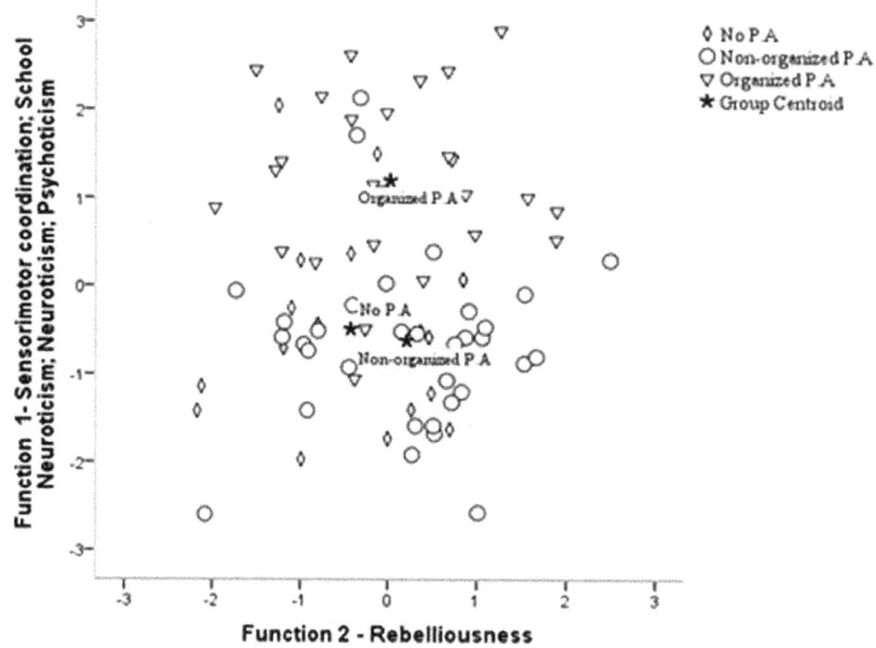

FIGURE 2 | Canonical discriminant function—distribution of physical activity groups based on the significant scores of sensorimotor coordination, school neuroticism, neuroticism, psychoticism, in first function and rebelliousness in the second function. OPA, Organized physical activity; NPA, No physical activity; NOPA, Non-organized physical activity.

neuroticism, rebelliousness, psychoticism, and neuroticism than adolescents with disabilities and/or the control group. Results also suggested that the risk of school in-adaptability (inferred from psychological and behavioral school outcomes) appeared to be higher among the adolescents with conduct disorders and on the adolescents who do not practice physical activity compared to those who are physically active. Hence, based on the facilitating role of organized physical activity regarding adolescents' psychological and behavioral school adaptability, it can be concluded that adolescents with conduct disorders could benefit the most from organized physical activity programs.

Organized Physical Activity on Sensorimotor Coordination

Regarding the sensorimotor coordination of the upper limbs, results of the present study showed a significant advantage for adolescents practicing organized physical activity. In particular, adolescents who practiced organized physical activity had significantly higher scores of sensorimotor coordination in comparison to the adolescents who practiced non-organized physical activity or who did not practice physical activity. However, contrary to our hypothesis, sensorimotor coordination in adolescents with conduct disorders was not significantly different from adolescents with disabilities. Even if the level of coordination seemed to be slightly less developed among Ds participants and CDs participants, adolescents who did not practice physical activity showed even lower scores of sensorimotor coordination. This result not only demonstrated the benefits of practicing physical activity for motor skills, as suggested in other studies (Dodge and Lambert, 2009; Walters et al., 2009; Mangerud et al., 2014; Mosoi and Balint, 2015), but also highlighted that not practicing physical activity may restrict the level of sensorimotor coordination in adolescents period (Quatman-Yates et al., 2012). These results are once again consistent with the risks for adolescents who do not practice physical activity found in previous studies (Burnett-Zeigler et al., 2012; Eime et al., 2013).

Overall, practicing physical exercise in after school programs with an organized framework should be an interactive way for adolescents to manage their free time. One benefit for taking part in an organized physical activity after school program could be the improvement of friendships between peers, as well as the reduction of risk for aggressive behavior or arrest, especially for adolescents with conduct disorders (Jewell et al., 2015; Simplican et al., 2015). These benefits likely develop the usefulness and responsibility of the individual in the team and in the competitive environment.

Limitations

To the best of our knowledge, the present study is the first survey on school integration via organized physical activities involving adolescents with disabilities and conduct disorders. Therefore, the generalizability of its results is subject to a number of limitations. For example, the cross–sectional nature of this study does not allow for examination of directionality, therefore it remains unclear whether or not the organized school physical activity caused a change in school behavior. Furthermore, the relatively small number of participants in each of the groups (of adolescents and physical activities) and the use of self-reports could limit the generalizability of the results. In this study, the participants with conduct disorders were limited to unstructured activities due to their hospitalization status, which means the after school organized activities were missing. Therefore, in particular, future studies would need to include participants with conduct disorder who do not participate in any form of physical activity. Hence, applied research should conduct a longitudinal study with larger samples. This could provide deeper insights for understanding the effect of organized physical activities in after school programs on school adjustment, especially among adolescents with disabilities and conduct disorders. Another limitation refers to the cultural context in which the study was conducted (i.e., Romanian schools). Our results should not be interpreted in isolation especially about disadvantaged adolescents groups but rather under consideration of previous studies as a contribution to the growing body of evidence on the importance of participating in organized physical activity at school and in after school program. Additionally, futures studies should attempt to replicate these findings in other countries or different types of schools.

Implications for School Health

In order to foster adolescents' adaptability to school, personality traits, school behavior and sensorimotor coordination need to be observed and addressed concurrently. Sessions of organized physical activities could prevent the development of antisocial behavior, as well as the aggravation of the school environment. Involvement of adolescents in an organized physical activity after school program might be a particularly promising prevention strategy. Hence, to promote school adjustment, teachers should include didactic strategies for sport physical activities to increase the involvement of adolescents with conduct disorders, as well as disabled adolescents, in organized physical activities with help from families as well as the community (Edwards, 2015; Simplican et al., 2015). The adaptation and implementation of organized physical activities grounded within school programs represents one of the most important social desiderata in order to attract adolescents who do not practice any physical activity (Butler-Kort and Hagewann, 2011; Jewett et al., 2014; Nair et al., 2015). The development of organized physical activity within educational settings could represent a successful approach to public health in the long run (Abula et al., 2016; Marques et al., 2016) for a better adaptation of adolescents to the school and social environment (Bacarro et al., 2012; Drake et al., 2015 Hills et al., 2015), therefore preventing poor mental and physical health in young adulthood (Jewett et al., 2014).

CONCLUSION

In conclusion, the results of the present study point out the importance of being physically active as well as being involved in physical activity programs during adolescent years. Particularly, for behavioral problems of adolescents such as rebelliousness and school neuroticism as well as deficits in motor functions (poor sensorimotor coordination), organized physical activity in after school programs seem to offer potential for ameliorating these problems. Despite some limitations, our results also provide valuable information about the risks of adolescents who do not practice any physical activity. Arguably, decreasing strategies to manage organized physical activity decline may favor negative adaptive psychological and motor coordination outcomes similar to adolescents in Ds group and CDs group. Additional, applied research needs to be conducted, that focuses on personality traits (i.e., psychoticism and neuroticism) and school behavior (i.e., school neuroticism) among adolescents who did not practice physical activity in comparison to Ds and CDs adolescents who practiced physical activity. Future research concerning school behavior and organized physical activity could provide insight into whether participating in physical activities is associated with developing antisocial behavior. Furthermore, additional research could also potentially find a relationship between the reduction of sensorimotor coordination and the amount of free time experienced in adolescence. With this knowledge, adolescents could spend their free time furthering their development of sensorimotor coordination.

ETHICS STATEMENT

This study was conducted in accordance with the Declaration of Helsinki. Written informed consent from all subjects was obtained and all data were rendered completely anonymous. The data of this study are open to the public and made available by the Transilvania University of Braşov through the project POSDRU/159/1.5/S/134378.

AUTHOR CONTRIBUTIONS

The original research was part of the post Ph.D. thesis of AAM, supervised by LB. AAM, wrote the first draft of the manuscript. GM, JB, and AM wrote sections of the manuscript. All authors made substantial contributions in conceptualization, methodology, to analysis and interpretation of the data, contributed to manuscript revision, read and approved the submitted version.

ACKNOWLEDGMENTS

We would like to thank all the adolescents, parents, and schools for their participation and school health facilitators for their contributions to data collection. We thank Madison Ehmann (research assistant at Technical University of Munich) for proofreading and editing the manuscript.

REFERENCES

Abula, K., Gröpel, P., Chen, K., and Beckmann, J. (2016). Does knowledge of physical activity recommendations increase physical activity among Chinese college students? Empirical investigations based on the transtheoretical model. *JSHS* 7, 77–82. doi: 10.1016/j.jshs.2016.10.010

American Psychiatric Association [APA] (2013). *Diagnostic and Statistical Manual of Mental Disorders*, 5th Edn. Washington, DC: American Psychiatric Association.

Archie, S. M., Goldberg, J. O., Akhtar-Danesh, N., Landeen, J., McColl, L., and McNiven, J. (2007). Psychotic disorders, eating, habits and physical activity: who is ready for life style changing? *Psychiatric Serv.* 58, 233–239. doi: 10.1176/ps.2007.58.2.233

Bacarro, J. N., Kanters, M. A., Cerin, E., Floyd, M. F., Casper, J. M., Suau, L. J., et al. (2012). School sport policy and school-based physical activity environments and their association with observed physical activity in middle school children. *Health Place* 18, 31–38. doi: 10.1016/j.healthplace.2011.08.007

Beckmann, J., and Elbe, A. M. (2015). *Sport Psychology Intervention in Competitive Sports*. Newcastle upon Tyne: Cambridge Scholars Publishing.

Berse, T., Barenberg, J., Urban, V., and Dutke, S. (2014). Agentic extraversion moderates the effect of physical exercise on executive shifting performance. *J. Res. Pers.* 52, 37–41. doi: 10.1016/j.jrp.2014.06.007

Biddle, S. J., and Asare, M. (2011). Physical activity and mental health in children and adolescents: a review of reviews. *Br. J. Sport Med.* 44, 886–895. doi: 10.1136/bjsports-2011-090185

Booth, J. N., Leary, S. D., Joinson, C., Ness, A. R., Tomporowski, P. D., Boyle, J. M., et al. (2014). Associations between objectively measured physical activity and academic attainment in adolescents from a UK cohort. *Br. J. Sports Med.* 48, 265–270. doi: 10.1136/bjsports-2013-092334

Bult, M. K., Verschuren, O., Jongmans, M. J., Lindeman, E., and Ketelaar, M. (2011). What influences participation in leisure activities of children and youth with physical disabilities? A systematic review. *Res Dev Disabil.* 32, 1521–1529. doi: 10.1016/j.ridd.2011.01.045

Burnett-Zeigler, I., Walton, M. A., Ilgen, M., Barry, K. L., Chermack, S. T., Zucker, R. A., et al. (2012). Prevalence and correlates of mental health problems and treatment among adolescents seen in primary care. *J. Adolesc. Health* 50, 559–564. doi: 10.1016/j.jadohealth.2011.10.005

Butler-Kort, L. A., and Hagewann, K. J. (2011). School-based extracurricular activity involvement and adolescents self-esteem: a growth-curve analysis. *J. Youth Adolesc.* 40, 568–581. doi: 10.1007/s10964-010-9551-4

Carrasco, M., Barker, E. D., Tremblay, R. E., and Vitaro, F. (2006). Eysenck's personality dimensions as predictors of male adolescents trajectories of physical aggression, theft and vandalism. *Pers. Indiv. Differ.* 41, 1309–1320. doi: 10.1016/j.paid.2006.05.005

Clinciu, A. I. (2014). Validation study of school inadaptability questionnaire. *Soc. Behav. Sci.* 127, 154–158. doi: 10.1016/j.sbspro.2014.03.231

Clow, A., and Edmunds, S. (2014). *Physical Activity and Mental Health*. Leeds: Human Kinetics.

Dahan-Oliel, N., and Shikako-Thomas, K. (2012). Quality of life and leisure participation in children with neurodevelopment disabilities: a thematic analysis of the literature. *Qual. Life Res.* 21, 427–439. doi: 10.1007/s11136-011-0063-9

Davis, L. C., Tomporowski, D. P., McDowell, E. J., Austin, P. B., Miller, H. P., Yanasak, E. N., et al. (2011). Exercise improves executive function and achievement and alters brain activation in overweight children: a randomized controlled trial. *J. Health Psychol.* 30, 91–98. doi: 10.1037/a0021766

Delisle, T. T., Werch, E. C., Wong, H. A., Bian, H., and Weiler, R. (2010). Relationship between frequency and intensive of physical activity and health. *J. Sch. Health* 80, 134–140. doi: 10.1111/j.1746-1561.2009.00477.x

Desha, L. N., Ziviani, J. M., Nicholson, J. M., Martin, G., and Darnell, R. E. (2007). Physical activity and depressive symptoms in American adolescents. *J. Sport Exerc. Psycol.* 29, 534–543. doi: 10.1123/jsep.29.4.53

DeVellis, R. F. (2003). *Scale Development: Theory and Applications*, 2nd Edn. London: Sage Publications.

Dodge, T., and Lambert, S. F. (2009). Positive self – beliefs as a mediator of the relationship between adolescents' sports participation and health in young adulthood. *J. Youth Adolesc.* 38, 813–825. doi: 10.1007/s10964-008-9371-y

Drake, K. M., Longacre, M. R., MacKenzie, T., Titus, L. J., Beach, M. L., Rundle, A. G., et al. (2015). High school sports programs deferentially impact participation by sex. *J. Sports Health Sci.* 4, 282–288. doi: 10.1016/j.jshs.2013.11.006

Edwards, M. E. (2015). The role of sport in community capacity building: an examination of sport for development research and practice. *Sport Manag. Rev.* 18, 6–19. doi: 10.1016/j.smr.2013.08.008

Eime, R. M., Young, J. A., Harvey, J. T., Charity, M. J., and Payne, W. R. (2013). A systematic review of the psychological and social benefits of participation in sport for children and adolescents: informing development of conceptual model of health through sport. *Int. J. Behav. Nutr. Phys.* 10, 1–21. doi: 10.1186/1479-5868-10-98

Elinder, L. S., Sundblon, E., and Rosendahl, I. K. (2011). Low physical activity is a predictor of thinness and low self-rated health: gender differences in a Swedish cohort. *J. Adolesc. Health* 48, 481–486. doi: 10.1016/j.jadohealth.2010.08.005

Erskine, H., Baxter, A., Patton, G., Moffitt, T., Patel, V., Whiteford, H., et al. (2017). The global coverage of prevalence data for mental disorders in children and adolescents. *Epidemiol. Psychiatr. Sci.* 26, 395–402. doi: 10.1017/S2045796015001158

Esteban-Cornejo, I., Tejero-Gonzales, C., Sallis, J., and Veiga, O. L. (2015). Physical activity and cognition in adolescents: a systematic review. *J. Sci. Med. Sport* 18, 534–539. doi: 10.1249/MSS.0000000000000706

Eysenck, H. J., and Eysenck, S. B. G. (1975). *). Eysenck Personality Questionnaire (Junior and Adult), Manual*. San Diego, CA: Educational and Industrial Testing Services.

Ferguson, C. J. (2009). An effect size primer: a guide for clinicians and researchers. *Prof. Psychol.* 40, 532–538. doi: 10.1037/a0015808

Field, A. (2013). *Discovering Statistics Using SPSS*, 4th Edn. London: SAGE Publications, 623–664.

Fox, C. K., Barr-Anderson, D., Neumark-Sztainer, D., and Wall, M. (2010). Physical activity and sports team participation: associations with academic outcomes in middle school and high school students. *J. Sch. Health* 80, 31–37. doi: 10.1111/j.1746-1561.2009.00454.x

Grigoriu-Şerbănescu, M. (1984). Junior eysenck personality questionnaire based on a romanian sample. *Int. J. Psychol.* 21, 141–151. doi: 10.1080/00207598608247580

Hands, B., Larkin, D., Parker, H., Straker, L., and Perry, M. (2009). The relationship among physical activity, motor competence and health-related fitness in 14-year-old adolescents. *Scand. J. Med. Sci. Spor* 19, 655–663. doi: 10.1111/j.1600-0838.2008.00847.x

Heaven, P. C. L., Ciarrochi, J., and Vialle, W. (2008). Self-nominated per crowds, school achievement and psychological adjustment in adolescents: longitudinal analysis. *Pers. Indiv. Differ.* 44, 977–988. doi: 10.1016/j.paid.2007.10.031

Henderson, G., and Bryan, V. W. (1997). *Psychosocial Aspects of Disability*, 3rd Edn. Illinois: Springfield.

Hills, A. P., Dengel, D. R., and Lubans, D. R. (2015). Supporting public health priorities: recommendations for physical education and physical activity promotion in schools. *Prog. Cardiovasc. Dis.* 57, 368–374. doi: 10.1089/chi.2015.0024

Hoolis, J. L., Wiliams, A. J., Sutherland, R., Campbell, E., Nathan, N., Wolfenden, L., et al. (2014). A systematic review and meta-analysis of moderate-to-vigorous physical activity levels in elementary school physical education lessons. *Prev. Med.* 86, 34–54. doi: 10.1016/j.ypmed.2015.11.018

Jewell, L., Abtan, R., Scavone, A., Timmins, V., Swampillai, B., and Goldstein, B. I. (2015). Preliminary evidence of disparities in physical activity among adolescents with bipolar disorder. *Ment. Health Phys Act.* 8, 62–67. doi: 10.1016/j.mhpa.2015.04.001

Jewett, R., Sabiston, C. M., Brunet, J., O'Loughlin, E. K., Scarapicchia, T., and O'Loughlin, J. (2014). School sport participation during adolescence and mental health in early adulthood. *J. Adolesc.Health* 55, 640–644. doi: 10.1016/j.jadohealth.2014.04.018

Johnson, C. C. (2009). The benefits of physical activity for youth with developmental disabilities: a systematic review. *Am. J. Health Prom.* 23, 157–167. doi: 10.4278/ajhp.070930103

Kasser, S. L., and Lytle, R. K. (2013). *Inclusive Physical Activity: Promoting Health for a Life Time*. Leeds: Human Kinetics.

Mahoney, J. L., and Stattin, H. (2000). Leisure activities and adolescent antisocial behavior: the role of structure and social context. *J. Adolesc.* 23, 113–127.

doi: 10.1006/jado.2000.0302

Malone, L. A., Barfield, D. A., and Brasher, J. D. (2012). Perceived benefits and barriers to exercise among persons with physical disabilities or chronic health conditions within action or maintenance stages of exercise. *Disabil. Health J.* 5, 254–260. doi: 10.2522/ptj.20120279

Mangerud, W. L., Bjerkeset, O., Lydersen, S., and Indredavik, M. S. (2014). Physical activity in adolescents with psychiatric disorders and in the general population. *Child Adolesc Psychol. Men. Health* 8, 1–10. doi: 10.1186/1753-2000-8-2

Marcus, H. B., Dubbert, M. P., Forsyth, A. L., McKenzie, L. T., Stone, J. E., Dunn, L. A., et al. (2000). Physical activity behavior change: issues in adoption and maintenance. *Health Psychol.* 19, 32–41. doi: 10.1037/0278-6133.19.suppl1.32

Marques, A., Ekelund, U., and Sardinha, L. B. (2016). Associations between organized sports participation and objectively measured physical activity, sedentary time and weight status in youth. *J. Sci. Med. Sport* 19, 154–157. doi: 10.1016/j.jsams.2015.02.007

McIntyre, F., Chivers, P., Larkin, D., Rose, E., and Hands, B. (2015). Exercise can improve physical self perceptions in adolescents with low motor competence. *Hum. Mov.Sci.* 42, 333–343. doi: 10.1016/j.humov.2014.12.003

Moore, M. J., and Werch, C. E. (2005). Sports and physical activity participation and substance use among adolescents. *J. Adolesc. Health* 36, 486–493. doi: 10.1016/j.jadohealth.2004.02.031

Mosoi, A. A., and Balint, L. (2015). Sport – a solution to the social integration of children with conduct disorders? Pilot study. *Soc. Behav. Sci.* 180, 1297–1303. doi: 10.1016/j.sbspro.2015.02.267

Nair, M., Baltag, V., Bose, K., Boschi-Pinto, C., Lambrechts, T., and Mathai, M. (2015). Improving the quality of health care services for adolescents, globally: a standards-driven approach. *J. Adolesc. Health* 57, 288–298. doi: 10.1016/j.jadohealth.2015.05.011

Naylor, P. J., Nettlefold, L., Race, D., Hoy, C., Ashe, M. C., Wharf Higgins, J., et al. (2015). Implementation of school based physical activity interventions: a systematic review. *Prev. Med.* 72, 95–115. doi: 10.1016/j.ypmed.2014.12.034

Owen, K. B., Smith, J., Lubans, D. R., Ng, Y. Y. J., and Lonsdale, C. (2014). Self-determined motivation and physical activity in children and adolescents: a systematic review and meta-analysis. *Prev. Med.* 67, 270–279. doi: 10.1016/j.ypmed.2014.07.033

Pan, C., Liu, C., Chung, I., and Hsu, P. (2015). Physical activity levels of adolescents with and without intellectual disabilities during physical education and recess. *Res. Dev. Disabil.* 36, 579–586. doi: 10.1016/j.ridd.2014.10.042

Perkins, D. F., and Noam, G. G. (2007). Characteristics of sports-based youth development program. *New Dir Youth Develop.* 115, 75–106. doi: 10.1002/yd.224

Piedmont, R. L. (2014). "Inter-item correlations," in *Encyclopedia of Quality of Life and Well-Being Research*, ed. A. C. Michalos (Dordrecht: Springer), 3303–3304. doi: 10.1007/978-94-007-0753-5_1493

Poitras, V. J., Gray, C. E., Borghese, M. M., Carson, V., Chaput, J.-P., Janssen, I., et al. (2016). Systematic review of the relationships between objectively measured physical activity and health indicators in school-aged children and youth. *Appl. Physiol. Nutr. Metab.* 41, 197–239. doi: 10.1139/apnm-2015-0663

Quatman-Yates, C. C., Quatman, C. E., Meszaros, A. J., Paterno, M. V., and Hewett, T. E. (2012). A systematic review of sensorimotor function during adolescence: a developmental stage of increased motor awkwardness? *Br. J. Sports Med.* 46, 649–655. doi: 10.1136/bjsm.2010.079616

Rasberry, C. N., Lee, S. M., Robin, L., Larris, B. A., Russell, L. A., Coyle, K. K., et al. (2011). The association between school-based physical activity, including physical education, and academic performance: a systematic review of the literature. *Prev. Med.* 52, 10–20. doi: 10.1016/j.ypmed.2011.01.027

Reiss, S. (2009). Six motivational reasons for low school achievement. *Child Youth Care For.* 38, 219–225. doi: 10.1007/s10566-009-9075-9

Rhodes, R. E., and Smith, N. E. (2006). Personality correlates of physical activity: a review and meta-analysis. *Br. J. Med.* 40, 958–965. doi: 10.1136/bjsm.2006.028860

Rockhill, C. M., Vander Stoep, A., McCauley, E., and Katon, W. J. (2009). Social competence and social support as mediators between comorbid depressive and conduct problems and functional outcomes in middle school children. *J. Adolesc.* 32, 535–553. doi: 10.1016/j.adolescence.2008.06.011

Sachlin, B., and Lexell, J. (2015). Impact of organized sport on activity, participation, and quality of life in people with neurologic disabilities. *J. Phys. Med. Rehabil.* 7, 1081–1088. doi: 10.1016/j.pmrj.2015.03.019

Sadock, B. J., and Sadock, A. V. (2007). Synopsis of psychiatry. *Behav. Sci. Clin. Psychiatry.* 10, 1234–1238.

Samek, D. R., Elkins, I. J., Keyes, M. A., Iacono, W. G., and McGue, M. (2015). High school sports involvement diminishes the association between childhood conduct disorder and adult antisocial behavior. *J. Adolesc. Health* 57, 107–112. doi: 10.1016/j.jadohealth.2015.03.009

Schuhfried, G. (2013). *Vienna Test System: Psychological Assessment.* Moedling: Schuhfried.

Shapiro, D. R., and Martin, J. J. (2014). The relationships among sport self-perceptions and social well-being in athletes with physical disabilities. *Disabil. Health J.* 7, 42–48. doi: 10.1016/j.dhjo.2013.06.002

Simplican, S. C., Leader, G., Kosciulek, J., and Leahy, M. (2015). Defining social inclusion of people with intellectual and developmental disabilities: an ecological model of social networks and community participation. *Res. Dev. Disabil.* 38, 18–29. doi: 10.1016/j.ridd.2014.10.008

Skinner, R. A., and Piek, J. P. (2001). Psychosocial implications of poor motor coordination in children and adolescents. *Hum. Mov. Sci.* 20, 73–94. doi: 10.1016/S0167-9457(01)00029-X

Stathopoulou, G., Powers, M. B., Berry, A. C., Smits, J. A. J., and Otto, M. W. (2006). Exercise interventions for mental health: a quantitative and quality review. *Clin. Psychol. Sci. Pract.* 13, 179–190. doi: 10.1111/j.1468-2850.2006.00021.x

Taliaferro, L. A., Rienzo, B. A., Miller, D. M., Pigg, M. R. Jr., and Dodd, V. J. (2008). High school youth and suicide risk: exploring protection afforded through physical activity and sport participation. *J. Sch. Health* 78, 545–553. doi: 10.1111/j.1746-1561.2008.00342.x

Timo, J., Sami, Y. P., Anthony, W., and Jarmo, L. (2016). Perceived physical competence towards physical activity, and motivation and enjoyment in physical education as longitudinal predictors of adolescents' self reported physical activity. *J. Sci. Med. Sport* 19, 750–754. doi: 10.1016/j.jsams.2015.11.003

Vella, S. A., Schranz, N. K., Davern, M., Hardy, L. L., Hills, A. P., Morgan, P. J., et al. (2016). The contribution of organized sports to physical activity in Australia: results and directions from the Active Healthy Kids Australia 2014 Report Card on physical activity for children and young people. *J. Sci. Med. Sport* 19, 407–412. doi: 10.1016/j.jsams.2015.04.011

Walters, S., Barr-Anderson, D. J., Wall, M., and Neumark-Sztainer, D. (2009). Does participation in organized sports predict future physical activity for adolescents from diverse economic backgrounds? *J. Adolesc. Health* 44, 268–274. doi: 10.1001/jamapediatrics.2015.0327

Yazicioglu, K., Yavuz, F., Goktepe, A., and Tan, A. (2012). Influence of adapted sports on quality of life and life satisfaction in sport participants and non-sport participants with physical disabilities. *Disabil. Health J.* 5, 249–253. doi: 10.1016/j.dhjo.2012.05.003

2

Self-Determined Motivation and Competitive Anxiety in Athletes/Students: A Probabilistic Study Using Bayesian Networks

Francisco Javier Ponseti[1], Pedro L. Almeida[2], Joao Lameiras[3], Bruno Martins[4], Aurelio Olmedilla[5], Jeanette López-Walle[6]*, Orlando Reyes[6] and Alexandre Garcia-Mas[7]*

[1] Department of Pedagogy, University of the Balearic Islands, Palma, Spain, [2] Departamento de Psicologia Social e Organizacional, ISPA – Instituto Universitario, Lisbon, Portugal, [3] Portuguese Athletics Federation, Lisbon, Portugal, [4] GICAFE de la UIB, University of Lisbon, Lisbon, Portugal, [5] Departamento de Personalidad, Evaluación y Tratamiento Psicológicos, University of Murcia, Murcia, Spain, [6] Facultad de Organización Deportiva, Universidad Autónoma de Nuevo León, Nuevo León, Mexico, [7] Department of Psychology, University of the Balearic Islands, Palma, Spain

***Correspondence:**
Jeanette López-Walle
jeanette.lopezw@gmail.com
Aurelio Olmedilla
olmedilla@um.es

This study attempts to analyze the relationship between two key psychological variables associated with performance in sports – Self-Determined Motivation and Competitive Anxiety – through Bayesian Networks (BN) analysis. We analyzed 674 university students that are athletes from 44 universities that competed at the University Games in Mexico, with an average age of 21 years (SD = 2.07) and with a mean of 8.61 years' (SD = 5.15) experience in sports. Methods: Regarding the data analysis, firstly, classification using the CHAID algorithm was carried out to determine the dependence links between variables; Secondly, a BN was developed to reduce the uncertainty in the relationships between the two key psychological variables. The validation of the BN revealed AUC values ranging from 0.5 to 0.92. Subsequently, various instantiations were performed with hypothetical values applied to the "bottom" variables. Results showed two probability trees that have extrinsic motivation and amotivation at the top, while the anxiety/activation due to worries about performance was at the bottom of the probabilities. The instantiations carried out support the existence of these probabilistic relationships, demonstrating their scarce influence on anxiety about competition generated by the intrinsic motivation, and the complex probabilistic effect of introjected and identified regulation regarding the appearance of anxiety due to worry about performance.

Keywords: Bayesian networks, self-determined motivation, competitive anxiety, athletes, students

INTRODUCTION

One of the biggest problems facing social science is the great difficulty involved in predicting human behavior. It may be due to the large number of variables that bear influence on it, however, other explanations have also been proposed within the framework of information theory (IT) and the entropy inherent in the development of open and closed systems, although they do not form part of the currently valid paradigm in psychological research (Luce, 2003; Chen and Huang, 2018; Olmedilla et al., 2018). As far as statistical methods in Psychology are concerned, something very similar to the analysis derived from Bayes' theorem has arisen, which has a very direct relationship with the classic concept of Entropy (Laming, 2001; Farr et al., 2018). Adding sense to the similarity between these two concepts, we can argue that "IT provides a constructive criterion for setting up probability distributions on the basis of partial knowledge, and leads to a type of statistical inference that is called the (Jaakkola et al., 2000).

Therefore, it is plausible to assume that the conceptual framework of entropy is quite fitting when attempting to explain the situation of an athlete before a competition at a given moment in time. The so-called entropic "time arrow" - which implies irreversibility of events, by prohibiting the symmetry between past and future - understood psychologically, implies the generation of a past, through past events recall and memory-building, in the face of a mobile future that is configured mainly on the basis of expectations and a broad spectrum of emotions ranging from hope to fear.

In the case of sports psychology, one of the most relevant issues already extensively studied but still open to discussion affects precisely these two aspects of the "time arrow": how do emotions associated with future performance combine with the athletes' motivational past?

Motivation is one of the most studied variables in the context of sport (Lindahl et al., 2015; Clancy et al., 2016), and it is defined as the cause of a behavior, which operates at a psychological level within the individual and determines the execution or not of a certain activity (Tohidi and Jabbari, 2012). Intrinsic motivation can be defined as one in which individuals move autonomously toward new challenges, broader experience frameworks, and greater coherence in understanding. It represents a behavior that interests them, seeks encouragement, limits evidence, and openly assimilates novelty. On the other hand, there are four motivational norms that offer a broader framework on external motivation. The first of these is external regulation, in which the individual regulates his behavior through externally controlled rewards and punishments; the second is introjected regulation; in that regulation, the individual, by complying with internal demands, can develop certain forms of self-esteem, self-satisfaction and feelings of pride about himself; in identified regulation people value the importance of certain behavior and see it as something important for themselves; in integrated regulation, it implies that the individual brings a value or regulation in congruence with the other aspects of himself; with his basic psychological needs and with his other identifications. Finally, a motivation describes a state in which the individual is not motivated to behave or behaves in a way that is not mediated by intentionality (Ryan and Deci, 2017).

On the other hand, another of the most widely studied variables in regard to the activation of individual and sports performance is anxiety (Patel et al., 2010; Ponseti F. et al., 2016). This is defined as an immediate emotional state, characterized by apprehension and tension, associated with the activation of the organism that occurs in situations of competition (Martens, 1977). Also, competitive anxiety has been characterized by two cognitive components. One of these is worry, which is understood as restlessness about the potentially negative consequences associated with poor performance; and the second is de-concentration, which is associated with the athlete's difficulty to focus on key aspects of the task to be performed that impede clarity of thought during the competitive situation (Grossbard et al., 2009).

That is why, in view of the scarcity of relevant literature (Fuster-Parra et al., 2015), the objective of this paper is to investigate the relationships that exist between motivational regulations (intrinsic regulation, integrated regulation, identified regulation, introjected regulation, external regulation, and amotivation) and anxiety (cognitive anxiety, worry, and de-concentration), in relation to competition in sports. The study of the relationship between these variables is of particular importance, since some authors (Nuñez and García-Mas, 2017) even affirm the possibility that anxiety in its different dimensions (e.g., cognitive, somatic, and motor) in certain conditions and based on the intrinsic characteristics of the individuals, such as their motivational regulation, can play a facilitating role of performance in competitive contexts.

In our study, framed within a closed IT system (a sports competition directed at a homogenous sample of athletes/students), we decided in favor of using a tool recommended for this type of situation, namely analysis through a machine learning classification and Bayesian networks (BN) (Puga et al., 2007; Trafimow and Marks, 2015). This approach should allow us - in part - to simulate the reversal of the "time arrow" when modifying parameters in the temporal succession of events based on the principles of probability inherent to the BNs, which presuppose independence between the events under study.

Bayesian networks are beginning to be more widely used in the field of Social Science (Ranganathan et al., 2014; Lewandowski et al., 2015; Fuster-Parra et al., 2017; Chen and Huang, 2018) and, more recently, they have been introduced as a useful methodology in Sports Psychology, given their ability to provide information on the probability of occurrence of events (some of them psychological) related to performance in sports or, for example, the likelihood of sports injuries. BN have been used to discover relationships between negative features in sport, co-operative team work, motivation and types of sporting cooperation among players on competing teams, motivational climate and anxiety (Jones and Hanton, 2001) and relative age effect (Fuster-Parra et al., 2014, 2016; Ishigami, 2016; Ponseti F.J. et al., 2016).

Before the application of the BN, a machine learning classification model, namely CHAID (Chi-squared Automatic Interaction Detector), is used to discover the dependence links between anxiety and motivation.

As indicated, the psychological variables selected (the motivational and anxiety features of competing athletes/students) are located on both sides of the fulcrum of the present, between past and future. On the basis of the rationale expressed above, our aim in this study is to ascertain the probabilistic links between the different factors of self-determined motivation (Li et al., 2017) and those related to the anxiety associated with competition in young athletes from different sports specialties, especially to attempt to reduce the likelihood of anxiety occurring, and then to interpret the results obtained according to the entropy inherent in the system under study.

MATERIALS AND METHODS

Participants

The study was performed in Mexico with 674 university students that are athletes who competed in the University Games (Universiade) in 2017. They were from 44 universities, at least one athlete from each participating university, with a mean age of 21 years old (SD = 2.07) and a mean sports experience of 8.61 years (SD = 5.15). All universities took part in this study. All participants were previously informed about the protocol and purposes of the study. The study protocol was approved by the local ethics committee of the Universidad Autónoma de Nuevo León (Mexico) in accordance with current ethical standards in sport and scientific research.

Instruments

Competitive anxiety in sport was measured using the Spanish language adaptation (*Escala de Ansiedad Competitiva*), (Pineda-Espejel et al., 2016) of the Sport Anxiety Scale 2 (SAS-2) (Smith et al., 2006). The SAS-2 consists of three 5-item scales to measure three factors: somatic anxiety, worry, and lack of concentration or de-concentration. Each item was answered on a 4-point Likert scale with a range between "not at all" and "very much."

Self-determined motivation. An adapted version of the Sports Motivation Scale (Pelletier et al., 2013) was used in this study. This measure had been previously translated into Spanish cpssnm(Martín-Albo et al., 2006). The SMS-II is an 18-item inventory comprising six factors of behavioral regulation. These factors were extracted from the Self-determination Theory to test a model that would enable us to assess Autonomous and Controlled Motivation. The subscales are intrinsic motivation (e.g., "*for the pleasure it gives me to know more about the sport I play*"); identified regulation (e.g., "*because in my opinion it is one of the best ways to meet people*"); introjected regulation (e.g., "*because it is absolutely necessary to do sports if one wants to be in shape*"); external regulation (e.g., "*because it makes me better regarded by people I know*"); and a-motivation (e.g., "*I used to have good reasons for doing sports, but now I am wondering whether to carry on doing it*"). Each item was answered on a 7-point Likert scale with a range between "not at all" and "very much."

Procedure

The data was collected during the University Games (Universiade). Personal contact was first made with team coaches to inform them about the project. Instruments were applied in the concentration hotels, prior to their participation in the sporting event, at least one researcher was present to give instructions and answer athletes' questions. Emphasis was placed on the confidentiality of athletes' individual responses as well as on the need to answer honestly. In addition, the researcher explained to them that responding to the questionnaires implied voluntarily accepting to participate in the research.

Data Analysis

The CHAID (Chi-squared Automatic Interaction Detector) algorithm is used to discover relationships between a categorical or ordinal dependent variable and other categorical predictors. It computes a decision tree, which includes meaningful nodes that classify a nominal or ordinal dependent variable (Magidson and Vermunt, 2005). It is a convenient way to summarize data since it makes it easy to view relationships. It relies on the Chi-square test to determine the best next split at each node of the tree. To obtain the decision tree, the R package "CHAID" was used in the dataset. To apply the algorithm, a dependent variable and the independent variables need to be chosen beforehand. We selected "somatic anxiety" as the dependent variable and the remaining variables as the independent variables.

To obtain a BN (Bayesian network), it was necessary to determine a structure (defined by a twofold method). First, through a Directed Acyclic Graph (DAG) and the conditional probabilities assigned to each node of the DAG, and secondly, restricting pathways by using the CHAID algorithm on the resulting graph. Therefore, learning a BN implies the following two tasks: (i) structural learning, i.e., the identification of the topology of the BN, and (ii), parametric learning, i.e., the estimation of numerical parameters (conditional probabilities) given a network topology.

Structural learning was used to obtain the BN, the bnlearn package (Scutari, 2010) of the R language (Rosselet, 1987). To obtain the structure, we could follow either a search and score algorithm (Korb and Nicholson, 2010), which assigns a score to each BN structure and selects the model structure with the highest score, or a constraint-based search algorithm (Spirtes et al., 1993), which establishes conditional independence analysis on the data where an undirected graph is generated and converted into a BN using an additional independence test. We used the score-based algorithm Tabu (Korb and Nicholson, 2010), which gave us a plausible model for our data. The search procedure finds the structure that best improves the score, i.e., using the highest score (Bayesian Information Criterion – BIC).

RESULTS

In regard to the values found in the variables under study, the lack of importance of external regulation compared with the values of intrinsic motivation, and, to a lesser extent, with those of amotivation, are relevant. The subscales of the intrinsic and internalized regulation values are high, with regulation being identified as the one with the lowest values. Descriptive data of the variables studied are shown in **Table 1**.

When we observe the values of anxiety related to competition, we can see that they are below the average in the ranges. Anxiety related to competition shows values below the mean scores in the possible ranges in all cases. Somatic anxiety and lack of concentration are the dimensions with the lowest values, while worry about performance is higher than the average. SD values – with the exception of one case – are consistent with a relatively homogeneous sample and none of the values found is especially significant. The SD value of amotivation is very close to the

TABLE 1 | Descriptive data of the variables studied, mean and standard deviation (*N* = 674).

Variables	*M*	*SD*
Somatic anxiety	1.71	0.62
Worry anxiety	2.75	0.80
Lack of concentration anxiety	1.73	0.63
Intrinsic regulation	6.22	0.18
Integrated regulation	6.13	0.56
Identified regulation	4.17	0.74
Introjected regulation	5.83	0.15
External regulation	1.61	0.65
Amotivation	2.59	0.98

mean values, indicating that answers about this variable were not overly homogeneous.

When the values for anxiety related to competition are observed, one can see that they are below the average in each range. Anxiety related to competition returns values in all cases below the mean score in the possible ranges. Somatic anxiety and lack of concentration are the dimensions with the lowest values, while concern about performance is above average. The SD in all cases are consistent with a relatively homogeneous population, and none of the values found is especially remarkable.

Figure 1 shows the result of applying the CHAID algorithm, which revealed a tree prediction model for the "Somatic Anxiety" variable; therefore, uncertainty in the data obtained was reduced, allowing for BN analysis with restrictions and thus reducing the complexity of the entire system. Five variables were found to predict "Somatic Anxiety." Four of these were motivational: intrinsic and external global regulations, and two subscales of intrinsic motivation, identified and integrated regulation; and the last one being anxiety related to performance.

The CHAID tree starts with the top "External Regulation" decision node, with the 674 instances of the data set divided into two partitions, based on the result of splitting this node into two categories – "High" ($n = 67$) and "Low" ($n = 607$). The "Low" category shows the majority of cases are associated with "Somatic Anxiety." This node is further split on the basis of the value of the "Anxiety from Worry about performance" predictor variable, resulting into two more nodes based on this category. Splitting continues until either the new split does not help to improve prediction accuracy, or a node contains less instances than a pre-defined size.

As for the BN, validation was performed using a 10-fold cross validation, taking into consideration the area under the curve (AUC), which is defined as the probability of correctly identifying a pair of cases (positive and negative). As can be seen in **Table 2**, the validation values generated in the BN with all the variables under study are acceptable. However, in the same line as the descriptive values, the minor AUC values correspond to amotivation, the identified regulation, as well as to anxiety from worry about performance. To achieve a better understanding of the accuracy of the classification, sensitivity and specificity were calculated. While it is possible to find high accuracy in some variables, when sensitivity and specificity are observed, we detect a null positive classification ability on identified regulation, low classification on intrinsic and integrated regulation, and a generally high negative classification ability.

Figure 2 shows the BN generated with the restrictions found after the CHAID analysis using an acyclic graph. The top variable is the external regulation, showing low probability, while the bottom variables (probabilistically dependent on the others) are the identified regulation, which in turn is dependent on global intrinsic regulation. The two intermediate variables – no nodes were found – are Anxiety from Worry about performance and the sub-variable of Identified Intrinsic regulation. The probability values found in the sample group indicate that the participants in our study have a high probability of being intrinsically motivated, with a low probability of perceiving external rewards or benefits (although this variable is shown as key to triggering the likelihood of the other variables occurring), as well as the presence of mean probability of anxiety from worry about performance, which acts as a buffer for the other variables.

BN Instantiations With Hypothetical Data

The global Markov property was applied to maximize and minimize the likelihood values for different variables. The global Markov property states that any node X is conditionally independent of any other node given its Markov blanket (a Markov blanket of X in a BN is the set of nodes consisting of X's parents, X's children and other parents of X's children). The features instantiated were in the Markov blanket of different features, therefore given its Markov blanket, each feature is independent of the remaining features. The two variables selected are: (1) the most relevant Anxiety subscale found, the one relating to worry about performance, as appears in the BNs; and (2) overall intrinsic motivation, which is the most significant node in the two BNs.

We began by attempting to maximize the likelihood of anxiety due to worry about performance occurring, in this case, on the CHAID restricted BN (see **Table 3**). The first two steps are the ones that produce the most significant changes; indeed, probability of "lack of concentration" and "introjected regulation" decrease to give an 18% increase in low level probability of anxiety from worry, which comes from a low value: one third of detected likelihood. The following steps have less weight and, in order of significance, include a reduction in somatic anxiety and different sub-scales for self-determined success motivation, although the latter represents a reduction of less than one tenth of the likelihood, which reaches a maximum of 64.83% (barely double the probability actually obtained in the sample, which is 35.88%). This indicates that the existence of anxiety from worry about performance is very strong and cannot be reduced even if it is forced by using hypothetical "anti-entropic" values and will only return values within the average likelihood of occurrence.

In **Table 4**, it can be seen that when trying to reach the maximum probability of the identified intrinsic motivation sub-scale (which is the most relevant bottom motivational variable in the NB with restrictions), the reversed BN only achieves an increase of 6%. In this sense, it is unquestionably a very solid variable. This maximum value is reached in three

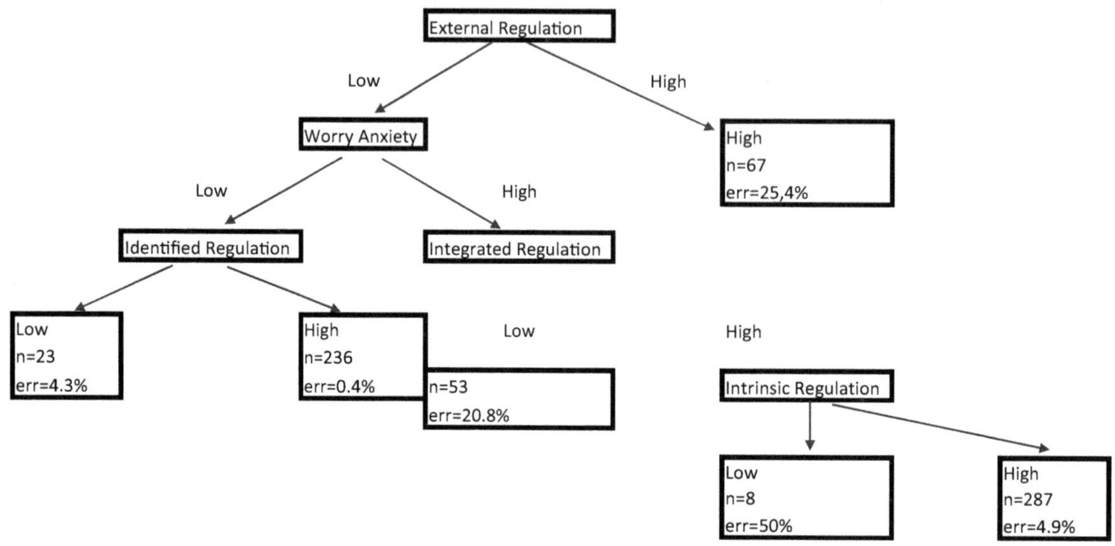

FIGURE 1 | Chi-squared Automatic Interaction Detector algorithm defining the inter-dependent variables.

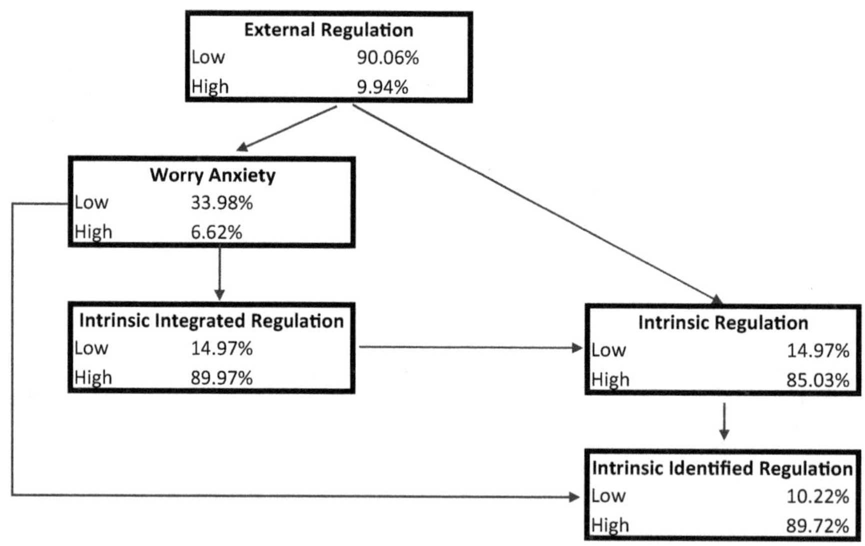

FIGURE 2 | Bayesian Networks generated using the restrictions made after the CHAID algorithm (inter-dependent variables only).

steps, with very similar values, two of them imply reaching the maximum probability of overall intrinsic motivation and introjected regulation, and then to the minimum value for anxiety from worry about performance.

DISCUSSION

Our aim in this study was to ascertain the probabilistic links between the different factors of self-determined motivation and those related to anxiety, particularly attempting to reduce the likelihood of anxiety occurring. Firstly, in response to the objective and question posed, it should be noted that all the analyses carried out demonstrate that it is possible to reduce uncertainty in the relationships between motivation and anxiety in the field of competitive sports.

The main findings can be summarized by the statement that competitive anxiety is completely "disassembled" in its three factors with respect to its probabilistic weight of occurrence: the predecessor variable of the others is worry about performance, while the other two dimensions have occupied some key positions as well. De-concentration (or lack of concentration) anxiety (the one most responsible for diminished performance) acts as a "modulator" on anxiety from worry triggered by the weight of the probability of external motivation, while somatic anxiety becomes the "final" sub-product of the other variables. Further studies on our group have demonstrated the caution with which somatic signs of anxiety must be taken by external observers

TABLE 2 | Validation of the BN developed with the variables studied: AUC values, accuracy, sensitivity, and specificity.

Variables	AUC	Accuracy	Sensitivity	Specificity
Somatic anxiety	0.79	0.93	0.97	0.62
Worry anxiety	0.59	0.64	0.39	0.80
Lack of concentration anxiety	0.83	0.94	0.98	0.68
Intrinsic regulation	0.60	0.94	0.25	0.98
Integrated regulation	0.61	0.86	0.24	0.98
Identified regulation	0.51	0.90	0.00	1
Introjected regulation	0.63	0.80	0.31	0.96
External regulation	0.84	0.95	0.98	0.70
Amotivation	0.54	0.78	0.96	0.11

TABLE 3 | Step-by-step instantiations leading to maximization of the likelihood of low perfomance' Worry anxiety in the BN with CHAID restrictions.

Step	Instantiaded variable	Level	Value
1	None (initial value)	Low	35.88
2	Lack of concentration	Low	43.44
3	Introjected regulation	Low	51.00
4	Somatic anxiety	Low	54.05
5	Identified regulation	Low	57.55
6	Integrated regulation	Low	64.07
7	External regulation	Low	64.42
8	Amotivation	Low	64.83

TABLE 4 | Step-by-step instantiations leading to maximization of the likelihood of high identified intrinsic regulation in the BN with CHAID restrictions.

Step	Instantiaded variable	Level	Value
1	None (initial value)	high	89.16
2	Global intrinsic motivation	high	91.07
3	Perfomance worry anxiety	low	92.99
4	Introjected motivation	high	95.19

when determining the ability of subjects to perform their tasks (García-Mas et al., 2016).

All the analyses carried out demonstrate that it is possible to reduce uncertainty in the relationships between motivation and anxiety when in the performance of competitive sport. Participants in the sample have a high probability of being intrinsically motivated, with a low probability of perceiving external rewards or benefits.

However, it should be noted that this sample – composed of young student/athletes of medium rather than top performance level – presents several clear biases: low probability of anxiety and external regulation and amotivation, contrasting with high probability of emergence of self-determined motivation, without any clear predominance of the source of intrinsic regulation (Ntoumanis, 2001; Standage et al., 2003). As indicated in other studies (Wolf et al., 2015), competition-related anxiety cannot be taken as a whole but, rather, its three factors must be considered separately in both the psychological evaluation and intervention, as is clearly shown in the BN without restrictions for somatic anxiety.

The results found in the BN with restrictions showed that there were five variables to predict somatic anxiety. Four of them are motivational: intrinsic and external global regulations, and two sub-scales of intrinsic motivation, identified and integrated regulation, with the last one being anxiety related to performance.

The probability values found in our study group indicate that the participants in the sample have a high probability of being intrinsically motivated, with a low probability of perceiving external rewards or benefits, although this variable triggers the probability of the other variables occurring, as well as the presence of average likelihood of anxiety related to performance, which acts as a buffer for the other variables.

Working with instantiations leaves the probability landscape much clearer. To obtain the lowest possible probability value for Anxiety from Worry (which is the one least associated with decreased performance (Pulido et al., 2018), several variables need to change their likelihood. The two variables whose probable occurrence is most likely to be reduced are de-concentration and introjected regulation [which is usually accompanied by "negative" emotions, such as guilt (Fenton et al., 2016)]. To a lesser extent, the likelihood of occurrence should also be reduced for somatic signs of anxiety and for high levels of motivation, both intrinsic and extrinsic. If we combine this data with the "actual" probabilities found in the BNs and the nodal or predecessor position that anxiety from worry about performance holds, we can see that perhaps the latter is indeed the key element in the system under study. Further support for this idea is given by the fact that zero probability (100% Low) cannot be achieved, which may perhaps be indicative of a specific characteristic in this type of athlete, namely athletes that are also concerned about their academic careers (Aquilina, 2013; Vilanova and Puig, 2016) and who may have some kind of "immunity" toward external regulation, which in turn triggers a lower likelihood of somatic anxiety.

Further to the previous argument, by obtaining the maximum intrinsic regulation [the one identified as the bottom variable in both BN and which is based on a high probability value (almost 90%)], it is possible to increase its likelihood when introjected and global intrinsic regulations reach 100% probability of occurrence, and when anxiety due to worry about performance is at 100% low probability, i.e., zero. Therefore, strong opposition clearly exists between the emotion of guilt and anxiety due to worry about performance in athletes' minds.

In an attempt to summarize the results obtained more succinctly, we can conclude that the athletes in our survey start with high values of self-motivation and low anxiety associated with competition; that the BNs performed show a probabilistic "constellation" that situates anxiety due to worry about performance and external regulation as the basic predecessors, and intrinsic regulation and somatic anxiety as the bottom variables, while amotivation and the de-concentration lack any informative value. All these findings are confirmed when hypothetical values are inserted in these key variables and we are able to see how the likelihood of other variables need to be changed in order to reach their maximum or minimum probability of occurrence. Also, the obtained results reinforce that the adapted version of the Sport Anxiety Scale (SAS-2) is an adequate and valid measure for the assessment of anxiety in young athletes.

The reduction of uncertainty derives from the successive application of two statistical models. First, the CHAID algorithm has made clear the relationships (or not) of the variables studied, simplifying the subsequent probabilistic analysis. Once the BN has been carried out, the uncertainty has been further reduced by making clear the "chains" of probabilistic impact of each variable with respect to the other relevant ones. In addition, in the same sense, the instantiations have further clarified the landscape (reinforcing some of the results and weakening some others), so that the ambiguity in the probability of occurrence of the variables has been reduced in a very relevant way.

From a practical point of view, thanks to this study we know more about how to cope with Dual Career students/athletes, regarding their motivation (mostly intrinsic, which affects the type of reinforcements and incentives to use with them); or to the relevant importance of the Worry anxiety in contrast with the lower importance of the somatic anxiety in terms of detrimental performance, which is paradoxically often the one that receives the most attention from sports professionals, including psychologists.

This study entails certain limitations, the most important being those derived from the characteristics of the sample studied, as well as the impossibility of relating the variables under study to the performance (either subjectively and/or objectively evaluated) of the athletes/students. Also, the bias that these athletes reveal in regard to their type of motivation and competitive anxiety have limited the results obtained when BNs are used with limited hypothetical values.

When considering the study as a whole, the next step in the research should be to structure the system under study in a more useful manner, firstly, to analyze the concept of "dual career" completely "from the inside," which would be useful to understanding our athletes' specific motivational features; and secondly, to improve the quality of the instantiations made through longitudinal and "survival" studies in order to confirm the predictions derived from this use of probabilistic BNs.

ETHICS STATEMENT

The studies involving human participants were reviewed and approved by the local ethics committee of the Universidad Autónoma de Nuevo León (Mexico). The patients/participants provided their written informed consent to participate in this study.

AUTHOR CONTRIBUTIONS

FP, PA, AO, and AG-M: conceptualization of the study. BM and AG-M: methodology, software, validation, and formal analysis. OR and JL-W: investigation. JL-W, AO, and BM: resources. FP: writing - original draft preparation and visualization. FP, JL, PA, and AG-M: writing - review and editing. AG-M, JL-W, and AO: supervision. All the authors contributed to the revision of the manuscript, and read and approved the presented version.

REFERENCES

Aquilina, D. (2013). A study of the relationship between elite athletes' educational development and sporting performance. *Int. J. Hist. Sport* 30, 374–392. doi: 10.1080/09523367.2013.765723

Chen, W., and Huang, S. (2018). Evaluating flight crew performance by a bayesian network model. *Entropy* 20:178. doi: 10.3390/e20030178

Clancy, R. B., Herring, M. P., MacIntyre, T. E., and Campbell, M. J. (2016). A review of competitive sport motivation research. *Psychol. Sport Exerc.* 27, 232–242. doi: 10.1016/j.psychsport.2016.09.003

Farr, C., Ruggeri, F., and Mengersen, K. (2018). Prior and posterior linear pooling for combining expert opinions: uses and impact on Bayesian networks-the case of the wayfinding model. *Entropy* 20:209. doi: 10.3390/e20030209

Fenton, S. A. M., Duda, J. L., and Barrett, T. (2016). Optimising physical activity engagement during youth sport: a self-determination theory approach. *J. Sports Sci.* 34, 1874–1884. doi: 10.1080/02640414.2016.1142104

Fuster-Parra, P., García-Mas, A., Cantallops, J., Ponseti, F. J., and Luo, Y. (2016). Ranking features on psychological dynamics of cooperative team work through Bayesian networks. *Symmetry* 8:34. doi: 10.3390/sym8050034

Fuster-Parra, P., García-Mas, A., Ponseti, F. J., and Leo, F. M. (2015). Team performance and collective efficacy in the dynamic psychology of competitive team: a Bayesian network analysis. *Hum. Mov. Sci.* 40, 98–118. doi: 10.1016/j.humov.2014.12.005

Fuster-Parra, P., García-Mas, A., Ponseti, F. J., Palou, P., and Cruz, J. (2014). A Bayesian network to discover relationships between negative features in sport: a case study of teen players. *Qual. Quant.* 48, 1473–1491. doi: 10.1007/s11135-013-9848-y

Fuster-Parra, P., Vidal-Conti, J., Borràs, P. A., and Palou, P. (2017). Bayesian networks to identify statistical dependencies. A case study of Spanish University students' habits. *Inform. Health Soc. Care* 42, 166–179. doi: 10.1080/17538157.2016.1178117

García-Mas, A., Ortega, E., Ponseti, J., De Teresa, C., and Cárdenas, D. (2016). Workload and cortisol levels in helicopter combat pilots during simulated flights. *Rev. Andal. Med. Deport.* 9, 7–11. doi: 10.1016/j.ramd.2015.12.001

Grossbard, J. R., Smith, R. E., Smoll, F. L., and Cumming, S. P. (2009). Competitive anxiety in young athletes: differentiating somatic anxiety, worry, and concentration disruption. *Anxiety Stress Coping* 22, 153–166. doi: 10.1080/10615800802020643

Ishigami, H. (2016). Relative age and birthplace effect in Japanese professional sports: a quantitative evaluation using a Bayesian hierarchical poisson model. *J. Sports Sci.* 34, 143–154. doi: 10.1080/02640414.2015.1039462

Jaakkola, T., Meila, M., and Jebara, T. (2000). "Maximum entropy discrimination," in *Proceedings of the 12th International Conference on Neural Information Processing Systems* (Cambridge: MIT Press), 470–476.

Jones, G., and Hanton, S. (2001). Pre-competitive feeling states and directional anxiety interpretations. *J. Sports Sci.* 19, 385–395. doi: 10.1080/026404101300149348

Korb, K. B., and Nicholson, A. E. (2010). Bayesian artificial intelligence. in *Bayesian Artificial Intelligence*, eds K. B., Korb, & A. E., Nicholson, (Boca Raton, FL: CRC Press).

Laming, D. (2001). "Statistical information, uncertainty, and Bayes' theorem: some applications in experimental psychology," in *Proceedings of the 6th*

European Conference on Symbolic and Quantitative Approaches to Reasoning with Uncertainty: ECSQARU 2001, Toulouse.

Lewandowski, C. M., Co-investigator, N., and Lewandowski, C. M. (2015). Self-directed learning oriented assessments in the asia-pasific. *Eff. Br. Mindfulness Interv. Acute Pain Exp. An Exam. Individ. Differ.* 1, 1689–1699. doi: 10.1017/CBO9781107415324.004

Li, C., Wang, C. K. J., and Pyun, D. Y. (2017). Impacts of talent development environments on athlete burnout: a self-determination perspective. *J. Sports Sci.* 35, 1838–1845. doi: 10.1080/02640414.2016.1240370

Lindahl, J., Stenling, A., Lindwall, M., and Colliander, C. (2015). Trends and knowledge base in sport and exercise psychology research: a bibliometric review study. *Int. Rev. Sport Exerc. Psychol.* 8, 71–94. doi: 10.1080/1750984x.2015.1019540

Luce, R. D. (2003). Whatever happened to information theory in psychology? *Rev. Gen. Psychol.* 7, 183–188. doi: 10.1037/1089-2680.7.2.183

Magidson, J., and Vermunt, J. K. (2005). An extension of the CHAID tree-based segmentation algorithm to multiple dependent variables. in *Classification: The Ubiquitous Challenge*, eds C. Weihs, & W. Gaul (Heidelberg. Springer).

Martens, R. (1977). *Sport Competition Anxiety Test.* Champaign: Human Kinetics Publishers.

Martín-Albo, J., Lucas Núñez, J. L., Navarro, J., and González, V. (2006). Validación de la versión española de la escala multidimensional de orientaciones a la deportividad. *Rev. Psicol. Deport.* 15, 9–22.

Ntoumanis, N. (2001). Empirical links between achievement goal theory and self-determination theory in sport. *J. Sports Sci.* 19, 397–409. doi: 10.1080/026404101300149357

Nuñez, A., and García-Mas, A. (2017). Relationship between performance and anxiety in sports: a systematic review. *Retos* 32, 172–177. doi: 10.1371/journal.pone.0186100

Olmedilla, A., Rubio, V. J., Fuster-Parra, P., Pujals, C., and García-Mas, A. (2018). A Bayesian approach to sport injuries likelihood: does player's self-efficacy and environmental factors plays the main role? *Front. Psychol.* 214:631–647. doi: 10.3389/fpsyg.2018.01174

Patel, D. R., Omar, H., and Terry, M. (2010). Sport-related performance anxiety in young female athletes. *J. Pediatr. Adolesc. Gynecol.* 23, 325–335. doi: 10.1016/j.jpag.2010.04.004

Pelletier, L. G., Rocchi, M. A., Vallerand, R. J., Deci, E. L., and Ryan, R. M. (2013). Validation of the revised sport motivation scale (SMS-II). *Psychol. Sport Exerc.* 14, 329–341. doi: 10.1016/j.psychsport.2012.12.002

Pineda-Espejel, H. A., Alarcón, E., López-Ruiz, Z., Trejo, M., and Chávez, C. (2016). Propiedades psicométricas de la escala de motivación en el deporte revisada (SMS-II) adaptada al español hablado en méxico. *Rev. Int. Ciencias Deport.* 12, 107–120. doi: 10.5232/ricyde2016.04402

Ponseti, F., Sese, A., and Garcia-Mas, A. (2016). The impact of competitive anxiety and parental influence on the performance of young swimmers. *Revista Iberoamericana de Psicologia Del Ejercicio y El Deporte* 11, 229–237. doi: 10.1111/j.1600-0838.2010.01277.x

Ponseti, F. J., Garcia-Mas, A., Palou, P., Cantallops, J., and Fuster-Parra, P. (2016). Self-determined motivation and types of sportive cooperation among players on competitive teams A Bayesian network analysis. *Int. J. Sport Psychol.* 47, 428–442. doi: 10.7352/IJSP-2016.47.428

Puga, J. L., García, J. G., De, L., Sánchez, F., De, I., and Solana, F. (2007). Las redes bayesianas como herramientas de modelado en psicología. *An. Psicol.* 23, 307–316.

Pulido, D., Borrás, P. A., Salom, M., and Ponseti, F. J. (2018). Competitive anxiety in grassroots sport in the balearic islands. *Rev. Psicol. Deport.* 27, 5–9.

Ranganathan, S., Spaiser, V., Mann, R. P., and Sumpter, D. J. T. (2014). Bayesian dynamical systems modelling in the social sciences. *PLoS One* 9:e86468. doi: 10.1371/journal.pone.0086468

Rosselet, A. (1987). Language definition-based compiler development. *J. Syst. Softw.* 7, 145–161. doi: 10.1016/0164-1212(87)90019-7

Ryan, R. M., and Deci, E. L. (2017). *Self-Determination Theory: Basic Psychological Needs in Motivation Development and Wellness.* New York, NY: Guilford Publishing.

Scutari, M. (2010). Learning Bayesian networks with the bnlearn r package. *J. Stat. Softw.* 35, 1–22. doi: 10.18637/jss.v035.i03

Smith, R. E., Smoll, F. L., Cumming, S. P., and Grossbard, J. R. (2006). Measurement of multidimensional sport performance anxiety in children and adults: the sport anxiety scale-2. *J. Sport Exerc. Psychol.* 28, 479–501. doi: 10.1123/jsep.28.4.479

Spirtes, P., Glymour, C., and Scheines, R. (1993). *Causation, Prediction, and Search*, Vol. 81. New York, NY: Springer.

Standage, M., Duda, J. L., and Ntoumanis, N. (2003). Predicting motivational regulations in physical education: the interplay between dispositional goal orientations, motivational climate and perceived competence. *J. Sports Sci.* 21, 631–647. doi: 10.1080/0264041031000101962

Tohidi, H., and Jabbari, M. M. (2012). The effects of motivation in education. *Proc. Soc. Behav. Sci.* 31, 820–824. doi: 10.1016/j.sbspro.2011.12.148

Trafimow, D., and Marks, M. (2015). Editorial. *Basic Appl. Soc. Psychol.* 37, 1–2. doi: 10.1080/01973533.2015.1012991

Vilanova, A., and Puig, N. (2016). Personal strategies for managing a second career: the experiences of Spanish olympians. *Int. Rev. Sociol. Sport* 51, 529–546. doi: 10.1177/1012690214536168

Wolf, S. A., Evans, M. B., Laborde, S., and Kleinert, J. (2015). Assessing what generates precompetitive emotions: development of the precompetitive appraisal measure. *J. Sports Sci.* 33, 579–587. doi: 10.1080/02640414.2014.951873

3

"Cooperative Learning does not Work for me": Analysis of its Implementation in Future Physical Education Teachers

David Hortigüela-Alcalá[1], Alejandra Hernando-Garijo[1], Sixto González-Víllora[2], Juan Carlos Pastor-Vicedo[3] and Antonio Baena-Extremera[4]*

Faculty of Education, University of Burgos, Burgos, Spain, [2] Faculty of Education of Cuenca, University of Castilla-La Mancha, Cuenca, Spain, [3] Faculty of Education of Toledo, University of Castilla-La Mancha, Toledo, Spain, [4] Faculty of Education of Granada, University of Granada, Granada, Spain

***Correspondence:**
David Hortigüela-Alcalá
dhortiguela@ubu.es

Cooperative learning (CL) is one of the pedagogical models that has had more application in the area of Physical Education (PE), being highly worked in the initial training of teachers. The aim of the study is to check to what extent future PE teachers are able to apply in the classroom the PE training they have received at university, deepening their fears, insecurities and problems when carrying it out. Thirteen future PE teachers (7 girls and 6 boys) aged 20.87 ± 1.43 participated and, after having been trained in CL in various subjects, applied it in the classroom during their internship. They were selected through purposeful non-probability sampling. A qualitative methodology was used, being the interviews, the teaching diaries and the seminars with the tutor the instruments of data collection used. Three categories of analysis were used: (a) initial expectations in the application of the CL; (b) problems encountered in its implementation; (c) reflection about its application in the future. The results showed how the future teachers did not see their expectations of success fulfilled, encountering resistance from both students and teachers in PE. Furthermore, they reflect the need to continue training in a model that has infinite nuances so that it can be implemented satisfactorily. It is necessary to continue researching a pedagogical model with so many possibilities in the area of PE and with so much transversality on a social level.

Keywords: physical education, cooperative learning, pedagogical model, models-based practice, initial teacher training

INTRODUCTION

Society is constantly evolving, transforming different implicit realities under concrete socio-cultural factors (Sudakova and Astafyeva, 2019). In the face of this, the school cannot remain in the background, and concrete mechanisms of permanent formation must be established that are in line with the current situation. This connection between society and school must be closely linked to the role played by the university, intentionally addressing research-action processes that favor and promote true educational innovation (Roffeei et al., 2018). If continuing education is especially relevant to educational advancement, initial training takes on special significance, due to its great impact on the creation of the professional identity of teachers (Androusou and Tsafos, 2018). In this sense, without a doubt, one of the greatest challenges lies in seeing how this university training can be successfully replicated by future teachers in schools. It is also necessary to focus on other factors that may be important in the development of a teacher's identity, such as the transferability of learning, academic motivation or the teacher's perception of competence.

This relevance of initial teacher training takes on an even greater dimension when it comes to PE, where the use of corporeality is present. The body is an indissoluble element of the individual, and for this reason, from the PE it must be worked on with clear pedagogical purposes that go beyond biomedical and physiological parameters (Kennedy et al., 2019). The acquisition of values in the practice of physical activity is not achieved by the mere fact of doing it, but rather there must be an ethical base built under very clear and defined social purposes (Schenker, 2019). This is where pedagogical models of teaching come into play, especially that of CL, which has already demonstrated benefits in the relational, motivational and learning environments of students (Casey and MacPhail, 2018). Applying the CL model in PE with guarantees ensures a climate of respect, empathy and initial solidarity on which to base motor practice, something that favors the self-concept and autonomy of students when carrying out their daily activities in the classroom. This relates to the theory of self-determination, demonstrating how a good social climate in the group affects the intrinsic motivation of students, the identified regulation and task orientation (Sevil et al., 2016). Starting from a climate of equality in the PE classroom is essential, since corporal exposure to others is constant, which on many occasions generates fears and insecurities in the face of failure and the consequent mockery of one's classmates (Duncan and Bellar, 2015). This has a direct consequence in society, where on many occasions the criteria of honesty and nobility have been lost, with the ego taking precedence and the search for individual benefit over the common good.

However, applying the CL model in PE effectively is not easy, since it requires a high level of mastery in the knowledge of its implementation phases and the elements that constitute it. In certain cases, faculty believe that they are applying it adequately, when in reality what they are doing are only isolated activities of a cooperative nature that are not integrated into a specific methodology (Morgan, 2019). And if it is not easy to apply it consistently, it is even more complex to teach it with guarantees of replicability in the classroom. On various occasions, the initial training of teachers, due to the idyllic context in which the teaching takes place, can lead to a feeling of control over the learning acquired by the student, something that is not always corroborated when he or she tries to apply it in the classroom (Jones, 2019). Studies carried out with future PE teachers, with a pre-test design, showed that the CL is fundamental to apply it as a scaffolding in the teaching process. Specifically, this scaffolding favors variables such as practical knowledge, teaching skills and self-efficacy (Legrain et al., 2019). However, it was shown that when this scaffolding is not structured and applied in a transversal way in the training, problems related to teaching skills appear. Research has shown the difficulties PE teachers have in introducing new technologies into cooperative learning (CL) when they do not intentionally use them throughout the course (Bodsworth and Goodyear, 2017). Sometimes PE teachers confuse the implementation of CL with the implementation of specific activities and games, which causes problems for the class to act truly as a group (Casey et al., 2015). Another of the main problems of teachers in the application of the CL is found in the difficulties that students have in solving their problems, so it is necessary to establish longitudinal programs of intervention (Gorucu, 2016). On some occasions, in the teacher's eagerness to apply the CL in the classroom, they forget what the didactic purposes of the proposed interventions are (Wallhead and Dyson, 2017). Another major problem is generated around the power relationships established in the classroom. The qualitative research of Barker and Quennerstedt (2017), through the work of dance in PE, showed how CL can favor the group climate over the students' motor skills. Another of the most common reticence among PE teachers to apply CL is the reduction of motor commitment it entails in the classroom. However, research such as that of Altinkok (2017), applied with 6–7 year-old students, in 12 weeks and with a pre-test, showed a greater development of motor skills in the experimental group.

Therefore, and considering the different social benefits that the implementation of the CL in the school PE has demonstrated, it is necessary to verify the effects of replicability that its teaching has on the future PE teachers. Therefore, the objective of the study is to analyze to what extent future PE teachers are able to apply in the classroom the training on CL that they have received at the university, deepening in their fears, insecurities and problems when carrying it out. This is a significant contribution to the existing literature on the subject, since, in addition to generating new evidence on the applicability of this model, it uses a contrast of qualitative instruments that allow for reflection and redirection of the practices of teachers throughout their process of implementation in the classroom.

Cooperative Learning as an Essential Element in the Initial Training of Physical Education Teachers

In the initial training of PE teachers, in addition to the specific contents of the discipline, it is necessary to intentionally address a diversity of methodological aspects that are transferable to the classroom in which they carry out their professional activity (Capel et al., 2018). These are related to the design of classes, the organization of groupings, time management or the application of assessment. All of them are clearly immersed in the development of pedagogical models, within which the CL is essential for several reasons. It starts from an important social base, which makes dialogue and consensus building a priority in its implementation. In addition, and starting from the empowerment of the capacities of the group members, the achievement of challenges is sought jointly, which favors the feeling of affiliation (Hortigüela-Alcalá et al., 2019). This process must be articulated under the promotion of the generation of positive motor experiences, proposing activities where the level of achievement is perceived as affordable and motivating by the students (Koka, 2013). All the typology of contents that includes the subject of PE has a place in the CL, always being implicit the values of solidarity, empathy and respect for others. These fundamental premises of action in the classroom have a clear connection with the behavioral patterns of today's society, which allows the establishment of a binomial with the school and with the connection of its learning. Furthermore, it can be applied in a transversal way to other curricular areas, establishing common action protocols regarding student responsibility and autonomy.

Another of the fundamental aspects that justify the teaching of the CL in the initial training of teachers is the increase of the motor possibilities that it entails in the student, since it does not reduce the learning objectives to the achievement of a determined motor performance in an isolated test. Its vision and application is carried out in its widest spectrum, being applicable in diversity of contents, tasks and contexts (Casey and Goodyear, 2015). In addition, it allows the development of emotional bonds between the members of the class, putting themselves in the place of others when it comes to making decisions. This causes that as future PE teachers they rethink how to promote social interactions in the classroom in a positive way, improving the group climate, self-esteem and self-concept of the students. Under this prism of pedagogical action, one of the main purposes of school PE is achieved, which is the generation of positive learning experiences around motor skills. This is connected to what has been called transcontextual analysis, defined as the impact that PE classes have on students so that they later decide to practice physical activity autonomously in their free time (Hagger and Chatzisarantis, 2016). The CL model is also very interesting to be applied from the sports teaching, since it teaches that everyone has to play with everyone in different conditions and situations, going far beyond the mere competition where someone is always defeated (Kolovelonis, 2019). It establishes procedures for playful performance in which everyone has the right and opportunity to win, and the fact of not winning does not mean that someone is eliminated. For this purpose, techniques such as 1-2-4, numbered heads together, Aronson's puzzle or the collective score are applied.

It is necessary to emphasize from the initial training of the teaching staff that the CL is not only applied in a punctual way through isolated activities, since the key to the success of its implementation is found in delimiting temporary phases in the medium term that allow the class to act in a cohesive way around motor skills (Lafont et al., 2016). This pedagogical awareness leads the future PE teacher to create a professional identity of a cooperative nature, generating an idiosyncrasy and a behavior that defines him/her as a teacher. This has repercussions on such relevant aspects as the selection of content to be developed in the classroom, time management in tasks, the way of carrying out groupings or the proposal and typology of the approach to objectives. Therefore, the transversality that characterizes the CL is usually well accepted among future PE teachers, since their previous experiences do not limit or bias their applicability in the classroom (Yuksel et al., 2019). The design, preparation and evaluation of activities are essential for PE teacher to gain confidence in their professional practice. To this end, it is essential that, in addition to knowing about the diversity of activities, they are able to structure them within a methodology that can be adapted in a variety of contexts (Lafont et al., 2016). However, a novice teacher's professional beginnings are not easy. Considering the level of teaching experience, it can be seen that new teachers are excessively dependent on the curriculum. Therefore, it is necessary that initial training of PE teachers include more support from experienced teachers in the subject (Viciana and Mayorga-Vega, 2017). While teachers say they are confident in aspects related to health and fitness, they are more hesitant in those related to assessment and classroom control (Randall, 2020). Another of the training deficiencies that future PE teachers admit to have is that related to Special Educational Needs. This subsequently generates problems in the actual treatment of inclusion in the classroom (Maher and Fitzgerald, 2020). It is necessary to work from the initial training of teachers to question the hegemonic practices associated with PE, establishing pedagogical lines that can respond to the needs of a new type of physical education (PE) teacher (Wrench and Garrett, 2015).

All of the above-mentioned benefits are key to the initial training of teachers, thus increasing the guarantees of implementing it in their professional future and thus achieving educational and social transformation. And this is precisely what this study aims to prove, analyzing the effectiveness of its application in the specific school context by new teachers.

MATERIALS AND METHODS

Participants

Thirteen future PE teachers (7 girls and 6 boys) aged 20.87 ± 1.43 participated. This number of participants is ideal in relation to the type of study, instruments and analysis used. All of them had received CL training throughout their university career. This qualification is the Degree in Primary Education, with the speciality in CL, given at the University of Burgos (Spain). There are 5 subjects (30 ECTS or 750–900 h the student spends on the study activity) that make up the specialty, taken in the third and fourth years. Specifically, in the third year there is a subject called pedagogical models in PE, whose main objectives revolve around the teaching of the school PE, with the teaching of the CL model having great weight. It is in this subject that future PE teachers were specifically trained in the application of the CL in the classroom. The model was approached in a theoretical-practical way, analyzing each of its elements and phases and applying them later in the classroom through a diversity of contents. A model of formative assessment and feedback was established in each of the classes, influencing in a reflexive way their learning possibilities. However, in previous subjects, different methodological approaches had been dealt with in PE in a transversal way. These subjects are called "Educational Game in PE" "Inclusive PE" and "Sports Initiation." The main idea is that future teachers acquire the necessary knowledge to be able to apply the model with guarantees within the classroom in the near future. This was verified in their school practice phase carried out in the third and fourth grades. These practices were developed in 8 public schools in the city of Burgos (Spain). The choice of these 13 participants was intended to meet a double criterion: (a) the participants' voluntariness; (b) the best academic record in the subject of pedagogical models in PE. These criteria guarantee the correct acquisition of the CL by the participants, which ensures greater reliability of the results. The students with the best grades proved to have a better understanding of the essence of the CL, which ensured better replicability of the model in schools. Three schools where the internships took place were subsidized, while the rest were publicly owned. Two schools were in municipalities near the capital, while the others were in the city itself. None of them had more than 600 students. There was no substantial difference in the characteristics of the student in all of the schools, except for two schools located in a neighborhood with a lower socio-economic level. This did not decisively influence the application of the CL by the future teachers. In none of the schools was the CL being applied as a PE methodology, which eliminated the possible bias of the interventions. These interventions were carried out with students from all grades of the primary stage.

The training given on CL was carried out by a 34 years old teacher, doctor, with 10 years of experience in the university field in the same degree and university, and specialist in the teaching of school PE.

Instruments

Three different instruments were used for the collection of information: interviews, teaching diaries and the seminars with the teacher. The questions in each instrument are clearly connected to the objectives of the study and to the categories that structure the results, thus giving reliability to the study (Swaminathan and Mulvihill, 2018). These tools make it possible to gather in a detailed and in-depth way all the information concerning the experiences of future EP teachers on the implementation of the CL. In addition, the use of Teachers' Diaries and Seminars with the professor allowed for reflection throughout the intervention, redirecting professional practice according to the problems encountered. Teachers' Diaries have proven to be an ideal qualitative tool for building the professional identity of novice teachers (Gut et al., 2016).

Interviews: These were carried out individually with the participants at the end of the intervention and were of a semi-structured nature (**Table 1**). Issues related to the initial expectations generated, to the results obtained after the implementation of the CL in the classroom and to the main benefits and problems found for its future replicability were addressed.

Teachers' diaries: each participant made his or her own. They had a structured character based on the categories of analysis of the results: (a) initial expectations in the application of the CL; (b) problems encountered in its implementation; (c) reflection on its application in the future. The participants were writing in the same weekly throughout the 12 weeks that the intervention lasted. It is a tool that allows the teacher to take a perspective on the development of his/her own practice, and that, applied over time, favors a greater understanding of the context in which one acts (Safronov et al., 2020).

Seminars with the professor: were carried out throughout the intervention. Before the beginning of the application in the classroom, the professor who taught them about C established with the participants four seminars, spaced approximately every three weeks. They were conducted together, in order to exchange opinions and experiences about the results that were being found in each of the contexts. It is a clearly reflective instrument of great utility within the educational action-research process (Liu and Wang, 2018).

TABLE 1 | Basic script used for semi-structured interviews with participants.

- What were your initial intentions before you carried out the process?
- How did you organize the work in the classroom based on cooperative learning?
- What has the application of the CL in the classroom brought you?
- What have been the main problems you have encountered?
- What would you change if you had to make a new intervention with the CL?
- Will you continue applying the CL in your professional future? Why?

Design and Procedure

The research has been structured in four distinct phases throughout the 2018–2019 school year:

Phase 1. Structuring of the study and establishment of the schedule: the study arose from the need to verify to what extent the initial training received by PE teachers on CL was subsequently replicated in the classroom. The usefulness and contribution of the research was confirmed since, through a qualitative approach, the aim was to check the experiences of future teachers in their practice contexts.

Phase 2. Contact with the participants and delimitation of the CL intervention in the classroom: having taught about CL to all the participants, it was easy to contact them to carry out the research. They were summoned before the start of their 12-week internship in order to record data from the schools they were going to work in. In addition, the intervention to be carried out was specified to be homogeneous in all cases. The intervention of all participants was based on three basic principles: (a) to respect the five elements that make up the CL; (b) to eliminate competitive proposals within the classroom; (c) to carry out the same didactic units in the intervention. The choice of these criteria was made in view of the importance of respecting the structure that gives the CL its essence, thus giving it sufficient rigor in its application (Fernández-Río et al., 2018). In this way, it was guaranteed that any possibility of competition would be eliminated. It was agreed to carry out the pedagogical interventions through the same contents, in order to maintain the fidelity in the totality of the interventions. These units were three. The first one was about games and cooperative activities, where a series of group challenges were posed to be solved in a motor way. These activities were related to transporting objects, overcoming obstacles, passing and receiving mobile elements and trusting one's peers. The second unit of work was body expression, specifically shadow theater, where groups worked with a light bulb and a white cloth to make different shadows and create a narrative story. The third didactic unit focused on the work of motor skills and physical condition, where the four basic physical capacities were worked on through cooperative team challenges, thus obtaining rewards to overcome different levels. The aim of this program was to implement CL through a diversity of contents, demonstrating in a practical way how the phases and elements that structure the model were applied. This training was related to the previous learning that the students had in relation to other models, deriving in the possibility of its hybridization. The characteristics of the intervention are based on reflection, action research and the replicability of learning. The theory was clearly linked to practice, establishing constant reflections on what happened in each of the activities. This would allow them to act with greater rigor when they were in the schools.

Before carrying out the field work, the teacher prepared a script with the timing of the sessions to be carried out by the participants. This made it possible to guarantee a reliable and homogeneous intervention. Throughout the intervention in the schools it was corroborated that this script was respected.

Phase 3. Carrying out of the seminars with the participants: these seminars were carried out throughout the 12 weeks of intervention. A total of four were held. A seminar was established every three weeks. This was considered to be an adequate time, maintaining the balance between autonomous classroom practice of future teachers and the need for advice. All the participants were summoned to a seminar at the university in order to dialogue, share, advise and guide their interventions. The teacher used a script, divided into four parts, to maintain the monitoring structure: (a) compliance with the established plan; (b) type of problems encountered in the classroom; (c) how to solve these problems; (d) comments, questions and suggestions. In these seminars, in rotational order, each participant presented the main problems they had encountered in the classroom, in order to find common patterns of action that could be useful to all. Subsequently, decisions were made to try to reverse these problems found in the classroom. Each seminar lasted approximately 2 h. All were recorded on audio, for later listening when recapitulating the data.

Phase 4. Conducting the interviews and data analysis: at the end of the intervention, individual interviews were conducted with each of the participants. These interviews were carried out in the teacher's office. Each one had a duration of 45 min and they were recorded in audio. In this last phase the teacher also received the teachers' diary. From here, all the data obtained was transcribed and dumped into the text analysis computer program and the data was analyzed. In addition, the researchers reflected deeply on the purpose of the study, the procedure carried out and its adequacy to the objective set.

Data Analysis

A qualitative approach was used to gain an in-depth understanding of how future teachers were able to apply the CL learned at university in the classroom. To do so, it was essential to know in first person the perception of the participants throughout the process, verifying how they were gradually transforming their school contexts and creating their professional identity. The fact that the main source of data was the assessments and experiences of those involved in the process allowed us to approach the study phenomenon in a real and interpretative way (Rubel and Okech, 2017). A triangulation was carried out between the information obtained in the data collection instruments with the aim of guaranteeing the reliability, transferability and credibility of the results. In addition, the most significant text extracts were coded in each of the instruments, using cross matching patterns (Saldaña, 2009). The researchers took an active part in the field work, reflecting throughout the process on the linearity of the results with the objectives of the study. The information was articulated, grouping it by thematic axes in the categories generated by means of a selective, open and axial codification (Strauss and Corbin, 2002).

Generation of Categories and Their Categorization

Once the data from each instrument used was transcribed, it was dumped into the WEFT QDA computer and analysis program. Through the saturation of coinciding texts and ideas and the treatment of thematic axes, the information was grouped into the three initial categories of the study: (a) initial expectations in the application of the CL; (b) problems encountered in its implementation; (c) reflection on its application in the future. These categories are common to all the data collection instruments used, and are used to structure the analysis of the results. They are related to the object of study and the design of research, thus respecting the criteria of specificity and coherence that all qualitative research must have (Le Roux, 2017).

Initial expectations in the application of the CL: aspects related to the way of understanding and applying CL in the classroom, its educational purposes and the factors that directly influence its school treatment are addressed.

Problems encountered in its implementation: information regarding the problems encountered when applying the CL in the classroom and the guidelines and orientations established to successfully redirect the process are analyzed.

Reflection about its application in the future: the data linked to which are the positions and attitudes that future FE teachers have in relation to the application of the CL in the future are integrated, taking into account what happened after their first experience.

Coding of Data Collection Instruments

Different acronyms are used to identify the text extracts with the data collection instrument from which they come. In relation to the interviews, it is used (EP1, EP2, EP3...) depending on the participant interviewed. Likewise, with regard to the teaching diaries, it is used (DD1, DD2, DD3...). For the seminars with the teacher, the acronym (SP1, SP2, SP3, and SP4) is used, taking into account the four seminars held throughout the intervention.

RESULTS

With regard to data coding, the following primary and secondary issues were obtained:

Initial expectations in the application of the CA: The primary issues were the understanding and application of the CL, while the secondary issues were the expectations, fears and uncertainty generated about the functioning of the model.

Problems encountered in its implementation: The primary issues were the excessive competitiveness of the students and their lack of experience, while the secondary issues were the lack of motor commitment, and the use of adequate space and materials.

Reflection on its future application: The primary was the need for further training in the model, while the secondary was the importance of reflection throughout the process and confidence in the model's potential. All the information extracted from the three data collection instruments is grouped into the three categories of the study. Through the analysis of crossed patterns, the number of resulting literal text extracts is presented, showing the most significant and coinciding ones. Presenting the most consistent text extracts in each of the categories, in relation to the objectives of the study, favors the elimination of possible biases on the part of the researchers and guarantees the reliability of qualitative studies (Peterson, 2019). The qualitative methodology must have its main strength in the analysis of the participants' experiences through the text, being not at all less rigorous than the quantitative one (Wallace and Kuo, 2020). In this case, the results follow a research structure linked to four of the five qualitative approaches (Creswell, 2007; Creswell et al., 2007): case study, narrative, phenomenology and action research.

Initial Expectations in the Application of the CA (302 Text Extracts)

It can be seen how the expectations that the future teachers had at the beginning were not completely satisfied, finding problems in practice such as student boredom and lack of control over the classroom:

> *"I honestly thought that the students would respond very well to cooperative learning activities, however, many of them said that they were bored and wanted to do something else" (EP5). "I go home frustrated, because I had prepared the session very well, I thought it would be fun for them, but I spent the whole class trying to motivate them towards the activities [...] (DD9)." "It was a direct hit with reality. From the beginning I lost control of the class, and I was more concerned about being attended and listened to than actually doing the activities. The students disconnected as soon as the explanations were a little long" (SP1).*

It also reflects how future teachers thought they knew the CL model, although later in the classroom many doubts and uncertainties were generated when applying it in terms of aspects such as group management, application of content and time management:

> *"I thought I was clear about the principles of the CL, and how through them the class was going to cooperate. However, from the first day I realized that it was not going to be easy, as I found it difficult to adapt the activities to the characteristics of the groups" (EP10). "In principle I thought that the application of the CL could be carried out through any content, but for example in those of a sporting nature I find it difficult to eliminate competition" (DD5). "One of the main ones for me is managing class time. I think that in one class I will be able to do three or four activities, when at most I have time for two" (SP2).*

Participants highlight how the reality of the classroom with children differs greatly from what was learned and experienced at the university:

> *"When they tell you about the benefits of CL in the university you only see advantages, everything seems very nice and you think it will be easy to apply" (EP1). "They show you videos of the kids doing activities and you are shocked [...]. You can't wait to get to the classroom to try them out" (EP6). "When you get to class everything changes, you realize that everything in college was too idyllic" (DD9). "Among us adults, there was silence, more autonomy and when something was proposed everyone did it without a problem [...] When you put it to the children it is a totally different reality, more complex" (SP3).*

Problems Encountered in Their Implementation (318 Text Extracts)

One of the main problems perceived by future teachers was the excessive competition among students:

> *"Children are very used to competing in PE, and this is noticeable from day one" (EP7). "They always want to win above all else and this makes it very difficult for them to enter into the logic of cooperation" (EP12). "Whenever I propose a cooperative activity there are always a couple of students in class who want to solve it by themselves as soon as possible, and they also tend to make fun of those who are not capable" (DD13). "They are so used to winning and losing that when they have to think as a team there are some who tend to get bored [...] There is also a group of students who do not talk for fear of being laughed at" (DD6). "Some class members are not able to respect each other's waiting times and different learning rhythms... they think more individually than collectively and this is hard to change" (SP4).*

It was also observed how future teachers perceived greater ease in applying the model to those contents more linked to cooperative activities than to those related to physical condition:

> *"When you are doing team activities it is much easier to apply the model, as the guidelines are much clearer" (EP9). "I realized how in physical fitness activities we act more competitively and it becomes more difficult." (DD10). "In some content related to games I usually go to win individually, so implementing the model sometimes becomes more complicated" (DD5). "The main challenge is to be able to apply the cooperative learning model above any content" (SP2).*

Another problem expressed by the future teachers was the lack of motor commitment involved in the implementation of the CL:

> *"I am aware that the CL involves reflection and dialogue among participants [...]. The problem is when this time is too long, which causes the time of motor practice to be reduced" (EP4). "You can see how some children disconnect when the explanation is too long" (EP8). "On the one hand I know that the methodology has these characteristics, but on the other hand I think that from the PE we should encourage movement and the practice of physical activity, so I am faced with an eternal dilemma" (DD12). "It is the students themselves who often say that they are bored, commenting that when we practice a sport [...] Many times you think that what you are doing makes no sense and does not motivate them. This makes me very angry, since I prepare my classes a lot" (SP3).*

Reflection on Its Future Application (324 Text Extracts)

The results of this variable indicate how future teachers express the need for further training in the model:

> *"This classroom experience has helped me realize what I still need to learn from cooperative learning" (EP10) "I thought I already knew a lot about cooperative learning, but reality has shown me that I still have to justify the tasks much better, their adaptation to the students, to the space [...]" (EE8) "Some things are not going well for me, but the most important thing is that I am aware of why, so I*

will be able to change it the next times I develop these tasks in class." (DD7) "This is to be taken as an apprenticeship in our training [...]. We must not despair, it is our first experience in the classroom, and we still have a long way to go in our formation" (SP2).

They also highlighted the satisfaction and importance of the seminars held with the professor throughout the intervention:

"The seminars have helped me to know that I was not the only person who had problems, and that things were happening to the rest of my classmates in class that were very similar to mine" (EE2). "We have always been told at the university about the importance of teaching reflection on practice, and the seminars we have done have helped me to realize this" (DD13) "I was looking forward to this seminar to share with you everything that is happening to me and see how the intervention is going [...]. It is an ideal way to share and look for common strategies" (SS3).

Although the participants have reflected a diversity of problems in the implementation of the model in the classroom, they remain confident in their potential and in continuing to apply it in their professional future:

"Having had certain problems at the beginning is normal, but I still believe that this model is fundamental in contributing to the type of physical education that we want" (EE1) "Problems in the classroom are normal with this methodology and with any other [...] Mistakes serve to continue learning" (EE4) "Although I have had problems, there have been more positive than negative things, and I honestly want to continue applying this methodology in my future" (DD8) "If you believe in participatory physical education, you must use models such as the cooperative model, otherwise the principles behind the subject are totally different" (SS4).

DISCUSSION

The aim of the study was to analyze to what extent future PE teachers were able to apply the CL training they have received at university in the classroom, by exploring their fears, insecurities and problems in doing so. The results show how the initial expectations that future PE teachers had are not matched in reality, finding a variety of problems when applying the C model in the classroom. However, they show that they understand the difficulty involved and intend to continue applying it in their professional future. The results obtained connect perfectly with the theory of occupational socialization (Richards et al., 2014), which tries to connect the initial training of teachers with the professional reality they will find in the classroom. To do so, it is essential to pay attention to the pedagogy of dialogue, actively following up on the future teachers in their first contacts with the classroom. This will allow them to achieve confidence and competence in themselves to create their own professional identity (Eather et al., 2019).

In relation to the first category of the study, related to the initial expectations, the reality in the school showed them the complexity that has to apply the CL with the children, manifesting how different everything is in relation to what was experienced in the university. This is one of the main problems that exist today in the initial training of teachers, where they are trained more on theoretical aspects than on the acquisition of practical resources for application in the classroom (Richards et al., 2013). From the perspective of pedagogical coherence, university teachers must maintain a close relationship with what is happening in the schools, showing scientific evidence of which methods, strategies and protocols are the best to follow in each context. As indicated by Greaves et al. (2019), the university must provide channels so that future teachers can apply what they have learned in their subjects, with the possibility of experimentation and above all with guarantees of redirecting teaching processes. The data from the study have reflected the perceived shortcomings in managing groups and class time well according to the content selected. It is common for new teachers to fall into the error of "more is better," considering that many activities are necessary in order to generate more learning. In fact, the CL is characterized by a high component of group reflection, which means that in many cases the number of activities is not the most relevant element in the teacher's planning (Walker and Johnson, 2018). On the other hand, the participants in the study have reflected the frustration they felt when students were sometimes bored in class. This is common when students first receive the CL in PE, as they are usually more accustomed to traditional PE models in which physiological activation takes precedence over social and learning aspects. Dyson et al. (2016) indicate that despite the initial resistance that we may encounter in schools, students and even families when applying the CL, we must be consistent in its application until the student acts under the logic of cooperation. This full conviction can serve as a stimulus for the professional development of teachers, thus increasing the possibilities of applying the pedagogical model correctly.

With regard to the second category of the study concerning the problems encountered, two were the main axes found. On the one hand, the excessive competitiveness of students, and on the other, the perceived lack of motor commitment. It is usual that the activities applied in the PE are based on the immediacy of the objective to be achieved from an individual approach (throwing faster, arriving running before the colleagues, making more jumps than the others...). This type of conception of the subject, applied year after year, creates in the student a driving culture, where what matters is individuality above any collective, creative and social criteria (Pill and SueSee, 2017). When this logic of acting is imposed, the students with more individual success reject any kind of change in the subject, since the protagonism to which they were accustomed is reduced. This is why new teachers must be guided and accompanied throughout these training processes, since they produce great contrasts with respect to their initial pretensions (Richards and Templin, 2011). In this sense, even today the "wet T-shirt syndrome" still prevails within the PE classes, understanding that if the student does not sweat in the PE classes is not generating real learning. However, several studies (Hortigüela-Alcalá et al., 2017, 2018) indicate that the motivation and predisposition of PE teachers to teach one content or another is not linked to the intensity of the level of physical practice required by the content. Therefore, teaching programs must be aimed at reducing the competitiveness of students, designing protocols to monitor each of the strategies implemented (Johnson and Johnson, 2009). Connecting with the ideas addressed in the theoretical framework, the results have shown the various problems encountered by future PE teachers. This is why CL must be taught in universities as an in-depth pedagogical model, and not in isolation at specific moments. Its possibilities are infinite, but if it is not properly focused, it can have the opposite effect to that intended at the beginning, for example in the dialogue that it requires among students for learning sports (Darnis and Lafont, 2015). It is essential to have clear teaching structures that can be applied transversely to any content, with the objective of fostering social relations through motor skills (O'Leary et al., 2015).

The last category of the study has been about the reflection of the future PE teachers to apply the CL in their professional future. Firstly, the future teachers express the need to continue being trained in the model, assuming its complexity and considering the experience a key factor to be able to continue evolving as professionals. In this sense, Bores-García et al. (2020) highlight the importance of the activities carried out in the classroom being governed by the principles that give meaning to the CL model, and for this, teachers must ensure that these activities can be extrapolated to a variety of contexts. In this sense, the participants of the study highlighted as very relevant and necessary the seminars that were held with the teacher throughout the intervention, since they allowed them to reconstruct their steps in the school and to reflect on the problems that were encountered throughout the process. Lynch and Curtner-Smith (2019) criticize the poor connection that in many cases exists between education faculties and schools, explaining how an education system is broken if the predominant socio-cultural influences in each context are not intentionally addressed. There is still a large gap between initial teacher training and the reality of schools, which creates a tension between theory and practice. In order to reduce this tension, it is essential that teacher trainers develop auto-ethnographic processes in order to understand the applicability of learning (Yung, 2020). Some authors advocate the need for an intense reformulation of initial teacher training, establishing innovative training plans that adapt to an increasingly changing educational reality (Yeigh and Lynch, 2017). Finally, the results show how future teachers, after the experience, continue to trust in the potential derived from the CL, hoping to continue applying it in their professional future. This is why, from the initial teacher training, the development of practices in real contexts must be guaranteed, thus contributing to the generation of the construction of a clear professional identity that can be transferred to their daily life at school (Androusou and Tsafos, 2018). In the present investigation, a 12-week intervention has been carried out, addressing the entire duration of the course. It is ideal to be able to establish interventions of the longest possible duration, thus guaranteeing the establishment of significant learning (Watts et al., 2019).

CONCLUSION

In relation to the objective of the study, it has been verified how the future teachers of PE have not seen their initial expectations fulfilled in the application of the CL in the school, finding diverse problems like the management of the time, the motivation of the student or the scarce motor commitment of the activities. However, they consider the experience to be very positive, hoping to continue applying the model in their professional future. The main contribution of this research, besides generating new evidences about the applicability of the CL, has been the use of a contrast of qualitative instruments that allow to reflect and redirect the practices of the future PE teachers. In addition, seminars were carried out with the participants throughout the intervention process, thus contributing to the pedagogy of dialogue and the theory of occupational socialization. This is a contribution to the previous literature, since it allows for the establishment of connections between the initial training of PE teachers and schools, through designs based on reflection and the construction of professional identity.

However, the article has some limitations. On the one hand, only one intervention is measured. On the other hand, only the assessments experienced by future PE teachers are taken into account. Therefore, it would be interesting to contrast these results with future interventions of a longitudinal nature, thus verifying the level of evolution of the participants with respect to the application of the CL. In this sense, it would also be possible to attend to the students' assessments. In addition, it would be interesting to make interventions by increasing the number of participants, as well as the establishment of teaching programs based on a diversity of research.

We consider this research of special interest for all those PE teachers who work the CL in the school. Also for all those responsible for the elaboration of school curricula or for the management of physical activity programs, understanding that the cooperation has to be closely linked to the sport field. It is necessary to continue investigating in this line and throwing light on the bonanzas and guarantees of the application of the CL in PE.

ETHICS STATEMENT

The studies involving human participants were reviewed and approved by the Bioethics Committee of the University of Burgos. The participants provided written informed consent to participate in this study.

AUTHOR CONTRIBUTIONS

DH-A: conceptualization, validation, and investigation. AH-G: investigation and visualization. SG-V: investigation and formal analysis. JP-V: investigation and resources. AB-E: review and editing. All authors contributed to the article and approved the submitted version.

REFERENCES

Altinkok, M. (2017). The effect of movement education based on cooperative learning method on the development of basic motor skills of primary school 1st grade learners. *J. Baltic Sci. Educ.* 16, 241–249.

Androusou, A., and Tsafos, V. (2018). Aspects of the professional identity of preschool teachers in Greece: investigating the role of teacher education and professional experience. *Teachnol. Dev.* 22, 554–570. doi: 10.1080/13664530.2018.1438309

Barker, D. M., and Quennerstedt, M. (2017). Power and group work in physical education: a foucauldian perspective. *Eur. Phys. Educ. Rev.* 23, 339–353. doi: 10.1177/1356336x15620716

Bodsworth, H., and Goodyear, V. (2017). Barriers and facilitators to using digital technologies in the cooperative learning model in physical education. *Phys. Educ. Sport Pedagogy* 22, 563–579. doi: 10.1080/17408989.2017.1294672

Bores-García, D., Hortigüela-Alcalá, D., Fernandez-Rio, F. J., González-Calvo, G., and Barba-Martín, R. (2020). Research on cooperative learning in physical education. Systematic review of the last five years. *Res. Q. Exerc. Sport.* 1–10. doi: 10.1080/02701367.2020.1719276

Capel, S., Bassett, S., Lawrence, J., Newton, A., and Zwozdiak-Myers, P. (2018). How trainee physical education teachers in England write, use and evaluate lesson plans. *Eur. Phys. Educ. Rev.* 25, 964–982. doi: 10.1177/1356336X18785053

Casey, A., Goodyear, V., and Dyson, B. (2015). Model fidelity and students'responses to an authenticated unit of cooperative learning. *J. Teach. Phys. Educ.* 34, 642–660. doi: 10.1123/jtpe.2013-0227

Casey, A., and Goodyear, V. A. (2015). Can cooperative learning achieve the four learning outcomes of physical education? A review of literature. *Quest* 67, 56–72. doi: 10.1080/00336297.2014.984733

Casey, A., and MacPhail, A. (2018). Adopting a models-based approach to teaching physical education. *Phys. Educ. Sport Pedagogy* 23, 294–310. doi: 10.1080/17408989.2018.1429588

Creswell, J. W. (2007). *Research Design: Qualitative, Quantitative, and Mixed Methods Approaches*, 2nd Edn. Thousand Oaks, CA: Sage.

Creswell, J. W., Hanson, W. E., Clark, V. L., and Morales, A. (2007). Qualitative research designs: selection and implementation. *Counsel. Psychol.* 35, 1–12.

Darnis, F., and Lafont, L. (2015). Cooperative learning and dyadic interactions: two modes of knowledge construction in socio-constructivist settings for team-sport teaching. *Phys. Educ. Sport Pedagogy* 20, 459–473. doi: 10.1080/17408989.2013.803528

Duncan, C. A., and Bellar, D. M. (2015). Let's make physical education more physical and more educational. *Strategies* 28, 3–6. doi: 10.1080/08924562.2014.1001103

Dyson, B. P., Colby, R., and Barratt, M. (2016). The co-construction of cooperative learning in physical education with elementary classroom teachers. *J. Teach. Phys. Educ.* 35, 370–380. doi: 10.1123/jtpe.2016-0119

Eather, N., Riley, N., Miller, D., and Imig, S. (2019). Evaluating the impact of two dialogical feedback methods for improving pre-service teacher's perceived confidence and competence to teach physical education within authentic learning environments. *J. Educ. Train. Stud.* 7:32. doi: 10.11114/jets.v7i8.4053

Fernández-Río, J., Hortigüela, D., and Pérez-Pueyo, A. (2018). Revisando los modelos pedagógicos en educación física. Ideas clave para incorporarlos al aula. *Rev. Española Educ. Física y Deportes* 423, 57–80.

Gorucu, A. (2016). The investigation of the effects of physical education lessons planned in accordance with cooperative learning approach on secondary school students' problem solving skills. *Educ. Res. Rev.* 11, 998–1007. doi: 10.5897/ERR2016.2756

Greaves, E., Belfield, C., and Allen, R. (2019). Do trainee teachers harm pupil attainment? Isolating the effect of pre-service teachers on contemporaneous pupil performance in 'high-stakes' tests. *Br. Educ. Res. J.* 45, 458–482. doi: 10.1002/berj.3507

Gut, D. M., Dianne, M., Wan, G., Beam, P. C., and Burgess, L. (2016). Reflective Dialog journals: a tool for developing professional competence in novice teachers. *Sch. Univ. Partnerships* 9, 60–70.

Hagger, M. S., and Chatzisarantis, N. L. D. (2016). The trans-contextual model of autonomous motivation in education: conceptual and empirical issues and meta-analysis. *Rev. Educ. Res.* 86, 360–407. doi: 10.3102/0034654315585005

Hortigüela-Alcalá, D., Hernando-Garijo, A., Pérez-Pueyo, Á, and Fernández-Río, J. (2019). Cooperative learning and students' Motivation, social interactions and attitudes: perspectives from two different educational stages. *Sustainability* 11:7005. doi: 10.3390/su11247005

Hortigüela-Alcalá, D., Salicetti, A., and Hernández, J. (2017). Motivational contrast in physical education depending on caloric expenditure. *Rev. Int. Med. Ciencias la Act. Física y del Deport.* 18, 621–635. doi: 10.15366/rimcafd2018.72.002

Hortigüela-Alcalá, D., Salicetti, A., Hernando-Garijo, A., and Pérez Pueyo, Á (2018). Relationship between the level of physical activity and the motivation of physical education teachers. *Sport. Sci. J. Sch. Sport. Phys. Educ. Psychomot.* 4:331. doi: 10.17979/sportis.2018.4.2.3291

Johnson, D. W., and Johnson, R. T. (2009). An educational psychology success story: social interdependence theory and cooperative learning. *Educ. Res.* 38, 365–379. doi: 10.3102/0013189x09339057

Jones, L. (2019). The 'C-Word': novice teachers, class identities and class strategising. *Pedagog. Cult. Soc.* 27, 595–611. doi: 10.1080/14681366.2019.1566161

Kennedy, A. K., Ramseyer Winter, V., and Corbin, M. M. (2019). Physical Education Class and Body Image perception: are they related? *Phys. Educ.* 76:2. doi: 10.18666/TPE-2019-V76-I2-8766

Koka, A. (2013). The relationships between perceived teaching behaviors and motivation in physical education: a one-year longitudinal study. *Scand. J. Educ. Res.* 57, 33–53. doi: 10.1080/00313831.2011.621213

Kolovelonis, A. (2019). Relating students' participation in sport out of school and performance calibration in physical education. *Issues Educ. Res.* 29, 774–789.

Lafont, L., Rivière, C., Darnis, F., and Legrain, P. (2016). How to structure group work? Conditions of efficacy and methodological considerations in physical education. *Eur. Phys. Educ. Rev.* 23, 327–338. doi: 10.1177/1356336X15626639

Le Roux, C. S. (2017). Exploring rigour in autoethnographic research. *Int. J. Soc. Res. Methodol.* 20, 195–207. doi: 10.1080/13645579.2016.1140965

Legrain, P., Escalié, G., Lafont, L., and Chaliès, S. (2019). Cooperative learning: a relevant instructional model for physical education pre-service teacher training? *Phys. Educ. Sport Pedagogy* 24:73–86. doi: 10.1080/17408989.2018.1561838

Liu, W., and Wang, Q. (2018). The processes of teachers' engagement in action research: an ethnographic study in Beijing. *Educ. Action Res.* 26, 258–272. doi: 10.1080/09650792.2017.1307128

Lynch, S., and Curtner-Smith, M. D. (2019). "The education system is broken:" the influence of a sociocultural foundations class on the perspectives and practices of physical education preservice teachers. *J. Teach. Phys. Educ.* 38, 377–387. doi: 10.1123/jtpe.2018-0258

Maher, A. J., and Fitzgerald, H. (2020). Initial teacher education and continuing professional development: the perspectives of special school physical education teachers. *Curr. Stud. Health Phys. Educ.* 11, 18–33. doi: 10.1080/25742981.2019.1696687

Morgan, K. (2019). Applying mastery TARGET structures to cooperative learning in physical education. *J. Phys. Educ. Recreat. Dance* 90, 27–32. doi: 10.1080/07303084.2019.1559677

O'Leary, N., Wattison, N., Edwards, T., and Bryan, K. (2015). Closing the theory-practice gap: physical education students' use of jigsaw learning in a secondary school. *Eur. Phys. Educ. Rev.* 21, 176–194. doi: 10.1177/1356336x14555300

Peterson, J. S. (2019). Presenting a qualitative study: a reviewer's perspective. *Gifted Child Quart.* 63, 147–158. doi: 10.1177/0016986219844789

Pill, S., and SueSee, B. (2017). Including critical thinking and problem solving in physical education. *J. Phys. Educ. Recreat. Dance.* 88, 43–49. doi: 10.1080/07303084.2017.1367741

Randall, V. (2020). Becoming a primary physical educator. *Education* 48, 133–146. doi: 10.1080/03004279.2019.1594330

Richards, K. A., and Templin, T. J. (2011). The influence of a state mandated induction assistance program on the socialization of a beginning physical education teacher. *J. Teach. Phys. Educ.* 30, 340–357. doi: 10.1123/jtpe.30.4.340

Richards, K. A. R., Templin, T. J., and Gaudreault, K. L. (2013). Understanding the realities of school life: recommendations for the preparation of physical education teachers. *Quest* 65, 442–457. doi: 10.1080/00336297.2013.804850

Richards, K. A. R., Templin, T. J., and Graber, K. (2014). The socialization of teachers in physical education: review and recommendations for future works. *Kinesiol. Rev.* 3, 113–134. doi: 10.1123/kr.2013-0006

Roffeei, S. H. M., Yusop, F. D., and Kamarulzaman, Y. (2018). Determinants of innovation culture amongst higher education students. *Turk. Online J. Educ. Technol. - TOJET* 17, 37–50.

Rubel, D., and Okech, J. E. A. (2017). Qualitative research in group work: status, synergies, and implementation. *J. Spec. Gr. Work* 42, 54–86. doi: 10.1080/01933922.2016.1264522

Safronov, P., Bochaver, A., Nisskaya, A., and Koroleva, D. (2020). Together apart: field notes as artefacts of collaborative ethnography. *Ethnogr. Educ.* 15, 109–121. doi: 10.1080/17457823.2019.1600154

Saldaña, J. (2009). *The Coding Manual for Qualitative Researchers*. Thousand Oaks, CA: Sage.

Schenker, K. (2019). Teaching physical activity—a matter of health and equality? *Scand. J. Educ. Res.* 63, 53–68. doi: 10.1080/00313831.2017.1324903

Sevil, J., Abós, A., Aibar, A., Julián, J. J., and García-González, L. (2016). Gender and corporal expression activity in physical education: effect of an intervention on students' motivational processes. *Eur. Phys. Educ. Rev.* 22, 372–389. doi: 10.1177/1356336X15613463

Strauss, A. L., and Corbin, J. M. (2002). *Bases de la Investigación Cualitativa: Técnicas y Procedimientos Para Desarrollar la Teoría Fundamentada*. Colombia: Universidad de Antioquia.

Sudakova, N. E., and Astafyeva, O. N. (2019). Inclusion as a modern cultural universal: reflection and conceptualization. *J. Soc. Stud. Educ. Res.* 10, 212–235.

Swaminathan, R., and Mulvihill, T. M. (2018). *Teaching Qualitative Research: Strategies for Engaging Emerging Scholars*. New York, NY: The Guilford Press.

Viciana, J., and Mayorga-Vega, D. (2017). Influencing factors on planning decision-making among spanish in-service physical education teachers. a population-based study. *Electron. J. Res. Educ. Psychol.* 3, 491–509. doi: 10.14204/ejrep.43.16112

Walker, E., and Johnson, I. L. (2018). Using best practices when implementing the cooperative-learning theory in secondary physical education programs. *Strategies* 31, 5–11. doi: 10.1080/08924562.2018.1465870

Wallace, T. L., and Kuo, E. (2020). Publishing qualitative research in the "journal of educational psychology": synthesizing research perspectives across methodological silos. *J. Educ. Psychol.* 112, 579–583. doi: 10.1037/edu0000474

Wallhead, T., and Dyson, B. (2017). A didactic analysis of content development during cooperative learning in primary physical education. *Eur. Phys. Educ. Rev.* 23, 311–326. doi: 10.1177/1356336x16630221

Watts, T. W., Bailey, D. H., and Drew, C. (2019). Aiming further: addressing the need for high-quality longitudinal research in education. *J. Res. Educ. Effect.* 12, 648–658. doi: 10.1080/19345747.2019.1644692

Wrench, A., and Garrett, R. (2015). Emotional connections and caring: ethical teachers of physical education. *Sport Educ. Soc.* 20, 212–227. doi: 10.1080/13573322.2012.747434

Yeigh, T., and Lynch, D. (2017). Reforming initial teacher education: a call for innovation. *Austr. J. Teacher Educ.* 42, 112–127. doi: 10.14221/ajte.2017v42n12.7

Yuksel, H. S., Sutcu, O., and Ozdemir, B. (2019). Exploring of prospective teachers' metaphoric perceptions about the concepts of "physical education course" and "physical education teacher." *J. Educ. Learn.* 8, 58–68.

Yung, K. W. (2020). Becoming a teacher educator through being a student teacher: an autoethnography in the practicum. *J. Educ. Teach. Int. Res. Pedagogy* 46, 248–250. doi: 10.1080/02607476.2020.1724655

4

Physical Activity in Natural Environments is Associated with Motivational Climate and the Prevention of Harmful Habits

*Manuel Castro-Sánchez[1], Félix Zurita-Ortega[1], José Antonio Pérez-Turpin[2], Javier Cachón-Zagalaz[3], Cristian Cofre-Bolados[4,5], Concepción Suarez-Llorca[6] and Ramón Chacón-Cuberos[7]**

[1] Department of Didactics of Musical, Plastic and Body Expression, Faculty of Fine Arts, University of Granada, Granada, Spain, [2] Department of Didactic General and Specific Training, University of Alicante, Alicante, Spain, [3] Department of Didactics of Musical, Plastic and Body Expression, University of Jaén, Jaén, Spain, [4] School of Physical Activity, Sports and Health Sciences, University of Santiago-Chile, Santiago, Chile, [5] Escuela de Ciencias del Deporte, Facultad de Salud, Universidad Santo Tomás (UST), Santiago, Chile, [6] Department of Evolutionary Psychology and Didactic, University of Alicante, Alicante, Spain, [7] Departamento de Métodos de Investigación y Diagnóstico en Educación, Universidad de Granada, Granada, Spain

***Correspondence:**
Ramón Chacón-Cuberos
rchacon@ugr.es

Background: Practicing physical activity in a natural environment has various benefits that make it an ideal setting to develop healthy behaviors and thereby diminish unhealthy habits. The objective of this study was to develop and verify an explicative model for motivational climate in sport, considering its potential influence on alcohol and tobacco consumption.

Methods: The study included 2273 adolescents from Granada (Spain), analyzing motivational climate (PMCSQ-2), alcohol consumption (AUDIT) and tobacco consumption (FTND). Multi-group structural equation modeling was conducted, yielding an excellent fit ($\chi 2$ = 168.170; gl = 32; p = 0.00; CFI = 0.972; NFI = 0.966; IFI = 0.972; RMSEA = 0.045).

Results: The main findings were: a negative relationship between task climate and alcohol consumption among students practicing physical activities in a natural environment; a positive relationship between ego climate and alcohol consumption among those practicing other types of physical activity; and a positive and direct relationship between alcohol and tobacco consumption, which was stronger among those who did not practice physical activity in a natural environment.

Conclusion: We conclude that physical-sport activity practiced in nature is a key to acquiring healthy patterns characterized by intrinsic motivations in sport and lower consumption of harmful substances.

Keywords: motivation, physical activity, natural environment, alcohol, tobacco

INTRODUCTION

Adolescence represents a key stage in the development and acquisition of healthy and/or harmful habits that will endure throughout adulthood (Urrutia-Pereira et al., 2017). According to Lindgren et al. (2017) it is crucial to understand why tobacco and alcohol consumption begins during adolescence and to determine motivating factors, with the aim of avoiding the emergence of these behaviors and encouraging young people to acquire healthy life habits that persist during adulthood (Taylor et al., 2017).

Most of the research proposes the practice of healthy physical activity as a main alternative to these harmful habits (Barrett et al., 2017). In fact, it has been found a negative relationship between the levels of physical activity and the consumption of alcohol and tobacco, showing benefits at a physical, psychological and social level (Donoghue et al., 2017; Lewis et al., 2017). For these reasons, it is necessary to promote habits related to the practice of physical activity in children and adolescents towards in order to create healthy patterns that could be repeated in adulthood and avoid the development of maladaptative behaviors (Hatano et al., 2017; Montero-Duarte et al., 2019). There is a need to involve the peer group, educational institutions and family in the control of the multiple risk factors for this consumption in adolescents (Lebron et al., 2017).

Various researchers have proposed physical and sports activities as an alternative to these damaging behaviors and as a means of distancing young people from harmful substances (Cerkez et al., 2015). Ayán et al. (2017) reported that tobacco/alcohol consumption was inversely related to sports practice, which provides multiple psychological, physical and social benefits (Kose et al., 2015).

Physical activities in a natural environment have major hedonistic effects and involve interaction with nature in novel surrounds, while they are characterized by less strict rules in comparison to more competitive sports (Lawton et al., 2017). They may therefore be an ideal means for adolescents to acquire healthy habits, improving the physical condition of their whole body (Pretty et al., 2017; World Health Organization, 2017) and enhancing their psychological development in previously unknown settings that promote wellbeing and autonomy. Moreover, the socializing component of this type of activity fosters a feeling of belonging to the group and often requires collaboration to achieve its objectives (Sims-Gould et al., 2017).

Therefore, activities in natural environments appear to be an ideal way to get to know and enjoy the environment while performing motor activities that generate physical, cognitive and social benefits. This is because the natural environment has characteristics that make it conducive to fun, enhancing the sport's hedonistic component (Lorenz et al., 2017). This type of physical activity has a strong motivational component, which is key to modifying the intensity and direction of behavior, because the activities carried out in the natural environment focus on fun and pleasure, eliminating the negative connotations of excessive competitiveness that is sometimes present in sports (Calogiuri and Elliott, 2017). Psychologists consider motivation as one of the most influential factors to explain human behaviors (Gutiérrez and López, 2012).

Various studies identified the benefits derived from the practice of physical activity in nature, classified as follows: a decrease in cardiovascular diseases, a decrease in the rates of overweight and obesity, preventive effect against type 2 diabetes, various psychosocial benefits such as reduced levels of anxiety, depression, stress and emotional distress (Casper and Pfahl, 2015; Moreno et al., 2015; Cox et al., 2017; Gómez et al., 2018).

The practice of physical activity carried out in the natural environment in a non-competitive way, in which the subject focuses on the achievement of intrinsic goals, orienting itself more towards intrinsic motivations, constitutes a factor of prevention against the consumption of alcohol and tobacco. Nevertheless, physical activity focused on the achievement of extrinsic goals, in which a motivational orientation towards the ego is adopted, may represent a risk for the consumption of these substances (Bengoechea et al., 2017).

The importance of motivation in people's daily lives lies in their influence to perform certain behaviors or not, providing a theoretical basis to understand human behavior (Ryan and Deci, 2017). In the case of physical activity and sports, it will be valid to understand a multitude of psychological and behavioral factors related to their practice (Dweck, 1986). This study is focused on the motivational climate in sport, based on the Achievement Goal Theory (Nicholls, 1989) derived from the Self-determination Theory of Deci and Ryan (2008). According to this model, physical activities can be either ego-oriented, focused on demonstrating skills, competing with group members and defeating rivals, or task-oriented, centring on personal effort and self-improvement with greater self-determined motivation and enjoyment of the activity, enhancing adherence to physical activity practice (Newton et al., 2000; Palmer et al., 2017).

After reviewing the existing literature, the existence of an association between motivational climates and the development of healthy or maladaptive behaviors related to the consumption of harmful substances is observed. Therefore, it is important to analyze the possible relationship between the motivational climate in sports and the consumption of alcohol and tobacco, as well as to analyze the differences according to whether physical activity practice is performed in a standard way or in the natural environment because this can be constituted as a protective factor against this type of unhealthy habits. For these reasons, the objective of this study was to develop an explicative model for motivational climate in sport, considering its potential influence on alcohol and tobacco consumption. We performed multi-group structural equation modeling (SEM) as a function of the type of physical activity practiced by adolescents, comparing between activities in a natural environment and those in other settings.

MATERIALS AND METHODS

Subjects and Design

A quantitative, descriptive and cross-sectional study was undertaken, followed by a relational study developed using Structural Equation Modeling to analyze the degree of dependence among the different study variables.

Participants were selected from among the 11030 secondary school students in the city of Granada in southern Spain (data provided by the Education Ministry of the Junta de Andalucía). A representative sample (0.02 error; 95.5% CI) was selected by stratification, proportionality and randomization techniques, considering sex (male-female) and cycle (first-second). The inclusion criteria were: a) that the adolescents attended Compulsory Secondary Education in the city of Granada; b) not have any type of pathology that prevents them from participating in the research: c) have the informed consent of the parents or legal guardians to participate in the study. The final sample included 2273 adolescents, aged between 13 and 17 years (M = 14.94 years; SD = 1.25). The study was approved by the Research Ethics Committee of the University of Granada (641/CEIH/2018) and followed the principles of the 1975 Helsinki Declaration. Informed consent was obtained from all participants and their guardians. The anonymity of the participants was preserved at all times.

Measures

The perceived motivational climate in sport was evaluated with the 33-item Perceived Motivational Climate in Sport Questionnaire (PMCSQ-2), alongside the Spanish validation form González-Cutre et al. (2008). Participants responded to each item on a five-point scale from 1 (strongly disagree) to 5 (strongly agree). The questionnaire comprised two higher-order scales, each containing three subscales (task: cooperative learning [CL], effort/improvement [EI] and important role [IR]; ego: member rivalry [MR], unequal recognition [UR] and punishment for mistakes [PM]). Internal consistency of the data was assessed using Cronbach's alpha and was acceptable for both perceived task-involved climate (TC) and perceived ego-involved climate (EC) subscales ($\alpha = 0.860$ and $\alpha = 0.810$, respectively).

Alcohol consumption was assessed using the Spanish adaptation by Rubio (1998) of the Alcohol Use Disorders Identification Test (AUDIT) (Saunders et al., 1993). AUDIT comprises ten items, the first eight are evaluated on a five-point Likert scale (0 = Never; 4 = Daily) and the last two items on a three-point Likert scale, yielding a score of 0, 2, or 4 points. The first three items of the AUDIT describe the frequency of consumption, the next three describe the level of dependence and the remaining four items are related to harmful consumption. Item scores are added together to produce an overall score for each dimension. Cronbach's alpha for the data was $\alpha = 0.832$.

Tobacco consumption was assessed using the Spanish adaptation by Villareal-González (2009) of the Fagerström Test for Nicotine Dependence (FTND) (Heatherton et al., 1991). This instrument evaluates the number or amount of cigarettes,

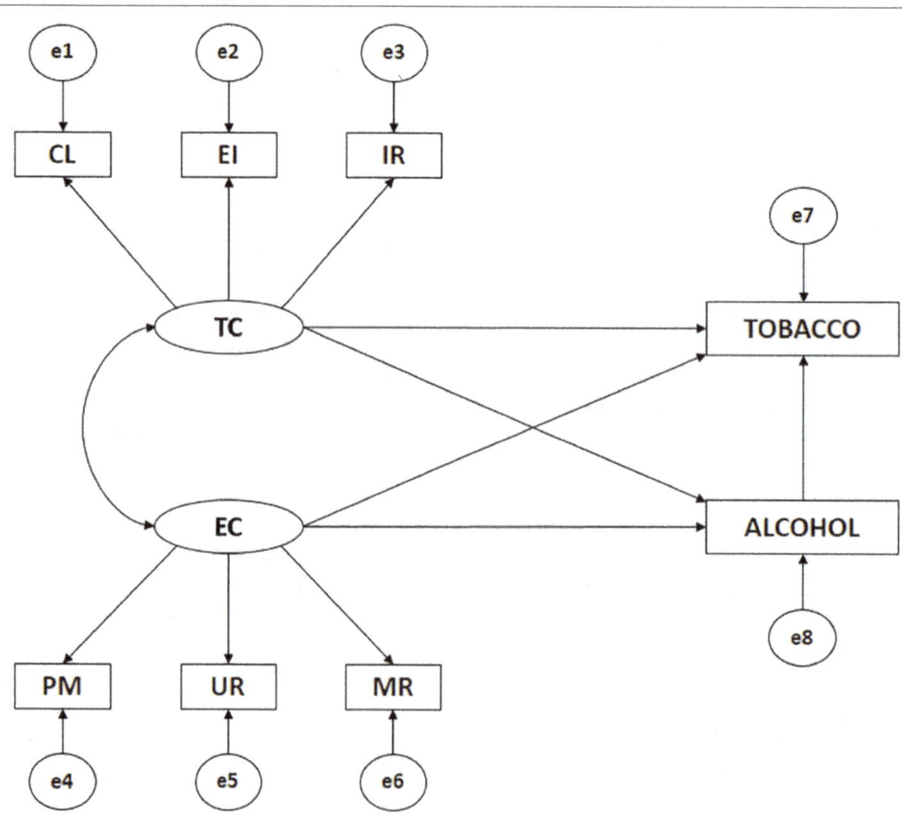

FIGURE 1 | Model theories: Task climate, ego climate, alcohol consumption and tobacco consumption. TC, Climate-Task; CL, Climate-Task Cooperative Learning; EI, Climate-Task Effort/Improvement; IR, Climate-Task Important Role; EC, Climate-Ego; MR, Climate-ego Intra-team Member rivalry; UR, Climate-ego Unequal Recognition; PM, Climate-ego Punishment for Mistakes; TOBACCO, Tobacco Consumption; ALCOHOL, Alcohol Consumption.

impulse to smoke and nicotine dependency. It includes six questions, the first four are dichotomous (0 = No and 1 = Yes), and the other two follow a four-option Likert-type scale (0 = Never and 3 = Always). The sum of items ranges between 0 and 10, establishing four categories (0 = Non-smoker, 1–4 = Low dependency, 5–6 = Moderate dependency and >6 = High dependency). The reliability determined for this investigation was α = 0.956.

Procedure

Permission was obtained from the Education Office of the Junta de Andalucía for the participation of secondary schools in the city of Granada, selected according to convenience sampling of the study categories. The management of each educational centre was informed about the nature of the research and the need for the collaboration of students. Authorisation forms were provided to obtain the informed consent of legal guardians.

Participants were guaranteed the anonymity of the information gathered, clarifying that it would only be used for scientific purposes. Interviewers were present during data gathering to solve any possible doubts, and no problems were reported. Teachers, counselors and other collaborators were thanked and promised a report on the data obtained, respecting confidentiality.

Statistical Analysis

SPSS® version 22.0 (IBM Corp, Armonk, NY, United States) was used for data analyses. Descriptive analysis was performed, determining frequencies and mean values. Associative analysis was conducted using Pearson's chi-square test. The significance level was set at 0.05. AMOS version 23.0 was used to create statistical models with instructive equations at the latent variable level. SEM was used to analyze the relationships between perceived motivational climate in sport, alcohol consumption and tobacco consumption (**Figure 1**). After developing the theoretical model, path analysis was conducted, considering the relationships of the matrix based on a multi-group analysis classifying participants in terms of the type of physical activity practiced as grouping variable (Marsh, 2007). Thus, two different structural models were configured to verify whether relationships among study variables varied as a function of the type of physical activity practiced: "physical activity in a natural environment" and "other type of physical activity."

The SEM for these data is characterized by eight observed variables and two latent variables. This model provides causal explanations for the latent variables from the relationships observed between indicators. Squares represent the observed variables, circles the error terms, and ovals the latent variables. The exogenous latent variables, TC and EC, were each inferred

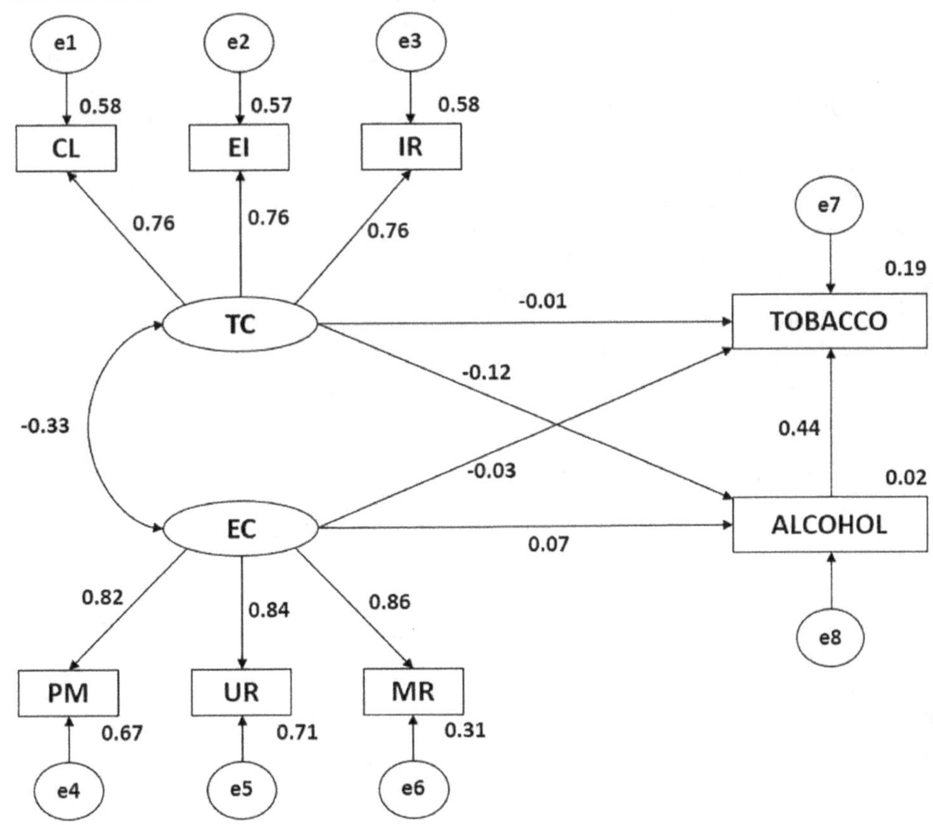

FIGURE 2 | Structural equation model in those who practice physical activity in a natural environment. TC, Climate-Task; CL, Climate-Task Cooperative Learning; EI, Climate-Task Effort/Improvement; IR, Climate-Task Important Role; EC, Climate-Ego; MR, Climate-ego Intra-team Member rivalry; UR, Climate-ego Unequal Recognition; PM, Climate-ego Punishment for Mistakes; TOBACCO, Tobacco Consumption; ALCOHOL, Alcohol Consumption.

using three indicators; for TC: CL, EI and IR; and for EC: MR, UR and PM. Alcohol consumption (ALCOHOL) and tobacco consumption (TOBACCO) were observed endogenous variables.

The bi-directional arrow (covariance) relates exogenous variables, while the unidirectional arrows are lines of influence between the latent and observable indicators, and are interpreted as multivariate regression coefficients. In addition, error prediction terms are associated with endogenous variables. The maximum likelihood (ML) method was used to estimate relationships between variables. We chose this method because it is consistent, unbiased and invariant to types of scale for variables with normal distribution.

Model fit was examined to verify the compatibility of the proposed model and the empirical information gathered. Goodness of fit was tested using a number of indexes briefly described here Chacón et al. (2018). Chi-square analysis was conducted when non-significant p-values indicated a good model fit. Comparative fit index (CFI), normalized fit index (NFI) and increase fit index (IFI) values >0.90 indicate acceptable model fit while values >0.95 indicate excellent model fit. Root mean square error of approximation (RMSEA) values <0.08 indicate acceptable model fit while values <0.05 indicate excellent model fit (Marsh, 2007).

RESULTS

Almost all model fit indexes indicated an excellent fit. A significant chi-square value was obtained ($\chi 2 = 168.170$; gl = 32; $p < 0.001$); however, given that this index has no upper limit and may also be sensitive to sample size, we also considered other standardized indexes less sensitive to sample size (Jöreskog, 1997). The NFI was 0.96, indicating an acceptable model fit. The CFI and the IFI yielded a value of 0.97 for both, indicating an excellent model fit. The RMSEA value was 0.45, indicating excellent fit (Browne and Cudeck, 1993). In summary, the data suggest that the model fits the empirical data well.

Figure 2 and **Table 1** exhibit the estimated values of the structural model parameters for students who practiced physical activity in a natural environment. They should present adequate magnitude, and the effects should significantly differ from zero. Likewise, improper estimations should not be obtained, such as negative variances. Statistically significant positive and direct relationships ($p < 0.005$) were observed among all categories of motivational climate and its dimensions. There was a significant ($p < 0.005$) negative indirect relationship between TC and EC ($r = -0.331$).

Analysis of the influence of indicators on each latent variable showed statistical significance in all cases ($p < 0.005$), with all relationships being positive and direct. In the case of TC, the highest correlation coefficient was obtained with IR ($r = 0.763$), followed by CL ($r = 0.760$) and EI ($r = 0.756$). In the case of EC, the highest correlation was with UR ($r = 0.842$), followed by PM ($r = 0.819$) and MR ($r = 0.556$).

A significant negative and direct association ($p < 0.005$) was observed between TC and alcohol consumption ($r = -0.121$), which was not associated with EC. No association was found

TABLE 1 | Weights and standardized regression weights of those who practice physical activity in a natural environment.

Relationship between variables	RW				SRW
	Estimations	SE	CR	P	Estimations
ALCOHOL ← EC	0.736	0.334	2.206	0.027	0.069
ALCOHOL ← TC	−1.008	0.264	−3.811	***	−0.121
CL ← TC	1.000	–	–	***	0.760
EI ← TC	0.845	0.035	24.109	***	0.756
IR ← TC	0.953	0.039	24.174	***	0.763
MR ← EC	1.000	–	–	***	0.556
UR ← EC	1.560	0.080	19.387	***	0.842
PM ← EC	1.396	0.071	19.537	***	0.819
TOBACCO ← TC	−0.058	0.120	−0.485	0.627	−0.014
TOBACCO ← ALCOHOL	0.220	0.012	18.289	***	0.441
TOBACCO ← EC	−0.153	0.151	−1.011	0.312	−0.029
EC ↔ TC	−0.102	0.011	−8.893	***	−0.331

*RW, Regression Weights; SRW, Standardized Regression Weights; SE, Estimation of Error; CR, Critical Ratio. TC, Task-involved Climate; EC, Ego-involved Climate; CL, Cooperative Learning; EI, Effort/Improvement; IR, Important Role; PM, Punishment for Mistakes; UR, Unequal Recognition; MR, Member Rivalry. *p < 0.05; **p < 0.01; ***p < 0.001.*

between EC or TC and tobacco consumption. A statistically significant ($p < 0.005$) positive and direct association was found between tobacco and alcohol consumption ($r = 0.441$).

Figure 3 and **Table 2** exhibit the estimated values of structural model parameters for students who practice another type of physical activity. They should present an adequate magnitude, thee effects should significantly differ from zero and improper estimations should not be obtained, including negative variances. Statistically significant ($p < 0.005$) positive and direct relationships were observed between both TC and EC and their dimensions. There was a significant ($p < 0.005$) negative and indirect relationship between TC and EC ($r = -0.325$).

Analysis of the influence of indicators on each latent variable found statistically significant ($p < 0.005$) positive and direct relationships in all cases. In the case of TC, IR showed the highest correlation coefficient ($r = 0.790$), followed by CL ($r = 0.753$) and EI ($r = 0.750$), while EC showed the highest association with UR ($r = 0.860$), followed by PM ($r = 0.809$) and MR ($r = 0.524$), as in the model for physical activity in a natural environment.

A significant ($p < 0.005$) positive and direct association was found between EC and alcohol consumption ($r = 0.196$), which showed no association with TC. As in the model for physical activity in a natural environment, no association was found between EC or TC and tobacco consumption.

A statistically significant ($p < 0.005$) positive and direct relationship was observed between tobacco consumption and alcohol consumption ($r = 0.497$). The relationship was stronger in the case of those practicing activities in a natural environment.

DISCUSSION

The SEM developed in this study reveals an excellent fit in all evaluation indexes, as a function of the number

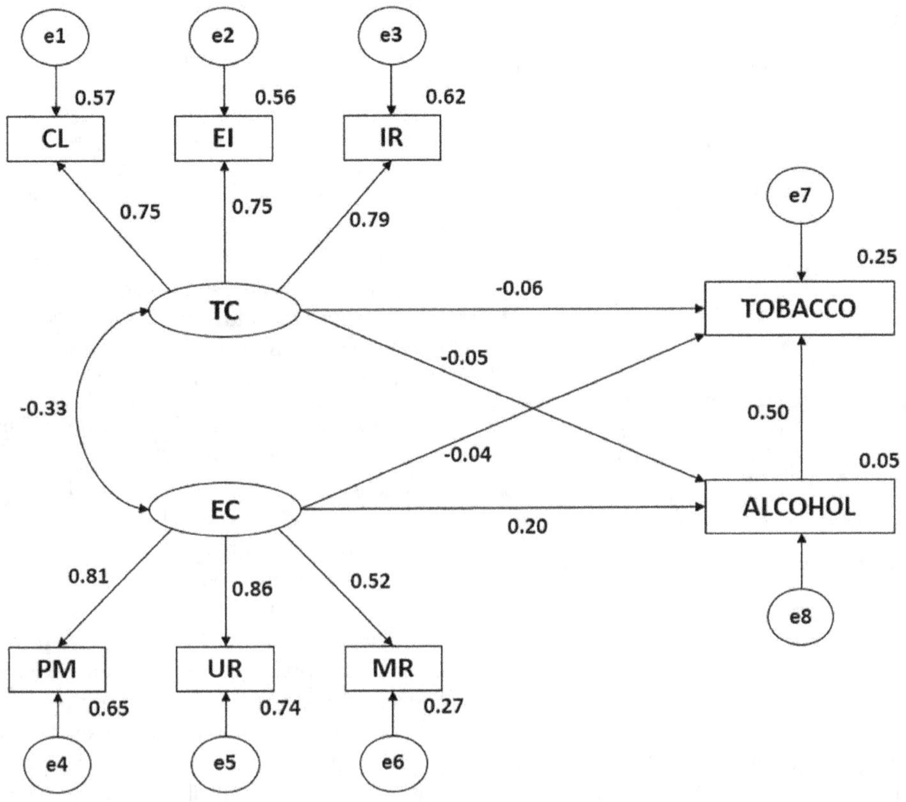

FIGURE 3 | Structural equation model in those practicing another type of physical activity. TC, Climate-Task; CL, Climate-Task Cooperative Learning; EI, Climate-Task Effort/Improvement; IR, Climate-Task Important Role; EC, Climate-Ego; MR, Climate-ego Intra-team Member rivalry; UR, Climate-ego Unequal Recognition; PM, Climate-ego Punishment for Mistakes; TOBACCO, Tobacco Consumption; ALCOHOL, Alcohol Consumption.

of participants, and significance was reached. A multigroup analysis of structural equations was conducted to compare the associations between sport-related motivational climate and harmful substance consumption according to the type of physical activity (in natural environments or otherwise). The path model developed achieved excellent fit indexes and represents a valid explicative model to elucidate the relationships between motivational factors and alcohol and tobacco consumption in Spanish secondary school students, in line with various national and international studies (Jaakkola et al., 2016; Lee and Chelladurai, 2016; Stenling et al., 2017; Chacón et al., 2018; Chacón-Cuberos et al., 2018).

Analyzing motivational climate, the proposed structural model revealed a significant inverse relationship between TC and EC among students practicing physical exercise either in a natural environment or in other settings, observing a stronger and more differentiated association among the former. Thus, individuals who practice physical-sports activities in a natural environment perceive a high climate of involvement with the task and a low climate of involvement with the ego, the opposite of the perceptions of those practicing activities in other settings (Navarro-Patón et al., 2018; Ring and Kavussanu, 2018). It appears that students adopt a predominant orientation, either towards the task, rewarding effort and self-improvement, or towards the ego, fomenting rivalry among group members and the pure demonstration of skills (Gano-Overway et al., 2017; Erturan-Ilker et al., 2018). In the case of those practicing sport in a natural environment, this inverse relationship is stronger, explained by the greater group cohesion and the ludic component of physical activities in this environment, promoting cooperation among group members. In contrast, physical activities in other environments place a higher value on the defeat of rivals and the exhibition of their skills (Arslanoglu, 2016; Amaro et al., 2017; Castro-Sánchez et al., 2019).

The most influential category for the TC dimension was IR, while the most influential indicator for EC was UR, especially in the case of students who did not practice physical activity in a natural environment. Harwood et al. (2015), reported that students who assign greater importance in their physical activity practices to social relationships, characteristic of activities developed in a natural environment, show a higher task orientation, prioritizing the ludic component of this type of activity. In activities developed in natural environments, the competitive desire to stand out in the group is attenuated in favor of a greater enjoyment of the activity, focusing on the fun and play it offers, dissociated from the competitive component characteristic of sports (Gerdin and Pringle, 2017).

Adolescents who practice physical activity in nature show a lower tendency to consume harmful substances (alcohol and tobacco) than adolescents who do physical activity in

TABLE 2 | Weights and standardized regression weights of those who practice another type of physical activity.

Relationship between variables	RW				SRW
	Estimations	SE	CR	P	Estimations
ALCOHOL ← EC	2.327	0.541	4.304	***	0.196
ALCOHOL ← TC	−0.418	0.387	−1.080	0.280	−0.048
CL ← TC	1.000	–	–	***	0.753
EI ← TC	0.839	0.049	17.076	***	0.750
IR ← TC	1.001	0.058	17.323	***	0.790
MR ← EC	1.000	–	–	***	0.524
UR ← EC	1.618	0.127	12.771	***	0.860
PM ← EC	1.469	0.113	12.984	***	0.809
TOBACCO ← TC	−0.311	0.189	−1.642	0.101	−0.065
TOBACCO ← ALCOHOL	0.274	0.019	14.760	***	0.497
TOBACCO ← EC	−0.273	0.259	−1.053	0.292	−0.042
EC ↔ TC	−0.099	0.016	−6.092	***	−0.325

*RW, Regression Weights; SRW, Standardized Regression Weights; SE, Estimation of Error; CR, Critical Ratio. TC, Task-involved Climate; EC, Ego-involved Climate; CL, Cooperative Learning; EI, Effort/Improvement; IR, Important Role; PM, Punishment for Mistakes; UR, Unequal Recognition; MR, Member Rivalry. *p < 0.05; **p < 0.01; ***p < 0.001.*

other environments. This association is fulfilled with alcohol, but not with the consumption of tobacco. In terms of the relationship between motivational climate and alcohol consumption, a negative and direct association was observed between TC and alcohol consumption in students practicing sport in a natural environment, while a positive relationship between EC and alcohol consumption was found in students practicing other types of physical activity. Accordingly, physical activity in natural environments is related to lower alcohol consumption, associated with task orientation, while activities in other settings is related to higher alcohol consumption, associated with ego orientation. It is considered that the practice of physical activity in natural environments is a protective factor against the consumption of harmful substances, including alcohol and tobacco (Dodge et al., 2017). This is explained by the generally hedonistic aim of physical activity in a natural environment, geared to enjoyment, contrasting with the performance-oriented objective of other physical-sport activities, leading to possible frustrations when the individual fails, favoring the consumption of alcohol and tobacco, among other harmful behaviors.

The relationship between tobacco and alcohol consumption was positive and direct but was stronger and more differentiated among students practicing physical activity in settings other than nature. This is consistent with the aforementioned proposition that physical-sport activities not developed in natural environments may pose a risk of alcohol consumption due to its higher competitive component (Cronholm et al., 2017). In addition, the state of euphoria generated by the positive results in sports competition causes some young people consume alcohol in order to celebrate the achievements. The natural environment enhances the enjoyment and involvement of adolescents in their activities, hence prioritizing task orientation and favoring lower levels of alcohol consumption (Nooijen et al., 2017) and higher adherence to physical activity during adulthood (Mäkelä et al., 2017).

This investigation permitted analysis and verification of the relationships between motivational factors and harmful substance consumption. However, it was not possible to infer cause-effect relationships due to its cross-sectional design, and longitudinal interventional studies are warranted based on programs of physical activity in a natural environment. It would be interesting for future studies that use the mixed methods study designs would be interesting to address this topic, qualitative research design is needed.

The main conclusion of this study is that physical activity in nature has a ludic component that favors a more self-determined motivation that may be related to lower alcohol consumption. Enjoyment and group cohesion prevail in this environment, whereas there is a greater motivational ego orientation in other settings, which may be related to higher alcohol consumption. The task motivational climate, both in sporting contexts and those linked to the practice of healthy physical activity in nature, constitutes a protective factor against the development of harmful behaviors such as the consumption of harmful substances, the development of sedentary habits or poor diet. Therefore, physical-sport activities in a natural environment are considered important to acquire healthy behaviors associated with adherence to physical activity practice and a lower consumption of harmful substances.

We propose the incorporation of activities in natural environments in school programs with the aim of reducing harmful behaviors and improving the health of adolescents through enjoyment-centered physical activities. In addition, it is necessary to promote task-oriented motivational climates in the adolescent stage, both in the context of the practice of daily physical activity and in competitive sport. This is because it relates to healthier behaviors and greater adhesion to the practice of physical activity that will last over time. To achieve this, teamwork should be encouraged, rewarding the effort to learn and personal improvement. On the contrary, excessive competitiveness must be suppressed, linking sports achievement to progress and not results. In this sense, the playful component of physical activity should be given special importance.

ETHICS STATEMENT

The research Ethics Committee of the University of Granada approved this study with code 641/CEIH/2018. Written informed consent was obtained from the parents/legal guardians of all participants.

AUTHOR CONTRIBUTIONS

RC-C, FZ-O, JP-T, and MC-S conceived the hypothesis of this study. FZ-O, MC-S, and CC-B participated in data collection.

RC-C, MC-S, and CS-L analyzed the data. RC-C, JC-Z, and JP-T wrote the manuscript with significant input from MC-S. All authors contributed to data interpretation of the statistical analysis, and read and approved the final manuscript.

REFERENCES

Amaro, L. A., Prado, P. A., Paiano, R., Verardi, C. E., Larizzatti, M. F., and Hirota, V. B. (2017). Correlation between goal orientation and attitudes of Brazilian elite swimmers. *J. Phys. Educ. Sport* 17, 783–788. doi: 10.7752/jpes.2017.02118

Arslanoglu, C. (2016). Relationship between target orientations and perceived motivational climate levels of students engaged in individual and team sports activities. *Int. J. Environ. Sci. Educ.* 11, 3311–3318.

Ayán, C., Molina, A. J., Varela, V., Cancela, J. M., Barrio, J. P., and Martín, V. (2017). Relationship between tobacco consumption and sport practice among health and education science university students. *Enfermería Clin.* 27, 21–27. doi: 10.1016/j.enfcle.2016.08.003

Barrett, P., Imamura, F., Brage, S., Griffin, S. J., Wareham, N. J., and Forouhi, N. G. (2017). Sociodemographic, lifestyle and behavioral factors associated with consumption of sweetened beverages among adults in cambridgeshire, UK: the fenland study. *Public Health Nutr.* 20, 2766–2777. doi: 10.1017/S136898001700177X

Bengoechea, E. G., Wilson, P. M., and Dunn, S. (2017). From liability to challenge: complex environments are associated with favorable psychosocial outcomes in adolescent sport participants. *J. Adolesc.* 58, 74–83. doi: 10.1016/j.adolescence.2017.05.004

Browne, M. W., and Cudeck, R. (1993). *Testing Structural Equation Models.* Beverly Hills, CA: Sage.

Calogiuri, G., and Elliott, L. R. (2017). Why do people exercise in natural environments? Norwegian adults' motives for nature-, gym-, and sports-based exercise. *Int. J. Environ. Res. Public Health* 14, 377–386. doi: 10.3390/ijerph14040377

Casper, J. M., and Pfahl, M. E. (2015). *Sport Management and the Natural Environment: Theory and Practice.* New York, NY: Routledge.

Castro-Sánchez, M., Zurita-Ortega, F., and Chacón-Cuberos, R. (2019). Motivation towards sport based on socio-demographic variables in university students from Granada. *J. Sport Health Res.* 11, 55–68.

Cerkez, I., Culjak, Z., Zenic, N., Sekulic, D., and Kondric, M. (2015). Harmful alcohol drinking among adolescents: the influence of sport participation, religiosity, and parental factors. *J. Child Adolesc. Subst. Abuse* 24, 94–101. doi: 10.1080/1067828x.2013.764372

Chacón, R., Zurita, F., Puertas, P., Knox, E., Cofré, C., Viciana, V., et al. (2018). Relationship between healthy habits and perceived motivational climate in sport among university students: a structural equation model. *Sustainability* 10:938. doi: 10.3390/su10040938

Chacón-Cuberos, R., Castro-Sánchez, M., González-Campos, G., and Zurita-Ortega, F. (2018). Victimization in the school, digital leisure and irritability: analysis using structural equations. *Relieve* 24, 1–12. doi: 10.7203/relieve.21.1.12614

Cox, D. T., Shanahan, D. F., Hudson, H. L., Plummer, K. E., Siriwardena, G. M., Fuller, R. A., et al. (2017). Doses of neighborhood nature: the benefits for mental health of living with nature. *BioScience* 67, 147–155. doi: 10.1093/biosci/biw173

Cronholm, F., Rosengren, B. E., Karlsson, C., and Karlsson, M. K. (2017). A physical activity intervention program in school is also accompanied by higher leisure-time physical activity: a prospective controlled 3-year study in 194 prepubertal children. *J. Phys. Activ. Health* 14, 301–307. doi: 10.1123/jpah.2016-0213

Deci, E. L., and Ryan, R. M. (2008). Self-determination theory: a macrotheory of human motivation, development, and health. *Can. Psychol.* 48, 182–185. doi: 10.1037/a0012801

Dodge, T., Clarke, P., and Dwan, R. (2017). The relationship between physical activity and alcohol use among adults in the united states: a systematic review of the literature. *Am. J. Health Promot.* 31, 97–108. doi: 10.1177/0890117116664710

Donoghue, K., Rose, H., Boniface, S., Deluca, P., Coulton, S., Alam, M. F., et al. (2017). Alcohol consumption, early-onset drinking, and health-related consequences in adolescents presenting at emergency departments in England. *J. Adolesc. Health* 60, 438–446. doi: 10.1016/j.jadohealth.2016.11.017

Dweck, C. S. (1986). Motivational processes affecting learning. *Am. Psychol.* 41, 1040–1048. doi: 10.1037/0003-066X.41.10.1040

Erturan-Ilker, G., Yu, C., Alemdaroğlu, U., and Köklü, Y. (2018). Basic psychological needs and self-determined motivation in PE to predict health-related fitness level. *J. Sport Health Res.* 10, 91–100.

Gano-Overway, L. A., Steele, E., Boyce, B. A., and Whaley, D. (2017). Exploring relationships between the coach-initiated motivational climate and psychological coping skills over the high school American football season. *Int. J. Sports Sci. Coaching* 12, 790–794. doi: 10.1177/1747954117738873

Gerdin, G., and Pringle, R. (2017). The politics of pleasure: an ethnographic examination exploring the dominance of the multi-activity sport-based physical education model. *Sport Educ. Soc.* 22, 194–213. doi: 10.1080/13573322.2015.1019448

Gómez, E. A., Ceballos, O., and Enríquez, M. C. (2018). Physical activity level, energy balance and excess weight in university students. *Sport* 7, 101–108.

González-Cutre, D., Sicilia, A., and Moreno, J. A. (2008). Cognitive-social model of achievement motivation in physical education. *Psicothema* 20, 642–651.

Gutiérrez, M., and López, E. (2012). Motivation, student behavior and academic performance. *Infancia Aprendizaje* 35, 61–72. doi: 10.1174/021037012798977421

Harwood, C. G., Keegan, R. J., Smith, J. M., and Raine, A. S. (2015). A systematic review of the intrapersonal correlates of motivational climate perceptions in sport and physical activity. *Psychol. Sport Exerc.* 18, 9–25. doi: 10.1016/j.psychsport.2014.11.005

Hatano, K., Sugimura, K., and Klimstra, T. A. (2017). Which came first, personality traits or identity processes during early and middle adolescence? *J. Res. Pers.* 67, 120–131. doi: 10.1016/j.jrp.2016.06.014

Heatherton, T., Kozlowski, L., Frecker, R., and Fagerström, K. O. (1991). The fagerström test of nicotine dependence: a revision of the fagerström tolerance questionnaire. *Br. J. Addict.* 86, 1119–1127. doi: 10.1111/j.1360-0443.1991.tb01879.x

Jaakkola, T., Ntoumanis, N., and Liukkonen, J. (2016). Motivational climate, goal orientation, perceived sport ability, and enjoyment within Finnish junior ice hockey players. *Scand. J. Med. Sci. Sports* 26, 109–115. doi: 10.1111/sms.12410

Jöreskog, K. G. (1997). "Structural Equation Models in the Social Sciences: Specification estimation and testing," in *Applications of Statistics*, ed. P. R. Krishnaiah (Amsterdam: North Holland Publishing Company), 265–287.

Kose, S., Steinberg, J., Moeller, F., Gowin, J., Zuniga, E., Kamdar, Z., et al. (2015). Neural correlates of impulsive aggressive behavior in subjects with a history of alcohol dependence. *Behav. Neurosci.* 129, 183–196. doi: 10.1037/bne0000038

Lawton, E., Brymer, E., Clough, P., and Denovan, A. (2017). The relationship between the physical activity environment, nature relatedness, anxiety, and the psychological well-being benefits of regular exercisers. *Front. Psychol.* 8:1058. doi: 10.3389/fpsyg.2017.01058

Lebron, C., Stoutenberg, M., Janowsky, M., Asfour, L., Huang, S., and Prado, G. (2017). The role of physical activity and sedentary behavior in substance use and risky sex behaviors in hispanic adolescents. *J. Early Adolesc.* 37, 910–924. doi: 10.1177/0272431616636230

Lee, Y. H., and Chelladurai, P. (2016). Affectivity, emotional labor, emotional exhaustion, and emotional intelligence in coaching. *J. Appl. Sport Psychol.* 28, 170–184. doi: 10.1080/10413200.2015.1092481

Lewis, B. A., Napolitano, M. A., Buman, M. P., Williams, D. M., and Nigg, C. R. (2017). Future directions in physical activity intervention research: expanding our focus to sedentary behaviors, technology, and dissemination. *J. Behav. Med.* 40, 112–126. doi: 10.1007/s10865-016-9797-8

Lindgren, K. P., Neighbors, C., Gasser, M. L., Ramirez, J. J., and Cvencek, D. (2017). A review of implicit and explicit substance self-concept as a predictor of alcohol and tobacco use and misuse. *Am. J. Drug Alcohol Abuse* 43, 237–246. doi: 10.1080/00952990.2016.1229324

Lorenz, K. A., Van Der Mars, H., Kulinna, P. H., Ainsworth, B. E., and Hovell, M. F. (2017). Environmental and behavioral influences of physical activity in junior high school students. *J. Phys. Act. Health* 14, 785–792. doi: 10.1123/jpah.2016-0709

Mäkelä, S., Aaltonen, S., Korhonen, T., Rose, R. J., and Kaprio, J. (2017). Diversity of leisure-time sport activities in adolescence as a predictor of leisure-time physical activity in adulthood. *Scand. J. Med. Sci. Sports* 27, 1902–1912. doi: 10.1111/sms.12837

Marsh, H. W. (2007). "Application of confirmatory factor analysis and structural equation modeling in sport/exercise psychology," in *Handbook of Sport Psychology*, 3rd Edn, eds G. Tenenbaum and R. C. Eklund (New York, NY: Wiley), 774–798. doi: 10.1002/9781118270011.ch35

Montero-Duarte, A., Bogas, R., Barradas, J. M., Gómez, S., and Chacón-Cuberos, R. (2019). Analysis and relationship between the problematic use of video games and the level of physical activity in adolescents of Huelva. ducation, Sport, Health and Physical Activity (ESHPA). *Int. J.* 3, 95–106.

Moreno, L., Cano, M., Orellana, Y., and Kain, J. (2015). Grado de cumplimiento de niños chilenos de bajos recursos con la recomendación diaria de actividad física: diferencia entre semana y fin de semana según estado nutricional. *Nutr. Hosp.* 31, 2195–2201. doi: 10.3305/nh.2015.31.5.8058

Navarro-Patón, R., Lago-Ballesteros, J., Basanta-Camiño, S., and Arufe Giráldez, V. (2018). Assessment of the basic psychological needs in physical education according to age, gender and educational stage. *J. Hum. Sport Exerc.* 13, 710–719. doi: 10.14198/jhse.2018.133.20

Newton, M., Duda, J. L., and Yin, Z. (2000). Examination of the psychometric properties of the perceived motivational climate in sport questionnaire-2 in a sample of female athletes. *J. Sports Sci.* 18, 275–290. doi: 10.1080/026404100365018

Nicholls, J. G. (1989). *The Competitive Ethos and Democratic Education*. London: Harvard University Press.

Nooijen, C. F., Möller, J., Forsell, Y., Ekblom, M., Galanti, M. R., and Engström, K. (2017). Do unfavourable alcohol, smoking, nutrition and physical activity predict sustained leisure time sedentary behavior? A population-based cohort study. *Prev. Med.* 101, 23–27. doi: 10.1016/j.ypmed.2017.05.019

Palmer, K. K., Chinn, K. M., and Robinson, L. E. (2017). Using achievement goal theory in motor skill instruction: a systematic review. *Sports Med.* 47, 2569–2583. doi: 10.1007/s40279-017-0767-2

Pretty, J., Rogerson, M., and Barton, J. (2017). Green mind theory: how brain-body-behavior links into natural and social environments for healthy habits. *Int. J. Environ. Res. Public Health* 14, 706–711. doi: 10.3390/ijerph14070706

Ring, C., and Kavussanu, M. (2018). The impact of achievement goals on cheating in sport. *Psychol. Sport Exerc.* 35, 98–103. doi: 10.1016/j.psychsport.2017.11.016

Rubio, G. (1998). Validation of the test for the identification of alcohol use disorders (AUDIT) in primary care. *Rev. Clín. Española* 198, 11–14. doi: 10.1016/S0212-6567(05)70552-7

Ryan, R. M., and Deci, E. L. (2017). *Self-Determination Theory: Basic Psychological Needs in Motivation, Development, and Wellness*. New York, NY: Guilford Publications.

Saunders, J., Aasland, O., Babor, T., De la Fuente, J., and Grant, M. (1993). Development of the alcohol use disorders identification test (AUDIT): who collaborative project on early detection of persons with harmful alcohol consumption-II. *Addiction* 88, 791–804. doi: 10.1111/j.1360-0443.1993.tb02093.x

Sims-Gould, J., Vazirian, S., Li, N., Remick, R., and Khan, K. (2017). Jump step-a community based participatory approach to physical activity & mental wellness. *BMC Psychiatry* 17:319. doi: 10.1186/s12888-017-1476-y

Stenling, A., Ivarsson, A., Hassmén, P., and Lindwall, M. (2017). Longitudinal associations between athletes' controlled motivation, ill-being, and perceptions of controlling coach behaviors: a bayesian latent growth curve approach. *Psychol. Sport Exerc.* 30, 205–214. doi: 10.1016/j.psychsport.2017.03.002

Taylor, E. A., Ward, R. M., and Hardin, R. (2017). Examination of drinking habits and motives of collegiate student-athletes. *J. Appl. Sport Manag.* 9, 56–77. doi: 10.18666/JASM-2017-V9-I1-7470

Urrutia-Pereira, M., Oliano, V. J., Aranda, C. S., Mallol, J., and Solé, D. (2017). Prevalence and factors associated with smoking among adolescents. *J. Pediatr.* 93, 230–237. doi: 10.1016/j.jped.2016.07.003

Villareal-González, M. E. (2009). *Un Modelo Estructural del Consumo de Drogas y Conducta Violenta en Adolescentes Escolarizados*. Ph.D. thesis, Universidad Autónoma de Nuevo León, México.

World Health Organization (2017). *Global Recommendations on Physical Activity for Health*. Geneva: WHO.

5

Mexican Basic Psychological Need Satisfaction and Frustration Scale in Physical Education

Jorge Zamarripa[1], René Rodríguez-Medellín[1], José Alberto Pérez-Garcia[1], Fernando Otero-Saborido[2] and Maritza Delgado[3]*

[1] Facultad de Organización Deportiva, Universidad Autónoma de Nuevo León, Nuevo León, Mexico, [2] Facultad de Ciencias del Deporte, Universidad Pablo de Olavide, Seville, Spain, [3] Facultad de Psicología, Universidad Autónoma de Nuevo León, Monterrey, Mexico

***Correspondence:**
Jorge Zamarripa
jorge.zamarriparv@uanl.edu.mx

Basic psychological needs are an energizing state that, if satisfied, will produce an increase in confidence and a healthy motivational orientation that leads to wellness. Frustration of these needs is the opposite concept of satisfaction, which refers to the negative sensation experimented by an individual when he or she perceives that their psychological needs are being actively limited by the actions of the significant other. To date, we have not found instruments validated in Spanish that measure both the satisfaction and the frustration of basic psychological needs in the physical education (PE) context. Therefore, the aims of this study are adapting the Basic Psychological Need Satisfaction and Frustration Scale (BPNSFS) to the PE context in Mexico; and examine its psychometric properties, structure, and factorial invariance by gender in a sample of fifth- and sixth-grade elementary school students. This study included a total of 1,470 fifth- and sixth-grade students from elementary schools in the metropolitan area of Monterrey, Nuevo Leon, Mexico. The results support the reliability, validity, structure, and strict invariance of the sixth Mexican version of the BPNSFS in physical education (BPNSFS-PE). The BPNSFS-PE can be used to measure the satisfaction and/or frustration of the basic psychological needs of students in PE class and to perform comparisons between groups of boys and girls.

Keywords: self-determination theory, autonomy, competence, relatedness, physical education, invariance, gender, Mexico

INTRODUCTION

The self-determination theory (SDT) (Deci and Ryan, 1985, 2002, 2014; Ryan and Deci, 2017) is a macro theory that provides a clear overview of motivational processes and their consequences in different contexts, such as education. It proposes that in individuals that develop a motivation that brings them closer to an activity (e.g., actively participate in classes), their participation in the said activity will satisfy three basic psychological needs (BNP), which are autonomy, competence, and relatedness.

Autonomy refers to the feeling of willfulness that can accompany any act, whether dependent or independent, collective, or individual (Ryan and Deci, 2000); in other words, it refers to the desire of the individual to be the origin of their behavior, and therefore, it is related with the freedom granted to make decisions while the activity takes place.

Competence refers to the ability to effectively interact with their environment to assure the conservation of the organism. Satisfaction of the need for competence provides the energy for learning (Deci and Ryan, 1985). This leads people to look for challenges that are optimal for those skills and abilities related to the activity (e.g., the skills and content of subjects); in the same way, the need for competence refers to the feeling people have to act effectively in the environment surrounding them with the aim of developing feelings of achievement.

Relatedness refers to being connected and respected by others (e.g., with the professor and classmates) and having a feeling of belonging to the group (Ryan, 1995).

By definition, *basic psychological needs* are an energizing state that, if satisfied, will produce an increase in confidence and a healthy motivational orientation that leads to wellness and facilitates the development of enjoyment, effort, persistence, commitment, and well-being (Deci and Ryan, 2000).

But these needs can also be decreased by a negative context. Therefore, for several years, a construct of frustration of the psychological needs has been developed by Bartholomew et al. (2011), which refers to the negative sensation experimented by an individual when he or she perceives that their psychological needs are being actively limited by the actions of a significant other (e.g., the class teacher).

The *frustration* of these needs is the opposite concept to their *satisfaction* (Bartholomew et al., 2011). For example, a student may not have a good social relationship with his or her classmates because he or she does not feel close and is not compatible with them; however, another student may not have a good relationship with his or her classmates because they reject or bother him or her. Obviously, both cases are different: the first case refers to low satisfaction of the need for a relationship, while the second is related to the frustration of this need. Thus, to value the frustration of the psychological needs, it is necessary to refer to the effect caused by the significant others in these needs.

In recent years, different instruments have been used to measure the satisfaction of basic psychological needs (BPNS) in physical education (PE), and these have been validated in different cultures, such as British (Standage et al., 2005), Spanish (Moreno Murcia et al., 2008), Brazilian (Pires et al., 2010), Greek (Vlachopoulos et al., 2011), Chinese (Liu and Chung, 2014), and Mexican (Zamarripa et al., 2017).

On the other hand, to measure the frustration of basic psychological needs (BPNF), the *Psychological Need Thwarting Scale (PNTS)* has been used (Bartholomew et al., 2011), which has been adapted and used in the context of PE in the Chinese (Liu and Chung, 2015) and Spanish populations (Cuevas et al., 2015, 2016).

The number of items that must be used to measure satisfaction, on the one hand, and frustration, on the other, limits the studies along these lines. Instruments that measure BPNS use a considerable number of items that vary from 16 to 33. If we add the 12 items needed to measure BPNF, the number of items needed to measure both constructs would vary between 28 and 45.

As an alternative to these instruments, Chen et al. (2015) created an instrument that measures both constructs with a smaller number of items. The instrument called the *Basic Psychological Need Satisfaction and Need Frustration Scale* (BPNSNFS) was validated with a sample in four different cultures and languages (Belgium, China, United States, and Peru). The sample consisted of 1,051 university students with a mean age of 20 years. The study authors showed evidence that the scale, composed of 24 items, presented a multidimensional structure of six factors that measure satisfaction and frustration, respectively, in each of the psychological needs. The results obtained in a cross-validation recognized four necessary items, such as an internal consistency for each dimension that ranged from 0.64 to 0.89. The model of the six factors proposed by the authors had a good fit, $SB\chi^2$ (231) = 441.99, CFI = 0.95, RMSEA = 0.04, and SRMR = 0.04.

Within the educational context, the PE class was one subject that was intimately linked to adopting a healthy lifestyle. In line with Telama et al. (2005), the main objective of PE in many countries must be the promotion of health in young population, and Mexico is not an exception. The high rates of sedentary and obesity in the population, in addition to a large number of children and teens that can be accessed through PE, makes this the ideal medium for promoting health and healthy fitness from an early age. For this reason, the study of the BNP in PE could contribute to achieving this objective since different studies have demonstrated that satisfying these needs leads to more positive results of physical activity; in other words, PE students that have their needs satisfied show greater commitment (Parish and Treasure, 2003), effort (Bagøien et al., 2010; Taylor and Lonsdale, 2010; Taylor et al., 2010), and amount of physical activity, as well as a better perception of quality of life related to health (Standage et al., 2012).

In this sense, Haerens et al. (2015) translated the BPNSNFS into Dutch and adapted it to the context of PE. A total of 499 students (boys = 43.8%, M_{age} = 15.76, SD = 1.16) from secondary schools in Flanders, Belgium participated. The structure of the instrument was examined with a high-order confirmatory factorial analysis (CFA) where the items were used as indicators of six first-order factors (satisfaction of autonomy, competence, and relatedness, and frustration of autonomy, competence, and relatedness), which also served as indicators of two higher-order factors, that is, BPNS and BPNF. The two-dimension model (BPNS and BPNF) had acceptable fit indexes, χ^2 (243) = 530.49, $p < 0.001$, RMSEA = 0.05, CFI = 0.91, and SRMR = 0.06. The internal consistency of the high-order factors of satisfaction (α = 0.87) and frustration (α = 0.84) was acceptable, as well as each one of the six first-order factors (α = 0.71–0.80).

To date, we have not found instruments validated in Spanish that measure both the satisfaction and BPNF in the context of PE. The aforementioned limits the study of this area in Spanish-speaking cultures such as Mexico, and due to the importance and repercussion that the BPNS has on different aspects related to the learning and well-being of students, it becomes necessary to have reliable instruments with an adequate number of items and that measures both constructs in the context of PE. Therefore, the aims of this study are to adapt the Basic Psychological Need Satisfaction and Frustration Scale (BPNSFS) (Chen et al., 2015) to the context of PE in Mexico and examine its psychometric properties, structure, and factorial invariance by gender, in a sample of fifth- and sixth-grade Mexican elementary school students.

MATERIALS AND METHODS

Design and Type of Study

This was a quantitative study with an instrumental design to evaluate the psychometric properties of a scale that measures the satisfaction and BPNF in the context of PE (Ato et al., 2013). This was a non-probabilistic convenience sample.

Participants

Study participants included 1,470 students (boys = 50.6% and girls = 49.4%) from fifth (49.3%) and sixth (50.7%) grade from federal (89.3%) and state (10.7%) elementary schools of the metropolitan area of Monterrey in the morning (70.6%), afternoon (24.3%), and (5.2%) fulltime shift, with ages from 10 to 14 years ($M_{\text{age}} = 10.56$; SD = 0.77) who attended PE class twice a week with a duration of 50 min per session, and in which 68% said they practiced at least one sport outside of school. Fifth- and sixth-grade students were chosen because children who belong to the final years of third childhood and early adolescence are at the highest level of cognitive development and will not have any complications when responding to the instruments (Papalia et al., 2009).

Instrument

To measure the students' satisfaction and frustration, the BPNSFS (Chen et al., 2015) was translated and adapted to the PE context. The scale is composed of 24 items grouped into two factors: basic psychological needs satisfaction (BPNS) and basic psychological needs frustration (BPNF). These two factors are composed of three variables each; the BPNS is composed of satisfaction of autonomy (SA), satisfaction of competence (SC), and satisfaction of relatedness (SR). In contrast, the BPNF is composed of frustration of autonomy (FA), frustration of competence (FC), and frustration of relatedness (FR). Each one of these variables was measured by four items. The instrument has as a heading "En mi clase de Educación Física." One example of a SA item is "...siento que tengo la libertad y posibilidad de elegir las actividades de la clase." and of the FA "...siento que la mayoría de las actividades que hago, las hago porque tengo que hacerlas." One example of an SC item is "...siento que puedo hacer bien las actividades." and of FC "...tengo serias dudas acerca de que pueda hacer bien las actividades.". One example of an SR item is "...siento que le importo a mis compañeros que me importan." and of the FR "...me siento excluido del grupo al que quiero pertenecer." The 24 items are answered on a Likert scale of five points that go from 1 (*Not True at All*) to 5 (*Completely True*).

Procedure

This study was carried out according to the ethical guidelines recommended by the American Psychological Association (APA). Authorization was requested in writing from the school zone authorities and from each of the principals of the schools explaining the objectives of the research and the procedure that would be performed together with a model of the instrument. Afterward, authorization was requested for application from the teachers of each group and from the selected students taking into consideration the inclusion criteria: be a regular student in their respective group, regularly have PE class at least twice a week, be voluntarily willing to complete the questionnaire, and deliver the informed consent to participate in the research signed by their parents or tutors. The students were informed of the objective of the study, their willingness to volunteer, the absolute confidentiality of their answers, and the management of the data. They were also told that there were no correct or incorrect answers and they were asked for maximum sincerity and honesty. The questionnaire was anonymous and self-administered collectively in the classroom during school hours. To homogenize the data collection conditions, the administrators received prior preparation and training. The protocol was approved by the Ethics Committee of the Universidad Autónoma de Nuevo León (No. 16CI19039021). All subjects gave written informed consent in accordance with the Declaration of Helsinki.

The BPNSFS was translated into Mexican Spanish following the translation-back-translation procedure (Hambleton and Kanjee, 1995). The translation was carried out by a professional translation agency hired by the study team. To adapt the translation to the context of PE, a group of experts was formed with two Ph.D. specialists and with previous experience in the validation of psychological instruments, a PE teacher, and a translator specialized in the area of physical activity and sports; they discussed the translation discrepancies until the first version of the Mexican Spanish-language instrument was achieved. This version was retranslated into English by a professional translation agency different from the first and both versions were contrasted: the original and the translation. Again, the differences in the versions were analyzed and necessary changes were introduced to facilitate the comprehension of the items achieving a final version of each of the scales. This version was administered as a pilot application to a group of 72 students of different school levels to verify comprehension of each of the items; the results of this pilot application did not show any comprehension problems. The items that comprise the scale are presented in **Table 1**.

Data Analysis

First, a descriptive analysis was performed for all the scales and the factors that comprise them. To test the factorial structure of the questionnaire, a confirmatory factor analysis (CFA) was performed of the two proposed models (of two and four factors). Taking into consideration its ordinal nature, the sample size, the number of response options (k = 5), and the symmetry and kurtosis values of the items (see **Table 1**), the CFA was performed with the *maximum likelihood* (ML) method and

TABLE 1 | Descriptive and standardized solution of the items and subscales of the instrument.

Subscales						Factorial saturations	
	En mi clase de Educación Física... [In my Physical Education class...]	***M***	**SD**	**Asymmetry**	**Kurtosis**	**Two factors**	**Six factors**
	Basic psychological needs satisfaction	3.73	0.69	−0.61	0.63		
	Autonomy satisfaction	3.56	0.83	−0.54	0.14		
1	... siento que tengo la libertad y posibilidad de elegir las actividades de la clase. (...I feel a sense of choice and freedom in the things I undertake.)	3.19	1.40	−0.25	−1.19	0.33	0.29
7	... siento que mis decisiones reflejan lo que realmente quiero. (...I feel that my decisions reflect what I really want.)	3.69	1.17	−0.74	−0.16	0.54	0.51
13	... siento que mis elecciones expresan lo que realmente soy. (... I feel my choices express who I really am.)	3.63	1.27	−0.72	−0.48	0.61	0.57
19	... siento que he estado haciendo lo que realmente me interesa. (...I feel I have been doing what really interests me.)	3.76	1.22	−0.83	−0.26	0.63	0.61
	Relatedness satisfaction	3.67	0.87	−0.53	−0.06		
3	... siento que le importo a mis compañeros que me importan. (... I feel that the people I care about also care about me.)	3.70	1.22	−0.79	−0.25	0.54	0.57
9	... me siento conectado con los compañeros que se preocupan por mí y por los cuales yo me preocupo. (... I feel connected with people who care for me, and for whom I care.)	3.74	1.24	−0.81	−0.33	0.56	0.60
15	... me siento cerca y conectado(a) con otros compañeros que son importantes para mí. (... I feel close and connected with other people who are important to me.)	3.73	1.24	−0.80	−0.31	0.66	0.68
21	... tengo una sensación de calidez cuando estoy con los compañeros con los que paso tiempo. (... I experience a warm feeling with the people I spend time with.)	3.51	1.29	−0.53	−0.76	0.58	0.59
	Competence satisfaction	3.94	0.81	−0.79	0.47		
5	... siento que puedo hacer bien las actividades. (...I feel confident that I can do things well.)	4.15	1.05	−1.35	1.34	0.60	0.62
11	... me siento capaz en las actividades que hago. (...I feel capable at what I do.)	3.92	1.15	−1.00	0.24	0.63	0.67
17	... siento que soy capaz de alcanzar los objetivos de la clase. (...I feel competent to achieve my goals.)	3.88	1.20	−0.93	−0.06	0.64	0.66
23	... siento que puedo cumplir con éxito las actividades difíciles. (...I feel I can successfully complete difficult tasks.)	3.81	1.20	−0.88	−0.10	0.60	0.62
	Basic psychological needs frustration	2.75	0.81	0.02	−0.30		
	Autonomy frustration	2.83	0.95	−0.12	−0.54		
2	... siento que la mayoría de las actividades que hago, las hago porque tengo que hacerlas. (...most of the things I do feel like "I have to".)	3.26	1.35	−0.37	−1.06	0.41	0.43
8	... me siento obligado(a) a hacer muchas actividades que yo no elegiría hacer. (...I feel forced to do many things I wouldn't choose to do.)	2.73	1.37	0.16	−1.22	0.52	0.56
14	... me siento presionado(a) a hacer muchas actividades. (...I feel pressured to do too many things.)	2.58	1.38	0.38	−1.12	0.68	0.72
20	... siento que las actividades de la clase son una serie de obligaciones. (...my daily activities feel like a chain of obligations.)	2.75	1.40	0.17	−1.25	0.56	0.62
	Relatedness frustration	2.75	0.94	0.12	−0.62		
4	... me siento excluido del grupo al que quiero pertenecer. (...I feel excluded from the group I want to belong to.)	2.75	1.45	0.14	−1.38	0.51	0.53
10	... siento que los compañeros que son importantes para mí son fríos y distantes conmigo. (...I feel that people who are important to me are cold and distant toward me.)	2.59	1.35	0.34	−1.08	0.61	0.65
16	... tengo la impresión de que le disgusto a los compañeros con los que paso tiempo. (...I have the impression that people I spend time with dislike me.)	2.67	1.35	0.29	−1.11	0.62	0.65
22	... siento que la relación con mis compañeros es superficial. (...I feel the relationships I have are just superficial.)	2.98	1.34	−0.09	−1.15	0.49	0.51
	Competence frustration	2.68	0.98	0.14	−0.70		
6	... tengo serias dudas acerca de que pueda hacer bien las actividades. (...I have serious doubts that I can do the activities well.)	3.14	1.38	−0.25	−1.18	0.51	0.51
12	... me siento decepcionado(a) con muchas de mis participaciones. (...I feel disappointed with many of my performance.)	2.57	1.35	0.35	−1.11	0.66	0.67
18	... me siento inseguro(a) de mis habilidades. (...I feel insecure about my abilities.)	2.60	1.38	0.31	−1.20	0.69	0.70
24	... me siento como un(a) fracasado(a) por los errores que cometo. (...I feel like a failure because of the mistakes I make.)	2.41	1.42	0.53	−1.09	0.61	0.62

All saturations were significant, $t > 1.96$, $p < 0.05$

as output the asymptotic covariance matrix of the polychoric correlations was used.

Model adequacy was analyzed with different fit indexes, such as the CFI, NNFI, and RMSEA. CFI and NNFI values greater than or equal to 0.95 indicate an acceptable fit (Hu and Bentler, 1999). For RMSEA, negative values or equal to or lower than 0.08 are considered satisfactory (Cole and Maxwell, 1985).

To determine which of the two models (two and six factors) adjusted better to the data, the differences between the goodness-of-fit indexes of the models were analyzed. Differences no greater than 0.01 between the CFI and NNFI values (Widaman, 1985; Cheung and Rensvold, 2002) and of 0.015 between the RMSEA values (Chen, 2007) were considered irrelevant in the models comparison, and therefore, claim support for the more constrained (parsimonious) model.

To determine if the Mexican version of the BPNSFS in physical education (BPNSFS-PE) shows invariance by gender, a multigroup CFA was performed. Incremental goodness-of-fit indexes of the alternative models were estimated. A difference of 0.01 or less between the CFI (Cheung and Rensvold, 2002) and of 0.05 between the NNFI values (Little, 1997) reflects practically irrelevant differences between the models. Regarding the RMSEA, a value of 0.015 or less between the alternative models indicates irrelevant differences (Chen, 2007).

Internal consistency of the instruments was evaluated with Cronbach's alpha (Cronbach, 1951); also, Pearson's correlation analysis was performed between all the variables. These were carried out using the statistical package SPSS Statistics V.21 and the program LISREL 8.80 (Jöreskog and Sörbom, 2006).

RESULTS

Descriptive Analysis and Normality

The descriptive analysis (mean, standard deviation, asymmetry, and kurtosis) of each of the items, variables, and factors that compose the scale is shown in **Table 1**. The results reveal that BPNS values are higher than the BPNF in the PE class. Particularly, competence is the psychological need that had the highest satisfaction values. On the other hand, autonomy was the psychological need that had the highest frustration values. Most of the asymmetry and kurtosis values were outside the range (−1.5 to 1.5), indicating a normal distribution of data (Shumacker and Lomax, 2004).

Confirmatory Factorial Analysis and Model Comparison

The goodness-of-fit of the two- ($SB\chi^2/df = 5.112$, NNFI = 0.951, CFI = 0.955, and RMSEA = 0.053) and six-factor model ($SB\chi^2/df = 4.94$, NNFI = 0.953, CFI = 0.960, y RMSEA = 0.052) was satisfactory. The values obtained from the differences between the fit indexes of both were irrelevant (ΔNNFI = 0.002, ΔCFI = 0.005, y ΔRMSEA = 0.001), which suggests that both models fit in a similar way; therefore, a more parsimonious model should be selected, in this case, the two-factor model (see **Table 2**). All estimated factorial saturations for the two- and six-factor model were significant (see **Table 1**).

Reliability

The results of the reliability analysis revealed alpha values of 0.55–0.66 for the SA, SR, and SC. This situation was similar to those of the FA, FR, and FC, which had alpha values of 0.62–0.66. Nevertheless, the internal consistency of the scales that measure BPNS and BPNF as a global measure presented good reliability with alpha values of 0.81 and 0.83, respectively.

Correlation Between Factors

The Pearson correlation analysis between the study variables revealed that BPNS had strong positive and significant correlations with SA, SR, and SC, and weak negative correlations with BPNF and FC. On the other hand, BPNF had strong positive and significant correlations with FA, FR, and FC; weak with SA; and negative with SC and SR (see **Table 3**).

Measurement Invariance

Based on the results of the CFA, invariance was evaluated based on the gender of the two-factor model. A preliminary analysis was performed that separately examined the structure of the BPNSFS-PE in the sample of boys (Model M0a) and girls (Model M0b). As shown in **Table 4**, the goodness-of-fit indexes of the models M0a and M0b were satisfactory with all the estimated parameters being statistically significant ($p < 0.01$).

Later, a multisample analysis was carried out. Model 1 (M1) examined the structural invariance of the BPNSFS-PE in both of the analyzed groups showing that the goodness-of-fit was satisfactory; therefore, we concluded that the factorial structure of the instrument is invariant in the two compared groups (see **Table 4**). The M1 was used as the basis for the nesting of restrictions.

Model 2 (M2), which tested the equivalence of factor saturations across the group of boys and girls, showed adequate fit indexes. After comparing these indexes with those of M1, the differences did not exceed the criteria values (ΔCFI < 0.01 and ΔNNFI < 0.05; ΔRMSEA < 0.015); therefore, this work presents evidence of the invariance of the factorial saturations of BPNSFS-PE across the evaluated sample.

Model 3 (M3) or the "strong factorial invariance model" (Meredith, 1993), which adds the equivalence of the intercepts, showed satisfactory goodness-of-fit indexes. The values obtained from the differences between the NNFI and the RMSEA from M3 and M1 did not exceed the criterion values. However, this did not happen with the CFI (see **Table 4**); nevertheless, it can be concluded that the equivalence of factorial saturations and

TABLE 2 | Goodness of fit indices of the confirmatory factor analysis of the two proposed models.

Models	χ^2/df	RMSEA	ΔRMSEA	CFI	ΔCFI	ΔNNFI	ΔNNFI
Two factors	5.11	0.053		0.955		0.951	
Six factors	4.94	0.052	0.001	0.960	0.005	0.953	0.002

df, degrees of freedom; RMSEA, root mean square error of approximation; NNFI, non-normed fit index; CFI, comparative fit index.

TABLE 3 | Bivariate correlations and internal consistency of the all variables of study.

	α	1	2	3	4	5	6	7
1. BPN. S	0.81	1						
2. Autonomy satisfaction	0.55	0.82**	1					
3. Relatedness satisfaction	0.65	0.85**	0.53**	1				
4. Competence satisfaction	0.66	0.83**	0.51**	0.58**	1			
5. BPN. F.	0.83	−0.06*	0.05*	−0.08**	−0.14**	1		
6. Autonomy frustration	0.64	−0.05	0.06*	−0.05*	−0.12**	0.83**	1	
7. Relatedness frustration	0.62	−0.02	0.06*	−0.04	−0.08**	0.84**	0.52**	1
8. Competence frustration	0.66	−0.10**	0.01	−0.10**	−0.15**	0.87**	0.58**	0.63**

*S, satisfaction; F, frustration; BPN, basic psychological needs; α, Cronbach alpha; *p < 0.05; **p < 0.01.*

TABLE 4 | Goodness of fit indexes of invariance models.

Model	Model description	*df*	$SB\chi^2$	RMSEA	90% CI	NNFI	CFI	ΔNNFI	ΔCFI	ΔRMSEA
M0a	Baseline model boys	251	815.88**	0.055	0.051–0.059	0.950	0.955			
M0b	Baseline model girls	251	737.67**	0.052	0.048–0.056	0.950	0.955			
M1	Structural invariance (baseline model)	503	1554.54**	0.053	0.050–0.056	0.950	0.955			
M2	FL invariance	526	1694.45**	0.055	0.052–0.058	0.947	0.950	0.003	0.005	0.002
M3	FL + INT invariance	548	2009.23**	0.060	0.058–0.063	0.937	0.937	0.013	0.018	0.007
M4	SF + Inv. + Error invariance	572	2305.58**	0.064	0.062–0.067	0.928	0.925	0.022	0.03	0.011

*df, degrees of freedom; RMSEA, root mean square error of approximation; 90% CI, 90% confidence interval for the RMSEA; NNFI, non-normed fit index; CFI, comparative fit index; Inv., Invariance; FL, factor load; INT, intercepts. All comparisons in the Δ indices are made with respect to the baseline model (M1). **p < 0.01.*

intercepts can be accepted when the invariance is fulfilled for two parameters, although not for the CFI.

Finally, Model 4 (M4) or the "strict factorial invariance model" (Meredith, 1993), which adds invariance to the factorial saturations, intercepts, and errors, also presented satisfactory fit indexes. As in the previous comparison, the difference obtained between the NNFI and the RMSEA of the M4 and M1 did not exceed the criterion values, except for the CFI; however, it can be concluded that the strict factor equivalence of the BPNSFS-PE is accepted across gender when the invariance in two of the three parameters examined is fulfilled.

DISCUSSION

The aims of this study were to adapt the BPNSFS (Chen et al., 2015) to the context of PE in Mexico and examine its psychometric properties, structure, and factorial invariance by gender, in a sample of fifth- and sixth-grade Mexican elementary school students.

The results of the CFA revealed a good fit of the data for the two proposed models (two and six dimensions). Regarding the two-dimensional model (BPNS and BPNF), our results were consistent with those obtained from the Dutch translation adapted to PE by Haerens et al. (2015). Likewise, the goodness-of-fit indexes of the six-factor model (SA, SR, SC, FA, FR, and FC) found in this study were also consistent with the satisfactory fit of the PE version used by Cuevas et al. (2018) and in the version for the general context developed by Chen et al. (2015).

Regarding model comparison (two and six factors), the product obtained from the incremental differences of both models did not exceed the criterion values; this indicates irrelevant differences between both models; therefore, the most parsimonious model was selected, that is, the two-factor model for the invariance analysis. These results differ from those found by Cordeiro et al. (2016), where the six-factor model presented better goodness-of-fit indexes that coincide with those found by Chen et al. (2015). However, the instrument used in both studies measured need satisfaction and frustration in a general context (instead of a specific domain). Nevertheless, within the context of PE, the results of the study by Haerens et al. (2015) coincide with this work using the two-factor model (satisfaction and frustration).

The internal consistency of the factors that correspond with satisfaction (SA, SR, and SC) and frustration (FA, FR, and FC) did not reach the criterion value recommended by some authors (Nunnally and Bernstein, 1994; Bland and Altman, 1997). Schmitt (1996) has suggested that there is no general level (e.g., 0.70) in which the alpha becomes "acceptable," but the instruments with a very low alpha can still be useful in some circumstances, for example, when a scale is composed of a small number of items (Dall'oglio et al., 2010) and in the first stages of studies such as in this work (Nunnally, 1967). However, the internal consistency of the scales that measure BPNS and BPNF presented adequate reliability, even without reaching the maximum acceptable alpha, since according to Streiner (2003), instruments with high values (e.g., >0.90) could suggest that the items are redundant and that they are measuring the same question but in a different way.

The results of the correlation analysis between dimensions (BPNS and BPNF) and their respective factors (SA, SR, SC, FA, FR, and FC) revealed positive and significant relatedness between them, as well as a negative and significant correlation between BPNS and BPNF. These correlations similarly coincide with the results reported in other studies that have used the same instrument (Chen et al., 2015; Haerens et al., 2015; Nishimura and Suzuki, 2016; Cuevas et al., 2018).

Finally, the results of the multigroup CFA revealed a strict factorial invariance of the BPNSFS-PE across sex in the two-factor structure. No recent studies have been found that examine the invariance of this instrument through gender groups in the context of PE. In the general context, the results of the study by Tóth-Király et al. (2018) revealed invariance by gender in the Hungarian version of the instrument; however, this analysis was performed on a model composed of two factors (BPNS and BPNF) and on a global one called *global need fulfillment*, which differs from the model we propose.

CONCLUSION

After examining the psychometric properties, structure, and factorial invariance of the Mexican version of the BPNSFS in the context of PE (BPNSFS-PE), it can be concluded that it is a reliable and valid instrument that can be used to measure the satisfaction and/or frustration of students' BPNs in PE class and make comparisons between groups of boys and girls, either as a two-factor (BPNS and BPNF) or a six-factor (SA, SR, SC, FA, FR, and FC) model according to the research purpose and question of each study, in order to increase the generation of knowledge and scientific production of this area in Mexico, since its factorial structure coincides with that used in previous studies and it is consistent with the assumptions of the SDT (Deci and Ryan, 1985, 2002, 2014; Ryan and Deci, 2017).

This study also has some limitations. The study participants only include fifth- and sixth-grade students from elementary schools in the metropolitan area of Monterrey; therefore, future research should include population from different school levels and sectors in the country. In addition, the study of the psychometric properties of the instrument could be expanded to include population from other Spanish-speaking countries, and in this way, contribute to the conduction of cross-cultural studies. Lastly, we suggest including in the study of factorial invariance the educational grades and levels, areas and populations of other sectors of the country, as well as population from different Spanish-speaking countries to determine its function and facilitate the comparison of results.

PRACTICAL APPLICATIONS

This instrument can be used by teachers, school principals, institutions responsible for PE, and researchers to perform studies with Mexican population with the aim of knowing the levels of satisfaction and frustration of students during PE class and to make comparisons between boys and girls. The aforementioned is of vital importance for learning because, as mentioned before, when needs are satisfied, there is an increase in confidence and a healthy motivational orientation that leads to health and that facilitates the development of enjoyment, effort, persistence, commitment, and well-being (Deci and Ryan, 2000).

ETHICS STATEMENT

The studies involving human participants were reviewed and approved by Ethics Committee of the Universidad Autónoma de Nuevo León (No. 16CI19039021). Written informed consent to participate in this study was provided by the participants' legal guardian/next of kin.

AUTHOR CONTRIBUTIONS

JZ, RR-M, and FO-S conceived the hypothesis of this study. JP-G and MD participated in data collection and methodology. JZ and MD analyzed the data. JZ and RR-M wrote the manuscript with significant input from JZ. JZ took charge of funding acquisition. All authors contributed to data interpretation of statistical analysis, and read and approved the final manuscript.

REFERENCES

Ato, M., López, J. J., and Benavente, A. (2013). Un sistema de clasificación de los diseños de investigación en psicología. *An. Psicol.* 29, 1038–1059. doi: 10.6018/analesps.29.3.178511

Bagøien, T. E., Halvari, H., and Nesheim, H. (2010). Self-determined motivation in physical education and its links to motivation for leisure-time physical activity, physical activity, and well-being in general. *Percept. Mot. Skills.* 111, 407–432. doi: 10.2466/06.10.11.13.14.Pms.111.5.407-432

Bartholomew, K. J., Ntoumanis, N., Ryan, R. M., and Thogersen-Ntoumani, C. (2011). Psychological need thwarting in the sport context: assessing the darker side of athletic experience. *J. Sport. Exerc. Psychol.* 33, 75–102. doi: 10.1123/jsep.33.1.75

Bland, J. M., and Altman, D. G. (1997). Statistics notes: cronbach's alpha. *Br. Med. J.* 314:572. doi: 10.1136/bmj.314.7080.572

Chen, B., Vansteenkiste, M., Beyers, W., Boone, L., Deci, E., Van Der Kaap-Deeder, J., et al. (2015). Basic psychological need satisfaction, need frustration, and need strength across four cultures. *Motiv. Emot.* 39, 216–236. doi: 10.1007/s11031-014-9450-1

Chen, F. F. (2007). Sensitivity of goodness of fit indexes to lack of measurement invariance. *Struct. Equ. Modeling* 14, 464–504. doi: 10.1080/10705510701301834

Cheung, G. W., and Rensvold, R. B. (2002). Evaluating goodness-of-fit indexes for testing measurement invariance. *Struct. Equ. Modeling* 9, 233–255. doi: 10.1207/S15328007SEM0902_5

Cole, D. A., and Maxwell, S. E. (1985). Multitrait-multimethod comparisons across populations: a confirmatory factor analytic approach. *Multivariate. Behav. Res.* 20:389. doi: 10.1207/s15327906mbr2004_3

Cordeiro, P., Paixao, P., Lens, W., Lacante, M., and Luyckx, K. (2016). the portuguese validation of the basic psychological need satisfaction and frustration scale: concurrent and longitudinal relations to well-being and Ill-being. *Psychol. Belg.* 56, 193–209. doi: 10.5334/pb.252

Cronbach, L. (1951). Coefficient alpha and the internal structure of tests. *Psychometrika* 16, 297–334. doi: 10.1007/BF02310555

Cuevas, R., García López, L., and Olivares, J. (2016). Sport education model and self-determination theory: an intervention in secondary school children. *Kinesiology* 48, 30–38. doi: 10.26582/k.48.1.15

Cuevas, R., García-Calvo, T., González, J., and Fernández-Bustos, J. G. (2018). Basic psychological needs, motivation and engagement in adolescent students. *Rev. Psicol. Deporte.* 27, 97–104.

Cuevas, R., Sánchez-Oliva, D., Bartholomew, K. J., Ntoumanis, N., and García-Calvo, T. (2015). Adaptation and validation of the psychological need thwarting scale in spanish physical education teachers. *Span. J. Psychol.* 18, E53. doi: 10.1017/sjp.2015.56

Dall'oglio, A. M., Rossiello, B., Coletti, M. F., Caselli, M. C., Rava, L., Di Ciommo, V., et al. (2010). Developmental evaluation at age 4: validity of an Italian parental questionnaire. *J. Paediatr. Child. Health.* 46, 419–426. doi: 10.1111/j.1440-1754.2010.01748.x

Deci, E., and Ryan, R. (1985). *Intrinsic Motivation and Self-Determintion in Human Behavior.* New York, NY: Plenum Press.

Deci, E., and Ryan, R. (2000). The "what" and "why" of goal pursuits: human needs and the self-determination of behaviour. *Psychol. Inq.* 11, 227–268. doi: 10.1207/S15327965PLI1104_01

Deci, E., and Ryan, R. (2002). *Handbook of Self-Determination Research.* New York, NY: The University Rochester Press.

Deci, E., and Ryan, R. (2014). "Autonomy and need satisfaction in close relationships: relationships motivation theory," in *in Human Motivation and Interpersonal Relationships*, ed. N. Weinstein (Netherlands: Springer), 53–73. doi: 10.1007/978-94-017-8542-6_3

Haerens, L., Aelterman, N., Vansteenkiste, M., Soenens, B., and Van Petegem, S. (2015). Do perceived autonomy-supportive and controlling teaching relate to physical education students' motivational experiences through unique pathways? Distinguishing between the bright and dark side of motivation. *Psychol. Sport. Exerc.* 16, 26–36. doi: 10.1016/j.psychsport.2014.08.013

Hambleton, R. K., and Kanjee, A. (1995). Increasing the validity of cross-cultural assessments: use of improved methods for test adaptations. *Eur. J. Psychol. Assess.* 11, 147–157. doi: 10.1027/1015-5759.11.3.147

Hu, L.-T., and Bentler, P. M. (1999). Cutoff criteria for fit indexes in covariance structure analysis: conventional criteria versus new alternatives. *Struct. Equ. Modeling* 6, 1–55. doi: 10.1080/10705519909540118

Jöreskog, K., and Sörbom, D. (2006). *LISREL 8.80. Structural Equation Modeling With the Simplis Command Language (Software de cómputo).* Chicago, EU: Scientific Software International.

Little, T. D. (1997). Mean and covariance structures (MACS) analyses of cross-cultural data: practical and theoretical issues. *Multivariate. Behav. Res.* 32, 53–76. doi: 10.1207/s15327906mbr3201_3

Liu, J. D., and Chung, P. K. (2014). Development and initial validation of the psychological needs satisfaction scale in physical education. *Meas. Phys. Educ. Exerc. Sci.* 18, 101–122. doi: 10.1080/1091367X.2013.872106

Liu, J. D., and Chung, P.-K. (2015). Development and initial validation of the chinese version of psychological needs thwarting scale in physical education. *J. Teach. Phys. Educ.* 34:402. doi: 10.1123/jtpe.2014-0053

Meredith, W. (1993). Measurement invariance, factor analysis and factorial invariance. *Psychometrika.* 58, 525–543. doi: 10.1007/bf02294825

Moreno Murcia, J. A., Gonzalez-Cutre Coll, D., Chillón Garzón, M., and Parra Rojas, N. (2008). Adaptación a la educación física de la escala de las necesidades psicológicas básicas en el ejercicio. *Rev. Mex. Psicol.* 25, 295–303.

Nishimura, T., and Suzuki, T. (2016). Basic psychological need satisfaction and frustration in japan: controlling for the big five personality traits. *Jpn. Psychol. Res.* 58, 320–331. doi: 10.1111/jpr.12131

Nunnally, J. C. (1967). *Psychometric Theory.* New York, NY: McGraw-Hill.

Nunnally, J. C., and Bernstein, I. H. (1994). "The assessment of reliability," in *Psychometric Theory*, 3rd Edn, eds J. Vaicunas and J. R. Belser (New York, NY: McGraw-Hill).

Papalia, D. E., Olds, S. W. E., and Felman, R. D. (2009). *Psicología del Desarrollo. De la Infancia a la Adolescencia.* México: McGraw-Hill.

Parish, L. E., and Treasure, D. C. (2003). Physical activity and situational motivation in physical education: influence of the motivational climate and perceived ability. *Res. Q. Exercise. Sport.* 74, 173–182. doi: 10.1080/02701367.2003.10609079

Pires, A., Cid, L., Borrego, C., Alves, J., and Silva, C. (2010). Preliminary validation of a questionnaire to measure basic psychological needs in Physical education. *Motri* 6, 33–51. doi: 10.6063/motricidade.157

Ryan, R. (1995). Psychological Needs and the Facilitation of Integrative processes. *J. Pers.* 63, 397–427. doi: 10.1111/j.1467-6494.1995.tb00501.x

Ryan, R., and Deci, E. (2000). Self-determination theory and the facilitation of intrinsic motivation. social development, and well-being. *Am. Psychol.* 55, 68–78. doi: 10.1037//0003-066x.55.1.68

Ryan, R. M., and Deci, E. L. (2017). *Self-Determination Theory: Basic Psychological Needs in Motivation, Development, and Wellness.* New York, NY: Guilford Press.

Schmitt, N. (1996). Uses and abuses of coefficient alpha. *Psychol. Assess.* 8, 350–353. doi: 10.1037/1040-3590.8.4.350

Shumacker, R. E., and Lomax, R. G. (2004). *A Beginner's Guide to Structural Equation Modeling.* New Jersey: Lawrence Erlbaum Associates, Inc., Publishers.

Standage, M., Duda, J. L., and Ntoumanis, N. (2005). A test of self-determination theory in school physical education. *Br. J. Educ. Psychol.* 75, 411–433. doi: 10.1348/000709904X22359

Standage, M., Gillison, F. B., Ntoumanis, N., and Treasure, D. C. (2012). Predicting students' physical activity and health-related well-being: a prospective cross-domain investigation of motivation across school physical education and exercise settings. *J. Sport. Exerc. Psychol.* 34, 37–60. doi: 10.1123/jsep.34.1.37

Streiner, D. L. (2003). Starting at the beginning: an introduction to coefficient alpha and internal consistency. *J. Pers. Assess.* 80, 99–103. doi: 10.1207/S15327752JPA8001_18

Taylor, I. M., and Lonsdale, C. (2010). Cultural differences in the relationships among autonomy support, psychological need satisfaction, subjective vitality, and effort in British and Chinese physical education. *J. Sport. Exerc. Psychol.* 32, 655–673. doi: 10.1123/jsep.32.5.655

Taylor, I. M., Ntoumanis, N., Standage, M., and Spray, C. M. (2010). Motivational predictors of physical education students' effort, exercise intentions, and leisure-time physical activity: a multilevel linear growth analysis. *J. Sport. Exerc. Psychol.* 32, 99–120. doi: 10.1123/jsep.32.1.99

Telama, R., Nupponen, H., and Piéron, M. (2005). Physical activity among young people in the context of lifestyle. *Eur. Phys. Educ. Rev.* 11, 115–137. doi: 10.1177/1356336X05052892

Tóth-Király, I., Morin, A. J. S., Böthe, B., Orosz, G., and Rigó, A. (2018). Investigating the multidimensionality of need fulfillment: a bifactor exploratory structural equation modeling representation. *Struct. Equ. Modeling* 25, 267–286. doi: 10.1080/10705511.2017.1374867

Vlachopoulos, S. P., Katartzi, E. S., and Kontou, M. G. (2011). The basic psychological needs in physical education scale. *J. Teach. Phys. Educ.* 30, 263–280. doi: 10.1123/jtpe.30.3.263

Widaman, K. F. (1985). Hierarchically nested covariance structure models for multitrait-multimethod data. *Appl. Psychol. Meas.* 9, 1–26. doi: 10.1177/014662168500900101

Zamarripa, J., Castillo, I., Tomas, I., Delgado, M., and Álvarez, O. (2017). Escala Mexicana de Satisfacción de las Necesidades Psicológicas Básicas en Educación Física. *Revista De Psicología Del Deporte* 26, 79–84.

6

Gendered Career Choices: Paths Toward Studying a Degree in Physical Activity and Sport Science

Pedrona Serra[1,2], Susanna Soler[1]*, María José Camacho-Miñano[3], Ana Rey-Cao[4] and Anna Vilanova[1]

[1] Institut Nacional d'Educació Física de Catalunya (INEFC), Universitat de Barcelona (UB), Barcelona, Spain, [2] Department of Specific Didactics and Pedagogy, University of the Balearic Islands, Palma, Spain, [3] Department for Languages, Arts and Physical Education, Feminist Research Institute, Complutense University of Madrid, Madrid, Spain, [4] Department of Special Didactics, Universidade de Vigo, Pontevedra, Spain

***Correspondence:**
Susanna Soler
ssoler@gencat.cat

Drawing on Social Cognitive Career Theory (SCCT), we examined factors affecting interest in pursuing a degree in Physical Activity and Sport Science (PASS) among Spanish teenage students. Although women were awarded 55.1% of all bachelor degrees in Spain in 2017–2018, female enrollment in PASS degrees is decreasing and currently stands below 20% across the country. To better understand the under-representation of women in this field, 4146 students (50.2% girls; mean age = 16.82 years; *SD* = 0.837) participated in a survey designed to measure a series of SCCT constructs: interest in studying a PASS degree, career outcome expectations, goal representations, and perceived social supports. With these data, we tested a set of path analysis models to explain gender differences in interest in studying a degree in PASS. These models tested the assumption that interest in PASS would mediate the paths from outcome expectations and social supports to goal representations. Model 1 assumed that interest would partially mediate the path from outcome expectations to goal representations, Model 2 assumed complete mediation, and Model 3 assumed absence of mediation. All models were tested separately for boys and girls. Our results provide information on how male and female students set personal goals based on expected career outcomes and show that this process is affected by gender stereotypes. The lack of interest by young women in studying a degree in PASS (only 7.8% of girls expressed this interest compared with 19.0% of boys), together with the gender differences observed in perceived social supports, outcome expectations, and goal representations, have several important theoretical and practical implications. The present research suggests that interventions that foster positive outcome expectations and social support are necessary to increase interest in studying PASS among teenage girls.

Keywords: career choice, social support, gender differences, young people, physical education, interest

INTRODUCTION

Although women were awarded 55.09% of all bachelor's degrees in Spain in 2017/18, they remain under-represented in science, technology, engineering, and mathematics (STEM) fields (Ministerio de Educación Cultura y Deporte, 2019). Female enrollment in physical activity and sport science (PASS) degrees in Spain is also worryingly low, at 18% (Serra et al., 2019). This tendency is even more alarming considering the fact that enrollment has been falling since 2000, when women accounted for 40% of all PASS students (Serra et al., 2019). This female under-representation is logically linked to a predominant male presence in sport professions additionally characterized by considerable horizontal and vertical gender segregation (Moragas, 2014; Viñas and Pérez, 2014; Pérez-Villalba et al., 2018). Women have also been found to be under-represented in coaching positions and similar professions in countries with different higher education and sports systems (Cunningham et al., 2005, 2007; Cunningham and Singer, 2010; Moran-Miller and Flores, 2011; Acosta and Carpenter, 2012; Hinojosa-Alcalde et al., 2017). A number of studies have addressed obstacles facing women interested in pursuing sporting careers, such as refereeing (Azurmendi, 2016; Kim and Hong, 2016), or occupying management and leadership positions in sporting organizations (Elling et al., 2019). This situation is not new, as in a study published over 10 years ago, Webb and Macdonald (2007) highlighted the difficulties faced by women in pursuing a successful career in physical education. In short, sport is largely characterized by gender biases, with a predominance of men and discrimination against women.

While Porto (2009) and Serra et al. (2019) have documented a downward trend in female enrollment in PASS degrees in recent years, no studies to date have explored the factors underlying the low presence of females in these degrees. To better understand the under-representation of women in this field, the aim of this study was to explore factors that influence male and female teenagers' decisions to choose or not to choose to study a degree in PASS. The ultimate aim is to identify factors that need to be corrected in order to reduce the gender gap in PASS degrees and improve women's representation in professional paths. Identification of these factors will guide corrective strategies aimed at improving female enrollment rates in this university degree and ultimately their presence in related professions.

THEORETICAL FRAMEWORK

Prior research has shown that social cognitive career theory (SCCT) (Lent et al., 1994) is a useful framework for investigating career choice processes. It has been widely applied in STEM research and is also used to investigate student intentions to enter the sports and leisure industry. As indicated by Alexander et al. (2011) and Cunningham et al. (2005, 2007), SCCT offers a social and heuristic framework for investigating academic and career choices, recognizes the social forces underpinning these choices, and helps to understand how social influences impact actions and motivations. Numerous studies have, furthermore, attempted to shed light on gender disparities in other disciplines, such as STEM (e.g., Su and Rounds, 2015; Park et al., 2018).

General Social Cognitive Career Theory Framework

Social cognitive career theory emerged in 1994 (Lent et al., 1994) as a specification of Bandura (1986) general social cognitive theory to contribute to our understanding of how people develop academic and career interests from the perspective of three core tenets: self-efficacy, outcome expectations, and goal representations (Lent et al., 1994; Bandura, 1997; Lent, 2012; Lent and Brown, 2013).

Self-efficacy refers to a person's beliefs about their ability to achieve a desired outcome (Bandura, 1987; Lent et al., 1994; Lent, 2012). These beliefs are closely linked to the nature of the actions required to achieve the outcome, the conditions required for these actions to be successful, the person's perception of their abilities, and the efforts required to overcome setbacks (Bandura, 1987). Self-efficacy partly determines outcome expectations, as a person who believes he or she is capable of performing a task successfully is likely to expect a positive outcome.

Outcome expectations refer to what a person expects will happen if they act or behave in a specific way (Lent et al., 1994; Lent, 2012). They are related to the question "If I do this, what will happen?" These expectations can be physical (e.g., monetary rewards or job opportunities), social (e.g., social approval, status), or self-evaluative (e.g., self-satisfaction) (Bandura, 1987). According to Lent et al. (1994), self-evaluative expectations are the strongest determinants of actions a person will take toward the attainment of a goal (Lent et al., 1994). People's academic or career choices tend to be governed by how they envisage the outcomes of their choices (Everhart and Chelladurai, 1998; Cunningham et al., 2005). Outcome expectations, in turn, help to establish personal goals (Lent et al., 1994).

Goal representations have an important role in self-regulating behavior, as they help a person to organize and guide their behavior in relation to the goals they have set. In brief, a person's actions are not simply the result of automatic responses to given situations or stimuli. Lent et al. (1994) stressed that personal goals were always present, but were generally implicit. Goals drive motivation when perceived as attainable (Lent et al., 1994). Individuals pursuing a given academic or career path need goals in order to plan and direct their actions (Lent, 2012). How satisfied or dissatisfied they then feel with these actions will either strengthen their resolve or prompt them to revise their goals (Lent, 2012).

People develop interest in activities that they believe they can perform competently and that they expect will have a positive effect on their personal development and social status and esteem. As their interest grows, they will set goals accordingly. People who anticipate negative outcomes, however, or who do not believe themselves capable of achieving a given goal (Blanco, 2009), are unlikely to develop this interest. People, like their environments, are constantly changing, and therefore their actions and envisaged outcomes will influence their attitudes and opinions, and may even modify their environment (Alexander et al., 2011).

The three key determinants of academic interest development according to SCCT – self-efficacy, outcome expectations, and goal representations – are also strongly linked to social support received in relation to the pursuit of one path or another.

Social Support in Relation to the Development of Academic and Career Interest

Social cognitive career theory posits that contextual factors have an important impact on academic and career choices (Lent et al., 1994). These factors may include family aspirations, financial situation, and level of education (Lent, 2012).

Social agents can also have a major influence on teenagers navigating academic and career choices (Stake and Nickens, 2005), in particular, family and teachers (Turner and Lapan, 2002; Sáinz, 2007; Metheny et al., 2008; Sáinz and López-Sáez, 2010; Rogers and Creed, 2011; Buday et al., 2012). Having friends with similar interests positively influences outcome expectations regarding certain professions (e.g., science professions) (Stake and Nickens, 2005), and social support from teachers, family, or friends can enhance a person's self-efficacy beliefs, help them to set goals, and motivate them to pursue these goals (Buday et al., 2012).

Contextual factors also have an important effect on interest development. According to Holland (1997), people first tend to develop preferences for activities that are influenced by people they interact with in their social circles. These preferences gradually become interests as the person gains confidence in their ability to perform successfully (Nauta, 2013). Social supports can strengthen vocational interest and consequently drive motivation and goal pursuit, just as barriers can have the opposite effect (Cunningham et al., 2005).

All these contextual factors configure a strong gendered socialization process that mediate gender differences in vocational and career interests (Lent et al., 2001, 2010; Lent and Brown, 2013). According to Betz and Hackett (2006), young men and women differ in their vocational interests and goals because the opportunities presented to them from an early age also differ, and this affects self-efficacy beliefs. This theory would explain why boys and girls are generally less interested in careers that do not conform to traditional gender stereotypes (Lent, 2012).

Previous Research in Women's Career Development

Bandura (1986) self-efficacy theory was first applied to explain career choices in work by Betz and Hackett (2006) aimed at understanding career development in women. These authors hypothesized that career self-efficacy beliefs played a more powerful role than interests, values, or abilities in restricting women's career choices. Girls exposed to traditional gender-role attitudes during childhood would have limited access to the information they need to develop strong self-efficacy beliefs in relation to a wide range of occupational fields. Gender differences in academic and career self-efficacy beliefs are linked to past gender-role socialization, current gender-role pressures, and perceptions of the gender-relatedness of tasks, activities, or occupations (Betz and Hackett, 1981). Traditional gender role attitudes and sterotypes regarding "appropriate" careers can undermine women's beliefs that they can successfully pursue a non-traditional career. The stronger the perceived gender linkage of an activity or occupation, the more likely it is that gender differences in self-efficacy will arise (Bandura, 1997).

People are generally more likely to choose a particular academic or vocational path if they envision a favorable outcome (Cunningham et al., 2007). Girls and women often adopt "satisficing" strategies by choosing traditionally female occupations that are perceived to be easier to combine with home and family responsibilities rather than optimally translating their interests and abilities into career pursuits (Bandura, 1997). Furthermore, Betz and Hackett (2006) illustrated how the process of gender role socialization can bias access by both boys and girls to information they need to develop strong self-efficacy beliefs, particularly in relation to strongly gendered activities.

Research in the field of STEM has identified several factors that contribute to gender bias in academic and career choices (Morgan et al., 2001; Sáinz, 2007; Candela, 2008; Rogers et al., 2008; Eccles, 2011; Su and Rounds, 2015), with findings showing that girls largely choose a career based on personal preferences, while boys are more likely to be influenced by future prospects, such as earning a lot of money, doing or inventing new things, or becoming famous. Girls, by contrast, largely choose STEM careers where they can help others, reflecting the extent to which gender stereotypes influence career choice (Sallop and Kirby, 2007; Sáinz, 2007; Candela, 2008; López-Bonilla et al., 2012). Women thus are more likely to opt for social care or affiliated professions (Jones et al., 2000) and to gravitate away from traditionally male STEM professions (Sáinz, 2007).

The aim of the present study was to test a series of path models to detect factors that influence teenager boys' and girls' decisions to choose or not to choose to study a degree in PASS. In line with SCCT and our review of the literature, these models will be defined based on the following hypotheses: (H1) social supports will be significantly associated with interest; (H2) PASS outcome expectations will be positively related to interest; (H3) interest will partially mediate the paths from outcome expectations and social supports to goal representations; and (H4) gender differences will be observed for perceived social supports, outcome expectations, and goal representations. To test the last hypothesis, the path models were tested separately for boys and girls.

MATERIALS AND METHODS

Sample and Data Collection

We analyzed a representative sample of students from 39 randomly selected secondary schools in three regions of Spain: Catalonia, Galicia, and Madrid (95% confidence interval; ±3). The schools were representative of a wide range of socioeconomic conditions (different social classes and urban and rural settings) and school types (public and private schools with and without vocational PASS courses).

All students enrolled at these schools in their final year of junior secondary education (4° *ESO*, 15–16 years old) and in the first of 2 years of the pre-university course (1° *Bachillerato*, 16–17 years old) were invited to participate. A total of 4146 students from 13 schools in each region took part in this study. The questionnaires were administered during class time by members of the research team. Girls accounted for 50.3% of the participants and no gender differences were observed in the distribution of the sample. Mean age was 16.82 years (*SD* = 0.837). Overall, 87.2% of participants were of Spanish origin; 3.37% were from other European countries (3.37%) while 9.40% were from countries in other parts of the world (e.g., Latin America and Africa). In total, 74.2% of the adolescents were from a school located in an urban area, while 28.5% were from a school in a rural area. Over two-thirds of the participants (67.7%) engaged in sport or exercise in their free time, but the rate was significantly higher for boys (76.3%) than girls (59.3%) [$\chi^2(1) = 136.825$, $p < 0.0001$]. The students had not participated in any careers guidance sessions before completing the questionnaire or received information about career opportunities in this field.

Instruments and Measures

The instrument consisted of an *ad hoc* questionnaire designed to collect demographic information and data for measuring four variables in relation to studying a degree in PASS: (a) goal representations, (b) career outcome expectations, (c) perceived social support, and (d) interest in studying the degree.

The preliminary questionnaire was evaluated and validated by six experts in the field. Based on their feedback, it was then modified for the pilot test. The resulting questionnaire was piloted among 155 students from a school that did not participate in the study to ascertain length of completion and comprehensibility. It was then further refined for administration in the 39 schools. All results reported in this article are based on data collected in June 2014.

Goal representation and outcome expectations were measured using 15 items adapted from the scales developed by Everhart and Chelladurai (1998) and by Sáinz (2007), who translated Eccles and Harold (1991). Three of the variables were based on the outcome expectations described by Bandura (1986): social (e.g., to help other people), self-evaluative (e.g., to learn new things), and physical (e.g., to obtain power, monetary rewards, or status). Drawing on the work of Sáinz (2007), we added a fourth outcome expectation variable focused on job attributes that are specific to or characteristic of most jobs in the field of sport and exercise. The questions were worded in such a way that the students' answers would provide information about their personal goals (e.g., "I would like a job that would allow me to...") and their outcome expectations (e.g., "If I studied a degree in PASS, I think I would be able to get a job that allowed me to..."). Items were rated on a 5-point Likert-type scale that ranged from 1 (strongly disagree) to 5 (strongly agree).

Social supports perceived by the students in relation to their interest in studying a degree in PASS was assessed using two variables: one based on the work of Sáinz (2007) and another based on our review of the literature. The two questions were (1) Has anybody recommended that you study PASS when you finish school? and (2) Has anybody recommended that you don't study PASS when you finish school? The options were "my father," "my mother," "my friends," "my physical education teacher," "another teacher," "a coach," and "other," and the students had to answer "yes" or "no."

Interest in studying a degree in PASS was assessed by a single item: Are you interested in studying a degree in PASS? The response options were: "yes," "maybe," "I don't know yet," and "no." The first two options were grouped as indicating interest while the second two options were grouped as indicating a lack of interest.

Data Analysis

We first performed a missing data analysis and a descriptive analysis of all study variables. Using the software package SPSS 18.0, we compared all variables between boys and girls using the *t*-test and assessed the internal consistency of the scales using Cronbach's alpha.

Prior to the mediational analysis, we calculated the correlations between all the variables to be included in the path analysis models. Correlation coefficients were interpreted according to the criteria of Safrit and Wood (1995): no correlation (score of 0–0.19), low correlation (0.20–0.39), moderate correlation (0.40–0.59), moderately high correlation (0.60–0.79), and high correlation ($\geq$0.80). We then tested a path analysis model in which the students' interest in studying PASS was hypothesized to mediate the relationship (path) between outcome expectations and goal representations. In addition, we expected that perceived social support would act only as a predictor of interest. The correlations and path analysis models are presented separately for boys and girls.

According to MacKinnon (2008), a mediating variable "is intermediate in the causal path from an independent variable to a dependent variable" (p. 8). To test for mediation, we explored three *a priori* models: Model 1 to test for partial mediation (direct and indirect effects), Model 2 to test for complete mediation (indirect effects only, i.e., interest), and Model 3 to test for absence of mediation (direct effects only). All three models were tested using the maximum likelihood estimator. Goodness of fit to the data was assessed using the following model fit indices: χ^2, root mean square error of approximation (RMSEA), the comparative fit index (CFI), and the Tucker-Lewis index (TLI). CFI and TLI values $\geq$0.95 and RMSEA values $\geq$0.06 were considered indicators of excellent fit; the respective values of $\geq$0.90 and $\leq$0.08 were considered to indicate acceptable fit.

Model 1 was the least parsimonious model and was therefore compared to Models 2 and 3. The comparisons were based on differences in χ^2 and in CFI, TLI, and RMSEA values. The most parsimonious model was only selected when differences in CFI were $<$0.01 and when TLI or RMSEA values were as good as or better than those obtained for the least parsimonious model. Mediated effects were obtained using the Model Indirect command and the VIA instruction as defined in the Mplus 7.0 software (Muthén and Muthén, 2012).

TABLE 1 | Comparison between boys and girls for outcome expectations, perceived social supports, interest, and goal representations in relation to studying a degree in PASS.

	Boys, *M* (*SD*)	Girls, *M* (*SD*)	*t*-test: *t*(*df*), *p*
Outcome expectations			
1. Social	3.31 (0.58)	3.46 (0.56)	−8.456 (4079.778), <0.001
2. Self-evaluative	3.55 (0.83)	3.53 (0.84)	0.649 (4098), NS
3. Physical	3.23 (0.79)	3.10 (0.75)	5.342 (4076), <0.001
4. Specific job attributes	4.18 (0.76)	4.35 (0.80)	−6.880 (4102), <0.001
5. Perceived social supports	0.83 (1.43)	0.43 (1.06)	10.039 (3764.491), <0.001
6. Interest	1.65 (0.91)	1.31 (0.66)	13.811 (3720.206), <0.001
Goal representations			
7. Social	3.40 (0.72)	3.65 (0.71)	−10.846 (4055), <0.001
8. Self-evaluative	3.92 (0.74)	3.98 (0.69)	−2.611 (4046.626), 0.009
9. Physical	3.72 (0.75)	3.62 (0.75)	4.279 (4054), <0.001
10. Specific job attributes	2.97 (0.94)	2.53 (0.81)	15.723 (3966.968), <0.001

RESULTS

Missing Data, Descriptive Scale Statistics, and Internal Consistency

Missing data rates did not exceed 1.1% for any of the study variables and therefore, according to Graham (2009), will not have affected our data analyses because they were <5%. In subsequent analyses thus we used pairwise deletion of missing data. **Table 1** shows the descriptive statistics for each study variable. Although the differences were small, they were all statistically significant except for self-evaluative goal representations. Of particular note were the differences in goal representations in the social (M_{boys} = 3.40; M_{girls} = 3.65), physical (M_{boys} = 3.72; M_{girls} = 3.62), and specific job attribute (M_{boys} = 2.97; M_{girls} = 2.53) domains. The difference for perceived social supports was also significantly different (M_{boys} = 0.83 and M_{girls} = 0.43). **Table 2** shows Cronbach's alphas for all the variables except the interest variable.

Correlations Between Variables

Almost all the correlations were positive and statistically significant (**Table 2**), although most of them were below <0.20 (no correlation) or between 0.20 and 0.39 (low correlation). Differences between male and female students were observed for correlations between outcome expectations and perceived social supports and interest.

Mediational Models

For this study, we tested a series of mediated path models to study the predictors of interest among teenage boys and girls in studying a degree in PASS. Relationships between outcome expectations, social supports, interest, and goal representations were analyzed using three different path models. Model 1 assumed that the effect of outcome expectations on goal representations would be partially mediated by interest in studying a degree in PASS; Model 2 assumed complete mediation, while Model 3 assumed absence of mediation. This sequence of competing models was tested separately for boys and girls. The results depicting the fit of the models to the data are presented in **Table 3**.

Model 1 provided an adequate fit for both boys and girls [boys: χ^2 (*df*) = 12.567 (4), p < 0.001, RMSEA (90 CI) = 0.047 (0.019 −0.077), CFI = 0.995, TLI = 0.954; girls: χ^2 (*df*) = 16.455 (4), p < 0.001, RMSEA (90 CI) = 0.055 (0.029 −0.084), CFI = 0.990, TLI = 0.914], and outperformed Models 2 and 3, supporting thus the hypothesis that interest in studying PASS partially mediated the effect of outcome expectations on goal representations (**Figure 1**). The R^2 values for

TABLE 2 | Correlations between variables analyzed in relation studying a degree in PASS.

	1	2	3	4	5	6	7	8	9	10
Outcome expectations										
1. Social	*0.61*	0.388**	0.215**	0.541**	0.105**	0.124**	0.338**	0.294**	0.187**	0.145**
2. Self-evaluative	0.424**	*0.68*	0.572**	0.213**	0.183**	0.221**	0.371**	0.371**	0.207**	0.324**
3. Physical	0.312**	0.526**	*0.66*	0.057	0.184**	0.246**	0.360**	0.256**	0.310**	0.398**
4. Specific job attributes	0.537**	0.129**	−0.046	*0.73*	0.004	−0.007	0.134**	0.197**	0.158**	0.100**
5. Perceived social supports	0.008	0.138**	0.158**	−0.048	*0.79*	0.582	0.235**	0.024	0.069*	0.334**
6. Interest[1]	0.013	0.162**	0.176**	−0.048	0.580**		0.268**	0.015	0.056	0.438**
Goal representations										
7. Social	0.317**	0.297**	0.243**	0.110**	0.070*	0.094*	*0.63*	0.343**	0.331**	0.465**
8. Self-evaluative	0.248**	0.323**	0.174**	0.200**	0.022	0.030	0.283**	*0.59*	0.354**	0.168**
9. Physical	0.147**	0.117**	0.217**	0.090*	0.071*	0.041	0.290**	0.373**	*0.68*	0.271**
10. Specific job attributes	0.056	0.248**	0.257**	−0.026	0.330**	0.415**	0.288**	0.210**	0.148**	*0.64*

Correlations computed using data for girls are presented in the left/bottom triangle of the table. Correlations computed using data for boys are presented in the right/upper triangle of the table. The range for all variables is 1–5, except for social supports (1–6) and interest (1–4). Cronbach's alpha coefficients are presented in the diagonal in italic. [1]*Interest was measured using a single item and therefore no Cronbach's alpha coefficients are presented.* *p < 0.05, **p < 0.01.

TABLE 3 | Model fit statistics and standardized coefficient estimates for mediation path analysis models.

Model	χ^2 *(df)*	RMSEA (CI 90)	CFI	TLI	ΔRMSEA	ΔCFI	ΔTLI
Girls							
1. Partial	16.455* (4)	0.055 (0.029–0.084)	0.990	0.914			
2. Complete	318.726* (20)	0.121 (0.110–0.133)	0.763	0.585	0.066	−0.227	−0.329
3. Direct	185.569* (12)	0.119 (0.105–0.135)	0.862	0.598	0.064	−0.128	−0.316
Boys							
1. Partial	12.567* (4)	0.047 (0.019–0.077)	0.995	0.954			
2. Complete	427.946* (20)	0.144 (0.132–0.156)	0.752	0.567	0.097	−0.243	−0.387
3. Direct	227.967* (12)	0.135 (0.120–0.151)	0.869	0.618	0.088	−0.126	0.377

*1. Partial = Model 1, partial mediation model; 2. Complete = Model 2, complete mediation model; 3. Direct = Model 3, direct effects model. *$p < 0.05$.*

Model 1 were (a) boys – $R^2_{\text{social (goal representations)}} = 0.240$, $R^2_{\text{self-evaluative (goal representations)}} = 0.181$, $R^2_{\text{physical (goal representations)}} = 0.119$, $R^2_{\text{specific job attributes (goal representations)}} = 0.297$, and $R^2_{\text{interest}} = 0.370$; and (b) girls – $R^2_{\text{social supports (goal representations)}} = 0.138$, $R^2_{\text{self-evaluative (goal representations)}} = 0.127$, $R^2_{\text{physical (goal representations)}} = 0.057$, $R^2_{\text{specific job attributes (goal representations)}} = 0.215$, and $R^2_{\text{interest}} = 0.344$. Therefore, the boys' model explained slightly more variance than the girls' model.

The statistically significant effects observed in Model 1 (**Figures 1A,B** and **Table 4**) showed some differences between girls and boys. The boys' model contained more direct and indirect (i.e., mediated by interest) effects. The following effects, all significant, were observed in the boys' model only: (a) indirect effect of perceived support on social (0.087) and self-evaluative (−0.049) goal representations; (b) direct effect of social outcome expectations on self-evaluative goal representations ($\beta = 0.156$) and indirect effect on specific job attributes (0.022); (c) direct ($\beta = 0.094$) and indirect (−0.010) effect of physical outcome expectations on self-evaluative goal representations and indirect effect on social goal representations (0.018); (d) direct effect of specific job attribute outcome expectations on interest ($\beta = -0.063$) and specific job attribute goal representations ($\beta = 0.083$) and indirect effect on social (−0.010) and specific job attribute (−0.023) goal representations. In the girls' model, self-evaluative outcome expectations had an indirect effect on specific job attribute goal representations (0.025), while specific job attribute outcome expectations had a direct effect on self-evaluative goal representations ($\beta = -0.134$).

Some common paths were also observed for boys and girls in the form of the following effects: (a) direct effect of perceived social supports on interest ($\beta_{girls} = 0.556$, $\beta_{boys} = 0.549$) and indirect effect on specific job attributes ($\beta_{girls} = 0.201$; $\beta_{boys} = 0.199$); (b) direct effect of social outcome expectations on social goal representations ($\beta_{girls} = 0.249$, $\beta_{boys} = 0.240$); (c) direct effect of self-evaluative outcome expectations on interest ($\beta_{girls} = 0.069$, $\beta_{boys} = 0.061$) and on social ($\beta_{girls} = 0.144$, $\beta_{boys} = 0.138$), self-evaluative ($\beta_{girls} = 0.271$, $\beta_{boys} = 0.270$), and specific job attribute ($\beta_{girls} = 0.139$, $\beta_{boys} = 0.092$) goal representations; (d) direct effect of physical outcome expectations on interest ($\beta_{girls} = 0.064$, $\beta_{boys} = 0.112$) and social ($\beta_{girls} = 0.076$, $\beta_{boys} = 0.196$), physical ($\beta_{girls} = 0.216$, $\beta_{boys} = 0.302$), and specific job attribute ($\beta_{girls} = 0.136$, $\beta_{boys} = 261$) goal representations and indirect effect on specific job attribute goal representations ($\beta_{girls} = 0.023$, $\beta_{boys} = 0.040$); and (e) direct effect of specific job attribute outcome expectations on physical goal representations ($\beta_{girls} = 0.073$, $\beta_{boys} = 0.104$).

DISCUSSION

The findings of this study contribute to our understanding of why female teenagers are less interested in studying a degree in PASS than their male peers and have important theoretical and practical implications.

Perceived social support was an important predictor of interest in studying PASS in both the boys and girls analyzed. In agreement with the literature, the empirical model showed that perceived support was significantly associated with interest, confirming thus our first hypothesis (H1). As indicated by Lent et al. (2000), social context has an important role in the development of interest toward one academic track or another. Social support, however, differs for boys and girls. Therefore, the potential influence of significant others (e.g., teachers, trainers, families, and friends) on a teenagers' academic and career choices should not be overlooked (Turner and Lapan, 2002; Stake and Nickens, 2005; Sáinz, 2007; Metheny et al., 2008; Sáinz and López-Sáez, 2010; Rogers and Creed, 2011; Buday et al., 2012).

Social cognitive career theory (Lent et al., 1994) posits that outcome expectations predict academic and career interests and goal representations. Our findings show that these expectations were significantly associated with goal representations both directly and indirectly (with interest as a mediator), confirming thus our second and third hypotheses (H2 and H3). We also observed gender differences in specific outcome expectation and goal representation variables. Self-evaluative and physical outcome expectations were significant in the paths identified for both girls and boys, but the boys' model additionally featured expectations related to specific job attributes. SCCT also posits that outcome expectations will exert a direct effect on goal representations in relation to career choices (Lent et al., 2001; Lent, 2012). In our study, we observed gender differences for each of the variables in the model, and as expected, the specific job attribute outcome expectation was related to personal goal representations among boys only.

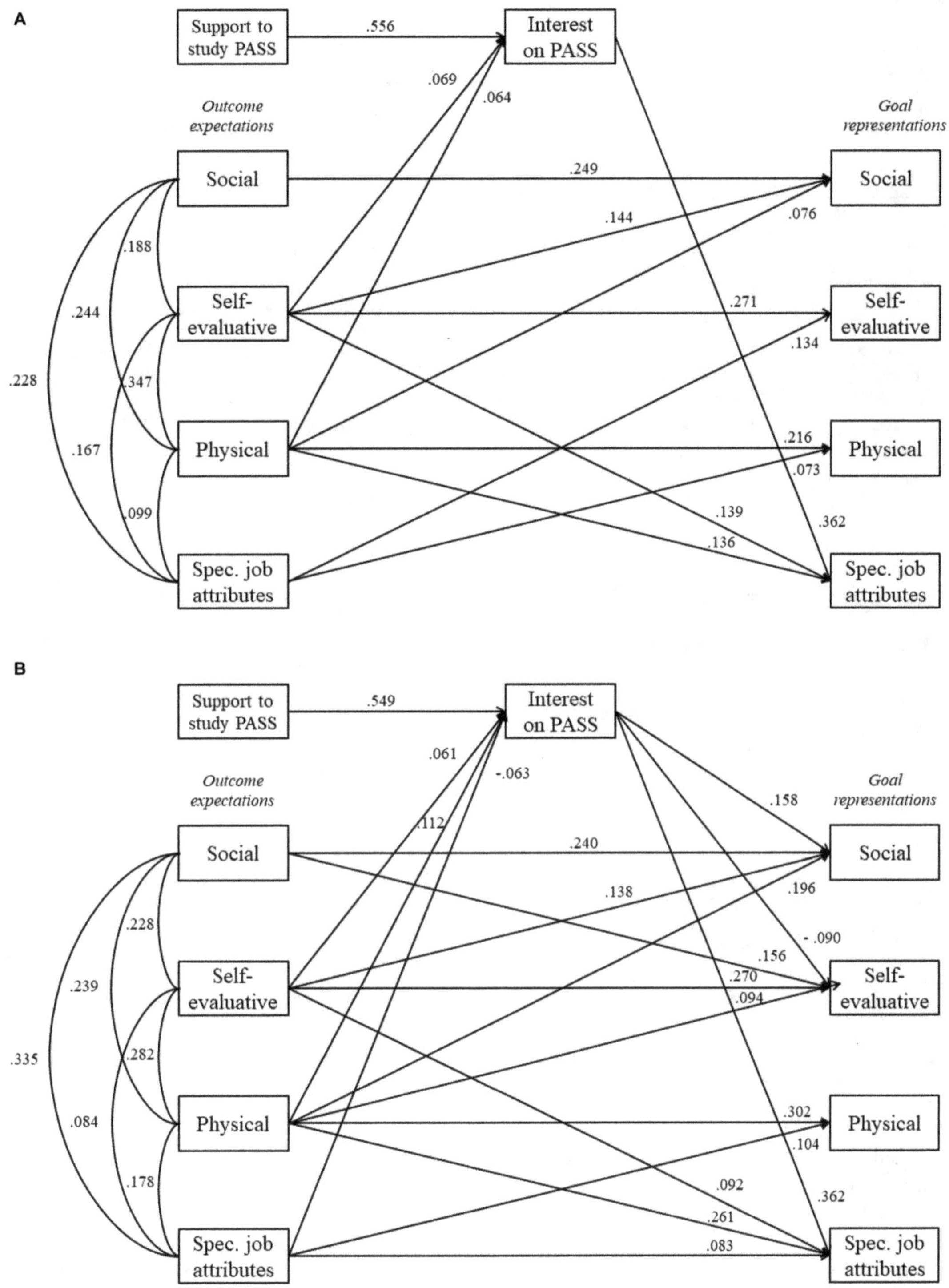

FIGURE 1 | Path analysis models showing the partial mediation of girls' **(A)** and boys' **(B)** interest in studying a degree in physical activity and sport science in the paths from perceived social supports and outcome expectations to goal representations. Only standardized statistically significant paths ($p < 0.05$) are shown. Spec. job attributes, specific job attributes.

The above findings provide insights into how teenage boys and girls establish personal goals based on the outcomes they envisage in relation to studying a degree in PASS. It has been well established that academic and career choices among both girls and boys are influenced by gender stereotypes. As observed in the literature review, female students are more likely to

TABLE 4 | Standardized indirect effects of outcome expectations on goal representations.

Independent variable	Mediator variable	Dependent variable	Boys		Girls	
			Mean indirect effect	95% CI for mean indirect effect	Mean indirect effect	95% CI for mean indirect effect
Perceived social supports	Interest	Social GRs	0.087*	0.053–0.120	0.026	−0.006–0.058
Perceived social supports	Interest	Self-evaluative GRs	−0.049*	−0.082 to −0.017	−0.003	−0.036–0.030
Perceived social supports	Interest	Physical GRs	−0.014	−0.044–0.016	0.005	−0.023–0.034
Perceived social supports	Interest	Specific job attribute GRs	0.199*	0.161–0.236	0.201*	0.149–0.253
Social OEs	Interest	Social GRs	0.010	−0.001–0.020	−0.001	−0.005–0.002
Social OEs	Interest	Self-evaluative GRs	−0.006	−0.012–0.001	0.000	−0.003–0.003
Social OEs	Interest	Physical GRs	−0.002	−0.006–0.002	0.000	−0.002–0.002
Social OEs	Interest	Specific job attribute GRs	0.022*	0.001–0.043	−0.010	−0.033–0.012
Self-evaluative OEs	Interest	Social GRs	0.008	−0.002–0.018	0.003	−0.002–0.008
Self-evaluative OEs	Interest	Self-evaluative GRs	−0.005	−0.011–0.002	0.000	−0.005–0.004
Self-evaluative OEs	Interest	Physical GRs	−0.001	−0.005–0.002	0.001	−0.003–0.005
Self-evaluative OEs	Interest	Specific job attribute GRs	0.019	−0.004–0.041	0.025*	0.005–0.045
Physical OEs	Interest	Social GRs	0.018*	0.005–0.030	0.003	−0.002–0.008
Physical OEs	Interest	Self-evaluative GRs	−0.010*	−0.018 to −0.002	0.000	−0.005–0.004
Physical OEs	Interest	Physical GRs	−0.003	−0.009–0.004	0.001	−0.003–0.004
Physical OEs	Interest	Specific job attribute GRs	0.040*	0.017–0.064	0.023*	0.001–0.045
Specific job attribute OEs	Interest	Social GRs	−0.010*	−0.020–0.000	−0.001	−0.005–0.003
Specific job attribute OEs	Interest	Self-evaluative GRs	0.006	−0.001–0.012	0.000	−0.002–0.002
Specific job attribute OEs	Interest	Physical GRs	0.002	−0.002–0.006	0.000	−0.002–0.002
Specific job attribute OEs	Interest	Specific job attribute GRs	−0.023*	−0.043 to −0.003	−0.007	−0.031–0.017

Perceived social support, perceived supports in relation to studying a degree in sport and exercise science; Interest, interest in studying a degree in sport and exercise science; OEs, outcome expectations; GRs, goal representations. $*p < 0.05$.

choose people-oriented careers, while male students are generally more interested in wealth and competitive positions (Sallop and Kirby, 2007; Sáinz, 2007; Candela, 2008; López-Bonilla et al., 2012). Our results also indicate that male and female teenagers are influenced by stereotyped portrayals of PASS studies and associated careers. Even though work in this field is largely people-oriented, it does not appear to be perceived as such by young people. Consequently, and in agreement with findings for STEM (Sáinz et al., 2014), misconceptions may discourage females from pursuing a career in this field.

Our results also support the theory that interest influences goal representations. SCCT predicts that interest in a given academic track or career will directly affect the setting of personal goals. In our study, goal representations were influenced by both interest and outcome expectations, confirming our third hypothesis (H3). However, again, the results for girls and boys differed. In the girls' model, interest in pursuing a degree in PASS was associated with job-specific attribute expectations only, while in the boys' model, it was associated with social, self-evaluative, and specific job attribute expectations.

Our fourth hypothesis (H4) was also confirmed, as we detected gender differences in perceived social supports, outcome expectations, and goal representations. We also found that the boy's model had greater explanatory power in relation to the SCCT than the girls'. While the girls' model provided an adequate and significant fit to the data, its paths were less elaborate than the boys'. Overall, and in support of work by Betz and Hackett (2006), our study confirms the importance of applying gender analysis to all the components of SCCT and its respective models.

Our findings support the applicability of SCCT to PASS studies and provide new insights into associated career choices among teenage boys and girls in their final years of school. They also support claims by Betz and Hackett (1981) that gender stereotypes influence perceptions of tasks, activities, and occupations, and extend current theories on social support. Social agents are known to exert a powerful influence on academic and career choices (Turner and Lapan, 2002; Sáinz, 2007; Sáinz and López-Sáez, 2010; Buday et al., 2012; Lent, 2012).

The results of our study confirm that male and female teenagers perceive different levels of support from their social environment in relation to their intention to study PASS at university. As expected, our path analysis showed gender differences along the path from social support to interest in these studies. Consistent with findings for research in the field of STEM, the effect of perceived social supports on the development of interest in studying PASS also differed between males and females (Sáinz and López-Sáez, 2010), with girls receiving less encouragement from people in their social circles to contemplate a career in PASS.

Practical Contributions

The findings of this study are relevant to educational institutions and career counselors seeking to bridge the gender gap in the field of PASS. PASS graduates can opt for a wide range of jobs in the fields of health, education, and care delivery, and while these professions have traditionally attracted women, female enrollment in PASS degrees has steadily declined over the past 25 years (Serra et al., 2019). Strategies targeting social agents are needed to break down gender-role stereotypes and encourage more young women to contemplate a career in this field. Institutions seeking to attract more women thus need to move away from the male-centered sports culture typically transmitted to society. Awareness-raising programs highlighting the myriad of job opportunities associated with PASS could also improve outcome expectations among young women.

People already working in this field, whether in academia or industry, can also play an important role in transforming overly simplistic and gendered conceptions of PASS. By serving as role models, they can foster positive outcome expectations and inspire young women to consider pursuing a career in this field. Training of these future professionals, however, needs to integrate a gender perspective, as otherwise, they may become agents of reproduction rather than change. The inclusion of gender issues in PASS studies and training programs for physical education instructors is crucial for breaking down gender stereotypes and widening the perspectives of future trainers. Numerous other factors in the teenagers' social and school environment, including positive experiences with sport and physical activity, can also help teenagers to develop an interest in studying PASS. If this dichotomous, male-centered vision of physical education, sport, and exercise continues, these degree courses will continue to be dominated by males.

Our findings are also relevant for sports policymakers and employers as sport and exercise permeate all levels of society; offer multiple job opportunities; and are of enormous economic, social, and cultural importance. If women are not encouraged to enroll in PASS and similar degrees, their participation in the workforce will decrease even further, resulting in a loss of richness and diversity that will only perpetuate existing gender gaps. Diversity drives innovation and creativity, and applied to the field of PASS, it may also provide inspiration to young women and other people from varying sociocultural backgrounds. A key practical implication of our study is that our findings can provide institutions and practitioners with insights into how best they can tailor initiatives to attract more women to PASS degrees (Serra et al., 2018; Soler et al., 2018).

Combating the under-representation of females in PASS degrees remains a challenge that, if correctly addressed, will contribute to eliminating gendered academic and career choices among young women and men.

Limitations and Future Directions

There are several limitations that should be noted in this study. First of all, we measured interest as an intention not a behavior. It would therefore be interesting to perform a longitudinal study of the adolescents who participated in this study to monitor their academic and career paths and see how they progress toward the attainment of their goals. It would also be interesting to perform a similar study from the perspective of the SCCT performance model, which analyzes persistence in educational and occupational pursuits and level of success achieved (performance outcomes, satisfaction, and well-being) (Lent et al., 1994). Analysis of these additional factors would help better understand the career choice process from a wider perspective. It would be particularly interesting to analyze how people who set themselves specific academic or career goals persist in the pursuit of these goals, regardless of positive or negative social influences or of perceived self-efficacy in physical activity and sport. Detailed comparisons of strategies followed by male and female adolescents could shed light on how and why the few girls interested in studying a degree in PASS actually go on to study this degree, despite perceived physical and social barriers. In relation to the academic/career satisfaction/well-being SCCT model (Lent and Brown, 2006; Lent, 2012), it would be interesting to analyze similarities and differences among male and female PASS students in terms of (1) value placed on the activity chosen, (2) awareness of progress toward personal goals, (3) beliefs in their ability to perform well in necessary tasks (self-efficacy), and (4) access to resources in their environment that enhance their self-efficacy beliefs and drive them to pursue their goals with greater energy (Lent and Brown, 2006).

Based on our findings, we suggest numerous areas for future research. Of particular interest is further investigation of external factors (social supports) that directly influence the development of interest in studying PASS among girls and boys. A closer analysis of the degree of influence exerted by different social agents (parents, siblings, trainers, teachers, etc.) will provide important insights into the relevance of each agent. Qualitative research based on interviews or women-only focus groups may also shed light on perceived social supports and barriers that encourage or discourage teenage girls from pursuing a career in PASS.

To conclude, the results of this study support many of the hypothesized relationships between the SCCT variables analyzed and suggest that both perceived social supports and positive conceptions of outcome expectations are important predictors of the formulation of personal goals in relation to studying a degree in PASS. Our findings contribute to a broader understanding of the SCCT model and show that while the basic relationships are generally confirmed, the different elements have a particular influence on social supports (environmental/external factors) and outcome expectations.

We have explored factors that influence male and female teenagers' interest in pursuing a degree in PASS. Trends from recent years indicate that if the current situation continues, female enrollment in these degrees will continue to decline and with it the number of potential role models for future generations.

By better understanding how teenage girls develop interest in PASS, we will be better equipped to create strategies that will attract women to this field and in doing so contribute to bridging the gender gap.

ETHICS STATEMENT

The study was reviewed and approved by the Research Ethics Committee of the Sports Administration of Catalonia, and ethical concerns were addressed throughout the research process. Written informed consent to participate in this study was provided by the participants' legal guardian/next of kin. Respondents and their families were provided with information about the study and were assured of confidentiality of identifiable information and were informed of their right to withdraw participation at any time without prejudice from any party. Informed signed consent was obtained from the students' parents and the school authorities prior to the study. No incentives were offered.

AUTHOR CONTRIBUTIONS

PS, SS, MC-M, AR-C, and AV: design of the study, analysis and interpretation of the data, and manuscript preparation. PS: acquisition of the data. SS: conceptualization and obtaining funding.

ACKNOWLEDGMENTS

The authors thank the Institut Nacional d'Educació Física de Catalunya (INEFC) de la Generalitat de Catalunya for providing the support.

REFERENCES

Acosta, R. V., and Carpenter, L. J. (2012). *Women in Intercollegiate Sport: A Longitudinal, National Study Thirty-five Year Update: 1977–2012.* Available at: http://www.acosta.org (accessed January 20, 2019).

Alexander, P. M., Holmner, M., Lotriet, H. H., Matthee, M. C., Pieterse, H. V., Naidoo, S., et al. (2011). Factors affecting career choice: comparison between students from computer and other disciplines. *J. Sci. Educ. Technol.* 20, 300–315. doi: 10.1007/s10956-010-9254-3

Azurmendi, A. (2016). *Obstáculos psicosociales para la participación de las mujeres en el deporte como entrenadoras y árbitras.* Tesis doctoral, Universidad del País Vasco, Donosti.

Bandura, A. (1986). *Social Foundations of Thought and Action: A Social Cognitive Theory.* Englewood Cliffs, NJ: Prentice-Hall.

Bandura, A. (1987). *Pensamiento y acción. Fundamentos sociales.* Barcelona: Ediciones Martínez Roca, S.A.

Bandura, A. (1997). *Self-Efficacy in Changing Societies.* Cambridge: Cambridge University Press.

Betz, N. E., and Hackett, G. (1981). The relationship of career-related self-efficacy expectations to perceived career options in college women and men. *J. Couns. Psychol.* 28, 399–410. doi: 10.1037/0022-0167.28.5.399

Betz, N. E., and Hackett, G. (2006). Career self-efficacy theory: back to the future. *J. Career Assess.* 14, 3–11. doi: 10.1177/1069072705281347

Blanco, Á. (2009). El modelo cognitivo social del desarrollo de la carrera: revisión de más de una década de investigación empírica. *Rev. Educ.* 350, 423–445.

Buday, S. K., Stake, J. E., and Peterson, Z. D. (2012). Gender and the choice of a science career: the impact of social support and possible selves. *Sex Roles* 66, 197–209. doi: 10.1007/s11199-011-0015-14

Candela, C. (2008). *Motivaciones y expectativas profesionales. Análisis desde la perspectiva de género.* Available at: http://roderic.uv.es/handle/10550/15419#.XJzhTLmEgBM.mendeley (accessed March 28, 2019).

Cunningham, G. B., Bruening, J., Sartore, M. L., Sagas, M., and Fink, J. S. (2005). The application of social cognitive career theory to sport and leisure career choices. *J. Career Dev.* 32, 122–138. doi: 10.1177/0894845305279164

Cunningham, G. B., Doherty, A. J., and Gregg, M. J. (2007). Using social cognitive career theory to understand head coaching intentions among assistant coaches of women's teams. *Sex Roles* 56, 365–372. doi: 10.1007/s11199-006-9175-z

Cunningham, G. B., and Singer, J. N. (2010). "You'll face discrimination wherever you go": student athletes' intentions to enter the coaching profession. *J. Appl. Soc. Psychol.* 40, 1708–1727. doi: 10.1111/j.1559-1816.2010.00636.x

Eccles, J. (2011). Gendered educational and occupational choices: applying the Eccles et al. Model of achievement-related choices. *Int. J. Behav. Dev.* 35, 195–201. doi: 10.1177/0165025411398185

Eccles, J. S., and Harold, R. D. (1991). Gender differences in sport involvement: applying the eccles' expectancy-value model. *J. Appl. Sport Psychol.* 3, 7–35. doi: 10.1080/10413209108406432

Elling, A., Hovden, J., and Knoppers, A. (2019). *Gender Diversity in European Sport Governance.* Abingdon: Routledge.

Everhart, C. B., and Chelladurai, P. (1998). Gender differences in preferences for coaching as an occupation: the role of self-efficacy, valence, and perceived barriers. *Res. Q. Exerc. Sport* 69, 188–200. doi: 10.1080/02701367.1998.10607683

Graham, J. W. (2009). Missing data analysis: making it work in the real world. *Annu. Rev. Psychol.* 60, 549–576. doi: 10.1146/annurev.psych.58.110405.085530

Hinojosa-Alcalde, I., Andrés, A., Serra, P., Vilanova, A., Soler, S., and Norman, L. (2017). Understanding the gendered coaching workforce in Spanish sport. *Int. J. Sports Sci. Coach.* 13, 485–495. doi: 10.1177/1747954117747744

Holland, J. L. (1997). *Making Vocational Choices: A Theory of Vocational Personalities and Work Environments*, 3rd Edn. Odessa, FL: Psychological Assessment Resources.

Jones, M. G., Howe, A., and Rua, M. J. (2000). Gender differences in students' experiences, interests, and attitudes toward science and scientists. *Sci. Educ.* 84, 180–192. doi: 10.1002/(SICI)1098-237X(200003)84:2<180:AID-SCE3<3.0.CO;2-X

Kim, M.-C., and Hong, E. (2016). A red card for women: female officials ostracized in South Korean football. *Asian J. Womens Stud.* 22, 114–130. doi: 10.1080/12259276.2016.1168156

Lent, R. W. (2012). "Social cognitive career theory," in *Career Development and Counseling: Putting Theory and Research to Work*, eds R. W. Lent, and S. D. Brown, (Somerset, NJ: John Wiley & Sons), 115–146.

Lent, R. W., and Brown, S. D. (2006). Integrating person and situation perspective on work satisfaction: a social-cognitive view. *J. Vocat. Behav.* 69, 236–247. doi: 10.1016/j.jvb.2006.02.006

Lent, R. W., and Brown, S. D. (2013). Social cognitive model of career self-management: toward a unifying view of adaptive career behavior across the life span. *J. Couns. Psychol.* 60, 557–568. doi: 10.1037/a0033446

Lent, R. W., Brown, S. D., Brenner, B., Chopra, S. B., Davis, T., Talleyrand, R., et al. (2001). The role of contextual supports and barriers in the choice of math/science educational options: a test of social cognitive hypotheses. *J. Couns. Psychol.* 48, 474–483. doi: 10.1037/0022-0167.48.4.474

Lent, R. W., Brown, S. D., and Hackett, G. (1994). Toward a unifying social cognitive theory of career and academic interest, choice, and performance. *J. Vocat. Behav.* 45, 79–122. doi: 10.1006/jvbe.1994.1027

Lent, R. W., Brown, S. D., and Hackett, G. (2000). Contextual supports and barriers to career choice: a social cognitive analysis. *J. Couns. Psychol.* 47, 36–49. doi: 10.1037/0022-0167.47.1.36

Lent, R. W., Paixão, M. P., da Silva, J. T., and Leitão, L. M. (2010). Predicting occupational interests and choice aspirations in Portuguese high school students: a test of social cognitive career theory. *J. Vocat. Behav.* 76, 244–251. doi: 10.1016/j.jvb.2009.10.001

López-Bonilla, J. M., Barrera, R. B., Serrano, M. Á. R., López-Bonilla, L. M., Florencio, B. P., Rodríguez, M. C. R., et al. (2012). Reasons which influence on the students' decision to take a university course: differences by gender and degree. *Educ. Stud.* 38, 297–308. doi: 10.1080/03055698.2011.598690

MacKinnon, D. P. (2008). *Introduction Statistical Mediation Analysis*. New York, NY: Taylor & Francis, doi: 10.1037/13620-13618

Metheny, J., McWhirter, E. H., and O'Neil, M. E. (2008). Measuring perceived teacher support and its influence on adolescent career development. *J. Career Assess.* 16, 218–237. doi: 10.1177/1069072707313198

Ministerio de Educación Cultura y Deporte (2019). *Datos y cifras del sistema universitario español*. Madrid: Secretaría General Técnica.

Moragas, M. (2014). *Les dones que presideixen els clubs esportius a Catalunya. Factors que incideixen en l'accés i en l'exercici del càrrec, i estil de lideratge* Barcelona: Universitat Ramon Llull.

Moran-Miller, K., and Flores, L. Y. (2011). Where are the women in women's sports? Predictors of female athletes' interest in a coaching career. *Res. Q. Exerc. Sport* 82, 109–117. doi: 10.1080/02701367.2011.10599727

Morgan, C., Isaac, J. D., and Sansone, C. (2001). The role of interest in understanding the career choices of female and male college students. *Sex Roles* 44, 295–320. doi: 10.1023/A:1010929600004

Muthén, L. K., and Muthén, B. O. (2012). *Mplus Editor (version 7.0) (software)*. Los Angeles, CA: Muthen & Muthen.

Nauta, M. (2013). "Holland's theory of vocational choice and adjustment," in *Career Development and Counseling: Putting Theory and Research to Work*, eds R. W. Lent, and S. D. Brown, (Somerset, NJ: John Wiley & Sons).

Park, I.-J., Kim, M., Kwon, S., and Lee, H.-G. (2018). The relationships of self-esteem, future time perspective, positive affect, social support, and career decision: a longitudinal multilevel study. *Front. Psychol.* 9:514. doi: 10.3389/fpsyg.2018.00514

Pérez-Villalba, M., Vilanova, A., and Soler, S. (2018). Sport labor market and gender: a comparative study on working conditions of physical activity and sport science graduates by Catalan universities. *Rev. Humanidades* 34:9. doi: 10.5944/rdh.34.2018.19731

Porto, B. (2009). Feminización y masculinización en los estudios de maestro y educación física en Galicia. *Rev. Investig. en Educ.* 6, 50–57.

Rogers, M. E., and Creed, P. A. (2011). A longitudinal examination of adolescent career planning and exploration using a social cognitive career theory framework. *J. Adolesc.* 34, 163–172. doi: 10.1016/j.adolescence.2009.12.010

Rogers, M. E., Creed, P. A., and Glendon, A. I. (2008). The role of personality in adolescent career planning and exploration: a social cognitive perspective. *J. Vocat. Behav.* 73, 132–142. doi: 10.1016/j.jvb.2008.02.002

Safrit, M. J., and Wood, T. M. (1995). *Introduction to Measurement in Physical Education and Exercise Science*, 3rd Edn. St. Louis, MO: Times Mirrow/Mosby.

Sáinz, M. (2007). *Aspectos psicosociales de las diferencias de género en actitudes hacia las nuevas tecnologías en adolescentes*. Madrid: Instituto de la Juventud.

Sáinz, M., and López-Sáez, M. (2010). Gender differences in computer attitudes and the choice of technology-related occupations in a sample of secondary students in Spain. *Comput. Educ.* 54, 578–587. doi: 10.1016/j.compedu.2009.09.007

Sáinz, M., Meneses, J., López, B-S., and Fàbregas, S. (2014). Gender stereotypes and attitudes towards information and communication technology professionals in a sample of spanish secondary students. *Sex Roles* 74, 154–168. doi: 10.1007/s11199-014-0424-2

Sallop, L. J., and Kirby, S. L. (2007). The role of gender and work experience on career and work force diversity expectations. *J. Behav. Appl. Manag.* 8, 122–140.

Serra, P., Soler, S., Prat, M., Vizcarra, M. T., Garay, B., and Flintoff, A. (2018). The (in)visibility of gender knowledge in the Physical activity and sport science degree in Spain. *Sport Educ. Soc.* 23, 324–338. doi: 10.1080/13573322.2016.1199016

Serra, P., Soler, S., Vilanova, A., and Hinojosa-Alcalde, I. (2019). Masculinización en estudios de las ciencias de la actividad física y el deporte. *Apunt. Educ. Física y Deport.* 4, 9–25. doi: 10.5672/apunts.2014-0983.es.(2019/1).135.01

Soler, S., Serra, P., and Vilanova, A. (2018). *La Igualtat en joc: guia de bones pràctiques de gènere en els estudis de la família de les ciències de l'activitat física i de l'esport*. Barcelona: Institut Nacional d'Educació Física de Catalunya.

Stake, J. E., and Nickens, S. D. (2005). Adolescent girls' and boys' science peer relationships and perceptions of the possible self as scientist. *Sex Roles* 52, 1–11. doi: 10.1007/s11199-005-1189-1184

Su, R., and Rounds, J. (2015). All STEM fields are not created equal: people and things interests explain gender disparities across STEM fields. *Front. Psychol.* 6:189. doi: 10.3389/fpsyg.2015.00189

Turner, S., and Lapan, R. T. (2002). Career self-efficacy and perceptions of parent support in adolescent career development. *Career Dev. Q.* 51, 44–55. doi: 10.1002/j.2161-0045.2002.tb00591.x

Viñas, J., and Pérez, M. (2014). *El mercat de treball de l'esport a Catalunya. Especial incidència a la província de Barcelona*. Barcelona: INDE.

Webb, L., and Macdonald, D. (2007). Techniques of power in physical education and the underrepresentation of women in leadership. *J. Teach. Phys. Educ.* 26, 279–297. doi: 10.1123/jtpe.26.3.279

7

Complementing the Self-Determination Theory with the Need for Novelty: Motivation and Intention to be Physically Active in Physical Education Students

Carlos Fernández-Espínola, Bartolomé J. Almagro*, Javier A. Tamayo-Fajardo and Pedro Sáenz-López

Department of Integrated Didactics, Faculty of Education, Psychology and Sports Sciences, Universidad de Huelva, Huelva, Spain

Correspondence:
Bartolomé J. Almagro
almagro@dempc.uhu.es

The theoretical framework of the self-determination theory establishes that the satisfaction of basic psychological needs and more self-determined motivational forms are related to positive behavioral consequences and, therefore, may increase the intention to be physically active in Physical Education students. In this sense, the need for novelty has been proposed as a psychological need by recent scientific evidence, so it is necessary to prove its possible contribution to the prediction of young people's behavior. Therefore, the main objective of the study was to test a model that analyzed the power of prediction of the satisfaction of the needs for autonomy, competence, relatedness, and novelty as well as the motivation experienced in Physical Education on the intention to be physically active. A questionnaire was administered to 1665 Physical Education students with an average age of 12.43 years (SD = 1.87), of which 835 were boys and 830 were girls. An adaptation of the Spanish educational context of the Basic Psychological Needs in Exercise Scale (BPNES) that includes the need for novelty, the Perceived Locus of Causality Scale (PLOC), and the Intention to be Physically Active Scale (IPAS) was used. Path analysis results showed that the satisfaction of the psychological needs for autonomy, competence, relatedness, and novelty predicted autonomous motivation. On the other hand, the need for autonomy positively predicted controlled motivation, while the satisfaction of relatedness did so negatively. The need for competence and autonomous motivation positively predicted the intention to be physically active in Physical Education students, obtaining an explained variance of 33%. However, controlled motivation was not related in a statistically significant way to the intention to be physically active. In conclusion, the results of the hypothesized model highlight the importance of satisfying all the basic psychological needs (including novelty) and give special emphasis to the need for competence, since it predicts autonomous motivation and the intention to be physically active outside of the educational context.

Keywords: self-determination theory, psychological needs, school education, secondary education, physically active

INTRODUCTION

Despite the multiple benefits that regular physical activity provides in children and adolescents (e.g., Janssen and LeBlanc, 2010), increasing adherence to it and reducing sedentariness among this demographic continues to be a major global health issue (WHO, 2019). In recent years, the study of motivation has been widely applied to the field of physical activity by being considered as that which energizes and gives direction to human behavior (Ryan and Deci, 2017) and, therefore, is very useful as a concept to analyze aspects related to adherence to activity (e.g., Ryan et al., 1997; Teixeira et al., 2012).

As such, one of the principal theories that focuses on the workings of motivational processes in human beings is the self-determination theory (SDT; Deci and Ryan, 1985, 2000; Ryan and Deci, 2017). SDT identifies the existence of three basic psychological needs which are universal and inherent in all individuals. These are autonomy, competence, and relatedness. "Autonomy" refers to a person's need to see themselves as the origin of their own actions and to experience actions of their own choosing; "competence" refers to the need to control the result and achieve efficiency; and "relatedness" refers to the need to be connected to others (Ryan and Deci, 2017). These three needs explain the regulation of people's behavior, established on a motivational continuum, which fluctuates between autonomous motivation (i.e., intrinsic regulation, integrated regulation, and identified regulation), passes through more controlled forms of motivation (i.e., introjected regulation and external regulation), and ends with the absence of regulation or amotivation (Deci and Ryan, 2000; Ryan and Deci, 2000, 2017; Vansteenkiste et al., 2010). Intrinsic motivation concerns activities carried out to generate pleasant sensations or for enjoyment and inherent interest. In identified regulation, the person consciously valors an activity and experiences a high degree of volition to act. In integrated regulation, the person valors the activity and finds it to be consistent with other interests. Introjected regulation refers to behaviors performed by avoidance of negative feelings (like shame or anxiety) for failure and by rewards of self-esteem for success. External regulation comprises behaviors which are imposed by a system of rewards and punishments. Finally, amotivation concerns to lacking intentionality (Ryan and Deci, 2020). SDT suggests that the satisfaction of these basic psychological needs is associated with autonomous motivation, while frustration of the same is related to controlled motivation and amotivation (Ryan and Deci, 2017).

As a complement to SDT, Vallerand (1997, 2001) developed the hierarchical model of intrinsic and extrinsic motivation (HMIEM), identifying the existence of three distinct levels of motivation: global (general motivation of the subject), contextual (motivation within a specific context, such as Physical Education classes), and situational (motivation experienced during the course of a Physical Education session or a particular activity). This model established that motivation at any of these levels is influenced by social factors (e.g., the interpersonal style of the teacher); that the perception of the three basic psychological needs mediates the effect between these social factors and motivation; and that motivation brings a series of consequences across a wide variety of contexts (Ryan and Deci, 2017), including in Physical Education (e.g., Van den Berghe et al., 2014). In this way, the scientific literature has shown how satisfaction of the needs for competence, autonomy and relatedness increases the most self-determined types of motivation (Ntoumanis, 2001; Standage et al., 2006; Fin et al., 2019), and this leads to positive behavioral consequences in students, some of which are associated with the practice of physical activity outside of the school context (e.g., the intention to be physically active; Hein et al., 2004; Mouratidis et al., 2008; Lim and Wang, 2009).

Within this context, González-Cutre et al. (2016) recently opened a new line of investigation concerning the functioning of motivational processes. These authors proposed that the need for novelty, understood as the need to experience something that has not been experienced previously or that diverges from the daily routine, could be considered as a new basic psychological need within SDT. In fact, several studies have proposed more new candidate-needs in the last few years (Vansteenkiste et al., 2020).

The fourth mini-theory of SDT, or in other words, the basic psychological needs theory (BPNT), analyze the relations between the basic psychological need satisfactions and frustrations on well-being and the ill-being (Ryan and Deci, 2017). Within BPNT, Ryan and Deci (2017) established six criteria that a candidate need should meet to be including as a basic psychological need: (1) the satisfaction of this candidate must be strongly associated with well-being, health and psychological integrity, while its frustration must be negatively associated with these consequences and positively related with ill-being; (2) it must specify the experiences and contents that lead to well-being; (3) candidate need should be a significant and constant mediator of the relationships between personal and social factors and the motivational and psychological functioning of the individual; (4) any new candidate should act as a growth need and not as a deficit need, meaning that the new basic psychological need must act in accordance with the three existing needs and not as a substitute for one of them when they become frustrated or threatened; (5) it should be a precursor and not a consequence within the motivational process of self-determination theory; and (6) it must work universally for all ages and cultures.

In this sense, Bagheri and Milyavskaya (2020) have proposed and analyzed a similar key-concept to novelty as candidate new. These authors showed how the novelty-variety (personal perception of doing or experimenting something new and the possibility of different combinations) fulfilled some criteria; since novelty-variety was a factor separated from the other needs, the findings did not depend on the age of the participants or novelty-seeking preferences, and when novelty-variety was thwarted, there was a reduction on well-being.

In this line, novelty (excluding the variety-feature) has also fulfilled some criteria. González-Cutre et al. (2016) showed through a confirmatory factor analysis that the need for novelty is a distinct construct to those of autonomy, competence, and relatedness. These results have coincided with recent findings by Trigueros et al. (2019) in a study to validate the Spanish version of the Basic Psychological Needs Satisfaction Scale for Physical Education classes. The confirmatory factor analysis also showed

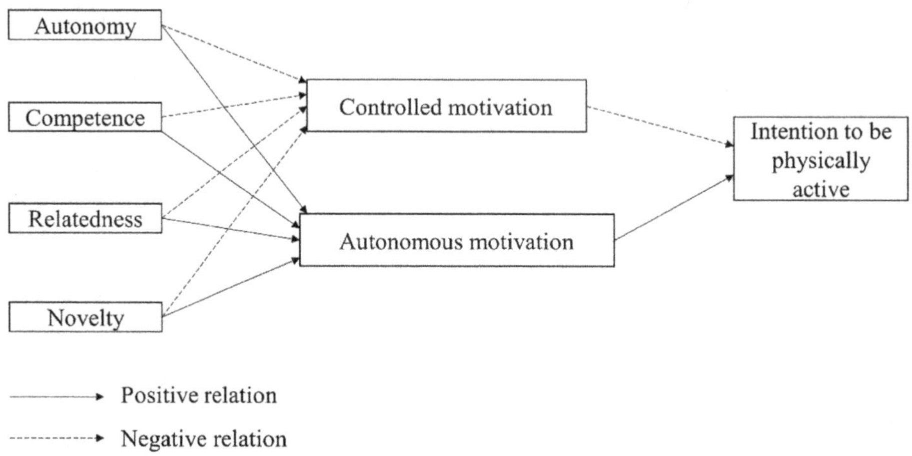

FIGURE 1 | Hypothesized model of the basic psychological needs, with autonomous and controlled motivation and the intention to be physically active.

the need for novelty as an independent factor. Likewise, the studies by González-Cutre et al. (2016, 2020) and González-Cutre and Sicilia (2019) have demonstrated how the aforementioned construct is positively associated with the most self-determined types of motivation and with positive consequences, such as life satisfaction, enjoyment, and vitality in Physical Education. González-Cutre et al. (2020) also showed the moderating role of openness to experience in the association between the novelty need satisfaction and well-being.

This existing relationship between the need for novelty and positive consequences has now become the object of study in other contexts. In particular, Birdsell (2018) has recently shown a positive correlation between the satisfaction of the need for novelty and the commitment to and satisfaction of learning English for a group of Japanese students. To this extent, the recent scientific evidence indicates that novelty could be a basic need within BPNT. However, it is still necessary to analyze whether similar benefits emerge at the cognitive, behavioral and physiological level, and in various contexts (Vansteenkiste et al., 2020).

In terms of the role played by the need for novelty with respect to physical activity, little is currently known. In fact, the study by Fernández-Espínola et al. (2020) is the only published investigation on the satisfaction of the need for novelty and its behavioral consequences in relation to the practice of physical activity (the intention to be physically active in the future). The results of this investigation showed that the need for novelty was associated with the intrinsic motivation of Physical Education students and the growth of their intention to be physically active in the future. However, the traditional basic psychological needs were not included in this study. Therefore, further study is required of the role of the need for novelty when combined with the other three psychological needs in a sequence that includes some variable related to the practice of physical activity as a consequence.

Thus, taking into account the importance that knowing young people's intention to be physically active could have for global health, just like the lack of studies that relate the need for novelty with behavioral consequences within SDT, the objective of the present study was to test the interrelations between the need for novelty and the basic psychological needs, autonomous motivation, controlled motivation and the intention to be physically active in the future. Using a model which hypothesizes that the three existing basic psychological needs, as well as novelty, would act as positive predictors of autonomous motivation and as negative predictors of controlled motivation. In turn, autonomous motivation would act as a positive predictor of the intention to be physically active, while controlled motivation would act as a negative predictor of the same (see **Figure 1**).

MATERIALS AND METHODS

Participants

The sample of this investigation was composed of 1665 students of Physical Education, who were studying between the 5th year of primary school up to the first year of the high school diploma (equivalent to first year of A-level study) and belonged to 15 educational institutions (12 public schools and three private schools) in the province of Huelva (Spain). Specifically, the sample constituted 835 boys and 830 girls, of ages ranging from 10 to 18 years old (M = 12.43, SD = 1.87). Convenience sampling was used to select the all the participants. Students received two physical education sessions per week.

Measures

Basic Psychological Needs

The most recent version of the Measurement of Psychological Needs Scale was employed (González-Cutre and Sicilia, 2019), which was adapted from the *Basic Psychological Needs in Exercise Scale* (BPNES; Vlachopoulos and Michailidou, 2006) for the Spanish educational setting, to which the authors added the need for novelty. The scale consisted of a total of 17 items grouped into four aspects (four items per aspect, except for the novelty aspect, which consisted of five items): autonomy (e.g., "I have the opportunity to choose how to exercise"), competence (e.g., "I exercise efficiently"), relatedness to others (e.g., "I feel very comfortable when I exercise with friends") and novelty (e.g., "I think that I often discover new things"). The preceding phrase was "In my Physical Education classes...". The responses were scored using a Likert scale with five options, from 1 (corresponding to *Totally agree)* to 5 (corresponding to *Totally disagree)*. The internal consistency of this scale was 0.83 for the need for novelty, 0.74 for the need for relatedness, 0.73 for the need for autonomy, and 0.70 for the need for competence. Factorial validity of the Psychological Needs Scale was examined using confirmatory factor analysis (CFA), which offered acceptable fit indices ($\chi^2 = 417.21$, $p = 0.00$, χ^2/g.l. = 3.69, CFI = 0.92, IFI = 0.92, TLI = 0.91, SRMR = 0.05, RMSEA = 0.06).

Autonomous and Controlled Motivation

The factors of intrinsic regulation, identified regulation, introjected regulation and external regulation were used from the Perceived Locus of Causality Scale in Physical Education, tested in the Spanish context by Moreno-Murcia et al. (2009) from the *Perceived Locus of Causality Scale* (PLOC; Goudas et al., 1994). Each factor is composed of 4 items: intrinsic regulation (e.g., "Because physical education is fun"), identified regulation (e.g., "Because I want to learn sporting skills"), introjected regulation ("Because I would feel bad about myself if I didn't do it") and external regulation (e.g., "Because I'll have problems if I don't do it"). The responses were scored using a Likert scale, with a scoring system range from 1 *(Totally disagree)* to 7 *(Totally agree)*. The phrase preceding the items was "I participate in Physical Education classes...". The internal consistency was 0.78 for intrinsic regulation, 0.78 for identified regulation, 0.69 for introjected regulation, and 0.70 for external regulation. The data from this study revealed adequate psychometric properties of the PLOC in PE using CFA ($\chi^2 = 520.60$, $p = 0.00$, χ^2 / g.l. = 3.25, CFI = 0.92, IFI = 0.92, TLI = 0.91, SRMR = 0.06, RMSEA = 0.06). In order to calculate autonomous motivation, the sum of intrinsic regulation subscale weighted by two and of identified regulation subscale was used. Similarly, in order to calculate controlled motivation, the sum of external regulation scale multiplied weighted by two and of introjected regulation scale was used (Hagger et al., 2014).

Intentionality to Be Physically Active

The adapted and translated (into Spanish) version (Moreno-Murcia et al., 2007) of *Intention to be Physically Active Scale* (IPAS) by Hein et al. (2004). The scale was introduced with the phrase "With respect to your intention to practice some form of physical activity...". The scale was composed of five items in order to measure the intention to be physically active (e.g., "I regularly practice sport in my free time"). The responses were scored using a Likert scale, ranging from 1 (*Totally disagree)* to 5 (*Totally agree*). Cronbach's alpha was 0.77. The CFA showed acceptable fit indices ($\chi^2 = 24.45$, $p = 0.00$, χ^2 / g.l. = 4.89, CFI = 0.99, IFI = 0.99, TLI = 0.98, SRMR = 0.02, RMSEA = 0.08).

Procedure

The present study was developed in accordance with current legislation in Spain concerning investigative studies of people and in line with the ethical principles of the American Psychological Association (2020). Firstly, the permission of the Ethics Committee of Biomedical Investigation of Andalusia (Spain) was obtained. The next measure completed to enable data collection was to establish contact with the management team of each of the educational institutions, with the intention of informing them about the aims of our investigation and to request their cooperation. Subsequently, given that the sample consisted of subjects who were minors, authorization in the form of a written signature was requested from their legal guardians so that they could participate in the study. Once authorization was granted, the questionnaires were distributed in the presence of the principal researcher, who gave a brief explanation of the objectives of the study, set out a series of guidelines on how to complete the questionnaires and addressed any issues that arose from the reading and comprehension of some of the items, emphasizing anonymity and the importance of providing honest answers. In general, the time required to complete the questionnaire was 15 minutes.

Data Analysis

Firstly, the data matrix was filtered, followed by an analysis of the reliability of the data and calculation of the variables. Then, descriptive statistics of said variables and bivariate correlations were calculated. Moreover, a path analysis was completed with the aim of analyzing the hypothesized predictive relationships between the study variables using the method of estimation of maximum authenticity. Regarding indirect effects, Preacher and Hayes' (2008) methods of multiple mediation were used, generating the limits of confidence for the indirect effects through bootstrapping. In order to verify the validity of the model, the following goodness-of-fit indices were taken into account: the CFI (*Comparative Fit Index*), the IFI (*Incremental Fit Index*), the TLI (*Tucker Lewis Index*), the ratio between chi-squared and degrees of freedom (χ^2 /g.l.), the SRMR (*Standardized Root Mean Square Residual*), and RMSEA (*Root Mean Square Error of Approximation*) combined with its confidence interval (CI) of 90%. The aforementioned goodness-of-fit indices are considered acceptable when the values of CFI, IFI, and TLI are greater than 0.90 (Hu and Bentler, 1995), 0.08 or lower for RMSEA (Browne and Cudeck, 1993) and SRMR (Hu and Bentler, 1999), and between 2 and 3 for χ^2 /g.l. (Schermelleh-Engel et al., 2003). This analysis was completed with the statistical programs SPSS 23.0 and Amos 23.0.

RESULTS

Descriptive Analysis and Bivariate Correlations

In **Table 1**, the descriptive statistics (mean, standard deviation, skewness and kurtosis) and bivariate correlations are shown. In terms of the mean scores of the motivational regulations,

TABLE 1 | Descriptive statistics and bivariate correlations of the study variables.

Variables	RG	*M*	SD	S	C	1	2	3	4	5	6	7	8	9	10	11
1. Autonomy	1–5	3.40	0.86	−0.27	−0.30	–	0.53**	0.34**	0.64**	0.47**	0.47**	0.33**	0.08**	0.50**	0.18**	0.33**
2. Competence	1–5	3.96	0.76	−0.67	0.01	–	–	0.46**	0.54**	0.59**	0.60**	0.27**	−0.03	0.63**	0.08**	0.52**
3. Relatedness	1–5	4.18	0.79	−0.91	0.16	–	–	–	0.46**	0.43**	0.41**	0.11**	−0.07**	0.45**	−0.17	0.34**
4. Novelty	1–5	3.83	0.89	−0.76	0.19	–	–	–	–	0.54**	0.55**	0.27**	0.01	0.58**	0.11**	0.37**
5. Intrinsic R	1–7	5.83	1.15	−1.21	1.36	–	–	–	–	–	0.76**	0.26**	−12**	0.98**	0.00	0.48**
6. Identified R	1–7	5.84	1.13	−1.33	1.86	–	–	–	–	–	–	0.36**	−0.02	0.89**	0.11**	0.53**
7. Introjected R	1–7	4.39	1.43	−0.21	−0.54	–	–	–	–	–	–	–	0.51**	0.31**	0.75**	0.24*
8. External R	1–7	3.87	1.54	−0.06	−0.79	–	–	–	–	–	–	–	–	−0.09**	0.95**	−0.04
9. Autonomous M	3–21	17.50	3.26	−1.30	1.73	–	–	–	–	–	–	–	–	–	0.04	0.53**
10. Controlled M	3–21	12.12	4.00	– 0.04	0.74	–	–	–	–	–	–	–	–	–	–	0.05*
11. Intention	1–5	4.22	0.80	−1.18	0.96	–	–	–	–	–	–	–	–	–	–	–

** $p < 0.05$ ** $p < 0.01$; M, mean; SD, standard deviation; S, skewness; C, kurtosis; R, regulation; RG, range; M, motivation.*

identified regulation, followed by intrinsic motivation, showed the highest value. Autonomous motivation showed higher mean score than controlled motivation. With respect to the mean scores of the basic psychological needs, the need for relatedness, followed by the need for competence, displayed the highest score.

In turn, in the correlation analysis it was observed that all the basic psychological needs correlated positively and significantly with the intention to be physically active and with all types of motivation, except for external regulation, where the need for autonomy correlated positively and significantly, whilst the need for relatedness correlated negatively and significantly. Regarding the correlation of motivational regulations and the intention to be physically active, all types of motivation correlated positively and significantly, except for external regulation.

Path Analysis

The results of the hypothesized model, where autonomous motivation and controlled motivation, respectively interceded positively and negatively between the satisfaction of the basic psychological needs and the intention to be physically active, showed that the need for novelty and the three basic psychological needs were positive and significant predictors of autonomous motivation, and that the latter also behaved as a positive predictor of intention. In turn, controlled motivation was only predicted significantly by the needs for relatedness (negatively) and autonomy (positively), and contrary to what was expected, behaved as a positive but insignificant predictor of intention. However, this model did not show adequate goodness-of-fit indices, $\chi^2 = 144.99$, $p < 0.05$, χ^2 /g.l. = 28.99, CFI = 0.97, IFI = 0.97, TLI = 0.85, SRMR = 0.043, RMSEA = 0.13, 90% CI [0.11, 0.14].

In this regard, with the aim of obtaining an improved fit of the model, the three relationships that showed an insignificant weight of regression (between the needs for competence and novelty with controlled motivation, and between the latter and the intention to be physically active) were eliminated, and the modified indices of the model were then observed. These suggested that the model could be improved, adding a direct relationship between the need for competence and the intention to be physically active. Thus, considerable improvements were achieved for the goodness-of-fit indices: $\chi^2 = 14.59$, $p < 0.05$, χ^2/g.l. = 2.09, CFI = 0.99, IFI = 0.99, TLI = 0.99, SRMR = 0.011, RMSEA = 0.026, 90% CI [0.005, 0.044].

The results of this model (see **Figure 2**) showed that satisfaction of the needs for autonomy ($\beta = 0.08$, $p < 0.001$), competence ($\beta = 0.39$, $p < 0.001$), relatedness to others ($\beta = 0.12$, $p = 0.001$) and novelty ($\beta = 0.26$, $p < 0.001$) were positive and significant predictors of autonomous motivation. In turn, with regard to controlled motivation, the need for autonomy acted as a positive predictor ($\beta = 0.21$, $p < 0.001$), and the need for relatedness as a negative predictor ($\beta = -0.09$, $p < 0.001$).

With respect to the intention to be physically active, this was predicted by autonomous motivation ($\beta = 0.34$, $p < 0.001$) and the need for competence (direct effect: $\beta = 0.30$, $p < 0.001$; indirect effect: $\beta = 0.13$, $p < 0.001$). Likewise, other indirect effects of intention to be physically active were found with respect to the need for autonomy ($\beta = 0.03$, $p < 0.001$), novelty ($\beta = 0.09$, $p < 0.001$) and relatedness to others ($\beta = 0.04$, $p < 0.001$). The explained variances were 49% for autonomous motivation, 4% for controlled motivation, and 33% for the intention to be physically active.

DISCUSSION

The objective of this study was to test the interrelationships between the need for novelty and the basic psychological needs, as well as motivation and the intention to be physically active in the future, through the use of a model which hypothesized that all the needs would act as positive predictors of autonomous motivation, and as negative predictors of controlled motivation. Equally, autonomous motivation would act as a positive predictor of the intention to be physically active, while controlled motivation would act as a negative predictor of the same. The results obtained have demonstrated partial support for the hypothesized model.

Firstly, the need for novelty and the three existing basic psychological needs predicted autonomous motivation both positively and significantly. These results were consistent with our model and the findings of González-Cutre and Sicilia (2019),

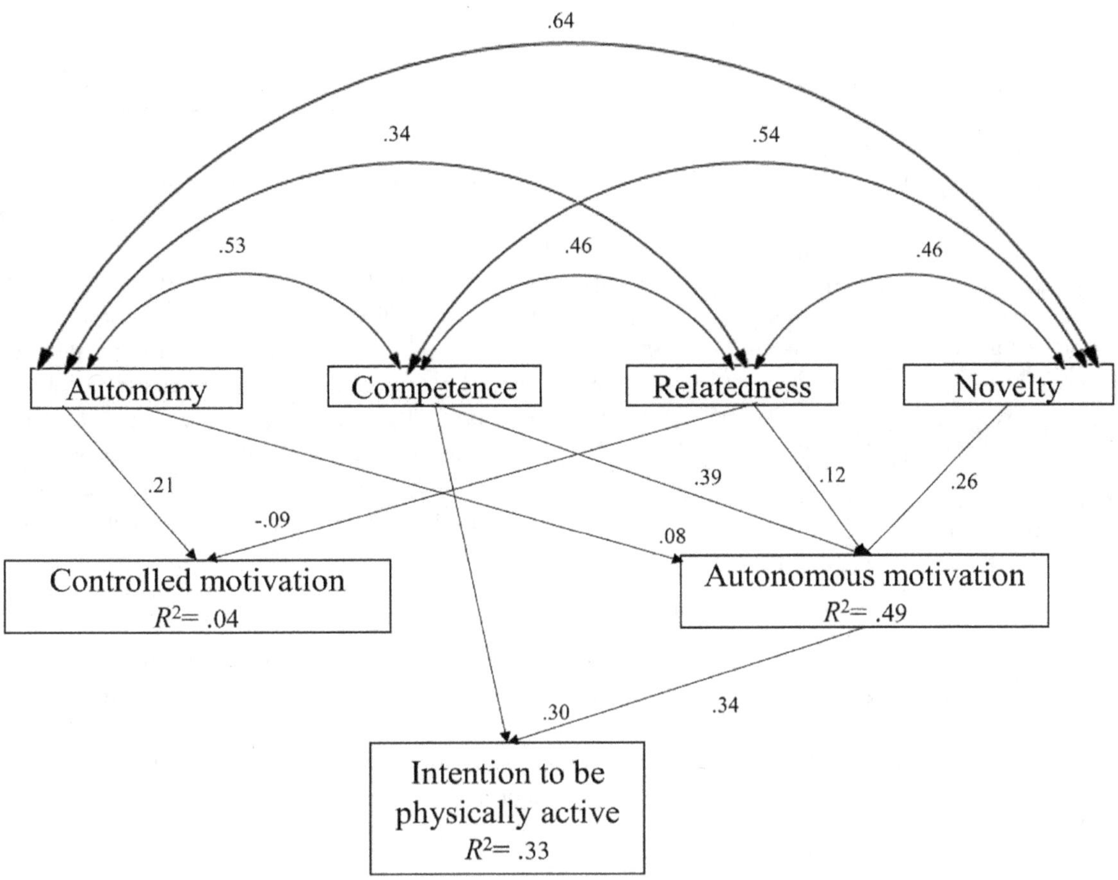

FIGURE 2 | Final path model of existing relationships between the four basic psychological needs, autonomous motivation, controlled motivation, and the intention to be physically active in the future. R^2 = explained variances.

Trigueros et al. (2019), and González-Cutre et al. (2020), where the types of autonomous motivation were positively predicted by the satisfaction of the four needs. This supports the idea that the need for novelty acts in synergy with the other three basic psychological needs, thus fulfilling one of the criteria established by Ryan and Deci (2017). For these authors, the fourth criterion that a proposed need must fulfill in order to be included in BPNT is that it acts as a growth need and not as a deficit need, meaning that the new basic psychological need must act in accordance with the three existing needs and not as a substitute for one of them when they become frustrated or threatened.

On the other hand, with respect to controlled motivation, the results obtained were not the same as those hypothesized. Only the needs for autonomy and relatedness were associated with it. The need for relatedness predicted controlled motivation negatively, while, contrary to what was expected, autonomy behaved as a positive predictor of the same. Currently, it is possible to compare these results only with the findings of González-Cutre et al. (2020), because this is the only study to have included controlled motivation within a similar motivational sequence. The results of the investigation by González-Cutre et al. (2020) showed that the need for competence acted as a negative predictor of controlled motivation, in accordance with the hypothesis of the proposed model. The satisfaction of a basic psychological need as a predictor of controlling motivation may be due to the fact that supporting autonomy, competence, and relatedness is positively correlated with introjected regulation and negatively and weakly correlated with external regulation (Vasconcellos et al., 2019).

Finally, with regard to the intention to be physically active, the results partially supported those proposed in the hypothesized model. In this regard, intention was predicted positively and directly by autonomous motivation, while no significant relationship was found with controlled motivation. These results agree with previous investigations (Hein et al., 2004; Taylor et al., 2010), where the most self-determined types of motivation behaved as positive predictors of the intention to be physically active in the future, providing evidence which supports the idea that what happens in Physical Education classes can affect students' behavior in their free time (Hagger et al., 2003; Hagger and Chatzisarantis, 2012; Ferriz et al., 2016). Moreover, it was found that satisfaction of the need for competence was the only one that directly affected this variable. In the study by González-Cutre et al. (2020), the need for competence was also the only one to present direct effects on the two consequences concerned (enjoyment and vitality). In this line, the recent systematic review and meta-analysis by Vasconcellos et al. (2019) has showed that the need for competence presents higher direct effects on adaptive outcomes than the need for autonomy or need for relatedness. As a result, it seems that the need to control and succeed in tasks by themselves could be a key factor in determining whether the practice of physical activity during childhood and adolescence is continued into adult life.

Likewise, the intention to be physically active was also indirectly predicted by the needs for autonomy, relatedness and novelty, the last of which presented the largest indirect effect. These results support the mediating role played by motivation in the existing relationship between the satisfaction of basic psychological needs, including the need for novelty, and its consequences, thus partially fulfilling another of the criteria established by Ryan and Deci (2017) to be able to include a new need in their theory. For these authors, any new need should behave as a constant and significant mediator of relationships between personal and social factors and the motivational functioning and psychology of the individual.

On the other hand, the principal limitations found in the study must be addressed, as well as future lines of investigation. Firstly, being of cross-sectional design, this study has not been able to analyze whether the satisfaction of the need for novelty is associated with positive consequences over a long period of time. It would be interesting for future studies to utilize a longitudinal design in order to explore this. Secondly, no social factors (e.g., interpersonal style of the teacher) have been measured in this study, and so it has not been able to assess the effect of measuring satisfaction of the need for novelty against social factors, motivation and their consequences. Future studies should analyze the role played by the need for novelty together with the three basic psychological needs in the complete sequence proposed by the theory of self-determination. Thirdly, neither integrated regulation nor amotivation was measured in this study. Finally only the relations of the satisfaction of the basic psychological needs have been analyzed in this study. It would be interesting for future investigations to explore the importance that the frustration of these needs has upon the intention to be physically active in the future.

CONCLUSION

In conclusion, the results of the hypothesized model have shown the importance of satisfying the need for novelty together with the other basic psychological needs (with special emphasis on the need for competence) in Physical Education classes, because this predicts the autonomous motivation and intention to be physically active of students in the future, outside of the school context.

As the results of the present study indicate, if teachers of Physical Education wish to increase the intention of their students to be physically active in the future, they must consciously try to generate a learning atmosphere in their classes that satisfies both the traditional basic psychological needs and the need for novelty (setting novel tasks and challenges that go beyond the daily routine), because said satisfaction predicts autonomous motivation and, consequently, grows the intention to practice physical activity in the future, outside of the educational context. In line with what is proposed by González-Cutre and Sicilia (2019), we suggest that, in order to introduce novel themes in Physical Education classes, teachers could apply methodologies unrelated to traditional approaches (e.g., gamification), use different materials, introduce the use of TIC, take students away from the school in order to practice physical activity (e.g., climbing and hiking), or call in experts so that students can take part in activities that are different to those typically taught in the educational center (e.g., parkour and zumba). Furthermore, the results of the study highlight the satisfaction of the need for competence above the other needs, because this directly predicts intention. Therefore, it is necessary for teachers to put special emphasis on proposing motor tasks and challenges that are achievable for the students, in order to help them to establish personal improvement as a principal objective, to allow them sufficient time to practice, to offer fundamentally positive encouragement, etc.

ETHICS STATEMENT

The studies involving human participants were reviewed and approved by the Portal de Ética de la Investigación Biomédica de Andalucía (Spain) (https://www.juntadeandalucia.es/salud/portaldeetica/). Written informed consent to participate in this study was provided by the participants' legal guardian/next of kin.

AUTHOR CONTRIBUTIONS

CF-E was responsible for conducting the study process, collaborating in the design of the study, collecting the data, conducting a preliminary analysis, and writing part of the manuscript. BA collaborated in the design of the study, was responsible for carrying out the analysis of the data and writing the results, collaborated in writing various sections of the manuscript, and has reviewed the final version. JT-F collaborated in the writing of the article and reviewed the final version. PS-L had primary responsibility for the design of the study, collaborated in the writing of the article, and reviewed the final version. All the authors collaborated significantly in the preparation of the manuscript and have given their approval to the final version of the article.

in the classroom," financed by *Programa Operativo FEDER Andalucía 2014-2020* (UHU-1259909. Ref.: PID2019-106918GB-I00), which made this study possible. This work was supported too by the *Grupo de Educación, Motricidad e Investigación Onubense* (HUM643) and by the *Centro de Investigación en Pensamiento Contemporáneo e Innovación para el Desarrollo Social* (COIDESO), of the *Universidad de Huelva*. In addition, the study has received aid to co-finance the payment of publication fees from the Vice-Rector's Office for Research at the *Universidad de Huelva*.

REFERENCES

American Psychological Association (2020). *Publication Manual of the American Psychological Association*, 7th Edn. Washington, DC: American Psychological Association, doi: 10.1037/0000165-000

Bagheri, L., and Milyavskaya, M. (2020). Novelty–variety as a candidate basic psychological need: new evidence across three studies. *Motiv. Emot.* 44, 32–53. doi: 10.1007/s11031-019-09807-4

Birdsell (2018). Understanding students' psychological needs in an English learning context. *J. Lib. Arts Dev.* 2, 1–14.

Browne, M. W., and Cudeck, R. (1993). "Alternative ways of assessing model fit," in *Testing Structural Equation Models*, eds K. A. Bollen and J. S. Long (Newbury Park: Sage), 136–162.

Deci, E. L., and Ryan, R. M. (1985). *Intrinsic Motivation and Self-Determination in Human Behavior*. New York, NY: Plenum, doi: 10.1007/978-1-4899-2271-7

Deci, E. L., and Ryan, R. M. (2000). The "what" and "why" of goal pursuits: human needs and the self-determination of behavior. *Psychol. Inq.* 11, 227–268. doi: 10.1207/S15327965PLI1104_01

Fernández-Espínola, C., Almagro, B. J., and Tamayo Fajardo, J. A. (2020). Prediction of physical education students' intention to be physically active: a model mediated by the need for novelty. *Retos* 37, 442–448.

Ferriz, R., González-Cutre, D., Sicilia, A., and Hagger, M. S. (2016). Predicting healthy and unhealthy behaviors through physical education: a self-determination theory-based longitudinal approach. *Scand. J. Med. Sci. Sport.* 26, 579–592. doi: 10.1111/sms.12470

Fin, G., Moreno-Murcia, J. A., León, J., Baretta, E., and Nodari Júnior, R. J. (2019). Teachers' interpersonal style in physical education: exploring patterns of students' self-determined motivation and enjoyment of physical activity in a longitudinal study. *Front. Psychol.* 9:2721. doi: 10.3389/fpsyg.2018.02721

González-Cutre, D., Romero-Elías, M., Jiménez-Loaisa, A., Beltrán-Carrillo, V. J., and Hagger, M. S. (2020). Testing the need for novelty as a candidate need in basic psychological needs theory. *Motiv. Emot.* 44, 295–314. doi: 10.1007/s11031-019-09812-7

González-Cutre, D., and Sicilia, Á (2019). The importance of novelty satisfaction for multiple positive outcomes in physical education. *Eur. Phys. Educ. Rev.* 25, 859–875. doi: 10.1177/1356336X18783980

González-Cutre, D., Sicilia, Á, Sierra, A. C., Ferriz, R., and Hagger, M. S. (2016). Understanding the need for novelty from the perspective of self-determination theory. *Pers. Individ. Dif.* 102, 159–169. doi: 10.1016/j.paid.2016.06.036

Goudas, M., Biddle, S., and Fox, K. (1994). Perceived locus of causality, goal orientations, and perceived competence in school physical education classes. *Br. J. Educ. Psychol.* 64, 453–463. doi: 10.1111/j.2044-8279.1994.tb01116.x

Hagger, M. S., and Chatzisarantis, N. L. D. (2012). Transferring motivation from educational to extramural contexts: a review of the trans-contextual model. *Eur. J. Psychol. Educ.* 27, 195–212. doi: 10.1007/s10212-011-0082-5

Hagger, M. S., Culverhouse, T., Chatzisarantis, N. L. D., and Biddle, S. J. H. (2003). The processes by which perceived autonomy support in physical education promotes leisure-time physical activity intentions and behavior: a trans-contextual model. *J. Educ. Psychol.* 95, 784–795. doi: 10.1037/0022-0663.95.4.784

Hagger, M. S., Hardcastle, S. J., Chater, A., Mallett, C., Pal, S., and Chatzisarantis, N. L. D. (2014). Autonomous and controlled motivational regulations for multiple health-related behaviors: between- and within-participants analyses. *Heal. Psychol. Behav. Med.* 2, 565–601. doi: 10.1080/21642850.2014.912945

Hein, V., Müür, M., and Koka, A. (2004). Intention to be physically active after school graduation and its relationship to three types of intrinsic motivation. *Eur. Phys. Educ. Rev.* 10, 5–19. doi: 10.1177/1356336x04040618

Hu, L.-T., and Bentler, P. M. (1995). "Evaluating model fit," in *Structural Equation Modeling: Concepts, Issues, and Applications*, ed. R. H. Hoyle (Thousand Oaks, CA: Sage), 76–99.

Hu, L. T., and Bentler, P. M. (1999). Cutoff criteria for fit indexes in covariance structure analysis: conventional criteria versus new alternatives. *Struct. Equ. Model.* 6, 1–55. doi: 10.1080/10705519909540118

Janssen, I., and LeBlanc, A. G. (2010). Systematic review of the health benefits of physical activity and fitness in school-aged children and youth. *Int. J. Behav. Nutr. Phys. Act.* 7:40. doi: 10.1186/1479-5868-7-40

Lim, B. S. C., and Wang, C. K. J. (2009). Perceived autonomy support, behavioural regulations in physical education and physical activity intention. *Psychol. Sport Exerc.* 10, 52–60. doi: 10.1016/j.psychsport.2008.06.003

Moreno-Murcia, J. A., González-Cutre, D., and Chillón, M. (2009). Preliminary validation in spanish of a scale designed to measure motivation in physical education classes: the perceived locus of causality (PLOC) scale. *Span. J. Psychol.* 12, 327–337. doi: 10.1017/S1138741600001724

Moreno-Murcia, J. A., Moreno, R., and Cervelló, E. (2007). El autoconcepto físico como predictor de la intención de ser físicamente activo. *Psicol. Salud* 17, 261–267. doi: 10.25009/pys.v17i2.710

Mouratidis, A., Vansteenkiste, M., Lens, W., and Sideridis, G. (2008). The motivating role of positive feedback in sport and physical education: evidence for a motivational model. *J. Sport Exerc. Psychol.* 30, 240–268. doi: 10.1123/jsep.30.2.240

Ntoumanis, N. (2001). A self-determination approach to the understanding of motivation in physical education. *Br. J. Educ. Psychol.* 71, 225–242. doi: 10.1348/000709901158497

Preacher, K. J., and Hayes, A. F. (2008). Asymptotic and resampling strategies for assessing and comparing indirect effects in multiple mediator models. *Behav. Res. Methods* 40, 879–891. doi: 10.3758/BRM.40.3.879

Ryan, R. M., and Deci, E. L. (2000). Self-determination theory and the facilitation of intrinsic motivation, social development, and well-being. *Am. Psychol.* 55, 68–78. doi: 10.1037/0003-066X.55.1.68

Ryan, R. M., and Deci, E. L. (2017). *Self-Determination Theory: Basic Psychological Needs in Motivation, Development, and Wellness*. New York, NY: Guilford Press.

Ryan, R. M., and Deci, E. L. (2020). Intrinsic and extrinsic motivation from a self-determination theory perspective: definitions, theory, practices, and future directions. *Contemp. Educ. Psychol.* 2020:101860. doi: 10.1016/j.cedpsych.2020.101860

Ryan, R. M., Frederick, C. M., Lepes, D., Rubio, N., and Sheldon, K. M. (1997). Intrinsic motivation and exercise adherence. *Int. J. Sport Psychol.* 28, 335–354.

Schermelleh-Engel, K., Moosbrugger, H., and Müller, H. (2003). Evaluating the fit of structural equation models: tests of significance and descriptive goodness-of-fit measures. *Methods Psychol. Res. Online* 8, 23–74.

Standage, M., Duda, J. L., and Ntoumanis, N. (2006). Students' motivational processes and their relationship to teacher ratings in school physical education: a self-determination theory approach. *Res. Q. Exerc. Sport* 77, 100–110. doi: 10.1080/02701367.2006.10599336

Taylor, I. M., Ntoumanis, N., Standage, M., and Spray, C. M. (2010). Motivational predictors of physical education students' effort, exercise intentions, and leisure-time physical activity: a multilevel linear growth analysis. *J. Sport Exerc. Psychol.* 32, 99–120. doi: 10.1123/jsep.32.1.99

Teixeira, P. J., Carraça, E. V., Markland, D., Silva, M. N., and Ryan, R. M. (2012). Exercise, physical activity, and self-determination theory: a systematic review. *Int. J. Behav. Nutr. Phys. Act.* 9:78. doi: 10.1186/1479-5868-9-78

Trigueros, R., Mínguez, L. A., González-Bernal, J. J., Aguilar-Parra, J. M., Padilla, D., and Álvarez, J. F. (2019). Validation of the satisfaction scale of basic psychological needs in physical education with the incorporation of the novelty in the spanish context. *Sustain.* 11:6250. doi: 10.3390/su11226250

Vallerand, R. J. (1997). "Toward a hierarchical model of intrinsic and extrinsic motivation," in *Advances in Experimental Social Psychology*, ed. M. P. Zanna

(New York, NY: Academic Press), 271–360. doi: 10.1016/S0065-2601(08)60019-2

Vallerand, R. J. (2001). "A hierarchical model of intrinsic and extrinsic motivation in sport and exercise," in *Advances in Motivation in Sport and Exercise*, ed. G. C. Roberts (Champaign: Human kinetics), 263–319.

Van den Berghe, L., Vansteenkiste, M., Cardon, G., Kirk, D., and Haerens, L. (2014). Research on self-determination in physical education: key findings and proposals for future research. *Phys. Educ. Sport Pedagog.* 19, 97–121. doi: 10.1080/17408989.2012.732563

Vansteenkiste, M., Christopher, N., and Bart, S. (2010). "The development of the five mini-theories of self-determination theory: an historical overview, emerging trends, and future directions," in *The Decade Ahead: Theoretical Perspectives on Motivation and Achievement*, eds T. C. Urdan and S. A. Karabenick (Bingley: Emerald Group Publishing Limited), 105–165. doi: 10.1108/S0749-7423(2010)000016A007

Vansteenkiste, M., Ryan, R. M., and Soenens, B. (2020). Basic psychological need theory: advancements, critical themes, and future directions. *Motiv. Emot.* 44, 1–31. doi: 10.1007/s11031-019-09818-1

Vasconcellos, D., Parker, P. D., Hilland, T., Cinelli, R., Owen, K. B., Kapsal, N., et al. (2019). Self-determination theory applied to physical education: a systematic review and meta-analysis. *J. Educ. Psychol.* doi: 10.1037/edu0000420. [Epub ahead of print].

Vlachopoulos, S. P., and Michailidou, S. (2006). Development and initial validation of a measure of autonomy, competence, and relatedness in exercise: the Basic Psychological Needs in Exercise Scale. *Meas. Phys. Educ. Exerc. Sci.* 10, 179–201. doi: 10.1207/s15327841mpee1003_4

WHO (2019). *Global Action Plan On Physical Activity 2018-2030: More Active People for a Healthier Word.* Geneva: World Health Organization, doi: 10.1016/j.jpolmod.2006.06.007

8

The Hardiness of Adolescents in Various Social Groups

Valerii Malkin[1†], Liudmila Rogaleva[1], Alla Kim[2] and Natalya Khon[3]*

[1] Department of Theory of Physical Culture, Ural Federal University, Yekaterinburg, Russia, [2] Department of General and Applied Psychology, Al-Farabi Kazakh National University, Almaty, Kazakhstan, [3] Department of Psychology, Turan University, Almaty, Kazakhstan

***Correspondence:**
Natalya Khon
Natalya.khon@gmail.com
† Deceased

Hardiness is considered as one of the adaptation resources of personality to stressful situations, responsible for the mental health preservation. Adolescents as an age group is one of most susceptible to stress factors, so conducting research on the development of hardiness in adolescents becomes necessary. Due to difference in social conditions under which development of hardiness of adolescents takes place, the purpose of our research was to study the hardiness of adolescents included in different social groups: first group – athletes, students of sports schools, second – students of specialized schools for intellectually gifted individuals, third– students of regular schools. In total, 239 adolescents of 14–16 years old participated. The study revealed significant differences in the development of hardiness among all three groups of adolescents. The general and specific patterns of the development of hardiness components of adolescents in different social groups were identified. The article describes the main types of manifestation of hardiness and its components under different social conditions of activity and development in modern adolescents.

Keywords: hardiness, adolescents, social environment, activities, development

INTRODUCTION

The problem of adaptation to the requirements of the social environment is particularly acute in adolescence, which is traditionally regarded as a crisis age (Kalashnikova and Petrova, 2017; Benzi et al., 2019; Morinaj and Hascher, 2019). The desire of adolescents to experience their own strength, to succeed and to assert themselves in the peer group is associated with various kinds of difficulties that can lead to inappropriate forms of behavior (Sobkin et al., 2005; Echazu and Nocetti, 2018). Because of this, more and more research is connected with the study of factors that ensure the development of hardiness, which is considered as the main adaptation resource of a person responsible for preserving the mental health and well-being of adolescents (Kiva et al., 2016; Oschepkov, 2017; Mishina, 2018).

According to the studied literature, various interrelated factors (genetic, social, age) of the controversial development of adolescents' hardiness are distinguished (Ivanova, 2013; Kormushina, 2016; Gorkovaya and Miklyaeva, 2017; Bezgodova et al., 2018). At the same time, most authors believe that the development of the hardiness of adolescents is determined to a greater degree by the social environment (Shvareva, 2010; Gorkovaya et al., 2015; Casagrande et al., 2018; Fokina et al., 2018; Guerra et al., 2019, etc.).

This is confirmed by a number of studies that prove the positive or negative impact of various social groups on the development of hardiness (Borzilova and Solonchenko, 2017; Kalashnikova and Nikitina, 2017; Nikitina, 2017; Melisbek and Bodnar, 2018). In particular, it proves the positive role of a happy family in the development of hardiness compared with the unfavorable one (Archakova, 2016; Gulyaeva and Myagkaya, 2017).

In a number of works it has been revealed that hardiness is more pronounced among adolescents involved in sports, creative, intellectual, or vocal activities, compared to ordinary schoolchildren (Sultanbaeva and Chertykov, 2014; Chernyavskaya and Shabanova, 2016; Plotnikov et al., 2017; Shumakova and Shamardina, 2018). Without disputing the significance of these studies it should be noted that they were conducted on a small sample and are rather local.

We believe that to study the role of the influence of the social environment on the development of the hardiness of adolescents, it is necessary, first of all, to determine the methodological position. In our opinion, this approach can be the social activity approach of the Russian psychologists – classics such as Ananyev (2007) and Rubinstein (2015), as well as the works of foreign researchers – Deci and Ryan (2000), Bandura (2004), and Seligman (2013).

The essence of this approach is that the influence of the social environment on the development of adolescents is always mediated by the type of activity that is leading for them and the conditions in which this activity is carried out. In the course of mastering activities and adapting to social conditions adolescents will develop the qualities that will be more necessary for carrying out activities and adapting to a specific environment. This methodological approach was the basis of our research presented in this article.

In determining hardiness, we rely on the work of Kobasa (1979) and Leontiev and Rasskazova (2006), who understand hardiness as the measure of personality's ability to withstand a stressful situation, maintaining internal balance without reducing success. It includes three autonomous components: commitment, control and challenge.

Commitment includes interest in their activities. The opposite phenomenon is detachment from social interests and life in general. Control implies the presence of their own beliefs, ideas, even in case of unwarranted success. The opposite phenomenon of control is helplessness, inability to defend one's opinion, to deny or insist on it. Challenge is based on a person's ability to be aware of his/her actions and decisions, being aware of the degree of risk in a given case at the same time (Leontiev and Rasskazova, 2006).

Based on the foregoing, it is possible to consider the above presented approach in the form of a scheme, according to which the development of the hardiness of adolescents to a greater extent is determined by activity (**Figure 1**).

The methodological basis of the study allowed us to identify three social groups of adolescents, who, due to a certain specificity of the performing activity may differ in terms of the level of development and components of hardiness. The number of such groups included adolescents involved in sports schools and schools of the Olympic reserve, making up the first group, students of gymnasiums, lyceums as the second group, students of secondary schools made up the third group.

The specificity of each group is determined by the dominant orientation of the activity in which they are included. In the first and second group there were either achievements in sports activities or academic achievements, in the third group students were more focused on their individual needs. The purpose of the study was to identify the similarities and differences, the influence of various social environments on the development of hardiness of adolescents and its components (commitment, control, and challenge).

General Hypothesis

It is assumed that the inclusion of adolescents in different social conditions of life can affect the development of their level and components of hardiness (commitment, control, challenge).

It is assumed that obtaining objective knowledge on the impact of social conditions and activities on the development of hardiness may be helpful for the development of more effective strategies for working with adolescents and improving their well-being and mental health.

Particular Hypotheses

Sporting activity takes place in conditions of real competition, aiming at both immediate and distant goals, therefore it is associated with stress-competitive situations, with the need to overcome difficulties, so it can be assumed that the existence of hardiness, on the one hand, is one of their main conditions of success, and therefore all components of hardiness are of high importance and must be developed at a sufficiently high level.

Learning activity in gymnasiums, lyceums and specialized research centers is focused on high academic achievements with orientation on future perspectives, it seems to be impossible without self-control, and therefore we can assume that this component must be high.

At regular school adolescents are in more natural conditions of life, they are more left to themselves, have fewer commitments and more free time to meet their individual needs. At the same time lack of sufficiently clear and long-term goals, peculiar for the other two groups of adolescents, will affect the development of hardiness components. So, the specificity of each group is determined by the dominant orientation of the activity in which they are included. In the first group these are sports results, in the second group the main is orientation is academic knowledge, while in the third group students are more focused on meeting their individual needs.

MATERIALS AND METHODS

Research Design

The study was conducted on the basis of the Olympic Reserve School, the "Yunost" Children and Youth Sports School, the Specialized Educational and Specialized Educational and Scientific Center (lyceum) for Gifted Schoolchildren, the Gymnasium with in-depth study of English and several secondary schools in Yekaterinburg. The research Ethics Committee of the Ural Federal University of Yekaterinburg approved this study. Written informed consent was obtained from the parents/legal guardians of all participants. The distribution of participants by gender is, in our opinion, very important in terms of its significance for determining behavior and readiness to overcome stress in the social environment

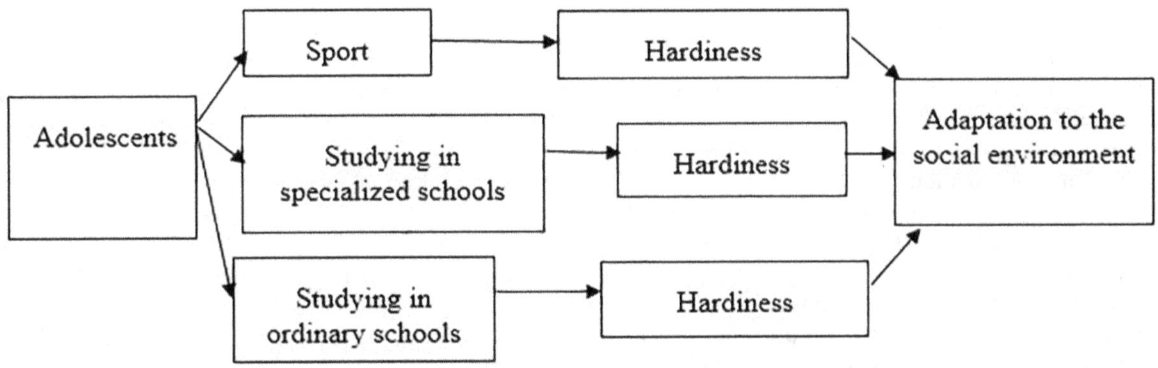

FIGURE 1 | Model of the influence of the social environment on the development of hardiness of adolescents.

(Gorkovaya et al., 2015; Kalashnikova and Petrova, 2017). The study involved 239 adolescents aged from 14 to 16 years, 80 adolescents-sportsmen (44 male and 36 female), 79 adolescents – lyceum students (39 male and 40 female), 80 adolescents- schoolchildren (37 male and 43 female).

Measures and Statistical Analysis

As a research method, we selected testing of adolescents from different social groups of 14–16 years old. To study hardiness, we used a questionnaire developed by the American psychologist Salvatore Maddy and adapted by Leontiev and Rasskazova (2006). The questionnaire consists of 45 questions, allow you to assess the level of hardiness, as well as indicators of 3 subscales (commitment, control, and challenge). The reliability determined for this investigation was α = 0.90.

To compare hardiness indicators the SPSS-23 program (Students *t*-test and the Kruskal–Wallis test) was used.

TABLE 1 | The level of development of hardiness of adolescents of different social groups.

Samples parameters	Number of participants with different level of hardiness (%)		
	Low level	**Middle level**	**High level**
For the sample as whole	14.2%	52.9%	32.9%
Adolescents girls	20.3%	54.3%	25.4%
Adolescents boys	7.3%	52.6%	40.1%
Adolescents- sportsmen	2%	53,5%	44.5%
Adolescents Lyceum students	15%	60%	25%
Adolescents-schoolchildren	23%	46%	31%
Boys athletes	2.2%	55.6%	42.2%
Lyceum students boys	5.1%	66.7%	28.2%
School boys	16.2%	32.5%	51.3%
Girls athletes	2.7%	54%	43.3%
Lyceum students girls	25%	52.5%	22.5%
Schoolgirls	31.7%	56.3%	12%

RESULTS

In the course of the study, we identified differences in the level of development of hardiness in adolescents of different social groups. The levels of development of resilience were determined in accordance with the data from the Leontiev and Rasskazova (2006), according to which the low level is less than 60 points, the average level is between 60 and 90 points, and the high level is above 90 points. The results of the study are presented in **Table 1**.

According to the data in **Table 1**, it is possible to note the differences in the indices of the development of hardiness both between three social groups and in the gender indicators within each group. First of all, talking about each group as a whole, we can conclude that 44.5% of adolescent -sportsmen have high level of hardiness, and only 2% have low rates. At the same time, if we talk about gender indicators, then indicators of the level of development of hardiness are almost the same in girls and boys.

The data obtained show that the competitive environment with a focus on achievement and a specific result, ensures the development of hardiness of adolescent- sportsmen at a sufficiently high level. In the group of lyceum students and schoolchildren the data obtained show similar to adolescent-sportsmen average indicators of hardiness. Number of adolescents with a high level (25%) is reduced and there is a clear increase in adolescents with a low level (15%). Moreover, the low values of hardiness are more pronounced in female lyceum students.

The analysis of the questionnaires of schoolchildren with high indicators of hardiness revealed interesting facts, in particular, young students of physical and mathematical classes, winners of scientific competitions, and young men of gymnasiums, but successfully combining sports with educational achievements, have high rates.

Thus, the findings confirm the fact that the competitive environment and focus on future achievements will increasingly develop the hardiness of adolescents. Relating the difficulties of adaptation in the gender aspect, it is obvious that in the academic environment girls find it harder to adapt.

There is a significant difference in the manifestation of hardiness in the two groups: only 22.5% of lyceum girls' students have high values vs. 43.3% in female athletes, 25% of them have low values vs. 2.7% in female athletes.

Thus, it can be concluded that the development of hardiness in the groups of adolescents of lyceum students differs from the group of adolescents-sportsmen.

In the third social group of adolescents –schoolchildren, the peculiarities of manifestation of hardiness are also noted, compared with the first and second groups. First, the level of high development of hardiness in this sample is lower (31%) than in the sample of adolescents sportsmen (44.5%), but slightly higher than that of adolescents lyceum students (25%).

At the same time, these high values are provided primarily by data on boys schoolchildren (51, 3%), which is higher than in other groups. The data obtained can be explained on the basis of questionnaires of adolescents with high rates, so they all have hobbies, in particular, go in for sports (recreational sports), but for them it's more a type of free leisure, not a focus on results, and secondly, they are quite independent in choosing activities and achieving their short-term goals, thirdly, they do not bear the burden of high responsibility imposed by adults.

Along with the pluses, we see that the number of adolescents schoolchildren with low values is also quite large (23%). This means that a fairly large group of adolescent schoolchildren do not develop hardiness, most likely due to the fact that these students are not involved in active forms of creative and sports activities. Low values throughout the sample were observed in 13.5% of adolescents, while it can be noted that the number of girls with a low level of hardiness exceeds boys, respectively 20, 3% and 7, 3%.

The group with low values includes not only girls schoolchildren (31.7%), but also boys schoolchildren (16.2%), and this means that a fairly large group of adolescents schoolchildren does not develop hardiness due to the fact that there are no conditions for its manifestation, these schoolchildren are not involved in active forms of creative and sports activities. Thus, the obtained data confirm the fact that a competitive environment and a focus on sporting achievements will contribute more to the development of the hardiness of adolescents than the academic environment focused on academic achievements, even if they are quite high. Thus, it can be concluded that all social groups

TABLE 2 | Data on hardiness and its components (commitment, control, challenge) in the group of adolescents-sportsmen and adolescents-lyceum students.

	Mean value		Standard deviation			
	Adolescents-sportsmen	Adolescents-lyceum students	Adolescents-sportsmen	Adolescents-lyceum students	*t*	Cohen coefficient
Commitment	35,4875	29,0127	7,23388	7,70530	5,461**	0.86
Control	33,0000	31,4684	7,30528	8,12693	1,250	0.27
Challenge	18,7375	17,4177	3,94180	5,17293	1,811	0.24
Hardiness	87,0250	77,5063	15,38862	18,34560	3,542**	0.60

*$p < 0.05$; **$p < 0.01$.

TABLE 3 | Data on hardiness and its components (commitment, control, challenge) in the group of adolescents lyceum students and adolescents schoolchildren.

	Mean value		Standard deviation			
	Adolescents-lyceyists	Adolescents-schoolchildren	Adolescents-lyceyists	Adolescents-schoolchildren	*t*	Cohen coefficient
Commitment	29,0127	33,3500	7,70530	8,73535	−3,321**	0.53
Control	31,4684	27,8500	8,12693	10,43254	2,441**	0.44
Challenge	17,4177	13,2125	5,17293	4,68959	5,368**	0.88
Hardiness	77,5063	74,4625	18,34560	19,97020	1,001	0.16

*$p < 0.05$; **$p < 0.01$.

TABLE 4 | Gender differences on hardiness and its components (commitment, control, challenge).

	Mean value		Standard deviation			Cohen coefficient
	Boys	Girls	Boys	Girls	*t*	
Commitment	33,9832	31,2231	8,15733	8,31914	2,595**	0.48
Control	32,6050	28,8926	8,20316	9,30663	3,276**	0.50
Challenge	16,8487	16,0000	5,31490	5,05140	1,268	0.24
Hardiness	83,7479	75,4545	17,82695	18,78874	3,507**	0.59

*$p < 0.05$; **$p < 0.01$.

have conditions for the development of the hardiness of adolescents, but it is the sports environment that has the most significant influence on its development. The presented results can be supplemented with data on the study of the development of components of hardiness, such as commitment, control, and challenge. To identify differences in the development of components of hardiness among adolescents from different social groups, mathematical data processing methods were used.

Analysis of the development of components of hardiness in the groups of adolescents - sportsmen and adolescents - lyceum students, presented in **Table 2**, suggests that there are significant differences in the component of commitment and general hardiness in these groups.

There are no significant differences in the components of control and challenge, this fact indicates that academic activities, as well as sports activities, contribute to the development of these components of hardiness. Cohen coefficient shows high effect for commitment (0.86) and middle effect for hardiness (0.60).

We can see in **Table 3** significant differences in control and challenge components in the studied groups. The indicator of hardiness, "control," is the conviction of adolescents that their efforts depend on personal results and they can influence the outcome of what is happening, even if this influence is not absolute and success is not guaranteed. Adolescents with a developed component of control feel that they choose their own activity, their own way. Thus, this suggests that in the framework of sports and academic activities, the development of control and challenge is higher than in the framework of general academic activities, whereby the development of hardiness is higher among adolescents-sportsmen and adolescents-lyceum students. Most likely, this is due to the fact that competition and a focus on achieving high sports or academic results require a greater manifestation of effort and readiness to work in conditions of both success and non-success. Cohen coefficient shows middle effect for commitment and control (0.53, 0.44) and high effect for challenge (0.88).

The obtained data confirmed the hypothesis put forward by us that in conditions of sports activity in adolescents the level of development of hardiness is higher than that of adolescents lyceum students and adolescents schoolchildren. At the same time, it can be noted that the influence of the academic environment and educational activities on the development of control and challenge in adolescents is quite high. Regarding adolescent schoolchildren, it can be said that in this environment there are conditions for developing the hardiness of adolescents, but only if they are included in active forms of leisure (sports, social, and creative groups).

Significant gender differences in commitment, control and general hardiness have been revealed. Boys in general have priority in **Table 4**. It can be concluded that it is the academic environment that is less conducive to the development of the hardiness of girls, while in the sports environment conditions are almost equal. Cohen coefficient shows middle effect for commitment and control (0.48, 0.50) and high effect for hardiness (0.59).

In fact, our data confirm studies indicating the important role of the social environment in the development of endurance of adolescents (Sultanbaeva and Chertykov, 2014; Archakova, 2016; Chernyavskaya and Shabanova, 2016; Malkin and Rogaleva, 2016; Borzilova and Solonchenko, 2017; Gulyaeva and Myagkaya, 2017; Plotnikov et al., 2017; Shumakova and Shamardina, 2018; Straub, 2019).

In our opinion, this can be explained that different types of activities do not equally affect the satisfaction of the needs for autonomy, competence and for relatedness (Deci and Ryan, 2000) and the achievement of self-efficacy (Bandura, 2004; Rubinstein, 2015; Nikitina, 2018; Rogaleva et al., 2018).

The data obtained can be used to develop strategies for educational programs for the correction of social conditions for the development of hardiness in adolescents of different social groups, ensuring their well-being. In particular, for adolescents of all social groups, one of the main conditions for increasing hardiness is the presence of involvement and interest in the implementation of activities or social interaction.

The second important aspect is the need to set short and long-range goals, which is typical for sports activities, and academic orientation schools and that are not sufficiently present in regular schools. Target attitudes and action to achieve them, can contribute to the development of self-control, risk-taking, acceptance of success and failure as an important experience that can increase adolescent confidence.

The third important component of the strategy for working with adolescents is to develop risk preparedness or the desire to actively acquire knowledge from experience for later use, this is achieved only if the substantive component of programs provides for linking activities with future professional activities, or with those skills which may be useful in mastering a particular profession, or have some real practical result that a teenager can be proud of and perceive it as kind of achievement significant for the future.

CONCLUSION

Thus, our study confirms the hypotheses put forward, according to which the development of the hardiness of adolescents depends on the activity they perform and the conditions in which the activity is carried out. The obtained new data can contribute to the construction of a strategy for working with adolescents and various social groups to achieve their well-being. In this regard, further studies may be aimed at studying the hardiness of adolescents in the context of availability of conditions for satisfying their needs in autonomy, competence and significant relationships, which are considered as factors of their well-being.

ETHICS STATEMENT

All procedures performed in studies involving human participants were in accordance with the ethical standards of the institutional and/or national research committee and with the 1964 Helsinki Declaration and its later amendments or comparable ethical standards.

AUTHOR CONTRIBUTIONS

VM, LR, AK, and NK conceived the hypothesis of this study, and wrote the manuscript with significant input from VM. VM and LR participated in data collection. All authors analyzed the data, contributed to data interpretation of the statistical analysis, and read and approved the final manuscript.

ACKNOWLEDGMENTS

We express our deep gratitude to Valerii Malkin in the preparation and writing of this article. Wide outlook and academic knowledge, humor and intelligence were the main features of this remarkable person. His ability to understand and support gave the strength and confidence, inspired and motivated to new ideas and projects.

REFERENCES

Ananyev, B. G. (2007). *Selected Works on Psychology*. St. Petersburg: Russia Publishing House of St. Petersburg University.

Archakova, T. O. (2016). *Viability and Hardiness of Children and Adolescents from Unfavorous Families. Human Viability: Individual, Professional and Social Aspects*. Moscow: Institute of Psychology RAE, 462–482.

Bandura, A. (2004). Health promotion by social cognitive means. *J. Health Educ. Behav.* 31, 143–164. doi: 10.1177/1090198104263660

Benzi, I. M. A., Preti, E., Di Pierro, R., Clarkin, J. F., and Madeddu, F. (2019). Maladaptive personality traits and psychological distress in adolescence: the moderating role of personality functioning. *J. Personal. Individ. Differ.* 140, 33–40. doi: 10.1016/j.paid.2018.06.026

Bezgodova, S. A., Miklyaeva, A. V., and Tereshchenko, V. V. (2018). Attitude to coming-of-age in adolescents of saint-petersburg and smolensk in context of their resiliency. *J. Bull. Kemerovo State University* 3, 77–84. doi: 10.21603/2078-8975-2018-3-77-84

Borzilova, N. S., and Solonchenko, S. S. (2017). Hardiness and adaptability of adolescents remaining without the support of parents, having and not having a significant adult. *J. Young Sci.* 1, 391–393.

Casagrande, P., Coimbra, D., and Andrade, A. (2018). Burnout in elite tennis players of different junior categories. *J. Revista Brasileira de Medicina do Esporte* 24, 121–124. doi: 10.1590/1517-869220182402181208

Chernyavskaya, V. S., and Shabanova, V. V. (2016). Resilience of teenagers with different levels of creativity (on the example of students at the vocational school of the industry of fashion and beauty of VGUES). *J. Sci. Method. Electr. J. Concept.* 11, 32–39.

Deci, E., and Ryan, R. (2000). Self-determination theory and the facilitation of intrinsic motivation, social development and well-being. *J. Am. Psychol.* 55, 68–78. doi: 10.1037//0003-066x.55.1.68

Echazu, L., and Nocetti, D. (2018). Understanding risky behaviors during adolescence: a model of self-discovery through experimentation. *Int. J. Int. Rev. Law Econ.* 57, 12–21. doi: 10.1016/j.irle.2018.11.001

Fokina, I. V., Sokolovskaya, O. K., and Nosova, N. V. (2018). Hardiness and its connection with values in adolescent age. *J. Probl. Mod. Teach. Educ.* 60, 468–471.

Gorkovaya, I. A., Isachenko, T. V., and Shmygareva, V. V. (2015). Impact of macrosocial factors on resilince in teenagers. *J. Mod. Probl. Sci. Educ.* 1:221.

Gorkovaya, I. A., and Miklyaeva, A. V. (2017). Characteristics of quality of life in adolescents with visual impairments in the context of their hardiness. *J. Clin. Psychol. Special Educ.* 6, 47–60. doi: 10.17759/psyclin.2017060404

Guerra, L. A., Rajan, S., and Roberts, K. J. (2019). The implementation of mental health policies and practices in schools: an examination of school and state factors. *J. School Health* 89, 328–338. doi: 10.1111/josh.12738

Gulyaeva, A. O., and Myagkaya, I. A. (2017). "Influence of family education on the formation of the components "hardiness" and viability in general," in *Proceedings of the V International Science Practical Conference of Questions of Modern Science: Problems, Trends and Prospects*, Penza, 25–27.

Ivanova, M. A. (2013). Life scenarios and hardiness of adolescents. *Fundam. Res.* 10, 875–878.

Kalashnikova, M. B., and Nikitina, E. V. (2017). *Vitality as a Necessary Personal Characteristics of Modern Adolescents*. Veliky Novgorod: Yaroslav-the-Wise Novgorod State University, 51–55.

Kalashnikova, M. B., and Petrova, E. A. (2017). The problem concerns of modern teenagers: risks and resources. *J. Pedagog. Rev.* 4, 166–174. doi: 10.23951/2307-6127-2017-4-166-174

Kiva, A. P., Perelygina, I. V., and Andrega, D. S. (2016). "Perception by modern teenagers of their own life and strategy of overcoming difficulties," in *Proceedings of the I International 71 All-Russian Scientific-Practical Conference Of Young Science and Students "Actual Problems Of Modern Medical Science and Public Health*, (Yekaterinburg: Ural State Medical University), 1914–1918.

Kormushina, N. G. (2016). "Hardiness as multiple phenomenon," in *Proceedings of International Interdisciplinary Scientific Conference Link of Modernity: The Hardiness of Individuals and Communities*, Yekaterinburg, 230–240.

Kobasa, S. C. (1979). Stressful life events, personality, and health: an inquiry into hardiness. *J. Personal. Soc. Psychol.* 57, 1–11. doi: 10.1037//0022-3514.37.1.1

Leontiev, D. A., and Rasskazova, E. I. (2006). *Test of Hardiness*. Moscow: Smisl.

Malkin, V. R., and Rogaleva, L. N. (2016). *Psychological Work in Sports School*. Yekaterinburg: Publishing house of the Ural University.

Melisbek, K. M., and Bodnar, E. L. (2018). Research of the hardiness of migrant adolescents. *Probl. Sci.* 6, 107–108.

Mishina, S. S. (2018). Resilience coefficient as a measure of risk of teenagers' suicide behaviour development. *J. Bull. Udmurt Univ. Ser. Philos. Psychol. Pedag.* 28, 308–312.

Morinaj, J., and Hascher, T. (2019). School alienation and student well-being: a cross-lagged longitudinal analysis. *Int. J. Eur. J. Psychol. Educ.* 34, 273–294. doi: 10.1007/s10212-018-0381-381

Nikitina, E. V. (2017). Phenomenon of hardiness: concept, modern views and research. *J. Acad.* 4, 100–103.

Nikitina, E. V. (2018). "The increasing of elder teenagers' viability level by means of socio-psychological training," in *Procedings of the All-Russian Scientific-Practical Conference with International Participation*, (Great Novgorod: Yaroslav), 144–151.

Oschepkov, A. A. (2017). "Human hardiness and resilience as factors of coping deviant behavior," in *Proceedings of the Congress of the Russian Psychological Society*, (Kazan: Kazan Federal University), 180–181.

Plotnikov, K. Y., and Kuzmin, M. Y. (2017). *The Hardiness of Adolescents Who are Engaged in Singing Activities*. Saratov: Collection of science, 317–321.

Rogaleva, L., Khaerzamanova, Y., and Mamaeva, I. (2018). "Motivational strategy of organization of psychology classes for senior school students," in *Proceedings of the 1st International Conference on Contemporary Education and Economic Development (CEED 2018)*, Bail, 1–5. doi: 10.2991/ceed-18.2018.1

Rubinstein, S. L. (2015). *Basics of General Psychology*. Saint Petersburg: Peter.

Seligman, M. (2013). *Path to Prosperity. New Understanding of Happiness and Well-being*. Moscow: Mann.

Shumakova, N. D., and Shamardina, M. V. (2018). Researches of the problems of intelligence in the context hardiness of teenage. *J. Trends Dev. Sci. Educ.* 34, 14–18.

Shvareva, E. V. (2010). Hardiness of adolescents in different educational environment. *J. Sci. Mod.* 6, 411–414.

Sobkin, V. S., Abrosimova, Z. B., Adamchuk, D. V., and Baranova, E. V. (2005). *Teenager: Norms, Risks, Deviations. Center of Sociology of Education*. Moscow: RAE.

Straub, G. (2019). Parental (over-)ambition in competitive youth sport: a multi-theoretical approach. *J. German J. Exerc. Sport Res.* 49, 1–10. doi: 10.1007/s1266201805619

Sultanbaeva, K. I., and Chertykov, I. N. (2014). "Hardiness as a moral feature of teenager-athlete," in *Proceedings of the V All-Russian Scientific-Practical Conference Human Development in the Modern World*, Moscow, 87–93.

9

The Effect of an Enriched Sport Program on Children's Executive Functions

Ambra Gentile[1,2], Stefano Boca[2], Fatma Neşe Şahin[3], Özkan Güler[3], Simona Pajaujiene[4], Vinga Indriuniene[5], Yolanda Demetriou[6], David Sturm[6], Manuel Gómez-López[7], Antonino Bianco[2] and Marianna Alesi[2]*

[1] Ph.D. Program in Health Promotion and Cognitive Sciences, University of Palermo, Palermo, Italy, [2] Department of Psychology, Educational Sciences and Human Movement, University of Palermo, Palermo, Italy, [3] Faculty of Sports Science, Ankara University, Ankara, Turkey, [4] Department of Coaching Science, Lithuanian Sports University, Kaunas, Lithuania, [5] Department of Physical and Social Education, Lithuanian Sports University, Kaunas, Lithuania, [6] Department of Sport and Health Sciences, Technical University of Munich, Munich, Germany, [7] Department of Physical Activity and Sport, Faculty of Sports Sciences, University of Murcia, Murcia, Spain

***Correspondence:**
Ambra Gentile
ambra.gentile01@unipa.it;
ambra.gentile91@gmail.com

Purpose: The effects of physical exercise on executive functions (EFs) are well-documented. EFs are involved in daily activities, and their development determines the quality of people's future life, both in terms of mental health and quality of life. The purpose of the current paper is to evaluate the effects of a physical education program, elaborated within the Enriched Sports Activity Program (ESA Program), an Erasmus + Project, on EFs, namely, visuospatial working memory, inhibitory control, cognitive flexibility, and task switching.

Method: Data were collected on November 2017 (t_1) and May 2018 (t_2). At t_1, a sample of 357 children from four European countries (Italy, Germany, Lithuania, and Turkey) performed a cognitive test battery made up of Digit Span Forward/Backward, Stroop Task, and Trail Making Test (TMT), whose order was randomized. From November until May, classrooms from the experimental group followed the ESA Program, while classrooms from the control continued with the ordinary physical education class. At t_2, children from both experimental and control groups performed again the cognitive battery.

Result: The repeated measures ANOVA showed a significant effect of the ESA Program on the TMT B and on Digit Span Backward, but no significant effects were found on Digit Span Forward and Stroop Task.

Conclusion: The introduction of a sport program enriched with cognitive stimuli has beneficial effects for children working memory and cognitive flexibility.

Keywords: training program, high-order cognitive abilities, cognitive flexibility, inhibitory control, physical education class, working memory

INTRODUCTION

In the past decades, cognition and exercise have been considered as separate domains and, for this reason, were treated independently (Diamond, 2000). In recent years, a close link between physical exercise and cognitive abilities has been recognized (Colcombe and Kramer, 2003), specifically for what concerns the influence of physical exercise on executive functions (EFs).

Many hypotheses have been provided for explaining this improvement as the increase of the catecholamine levels (Chmura et al., 1994; Verburgh et al., 2014), which is linked to prefrontal cortex activity as well as executive functioning (Mehren et al., 2019), or the increase of cerebral blood flow (CBF) due to exercise (Verburgh et al., 2014). During childhood, prefrontal cortex activation should be more dynamic, and brain plasticity should encourage a permanent improvement in cognitive functioning (Khan and Hillman, 2014; Erickson et al., 2015.

EFs relate to a set of cognitive abilities that supervise the information processing for the implementation of goal-directed actions and that require a certain amount of memory, attention, inhibition, and self-control (Eslinger, 1996; Best, 2010; Davis et al., 2011). Especially for children, EFs are involved in the learning process (Alloway and Alloway, 2010); therefore, they are considered crucial for successful performances at school and the development of academic skills (Nayfeld et al., 2013). A study of Visu-Petra et al. (2011) revealed that EFs significantly predict children's academic achievements. More specifically, working memory tasks forecast their performance in math tests, while the inhibition task is positively associated with the general semester grade. Haapala (2013) undertook a systematic literature review from 1966 to 2011 on physical activity, academic performance, and cognition in children and adolescents, providing evidences which showed positive effects of 14- to 36-week physical exercise training on mathematical, reading, and language achievement scores.

However, studies hypothesizing a connection between EFs and specific academic skills (e.g., math skills) found mixed results ranging from a positive influence of physical exercise to none on academic performances. A meta-analysis by de Greeff et al. (2018) found positive moderating effects of inhibition in the relationship between acute exercise and academic achievement, while no moderating effects were found concerning working memory and cognitive flexibility. Moreover, for what concerns physical activity programs, the meta-analysis revealed a significant moderating effect of working memory and cognitive flexibility, while no effects were detected concerning inhibition and planning. These inconsistent results, probably, are due to methodological difficulties in the EFs measurement that are, in turn, related to the complex conceptualization of the construct (Van der Ven et al., 2012). Indeed, the conceptualization of EFs has changed throughout time. In the past, the EF system was considered a unitary structure, while today, researchers have recognized the existence of different, distinguished, but interrelated functions (Miyake et al., 2000).

Hence, a good development in EF is crucial for youth, since problems encountered in EFs during childhood are related to problems in terms of health, social status, and quality of life later on in adult life (Jacka et al., 2011; Diamond, 2012). For this reason, EFs have been related to children with several health issues, as attention deficit hyperactivity disorder (ADHD) (Kempton et al., 1999; Holmes et al., 2010; Ziereis and Jansen, 2015), autism (McEvoy et al., 1993; Gilotty et al., 2002; Rosenthal et al., 2013), and brain injuries (McCarthy et al., 2005; Kesler et al., 2011).

A significant improvement in children's cognitive abilities due to physical exercise has been found by Sibley and Etnier (2003). Specifically, physical activity seems to have positive effects on EF inhibitory function, planning and problem solving, cognitive flexibility, and visuospatial attention (Bidzan-Bluma and Lipowska, 2018). To what concerns the amount and frequency of physical exercise, a meta-analysis by Verburgh et al. (2014) has shown that acute physical exercise, which is a single bout exercise whose duration lasts from 10 to 40 min, has an overall effect on EFs, while no effects were detected concerning chronic exercise; that is, an exercise program lasting between 6 and 30 weeks. According to the authors, two main explanations may be provided: on the one side, chronic exercise has a smaller positive effect on cognitive functioning if compared to the acute exercise; on the other side, the studies included in the meta-analysis might not be suitable in terms of intensity, frequency, and duration. Moreover, while in acute exercise studies, the cognitive assessment took place immediately after the physical exercise, no information was provided concerning chronic exercise. Concerning the age, for children from 6 to 12 years, the authors found a moderate improvement of cognitive function after acute exercise. The importance of physical exercise for children EFs is crucial especially for low performer children who register a greater improvement compared to normal performer children (Diamond, 2012).

Considering that physical exercise has beneficial effects on children's cognition, increasing attempts have been done to implement physical activity programs enriched with cognitive challenges (Hillman et al., 2008). Tuckman and Hinkle (1986) compared children's physical and cognitive performance in a specific running program and an ordinary physical education class, finding that runners also became more creative than children in the ordinary class condition. Concerning this topic, Memmert (2006) confirmed that a sport enriched program can improve sport-related creative thinking, since children learn to perform successful behavior and to act it through creative motor functions. Davis et al. (2007) tested a physical activity program for obese children, analyzing the potential benefits of the program on EFs, and finding positive effects related to planning ability in high dose of exercise condition (40 min/day) compared to the no-exercise control condition.

The success of a sports program depends on its structure and its features. Diamond (2012) maintains that an effective aerobic training program can reduce disparities in EFs produced by differences in social status and predicts further academic success. Nevertheless, the improvement in one EF can be transferred to another, given the abovementioned multidimensional structure of the EF system.

The forecasted physical activity should also challenge children throughout the program. From a motivational point of view (Deci and Ryan, 2008), if kids are not pushed to do better, they stop improving, and, on the other side, if the activity does not become challenging, children get bored and abandon the program. Finally, single bouts of aerobic activity have produced the best results on EFs, but programs that last over time show smaller effects, thus Diamond (2012) suggests to create combined programs of physical training and character development activities.

Considering these findings, the current paper analyzes the effect of Enriched Sports Activity Program (ESA Program) on children's EFs. The ESA Program is an enriched physical exercise protocol experimented within the Erasmus + Project *Enriched Sports Activity Program* (ESA Program; Agreement Nr.: Sport-579661-EPP-1-2016-2-IT-SPO-SCP). The project, which lasted 3 years, aimed at enhancing social inclusion, equal opportunity, and psychosocial well-being in children through an enriched protocol that introduced physical exercises able to stimulate cognitive growth (Alesi et al., 2017). The exercises were modified to stimulate the three core EFs, namely, inhibitory control, the ability to ignore one stimulus and concentrate on another; working memory, the goal-directed ability to monitor and manipulate mental representations stored in working memory; and task shifting, the ability to consciously switch from one task to another (Miyake et al., 2000; Diamond, 2013). The program was articulated into 27 units, divided into a 10-min baseline phase and a 15-min stimulation phase. The program is innovative since it standardized the warm-up session through the introduction of cognitive stimuli within exercises relating to several sports activities.

Considering the results retrieved from literature, the physical exercise protocol foreseen by the ESA Program should enhance EF performance in inhibitory control, working memory, and task shifting. Given the developmental phase of participants, ranging from 7 to 14 years, we expect a general improvement of all children's EFs, but a particular improvement in children who have followed the ESA protocol.

MATERIALS AND METHODS

Data collection took place in the first months of the school year in November (t_1) and in May (t_2), at the end of the same school year, within four different European countries (Italy, Lithuania, Turkey, and Germany) (**Table 1**). Four hundred twenty-two children were included in the sample, but 65 children did not complete the final evaluation. Thus, the research sample consisted of 357 children (48% males, 52% females) whose age was comprised between 7 and 14 years old (mean age = 9.55, SD = 1.77). The study was carried out according to the Helsinki Declaration (Hong Kong revision, September 1989). It also received permission from the Lithuanian Sports University's Research Ethics Committee in Social Sciences with approval No 579661-EPP-1-2016-2-IT-SPO-SCP (2018-02-05).

TABLE 1 | Selected participants per country.

Country	N	Intervention	Control
Italy	164	77	87
Lithuania	93	56	37
Turkey	80	40	40
Germany	85	38	36

Procedure

Cognitive data collection at t_1 took place within four European countries (Italy, Lithuania, Germany, and Turkey). After parents' signature of the consent form, children school classes were split in experimental and control groups. Children from both experimental group (ESA group) and control group completed a battery made up of three neuropsychological tasks derived by the Inquisit Lab platform: the Color Word Stroop Task (Stroop, 1935), the Trail Making Test (TMT) (Reitan, 1958), and the Digit Span Test (Lumley and Calhoon, 1934). One of the experimenters guided the children during the assessment, explaining the tasks they had to complete. Cognitive tasks were presented in a random order, and the data collection lasted about 30 min per respondent.

Children following the ESA Program completed 27 training units during physical education class, while children from the control group followed ordinary physical education class. At t_2, corresponding to the end of the school year, children repeated the same cognitive assessment in the same order presented at t_1.

Measures

Executive Functions

The following three EFs were measured: working memory, inhibitory control, cognitive flexibility and task-switching ability (Sánchez-Cubillo et al., 2009). For this purpose, Inquisit five by Millisecond© was employed, using the libraries available on the Millisecond© website. These scripts implemented the classic Stroop Task, TMT, and Digit Span Test with keyboard inputs.

Digit span forward/backward

Digit Span assesses working memory (Lumley and Calhoon, 1934; Woods et al., 2011). In the visual version, numeric sequences appear on the screen, and participants have to recall them (both in a forward and in a backward manner) by selecting with the mouse the digits from a circle of digits. Depending on performance, participants move up a level or down a level, and the assessment is over after 14 trials. The whole task lasts 15 min. The number of recalled digits before two consecutive errors was taken into consideration for data analysis. Scores are computed counting the number of recalled digits in the presented order and the number of recalled digits in the reversed order.

Stroop task

The Stroop Task is designed for assessing inhibitory control (Stroop, 1935). Participants are showed on the computer screen words written in four colors, such as red, green, blue, black. The task is made up of three conditions: in the congruent task (W), participants see some words on the screen and they have to indicate in which color the word is written that is congruent with its meaning, e.g., "red" word printed in red color. In the incongruent task (CW), participants have to indicate in which color the word is written and ignoring its meaning, e.g., "blue" word printed in red color. In the control condition (C), participants see some blocks on the screen, e.g., colored rectangles, and they have to indicate the color. Total trials are 84 derived by: 4 colors (red, green, blue, black) × 3 color-stimulus congruency (congruent, incongruent, control) × 7 repetitions. In the current study, the interference score was calculated considering the logarithmic difference between inhibitory reaction time and control reaction time (MacLeod, 1991).

Trail making test

The TMT is a test developed for assessing cognitive flexibility and task switching (Reitan, 1958). In the A version, participants have to link numbers in increasing order, while in the B version, participants have to connect a number and a letter in an increasing way alternatively (i.e., 1-A-2-B-3-C). The trails were 4:1. Only numbers from 1 to 5; 2. only numbers from 1 to 25; 3. numbers and letters from 1A to 5; 4. numbers and letters from 1A to 13. For the calculation of the scores, only the B version completion time was used since it is more sensitive to cognitive flexibility skill (Kortte et al., 2002).

Enriched Sport Program

ESA Program. The implementation lasted 14 consecutive weeks in the school and the sports center context. It involved children from 7 to 14 years who already practiced sport. The protocol aimed to enrich the warm-up of regular sports activities with cognitive stimuli (inhibition, working memory, task shifting) for improving children's EF. The program consisted of 27 units lasting 25 min. The unit was made up of a baseline phase and stimulation phase, and it was obtained through a combination of two features: cognitive stimulus and movement domain. The construct validity was assessed only qualitatively: four experts from psychology and sport science rated the extent to which an exercise could stimulate a specific cognitive function. The discrepancies were solved through discussion.

The cognitive stimuli for the stimulation phase could involve inhibitory control, working memory, or task shifting. In the activity stimulating inhibitory control, the coach's verbal command for an exercise corresponded to the execution of another movement previously associated. For example, the verbal command "Skip-ahead" corresponded to "Kicked-ahead" movement, and the command "Fore-foot gait-ahead" corresponded to "Rear-foot gait-ahead." The stimulation of working memory occurred through the explanation of a series of exercises that children had to perform in a reverse order. For example, the oral command "Balance on the line-ahead/behind" corresponded to the performance "Balance on the line-behind/ahead." Concerning the task shifting stimulation, a circuit of exercises was created, and each child had to perform a specific exercise that was different from the others' one. When the instructor whistled, children had to switch to the exercise that the kid ahead was performing, until all of them had performed all the exercises in the circuit.

All the three domains started with a beginning level (B), followed by an intermediate level (I), and finishing with an advanced level (A). The design of the protocol was the following: the first nine units concerned the beginner level of exercise, whose domain was alternatively athletic drill, then sports ball, and finally smart circuits, and whose stimulation concerned alternatively working memory, inhibition, and task shifting. The same structure was kept for intermediate level and advanced level (**Figure 1**).

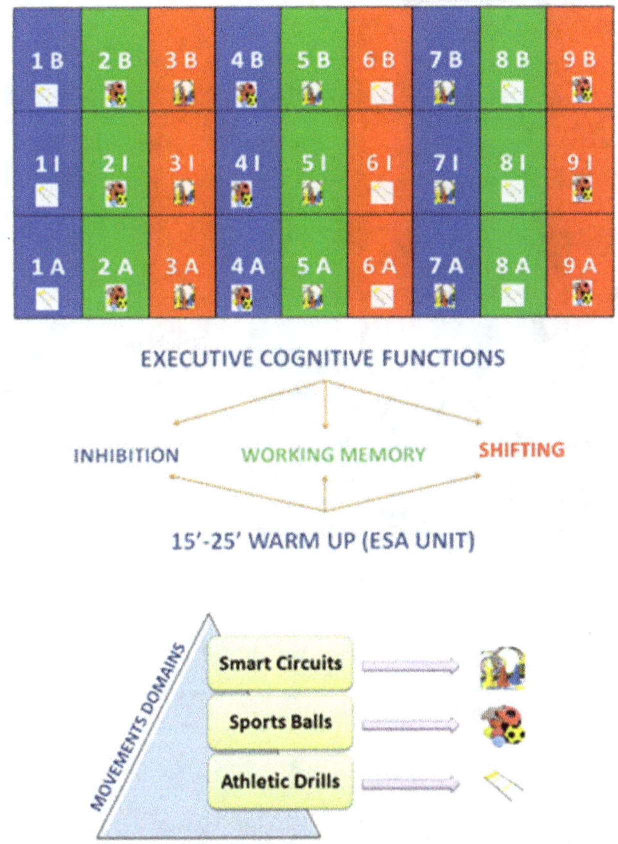

FIGURE 1 | The Enriched Sports Activity (ESA) Program Protocol.

A series of coaches' guidelines video tutorials were recorded to maximize the protocol standardization across the European administrators.

Data Analysis

Descriptive statistics was performed on the sample, including height and weight (**Tables 2**, **3**). Afterward, for evaluating the effects of the ESA Program on children's EFs, a repeated measures ANOVA model with Time × Group comparisons was performed. Specifically, the cognitive scores at the beginning and the end of the school year were compared, separating the general effect of improvement from the one induced by the ESA Program. The age of the participants was included as a covariate since the effects of physical exercise enhance executive function performance at different levels across ages (Ludyga et al., 2016).

RESULTS

For what concerns Digit Span Forward, repeated measures ANOVA showed a significant effect of Time between pre- and post-test conditions, while non-significant effects were found in the interaction between Time and Activity ($F_{1,355} = 2.26$, $p = 0.13$). No general performance improvement was observed in the Backward recall during time ($F_{1,351} = 0.21$, $p = 0.64$),

TABLE 2 | Distribution of height in different age ranges.

	Height (cm)	
Age	**Mean**	**SD**
7–8 years	131.0	6.19
9–10 years	140.0	8.62
11–12 years	154.0	9.58
13–14 years	165.0	5.42

TABLE 3 | Distribution of weight in different age ranges.

	Weight (kg)	
Age	**Mean**	**SD**
7–8 years	30.0	6.66
9–10 years	36.9	7.14
11–12 years	43.2	7.25
13–14 years	53.9	6.20

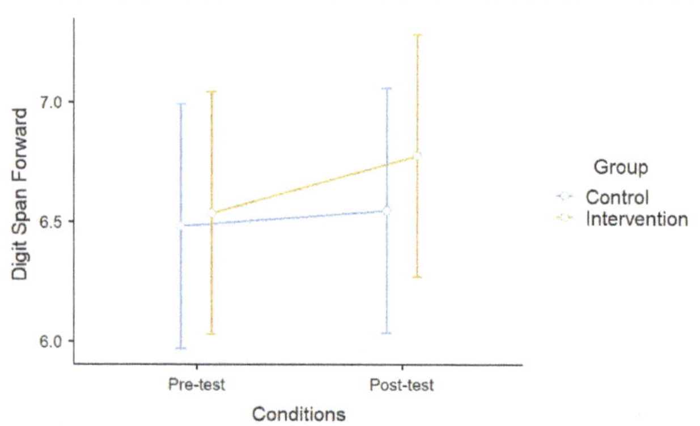

FIGURE 2 | Results on the Digit Span Forward.

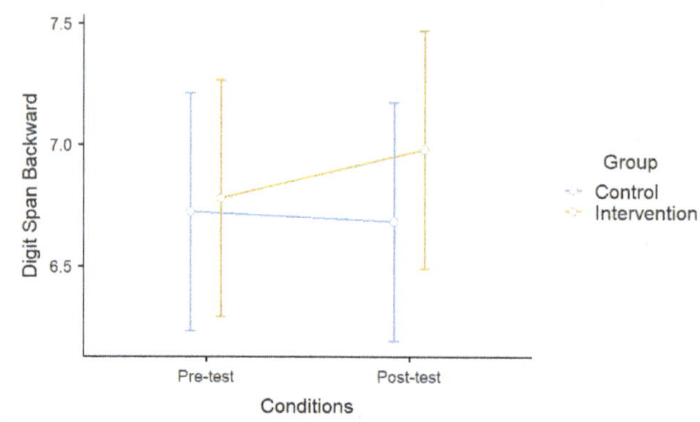

FIGURE 3 | Results on the Digit Span Backward.

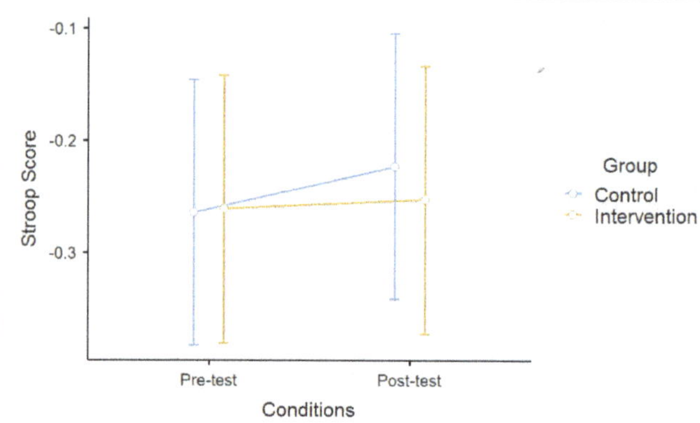

FIGURE 4 | Results on the Stroop Task.

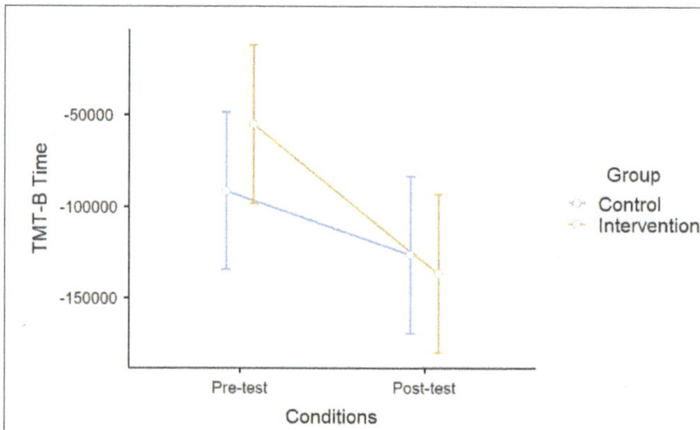

FIGURE 5 | Results on the Trail Making Test.

but children from the ESA Program significantly improved more their performance compared to the control group ($F_{1,351} = 4.58$, $p < 0.05$). No effects of Age were detected in both cases (Forward: $F_{1,355} = 1.04$, $p = 0.31$; Backward: $F_{1,351} = 0.05$, $p = 0.83$) (**Figures 2, 3**).

A significant effect of Age has been found on the Stroop Task ($F_{1,338} = 6.98$, $p < 0.01$), but both the Time effect and the interaction between the treatment and the group were non-significant (Time: $F_{1,335} = 2.34$; $p = 0.12$; Time × Group: $F_{1,335} = 0.87$, $p = 0.35$) (**Figure 4**). Concerning the TMT, a significant effect of the ESA Program between pre-test and post-test conditions was found ($F_{1,348} = 26.3, p < 0.00$), as well as the interaction between Time and Group ($F_{1,348} = 13.7$, $p < 0.001$) and the influence of Age ($F_{1,348} = 12.4, p < 0.001$) (**Figure 5**).

DISCUSSION

The purpose of the current study was to test the effectiveness of the ESA Program on children's cognitive performances, in particular, their EFs. The ESA Program is an enriched sports program containing warm-up physical exercises that were modified to stimulate three core EFs (inhibitory control, working memory, and task shifting) (Diamond, 2013).

Some studies have already proven that the introduction of an ESA program enhances cognitive functioning (Beck et al., 2016; Gheysen et al., 2018). In this study, we specifically tested changes in working memory and short-term memory through Digit Span

Forward and Backward Task, inhibitory control through the Stroop Task, cognitive flexibility and task shifting through the TMT that are EFs involved in daily life and relating to school performances (Visu-Petra et al., 2011).

Moreover, the ESA Program has already shown its effect concerning children's physical fitness, where moderate effects were found in relation to throwing, jumping, sprinting, and agility (Duda et al., 1991). Our sample was made up of children coming from four European countries that implemented the ESA Program within the same period and following the same protocol, shared with all the partners through video tutorials. In this way, the standardization of the procedures was ensured.

For the evaluation of the program effectiveness, repeated measures ANOVA was run, revealing a significant effect of the ESA Program on Digit Span Backward and TMT B version. No significant effect of the ESA Program was found on Digit Span Forward nor on the Stroop Task. To summarize our results, the enriched sport program produced positive effects for working memory, task switching, and cognitive flexibility, while no beneficial effects were detected on inhibitory control and short-time memory. Concerning the age of the sample, a significant interaction with the ESA Program was found in the Stroop Task and TMT, indicating that older children significantly reduced the completion time of the task, but the same effect was not detected for Digit Span Forward and Backward.

The positive effect of an enriched sports program on working memory is in line with ample research. Both longitudinal and cross-sectional studies underlie a positive association among structured physical activity in childhood with higher working memory performance (López-Vicente et al., 2017). Koutsandreou et al. (2016) found that 10 weeks of interventions based on cardiovascular and motor afterschool exercise programs enhanced working memory skills on a sample of 9- to 10-year-old children with a larger degree due to the motor exercise intervention rather the cardiovascular program.

Moreover, a study by Beck et al. (2016) employed a sport-enriched math program made up of three conditions, namely, gross motor math group, fine motor math group, and control condition. The results showed that children from all the conditions improved their performance, but the ones from gross motor condition enhanced their performance significantly more than the other groups when tested immediately after the program. This enhancement was not found after 8 weeks.

The ESA Program's effects on TMT B reduction of time is coherent with findings of a previous study carried out by Schmidt et al. (2016). The authors compared four experimental conditions characterized by an increasing cognitive load, ranging from low cognitive demand to high cognitive demand, and increasing physical demand. They found that following a period of 10 min of cognitive challenging tasks, children showed better focused attention and decreased processing speed. The speed component of the attention was highly influenced. These findings focus on the issue concerning the quality of intervention. Cognitive challenging physical activities revealed to be more suitable to improve children's attention compared to ordinary physical activities.

No improvements of the ESA Program were found upon inhibitory control, a result that contradicts other data in literature (Tsai, 2009; Drollette et al., 2014). However, the studies that found a positive effect of physical exercise on inhibitory control used clinical samples including children with specific problems, like ADHD (Chang et al., 2014), while our sample was made up of children from ordinary school class. It seems that children with poorer performance on EF tasks may experience more positive effects following sports programs compared to children exhibiting baseline normal performance on EFs (Ludyga et al., 2016).

The review by van der Fels et al. (2015) pointed out the interplay between cognitive and motor skills in childhood. The authors emphasized how challenging tasks stimulate the co-activation of prefrontal cortex, cerebellum, and basal ganglia and trigger common processes as inhibition, planning, and monitoring. The current study introduces many advantages, as the combination of different sport movement domains and cognitive stimulation that provide to the coaches an innovative structured warm-up characterized by an increasing cognitive load. A higher cognitive load task requires higher attention and regular physiological condition and muscular fatigue may impair cognitive performance. For this reason, the warm-up phase has been selected as the most appropriate exercise unit section for a suitable cognitive stimulation. Moreover, the physical assessment provided through the first phase of the Program has demonstrated its effectiveness also from a physical point of view (Thomas et al., 2020).

Some limitations of the present study should be noted. First of all, follow-up measurements were not implemented; thus, we do not have information about the stability of our results during time. Secondly, performances in EFs were detected, but an important limitation is that they were not linked to children's academic achievement or their reading, writing, and calculating skills. Finally, construct validity was only assessed qualitatively. Given these limitations, future research should investigate the effects of enriched sport programs with accurate construct validity measures on children's academic achievement with a follow-up period after the conclusion of the program.

Providing enriched programs, as the one suggested by the ESA Program, at school may significantly improve children's cognitive functioning that in turn should have beneficial effects on their academic performances.

ETHICS STATEMENT

The studies involving human participants were reviewed and approved by Lithuanian Sports University's Research Ethics Committee in Social Sciences. Written informed consent to participate in this study was provided by the participants' legal guardian/next of kin.

AUTHOR CONTRIBUTIONS

AG, AB, and MA contributed to the conceptualization. FŞ, ÖG, SP, VI, YD, DS, AB, and MA contributed to the data curation.

AG, SB, and MG-L contributed to the formal analysis. AB and MA contributed to the funding acquisition and contributed to the project administration. FŞ, ÖG, SP, VI, YD, DS, and MG-L contributed to the investigation. AG, MA, YD, DS, and MG-L contributed to the methodology. SP, VI, and MG-L contributed to the resources. FŞ and ÖG contributed to the software. SP, VI, and AB contributed to the supervision. YD and DS contributed to the validation. AG and MA contributed to the visualization. AG, SB, AB, MA, and MG-L contributed to the roles/writing of the original draft. FŞ, ÖG, SP, VI, YD, and DS contributed to the writing, reviewing, and editing.

REFERENCES

Alesi, M., Silva, C., Borrego, C., Monteiro, D., Genchi, R., Polizzi, V., et al. (2017). Cognitive and motivational monitoring during enriched sport activities in a sample of children living in Europe. The ESA Program. *J. Funct. Morphol. Kinesiol.* 2, 10–12.

Alloway, T. P., and Alloway, R. G. (2010). Investigating the predictive roles of working memory and IQ in academic attainment. *J. Exp. Child Psychol.* 106, 20–29. doi: 10.1016/j.jecp.2009.11.003

Beck, M. M., Lind, R. R., Geertsen, S. S., Ritz, C., Lundbye-Jensen, J., and Wienecke, J. (2016). Motor-enriched learning activities can improve mathematical performance in preadolescent children. *Front. Hum. Neurosci.* 10:645. doi: 10.3389/fnhum.2016.00645

Best, J. R. (2010). Effects of physical activity on children's executive function: contributions of experimental research on aerobic exercise. *Dev. Rev.* 30, 331–551. doi: 10.1016/j.dr.2010.08.001

Bidzan-Bluma, I., and Lipowska, M. (2018). Physical activity and cognitive functioning of children: a systematic review. *Int. J. Env. Res. Public Health* 15:800. doi: 10.3390/ijerph15040800

Chang, Y.-K., Hung, C.-L., Huang, C.-J., Hatfield, B. D., and Hung, T.-M. (2014). Effects of an aquatic exercise program on inhibitory control in children with ADHD: a preliminary study. *Arch. Clin. Neuropsychol.* 29, 217–223. doi: 10.1093/arclin/acu003

Chmura, J., Nazar, K., and Kaciuba-Uscilko, H. (1994). Choice reaction time during graded exercise in relation to blood lactate and plasma catecholamine thresholds. *Int. J. Sports Med.* 15, 172–176. doi: 10.1055/s-2007-1021042

Colcombe, S., and Kramer, A. F. (2003). Fitness effects on the cognitive function of older adults: a meta-analytic study. *Psychol. Sci.* 14, 125–130. doi: 10.1111/1467-9280.t01-1-01430

Davis, C. L., Tomporowski, P. D., Boyle, C. A., Waller, J. L., Miller, P. H., Naglieri, J. A., et al. (2007). Effects of aerobic exercise on overweight children's cognitive functioning: a randomized controlled trial. *Res. Q. Exerc. Sport* 78, 510–519. doi: 10.1080/02701367.2007.10599450

Davis, C. L., Tomporowski, P. D., McDowell, J. E., Austin, B. P., Miller, P. H., Yanasak, N. E., et al. (2011). Exercise improves executive function and achievement and alters brain activation in overweight children: a randomized, controlled trial. *Health Psychol.* 30, 91–98. doi: 10.1037/a0021766

de Greeff, J. W., Bosker, R. J., Oosterlaan, J., Visscher, C., and Hartman, E. (2018). Effects of physical activity on executive functions, attention and academic performance in preadolescent children: a meta-analysis. *J. Sci. Med. Sport* 21, 501–507. doi: 10.1016/j.jsams.2017.09.595

Deci, E. L., and Ryan, R. M. (2008). Self-determination theory: a macrotheory of human motivation, development, and health. *Can. Psychol.* 49, 182. doi: 10.1037/a0012801

Diamond, A. (2000). Close interrelation of motor development and cognitive development and of the cerebellum and prefrontal cortex. *Child Dev.* 71, 44–56. doi: 10.1111/1467-8624.00117

Diamond, A. (2012). Activities and programs that improve children's executive functions. *Curr. Direct. Psychol. Sci.* 21, 335–341. doi: 10.1177/0963721412453722

Diamond, A. (2013). Executive functions. *Annu. Rev. Psychol.* 64, 135–168. doi: 10.1146/annurev-psych-113011-143750

Drollette, E. S., Scudder, M. R., Raine, L. B., Moore, R. D., Saliba, B. J., Pontifex, M. B., et al. (2014). Acute exercise facilitates brain function and cognition in children who need it most: an ERP study of individual differences in inhibitory control capacity. *Dev. Cogn. Neurosci.* 7, 53–64. doi: 10.1016/j.dcn.2013.11.001

Duda, J. L., Olson, L. K., and Templin, T. J. (1991). The relationship of task and ego orientation to sportsmanship attitudes and the perceived legitimacy of injurious acts. *Res. Q. Exerc. Sport* 62, 79–87. doi: 10.1080/02701367.1991.10607522

Erickson, K. I., Hillman, C. H., and Kramer, A. F. (2015). Physical activity, brain, and cognition. *Curr. Opin. Behav. Sci.* 4, 27–32.

Eslinger, P. (1996). *Attention, Memory, and Executive Function.* Baltimore, MD: P.H. Brookes Publishing Company.

Gheysen, F., Poppe, L., DeSmet, A., Swinnen, S., Cardon, G., De Bourdeaudhuij, I., et al. (2018). Physical activity to improve cognition in older adults: can physical activity programs enriched with cognitive challenges enhance the effects? A systematic review and meta-analysis. *Int. J. Behav. Nutr. Phys. Act.* 15:63. doi: 10.1186/s12966-018-0697-x

Gilotty, L., Kenworthy, L., Sirian, L., Black, D. O., and Wagner, A. E. (2002). Adaptive skills and executive function in autism spectrum disorders. *Child Neuropsychol.* 8, 241–248. doi: 10.1076/chin.8.4.241.13504

Haapala, E. A. (2013). Cardiorespiratory fitness and motor skills in relation to cognition and academic performance in children–a review. *J. Hum. Kinet.* 36, 55–68. doi: 10.2478/hukin-2013-0006

Hillman, C. H., Erickson, K. I., and Kramer, A. F. (2008). Be smart, exercise your heart: exercise effects on brain and cognition. *Nat. Rev. Neurosci.* 9, 58–65. doi: 10.1038/nrn2298

Holmes, J., Gathercole, S. E., Place, M., Alloway, T. P., Elliott, J. G., and Hilton, K. A. (2010). The diagnostic utility of executive function assessments in the identification of ADHD in children. *Child Adolesc. Mental Health* 15, 37–43. doi: 10.1111/j.1475-3588.2009.00536.x

Jacka, F., Pasco, J., Williams, L., Leslie, E., Dodd, S., Nicholson, G., et al. (2011). Lower levels of physical activity in childhood associated with adult depression. *J. Sci. Med. Sport* 14, 222–226. doi: 10.1016/j.jsams.2010.10.458

Kempton, S., Vance, A., Maruff, P., Luk, E., Costin, J., and Pantelis, C. (1999). Executive function and attention deficit hyperactivity disorder: stimulant medication and better executive function performance in children. *Psychol. Med.* 29, 527–538. doi: 10.1017/s0033291799008338

Kesler, S. R., Lacayo, N. J., and Jo, B. (2011). A pilot study of an online cognitive rehabilitation program for executive function skills in children with cancer-related brain injury. *Brain Injury* 25, 101–112. doi: 10.3109/02699052.2010.536194

Khan, N. A., and Hillman, C. H. (2014). The relation of childhood physical activity and aerobic fitness to brain function and cognition: a review. *Pediatric Exerc. Sci.* 26, 138–146. doi: 10.1123/pes.2013-0125

Kortte, K. B., Horner, M. D., and Windham, W. K. (2002). The trail making test, part B: cognitive flexibility or ability to maintain set? *Appl. Neuropsychol.* 9, 106–109. doi: 10.1207/S15324826AN0902_5

Koutsandreou, F., Wegner, M., Niemann, C., and Budde, H. (2016). Effects of motor versus cardiovascular exercise training on children's working memory. *Med. Sci. Sports Exerc.* 48, 1144–1152. doi: 10.1249/MSS.0000000000000869

López-Vicente, M., Garcia-Aymerich, J., Torrent-Pallicer, J., Forns, J., Ibarluzea, J., Lertxundi, N., et al. (2017). Are early physical activity and sedentary behaviors related to working memory at 7 and 14 years of age? *J. Pediatr.* 188, 35.–41. doi: 10.1016/j.jpeds.2017.05.079

Ludyga, S., Gerber, M., Brand, S., Holsboer-Trachsler, E., and Puhse, U. (2016). Acute effects of moderate aerobic exercise on specific aspects of executive function in different age and fitness groups: a meta-analysis. *Psychophysiology* 53, 1611–1626. doi: 10.1111/psyp.12736

Lumley, F., and Calhoon, S. (1934). Memory span for words presented auditorially. *J. Appl. Psychol.* 18:773. doi: 10.1037/h0071977

MacLeod, C. M. (1991). Half a century of research on the Stroop effect: an integrative review. *Psychol. Bull.* 109, 163–203. doi: 10.1037/0033-2909.109.2.163

McCarthy, M. L., MacKenzie, E. J., Durbin, D. R., Aitken, M. E., Jaffe, K. M., Paidas, C. N., et al. (2005). The Pediatric Quality of Life Inventory: an evaluation of its reliability and validity for children with traumatic brain injury. *Arch. Phys. Med. Rehabil.* 86, 1901–1909. doi: 10.1016/j.apmr.2005.03.026

McEvoy, R. E., Rogers, S. J., and Pennington, B. F. (1993). Executive function and social communication deficits in young autistic children. *J. Child Psychol. Psychiatry* 34, 563–578. doi: 10.1111/j.1469-7610.1993.tb01036.x

Mehren, A., Ozyurt, J., Lam, A. P., Brandes, M., Muller, H. H., Thiel, C. M., et al. (2019). Acute effects of aerobic exercise on executive function and attention in adult patients with ADHD. *Front. Psychiatry* 10:132. doi: 10.3389/fpsyt.2019.00132

Memmert, D. (2006). Developing creative thinking in a gifted sport enrichment program and the crucial role of attention processes. *High Ability Stud.* 17, 101–115. doi: 10.1080/13598130600947176

Miyake, A., Friedman, N. P., Emerson, M. J., Witzki, A. H., Howerter, A., and Wager, T. D. (2000). The unity and diversity of executive functions and their contributions to complex "frontal lobe" tasks: a latent variable analysis. *Cognit. Psychol.* 41, 49–100. doi: 10.1006/cogp.1999.0734

Nayfeld, I., Fuccillo, J., and Greenfield, D. B. (2013). Executive functions in early learning: extending the relationship between executive functions and school readiness to science. *Learn. Individ. Differ.* 26, 81–88. doi: 10.1016/j.lindif.2013.04.011

Reitan, R. M. (1958). Validity of the Trail Making Test as an indicator of organic brain damage. *Percept. Mot. Skills* 8, 271–276. doi: 10.2466/pms.1958.8.3.271

Rosenthal, M., Wallace, G. L., Lawson, R., Wills, M. C., Dixon, E., Yerys, B. E., et al. (2013). Impairments in real-world executive function increase from childhood to adolescence in autism spectrum disorders. *Neuropsychology* 27:13. doi: 10.1037/a0031299

Sánchez-Cubillo, I., Perianez, J., Adrover-Roig, D., Rodriguez-Sanchez, J., Rios-Lago, M., Tirapu, J., et al. (2009). Construct validity of the Trail Making Test: role of task-switching, working memory, inhibition/interference control, and visuomotor abilities. *J. Int. Neuropsychol. Soc.* 15, 438–450. doi: 10.1017/S1355617709090626

Schmidt, M., Benzing, V., and Kamer, M. (2016). Classroom-based physical activity breaks and children's attention: cognitive engagement works! *Front. Psychol.* 7:1474. doi: 10.3389/fpsyg.2016.01474

Sibley, B. A., and Etnier, J. L. (2003). The relationship between physical activity and cognition in children: a meta-analysis. *Pediatr. Exerc. Sci.* 15, 243–256. doi: 10.1123/pes.15.3.243

Stroop, J. R. (1935). Studies of interference in serial verbal reactions. *J. Exp. Psychol.* 18:643. doi: 10.1037/h0054651

Thomas, E., Bianco, A., Tabacchi, G., Marques da Silva, C., Loureiro, N., Basile, M., et al. (2020). Effects of a physical activity intervention on physical fitness of schoolchildren: the enriched sport activity program. *Int. J. Environ. Res. Public Health* 17:1723. doi: 10.3390/ijerph17051723

Tsai, C.-L. (2009). The effectiveness of exercise intervention on inhibitory control in children with developmental coordination disorder: using a visuospatial attention paradigm as a model. *Res. Dev. Disabil.* 30, 1268–1280. doi: 10.1016/j.ridd.2009.05.001

Tuckman, B. W., and Hinkle, J. S. (1986). An experimental study of the physical and psychological effects of aerobic exercise on schoolchildren. *Health Psychol.* 5, 197–207. doi: 10.1037//0278-6133.5.3.197

van der Fels, I. M., Te Wierike, S. C., Hartman, E., Elferink-Gemser, M. T., Smith, J., and Visscher, C. (2015). The relationship between motor skills and cognitive skills in 4-16 year old typically developing children: a systematic review. *J. Sci. Med. Sport* 18, 697–703. doi: 10.1016/j.jsams.2014.09.007

Van der Ven, S. H., Kroesbergen, E. H., Boom, J., and Leseman, P. P. (2012). The development of executive functions and early mathematics: a dynamic relationship. *Br. J. Educ. Psychol.* 82, 100–119. doi: 10.1111/j.2044-8279.2011.02035.x

Verburgh, L., Konigs, M., Scherder, E. J., and Oosterlaan, J. (2014). Physical exercise and executive functions in preadolescent children, adolescents and young adults: a meta-analysis. *Br. J. Sports Med.* 48, 973–979. doi: 10.1136/bjsports-2012-091441

Visu-Petra, L., Cheie, L., Benga, O., and Miclea, M. (2011). Cognitive control goes to school: the impact of executive functions on academic performance. *Proc. Soc. Behav. Sci.* 11, 240–244. doi: 10.1016/j.sbspro.2011.01.069

Woods, D. L., Kishiyamaa, M. M., Lund, E. W., Herron, T. J., Edwards, B., Poliva, O., et al. (2011). Improving digit span assessment of short-term verbal memory. *J. Clin. Exp. Neuropsychol.* 33, 101–111. doi: 10.1080/13803395.2010.493149

Ziereis, S., and Jansen, P. (2015). Effects of physical activity on executive function and motor performance in children with ADHD. *Res. Dev. Disabil.* 38, 181–191. doi: 10.1016/j.ridd.2014.12.005

10

Levels of Physical Activity are Associated with the Motivational Climate and Resilience in University Students of Physical Education from Andalucía: An Explanatory Model

*Ramón Chacón-Cuberos[1], Manuel Castro-Sánchez[2], José Antonio Pérez-Turpin[3], Eva María Olmedo-Moreno[1] and Félix Zurita Ortega[2]**

[1] Department of Research Methods and Diagnosis in Education, University of Granada, Granada, Spain, [2] Department of Didactics of Musical, Plastic and Corporal Expression, University of Granada, Granada, Spain, [3] Department of Didactic General and Specific Training, University of Alicante, Alicante, Spain

***Correspondence:**
Félix Zurita Ortega
felixzo@ugr.es

Background: The practice of Physical Activity (PA) is a key factor for the improvement of physical and mental health, making the study of the motivational processes that take part in the development of active lifestyles of interest.

Methods: This cross-sectional study was conducted on 775 university students of Physical Education (PE) from Spain. This research aims to develop an explanatory model for the relationships between motivational climate and resilience according to the level of PA, using structural equations analysis. The main instrument used were the Perceived Motivational Climate in Sport (PMCSQ-2) and the Connor-Davidson Resilience Scale (CD-RISC).

Results: A negative relationship was observed between task-oriented climate (TC) and ego-oriented climate, which acquired greater correlation strength in the respondents who did less PA. Likewise, a positive relationship was obtained between TC and resilience, which was higher in participants who did more than 3 h of weekly PA. Finally, it was observed that resilience was highly correlated with personal competence, tenacity and control capacity in the most active respondents.

Conclusion: The importance of promoting task-oriented motivational climates in PA is highlighted, since this could develop a better resilience capacity in university students and will favor the tolerance to adversity and the positive acceptance of changes.

Keywords: resilience, motivational climate, physical activity, sport, university

INTRODUCTION

Given the benefits produced for physical and mental health, there's been an expansion in recent decades in the promotion of healthy lifestyles (Ekelund et al., 2016; Lewis et al., 2017). One of the main ways to achieve this aim is the practice of Physical Activity (PA). This is defined as all body movements that involve an energy expenditure, while the practice of physical exercise implies a prescription of PA with a specific load and rest periods. Moreover, sport is a more specific concept that can be defined as a regulated and institutionalized PA that can involve competition in different ways. Thus, an adequate prescription of these habits will provide multiple benefits at the physiological level, and its promotion is essential from an early age (Bouchard et al., 2018). Specifically, World Health Organization [WHO] (2010) recommends performing at least 150 min of moderate PA or 75 min of intense PA per week in adults aged between 18 and 64 years old. This recommendation is especially important in university students, which are approaching adulthood (Arnett and Tanner, 2016). This stage is a period of labor and social complexity, in which several harmful habits can arise due to peer influence. Some of these habits include the consumption of legal drugs, sedentary digital leisure or unhealthy food intakes (Chacón-Cuberos et al., 2018a; Erturan-Ilker et al., 2018).

Among the benefits provided by positive habits figures a decrease in the risk of suffering from diseases such as osteoporosis, cancer or obesity (Warburton and Bredin, 2017). PA produces an improvement in insulin sensitivity, develops cardiorespiratory fitness through adaptations in the cardiovascular system and helps decrease the percentage of fat mass (Fransson et al., 2018; López-Sánchez et al., 2018). In addition, PA also generates a multitude of benefits at a cognitive level, which are the focus of this research work. For example, Sink et al. (2015) demonstrated that older adults who followed an active lifestyle based on PA for 24 months improved cognitive function and reaction time. Likewise, Plotnikoff et al. (2015), Donnelly et al. (2016) revealed that adolescents who performed physical exercise improved their cerebral neuroplasticity, attention capacity and academic performance. In fact, the practice of PA is associated with improvements in several psychosocial factors, such as self-esteem, perceived well-being, self-concept or resilience (Kavosi et al., 2015; Plotnikoff et al., 2015; Prakash et al., 2015).

Due to the positive effects for the health linked to the practice of PA, it is interesting to study the motivational processes that promote its practice. The Self-Determination Theory (Ryan and Deci, 2017; Chacón-Cuberos et al., 2018b) and the Achievement Goals Theory (Mascret et al., 2015; Chacón-Cuberos et al., 2018a) represent the two main models that explain the development of behaviors in the sport context. The first theory states that the level of motivation linked to a behavior establishes a continuum which varies from higher to lower level of self-determination. The most self-determined area includes more autonomous and controlled forms of motivation such as intrinsic motivation, while amotivation is found in the less self-determined area. In the middle zone the extrinsic motivation can be found, which is characterized by behaviors which are done in order to obtain some separable outcome or rewards. It is also important to point out that this level of self-determination will be mediated by three basic components, such as competence, autonomy, and relationship with others (Ryan and Deci, 2000; Gorelik et al., 2018). Briefly, the need of competence is linked to the ability to control actions effectively in order to obtain the desired result. The need for autonomy is associated with the desire of the person to build and determine their own behavior and modify it according to the need of the context. Finally, the need of relationship is linked to behaviors that improve the social world of the athlete, integrating a socializing component (Ryan and Deci, 2017; Erturan-Ilker et al., 2018).

The second model establishes that the goals fixed by a person in the sport practice depend on the perception that people have of their abilities and skills (Harwood et al., 2015; Gorelik et al., 2018; Castro-Sánchez et al., 2019). The motivational climate is defined as the set of social and contextual signals through which social agents are related, which define the keys to success or failure (Moreno et al., 2008). Thus, two types of motivational climates can be developed as a result of the relationships between peers, rivals, coaches and other agents; the task-oriented motivational climate and the ego-oriented motivational climate. Moreover, several authors have demonstrated the link between the motivational climate and the theory of self-determination (Moreno et al., 2008; Jaakkola et al., 2017). The task-oriented climate (TC) is associated with intrinsic motivations that are related to teamwork, learning new skills and enjoying the PA. On the contrary, the ego-oriented climate (EC) is related to extrinsic motivations linked to competition and obtaining better results than rivals in sports practice (Chacón-Cuberos et al., 2018b; Monteiro et al., 2018; Cordo-Cabal et al., 2019).

Under this perspective, several studies have shown how the development of TCs in sport favors the promotion of healthy habits, while the ego-oriented motivational climate is associated with greater non-adaptive behaviors (Harwood et al., 2015; Chacón-Cuberos et al., 2018b). As an example of this basis, Reinboth and Duda (2006) show how people who practice collective sports, whose coach generates a task-oriented motivational climate, have higher levels of well-being. Similarly, Chacón-Cuberos et al. (2018a) reveal that the mastery climate is related to higher levels of PA and a better quality diet, while the EC is associated with greater alcohol consumption. Finally, and taking into account other psychological factors, Vitali et al. (2015) show that TC acts as a protective factor against burnout situations, as well as helping the development of resilience capacity.

The resilience capacity has been widely studied in the sport and academic context (Connor and Davidson, 2003; Doll et al., 2014; Vitali et al., 2015). This psychosocial factor refers to the ability to overcome situations of adversity (Connor and Davidson, 2003). In fact, resilience is closely associated with situations of stress and anxiety, since these negative factors are generated in situations in which an individual is not perceived with sufficient competence to overcome an event (Olmedilla et al., 2018; Zurita-Ortega et al., 2018). Therefore, it is of special interest to carry out actions that improve resilience capacity, since it acts as a protective factor against many vital experiences (Al-Haramlah, 2018). Sarkar and Fletcher (2014) show how the development of personal factors such as confidence, self-determined motivation and social support helps improve resilience and reduce the effect of stressors in the sport context. Moreover, Galli and Gonzalez (2015) highlight the importance of developing intervention programs based on the development of personal beliefs and the ability to control negative situations. In addition, and considering the association with the theoretical framework developed, it is interesting to know its association with PA and motivation. For example, the study conducted by Hegberg and Tone (2015) reveals through a linear regression analysis how the PA and the perceived resilience are positively related, which is mediated by the trait anxiety levels. Furthermore, Ka et al. (2015) point out in a study conducted in young people from China how PA was related to mental wellbeing, self-efficacy and resilience, which shows the potential of this psychosocial factor and its association with healthy habits.

This research considers the motivational orientations involved in PA and the relationships of the motivational climate on the resilience capacity in different context. The present study sought to answer the following research question: are there differences in the relationship between motivational climate and the capacity of resilience according to the level of PA done? Given the findings of previous research the following hypotheses are proposed:

- Hypothesis 1 (H1): TC will be directly related to the resilience capacity, while EC will be inversely associated with resilience.
- Hypothesis 2 (H2): University students who follow a more active lifestyle will show a stronger relationship between the TC and resilience capacity.

Thus, the following aims are set in the present study: (a) to develop an explanatory model about the relationships between motivational climate, resilience and its different indicators; (b) to contrast the structural equation model (SEM) developed according to the level of PA through multi-group analysis.

MATERIALS AND METHODS

Subjects and Design

This study presents a cross-sectional design with a single measurement in a single group. The study sample consisted of 775 university students of Physical Education (PE) from the eight provinces of the Autonomous Community of Andalusia (Spain), with 58.7% (n = 455) men and a 41.3% (n = 320) women. The age of the respondents was between 21 and 35 years old (22.22 $\pm$ 3.76). A total of 1167 students were enrolled in the mention of PE (degree in Primary Education) during the academic year 2016/2017 (data provided by the different universities). Considering the university centers that accepted to participate in this study and the selection criteria [(1) To study PE degree; (2) To attend regularly to university -at least 75% of attendance in class considering the check-list of their professors-; (3) Not to suffer from important pathologies], a sample of 829 subjects was considered using simple random sampling. A total of 54 questionnaires had to be eliminated because they were wrongly completed, obtaining a final sample of 775 university students. It can be considered that a representative sample was obtained for the studied population (university students of PE), with a sampling error of 0.05 and a CI of 95.5%. All the participants gave written informed consent.

Measures

This study used some main instruments as described below.

Perceived Motivational Climate in Sport Questionnaire (PMCSQ-2) (Walling et al., 1993). The Spanish version validated by González-Cutre et al. (2008) was used. This instrument allows to evaluate the motivational climate in sport and it is composed of 33 five-point items ranging from 1 to 5 (1 = Strongly Disagree; 5 = Strongly Agree). This scale establishes two dimensions (TC and ego-oriented climate), each containing three factors. These are Effort/Improvement, Cooperative learning, and Important role for the TC and Punishment for mistakes, Member rivalry, and Unequal recognition for the ego-oriented climate. This instrument has an acceptable value for Cronbach's alpha (α = 0.85), showing an appropriate internal consistency. For each dimension, TC showed an excellent value of α = 0.92, while EC ghas a value of α = 0.93.

Connor–Davidson Resilience Scale (CD-RISC), developed by Connor and Davidson (2003) and validated into Spanish by Olmo et al. (2017), which allows the assessment of the resilience capacity of respondents. This instrument is composed of 25 five-point items ranging from 0 to 4 (0 = I totally disagree; 4 = I totally agree). The 25 items conform to five factors related to resilient behavior, such as personal ability and tenacity, confidence and tolerance for adversity, positive acceptance of changes, capacity of control and spiritual influence. This instrument has an excellent reliability in the present study, showing an alpha value of α = 0.90. For each dimension the values were: Personal competence (α = 0.85), Tolerance to adversity (α = 0.71), Positive acceptance to changes (α = 0.72), Control capacity (α = 0.65), and Spirituality (α = 0.59).

International Physical Activity Questionnaire (IPAQ) (Craig et al., 2003), validated into Spanish by Mantilla and Gómez-Conesa (2007), allowed the evaluation of levels of PA done in the last week by respondents. This scale is scored through a five-point Likert scale with seven items (0 = Never; 4 = Always) obtaining a summation that establishes the global level of PA in the last 7 days. Subsequently, a variable of categorical type was created, which determined whether the participants performed more than 3 h per week of PA outside academic hours. This variable of dichotomous type (1 = Yes; 2 = No) was used for the multi-group analysis of the two structural equation models. This research obtained an acceptable reliability in this research (α = 0.86).

Procedure

First, the collaboration of the respondents was requested through an informative letter created by the Corporal Area of the University of Granada. This was provided to the university students who attended the Mention of PE of the degree of Primary Education of the eight Andalusian provinces. This document detailed the proposal of the research, as well as the objectives of the same. In addition, the informed consent of the participants was requested. This was obtained and written.

The application of the described instruments was subsequently done. A total of 829 university students took part in the study. Data collection was done during school hours in the different university centers without any type of incident. Moreover, researchers were present in order to ensure the correct application of the instruments. A total of 54 questionnaires had to be eliminated because they were wrongly filled out, leaving a final sample of 775 university students.

The anonymity of all subjects has been respected, as well as the Declaration of Helsinki of 1975 for studies with humans. Similarly, the Research Ethics Committee of the University of Granada (Spain) approved this study (462/CEIH/2017). Respondents participated voluntarily in this research.

Statistical Analysis

First, the IBM SPSS®23.0 (IBM Corp., Armonk, NY, United States) software was used to check the normal distribution of the sample through the values of asymmetry and kurtosis of the items of the scales. In this case, no value equal to or greater than 2 was obtained, showing a normal distribution. In addition, frequencies and means were used for the basic descriptive and the *T*-test to verify the existence of statistically significant differences between variables. On the other hand, the IBM AMOS®23 (IBM Corp., Armonk, NY, United States) software was used to analyze the relationships between the involved constructs of the structural model. Once the theoretical model is developed, a SEM is carried out considering the relationships of the matrix from a multi-group analysis according to the level of practice of PA. The SEM is made up of 11 observable variables and three latent variables to determine the indicators (**Figure 1**). In these, explanations of the associations between the latent variables are formulated from the observed relationships. Likewise, measurement errors (circles) are included in the observable variables so that they are directly controlled. The arrows are lines of relationships between the variables and these are interpreted as regression coefficients.

The SEM showed in **Figure 1** is composed of three latent variables (ovals) and 11 observed variables (squares). Task Climate (TC) and Ego Climate (EC) are the latent and exogenous variables. These two exogenous variables were inferred by the following six observed variables: Important Role (RI), Cooperative Learning (CL), and Effort/Improvement (EI) for Task Climate (TC), and Member Rivalry (MR), Unequal Recognition (UR), and Punishment for Mistakes (PM) for Ego Climate (EC). Another latent variable was Resilience (RES), which was inferred by Personal Competence (PC), Tolerance to Adversity (TA), Positive Acceptance to changes (PA), Control Capacity (CO), and Spirituality (S).

The method of maximum likelihood (ML) was used to estimate relationships between variables. We chose this method because it is consistent, unbiased and invariant to types of scale, given variables with a normal distribution. Model fit was examined to verify the compatibility of the proposed model and the empirical information gathered. Goodness of fit was tested using a number of indices described (Barrett, 2007). Chi-squared analysis followed when non-significant p-Values indicated a good model fit. Comparative fit index (CFI), normalized fit index (NFI) and increase fit index (IFI) values higher than 0.90 indicate acceptable model fit while values higher than 0.95 indicate excellent model fit. Root mean square error of approximation (RMSEA) values below 0.08 indicate acceptable model fit while values below 0.05 indicate excellent model fit.

RESULTS

First, descriptive data of the sample are shown in relation to the variables (motivational climate and resilience), considering the gender [men = 58.7% (n = 455); women = 41.3% (n = 320)] and the practice of more than 3 h per week of PA [+3 h/week = 74.1% (n = 574); −3 h/week = 25.9% (n = 201)]. Specifically, **Table 1** shows the differences between men and women for all sub-dimensions of the ego-oriented climate, being higher in men. Considering the practice of weekly PA, it was observed that those who practiced more than three weekly non-teaching hours had higher scores in the global TC, cooperative learning, unequal recognition and rivalry between members.

Table 2 shows the levels of resilience based on gender and the practice of PA. Statistically significant differences were observed in global resilience, personal competence and positive acceptance to change, with higher scores in men. In addition, statistically significant differences were revealed with regards to the levels of PA, with higher scores for those respondents who do more PA in global resilience, personal competence and tolerance to adversity.

Subsequently, the SEM was carried out, including the motivational climate and resilience, through a multi-group analysis according to the practice of PA. The path model showed correct fit indices in the parameters analyzed. *P*-value reveals a statistically significant value (χ^2 = 210.200, df = 82, $p < 0.001$). This index should not be interpreted in a standardized way due to its sensitivity to sample size. In this way, other fit indices were included as established by Marsh (2007). The NFI revealed an acceptable value of 0.94, while the CFI and the Increment Fit Index (IFI) showed excellent an value of 0.96 for both parameters. Moreover, an acceptable value of 0.05 was obtained for the RMSEA.

First, it is showed the SEM for respondents considered physically active (more than 3 hours of PA/week) (**Figure 2** and **Table 3**). Statistically significant differences were obtained at the $p < 0.001$ level in the associations given between the two dimensions of motivational climate and its indicators. In this sense, the indicator that had the greatest influence on TC was CL (b = 0.91), while the indicator that obtained the lowest regression weight was the Effort/Improvement (EI) (b = 0.83). For EC the highest correlation was showed by the UR (b = 0.91), while the indicator with the least influence was the Rivalry between members (MR) (b = 0.70). Likewise, the TC and EC were inversely related ($b = -0.54, p < 0.001$).

Statistically significant differences ($p < 0.001$) were observed between resilience capacity (RES) and all its indicators, showing direct relationships. The variable with the highest influence was Personal competence and tenacity (PC) (b = 0.92), while the one with the lowest regression weight was Spirituality (S) (b = 0.31). Moreover, the relationships between the motivational climate and the RES were positive and direct, acquiring a greater correlation strength for the TC (b = 0.52, $p < 0.001$) than for the EC (b = 0.16, $p < 0.05$).

Figure 3 and **Table 4** show the regression weights of the SEM designed for those university students who follow a less active lifestyle (less than 3 h of PA/week). Statistically significant differences were obtained for the relationships given between all

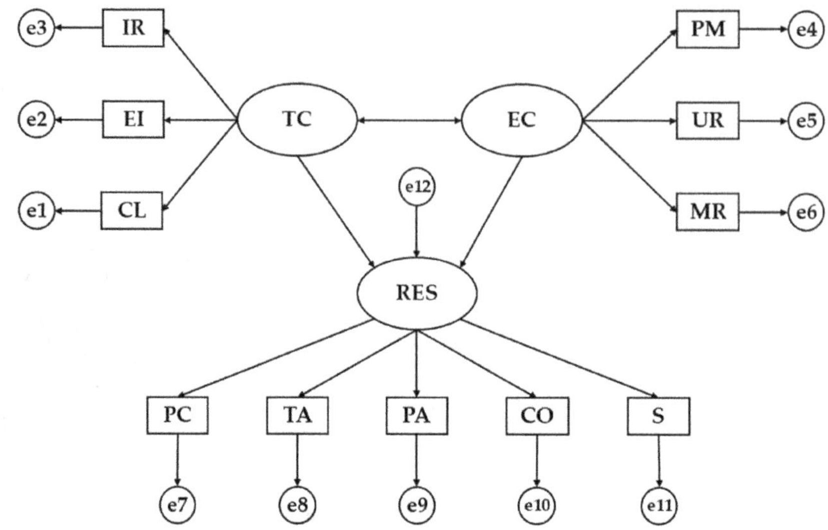

FIGURE 1 | Theoretical Model. TC, task-oriented climate; IR, important role; EI, effort/improvement; CL, cooperative learning; EC, ego-oriented climate; PM, punishment for mistakes; UR, unequal recognition; MR, member rivalry; RES, resilience; PC, personal competence; TA, tolerance to adversity; PA, positive acceptance to changes; CO, control capacity; S, spirituality.

the indicators and the two dimensions of the motivational climate ($p < 0.001$) as showed by the previous SEM. In this case, the indicator with the highest regression weight for the TC was the RI ($b = 0.91$), while the variable with the least association was the EI ($b = 0.76$). The highest correlation was shown with UR ($b = 0.93$) for the CE dimension, with the least regression weight for MR ($b = 0.65$).

In a similar line, statistically significant relationships ($p < 0.001$) are shown for all the indicators of the RES except for the S. The variable with the greatest regression weight was the PC ($b = 0.87$), while the one with the least influence was the CO ($b = 0.63$). Likewise, statistical associations were only observed for the relationship between TC and RES in the university students linked to a lower level of PA, showing a positive and direct association ($b = 0.30, p < 0.01$).

DISCUSSION

This research aims to analyze the relationships between motivational climate in sport and resilience capacity in university students using a SEM with multi-group analysis. This association

TABLE 1 | Levels of motivational climate according to gender and PA.

Motivational climate	Gender	Mean ± SD	Motivational climate	PA	Mean ± SD
TC	Men	3.90 ± 0.66	TC*	+3 h/week	3.91 ± 0.67
	Women	3.87 ± 0.65		−3 h/week	3.80 ± 0.59
CL	Men	3.90 ± 0.79	CL*	+3 h/week	3.92 ± 0.81
	Women	3.89 ± 0.81		−3 h/week	3.78 ± 0.80
EI	Men	3.93 ± 0.67	EI	+3 h/week	3.89 ± 0.65
	Women	3.86 ± 0.62		−3 h/week	3.83 ± 0.58
IR	Men	3.85 ± 0.76	IR	+3 h/week	3.88 ± 0.81
	Women	3.87 ± 0.80		−3 h/week	3.82 ± 0.69
EC*	Men	2.43 ± 0.78	EC	+3 h/week	2.30 ± 0.82
	Women	2.22 ± 0.84		−3 h/week	2.25 ± 0.83
PM*	Men	2.18 ± 0.80	PM	+3 h/week	2.07 ± 0.80
	Women	2.03 ± 0.83		−3 h/week	2.12 ± 0.91
UR*	Men	2.53 ± 0.98	UR*	+3 h/week	2.39 ± 1.02
	Women	2.29 ± 1.04		−3 h/week	2.27 ± 1.03
MR*	Men	2.71 ± 0.78	MR*	+3 h/week	2.54 ± 0.86
	Women	2.44 ± 0.86		−3 h/week	2.45 ± 0.78

*TC, task-oriented climate; IR, important role; EI, effort/improvement; CL, cooperative learning; EC, ego-oriented climate; PM, punishment for mistakes; UR, unequal recognition; MR, member rivalry; SD, standard deviation. *Statistically significant differences ($p < 0.05$).*

TABLE 2 | Levels of resilience according to gender and PA.

Resilience	Gender	Mean ± SD	Resilience	PA	Mean ± SD
RES*	Men	3.05 ± 0.56	RES*	+3 h/week	3.01 ± 0.50
	Women	2.96 ± 0.46		−3 h/week	2.90 ± 0.48
PC*	Men	3.21 ± 0.65	PC*	+3 h/week	3.16 ± 0.60
	Women	3.10 ± 0.57		−3 h/week	3.02 ± 0.56
TA	Men	2.98 ± 0.60	TA*	+3 h/week	2.88 ± 0.55
	Women	2.80 ± 0.53		−3 h/week	2.79 ± 0.59
PA*	Men	3.18 ± 0.62	PA	+3 h/week	3.18 ± 0.59
	Women	3.14 ± 0.59		−3 h/week	3.00 ± 0.64
CO	Men	3.00 ± 0.71	CO	+3 h/week	3.03 ± 0.69
	Women	3.02 ± 0.67		−3 h/week	2.94 ± 0.64
S	Men	2.42 ± 0.96	S	+3 h/week	2.39 ± 0.89
	Women	2.40 ± 0.83		−3 h/week	2.46 ± 0.77

*RES, resilience; PC, personal competence; TA, tolerance to adversity; PA, positive acceptance to changes; CO, control capacity; S, spirituality; SD, standard deviation. *Statistically significant differences ($p < 0.05$).*

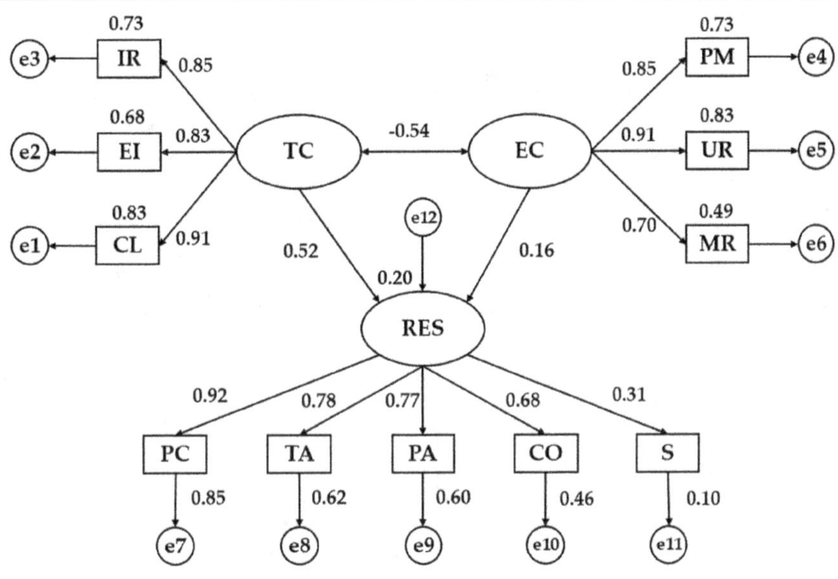

FIGURE 2 | Structural Equation Model for active students (>3 h/week of PA). TC, task-oriented climate; IR, important role; EI, effort/improvement; CL, cooperative learning; EC, ego-oriented climate; PM, punishment for mistakes; UR, unequal recognition; MR, member rivalry; RES, resilience; PC, personal competence; TA, tolerance to adversity; PA, positive acceptance to changes; CO, control capacity; S, spirituality.

is analyzed according to the level of PA in order to verify the relationship between these variables depending on the practice of more than 3 h per week of PA. Supporting this study, other similar researches are those carried out by Lee and Loke (2005), Schnettler et al. (2015), Chacón-Cuberos et al. (2018a), Zurita-Ortega et al. (2018), which address physical and mental health in university students as a risk group for harmful behaviors.

First, the influence exerted by the indicators of each dimension of the motivational climate is analyzed. The SEM showed that CL was the most influential indicator in the TC for students who practice more PA. The IR was the indicator with the higher regression weight for the respondents who did less than 3 h per week of PA. These results can be explained by the findings of Parish and Treasure (2003), who demonstrate how the most self-determined motivations favor higher levels of PA, which is linked to the TC as it is shown in the present research. Moreover, teamwork is more associated with intrinsic motivations given the hedonistic and social component involved in sports practice, which makes university students want to maintain this habit (Monteiro et al., 2018; Montero-Cobo et al., 2018). Nevertheless, the IR is established as an indicator that can be associated with both intrinsic and extrinsic motivations (Hodge and Gucciardi, 2015). For this reason, university students who are related to extrinsic motivations such as competition, practice sports with less frequency (Winter and Collins, 2015).

According to the ego-oriented climate, the UR obtained the greatest regression weight for active and non-active students, although this showed a higher score in the non-active students despite the difference being minimal. This lower influence can be justified by the premises previously explained, given that

TABLE 3 | Regression weights and standardized regression weights in active students (>3 h/week of PA).

Relationship between variables			RW				SRW
			EST	SE	CR	*P*-values	EST
RES	←	TC	0.388	0.052	7.398	***	0.517
RES	←	EC	0.131	0.056	2.349	*	0.161
CL	←	TC	1.000	–	–	***	0.912
EI	←	TC	0.724	0.036	19.942	***	0.826
IR	←	TC	0.940	0.045	21.058	***	0.855
PM	←	EC	1.000	–	–	***	0.853
UR	←	EC	1.368	0.074	18.375	***	0.910
MR	←	EC	0.891	0.063	14.241	***	0.698
PC	←	RES	1.000	–	–	***	0.920
TA	←	RES	0.789	0.044	17.831	***	0.784
PA	←	RES	0.827	0.047	17.441	***	0.773
CO	←	RES	0.857	0.059	14.462	***	0.681
S	←	RES	0.505	0.088	5.708	***	0.313
EC	↔	TC	−0.273	0.035	−7.712	***	−0.542

*TC, task-oriented climate; IR, important role; EI, effort/improvement; CL, cooperative learning; EC, ego-oriented climate; PM, punishment for mistakes; UR, unequal recognition; MR, member rivalry; RES, resilience; PC, personal competence; TA, tolerance to adversity; PA, positive acceptance to changes; CO, control capacity; S, spirituality; SRW, standardized regression weights; SE, estimation of Error; CR, critical ratio; RW, regression weights; EST, estimation. *p < 0.05 and ***p < 0.001.*

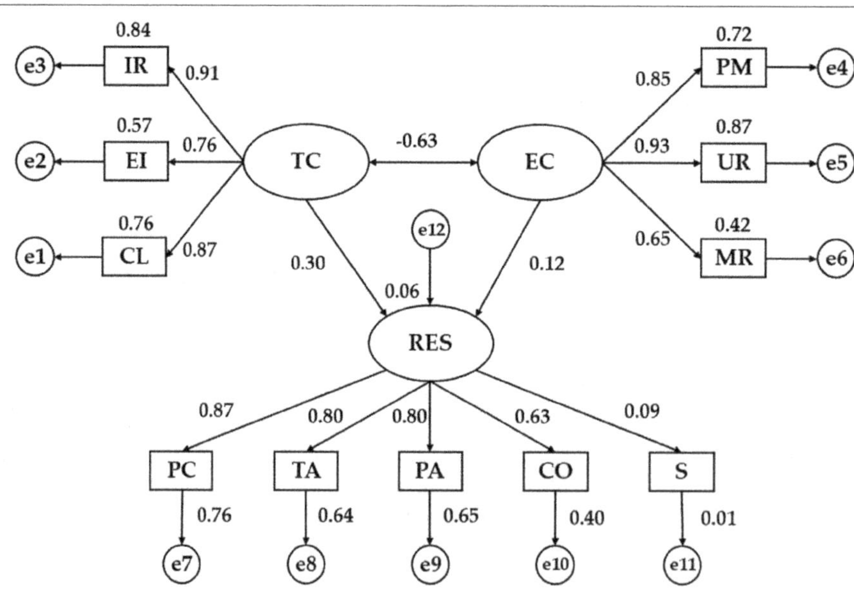

FIGURE 3 | Structural Equation Model for non-active students (<3 h/week of PA). TC, task-oriented climate; IR, important role; EI, effort/improvement; CL, cooperative learning; EC, ego-oriented climate; PM, punishment for mistakes; UR, unequal recognition; MR, member rivalry; RES, resilience; PC, personal competence; TA, tolerance to adversity; PA, positive acceptance to changes; CO, control capacity; S, spirituality.

university students who practice less PA are linked to external motivations associated with specific rewards and competition (Winter and Collins, 2015; McLaren et al., 2017). Specifically, Castro-Sánchez et al. (2018) established that the sport practice associated with competition can be linked to negative emotions that emerge from unwanted results, such as defeat, anxiety or frustration. This causes these individual to stop practicing sport due to these negative feelings, which make them less physically active (McLaren et al., 2017; Castro-Sánchez et al., 2018). Likewise, this type of motivation can be linked to non-adaptive behaviors, such as the consumption of harmful substances, the intensive use of technological devices or poor diets (Chacón-Cuberos et al., 2018b).

Personal competence and control capacity acquired a slightly higher regression weight for resilience in active people. These findings highlight that PA can be linked to an improvement of personal competence through tenacity and the ability to overcome negative situations. It is because the practice of PA

TABLE 4 | Regression weights and standardized regression weights in non-active students (<3 h/week of PA).

Relationship between variables			RW				SRW
			EST	**SE**	**CR**	***P*-values**	**EST**
RES	←	TC	0.215	0.072	2.970	**	0.300
RES	←	EC	0.086	0.071	1.220	0.222	0.122
CL	←	TC	1.000	–	–	***	0.871
EI	←	TC	0.633	0.047	13.525	***	0.758
IR	←	TC	1.047	0.061	17.176	***	0.915
PM	←	EC	1.000	–	–	***	0.851
UR	←	EC	1.383	0.089	15.550	***	0.930
MR	←	EC	0.729	0.068	10.676	***	0.650
PC	←	RES	1.000	–	–	***	0.871
TA	←	RES	0.947	0.069	13.698	***	0.802
PA	←	RES	0.916	0.067	13.719	***	0.804
CO	←	RES	0.839	0.083	10.051	***	0.631
S	←	RES	0.146	0.110	1.329	0.184	0.094
EC	↔	TC	−0.345	0.050	−6.859	***	−0.633

*TC, task-oriented climate; IR, important role; EI, effort/improvement; CL, cooperative learning; EC, ego-oriented climate; PM, punishment for mistakes; UR, unequal recognition; MR, member rivalry; RES, resilience; PC, personal competence; TA, tolerance to adversity; PA, positive acceptance to changes; CO, control capacity; S, spirituality; SRW, standardized regression weights; SE, estimation of error; CR, critical ratio; RW, regression weights; EST, estimation. **$p < 0.01$ and ***$p < 0.001$.*

generates endorphins and reduces stress, helps maintain levels of effort, allows the setting of attainable goals and favors the development of self-determined motivations (Mandolesi et al., 2018; Zurita-Ortega et al., 2018). In addition, Shoenfelt (2016) establish how the practice of sport improves the control capacity, since the athlete will learn to fight against situations of adversity such as defeat, and negative emotions such as anxiety, frustration or fear. In contrast, tolerance to adversity and positive acceptance of changes were the indicators more related to resilience in the respondents who practice fewer than 3 h of PA per week. This situation may be due to a lower capacity of these students to maintain behaviors when establishing goals, being less persistent and forced to accept the new events (Morgan et al., 2017). Thus, the respondents who practice more PA are more optimistic and empathic, which makes them more resilient without the need to achieve their objectives (Laborde et al., 2016).

The relationship between motivational climate and resilience revealed a positive relationship between TC and resilience capacity, which was higher in the more active respondents. From these results, it can be inferred that those students who practice more PA linked to intrinsic motivations such as hedonism, learning improvement or socialization, are more resilient. Specifically, Vitali et al. (2015) demonstrate how coaches who develop task-oriented motivational climates help improve the level of achievement in athletes, sports devaluation and burnout levels, acting as a protective factor and improving resilience. On a similar note, Martin and Dowson (2009) emphasize that positive psychology, which has certain elements in common with self-determined motivations, can be positively related to resilience. Specifically, it highlights the importance of favoring adaptive behaviors within the cognitive sphere such as goals oriented toward mastery, self-efficacy and the value of work (Crane et al., 2017; Chacón-Cuberos et al., 2018b). Likewise, within the field of behavior, emphasis is placed on developing persistence, planning and the ability to organize work tasks (Martin and Dowson, 2009; Secades et al., 2016).

The EC showed a lower association with resilience, and only in active people due to the relationship that exists between both motivational climates in those people who practice sports frequently. Specifically, Matosic et al. (2017) remember how the promotion of both motivational climates generates a positive effect on the adherence of university students to sports practice, justifying these findings. Nevertheless, the development of intrinsic motivations should not be neglected, since several works establish how motivational climates oriented exclusively to the ego are linked to situations of self-handicap, disgust, poor control and avoidance of failure (Martin and Dowson, 2009; Verner-Filion et al., 2014). This is due to situations in which the desired results are not achieved, when there is excessive competition or when these two factors lead to high levels of state anxiety, stress or sports burnout (Smith et al., 2007). Therefore, it can be concluded that the promotion of motivational climates oriented to the task could favor the resilient capacity and act in a preventive way with negative emotions in sports.

It is important to establish the main limitations of this study. The first is associated with the study design, since a cross-sectional research do not allow to show cause-effect relationships. However, the SEM is useful to know the associations between the psychosocial variables which have been studied. Moreover, multi-group analysis is used in order to compare the regression weights of this relationship according to a dichotomous variable as the practice of PA. Another limitation is linked to the study sample, since only university students who attend PE degrees were considered. Consequently, it can be established that this sample already has a relatively high level of PA. Therefore, there is a need to replicate this study in other types of university students, since students from other degrees may be more sedentary and may develop more harmful habits such as a poor diet or substance abuse. In this way, we could expand the vision of the existing relationships between PA level, resilience and motivation in sports as future perspectives. Finally, it would also be interesting to include other psychological factors associated with resilience, such as self-concept or burnout syndrome.

CONCLUSION

Considering the research question, it can be established that resilience is associated with the type of motivational climate in sport and the levels of PA of university students. Nevertheless, this relationship depends on the type of motivational climate, showing different types of influence in this capacity. Therefore, we should point out about the hypothesis:

- Hypothesis 1 (H1) was partially fulfilled, since TC was positively related to resilience. However, EC was not inversely associated with resilience, showing a positive relationship in respondents who practice more PA.
- Hypothesis 2 (H2) was fulfilled. The university students who practice more than 3 h per week of PA showed a stronger relationship between TC and resilience capacity.

As a main conclusion, it can be established that the practice of PA could be associated with more favorable motivational climates and levels of resilience capacity in university students. Specifically, respondents who do more than 3 h of PA per week showed slightly higher levels of TC, which were linked to a greater resilience. This factor was mainly influenced by a personal competence and the capacity of control.

ETHICS STATEMENT

All procedures performed in studies involving human participants were in accordance with the ethical standards of the institutional and/or national research committee and with the 1964 Helsinki Declaration and its later amendments or comparable ethical standards. Written informed consent was obtained from all individual participants included in this study.

AUTHOR CONTRIBUTIONS

RC-C, EO-M, and FZO conceived the hypothesis of this study. FZO, JP-T, and MC-S participated in the data collection. RC-C and MC-S analyzed the data. All authors contributed to the data interpretation of the statistical analysis, and read and approved the final manuscript. RC-C, EO-M, and MC-S wrote the manuscript with the significant input from FZO and JP-T.

REFERENCES

Al-Haramlah, A. R. (2018). Psychological stress, burnout and its relationship with decision making among table tennis referees: a case study. *Sport TK* 7, 103–110. doi: 10.6018/321951

Arnett, J. J., and Tanner, J. L. (2016). "The emergence of emerging adulthood: the new life stage between adolescence and young adulthood," in *Routledge Handbook of Youth and Young Adulthood*, ed. A. Furlong (Abingdon: Routledge), 50–56.

Barrett, P. (2007). Structural equation modelling: adjudging model fit. *Pers. Individ. Dif.* 42, 815–824. doi: 10.1016/j.paid.2006.09.018

Bouchard, C., Blair, S. N., and Haskell, W. L. (2018). *Physical Activity and Health.* Leeds: Human Kinetics.

Castro-Sánchez, M., Zurita-Ortega, F., and Chacón-Cuberos, R. (2019). Motivation towards sport based on socio-demographic variables in university students from Granada. *J. Sport Health Res.* 11, 55–68.

Castro-Sánchez, M., Zurita-Ortega, F., Chacón-Cuberos, R., López-Gutiérrez, C., and Zafra-Santos, E. (2018). Emotional intelligence, motivational climate and levels of anxiety in athletes from different categories of sports: analysis through structural equations. *Int. J. Environ. Res. Public Health* 15:894. doi: 10.3390/ijerph15050894

Chacón-Cuberos, R., Zurita-Ortega, F., Olmedo-Moreno, E., Padial-Ruz, R., and Castro-Sánchez, M. (2018a). An Exploratory model of psychosocial factors and healthy habits in university students of physical education depending on gender. *Int. J. Environ. Res. Public Health* 15:2430. doi: 10.3390/ijerph15112430

Chacón-Cuberos, R., Zurita-Ortega, F., Puertas-Molero, P., Knox, E., Cofré-Bolados, C., Viciana-Garófano, V., et al. (2018b). Relationship between healthy habits and perceived motivational climate in sport among university students: a structural equation model. *Sustainability* 10:938. doi: 10.3390/su10040938

Connor, K., and Davidson, J. (2003). Development of a new resilience scale: the connor-davidson RESILIENCE SCALE (CD-RISC). *Depress. Anxiety* 18, 76–82. doi: 10.1002/da.10113

Cordo-Cabal, L., Gómez-López, M., Granero-Gallegos, A., and Sánchez-Alcaraz, B. J. (2019). Relationship of the motivational climate generated by the coach and the causes of success in team sports players. Influence of gender, age and sport experience. *J. Sport Health Res.* 11, 139–150.

Craig, C. L., Marshall, A. L., Sjöström, M., Bauman, A. E., Booth, M. L., Ainsworth, B. E., et al. (2003). International physical activity questionnaire: 12-country reliability and validity. *Med. Sci. Sports Exerc.* 35, 1381–1395. doi: 10.1249/01.MSS.0000078924.61453.FB

Crane, M. F., Brabazon, G., Gucciardi, D. F., Loveday, T., and Wiggins, M. (2017). General self-efficacy and psychological resilience promote skill acquisition rate under psychological pressure. *Australas. J. Organ. Psychol.* 10:e3. doi: 10.1017/orp.2017.3

Doll, B., Brehm, K., and Zucker, S. (2014). *Resilient Classrooms: Creating Healthy Environments for Learning.* New York, NY: Guilford Publications.

Donnelly, J. E., Hillman, C. H., Castelli, D., Etnier, J. L., Lee, S., Tomporowski, P., et al. (2016). Physical activity, fitness, cognitive function, and academic achievement in children: a systematic review. *Med. Sci. Sports Exerc.* 48, 1197–1222. doi: 10.1249/MSS.0000000000000901

Ekelund, U., Steene-Johannessen, J., Brown, W. J., Fagerland, M. W., Owen, N., Powell, K. E., et al. (2016). Does physical activity attenuate, or even eliminate, the detrimental association of sitting time with mortality? A harmonised meta-analysis of data from more than 1 million men and women. *Lancet* 388, 1302–1310. doi: 10.1016/S0140-6736(16)30370-1

Erturan-Ilker, G., Yu, C., Alemdaroglu, U., and Köklü, Y. (2018). Basic psychological needs and self-determined motivation in PE to predict health-related fitness level. *J. Sport Health Res.* 10, 91–100.

Fransson, D., Nielsen, T. S., Olsson, K., Christensson, T., Bradley, P. S., Fatouros, I. G., et al. (2018). Skeletal muscle and performance adaptations to high-intensity training in elite male soccer players: speed endurance runs versus small-sided game training. *Eur. J. Appl. Physiol.* 118, 111–121. doi: 10.1007/s00421-017-3751-5

Galli, N., and Gonzalez, S. P. (2015). Psychological resilience in sport: a review of the literature and implications for research and practice. *Int. J. Sport Exerc. Psychol.* 13, 243–257. doi: 10.1080/1612197X.2014.946947

González-Cutre, D., Sicilia, A., and Moreno, J. A. (2008). Cognitive-social model of achievement motivation in physical education. *Psicothema* 20, 642–651.

Gorelik, V. V., Filippova, S. N., Belyaev, V. S., and Chumakov, B. N. (2018).

Individual and typological factors influencing the regulation of physiological adaptation to physical activity of schoolchildren with different age and gender. *J. Hum. Sport Exerc.* 13, 894–906. doi: 10.14198/jhse.2018.134.16

Harwood, C. G., Keegan, R. J., Smith, J. M., and Raine, A. S. (2015). A systematic review of the intrapersonal correlates of motivational climate perceptions in sport and physical activity. *Psychol. Sport Exerc.* 18, 9–25. doi: 10.1016/j.psychsport.2014.11.005

Hegberg, N. J., and Tone, E. B. (2015). Physical activity and stress resilience: considering those at-risk for developing mental health problems. *Ment. Health Phys. Act.* 8, 1–7. doi: 10.1016/j.mhpa.2014.10.001

Hodge, K., and Gucciardi, D. F. (2015). Antisocial and prosocial behaviour in sport: the role of motivational climate, basic psychological needs, and moral disengagement. *J. Sport Exerc. Psychol.* 37, 257–273. doi: 10.1123/jsep.2014-2225

Jaakkola, T., Yli-Piipari, S., Barkoukis, V., and Liukkonen, J. (2017). Relationships among perceived motivational climate, motivational regulations, enjoyment, and PA participation among Finnish physical education students. *Int. J. Sport Exerc. Psychol.* 15, 273–290. doi: 10.1080/1612197X.2015.1100209

Ka, F., Hung, L., Bong, C., Hing, W., and Ip, P. (2015). Physical activity improves mental health through resilience in Hong Kong Chinese adolescents. *BMC Pediatr.* 15:48. doi: 10.1186/s12887-015-0365-0

Kavosi, A., Saadati, M., Movahedi, A., Farahnia, M., Mohammadi, G., Aghababayan, A., et al. (2015). Physical activity enhances self-esteem of male college students, a randomized controlled trial. *Int. J. Travel Med. Glob. Health* 3, 49–52. doi: 10.20286/IJTMGH-030298

Laborde, S., Guillén, F., and Mosley, E. (2016). Positive personality-trait-like individual differences in athletes from individual-and team sports and in non-athletes. *Psychol. Sport Exerc.* 26, 9–13. doi: 10.1016/j.psychsport.2016.05.009

Lee, R. L., and Loke, A. J. (2005). Health-promoting behaviours and psychosocial well-being of university students in Hong Kong. *Public Health Nurs.* 22, 209–220. doi: 10.1111/j.0737-1209.2005.220304.x

Lewis, B. A., Napolitano, M. A., Buman, M. P., Williams, D. M., and Nigg, C. R. (2017). Future directions in physical activity intervention research: expanding our focus to sedentary behaviours, technology, and dissemination. *J. Behav. Med.* 40, 112–126. doi: 10.1007/s10865-016-9797-8

López-Sánchez, G. F., Ibáñez-Ortega, E. J., Camacho-Hidalgo, M. B., Sánchez-García, C., González-Carcelén, C. M., and Díaz-Suárez, A. (2018). Effects of a program through vigorous-intensity physical activity on blood pressure and heart rate of 6-7-year-old school children. *J. Sport Health Res.* 10, 173–180.

Mandolesi, L., Polverino, A., Montuori, S., Foti, F., Ferraioli, G., Sorrentino, P., et al. (2018). Effects of physical exercise on cognitive functioning and wellbeing: biological and psychological benefits. *Front. Psychol.* 9:509. doi: 10.3389/fpsyg.2018.00509

Mantilla, S., and Gómez-Conesa, A. (2007). International physical activity questionnaire. An adequate instrument in population physical activity monitoring. *Revista Iberoamericana de Fisioterapia y Kinesiologia* 10, 48–52. doi: 10.1016/S1138-6045(07)73665-1

Marsh, H. W. (2007). *Handbook of Sport Psychology*, Third Edn. New Jersey, NJ: Tenenbaum and R. C. Eklund, doi: 10.1002/9781118270011.ch35

Martin, A. J., and Dowson, M. (2009). Interpersonal relationships, motivation, engagement, and achievement: yields for theory, current issues, and educational practice. *Rev. Educ. Res.* 79, 327–365. doi: 10.3102/0034654308325583

Mascret, N., Elliot, A. J., and Cury, F. (2015). Extending the 3× 2 achievement goal model to the sport domain: the 3× 2 achievement goal questionnaire for sport. *Psychol. Sport Exerc.* 17, 7–14. doi: 10.1016/j.psychsport.2014.11.001

Matosic, D., Ntoumanis, N., Boardley, I. D., Sedikides, C., Stewart, B. D., and Chatzisarantis, N. (2017). Narcissism and coach interpersonal style: a self-determination theory perspective. *Scand. J. Med. Sci. Sports* 27, 254–261. doi: 10.1111/sms.12635

McLaren, C. D., Newland, A., Eys, M., and Newton, M. (2017). Peer-initiated motivational climate and group cohesion in youth sport. *J. Appl. Sport Psychol.* 29, 88–100. doi: 10.1080/10413200.2016.1190423

Monteiro, D., Borrego, C. C., Silva, C., Moutão, J., Marinho, D. A., and Cid, L. (2018). Motivational climate sport youth scale: measurement invariance across gender and five different sports. *J. Hum. Kinet.* 61, 249–261. doi: 10.1515/hukin-2017-2124

Montero-Cobo, J. L., Polaino-Rodríguez, C., Puertas-Molero, P., and González-Valero, G. (2018). Design of a diagnosis of needs for adolescent students: physical Education as an action resource. *Educ. Sport Health Phys. Act.* 2, 105–123.

Moreno, J. A., Cervelló, E., and González-Cutre, D. (2008). Relationships among goal orientations, motivational climate and flow in adolescent athletes: differences by gender. *Spanish J. Psychol.* 11, 181–191. doi: 10.1017/S1138741600004224

Morgan, P. B., Fletcher, D., and Sarkar, M. (2017). Recent developments in team resilience research in elite sport. *Curr. Opin. Psychol.* 16, 159–164. doi: 10.1016/j.copsyc.2017.05.013

Olmedilla, A., García-Alarcón, M., and Ortega, E. (2018). Relationships between sports injuries and stress in female football and indoor fotball. *J. Sport Health Res.* 10, 339–348.

Olmo, M., Olmedo, E., Cepero, M., Zurita, F., and Padial, R. (2017). Validation of resilience scale (CD-RISC) in elite athletes through a structual equation model. *Retos* 32, 96–100.

Parish, L. E., and Treasure, D. C. (2003). Physical activity and situational motivation in physical education: influence of the motivational climate and perceived ability. *Res. Q. Exerc.Sport* 74, 173–182. doi: 10.1080/02701367.2003.10609079

Plotnikoff, R. C., Costigan, S. A., Williams, R. L., Hutchesson, M. J., Kennedy, S. G., Robards, S. L., et al. (2015). Effectiveness of interventions targeting physical activity, nutrition and healthy weight for university and college students: a systematic review and meta-analysis. *Int. J. Behav. Nutr. Phys. Act.* 12:45. doi: 10.1186/s12966-015-0203-7

Prakash, R. S., Voss, M. W., Erickson, K. I., and Kramer, A. F. (2015). Physical activity and cognitive vitality. *Annu. Rev. Psychol.* 66, 769–797. doi: 10.1146/annurev-psych-010814-015249

Reinboth, M., and Duda, J. L. (2006). Perceived motivational climate, need satisfaction and indices of well-being in team sports: a longitudinal perspective. *Psychol. Sport Exerc.* 7, 269–286. doi: 10.1016/j.psychsport.2005.06.002

Ryan, R. M., and Deci, E. L. (2000). Self-determination theory and the facilitation of intrinsic motivation, social development, and well-being. *Am. Psychol.* 55, 68–78. doi: 10.1037//0003-066x.55.1.68

Ryan, R. M., and Deci, E. L. (2017). *Self-Determination Theory: Basic Psychological Needs in Motivation, Development, and Wellness.* New York, NY: Guilford Publications.

Sarkar, M., and Fletcher, D. (2014). Psychological resilience in sport performers: a review of stressors and protective factors. *J. Sports Sci.* 32, 1419–1434. doi: 10.1080/02640414.2014.901551

Schnettler, B., Miranda, H., Lobos, G., Orellana, L., Sepúlveda, J., Denegri, M., et al. (2015). Eating habits and subjective well-being. A typology of students in Chilean state universities. *Appetite* 89, 203–214. doi: 10.1016/j.appet.2015.02.008

Secades, X. G., Molinero, O., Salguero, A., Barquín, R. R., de la Vega, R., and Márquez, S. (2016). Relationship between resilience and coping strategies in competitive sport. *Percept. Mot. Skills* 122, 336–349. doi: 10.1177/0031512516631056

Shoenfelt, E. L. (2016). How much do we really know about employee resilience? More, if we include the sport psychology resilience research. *Ind. Organ. Psychol.* 9, 442–446. doi: 10.1017/iop.2016.36

Sink, K. M., Espeland, M. A., Castro, C. M., Church, T., Cohen, R., Dodson, J. A., et al. (2015). Effect of a 24-month physical activity intervention vs health education on cognitive outcomes in sedentary older adults: the LIFE randomized trial. *JAMA* 314, 781–790. doi: 10.1001/jama.2015.9617

Smith, R. E., Smoll, F. L., and Cumming, S. P. (2007). Effects of a motivational climate intervention for coaches on young athletes' sport performance anxiety. *J. Sport Exerc. Psychol.* 29, 39–59. doi: 10.1123/jsep.29.1.39

Verner-Filion, J., Vallerand, R. J., Donahue, E. G., Moreau, E., Martin, A., Mageau, G. A., et al. (2014). Passion, coping, and anxiety in sport: the interplay between key motivational and self-regulatory processes. *Int. J. Sport Psychol.* 45, 516–537. doi: 10.7352/IJSP2014.45.516

Vitali, F., Bortoli, L., Bertinato, L., Robazza, C., and Schena, F. (2015). Motivational climate, resilience, and burnout in youth sport. *Sport Sci. Health* 11, 103–108. doi: 10.1007/s11332-014-0214-9

Walling, M. D., Duda, J. L., and Chi, L. (1993). The perceived motivational climate in sport questionnaire: construct and predictive validity. *Int. J. Sport Exerc. Psychol.* 15, 172–183. doi: 10.1123/jsep.15.2.172

Warburton, D. E., and Bredin, S. S. (2017). Health benefits of physical activity: a systematic review of current systematic reviews. *Curr. Opin. Cardiol.* 32, 541–556. doi: 10.1097/HCO.0000000000000437

Winter, S., and Collins, D. (2015). Where is the evidence in our sport psychology practice? A United Kingdom perspective on the underpinnings of action. *Prof. Psychol. Res. Pr.* 46, 175–182. doi: 10.1037/pro0000014

World Health Organization [WHO], (2010). *Global Strategy on Diet, Physical Activity and Health.* Available at: https://www.who.int/dietphysicalactivity/pa/en/ (accessed November 22, 2018).

Zurita-Ortega, F., Chacón-Cuberos, R., Cofre-Bolados, C., Knox, E., and Muros, J. J. (2018). Relationship of resilience, anxiety and injuries in footballers: structural equations analysis. *PLoS One* 13:e0207860. doi: 10.1371/journal.pone.0207860

11

Applying the Personal and Social Responsibility Model as a School-Wide Project in all Participants

David Manzano-Sánchez, Luís Conte-Marín, Manuel Gómez-López and Alfonso Valero-Valenzuela*

Department of Physical Activity and Sport, Faculty of Sports Sciences, University of Murcia, Murcia, Spain

***Correspondence:**
Manuel Gómez-López
mgomezlop@um.es

The present study aims to apply a program based on Hellison's Teaching Personal and Social Responsibility Model (TPSR), traditionally used in Physical Education, to other educational participants and examine the assessment of the teachers who carried it out during the 2018–2019 school year. The program was applied over 8 months of one academic year and during at least 60% of the weekly class hours. Initially, 30 teachers participated, of whom 16 were involved in the interviews carried out, all of them being Secondary Education teachers. We used qualitative methodology through content analysis carried out with ATLAS.ti 7.1.3. The instruments used to collect information were semi-structured recorded group interviews. The conclusion is that the Personal and Social Responsibility Model can be applied to all participants in the curriculum and is adaptable to any content and type of student body. As a basis for future research, we suggest the application of the model by all teachers involved in the same school year and the participation of students' families.

Keywords: methodology, innovation, teacher training, education, physical education

INTRODUCTION

Social demand has led to formal education serving to provide tools for learners to be able to adapt to the constant changes demanded by society. To this end, it is necessary to develop the skills and competences that can help them adapt to these different demands (Larson, 2000). A fundamental aspect of responding to this demand is to promote learner autonomy and self-sufficiency (Oriol et al., 2016), improve the learning environment (Legault and Inzlicht, 2013) and influence learner behavior through Teaching Personal and Social Responsibility Model (TPSR) (Hellison and Wright, 2003) to reduce dependence on teachers' characteristics in traditional teaching in order to increase cooperative work with classmates (Walkey et al., 2013), in line with the Project Based Learning approach in Stentoft (2016) and Woods (2016) in which learners are significantly involved in their learning by working on joint projects.

In this regard, current education seeks to incorporate new teaching models that allow for a renewal of teaching methodologies that transform the process into meaningful experiences for students in which aspects such as reflection and active participation in classes are especially encouraged (Pérez-López and Rivera-García, 2017). Therefore, it is intended to focus on an approach that allows students to develop their skills and in which they are the real protagonists, rather than teachers' explicit teaching (Brockbank and McGill, 2002). In other words, teachers become facilitators of learning and students build their own training process (Pérez-López and Rivera-García, 2017).

Motivation is one of the most important variables for implementing an innovative methodology and achieving greater academic adherence and is fundamental to school performance and grades (Shim and Ryan, 2005). The lack of motivational strategies on the part of teachers results in poorer academic performance among students (Tejedor and García-Valcárcel, 2007).

In order to achieve improvements in teaching, new pedagogical models have been developed in recent years (Menéndez and Fernández, 2016), with the so-called TPSR (Hellison, 1978) being highlighted as one of the most appropriate for encouraging students to develop correctly in their social environment, learning to be responsible for themselves and others (Hellison, 1985). This model is currently one of the most powerful tools for the development of values in adolescents (Escartí et al., 2005), its main limitation is the lack of time to apply it, given that it is restricted to a few Physical Education hours a week, the beliefs of students regarding PE, and their difficulties in reflection and dialog (Llopis-Goig et al., 2011).

Furthermore, responsibility has been proven to have positive relationships with motivational constructs, especially with intrinsic motivation (Escartí et al., 2011; Belando et al., 2015; Ortiz et al., 2016), which may indicate that teaching based on the transfer of autonomy and the promotion of responsibility can be appropriate for the improvement of motivation and other social factors along with academic performance (Smithikrai, 2013; Baena-Extremera et al., 2016; Calderón et al., 2016; Granero-Gallegos et al., 2020).

The latest trends in TPSR seek to innovate the model, and thus some studies have hybridized it with Cooperative Learning to find out that TPSR is a very useful model when it comes to meeting the demands of the current educational system and the achievement of competencies through active methodologies (Merino-Barrero et al., 2017). The study by Gordon et al. (2016) implements TPSR with social and emotional learning (SEL) (Gould and Carson, 2008) in line with TPSR approaches and strategies and achieves very interesting results in student self-control. Furthermore, the study by Alcalá et al. (2019), in which they applied TPSR with Pre-school, Primary and Physical Education university students in Spain, Costa Rica and Chile is also worth highlighting. The participants' perception of the pedagogical possibilities was very positive with regard to their future as teachers, and they agreed on the capacity to promote their professional development in the study by Llopis-Goig et al. (2011).

Thus, teacher training is considered a dimension of capital importance because of its decisive impact on the quality of educational inclusion (León Guerrero, 2011). In this context, the professional development of teachers should be understood as any attempt to improve educational practice, beliefs and professional and personal knowledge with the aim of increasing the quality of teaching, research and management, individually and together with colleagues, in order to improve student learning (Imbernón, 2013). However, professional development is more than just training; it is the product of the pedagogical development that teachers acquire throughout their lives, their knowledge and understanding of themselves as teachers, the cognitive and emotional development that they carry out individually and with their colleagues at school, and the theoretical development of educational matters (Pegalajar-Palomino, 2014).

This work was preceded by one (Manzano and Valero-Valenzuela, 2019) in which a pilot study was carried out applying TPSR in a primary school, and which obtained improvements in students' self-concept, responsibility, motivation and autonomy, in addition to high levels of satisfaction with the methodology on the part of the students and teachers involved. In addition to this, there is study (Manzano-Sánchez and Valero-Valenzuela, 2019), in which more than 300 primary and secondary school students obtained improvements in responsibility, intrinsic motivation, basic psychological needs, classroom climate and pro-social behavior by applying the model and in which a series of teacher interviews were conducted with a very positive evaluation of the model by the students.

The main objective of the present study is to apply the TPSR in the general educational context, to examine the perception of the teachers involved in terms of its applicability, future perspectives and positive and negative aspects of the experience.

MATERIALS AND METHODS

Design

A qualitative research study was carried out by using a descriptive and cross-sectional method with semi-structured interviews with teachers participating in the implementation of the TPSR, which were carried out once the model application was completed and with sustained training and assessment for teachers (Montero and León, 2007).

Participants

Participants were selected according to accessibility and convenience. They included 30 Secondary Education teachers from public schools using the Personal and Social Responsibility Model. The teachers who participated in the interviews were a total of 16. None of the participants in the interviews had previous experience with the TPSR. The teachers were recorded in video and their behavior was analyzed by experts qualified in observational methodology and the TPSR.

Instruments

At the same time, a qualitative analysis of teachers was carried out at the end of the process through semi-structured interviews in order to obtain an internal perspective of their experience (Patton, 2002) in their own school, with 13 questions mainly coming from the study Sánchez-Alcaraz et al. (2019): (1) Do you feel that you have more tools available to teach in schools and deal with children with coexistence issues? (2) Do you feel that you are sufficiently trained to implement the TPSR? (3) What are the main problems that have arisen? (4) How do you feel when you apply the TPSR? (5) What are the most innovative aspects that you feel the TPSR is bringing to your classes? (6) What do you think can be improved in the application of the TPSR? (7) What characteristics of the students do you think could be more adequate for an appropriate application of the TPSR? Do you think teachers' previous experience is important? (8) What improvements do you think could be made to the contents of the TPSR? (9) Do you think that the TPSR actually works in terms of the inclusion of values, attitudes and socially adequate values? (10) Do you think that through the TPSR students learn the contents of the subject as well as attitudes and values? (11) What advantages have you found in the TPSR with respect to the methodology you have used until now? (12) Are the tasks better adapted to the interests of the students? (13) Is there anything else you would like to add?

Procedure

We included Informed consent (confidential treatment of data, participation in the study and filming of sessions) for parents and students and a letter of presentation was sent to schools along with the report of the Ethics Committee of the University of Murcia (1685/2017). The program covered 8 months. The contents were selected in accordance with current educational laws (State Agency State Gazette, 2013).

Intervention Program

The sessions featured a modification of Hellison's session format (Hellison, 2011) given that they included four parts rather than five: (1) initial greeting: the teacher interacted with students to create links with them, (2) awareness talk: the teacher presented the objectives of the session in academic and values terms according to the level of the responsibility model, (3) activity plan, where most of the practical class was carried out, integrating responsibility strategies in the various tasks, and (4) group meeting and self-evaluation: at the end of each session, the teacher and students shared their perceptions regarding responsibility and individual behaviors, the class and the teacher's performance by raising their thumb upward (positive evaluation), to the side (middle) or downward (negative evaluation). Teachers used both general strategies to implement the TPSR (e.g., assigning tasks, providing opportunities for success, defining roles) and specific strategies (e.g., reciprocal teaching, cooperative groups, personal work plan). Similarly, these strategies were also used to resolve individual (e.g., 5 Clean Days) and collective (e.g., Grandma's Law) conflicts, fully integrating the TPSR into all classes in addition to Physical Education (Escartí et al., 2013).

Teacher Training

The implementation of any educational program requires specific teacher training (Li et al., 2008). Teachers were trained in the TPSR in a two-phase approach: (1) A 5 h course on the model's theory and practice in which they were explained how to design classroom climates according to the model and were provided with comprehensive and specific strategies for accountability development, as well as a "model guide" so that they could review the various strategies undertaken as well as others. (2) Continuous training: during the implementation of the program (8 months) the principal researcher met with the teachers on several occasions and through different channels. In the first week, the teachers had to hand in a document reflecting the structure of a session of their own class applying the model at the first level, with their corresponding activities and strategies, with the principal researcher providing feedback to the teachers as appropriate. In the second week, the sessions were implemented in the different participants, and a minimum of one session per month was filmed and evaluated by the research team. In the following week, a report was given with the session and the aspects to be modified, and this sequencing was carried out throughout the intervention, as well as a quarterly meeting to discuss the intervention among the teachers. The students learned responsibility progressively, moving through the different levels (Escartí et al., 2013). However, level 5 was involved from the beginning, in an attempt to transfer it to students' lives.

Interview Preparation

To draw up the interview questions, the aspects covered in the TPSR were taken into account, as well as those that could be of interest as an object of the investigation. For this purpose, several questions were selected and analyzed by various researchers and/or teachers who had applied the TPSR, ending with the selection of the 13 questions above.

The interviews were carried out dividing the teachers into two groups of seven and nine people who were interviewed by two researchers who only intervened during the interview to formulate the questions in order to avoid possible biases. The duration of the interviews was 75 min and the answers were recorded through a wireless microphone in order to analyze the results later.

Data Analysis

The results were analyzed using ATLAS V. 7.1.3, powerful software for the qualitative analysis of large bodies of textual, graphical, audio and video data (Morales-Sánchez et al., 2014).

To analyze the qualitative content of the interviews, the video recordings of the interviews (primary documents) were incorporated for analysis in multimedia format, having been organized and stored in a single file (Hermeneutic Unit). This file contains all the information produced in the course of the analysis in addition to the primary documents and contains codes, notes and memos, quotations and network views.

Each of the primary documents corresponded to one of the participants and the answers they gave. It should be noted that the answers were recorded literally and that some participants did not contribute to all the answers by agreeing with the rest of the participants or not answering at all. The quotes are each of the phrases or sentences that have been included in the study. The notes or memos correspond to segments of the recordings that were noteworthy from the primary documents and that are associated with different codes. The codes were the different aspects of the main analysis, reflected in 13 families of codes corresponding to each of the questions and eight new codes referring to the analyzed variables that emerged from the previous ones that were the object of interest (**Figure 1**).

- Adaptation of the model to class-contents
- Specific characteristics of the teacher-students for the model
- Contents that go with the values
- Better contents
- Developing of values
- Development of model values
- Adequate training for the model
- Better teaching quality
- More teaching strategies
- More tools with the mode
- Tasks better adapted to the students
- Improved coexistence
- Possible improvements to the model
- All teachers must participate
- New aspects of the model
- Other comments
- Problems adapting the model
- Problems in adapting the model
- Teacher satisfaction with the model
- Feeling when the model is applied
- Evaluation of negative aspects of the model
- Advantages of the model with respect the previous (model?)

FIGURE 1 | Code families and new codes.

Finally, the network views reflect the connection between the different codes.

RESULTS

The analysis of the content of the interviews was carried by reducing the different citations in the different codes elaborated according to the objectives of the present research regarding the characteristics of the TPSR and the contributions for future research and aspects to be highlighted and improved (**Figure 2**).

The "Teacher Satisfaction with the Model" code had a frequency of 41 and was the one most reflected in the interviews. In this regard, it is worth noting some statements in relation to satisfaction such as, "Thanks to the model, I feel useful, I mean what we said before, I see that I am spending my energy or investing it in a productive way". Also noteworthy is the contribution in one of the interviews by a teacher who said that, "The Responsibility Model is the best-kept secret".

Worthy of further note are those least related to "Improving Coexistence", "Promoting Model Values" and "Positive Adaptation of the Model to the Class-Content". In this regard, it has been a very positive contribution to have a high level of rationale for this last code, given that one of the main objectives of the application of the TPSR to all participants is to determine its capacity to adapt to these and the different students, with some comments such as "I have not had to modify any content, nothing different, so really totally adapted to them and giving the contents" (sic) or others such as "It is valid for any course, it is necessary for motivation and attention and these are the two variables that we have to promote as much as possible".

On the other side of the coin is the fact that the negative aspects had a very low number of mentions. Specifically, the "Negative Assessment of Model Aspects" occurred on two occasions, specifically in reference to the systematic nature of the application and the importance of leaving time for the final part of the session, for example, "You have to be careful to really comply systematically with the structure of the session or it will remain that way, simply strategies that you apply as you can, you must be systematic". As for the "Model Adaptation Problems", only two results were found, with reflections related to the Second year of High School, "I have had problems with Second year of High School, they have difficulties in many areas. We have taught these students since they were little... and we always complain that they are good but very talkative".

Finally, another of the objectives was to see the future perspectives of the model and suggestions; we created a new Code called "Need for participation of all teachers" which had 29 mentions, 26 of these referring to teachers and three to the importance of including families. By way of example, the following reflection, "It should be a uniform thing and if possible, unify reward, levels... something essential, that they always know that from the beginning of the course they have an ID card that works for all the teachers and all the participants".

A co-occurrence analysis was also carried out, the relationships between codes with similar dimensions being reflected in Table format (**Figure 3**). The maximum co-occurrence was between "higher quality of teaching" and "More Strategies in teaching" with a frequency of 11 and an index of 0.31. Secondly, the co-occurrence between "Promotion of model values" and "Improvement of coexistence" with a frequency of 11 and an index of 0.20 and "Higher quality of teaching" with "Teacher satisfaction with the model", with a frequency of 10 and an index of 0.20 is worth noting.

Finally, it is important to note a network where all the co-occurrences were imported (**Figure 4**). **Figure 4** shows that the highest quality of teaching is associated with teacher satisfaction with the model. In this regard, various codes were part of the highest quality of teaching: the promotion of values, the improvement of coexistence, the greater adaptation of tasks, and the ease of providing content as well as the values of the model.

DISCUSSION

The main objective of the present study was to apply the TPSR in the general educational context to measure the perception of the teachers involved in terms of its application, future perspectives and positive and negative aspects of the experience.

In this regard, it should be noted that of all the codes generated, the one that had the greatest occurrence in the interviews was "satisfaction with the model". Furthermore,

Name	Mentions
Adaptation of the model to class-contents	30
Development of model values	32
Better teaching quality	18
More teaching strategies	28
Improved coexistence	33
All teachers must participate	29
Problems in adapting the model	2
Teacher satisfaction with the model	41
Evaluation of negative aspects of the model	2

FIGURE 2 | Justification for the codes.

	Adaptation of the model to class-contents	Development of model values	Better teaching quality	More teaching strategies	Improved coexistence	All teachers must participate	Problems in adapting the model	Teacher satisfaction with the model	Evaluation of negative aspects of the model
Adaptation of the model to class-contents		5 - 0.09	4 - 0.09	3 - 0.05	5 - 0.09	2 - 0.04	2 - 0.07	7 - 0.11	1 - 0.03
Development of model values	5 - 0.09		6 - 0.14	7 - 0.13	11 - 0.20	1 - 0.02	n/a	10 - 0.16	n/a
Better teaching quality	4 - 0.09	6 - 0.14		11 - 0.31	5 - 0.11	n/a	n/a	10 - 0.20	n/a
More teaching strategies	3 - 0.05	7 - 0.13	11 - 0.31		2 - 0.03	n/a	n/a	9 - 0.15	n/a
Improved coexistence	5 - 0.09	11 - 0.20	5 - 0.11	2 - 0.03		n/a	n/a	11 - 0.17	n/a
All teachers must participate	2 - 0.04	1 - 0.02	n/a	n/a	n/a		n/a	1 - 0.01	1 - 0.03
Problems in adapting the model	2 - 0.07	n/a	n/a	n/a	n/a	n/a		n/a	n/a
Teacher satisfaction with the model	7 - 0.11	10 - 0.16	10 - 0.20	9 - 0.15	11 - 0.17	1 - 0.01	n/a		n/a
Evaluation of negative aspects of the model	1 - 0.03	n/a	n/a	n/a	n/a	1 - 0.03	n/a	n/a	

FIGURE 3 | Code co-ocurrence table.

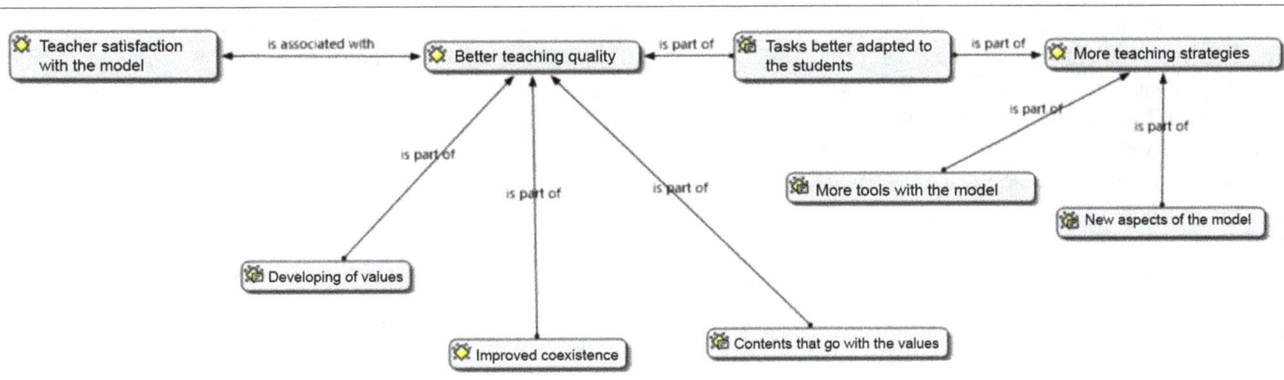

FIGURE 4 | Co-occurence network.

some of the interviews noted the importance of continuing to apply the model for a long time to improve performance and that it should last throughout the school year, in line with the study by Llopis-Goig et al. (2011) which indicates that improvements in the model in terms of responsibility require a long duration, as also indicated by Manzano-Sánchez et al. (2019) where, with an application period of 4 months, improvements were obtained in only some of the variables, its duration being a limitation. Similar is the case of Sánchez-Alcaraz et al. (2019) where the importance of applying the model throughout the school year and in all participants is highlighted in the interviews carried out. In addition to this, it should be noted that Llopis-Goig et al. (2011) have pointed out the importance of involving the entire educational community and the family environment, the latter also being reflected by the teachers participating in this study.

The TPSR was also perceived by the teachers as applicable to all contents and participants, with comments such as "All contents are adapted to one or other levels always, but the question is group level and how to adapt it to this", which is a positive assessment as to the capacity of the TPSR to adapt to the contents while working on educational values." You are no longer limited only to working on the contents of the subject, but you already have a system to measure, evaluate and work on other aspects related to behavior and conduct". All of this is in line with the study by Manzano and Valero-Valenzuela (2019), here the teacher who participated in the study indicated that he was able to adapt the model to all the areas he taught in his group in Primary Education.

It is worth noting that the teachers' perception was that TPSR can be suitable not only for difficult students but for any type of student. Furthermore, certain interviews reflected the importance of teachers participating in the methodology, and that this should increase the time students are taught through the model, "The time of exposure that the student has to the model has an impact and is important, of course". This does not coincide with the study by Sánchez-Alcaraz et al. (2013), in which teachers felt that content, student body and teacher experience are determining factors in the application of TPSR.

With regard to the classroom climate, very positive results were also obtained, with the code "improvement of coexistence" having a total of 33 mentions that represented the second-highest value behind satisfaction, with some comments such as that of a teacher with a difficult group, "With the model now they respect each other and these things, now they let others work and this is already an achievement in itself, it means reaching and surpassing level 1 and that is a lot", thus supporting the study by Caballero (2015) where in applying the TPSR the participants obtained improvements in students' classroom climate with activities in the natural environment. Several teachers referred to aspects related to better student behavior, following the line of the aforementioned author and Carreres (2014) where the TPSR improved not only personal and social responsibility but also pro-social behavior. The study by Escartì et al. (2010) confirms that it helped teachers to structure classes and promoted the learning of responsible student behaviors. A significant increase in self-regulatory and self-efficacy was also observed in the participants of the intervention group.

The only study that has applied the TPSR in secondary schools and that has carried out interviews with teachers found much in line with those of this intervention. Thus, Manzano-Sánchez and Valero-Valenzuela (2019), showed high satisfaction with the model in the interviews conducted, a positive evaluation in terms of its possibilities for promoting values and wanting to continue its application in future courses, aspects also reflected within the different reflections on this study by the teachers. We therefore do not agree with the study by García et al. (2014), where the teaching staff indicate that the innovative methodologies for promoting autonomy and responsibility are perceived as complex to apply due to the limited time available, given that there was only one comment that indicated "the day I get confused I don't get to the evaluation, or I set the alarm on my mobile phone 5 min before the end of the class". Furthermore, the possibility of hybridizing with other pedagogical models such as Cooperative Learning, could improve some of the potential or educational results that TPSR has in a unique way (González-Víllora et al., 2019).

It should be noted that the novelty of this study in terms of its scope (educational context in general) may serve as a reference point for future work in education, since although very good results have been obtained in terms of teacher assessment, they could only be contrasted with studies in Physical Education, extracurricular sports activities or other sports activities, with the exception of the studies by Manzano and Valero-Valenzuela (2019) and Manzano-Sánchez and Valero-Valenzuela (2019). Finally, the use of the mixed methods methodology helps to draw conclusions taking into account different points of view and perspectives.

CONCLUSION

The TPSR can be applied to all participants in the curriculum and is perceived as appropriate for teachers. Its applicability does not have more suitable content or more specific groups than others, but it can be used for any teacher or course independently of these aspects. It was perceived as appropriate to improve educational values without detriment of the contents, indicating even more simplicity to teach contents and a new motivation for teachers. It is suggested that the application of the TPSR should be carried out by all teachers participating with the same class group in order to improve the benefits and involve families in the process. Future lines of research could consider the possibility of replicating this study in other contexts within the educational system (for instance elementary or primary education), using a methodology similar to that of this study, combining quantitative and qualitative instruments.

ETHICS STATEMENT

The studies involving human participants were reviewed and approved by the Ethics Committee of the University of Murcia REF-1685/2017. Written informed consent to participate in this study was provided by the participants, participants' legal guardian/next of kin.

AUTHOR CONTRIBUTIONS

DM-S and AV-V developed the methodological proposal and data analysis. MG-L described the conclusions and references. DM-S realized the literature review and wrote the part of the theoretical frame. LC-M collaborated in data analysis and redaction of results.

REFERENCES

Alcalá, D., Rìo, J., Calvo, G., and Pueyo, A. (2019). Comparing effects of a TPSR training programme on prospective physical education teachers' social goals, discipline and autonomy strategies in Spain, Chile and Costa Rica. *Phys. Educ. Sport Pedagog.* 24, 220–232. doi: 10.1080/17408989.2018.1561837

Baena-Extremera, A., Gómez-López, M., Granero-Gallegos, A., and Martínez-Molina, M. (2016). Prediction model of satisfaction and enjoyment in physical education from the autonomy and motivational climate. *Univ. Psychol.* 15, 39–50. doi: 10.11144/Javeriana.upsy15-2.mpsd

Belando, N., Férriz-Morel, R., Rivas, S., Almagro, B., Sáenz-López, P., Cervelló, E., et al. (2015). Sport commitment in adolescent soccer players. *Motricidade* 11, 3–14. doi: 10.6063/motricidade.2969

Brockbank, A., and McGill, I. (2002). *Aprendizaje Reflexivo en la Educación Superior [Reflective Learning in Higher Education].* Madrid: Morata.

Caballero, P. (2015). Design, implementation and assessment of an outdoor activities programme to promote personal and social responsibility in professional training students. *Cuad. Psicol. Deporte* 15, 179–194.

Calderón, A., de Ojeda, D. M., Valverde, J. J., and Méndez-Giménez, A. (2016). Now we help ourselves more". Team-teaching and social classroom climate. Experience with Sport Education. *RICYDE Rev. Int. Cienc. Deporte* 12, 121–136. doi: 10.5232/ricyde2016.04403

Carreres, F. (2014). *Efectos, en los Adolescentes, de un Programa de Responsabilidad Personal y Social a Través del Deporte Extraescolar [Effects on Adolescents of a Programme of Personal and Social Responsibility Through Extracurricular Sport].* Alicante: University of Alicante.

Escartí, A., Gutiérrez, M., and Pascual, C. (2011). Psychometric properties of the Spanish version of the personal and social responsability questionnaire in physical education contexts. *Rev. Psicol. Deporte* 20, 119–130.

Escartí, A., Gutiérrez, M., Pascual, C., and Wright, P. (2013). Observation of the strategies that physical education teachers use to teach personal and social responsibility. *Rev. Psicol. Deporte* 22, 159–166.

Escartí, A., Pascual, C., and Gutiérrez, M. (2005). *Responsabilidad Personal y Social a Través de la Actividad Física y el Deporte [Personal and Social Responsibility Through Physical Activity and Sport].* Barcelona: Graó.

Escartì, A., Gutieìrrez, M., Pascual, C., and Llopis, R. (2010). Implementation of the personal and social responsibility model to improve self-efficacy during physical education classes for primary school children. *Int. J. Psychol. Psychol. Ther.* 10, 387–402.

García, D. M., Benavent, G. T., Cardo, V. D., Llopis, L. S., and López, E. T. (2014). The development of autonomy and responsibility in physical education: a collaborative case study in secondary. *Retos Nuevas Tendencias Educ. Física Deporte Recreac.* 26, 3–8.

González-Víllora, S., Evangelio, C., Sierra-Díaz, J., and Fernández-Río, J. (2019). Hybridizing pedagogical models: a systematic review. *Euro. Phys. Educ. Rev.* 25, 1056–1074. doi: 10.1177/1356336X18797363

Gordon, B., Jacobs, J. M., and Wright, P. M. (2016). Social and emotional learning through a teaching personal and social responsibility based after-school program for disengaged middle-school boys. *J. Teach. Phys. Educ.* 35, 358–369. doi: 10.1123/jtpe.2016-0106

Gould, D., and Carson, S. (2008). Life skills development through sport: current status and future directions. *Int. Rev. Sport Exerc. Psychol.* 1, 58–78. doi: 10. 1080/17509840701834573

Granero-Gallegos, A., Gómez-López, M., Baena-Extremera, A., and Martínez-Molina, M. (2020). Interaction effects of disruptive behaviour and motivation profiles with teacher competence and school satisfaction in secondary school physical education. *Int. J. Environ. Res. Public Health* 17:114. doi: 10.3390/ijerph17010114

Hellison, D. (1978). *Beyond Balls and Bats: Alienated (and Other) Youth in the gym* Washington, DC: AAHPER publications.

Hellison, D. (1985). *Goals and Strategies for Teaching Physical Education.* Champaign. IL: Human Kinetics Publishers Inc.

Hellison, D. (2011). *Teaching Personal and Social Responsibility through Physical Activity*, 3rd Edn. Champaign, IL: Human Kinetics Publishers Inc.

Hellison, D., and Wright, P. (2003). Retention in an urban extended day program: a process-based assesment. *J. Teach. Phys. Educ.* 22, 369–381. doi: 10.1123/jtpe.22.4.369

Imbernón, F. (2013). Formación y desarrollo de la profesión. De qué hablamos? [Formation and professional development. What are we talking about?]. *Aula Innovación Educ.* 218, 12–15.

Larson, R. (2000). Toward a psychology of positive youth development. *Am. Psychol.* 55, 170–183. doi: 10.1037/0003-066X.55.1.170

Legault, L., and Inzlicht, M. (2013). Self-determination, self-regulation and the brain: autonomy improves performance by enhancing neuroaffective responsiveness to self-regulation failure. *J. Pers. Soc. Psychol.* 105, 123–138. doi: 10.1037/a0030426

León Guerrero, M. J. (2011). Training in inclusive education in the new infant and primary education degrees in Spain. *REIFOP* 25, 145–163.

Li, W., Wright, P. M., Rukavina, P. B., and Pickering, M. (2008). Measuring students' perceptions of personal and social responsibility and the relationship to intrinsic motivation in urban physical education. *J Teach. Phys. Educ.* 27, 167–178. doi: 10.1123/jtpe.27.2.167

Llopis-Goig, R., Escartí, A., Pascual, C., Gutiérrez, M., and Marín, D. (2011). Strengths, difficulties and improvable aspects in the application of a personal and social responsibility program in physical education: an evaluation based on the implementers' perceptions. *Cult. Educ.* 23, 445–461. doi: 10.1174/113564011797330324

Manzano, D., and Valero-Valenzuela, A. (2019). The personal and social responsibility model (TPSR) in the different subjects of primary education and its impact on responsibility, autonomy, motivation, self-concept and social climate. *J. Sport Health Res.* 11, 273–288.

Manzano-Sánchez, D., and Valero-Valenzuela, A. (2019). Implementation of a model-based programme to promote personal and social responsibility and its effects on motivation, prosocial behaviours, violence and classroom climate in primary and secondary education. *Int. J. Environ. Res.* 16:4259. doi: 10.3390/ijerph16214259

Manzano-Sánchez, D., Valero-Valenzuela, A., Conde-Sánchez, A., and Ming-Yao, C. (2019). Applying the personal and social responsibility model-based program: differences according to gender between basic psychological needs, motivation, life and intention to be physically active. *Int. J. Environ. Res. Public Health* 16:2326. doi: 10.3390/ijerph16132326

Menéndez, J. I., and Fernández, J. (2016). Violencia, responsabilidad, amistad y necesidades psicológicas básicas: efectos de un programa de educación deportiva y responsabilidad personal y social [Violence, responsibility, friendship and basic psychological needs: effects of a program of sports education and personal and social responsibility]. *Rev. Psicodidact.* 21, 245–260. doi: 10.1387/RevPsicodidact.15269

Merino-Barrero, J. A., Valero-Valenzuela, A., and Belando-Pedreño, N. (2017). El modelo de responsabilidad personal y social: variables asociadas a su implementación [The personal and social responsibility model: variables associated with its implementation]. *EMasF Rev. Digit. Educ. Física* 49, 60–77.

Montero, I., and León, O. G. (2007). A guide for naming research studies in Psychology. *Int. J. Clin. Health Psychol.* 7, 847–862.

Morales-Sánchez, V., Pérez-López, R., and Anguera, M. T. (2014). Indirect observational methodology in managing sports services. *Rev. Psicol. Deporte* 23, 201–207.

Oriol, X., Amutio, A., Mendoza, M., Da Costa, S., and Miranda, R. (2016). Emotional creativity as predictor of intrinsic motivation and academic engagement in university students: the mediating role of positive emotions. *Front. Psychol.* 7:1243. doi: 10.3389/fpsyg.2016.01243

Ortiz, P., Gómez-López, M., Martín, I., Reigal, R. E., García-Mas, A., and Chirosa, L. J. (2016). Role played by the coach in the adolescent players'commitment. *Stud. Psychol.* 58, 184–198. doi: 10.21909/sp.2016.03.716

Patton, M. Q. (2002). *Qualitative Research and Evaluation Methods.* Thousand Oaks, CA: Sage.

Pegalajar-Palomino, M. C. (2014). Teacher professional development in special education centres. *REIFOP* 17, 177–192. doi: 10.6018/reifop.17.1.18 1731

Pérez-López, I., and Rivera-García, E. (2017). Developing teachers, developing people: analysis of the lessons learnt by university students from a gamification experience. *Signo Pensam.* 36, 112–129. doi: 10.11144/Javeriana.syp36-70.fdfp

Sánchez-Alcaraz, B. J., Cañadas, M., Valero-Valenzuela, A., Gómez, A., and Funes, A. (2019). Results, difficulties and improvements in the model of personal and social responsibility. *Apunts. Educ. Física Deporte.* 35, 66–82. doi: 10.5672/apunts.2014-0983.es.(2019/2).136.05

Sánchez-Alcaraz, B. J., Gómez-Mármol, A., Valero Valenzuela, A., and De la Cruz Sánchez, E. (2013). Aplicación de un programa para la mejora de la responsabilidad personal y social en las clases de educación física [Implementation of a program for the improvement of personal and social responsibility in physical education classes]. *Motricidad Eur. J. Hum. Mov.* 30, 121–129.

Shim, S., and Ryan, A. (2005). Changes in self-efficacy, challenge avoidance, and intrinsic value in response to grades: the role of achievement goals. *J. Exp. Educ.* 73, 333–349. doi: 10.3200/JEXE.73.4.333-349

Smithikrai, C. (2013). "The mediating roles of academic stress and life satisfaction in the relationship between personal responsibility and academic performance," in *Innovation. Communication and Engineering*, eds F. Lumban, S. Kadry, M. Taylor, and P. Shen, (London: Taylor & Francis Group), 383–387. doi: 10.1201/b16658-67

State Agency State Gazette, (2013). Organic Law 8/2013, of 9 December, for the improvement of educational quality (LOMCE). *Off. State Bull.* 295, 97858–97921.

Stentoft, D. (2016). *The Aalborg Model for Project Based Learning.* Aalborg: Aalborg University Press.

Tejedor, F. J., and García-Valcárcel, A. (2007). Causes for low performance in university students (according to teachersand students themselves). Proposals for improvement within the European area for higher education. *Rev. Educ.* 342, 443–473.

Walkey, F. H., McClure, J., Meyer, L. H., and Weir, K. F. (2013). Low expectations equal no expectations: aspirations, motivation, and achievement in secondary school. *Contemp. Educ. Psychol.* 38, 306–315. doi: 10.1016/j.cedpsych.2013.06.004

Woods, D. (2016). *Problem-Based Learning.* Hamilton, ON: McMaster University.

12

Self-Concept and Physical Activity: Differences Between High School and University Students

Wanesa Onetti-Onetti[1], José Luis Chinchilla-Minguet[2], Fernando Manuel Lourenço Martins[3,4] and Alfonso Castillo-Rodriguez[5]*

[1]Faculty of Education, UNIR, International University of La Rioja, Logroño, Spain, [2]Department of Languages, Arts and Sports, University of Málaga, Málaga, Spain, [3]Instituto Politécnico de Coimbra, Coimbra, Portugal, [4]Instituto de Telecomunicações, Covilhã, Portugal, [5]Department of Physical Education and Sports, University of Granada, Granada, Spain

***Correspondence:**
Alfonso Castillo-Rodriguez
acastillo@ugr.es

The period of adolescence stands out as a critical and decisive phase, first because it leaves its mark on personality development, which is affected by psychosocial factors, and second because the healthy lifestyle habits acquired during this stage form a foundation for adulthood. The objective of the present study was first to evaluate the levels of participation in physical activities (PA) and of self-concept in high school and university students, and second to find relationships between these psycho-physical variables. Four hundred and forty adolescents ranging in age from 16 to 20 years, from Spain and Portugal, participated in this study (cross-sectional design). The IPAQ and Self-Concept Form-5 questionnaires were used. The results demonstrated some differences; the Portuguese university students had lower scores in the academic, emotional and physical dimensions and vigorous PA but higher sitting time, walking and moderate PA compared to Portuguese high school students. In addition, Spanish university students had lower self-concept scores although higher practice of PA and lower sitting time than Spanish high school students ($p < 0.05$). On the other hand, a positive relationship was found between different dimensions of self-concept and levels of PA, while the relationship between these dimensions and the time the adolescent spent sitting was negative. In conclusion, the university students have lower scores of self-concept dimensions (in general), and the practice of PA is higher in Spanish university students, confirming the clear presence of differences between both educational stages. The relationship between the dimensions of self-concept in general and the level of PA was positive (following the contributions of Marsh).

Keywords: physical activity, self-concept, adolescents, educational stage, IPAQ

INTRODUCTION

The scientific literature has demonstrated that regular practice of moderate (MPA) and vigorous (VPA) physical activities (PA) provides health benefits for different ages (Reiner et al., 2013). Accordingly, the World Health Organization has recommended that adolescents between 15 and 17 years old should practice at least 60 min of MPA and VPA daily, and at later ages, at least 150 min of MPA or 75 min of VPA weekly (World Health Organization, 2010). These ages, which include adolescence as well as the start of adulthood, are particularly important due to their propensity for forming healthy lifestyle habits. For this reason, Hills et al. (2015) recommend programs to create such habits and to reduce physical inactivity, as the latter could lead to the onset of certain health risk factors such as overweight and obesity (Du et al., 2014).

More specifically, adhering to a practice of PA is considered one of the principal solutions to avoid these risk factors and cardiovascular diseases, thereby fostering good health and quality of life (Myers et al., 2002; Blair et al., 2012; Kokkinos, 2012). Nevertheless, adolescents do not regularly practice PA, neither in high school (Olds et al., 2009) nor in university (Pengpid et al., 2015). This lack of practice has become one of the major problems of today's society in general (World Health Organization, 2010; Kohl et al., 2012), as there exist a significant number of persons who are sedentary as compared to those who are physically active (Expósito et al., 2012).

The beginnings of unhealthy lifestyles seem to appear, predominantly, in the period of adolescence which coincides with the transition from high school to university, where these young adults are subjected to multiple changes because of their psychological instability (Smetana et al., 2006). The transition to university is seen as an exciting period for many students in their first year as it involves new challenges in their lives (Rach and Heinze, 2017) and also greater responsibility, which consequently poses risks for their self-concept (Salinas-Miranda et al., 2015). The changes in healthy lifestyle and habits that occur during this transition are manifested in a lower level of PA (Varela-Mato et al., 2012), in part due to the elimination of required physical education classes (Chen et al., 2014). These, along with a change of city for the majority of students, are factors that may make PA problematic during the university period (Rona and Gokmen, 2005).

The assessment of healthy habits at these ages is particularly important given that these habits could affect overall self-concept. Self-concept is composed of five dimensions: academic, social, emotional, family, and physical. The relationship of these dimensions with the healthy behavior of adolescents can determine self-improvement actions (Marsh, 1989; Pastor et al., 2006) such as taking part in PA and having adequate nutrition, in the pursuit of quality of life (Serra-Majem et al., 2004; Wanden-Berghe et al., 2015). The performance of PA is related to self-concept (Slutzky and Simpkins, 2009), even to the point of possible changes in the student's personality and his capacity to understand his own behavior (Marsh and Redmayne, 1994), his relationship with others, his deficiencies, and his motivations. Physical self-concept was both an effect and a cause of exercise behavior (Marsh and Martin, 2011). For their part, Cerkez et al. (2015) attest to the fact that regular participation in PA has a positive relation with physical self-concept. When there exist a low level of participation in PA, the person may be vulnerable in his social self-concept due to dissatisfaction with his body image (Annesi, 2010; Chen and Lee, 2013; Zschucke et al., 2013; Owen et al., 2014). On the other hand, VPA can affect the emotional dimension of self-concept during the transition. This dimension measures the perception of a person's emotions and the degree of control he has over them. It is a significant dimension to investigate in adolescents who are entering university because of the stress and fatigue that VPA, such as the practice of sports, can cause (Strong et al., 2005).

For these reasons, the importance of PA is stressed, as a means by which adolescents can improve their physical condition and competence, body image, self-esteem, and self-concept (Crocker et al., 2000; Moreno et al., 2007; Rojas et al., 2011). Our hypothesis is that the level of self-concept is related positively to the level of participation in PA, expressed as VPA and/or MPA.

Despite the numerous studies of adolescents and university students which look at self-concept and its relation with PA, there are none which analyze if this relationship is different for high school students as compared to university students in order to understand the effect this school transition may have on these young adults. A better understanding of these associations, and the differences found between university and high school students, would improve our current understanding and help in designing intervention strategies focused on increasing PA as a path toward improved self-concept. Accordingly, the present study proposes two objectives. The first objective was to assess the levels of PA and self-concept during the transition from high school to university. The second objective was to analyze relationships between the level of PA and the self-concept dimensions.

MATERIALS AND METHODS

Participants and Procedure

We selected the school participants by a cluster sampling, taking into account the population from high schools and colleges situated in the South of Spain and in the North of Portugal. Initially, the recruitment of students was carried out through the same protocol in both countries. Twelve high schools (six from Spain and six from Portugal) and eight colleges (four from Spain and four from Portugal) were selected at random. All of them agreed to participate in the study except for one college in Portugal. Subsequently, the web link was sent to 400 high school students (200 from Spain and 200 from Portugal) and 400 university students (200 from Spain and 200 from Portugal). Of the total number of students, 311 from Spain and 163 from Portugal completed it. Finally, 34 participants were eliminated because of insufficient completion of the different instruments, leaving an uncompleted response rate of 7.17% (**Figure 1**). Our final sample consisted of 300 Spanish students [mean (M) age = 17.9, standard deviation (SD) = 3.4 years; weight M = 65.1, SD = 12.0 kg; height M = 171.2, SD = 9.2 cm] and 140 Portuguese students (age M = 18.4, SD = 3.1 years; weight M = 64.2, SD = 9.7 kg; height M = 170.3, SD = 9.5 cm). The participants were studying from the last two grades of the high school (before the transition) until the first two grades of university (after the transition). Their ages ranged from 16 to 21 years.

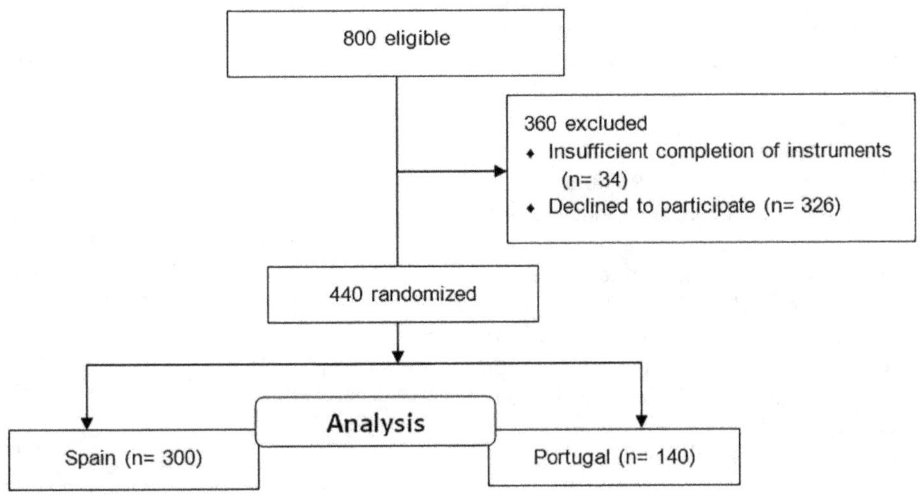

FIGURE 1 | Flow diagram of recruitment of participants.

A cross-sectional, descriptive, and observational quantitative methodology was used in this study. The parents, in the case of the high school students, were informed of the aims and signed the consent form prior to the participation of the students in this study, and all the participants also gave their written consent to voluntarily participate in the research. The study was approved by the Ethics Committee of the University of Granada (Spain) and followed the guidelines found in the Helsinki Declaration (2013) which establishes ethical principles for investigations using human beings and confidentiality. The authors sent an email invitation to participate in the study to the teachers of the institutions. When we received the acceptance to participate by the teacher, we sent the consent so they could sign it. All participants were measured for weight and height. In the case of high schools, these measurements were carried out by the physical education teacher, and in the colleges, the researchers of this study, always through the same instrument. Once we had the physical and socio-demographic characteristics, they were able to carry out the questionnaires *via* the Internet that were provided through the media of the groups. They received this email invitation that contained the web link to the study with aims and tests of the study. The identification of the student was never requested.

Instruments

Physical and social-demographic characteristics were collected from the participants through an ad-hoc test with questions regarding age, weight, height, sex, grade, and educational level. Electronic scale SECA (Hamburg, Germany) was used to measure body weight to the nearest 100 g and height was measured to the nearest 0.1 cm with a SECA electronic stadiometer (Seca Ltd., Medical Scales and Measurement Systems, Birmingham, United Kingdom). After that, we could calculate the overweight level of the participants using BMI according to Cole et al. (2000) and World Health Organization (2016) classification system (normal-weight if BMI < 25.0 kg·m^{-2}; overweight if BMI ≥ 25.0 kg·m^{-2}).

The Self-Concept Questionnaire, called Form 5, was validated for the Spanish sample (García and Musitu, 2001; level of reliability = 0.85), is based on the theoretical model created by Shavelson et al. (1976), and consists of five subscales, each one measured by six items: academic/occupational (items 1, 6, 11, 16, 21, and 26), social (items 2, 7, 12, 17, 22, and 27), emotional (items 3, 8, 13, 18, 23, and 28), family (items 4, 9, 14, 19, 24, and 29), and physical (items 5, 10, 15, 20, 25, and 30). In this way, using a Likert-type scale from 1 to 99, one single instrument measures the principal dimensions of self-concept (Grandmontagne and Fernández, 2004). In this study, the reliability level was $\alpha = 0.859$ (higher than original version with 0.810), where all the dimensions had optimized values (academic, $\alpha = 0.898$; social, $\alpha = 0.878$; emotional, $\alpha = 0.858$; family, $\alpha = 0.882$; physical, $\alpha = 0.779$).

To measure PA levels, participants completed the International Physical Activity Questionnaire-Short Form (IPAQ-SF; Booth, 2000). This questionnaire has been validated in different countries (Craig et al., 2003), and it has shown acceptable psychometric properties to assess PA levels with good reliability, as the Spearman correlation coefficient values are around 0.8. The Spanish IPAQ-SF reliability for measuring PA levels used for both high school and university students has been assessed and verified ($r = 0.49$, $p < 0.001$; Rodriguez-Muñoz et al., 2017). According to the official IPAQ scoring protocol, we calculated total daily PA by summing the product of reported time in PA level and sitting time.

Statistical Analysis

The influences of the country (Spain and Portugal) and the educational stage (high school and University) factors on academic, social, emotional, family, and physical dimensions of self-concept and PA variables [VPA, MPA, walking activities (WPA), and sitting time] were analyzed using two-way ANOVA after checking the normality and homogeneity assumptions (Pallant, 2011). A Bonferroni correction *post hoc* was performed to make comparisons between groups. Furthermore, an independent samples t-test (not paired samples t-test) was used for educational stage as an independent variable (using the last grade of high school and the first year at university) after validating normality and homogeneity assumptions (Pallant, 2011). The effect size was presented as η^2 for a two-way ANOVA test and interpreted using the follow criteria: minimum effect ($\eta^2 \leq 0.02$), moderate effect ($0.02 < \eta^2 \leq 0.09$), and strong effect ($\eta^2 > 0.09$) (Lakens, 2013). For the case of independent samples t-test, Cohen's d was executed as effect size using the follow criteria: small effect ($d < 0.20$), moderate effect ($0.20 \leq d < 0.80$), and large effect ($d \geq 0.80$) (O'Donoghue, 2013). Finally, correlational analysis (Pearson's test) was carried out in order to assess the relationship between the self-concept dimensions and the PA variables. The data analysis was conducted using IBM SPSS (version 24.0) software for Windows and a statistical significance of 5% ($p < 0.05$) was defined.

RESULTS

In this section, we consider high school Spanish students (HS), university Spanish students (US), high school Portuguese students (HP), and university Portuguese students (UP). There was significant interaction (**Table 1**) between country and educational stage for academic self-concept ($F_{(1,440)} = 5.828$; $p = 0.016$; $\eta^2 = 0.013$; small effect size); emotional self-concept ($F_{(1,440)} = 8.879$; $p = 0.003$; =0.020; small effect size); physical self-concept ($F = 26.135$; $p = 0.001$; $\eta^2 = 0.057$; moderate effect size); VPA ($F_{(1,440)} = 69.646$; $p = 0.001$; $\eta^2 = 0.138$; large effect size); MPA ($F_{(1,440)} = 25.416$; $p = 0.001$; $\eta^2 = 0.055$; moderate effect size); WPA ($F_{(1,440)} = 5.26$; $p = 0.022$; $\eta^2 = 0.012$; small effect size); and sitting time ($F_{(1,440)} = 28.234$; $p = 0.002$; $\eta^2 = 0.061$; moderate effect size). In this case, an independent sample t-test was used for educational stage, with the observed groups being the last grade of high school and the first year at the university [**Figure 2A** (self-concept dimensions) and **Figure 2B** (PA variables)]. The academic and emotional dimensions and the sitting time were lower at university, although the MPA was higher ($p < 0.05$).

Finally, correlational analysis is shown in **Table 2**. Bivariate correlation analysis revealed that physical self-concept was positively related to VPA and MPA and negatively related to sitting time both in high school and university (with a greater correlation coefficient for VPA). Furthermore, VPA and MPA were negatively associated with the academic (high school) and emotional self-concept dimensions.

DISCUSSION

The purpose of the present study was, first, to evaluate the levels of practice of PA and self-concept in high school and university students, and second, to find relationships between these psycho-physical variables. The results indicated that there are differences of self-concept dimensions and PA variables between countries and educational stages. On the one hand, university Spanish students had lower self-concept scores

TABLE 1 | t-Test between high school and university students for the self-concept and PA variables, and two-ways ANOVA test (the three final columns) between country and educational stage factors.

		Spain		p	d	Portugal		p	d	$F_{(1,440)}$	p^*	η^2
		High school	University			High school	University					
Academic	(Points)	76.58 ± 15.14[a]	75.43 ± 11.94[a]	0.452	0.082	77.23 ± 7.66	69.23 ± 13.04	0.000	0.734	5.665	0.001	0.038
Social	(Points)	79.51 ± 14.07	78.91 ± 12.22	0.691	0.045	71.37 ± 12.44	74.54 ± 12.43	0.161	0.254	7.247	0.000	0.047
Emotional	(Points)	49.36 ± 24.69[b]	42.98 ± 19.11[b]	0.010	0.280	67.90 ± 6.67	48.34 ± 17.55[b]	0.000	1.434	19.207	0.000	0.117
Family	(Points)	84.76 ± 13.36	86.04 ± 9.93	0.331	0.105	88.65 ± 4.24	86.05 ± 10.11	0.060	0.327	1.839	0.139	0.012
Physical	(Points)	66.36 ± 18.87[c,b]	74.23 ± 11.02[b]	0.000	0.481	81.43 ± 6.75	72.41 ± 16.05[b]	0.000	0.714	16.529	0.000	0.102
VPA	(min·day^{-1})	22.46 ± 18.53[c]	38.73 ± 13.75	0.000	0.481	24.81 ± 17.72[c]	18.99 ± 17.30[c]	0.068	0.333	71.452	0.001	0.330
MPA	(min·day^{-1})	13.23 ± 12.89[c]	24.77 ± 13.53	0.000	1.426	13.68 ± 7.99[c]	17.11 ± 17.41[c]	0.155	0.247	45.418	0.001	0.238
WPA	(min·day^{-1})	25.25 ± 10.55	30.13 ± 10.71[d]	0.000	1.216	10.75 ± 7.60[c,d]	18.57 ± 14.23[b,c,d]	0.000	0.672	66.651	0.001	0.314
Sitting time	(min·day^{-1})	397.7 ± 208.8	251.2 ± 114.5[d]	0.000	0.975	225.6 ± 88.49[d]	270.7 ± 166.6[d]	0.059	0.332	28.526	0.001	0.164

*VPA, Vigorous physical activity; MPA, Moderate physical activity; WPA, Walking physical activity. *Two-ways ANOVA: significantly different at p < 0.05 compared with (Bonferroni Post hoc). [a]UP (academic self-concept; WPA). [b]HP (emotional self-concept; physical self-concept). [c]US (physical self-concept; VPA; MPA; WPA). [d]HS (WPA; sitting time).*

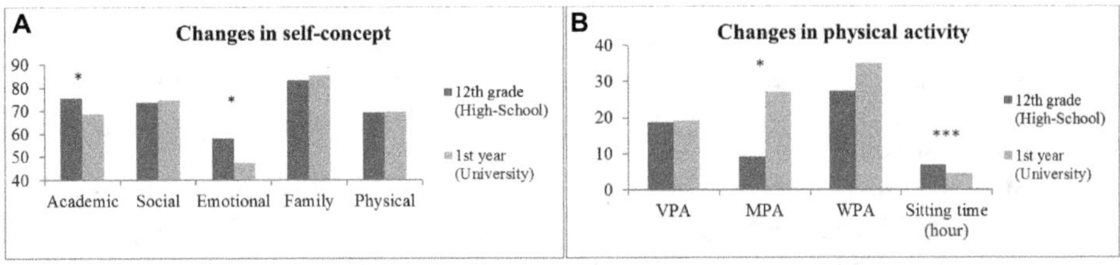

FIGURE 2 | (A) Changes in self-concept by grades. **(B)** Changes in physical activity by grades. *$p < 0.05$; ***$p < 0.001$.

TABLE 2 | Correlational analysis.

		Academic	Social	Emotional	Family	Physical
VPA	(High school)	−0.032	−0.020	−0.173**	0.059	0.288**
	(University)	0.153*	0.170*	−0.224**	0.112	0.204**
MPA	(High school)	−0.194**	−0.117	−0.160*	−0.016	0.129*
	(University)	0.029	0.017	−0.111	−0.076	0.019
WPA	(High school)	0.083	0.275**	−0.054	0.046	−0.161*
	(University)	0.251**	0.122	−0.215**	0.230**	0.126
Sitting time	(High school)	−0.075	0.044	0.082	−0.093	−0.283**
	(University)	−0.160*	−0.228**	−0.301**	−0.024	−0.056

*$p < 0.05$; **$p < 0.01$. VPA, Vigorous physical activity; MPA, Moderate physical activity; WPA, Walking physical activity.*

(small effect size) although higher practice of PA and lower sitting time (large effect size) than high school Spanish students. On the other hand, university Portuguese students had lower self-concept scores (large effect size) and VPA, although higher sitting-time, WPA, and MPA (moderate effect size) than high school Portuguese students. This is in accordance with the scientific literature which shows that this educational transition could suppose important changes in adolescents, especially psychological and emotional changes (Ullrich-French et al., 2013; Akos et al., 2015). The sources of these psychosocial changes are, among others, the appearance of stress, social problems (friends or family), and physical changes characteristic of this age, which all affect personality development. Hagger et al. (2005) indicated that although there were also some statistically significant decreases in self-concept ratings across grade, the effect sizes were small and offered little evidence for developmental changes in physical self-concept. In this study, the effect size was large in both populations, although the tendency in Spanish students was increasing, and in Portuguese students, it was decreasing with respect to physical self-concept.

The university Spanish students had higher practice of PA in general (VPA, MPA, and less time sitting). These results differ from those found in the studies by Cocca et al. (2014) and Sevil et al. (2018), who observed lower scores in the practice of PA in university students, as occurred with the Portuguese students in our study. This could be due to the students' discipline of studies (science vs. humanities), mode of transport from residence to the campus, and in general, available free time. These changes in lifestyle can provoke personal, emotional, and social changes which may be manifested in tobacco and alcohol consumption, diet, and time spent sitting in front of the television (Romaguera et al., 2011). This, in turn, has the immediate consequence of a reduction in the emotional dimension of self-concept (appearing in all the students) and in the academic dimension (seen in the Portuguese university students), which ends up producing a change in personality (Slutzky and Simpkins, 2009). Nevertheless, the Spanish university students, in comparison with their high school counterparts, reduced their sitting time in favor of increasing their practice of PA.

This study also examined the differences in the existing associations between the psycho-physical variables found in both educational stages (high school and university). In a concrete way, there are several correlations between specific dimensions of self-concept and PA variables. This fact has been studied through various contributions by Marsh (Marsh and Redmayne, 1994; Marsh and Martin, 2011; among others), which confirms the causal existence and effects between this construct and the PA or physical fitness of children and adolescents. However, until now, the differences and relationships of these variables have not been described taking into account the educational transition to university, having knowledge of the contextual variables and evolution that this population has. To start, the academic, social, and family self-concept dimensions were positively related to the level of the practice of PA in accordance with other studies (Annesi, 2006; Esnaola and Revuelta, 2009; Contreras et al., 2010; Bean et al., 2012). Higher levels of practice had a positive effect on the social behavior and health of the adolescents (Esnaola et al., 2018). However, these relationships were seen mostly in the university students. In high school students, only the social and physical dimensions were positively related to WPA and VPA, respectively. A possible explanation could be that the mandatory requirement of physical education classes in high school, as opposed to the voluntary practice of PA by university students for social and health reasons, produces a different effect on self-concept (Roberts et al., 2015). Sevil et al. (2018) conclude that intervention programs are needed to improve sports practice and the dimensions of self-concept in order to maintain or increase the levels of PA during the transition to university for the Portuguese students. On the other hand, the emotional dimension of self-concept was inversely related to VPA in all the students. This may have been due to the anxiety and stress associated with overtraining, or perhaps the type of sport practiced, given that repeated vigorous actions provoke a weakening of mental processes, which ultimately affects the emotional dimension (Strong et al., 2005). Finally, it is necessary to take into account the type of sport practiced, individually or as a team, the duration of the practice, the frequency of sports practice, and adherence. All of these are factors that can affect self-concept to a greater or lesser extent (Berger, 1996).

The present study has some limitations which should be considered in future research, one of which is the limited size of our sample. Even though our study included 440 participants from Spain and Portugal, this number should be increased in order to establish more robust statistical conclusions. Furthermore, the high rate of attrition in the Portuguese sample could be due to lack of interest to participate in the study, since the tests were provided through a web link and thus anonymity was maintained. This problem could have been solved by making some additional reminders or by expanding the sample bias in other universities even if they are more widely spaced. The results demonstrated that the university students had lower self-perceptions than students at the high school, and also it seems to have scarce relation to the practice of PA. Therefore, it is necessary to encourage future longitudinal studies to investigate intra-participant information. In this way, a cause-effect relationship could be confirmed on the generalizable fluctuation of the adolescent's self-concept. In addition, these results provided could be predetermined by other school stages, which strengthens the idea of carrying out future longitudinal studies. Another future line of research could be to investigate the effect of the university transition on males versus females. It is believed that there are differences to consider and discuss due to academic, emotional, and hormonal changes which occur in both sexes at these ages. Finally, it is possible to broaden the study by evaluating the relationship between levels of obesity and self-concept dimensions before and after the transition to university. The hypothesis would be that since these students have lower self-concept (than their normal-weight counterparts) in the physical, emotional, and social dimensions before the transition, the reduction in self-concept after the transition would possibly be lower.

In conclusion, the main findings of this study indicate that, on the one hand, the academic, emotional, and physical dimensions of self-concept and in the level of PA are lower in university students, admitting certain differences in the two countries studied. On the other hand, there exists a positive relationship between the self-concept dimensions in general and the level of practice of PA, and conversely, a negative relationship between the self-concept dimensions and the amount of time the adolescent spends sitting. In addition, all measures were self-reported and, as such, they could be biased upwards. For this reason, these results and the conclusions of this study should be taken into consideration with caution. Although the results provided correspond to different samples (inter-participant differences) where the independent variable has not been manipulated, we consider that these results could be supported by others whose study belongs to a longitudinal design. These results reinforce the need to promote active lifestyles in adolescents with the objective of enhancing his well-being and development in this stage of his life. The practical application of these findings is to serve as a stimulus for the promotion of the practice of PA during the transition to university, as it is a critical period in the life of adolescents.

ETHICS STATEMENT

The study was approved by the Ethics Committee of the University of Granada (Spain) and followed the guidelines found in the Helsinki Declaration (2013) which establishes ethical principles for investigations using human beings and confidentiality.

AUTHOR CONTRIBUTIONS

WO-O and AC-R contributed conceptualization, data curation, methodology, project administration, resources, supervision, validation, writing – original draft and review and editing. JC-M and FM contributed formal analysis, funding acquisition, investigation, methodology, project administration, resources, supervision, visualization, writing – original draft and writing – review and editing.

REFERENCES

Akos, P., Rose, R. A., and Orthner, D. (2015). Sociodemographic moderators of middle school transition effects on academic achievement. *J. Early Adolesc.* 35, 170–198. doi: 10.1177/0272431614529367

Annesi, J. J. (2006). Relations of physical self-concept and self-efficacy with frequency of voluntary physical activity in preadolescents: implications for after-school care programming. *J. Psychosom. Res.* 61, 515–520. doi: 10.1016/j.jpsychores.2006.04.009

Annesi, J. J. (2010). Relationship of physical activity and weight loss in women with class II and class III obesity: mediation of exercise-induced changes in tension and depression. *Int. J. Clin. Health Psychol.* 10, 435–444. doi: 10.1155/2010/171957

Bean, M. K., Miller, S., Mazzeo, S. E., and Fries, E. A. (2012). Social cognitive factors associated with physical activity in elementary school girls. *Am. J. Health Behav.* 36, 265–274. doi: 10.5993/AJHB.36.2.11

Berger, B. G. (1996). Psychological benefits of an active lifestyle: what we know and what we need to know. *Quest* 48, 330–353. doi: 10.1080/00336297.1996.10484201

Blair, S. N., Sallis, R. E., Hutber, A., and Archer, E. (2012). Exercise therapy–the public health message. *Scand. J. Med. Sci. Sports* 22, e24–e28. doi: 10.1111/j.1600-0838.2012.01462.x

Booth, M. L. (2000). Assessment of physical activity: an international perspective. *Res. Q. Exerc. Sport* 71, 114–120. doi: 10.1080/02701367.2000.11082794

Cerkez, I., Culjak, Z., Zenic, N., Sekulic, D., and Kondric, M. (2015). Harmful alcohol drinking among adolescents: the influence of sport participation, religiosity and parental factors. *J. Child Adolesc. Subst. Abuse* 24, 94–101. doi: 10.1080/1067828X.2013.764372

Chen, S., Kim, Y., and Gao, Z. (2014). The contributing role of physical education in youth's daily physical activity and sedentary behavior. *BMC Public Health* 14, 1–7. doi: 10.1186/1471-2458-14-110

Chen, J. J., and Lee, Y. (2013). Physical activity for health: evidence, theory, and practice. *J. Prev. Med. Public Health* 46(Suppl. 1), S1–S2. doi: 10.3961/jpmph.2013.46.S.S1

Cocca, A., Liukkonen, J., Mayorga-Vega, D., and Viciana-Ramírez, J. (2014). Healthrelated physical activity levels in Spanish youth and young adults. *Percept. Mot. Skills* 118, 247–260. doi: 10.2466/10.06.PMS.118k16w1

Cole, T. J., Bellizzi, M. C., Flegal, K. M., and Dietz, W. H. (2000). Establishing a standard definition for child overweight and obesity worldwide: international survey. *BMJ* 320, 1–6. doi: 10.1136/bmj.320.7244.1240

Contreras, O. R., Fernández, J. G., García, L. M., Palou, P., and Ponseti, J. (2010). Relationship in adolescents between physical self-concept and participating in sport. *Rev. Psicol. Deporte* 19, 23–39.

Craig, C. L., Marshall, A. L., Sjorstrom, M., Bauman, A. E., Booth, M. L., Ainsworth, B. E., et al. (2003). International physical activity questionnaire: 12-country reliability and validity. *Med. Sci. Sports Exerc.* 35, 1381–1395. doi: 10.1249/01.MSS.0000078924.61453

Crocker, P. R. E., Eklund, R., and Kowalski, K. C. (2000). Children's physical activity and physical self-perceptions. *J. Sports Sci.* 18, 383–394. doi: 10.1080/02640410050074313

Du, H., Li, L., Whitlock, G., Bennett, D., Guo, Y., Bian, Z., et al. (2014). Patterns and socio-demographic correlates of domain-specific physical activities and their associations with adiposity in the China Kadoorie Biobank study. *BMC Public Health* 14, 1–10. doi: 10.1186/1471-2458-14-826

Esnaola, I., and Revuelta, L. (2009). Relations between the physical activity, physical self-concept, expectations, perceived value and perceived difficulty. *Acción Psicol.* 6, 31–43. doi: 10.5944/ap.6.2.219

Esnaola, I., Sesé, A., Antonio-Agirre, I., and Azpiazu, L. (2018). The development of multiple self-concept dimensions during adolescence. *J. Res. Adolesc.* doi: 10.1111/jora.12451 [Epub ahead of print]

Expósito, C., Fernández, E. J., Bartolomé, J., and Sáenz-López, P. (2012). Validation of the scale measure of the intention to be physically active in the university context. *Cuad. Psicol. Deporte* 12, 49–56. doi: 10.4321/S1578-84232012000200006

García, F., and Musitu, G. (2001). *Autoconcepto forma 5. AF5. Manual.* (Madrid: TEA).

Grandmontagne, A. G., and Fernández, A. R. (2004). Eating disorders, sport practice and physical self-concept in adolescents. *Actas Esp. Psiquiatr.* 32, 29–36.

Hagger, M. S., Biddle, S. J., and John Wang, C. K. (2005). Physical self-concept in adolescence: generalizability of a multidimensional, hierarchical model across gender and grade. *Educ. Psychol. Meas.* 65, 297–322. doi: 10.1177/0013164404272484

Hills, A. P., Dengel, D. R., and Lubans, D. R. (2015). Supporting public health priorities: recommendations for physical education and physical activity promotion in schools. *Prog. Cardiovasc. Dis.* 57, 368–374. doi: 10.1016/j.pcad.2014.09.010

Kohl, H. W., Craig, C. L., Lambert, E. V., Inoue, S., Alkandari, J. R., Leetongin, G., et al. (2012). The pandemic of physical inactivity: global action for public health. *Lancet* 380, 294–305. doi: 10.1016/S0140-6736(12)60898-8

Kokkinos, P. (2012). Physical activity, health benefits, and mortality risk. *ISRN Cardiol.* 2012, 1–14. doi: 10.5402/2012/718789

Lakens, D. (2013). Calculating and reporting effect sizes to facilitate cumulative science: a practical primer for t-tests and ANOVAs. *Front. Psychol.* 4:863. doi: 10.3389/fpsyg.2013.00863

Marsh, H. W. (1989). Age and sex effects in multiple dimensions of self-concept: preadolescence to early adulthood. *J. Educ. Psychol.* 81, 417–430. doi: 10.1037/0022-0663.81.3.417

Marsh, H. W., and Martin, A. J. (2011). Academic self-concept and academic achievement: relations and causal ordering. *Br. J. Educ. Psychol.* 81, 59–77. doi: 10.1348/000709910X503501

Marsh, H. W., and Redmayne, R. S. (1994). A multidimensional physical self-concept and its relations to multiple components of physical fitness. *J. Sport Exerc. Psychol.* 16, 43–55. doi: 10.1123/jsep.16.1.43

Moreno, J. A., Moreno, R., and Cervelló, E. (2007). The physical self-concept as predictor of the intention of being physically active. *Psicol. Salud* 17, 261–267.

Myers, J., Prakash, M., Froelicher, V., Do, D., Partington, S., and Atwood, J. E. (2002). Exercise capacity and mortality among men referred for exercise testing. *N. Engl. J. Med.* 346, 793–801. doi: 10.1056/NEJMoa011858

O'Donoghue, P. (2013). *Statistics for sport and exercise studies: An introduction.* (New York: Routledge).

Olds, T., Wake, M., Patton, G., Ridley, K., Waters, E., Williams, J., et al. (2009). How do school-day activity patterns differ with age and gender across adolescence? *J. Adolesc. Health* 44, 64–72. doi: 10.1016/j.jadohealth.2008.05.003

Owen, N., Salmon, J., Koohsari, M. J., Turrell, G., and Giles-Corti, B. (2014). Sedentary behavior and health: mapping environmental and social contexts to underpin chronic disease prevention. *Br. J. Sports Med.* 48, 174–177. doi: 10.1136/bjsports-2013-093107

Pallant, J. (2011). *SPSS survival manual. A step b& step guide to data analysis using SPSS.* 4th edn. (Crows Nest NSW: Allen & Unwin).

Pastor, Y., Balaguer, I., and García-Merita, M. (2006). The relationship between self-concept and healthy lifestyle in adolescence: an exploratory model. *Psicothema* 18, 18–24.

Pengpid, S., Peltzer, K., Kassean, H. K., Tsala, J. P. T., Sychareun, V., and Müller-Riemenschneider, F. (2015). Physical inactivity and associated factors among university students in 23 low-, middle-and high-income countries. *Int. J. Public Health* 60, 539–549. doi: 10.1007/s00038-015-0680-0

Rach, S., and Heinze, A. (2017). The transition from school to university in mathematics: which influence do school-related variables have? *Int. J. Sci. Math. Educ.* 15, 1343–1363. doi: 10.1007/s10763-016-9744-8

Reiner, M., Niermann, C., Jekauc, D., and Woll, A. (2013). Long-term health benefits of physical activity–a systematic review of longitudinal studies. *BMC Public Health* 13:813. doi: 10.1186/1471-2458-13-813

Roberts, S., Reeves, M., and Ryrie, A. (2015). The influence of physical activity, sport and exercise motives among UK-based university students. *J. Furth. High. Educ.* 39, 598–607. doi: 10.1080/0309877X.2014.938265

Rodriguez-Muñoz, S., Corella, C., Abarca-Sos, A., and Zaragoza, J. (2017). Validation of three short physical activity questionnaires with accelerometers among university students in Spain. *J. Sports Med. Phys. Fitness* 57, 1660–1668. doi: 10.23736/S0022-4707.17.06665-8

Rojas, C., Brante, M., Miranda, E., and Perez-Luco, R. (2011). Anxiety, depression and self-concept among morbid obese patients before and after bariatric surgery. *Revista medica de Chile* 139, 571–578. doi: 10.4067/s0034-98872011000500002

Romaguera, D., Tauler, P., Bennasar, M., Pericas, J., Moreno, C., Martinez, S., et al. (2011). Determinants and patterns of physical activity practice among Spanish university students. *J. Sports Sci.* 29, 989–997. doi: 10.1080/02640414.2011.578149

Rona, M. S., and Gokmen, H. (2005). The perception level of Gazi university students concerning the objectives of physical education. *Hacettepe Univ. J. Sport Sci.* 3, 13–22.

Salinas-Miranda, A. A., Salemi, J. L., King, L. M., Baldwin, J. A., Austin, D. A., Scarborough, K., et al. (2015). Adverse childhood experiences and health-related quality of life in adulthood: revelations from a community needs assessment. *Health Qual. Life Outcomes* 13, 1–12. doi: 10.1186/s12955-015-0323-4

Serra-Majem, L., Ribas, L., Ngo, J., Ortega, R. M., García, A., Pérez-Rodrigo, C., et al. (2004). Food, youth and the mediterranean diet in Spain. Development of KIDMED, mediterranean diet quality index in children and adolescents. *Public Health Nutr.* 7, 931–935. doi: 10.1079/PHN2004556

Sevil, J., Sánchez-Miguel, P. A., Pulido, J. J., Práxedes, A., and Sánchez-Oliva, D. (2018). Motivation and physical activity: differences between high school and university students in Spain. *Percept. Mot. Skills* 125, 894–907. doi: 10.1177/0031512518788743

Shavelson, R., Hubner, J., and Stanton, J. (1976). Self-concept: validation of construct interpretation. *Rev. Educ. Res.* 46, 407–441. doi: 10.3102/00346543046003407

Slutzky, C., and Simpkins, S. (2009). The link between children's sport participation and self-esteem: exploring the mediating role of sport self-concept. *Psychol. Sport Exerc.* 10, 381–389. doi: 10.1016/j.psychsport.2008.09.006

Smetana, J. G., Campione-Barr, N., and Metzger, A. (2006). Adolescent development in interpersonal and societal contexts. *Annu. Rev. Psychol.* 57, 255–284. doi: 10.1146/annurev.psych.57.102904.190124

Strong, W. B., Malina, R. M., Blimkie, C. J., Daniels, S. R., Dishman, R. K., Gutin, B., et al. (2005). Evidence based physical activity for school-age youth. *J. Pediatr.* 146, 732–737. doi: 10.1016/j.jpeds.2005.01.055

Ullrich-French, S., Cox, A. E., and Bumpus, M. F. (2013). Physical activity motivation and behavior across the transition to university. *Sport Exerc. Perform. Psychol.* 2, 90–101. doi: 10.1037/a0030632

Varela-Mato, V., Cancela, J. M., Ayan, C., Martín, V., and Molina, A. (2012). Lifestyle and health among Spanish university students: differences by gender and academic discipline. *Int. J. Environ. Res. Public Health* 10, 2728–2741. doi: 10.3390/ijerph9082728

Wanden-Berghe, C., Martín-Rodero, H., Rodríguez-Martín, A., Novalbos-Ruiz, J. P., Martínez de Victoria, E., Sanz-Valero, J., et al. (2015). Quality of life and its determinants in Spanish university students of health sciences factors. *Nutr. Hosp.* 31, 952–958. doi: 10.3305/nh.2015.31.2.8509

World Health Organization (2010). *Oral health surveys: Basic methods*. Geneva: World Health Organization.

World Health Organization (2016). *Obesity and overweight 2016.* Available at: http://www.who.int/mediacentre/factsheets/fs311/en/ (accessed February 13, 2019).

Zschucke, E., Gaudlitz, K., and Ströhle, A. (2013). Exercise and physical activity in mental disorders: clinical and experimental evidence. *J. Prev. Med. Public Health* 46(Suppl. 1), S12–S21. doi: 10.3961/jpmph.2013.46.S.S12

13

Effects of Service Learning on Physical Education Teacher Education Students' Subjective Happiness, Prosocial Behavior and Professional Learning

Oscar Chiva-Bartoll[1]*, Pedro Jesús Ruiz Montero*[2,3]**, Carlos Capella-Peris*[4] *and Celina Salvador-García*[5]

[1] Department of Education and Specific Didactics, Jaume I University, Castellón, Spain, [2] Department of Physical Education and Sport, Faculty of Education and Sport Sciences, University of Granada, Melilla, Spain, [3] Faculty of Education, University of Málaga, Málaga, Spain, [4] Department of Physical Education and Sport, University of Valencia, Valencia, Spain, [5] Faculty of Education, Universidad Internacional de la Rioja, Logroño, Spain

Correspondence:
Pedro Jesús Ruiz Montero
pedrorumo@uma.es

Purpose: This study aims to analyze the effects of a service learning (SL) program on the subjective happiness (SH), prosocial behavior (PB), and professional learning (PL) perceptions of Physical Education Teacher Education (PETE) students as well as to examine the correlations among these variables.

Methods: The study used a quasi-experimental design of two non-equivalent groups (control and experimental) comparing pre-test and post-test data. The instruments used were the Subjective Happiness Scale, the Prosocial and Civic Competence questionnaire, and the Impact of Service Learning during Initial Training of Physical Activity and Sports questionnaire.

Results: Data indicated that SL only had a significant influence on SH when the students compared themselves with their peers. On the other hand, the effect of SL on promoting PB and PL perceived was significant in several of their dimensions. Finally, the results showed a greater correlation of the perceived PL with the PB than with the SH.

Discussion/Conclusion: The results of the study provide educational researchers with valuable information to better understand how SL influences the training of PETE students.

Keywords: physical education, service learning, teacher training, social skills, personality

---

Abbreviations: IMAPS-AFD-FI, impact of service learning during initial training of physical activity and sports; PB, prosocial behavior; PCC, prosocial and civic competence; PETE, physical education teacher education; PL, professional learning; SH, subjective happiness; SHS, subjective happiness scale; SL, service learning.

INTRODUCTION

Physical Education Teacher Education (PETE) students require a break from traditional methodologies and demand new avenues that give them maximum prominence. Furthermore, there is no doubt that one of the aims of the current Physical Education lies in responding to the needs of the society of the XXI century (Metzler, 2017). In accordance with this view, SL is a teaching methodology that seeks to develop academic and professional competencies while providing community service to meet social needs (Capella-Peris et al., 2020).

The framework of SL is mainly based on the experiential learning theory proposed by Dewey (1938), which states that learning happens within a particular environment. In this regard, SL stimulates the acquisition of knowledge in a constructive way, favoring sociocultural learning and promoting active learning with the promotion of social justice (Jones and Kiser, 2014).

Various works in the field of PETE have shown that SL increases the students' knowledge of the curriculum as well as perceived applied skills (Galvan et al., 2018). This fact reinforces the idea that SL represents a great opportunity to develop professional skills combining both theory and practice. Several studies have also analyzed the effect of SL academically and professionally (Galvan et al., 2018; Capella-Peris et al., 2020), while other works have focused on the impact of this teaching method from a social standpoint (Domangue and Carson, 2008; Gil-Gómez et al., 2015; Whitley et al., 2017).

The present work intends to go a step further, not only analyzing the social and professional skills developed through SL but also considering its influence on the subjective happiness of PETE students. The SL intervention analyzed in this study was implemented in the particular context of Melilla, an autonomous Spanish city located in the north coast of the African continent. Due to its geographical position, this city has many unique features, chief among which is the composition of its population. High immigration rates, together with a high number of people from disadvantaged sociocultural environments and/or at risk of social exclusion as disabled older adults, create a context where the well-being of a large segment of its inhabitants is in question.

In disadvantaged social contexts like this, SL could help students gain not only well-being but also a deeper understanding of the community they live in. In this sense, students who have participated in SL programs have improved on their engagement with and learning about the community (Pak, 2018). This issue is relevant because students learn to develop a sense of belonging to a place when they are given the opportunity to help build their community, and this process not only improves their well-being but also helps instill a belief that they can make a valuable impact in their community (Williams, 2016).

The most important aspect of well-being – but at the same time the most controversial – is happiness. It is subject to debate because it can vary according to each person. In addition, happiness is associated with other concepts such as satisfaction, pleasantness, goodness, positivity, and a meaningful and/or full life (Ruysschaert, 2014).

Some studies have confirmed a positive effect of SL on student happiness in different social environments, for example, a SL intervention carried out by university students with adolescents with low resources in Mongolia (Shu-Chin and Tzong-Heng, 2016) or a SL intervention carried out by pre-service teachers with minors with special educational needs in Spain (Capella-Peris et al., 2020).

On its part, PB in SL contexts refers to a wide range of attitudes motivated by a genuine desire to benefit others without any expectation of benefit to oneself (Gil-Gómez et al., 2016). These include altruism, empathy, cooperation, honesty, humility, kindness, the ability to share and help others, and the desire to volunteer and make donations (Padilla-Walker and Carlo, 2014). This leads to a positive relationship between the implementation of SL and the development of PB of the participant students (Gil-Gómez et al., 2016). In this vein, SL activities, even programs with limited intensity and duration, have been found to be related to a number of positive outcomes related to the participants' sense of social responsibility as well as self-efficacy and prosocial behavior (Lim, 2007). However, it is necessary to deepen our understanding of this issue by specifically focusing on PETE students in multicultural contexts.

In addition, in PETE training settings, evidence supports that SL can develop PL such as evaluation skills, emotional engagement, and cognitive readiness with the community (Chambers and Lavery, 2012; Seban, 2013), perceived competency as teachers, and several teaching strategies (Galvan et al., 2018). Moreover, SL stands as a favorable opportunity to develop Physical Education competencies, combining theory and practice in the same activity (Wilkinson et al., 2013).

The objective of the study is to analyze the effects of SL on the SH, PB, and PL perceptions of PETE students as well as to examine the correlations among these variables.

MATERIALS AND METHODS

Research Settings

This study follows the model-based practice within Physical Education to investigate pedagogical models. Thus, it presents the three key elements stated by Hastie and Casey (2014): description of the curricular elements, validation of model implementation, and a description of the program context.

The SL project was implemented at the Faculty of Education and Sport Sciences, Melilla campus, which is part of the University of Granada (Spain). The contents of the courses involved were: (1) body expression and games, (2) evaluation of teaching of Physical Education and Sport, and (3) planning and organizing sport systems and activities. These are the subjects of the PETE program and, among others, they aim to develop the following competencies detailed in the curriculum:

- Design, develop, and evaluate the teaching-learning processes related to physical activity and sport, considering the individual and contextual characteristics of people.
- Evaluate physical condition and prescribe health-oriented physical exercise.

- Promote and evaluate the creation of long-lasting and autonomous physical activity and sport habits among different populations.
- Plan, develop, and evaluate the performance of recreational physical activities.
- Select and know how to use appropriate sports equipment for each recreational physical activity.

The service that the students offered consisted of providing the disadvantaged population of Melilla with opportunities for the practice of healthy, recreational, and educational physical activity. The structure of the SL program, following the recommendations of Jacoby (2015), was based on Kolb's learning stages (Kolb, 1984). Initially, a stage of concrete experience was carried out, focused on establishing the students' initial contact with specific community problems (involving a broad range of cultural, social, religious, and physical characteristics). After this phase came the reflection stage, in which the pupils had to focus on observation and reflection to propose an action plan based on the academic subjects involved. After that, the students defined the specific needs to be met. Therefore, they theoretically examined the topics and concepts worked to link the tasks proposed with the academic contents. The execution of the tasks made up the program's active experimentation phase.

Design

Given the aims of the study, this work implemented a quasi-experimental design of two non-equivalent groups (experimental and control) with pre-test and post-test measures to compare how the participation in a SL program based on physical activity promotion affected the SH, PB, and PL of PETE students. In addition, to deepen on the analysis, the correlations among these variables were also analyzed.

Participants

A total of 104 students (average age was 22.9 ± 2.5 years) from the Sport Science and Primary School Bachelor Degree participated in the study. They belong to the fifth year – "Assessment of the Physical Activity and Sports Teaching" – and third year – "Body Expression and Games" – of the Bachelor Degree subjects. The control group, which took the course following traditional methodologies, consisted of 55 students (53%), with an average age of 22.7 ± 3.5 years. On the other hand, 49 students (47%), with an average age of 23.2 ± 1.4 years, participated in the SL program. These composed the experimental group. **Table 1** shows the most outstanding sociodemographic characteristics of the participants.

TABLE 1 | Sociodemographic characteristics of the sample.

	Control group (n = 55)	Experimental group (n = 49)
Sex		
Female	8 (15%)	6 (12%)
Male	47 (85%)	43 (88%)
Religion		
Catholic	37 (67%)	31 (63%)
Muslim	8 (15%)	3 (6%)
None	10 (18%)	15 (31%)
Attendance rate		
Has not attended class	–	–
Less than 25%	–	–
Between 25–50%	–	–
Between 50–75%	3 (6%)	2 (4%)
Between 75–90%	15 (27%)	6 (12%)
More than 90%	37 (67%)	41 (84%)
Previous experience of volunteering or SL		
With previous experience	19 (35%)	11 (22%)
No previous experience	36 (65%)	38 (78%)

Instrument and Procedures

Subjective Happiness Scale

The Spanish version of the SHS has been used to assess the degree of SH of the participating students (Extremera and Fernández-Berrocal, 2014). This version has been validated for use with youngsters and adults. The four-item instrument measures subjective happiness, asking the participants either to self-rate themselves or to compare themselves to others. Each item is scored on a Likert-type scale from one (the lowest value) to seven (the highest value).

Prosocial and Civic Competence

This instrument has been used to analyze the promotion of PB in the implementation of SL projects in the field by PETE students (Gil-Gómez et al., 2016); it was thus deemed to be an ideal tool for the current study. The PCC questionnaire consists of 31 items distributed along six dimensions: compliance with social norms (three items), social sensitivity (six items), help and collaboration (four items), security and firmness in interaction (eight items), prosocial leadership (four items), and social responsibility (six items). As in the previous case, the answer options are presented on a Likert-type scale from one (strongly disagree) to five (strongly agree).

Impact of Service Learning During Initial Training of Physical Activity and Sports

This questionnaire was designed specifically to assess the PL perceptions of students when participating in SL programs. The IMAPS-AFD-FI is a validated tool to analyze SL experiences in the context of Physical Education (García-Rico et al., 2019). This instrument consists of 41 items distributed across seven categories: context identification (nine open questions), learning (five items), pedagogical value (seven items), social impact (six items), professional development (four items), professional skills (seven items), and experience opinion (three items and one open-ended question). With the exception of the first part and the last open-ended question, the remainders of the items are answered using a five-point Likert-type scale from 1 (totally disagree) to 5 (totally agree). Given the quantitative nature of our research, the open questions of the IMAPS-AFD-FI were not used in this work.

Data Analysis

The Kolmogorov–Smirnov test was used to determine the normality of the data. After extracting the mean and standard deviation as descriptive statistics, the p-value was calculated using the Wilcoxon test for related samples in order to identify significant differences. Regarding the pre-test and post-test differences between the control and the experimental groups, the Mann–Whitney U test was used for two independent samples. This process was carried out with regard to the SHS and the PCC instrument in the control and the experimental groups and with respect to the PL perceived in the SL program (IMAPS-AFD-FI) in the experimental group. The effect size was calculated using Cohen's d value. It can be interpreted as small ($0.2 < d < 0.5$), medium ($0.5 < d < 0.8$), or large ($0.8 < d$) (Cohen, 1992). The Spearman correlation coefficient was used to determine the relationships between the dimensions of the SHS, PCC, and IMAPS-AFD-FI. The correlation can be interpreted as very weak ($0 < rp < 0.2$), weak ($0.2 \leq rp < 0.4$), moderate ($0.4 \leq rp < 0.6$), strong ($0.6 \leq rp < 0.8$), and very strong ($0.8 \leq rp < 1$). All statistical analyses were performed with the Statistical Package for the Social Sciences (SPSS, v.23.0 for Windows, SPSS Inc., Chicago, IL, United States).

RESULTS

The data analysis showed that the SL program slightly improved the SH of the students, obtaining significant results ($p < 0.05$) in one of the four items of the SHS scale ("compared with most of my peers, I consider myself."). In contrast, in the control group, there was no significant difference in any item. On the other hand, while analyzing the effect of SL on PB, it was found that improvement in the students of the experimental group was notable. There were significant differences in four of the six items of the PCC questionnaire: accordance with social norms and prosocial leadership (both $p < 0.01$), social sensitivity, and security and firmness in interaction (both $p < 0.05$). The improvement is much less noticeable in the control group, where significant improvements are obtained only with respect to compliance with social norms. All of these points to a marked effect of SL on the promotion of students' PB. **Table 2** presents the results of the different variables of the SHS and PCC questionnaires in both groups, analyzed before and after the intervention.

Regarding the PL perceptions of the SL program, the experimental group showed significant improvements ($p < 0.05$) in four of the six items of the IMAPS-AFD-FI instrument: learning, social impact perceived, professional skills, and opinion. This suggests that the impact of the SL program was notable in the PL perceived by the students. **Table 3** shows the results related to the analysis of this variable (IMAPS-AFD-FI) in the experimental group.

Regarding the relationship of the analyzed aspects, it was significant in 34 of 60 possible cases. Of those, 20 had a level of significance of $p < 0.01$, while 14 had a level of significance of $p < 0.05$. All were positive; there was a moderate degree of correlation ($0.4 \leq rp < 0.6$) in 25 cases and a strong degree of correlation ($0.6 \leq rp < 0.8$) in nine cases. When

TABLE 3 | Analysis of the satisfaction of SL on the experimental group.

	Experimental group (n = 49)			
	Pre-test	**Post-test**	p	d
Professional learning perceived (IMAPS-AFD-FI)				
Learning	3.84 (0.18)	4.45 (0.45)	0.001*	−0.664
Pedagogical value	4.12 (0.42)	4.33 (0.46)	0.147	−0.231
Social impact	3.91 (0.45)	4.02 (0.52)	0.027*	−0.112
Professional development	3.22 (0.81)	3.40 (0.78)	0.389	−0.112
Professional skills	3.71 (0.48)	4.01 (0.56)	0.031*	−0.276
Opinion	3.29 (1.02)	3.94 (0.83)	0.003*	−0.329

*$p < 0.05$.

TABLE 2 | Analysis of subjective happiness and prosocial and civic competencies in control and experimental groups.

	Control group (n = 55)				Experimental group (n = 49)			
	Pre-test	**Post-test**	p	d	**Pre-test**	**Post-test**	p	d
Subjective happiness (SH)								
In general, I consider myself...	4.58 (0.22)	4.74 (1.06)	0.769	−0.103	5.44 (0.65)	5.59 (0.87)	0.46	−0.097
Compared with most of my classmates, I consider myself...	4.43 (1.19)	4.76 (1.48)	0.316	−0.121	4.96 (1.01)	5.41 (1.42)	0.046*	−0.179
Some people are generally very happy...	4.91 (1.18)	5.01 (1.54)	0.714	−0.036	5.07 (1.69)	5.53 (1.71)	0.262	−0.134
Some people are generally not very happy...	2.67 (1.49)	2.83 (1.43)	0.144	−0.054	2.37 (1.34)	2.51 (1.55)	0.541	−0.048
Prosocial and civic competencies (PCC)								
Compliance with social norms	4.38 (0.39)	4.56 (0.34)	0.030*	−0.238	4.43 (0.33)	4.77 (0.55)	0.004**	−0.351
Social sensitivity	4.21 (0.35)	4.37 (0.46)	0.250	−0.192	4.02 (0.11)	4.34 (0.25)	0.039*	−0.637
Help and collaboration	4.03 (0.65)	4.34 (0.61)	0.126	−0.238	4.03 (0.31)	4.08 (0.41)	0.509	−0.068
Security and firmness in interaction	3.63 (0.61)	3.91 (0.67)	0.210	−0.213	3.74 (0.57)	3.87 (0.53)	0.024*	−0.117
Prosocial leadership	3.51 (0.90)	3.76 (0.64)	0.413	−0.158	3.61 (0.59)	3.92 (0.51)	0.008**	−0.271
Social responsibility	3.11 (0.24)	3.35 (0.43)	0.139	−0.325	3.19 (0.38)	3.35 (0.31)	0.152	−0.224

*$p < 0.05$; **$p < 0.01$.

analyzing separately the relationship between each scale of the IMAPS-AFD-FI and SHS, eight significant records of 24 possible are obtained, four of them with a level of significance of $p < 0.01$ and four with a level of significance of $p < 0.05$. All of them were positive, with a moderate degree of correlation ($0.4 \leq rp < 0.6$) in seven cases and with a strong degree of correlation ($0.6 \leq rp < 0.8$) in one case. In contrast, the relationship between IMAPS-AFD-FI and PCC instrument items was significant in 26 of 36 possible cases – 16 of them with a level of significance of $p < 0.01$ and 10 with a level of significance of $p < 0.05$; all of them were positive, with a moderate degree of correlation ($0.4 \leq rp < 0.6$) in 18 cases and strong degree of correlation ($0.6 \leq rp < 0.8$) in eight cases. When analyzing these data, it is verified that the results of the IMAPS-AFD-FI instrument show a greater link with the PCC questionnaire than with the SHS. **Table 4** presents the analysis performed which display the relation between the PL perceived in SL (IMAPS-AFD-FI) on SH and PCC in the experimental group.

DISCUSSION

Results related to SH indicated that, in our study, SL had a limited influence on it, although the literature presents mixed positions. On the one hand, several studies show that spending time helping other people is associated with improvements in one's well-being due to the promotion of social integration (Musick and Wilson, 2003; Gil-Gómez et al., 2016; Mesurado et al., 2019). On the other hand, there are studies in line with our results (i.e., indicating that SL is not always associated with an improvement in the students' well-being). These studies highlight different causes that can affect this variable. Standing out above all others, SL may make students recognize the problems suffered by the people receiving the service, which, consequently, could produce a feeling of unhappiness after the SL participation (Chiva-Bartoll et al., 2018). In the present investigation, the results could have been influenced by the fact that people who live in areas with higher rates of social inequality tend to consider themselves unhappier (Laurence, 2019). Thus, the fact that the SL program had been developed in a city with high rates of inequality could have affected the SH of the students, too.

Despite having found that SL has little influence on the SH of the students, it is interesting to emphasize that one of the four variables that comprise the SHS questionnaire obtained a significant improvement. It was the one that referred to the feeling of happiness compared with other people. In this case, as previously stated, it could be due to the increase of cultural and social awareness generated by the participation in the SL program (Sewry and Paphitis, 2018). In fact, one of the basic objectives of SL lies in the acquisition of a deeper knowledge of the problems that a disadvantaged sector of the population must face (Kronick et al., 2011). Thus, participating in the SL program could have made the students aware of the difficult situation in which the recipients of the service live, generating a rethinking of their own well-being in comparison to those of others (Sewry and Paphitis, 2018).

With regard to the effect of SL on the promotion of PB, the outcome for the members of the experimental group was notable. These findings are in line with those of other studies which have proposed that PB is incentivized through empathy and practical experience (Mesurado et al., 2019). Thus, this approach is also in line with various studies that found a positive impact of SL on the development of empathy (Lee et al., 2018).

Analyzing the elements of the PCC scale individually, the improvements in items relating to *security* and *firmness in interactions* are linked to a loss of uncertainty and fear caused by working with disadvantaged groups in the SL program as well as the breaking of preconceived stereotypes (Cabedo et al., 2018; Chiva-Bartoll et al., 2019, 2020). Previous studies have indicated effects in this regard when working with groups at risk of social exclusion in Uganda (Grain et al., 2019) and through raising the students' awareness of their similarities with the service beneficiaries (Andreoletti and Howard, 2018). Normally, the students tend to show prior suspicion toward the intervention. After several sessions though, their safety tends to increase and they end up requesting a greater number of SL practices (Reynaud et al., 2013). This fact also has precedents in the field of Physical Education.

Improvements in *prosocial leadership*, as were seen in this investigation, are thought to be closely linked to concepts such as humility and social equality (Owens et al., 2019). Moreover, effective communication is also key to promoting prosocial leadership when educational entities provide services to the community (Sanders et al., 2019). In our case, the development of both constructs was associated with the management and direction of game sessions and physical exercises with migrant children and youth and the older adults. The use of SL as well as the implementation of other active methodologies has also been reported to have positive effects on prosocial leadership skills (Celio et al., 2011; Dingel and Wei, 2014; Sun et al., 2017).

In relation to the improvement of the students' *social sensitivity*, the results of a study with Colombian university students who worked with 540 pupils point in the same direction as that of ours (Duque, 2018). In addition, due to indirect effects, the development of social sensitivity has been suggested to be linked to the development of social justice (Jones and Kiser, 2014) as well as social skills and citizen participation (Whitley et al., 2017). In any case, this result is not surprising since there are previous findings about the social impact of SL in the sensitivity and the social interpretation of the students involved (Mesurado et al., 2019).

Some studies have found improvements in the *accordance with social norms* (Gil-Gómez et al., 2016). Thus, the students could have understood and accepted the rules of coexistence that govern or function the recipients of the service. However, the control group also showed a significant improvement related to this dimension. This could be due to Melilla's special social context (i.e., in that living in a place with obvious social inequality can produce respect for people with authority and acceptance of the rules of coexistence) (Kronick et al., 2011). Therefore, it cannot be assumed that the improvements in the experimental group were exclusively due to the implementation of the SL program.

TABLE 4 | Spearman correlation between the PL perceived on SL (IMAPS-AFD-FI), subjective happiness (SH), and prosocial and civic competencies (PCC) in the experimental group (post-test).

SL impact (IMAPS-AFD-FI)	Subjective happiness (SH)				Prosocial and civic competencies (PCC)					
	1	2	3	4	5	6	7	8	9	10
Learning	0.553**	0.382	0.414*	−0.254	0.607**	0.752**	0.497*	0.534**	0.629*	0.409*
Pedagogical value	0.599**	0.276	0.372	−0.384	0.589**	0.744**	0.469*	0.491*	0.578**	0.331
Social impact	0.418*	0.204	0.340	−0.165	0.347	0.485*	0.398	0.298	0.436*	0.181
Professional development	0.247	0.169	0.376	−0.193	0.233	0.208	0.381	0.532**	0.430*	0.095
Professional skills	0.609**	0.423*	0.557*	−0.373	0.562**	0.681**	0.652**	0.637**	0.683**	0.419*
Opinion	0.563**	0.374	0.371	−0.245	0.555**	0.583**	0.522**	0.525**	0.487*	0.306

$^{*}p < 0.05$; $^{**}p < 0.01$. SH = 1 – In general, I consider myself . . .; 2 – Compared with most of my classmates, I consider myself . . .; 3 – Some people are generally very happy . . .; 4 – Some people are generally not very happy . . .; CCP = 5 – Compliance with social norms; 6 – Social sensitivity; 7 – Help and collaboration; 8 – Security and firmness in the interaction; 9 – Prosocial leadership; 10 – Social responsibility.

It would therefore be appropriate to carry out further research on this issue.

Finally, the results related to the factors of *help and collaboration* and *social responsibility* were surprising as no significant differences were found, while previous studies found improvements in both aspects after implementing SL (Whitley et al., 2017). As in the previous case, this result evinces a need for additional research on the topic.

Regarding the PL perceived by the students of the SL program, numerous works have addressed this issue before with similar results (Domangue and Carson, 2008; Ward et al., 2017; Whitley et al., 2017; Galvan et al., 2018; Capella-Peris et al., 2020).

A separate analysis of the elements of the IMAPS-AFD-FI scale revealed a prominent effect on student-applied learning (Kassabgy and El-Din, 2013). This improvement has been linked to the value of the practical experience gained from SL (Baldwin et al., 2007; Robinson and Meyer, 2012). Likewise, the interventions in small groups, where all members provide efficient solutions and give reciprocal feedback, lead to the consolidation of curricular learning in a globalized way (Short et al., 2019). Recent studies indicate that SL facilitates the acquisition of knowledge related to inclusive pedagogy and social values. In a more personal way, other studies argue that SL is very useful for students as it helps them imagine the future that awaits them in their work and/or social life and arouses curiosity about working with different groups in their closest social context. University students benefit the most from any type of SL intervention since it will help them step outside of their comfort zone (Kassabgy and El-Din, 2013). Thus, thanks to their participation in the project, PETE students were able to learn more about the different groups that make up Melilla's particular social reality.

Regarding *professional skills* – a dimension closely linked to learning – it appears that such competence has been developed thanks to the implementation of different teaching strategies (that allowed students to self-assess in real-life situations). Therefore, it is understood that real-world experiences play a decisive role in the development of professional skills (Brown and Bright, 2017). Another variable of great importance in this regard is the intrinsic motivation of the students, establishing that those with greater motivation can develop professional skills in a more effective way (Shin et al., 2018). However, not all SL programs stimulate professional skills in the same way. Some studies indicate that this improvement may be limited by a lack of connection between the curriculum of the course and the service provided (Segal-Engelchin et al., 2017). Therefore, the relationship between academic content and the intervention must be clear to maximize the benefits of SL.

The effect of SL on the *opinion* dimension refers to various issues. On the one hand, there is an improvement of *critical and reflective thinking*, a widely documented result in research on the application of SL (Carrington et al., 2015). On the other hand, there is a positive change regarding the students' vision on various issues, such as the beneficiaries of the service or the methodology itself. It is thus recommended that, in order to improve the opinion of students regarding the SL implementation, it must have the support of the institutions. In addition, collaboration agreements should be set up as soon as possible and students should be involved as much as possible in all decision processes (Playford et al., 2019).

The results across the three previous dimensions indicate the potentially significant impact of SL on PETE students. Such findings have been confirmed academically and socially, suggesting that SL is an optimal tool for educational institutions for addressing social transformation issues (Whitley et al., 2017; Capella-Peris et al., 2020). On the other hand, despite observing improvements in the variables of pedagogical value and professional development, they were not statistically significant. This was unexpected since they are closely related to the dimensions of both learning and professional skills. Thus, it seems to be appropriate to deepen on the investigation of these variables in order to derive new results.

Lastly, the results obtained by Spearman correlations reinforce the results described in the preceding lines. Thus, the results have shown that there are certain significant correlations between SH and SL, mainly, the one referring to their own *happiness* and *professional skills*. The reason for this may be that, as mentioned in previous paragraphs, participation in SL makes them reconsider their own happiness (Sewry and Paphitis, 2018). They recognize their comfortable social position in comparison to the recipients of the service and see the benefits related to the professional skills linked to their university studies they are gaining (Celio et al., 2011).

On the other hand, many correlations between the PCC and the impact of SL show a close relationship between the impact produced by SL and the development of PB (Lim, 2007). Although most of the components had significant correlations, the dimension of *professional skills* of the IMAPS-AFD-FI and *prosocial leadership* on the PCC obtained the strongest correlations. This suggests that SL can have a positive effect on prosocial leadership and the development of professional skills in the students. It also suggests that the greater the impact of SL, the more PB the student develops (Celio et al., 2011).

Although promising results have been obtained in this research, there are several limitations that must be considered. It is true that the results cannot be generalized categorically because of the sample size in the present study. In addition, the fact that the students were selected by means of convenience sampling must be considered, as a randomized controlled trial would have strengthened the validity of this study (Zirkel et al., 2015). However, this work – which used validated questionnaires – has allowed us to deepen our knowledge about the impact of SL in the field of teacher training and to provide relevant information to the academic world.

Regarding future research opportunities, these results also open the door to new research in the field of SL since, although there are clear improvements (especially in terms of the development of PB and about the impact of SL), it would be interesting to continue deepening on this field by analyzing SL programs of different lengths and intensities. It would also be helpful to use larger samples that would allow generalizing the results. In addition, in order to continue studying the relationship between SH and SL, investigations could be carried out in different social contexts. Those results could be contrasted with ours, which would help to reveal the circumstances where SL is an effective tool for helping to improve student welfare. Similarly, it would be promising to open research lines that analyze the impact of this educational approach throughout the entire teaching–learning process and analyzing its long-term effects on students, recipients, and society.

CONCLUSION

Overall the application of the SL program had a positive impact on PB and perceived PL of PETE students. In addition, it was found that both effects were highly interrelated, indicating a reciprocal relationship between them. On the other hand, there were no improvements in SH, which could be due to the awareness of the social problems that the SL caused in the students involved.

SL programs are being increasingly used at different levels and educational stages (Celio et al., 2011), so more research in order to deepen our understanding of its implications on PETE students is needed. The present study has contributed in this regard by providing relevant information for all those academics and/or professors interested in this pedagogical method. In addition, it has introduced new and interesting lines of research that can favor the improvement of SL, the understanding of the effects on the individuals' well-being, and the personal development of the students involved.

ETHICS STATEMENT

The studies involving human participants were reviewed and approved by Ethics Committee on Human Research of the University of Granada. The patients/participants provided their written informed consent to participate in this study.

AUTHOR CONTRIBUTIONS

OC-B and PR conceived the presented idea and designed the study. PR and CC-P organized the database and performed the statistical analysis. OC-B wrote the first draft of the manuscript. OC-B, PR, and CS-G reviewed the methodological sections of the manuscript. All of the authors contributed to the manuscript revision and read and approved the submitted version.

ACKNOWLEDGMENTS

We would like to specially thank to all of the students who participated in this study. We would also like to thank as well to the Social Service of Melilla (farm school "Gloria Fuertes"), youth center and residence for the elderly "Gota de Leche" and NGO "Melilla Acoge," "UGR-Solidarity Unit," and Plan FIDO 2018, Quality and Innovation Unit. Finally, thanks to the ENDAVANT group of the Universitat Jaume I (UJI-A2019-01).

REFERENCES

Andreoletti, C., and Howard, J. L. (2018). Bridging the generation gap: intergenerational service-learning benefits young and old. *Gerontol. Geriat.Educ.* 39, 46–60. doi: 10.1080/02701960.2016.1152266

Baldwin, S. C., Buchanan, A. M., and Rudisill, M. E. (2007). What teacher candidates learned about diversity, social justice, and themselves from service-learning experiences. *J. Teach. Educ.* 58, 315–327. doi: 10.1177/0022487107305259

Brown, K. M., and Bright, L. M. (2017). Teaching caring and competence: student transformation during an older adult focused service-learning course. *Nurse Educ. Pract.* 27, 29–35. doi: 10.1016/j.nepr.2017.08.013

Cabedo, L., Royo, M., Moliner, L., and Guraya, T. (2018). University social responsibility towards engineering undergraduates: the effect of methodology on a service-learning experience. *Sustainability* 10:1823. doi: 10.3390/su10061823

Capella-Peris, C., Gil-Gómez, J., and Chiva-Bartoll, O. (2020). Innovative analysis of service-learning effects in physical education: a mixed methods approach. *J. Teach.Phys. Educ.* 39, 102–110. doi: 10.1123/jtpe.2019-0030

Carrington, S., Mercer, K. L., Iyer, R., and Selva, G. (2015). The impact of transformative learning in a critical service-learning program on teacher development: building a foundation for inclusive teaching. *Reflective Pract.* 16, 61–72. doi: 10.1080/14623943.2014.969696

Celio, C. I., Durlak, J., and Dymnicki, A. (2011). A meta-analysis of the impact of service-learning on students. *J. Exp. Educ.* 34, 164–181. doi: 10.5193/JEE34.2.164

Chambers, D. J., and Lavery, S. (2012). Service-learning: a valuable component of pre-service teacher education. *Austr. J. Teach. Educ.* 37, 128–137. doi: 10.14221/ajte.2012v37n4.2

Chiva-Bartoll, O., Capella-Peris, C., and Salvador-García, C. (2020). Service-learning in physical education teacher education: towards a critical and inclusive perspective. *J. Educ. Teach.* 46. doi: 10.1080/02607476.2020.1733400

Chiva-Bartoll, O., Gil-Gómez, J., and Zorrilla-Silvestre, L. (2019). Improving the effective personality of preservice Teachers through service-learning: a physical education Approach. *Rev. Investig. Educ.* 2, 327–343. doi: 10.6018/rie.37.2.303331

Chiva-Bartoll, O., Pallarès-Piquer, M., and Gil-Gómez, J. (2018). Aprendizaje-servicio y mejora de la Personalidad Eficaz en futuros docentes de Educación Física. *Rev. Compl. Educ.* 29, 181–197. doi: 10.5209/RCED.52164

Cohen, J. (1992). A power primer. *Psychol. Bull.* 112, 155–159.

Dewey, J. (1938). *Experience and Education*. New York, NY: Macmillan.

Dingel, M., and Wei, W. (2014). Influences on peer evaluation in a group project: an exploration of leadership, demographics and course performance. *Assess. Eval. Higher Educ.* 39, 729–742. doi: 10.1080/02602938.2013.867477

Domangue, E., and Carson, R. L. (2008). Preparing culturally competent teachers: service-learning and physical education teacher education. *J. Teach. Phys. Educ.* 27, 347–367. doi: 10.1123/jtpe.27.3.347

Duque, E. (2018). Evaluando una experiencia de aprendizaje servicio en torno al aprendizaje de conceptos de la ciudadanía digital. *RIDAS Rev. Iberoam. Aprendizaje Servic.* 5, 12–23. doi: 10.1344/RIDAS2018.5.2

Extremera, N., and Fernández-Berrocal, P. (2014). The subjective happiness scale: translation and preliminary psychometric evaluation of a spanish version. *Soc. Ind. Res.* 119, 473–481. doi: 10.1007/s11205-013-0497-2

Galvan, C., Meaney, K., and Gray, V. (2018). Examining the reciprocal nature of service-learning for underserved students and preservice teachers. *J. Teach. Phys. Educ.* 37, 363–372. doi: 10.1123/jtpe.2018-0051

García-Rico, L., Santos-Pastor, M. L., and Martínez-Muñoz, L. F. (2019). "La perspectiva del alumnado universitario de actividad físico-deportiva sobre la repercusión del aprendizaje-servicio para su formación inicial," in *Metodologías Activas en Ciencias del Deporte*, Vol. II, eds P. J. Ruiz, and A. Baena, (Sevilla: Wanceulen Editorial.), 135–158.

Gil-Gómez, J., Chiva-Bartoll, Ò, and Martí-Puig, M. (2015). The impact of service learning on the training of pre-service teachers. Analysis from a physical education subject. *Eur. Phys. Educ. Rev.* 21, 467–484. doi: 10.1177/1356336x15582358

Gil-Gómez, J., Moliner-García, O., Chiva-Bartoll, O., and García, R. (2016). Una experiencia de aprendizaje-servicio en futuros docentes: desarrollo de la competencia social y ciudadana. *Rev. Compl. Educ.* 27, 53–73. doi: 10.5209/rev_RCED.2016.v27.n1.45071

Grain, K., Katumba, T., Kirumira, D., Nakasiita, R., Nakayenga, S., Nankya, E., et al. (2019). Co-constructing knowledge in Uganda: host community conceptions of relationships in international service-learning. *J.Exp. Educ.* 42, 22–36. doi: 10.1177/1053825918820677

Hastie, P. A., and Casey, A. (2014). Fidelity in models-based practice research in sport pedagogy: a guide for future investigations. *J. Teach. Phys. Educ.* 33, 422–431. doi: 10.1123/jtpe.2013-0141

Jacoby, B. (2015). *Service-Learning Essentials*. San Francisco, CA: Campus Compact-Jossey-Bass.

Jones, A. L., and Kiser, P. M. (2014). Conceptualizing criticality as a guiding principle for high quality academic service learning. *Int. J. Teach. Learn. Higher Educ.* 26, 147–156.

Kassabgy, N., and El-Din, Y. S. (2013). Investigating the impacts of an experiential service-learning course. *TESOL J.* 4, 571–586. doi: 10.1002/tesj.92

Kolb, D. (1984). *Experiential Learning: Experience as the Source of Learning and Development*. Englewood Cliffs, NJ: Prentice Hall.

Kronick, R. F., Cunningham, R. B., and Gourley, M. (2011). *Experiencing Service Learning*. Knoxville, TN: University of Tennessee Press.

Laurence, J. (2019). Community disadvantage, inequalities in adolescent subjective well-being, and local social relations: the role of positive and negative social interactions. *Soc. Sci. Med.* 237, 112442. doi: 10.1016/j.socscimed.2019.112442

Lee, S. J., Wilder, C., and Yu, C. (2018). Exploring students' perceptions of service-learning experiences in an undergraduate web design course. *Teach. Higher Educ.* 23, 212–226. doi: 10.1080/13562517.2017.1379486

Lim, K. M. (2007). "Development of prosocial values: service learning as a strategy," in *Youth guidance: Issues, Interventions & Reflections*, eds H. W. E. Lui, and S. S. Wong, (Singapore: Pearson Education), 28–40.

Mesurado, B., Distefano, M. J., Robiolo, G., and Richaud, M. C. (2019). The Hero program: development and initial validation of an intervention program to promote prosocial behavior in adolescents. *J. Soc. Pers. Relationsh.* 36, 2566–2584. doi: 10.1177/0265407518793224

Metzler, M. (2017). *Instructional Models in Physical Education. Routlegde*. London: Taylor and Francis Group, doi: 10.4324/9781315213521

Musick, M. A., and Wilson, J. (2003). Volunteering and depression: the role of psychological and social resources in different age groups. *Soc. Sci. Med.* 56, 259–269. doi: 10.1016/S0277-9536(02)00025-4

Owens, B. P., Yam, K. C., Bednar, J. S., Mao, J., and Hart, D. W. (2019). The impact of leader moral humility on follower moral self-efficacy and behavior. *J.Appl. Psychol.* 104, 146–163. doi: 10.1037/apl0000353

Padilla-Walker, L. M., and Carlo, G. (2014). "The study of prosocial behavior: past, present, and future," in *Prosocial Development: a Multidimensional Approach*, eds L. M. Padilla-Walker, and G. Carlo, (New York, NY: Oxford University Press), 3–16.

Pak, C. S. (2018). Linking service-learning with sense of belonging: a culturally relevant pedagogy for heritage students of Spanish. *J. Hispanic Higher Educ.* 17, 76–95. doi: 10.1177/1538192716630028

Playford, D., Bailey, S., Fisher, C., Stasinska, A., Marshall, L., Gawlinski, M., et al. (2019). Twelve tips for implementing effective service learning. *Med. Teach.* 41, 24–27. doi: 10.1080/0142159X.2017.1401217

Reynaud, E., Barrington, L., and Willard-Schmoe, E. (2013). "Integrated service-learning: students perspectives," in *120th ASEE Annual Conference and Exposition*, Atlanta, GA, 23767.1–23767.18.

Robinson, D. B., and Meyer, M. (2012). Health education and interactive drama: Findings from a service learning project. *Health Educ. J.* 71, 219–228. doi: 10.1177/0017896911398811

Ruysschaert, N. (2014). The use of hypnosis in therapy to increase happiness. *Am. J. Clin. Hypnosis* 56, 269–284. doi: 10.1080/00029157.2013.846845

Sanders, M., Galindo, C., and DeTablan, D. (2019). Leadership for collaboration: exploring how community school coordinators advance the goals of full-service community schools. *Child. Sch.* 41, 89–100. doi: 10.1093/cs/cdz006

Seban, D. (2013). The impact of the type of projects on preservice teachers' conceptualization of service learning. *Teach. Teach. Educ.* 32, 87–97. doi: 10.1016/j.tate.2013.01.009

Segal-Engelchin, D., Kaufman, R., Huss, E., and Amos, O. (2017). Impacts of an intensive macro-oriented social work programme on first-year students' values, practice preferences and sense of practice competence. *Br. J. Soc.Work* 47, 2346–2363. doi: 10.1093/bjsw/bcw127

Sewry, J. D., and Paphitis, S. A. (2018). Meeting important educational goals for chemistry through service-learning. *Chem. Educ. Res. Pract.* 19, 973–982. doi: 10.1039/C8RP00103K

Shin, J., Kim, M.-S., Hwang, H., and Lee, B.-Y. (2018). Effects of intrinsic motivation and informative feedback in service-learning on the development of college students' life purpose. *J. Moral Educ.* 47, 159–174. doi: 10.1080/03057240.2017.1419943

Short, V., Covey, J. A., Webster, L. A., Wadman, R., Reilly, J., Hay-Gibson, N., et al. (2019). Considering the team in team formulation: a systematic review. *Ment. Health Rev. J.* 24, 11–29. doi: 10.1108/MHRJ-12-2017-0055

Shu-Chin, S., and Tzong-Heng, C. (2016). A qualitative study of interdisciplinary cooperation on computer and English: a case study of Aletheia University participated in international volunteer service learning to inner Mongolia. *Syst. Pract. Act. Res.* 29, 485–516. doi: 10.1007/s11213-016-9375-6

Sun, J., Anderson, R. C., Perry, M., and Lin, T.-J. (2017). Emergent leadership in children's cooperative problem solving groups. *Cogn. Inst.* 35, 212–235. doi: 10.1080/07370008.2017.1313615

Ward, S., Pellett, H. H., and Perez, M. I. (2017). Cognitive disequilibrium and service-learning in physical education teacher education: perceptions of pre-service teachers in a study abroad experience. *J. Teach.Phys. Educ.* 36, 70–82. doi: 10.1123/jtpe.2015-0006

Whitley, M. A., Walsh, D., Hayden, L., and Gould, D. (2017). Narratives of experiential learning: students' engagement in a physical activity-based service-learning course. *J. Teach. Phys. Educ.* 36, 419–429. doi: 10.1123/jtpe.2016-0141

Wilkinson, S., Harvey, W. J., Bloom, G. A., Joober, R., and Grizenko, N. (2013). Student teacher experiences in a service-learning project for children with attention-deficit hyperactivity disorder. *Phys. Educ. Sport Pedagogy* 18, 475–491. doi: 10.1080/17408989.2012.690385

Williams, D. R. (2016). Service-learning and the hungry and homeless: tangible sensibilities of care among young urban adolescents. *Child. Youth Environ.* 26, 164–178. doi: 10.7721/chilyoutenvi.26.1.0164

Zirkel, S., Garcia, J. A., and Murphy, M. C. (2015). Experience-sampling research methods and their potential for education research. *Educ. Res.* 44, 7–16. doi: 10.3102/0013189x14566879

14

Motivation, Discipline and Academic Performance in Physical Education: A Holistic Approach from Achievement Goal and Self-Determination Theories

*Fernando Claver[1], Luis Manuel Martínez-Aranda[2,3], Manuel Conejero[4] and Alexander Gil-Arias[1]**

[1] Centre for Sport Studies, Rey Juan Carlos University, Fuenlabrada, Spain, [2] Faculty of Sport, Catholic University of San Antonio (UCAM), Murcia, Spain, [3] Neuroscience of Human Movement Research Group (Neuromove), UCAM, Murcia, Spain, [4] Faculty of Sport Science, University of Extremadura, Cáceres, Spain

***Correspondence:**
Alexander Gil-Arias
alexander.gil@urjc.es

The analysis of disciplined behaviors and academic performance in a school context has become one of the main concerns within the educational community. Physical Education is highlighted as a key subject to analyze students' behavior. Researchers and Physical Education teachers are interested on the motivational processes that predict positive student outcomes in order to support them. Thus, the main purpose was to determine a predictive model of disciplined behaviors and academic performance in Physical Education students. The Achievement Goal Theory and Self-Determination Theory acted as the theoretical framework. A total of 919 Spanish secondary school students participated in the study. The studied variables were task-oriented motivational climate, basic psychological needs, autonomous motivation, disciplined behavior, and academic performance. Data collection included Spanish validated questionnaires. The Mplus statistical program was used to perform a structural equation model of prediction. It included antecedents (task-oriented climate), motivational processes (basic psychological needs and autonomous motivation), and consequences (disciplined behavior, Physical Education and overall students' performance). The results revealed that positive outcomes (discipline and academic performance in Physical Education) were positively predicted by autonomous motivation; autonomous motivation was positively predicted by basic psychological needs and these, in addition, by the task-oriented climate. The results highlighted the importance of the task-oriented motivational climate and the mediating role of the basic psychological needs and autonomous motivation in order to generate these positive student outcomes in Physical Education. This study could be a useful resource for teachers, since it offers the motivational variables that lead students to achieve disciplined behaviors and academic performance in Physical Education. Intervention programs based on the results of the present study could be applied in Physical Education classes in order to obtain better behavioral as well as cognitive positive student outcomes.

Keywords: teacher climate, motivation, structural equations model, discipline, academic performance, Physical Education

INTRODUCTION

The understanding of cognitive mechanisms related to students' discipline behaviors and academic performance has become the most worrisome aspect to secondary Physical Education (PE) teachers (Gutiérrez and López, 2012b). Thus, discipline in the school environment has become one of the main concerns of the educational community since it is a key indicator that the teaching–learning process is carried out successfully. The educational structure aims to promote prosocial behaviors in order to generate the most favorable conditions for the teaching–learning process that will allow the student to achieve an adequate performance (Barkoukis et al., 2014; Sánchez-Oliva et al., 2014).

Teaching strategies are essential to create an adequate classroom context that enables the implementation of planned tasks. In fact, teachers who promote a conducive environment for learning and engagement, in which students collaborate in its development, will achieve the learning objectives (Noltemeyer et al., 2019; Núñez and León, 2019). On the contrary, those teachers who do not encourage a classroom context with involved, autonomous, and participatory students will have more difficulties in achieving the planned teaching objectives (Granero-Gallegos et al., 2020a). Regarding the teacher's contribution to the disciplined behaviors promotion, the proper application of teaching skills and attitudes reduces disciplinary problems. Teaching skills in PE allow a better group control and give the teacher more time for corrections and provide feedback to students, increasing their participation, autonomy, and effectiveness in the classroom, and consequently academic achievement (Gutiérrez et al., 2009; Wade et al., 2020).

The relationship between teacher skills and student academic performance has been extensively studied (Taylor et al., 2014). Participative methodologies that focus the teaching–learning process on the student, positive corrections, and giving autonomy to students are associated with positive consequences (Gil-Arias et al., 2020), such as disciplined behaviors (Gutiérrez et al., 2010) and academic performance in PE (Cid et al., 2019). However, the very complex reality of PE lessons in secondary education sometimes forces the teacher to stop focusing on the students' academic performance to give priority to more controlled instructional approaches in order to avoid disruptive behaviors (Granero-Gallegos et al., 2020a).

Among the difficult conditions of the classroom context, student motivation is highlighted as a key variable when analyzing secondary school discipline behaviors and academic achievement (León et al., 2015; Rahimi and Karkami, 2015; Chik and Abdullah, 2018) but also in PE achievement (Gutiérrez and López, 2012b; Sevil et al., 2017). In this regard, research in the psychosocial field provides an appropriate framework to integrate learning skills with coexistence skills. Conflict, disruptive behavior, disobedience to teachers' instructions, and non-compliance with sanctions are phenomena closely linked to school amotivation (Vera and Moreno-Murcia, 2016; Anderson et al., 2019). Thus, this research is based on the Achievement Goal Theory (AGT) (Nicholls, 1984) and the Self-Determination Theory (SDT) (Ryan and Deci, 2020) as the framework that allows to explain and predict how the PE students' behavior can be regulated (Vasconcellos et al., 2019).

The interpretation that people are intentional organisms, directed by certain objectives and acting rationally in accordance with them, is the fundamental idea of the AGT (Nicholls, 1984). In achievement contexts, beliefs consistently guide behavior. This theory assumes that the greatest point of interest for individuals in performance contexts such as PE lies in demonstrating competence and ability. Thus, the motivational climate transmitted by the teacher through the structuring and teaching pathway of PE classes may be a task-oriented motivational climate, where skill judgment is based on the level of task mastery being achieved (striving to improve), or an ego-oriented motivational climate, where social comparison between students is promoted, understanding success when they show greater skill than others (Wallhead et al., 2013).

On the other hand, the SDT has been one of the theoretical models that have contributed the most to a better understanding of the cognitive, emotional, and behavioral patterns related to student progress (Ryan and Deci, 2020), especially in PE (Van Den Berghe et al., 2014; Vasconcellos et al., 2019). According to this theory, the origin of motivation can be more internal or external for the student (more or less self-determined) depending on if they are freely engage in their activities (Ryan and Deci, 2017). Specifically, SDT distinguishes between different dimensions of motivation (autonomous, controlled, and amotivation). Autonomous motivation is the most self-determined one and involves the behavior regulation with the experiences of volition, psychological freedom, and reflective self-endorsement (Aelterman et al., 2012). Studies developed in secondary school PE students have linked the more self-determined motivation to positive and adaptive outcomes at affective (e.g., well-being) (Standage et al., 2012), cognitive (e.g., academic achievement) (Ntoumanis and Standage, 2009), and behavioral levels (e.g., discipline) (Moreno-Murcia et al., 2011; Zimmerman and Kitsantas, 2014). Within the SDT, three basic psychological needs (BPNs) lead to self-determined behaviors (Ryan and Deci, 2017). The BPN of autonomy is satisfied when the students have the initiative in their behavior and the opportunity to choose; the BPN of competence is linked to the effective interaction with the environment, while the BPN of relatedness is related to positive interactions and group membership. Previous research has demonstrated the positive predictive capacity of BPNs on autonomous motivation in PE (Koka, 2014; Sánchez-Oliva et al., 2014; Ferriz et al., 2016; Van Den Berghe et al., 2016).

Complementary to the SDT, the Hierarchical Model of Motivation (Vallerand and Ratelle, 2002; Vallerand, 2007) was created in order to improve and relate the constructs of the SDT and originated the integral analysis of motivational and cognitive processes (McCarthy, 2011). The Hierarchical Model of Motivation explains the determinants of motivation processes and its consequences, becoming the main theory to explain motivation in the PE, sport, and exercise field (Clancy et al., 2016). In this way, the motivational climate that the teacher promotes in PE lessons constitutes one of the fundamental elements influencing the satisfaction of BPNs, acting as mediators between social factors and the self-determined type of regulation experienced by students (Tessier et al., 2010). According to previous research, SDT and AGT could be integrated in order to achieve a better motivational process understanding and its positive consequences (Duda, 2013). Furthermore, in a PE context, the teacher encourages a motivational climate, characterized by a variety of challenging tasks at the personal level, where cooperation is necessary to achieve a common goal, and where the students can have their own initiative, covering their BPNs. This will lead to a more self-determined motivation, having positive affective, cognitive, and behavioral consequences (Cox and Williams, 2008; Abós et al., 2017).

Previous research on the teaching of PE has been limited by the analysis of antecedents, motivational processes, and consequences in an isolated manner (Cid et al., 2019). Although the discipline has been a well-studied construct in the general educational context (Zimmerman and Kitsantas, 2014), studies in the field of PE are less abundant. Research has pointed out that the perception of a task-oriented classroom environment was positively related to self-determined reasons to maintain disciplined behavior. It was also associated with the student's perception, mainly related to strategies based on responsibility and intrinsic reasons that the teacher used to maintain discipline (Spray and Wang, 2001; Gutiérrez and López, 2012a; Granero-Gallegos et al., 2020b). The study conducted by Spray and Wang (2001) in a group of English students reported that those who had a higher feeling of competence in PE expressed more self-determined reasons for maintaining and adequate behavior during the sessions. On the other hand, Moreno et al. (2011) analyzed a sample of Spanish secondary school students, determining that intrinsic motivation was positively related to the three BPNs, as well as with the discipline behavior. Other studies analyzed students' discipline and self-regulation measures as a predictor of academic performance and did not only analyze the disciplined behavior as a consequence (Zimmerman and Kitsantas, 2014).

Academic performance at school, measured as the final score of the student (Sternberg, 2015), has been traditionally studied and explained by individual variables, mainly intellectual, but also by personality and contextual factors. Some authors state that the cognitive variables are the most important for predicting academic achievement and explaining most of the phenomena (Poropat, 2011). However, other authors support that the study of contextual and personality variables provides a better and more complete explanation of academic performance. In a recent study, Baños et al. (2020) presented a predictive model of academic performance based on the individual's satisfaction. Student motivation is shown as a relevant variable because motivation is related to the learning goals that students have, which, in turn, evoke different mental situations in students, resulting in them having a positive or negative attitude toward study. This determines the effort invested to achieve learning and academic performance. A meta-analysis presented by Taylor et al. (2014) highlighted the role of motivation on school achievement. They also found that self-determined motivation was associated with higher academic performance. In PE, academic performance and metacognitive skills have been predicted by motivational variables in previous research (Chatzipanteli et al., 2015; Kirby et al., 2015; Sevil et al., 2017). In a longitudinal study, Barkoukis et al. (2014) indicated that a more self-determined motivation obtained higher academic performance in PE and, in addition, a less self-determined motivation explained lower qualifications.

Finally, several studies demonstrated the association between academic performance and disciplined behaviors in a high school context (Zimmerman and Kitsantas, 2014; Noltemeyer et al., 2019), but scientific research testing predictive models of both disciplined behavior and academic achievement in PE (Gutiérrez and López, 2012b) is limited. To our knowledge, these studies do not integrate AGT and SDT constructs. At this point, and given the relevance of motivational variables to regulate behavioral and cognitive outcomes of students in PE, the aim of this study was to determine a predictive model of disciplined behaviors and academic performance (overall and specific) in PE secondary school. We hypothesized that (1) task-oriented climate will predict autonomous motivation through the BPNs (Cox and Williams, 2008) and that (2) autonomous motivation will predict disciplined behaviors (Spray and Wang, 2001) and (3) academic performance (Cid et al., 2019).

MATERIALS AND METHODS

Design and Participants

A cross-sectional study design with on-probability-based sampling was used. The sample consisted of 919 secondary school students, from 10 educational centers from two regions in Spain, aged between 12 and 18 years old (M = 14.63; SD = 1.54). The sample was composed of students from both genders, male (n = 433, M_{age} = 14.62, SD_{age} = 1.61) and female (n = 486, M_{age} = 14.64, SD_{age} = 1.49). In order to represent the different characteristics of the population, 42 classes (clusters) were randomly selected. Each cluster consisted of a group of approximately 21 students.

Measurements

The Spanish version (Cervelló et al., 2010) of the Learning and Performance Orientation in PE Classes Questionnaire (Papaioannou, 1994) was used to measure task-oriented motivational climate in PE classes, as in previous research (Gil-Arias et al., 2020). The questionnaire begins with the sentence "In my PE classes..." and the factor is composed of 13 items (e.g., "The PE teacher is most satisfied when all the students learn something new" or "I am very satisfied when I learn new skills and games"). The factor reported a McDonald's Omega of 0.86. Confirmatory factor analysis showed adequate adjustment indexes: χ^2 = 749.90; p < 0.001; χ^2/df = 2.44, CFI = 0.93, TLI = 0.92, RMSEA = 0.04, SRMR = 0.07.

The Spanish version (Moreno-Murcia et al., 2008b) of the BPNs in the Exercise Scale (Vlachopoulos and Michailidou, 2006) was applied to measure BPNs in the PE context, as in previous research (Jiménez et al., 2015). The questionnaire begins with the initial question "In my PE classes..." and it is composed of a total of 12 items, of which four measured autonomy (e.g., "The way I conduct classes is an expression of myself"), four related to competence (e.g., "I am able to manage the demands of a PE class"), and the other four measured the relatedness factor (e.g., "I interact in a very friendly way with the rest of the class"). Each factor reported a McDonald's Omega of 0.81, 0.81, and 0.91, respectively. Confirmatory factor analysis showed adequate adjustment indexes: χ^2 = 168.172; $p < 0.001$; χ^2/df = 3.36, CFI = 0.96, TLI = 0.95, RMSEA = 0.05, SRMR 0.05.

The Spanish version (Moreno-Murcia et al., 2009) of the Perceived Locus of Causality Scale (Goudas et al., 1994) was used to measure autonomous motivation in PE, as in previous research (Ferriz et al., 2016). The questionnaire begins with the question "I participate in the PE classes..." and the factor is composed of eight items (e.g., "because PE is stimulating"). Autonomous motivation was calculated through intrinsic regulation (e.g., "because I enjoy learning new skills") and identified regulation (e.g., "because I can learn skills that could be used in other areas of my life") (Haerens et al., 2010). The factor reported a McDonald's Omega of 0.97. Confirmatory factor analysis showed adequate adjustment indexes: χ^2 = 452.908; $p < 0.001$; χ^2/df = 2.96, CFI = 0.95, TLI = 0.94, RMSEA = 0.05, SRMR = 0.07.

The Spanish version (Cervelló et al., 2004) of the Discipline and Indiscipline Behavior in PE Inventory was used to measure discipline behaviors in PE classes, as in previous research (Gutiérrez and López, 2012b). The questionnaire begins with the statement "In my PE classes..." and the factor consists of 10 items (e.g., "you address yourself with respect to the teacher"). The factor reported a McDonald's Omega value of 0.87. Confirmatory factor analysis showed adequate adjustment indexes: χ^2 = 399.68; $p < 0.001$; χ^2/df = 2.42, CFI = 0.99, TLI = 0.99, RMSEA = 0.04, SRMR = 0.04.

All the instruments were anchored on a Likert scale ranging from 1 (*strongly disagree*) to 5 (*strongly agree*).

PE academic performance and *Overall academic performace* were measured through a single item that reported the qualifications in the previous evaluation in PE and the rest of the subjects, respectively. This type of measure has been used in previous research (Baños et al., 2020).

Procedures

The research was fully approved by the Ethics Committee of the local University following the guidelines of the Helsinki Declaration. In order to carry out the research, PE teachers and directors of the secondary schools were contacted. All students and their parents or legal tutors were informed about the study, which was anonymous. Subsequently, they signed a consent form to voluntarily participate in the study. Data collection occurred directly in the PE classes. An investigator provided questionnaires to the participants and informed them about how to fill them in, solving the questions that might appear during the process, ensuring an adequate concentration climate and avoiding the presence of the PE teacher. The estimated time to complete the instruments was 15 min.

Statistical Analysis

Data analysis was performed using the statistical programs IBM SPSS Statistics 25.0 (IBM Corp, 2017) and MPlus 7.4 (Muthén and Muthén, 2012). The psychometric properties of the questionnaires were calculated, including an initial exploratory factor analysis (EFA) and confirmatory factor analysis (CFA) to test the instruments' factor structure. The reliability of the study measurements was analyzed through McDonald's Omega because Cronbach's Alpha requires equal loads for all items in the same factor (Zhang and Yuan, 2016) and also that the numerical data should be continuous. Moreover, McDonald's Omega has shown evidence of better accuracy to Likert-type ranging responses and values above 0.70–0.80 implying reliable measures (Revelle and Zinbarg, 2009).

The structural equation model (SEM) proposed was analyzed with the aim of testing the association between the study variables. The indicators of the latent variables in the SEM were the items of the different scales. To estimate the value of the parameters and the adjustment indexes in both CFA and SEM, robust maximum likelihood (MLR) estimation method was employed due to the Likert nature of the items. Model adjustment was assessed with a combination of the χ^2/df test (<5) and the adjustment indexes (Kline, 2011). The *P*-value was established at level 0.05. A comparative adjustment index (CFI) and Tucker–Lewis index (TLI) close to or above 0.90 together with a root mean square error of approximation value close to or below 0.06 and the standard root mean square residual (SRMR) close to or below 0.08, respectively, were considered indicative of an acceptable model fit (Hu and Bentler, 1999).

RESULTS

Preliminary Analyses

Descriptive statistics, correlation matrix, means and standard deviations of all major variables, as well as Pearson's correlations among the study variables are shown in **Table 1**. Results revealed a positive and significant relationship between task-oriented climate, the three BPNs, autonomous motivation, and disciplined behavior. Academic performance in PE was significantly positively associated with task-oriented climate, the three BPNs, and discipline, while overall academic performance was significantly positively associated with relatedness and PE academic performance.

Structural Equation Modeling

A complete structural regression model was presented to test the study hypothesis, including antecedents (task climate), predicting BPNs (which in turn will predict motivational process), and, thereafter, the consequences (discipline, PE academic performance, and overall academic performance). The model shows adequate adjustment indexes: χ^2 = 2464.38; $p \leq 0.001$; χ^2/df = 2.56, CFI = 0.90, TLI = 0.90, SRMR = 0.07, and RMSEA = 0.04. The model explained 46% of the variance in discipline, 2% in PE academic performance, and 1% in overall academic performance.

Figure 1, which shows the latent variables, illustrates that the task climate has a positive effect on BPNs (autonomy $\beta = 0.73$, $p < 0.001$; competence $\beta = 0.91$, $p < 0.001$; and relatedness $\beta = 0.60$, $p < 0.001$). BPNs have a positive effect on autonomous

TABLE 1 | Descriptive analyses, values, and correlations.

	M	*SD*	1	2	3	4	5	6	7
(1) Task climate	4.09	0.65							
(2) BPN autonomy	3.19	0.84	0.52**						
(3) BPN competence	3.79	0.82	0.49**	0.58**					
(4) BPN relatedness	4.18	0.84	0.42**	0.47**	0.50**				
(5) Autonomous motivation	3.82	0.92	0.67**	0.55**	0.61**	0.43**			
(6) Discipline	4.26	0.59	0.63**	0.42**	0.48**	0.50**	0.50**		
(7) PE performance	3.72	1.07	0.13*	0.12*	0.28*	0.27**	0.08	0.26**	
(8) Academic performance	3.65	1.02	0.10	−0.01	0.03	0.15**	−0.04	0.24**	0.63**

**Correlation is significant at 0.05 level; **Correlation is significant at 0.01 level. BPN, basic psychological need; PE, Physical Education.*

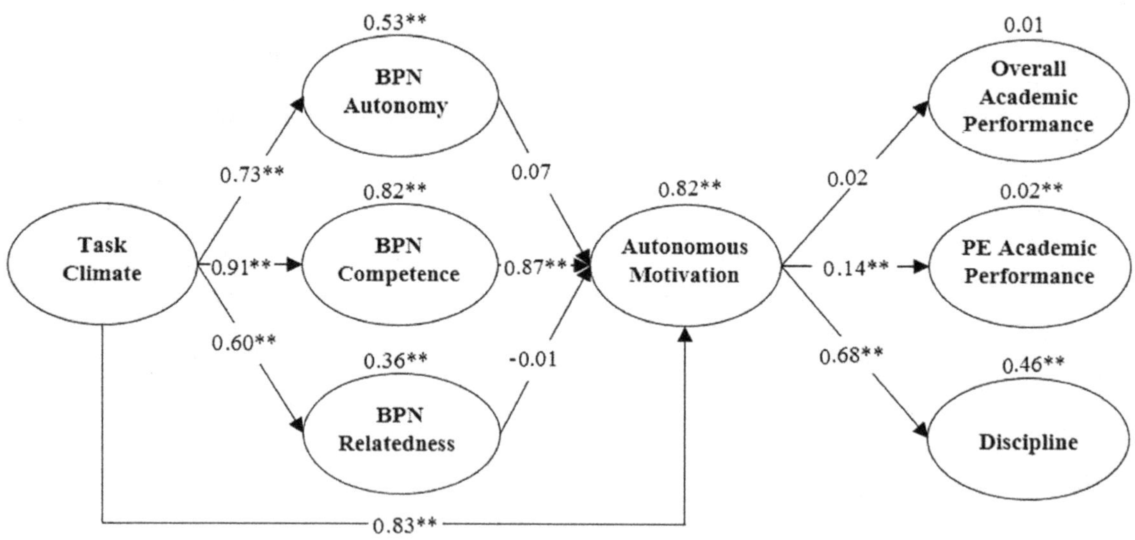

FIGURE 1 | Structural equation model with standardized weights, variances and significance. *Significance level at $p < 0.05$, **significance level at $p < 0.01$; BPN, basic psychological need; PE, Physical Education.

motivation (autonomy $\beta = 0.07$, $p = 0.77$; competence $\beta = 0.86$, $p < 0.001$; relatedness $\beta = -0.01$, $p = 0.85$). Autonomous motivation has a positive effect on PE academic performance ($\beta = 0.14$, $p < 0.001$) and discipline ($\beta = 0.68$, $p < 0.001$), but with no effect on overall academic performance ($\beta = 0.02$, $p = 0.32$). Moreover, there is an indirect effect of basic task climate and autonomous motivation, mediated by the three BPNs ($\beta = 0.83$, $p < 0.001$).

DISCUSSION

The aim of this study was to determine a predictive model of disciplined behaviors and academic performance in PE secondary school, integrating AGT and SDT constructs. A SEM was tested in order to determine the hypothesis of the study. The results showed the relevance of task-oriented climate and the mediating role of BPNs and autonomous motivation to predict students' disciplined behavior and PE academic performance. The study could support PE teachers' interventions in order to achieve student adaptative consequences.

The first hypothesis, stating that *task climate will predict autonomous motivation through the basic psychological needs*, was confirmed by the results. The task-oriented climate predicted BPNs, which, in turn, predicted autonomous motivation. Our findings are consistent with previous research integrating AGT and SDT frameworks, evidencing the relationship between motivational climate and student motivation (Braithwaite et al., 2011; Duda, 2013; Cid et al., 2019). As an example, Standage et al. (2006) found a positive relationship between the motivational climate involving the task and self-determined motivation (intrinsic). In a predictive study, Gutiérrez et al. (2010) examined the relationship among pupils' perceptions of the motivational climate, and pupils' intrinsic motivation in PE in a sample of 2189 Spanish adolescents, aged between 13 and 17 years. They tested a SEM, and the most important predictors of pupils' intrinsic motivation were the perceived mastery climate. In the same line, Baena-Extremera et al. (2015) and Jaakkola et al. (2017) tested other SEMs and also task-oriented climate predicted self-determined motivation. In addition, a motivational climate intervention has produced changes in students' self–determined motivation in school PE classes (Bortoli et al., 2017). In a recent study, Cecchini et al. (2020) proposed an intervention throughout an academic year in PE to encourage a task-oriented climate, in which an increase in self-regulated forms of motivation was found.

Basic psychological needs are considered to modulate the effects of socio-contextual factors (e.g., PE teacher attitude) on the students' self-determined motivation (Vasconcellos et al., 2019; Ryan and Deci, 2020). In a previous study involving 155 high school students, Moreno et al. (2011) stated that task-oriented climate was positively and significantly associated with the three BPNs, as in the present study. In the same line, the work developed by Kirby et al. (2015) showed that the style and the intervention of the teacher in the PE classes determined the satisfaction of the three BPNs. Another example was the intervention study conducted by Abós et al. (2017) in which the experimental group reported significant improvements on the three BPNs through an acrosport teaching unit based on developing a task-oriented motivational climate. Similarly, Bechter et al. (2019) demonstrated the positive effects of a teacher training-based program on student-centered learning intervention on BPNs in 554 Australian PE students. Following the same line, Gil-Arias et al. (2020) compared a student-centered intervention to a traditional teacher-centered one using AGT and SDT as a framework to explain how the social–contextual factors surrounding one teacher's employment of these two pedagogical approaches influenced students' motivation levels. They found that student-centered learning context improves the BPNs as in the present study, where the task-oriented climate improved the BPNs satisfaction of autonomy, competence, and relatedness.

However, despite the fact that many studies highlighted the role of classroom climates in catalyzing a higher student autonomous motivation and the modulating effect of BPNs on student autonomous motivation (Braithwaite et al., 2011; Duda, 2013; Vasconcellos et al., 2019), only some of them analyzed the task-oriented motivational climate as an antecedent of the motivational process in PE, including the mediating role of BPNs (Cox and Williams, 2008; Sevil et al., 2016; Abós et al., 2018). An intervention program based on task-oriented climate was applied by Sevil et al. (2016), and they found that a student-centered learning context enhances BPNs of autonomy and competence, as well as students' intrinsic motivation. Moreover, Cox and Williams (2008) tested structural equation modeling, showing that competence, autonomy, and relatedness satisfaction mediated the relationship between teacher climate and self-determined motivation as well as in our current study. However, in the study by Cox and Williams (2008), the BPN of satisfaction significantly and positively predicted the self-determined motivation, while in the present study, only competence acted as a significant predictor of autonomous motivation. These results are also in line with those of Sevil et al. (2016) in that the BPN of competence significantly increased after an intervention program. As competence satisfaction refers to the people's need to believe that they are effective in a specific situation context, and based on the obtained results, teachers should prioritize its support by using positive feedback, questioning and adapting the tasks to the student developmental needs and competence level (Abós et al., 2018).

In summary, the developed studies in PE (as well as in sport context) reveal the importance of the task-oriented climate and the role of BPNs in the emergence of more self-determined forms of motivation (Aelterman et al., 2013). Teacher intervention should have a strong influence on the BPNs and consequently on the students' autonomous motivation. Thus, the PE teacher must involve students in decision-making in the process of organizing and directing the sessions, favoring their autonomy and leadership; success must be defined and evaluated in terms of effort and personal progress; mistakes should be part of the teaching–learning process; participation and commitment to the proposed activities should be emphasized; the tasks set must be varied and adjusted to the level of competence of the students; a wide range of teaching styles should be employed (cognitive, creative, socializing, individualizing, and participatory teaching styles); different strategies for grouping students, as well as a private evaluation, meaningful and relative to personal progress and mastery of the task, should be used (Moreno et al., 2011; Bortoli et al., 2017; Cecchini et al., 2020).

The second hypothesis stated that *autonomous motivation will positively predict disciplined behaviors*. The results of the study confirmed the second hypothesis. Autonomous motivation positively predicted disciplined behaviors. Our findings are in line with previous research that demonstrated the predictive capacity of self-determined motivation on prosocial behaviors (Hodge and Lonsdale, 2011; Adie et al., 2012; Sánchez-Oliva et al., 2014). Based on SDT, Sánchez-Oliva et al. (2014) tested a complete model of structural regression in PE students by analyzing antecedents, motivational process, and positive disciplined behaviors. The results showed how BPNs support predicted student autonomous motivation through the BPNs satisfaction, and the self-determined motivation predicted positive discipline behaviors in PE (respect, self-control, cooperation, and tolerance). The role of the teacher should be based on the establishment of different sets of strategies aimed at increasing the students' confidence, being able to contribute to the teaching–learning process with a number of positive aspects. Among these aspects, the participation in the tasks by the students with an optimal level of self-esteem, the development of a proactive attitude, the promotion of the capacity for teamwork, and the perception of having less fear for making mistakes among the rest of colleagues are worth mentioning. All these aspects will lead to a greater feeling of union and belonging among the students, as well as the perception of a task-oriented motivational climate that will incite the students to have a positive predisposition toward the learning tasks, leading to disciplined behaviors (Tessier et al., 2010; Sánchez-Oliva et al., 2015).

Most of the research on disciplined behaviors has been based on AGT, finding a strong relationship between students' perception of a motivational climate involving the task and discipline in PE (Spray, 2002; Cervelló et al., 2004; Moreno et al., 2011). The study developed by Vera and Moreno-Murcia (2016) revealed that students with motivational profiles oriented to the task showed more self-determined reasons to be disciplined. Similarly, Martínez-Galindo et al. (2012) showed that the strategies based on the teacher's responsibility and intrinsic reasons to maintain discipline were related to the perception of a task-oriented motivational climate and with the students' disposition to be disciplined. Task-oriented motivational climate also predicted the student identified and intrinsic reasons for being disciplined. Similarly, Moreno-Murcia et al. (2008a) found that task-oriented students perceived the strategies used by the teacher to maintain discipline in the classroom based on cooperation with others and responsibility in their own behavior, resulting in an increased self-determined motivation. The authors pointed out the importance of creating learning-oriented classroom environments because it also guided students toward a positive discipline, due to the high predictive capacity that this type of climate has shown in the tested model. Likewise, teachers must transmit implicit and explicit keys oriented toward effort, personal improvement, and acquisition of skills, which will lead to an increase in self-determined motivation. As a consequence, students will show more disciplined behavior (Adie et al., 2012).

In PE school context, disciplined behaviors have been approached from different motivational theories in an isolated manner (AGT or SDT). There are few studies that have been carried out integrating the constructs of the AGT and the SDT. We could find only one study where both constructs are integrated (Moreno et al., 2011), but they observed that the motivational climate was the main predictor of the discipline, rather than autonomous motivation in a regression analysis. This is why the present study represents an improvement when evaluating how the classroom climate predicts disciplined behaviors of the students, mediated by the autonomous motivational processes of the students in a complete predictive model. In brief, the main purpose for teachers would be to favor the appearance of disciplined behaviors through the application of interactive skills (e.g., open tasks in the form of problem situations, which encouraged personal challenge and self-regulation of learning) that allow students to perceive a task-oriented motivational climate. This perception will lead to a better achievement of BPNs and, as a consequence, a more autonomous motivation leading to disciplined behaviors.

The third hypothesis stating that *autonomous motivation will positively predict academic performance* was further confirmed by the results. Autonomous motivation positively predicted PE academic performance. Our findings are consistent with previous research based on SDT such as the longitudinal study by Barkoukis et al. (2014), which, after a 3-year intervention period, demonstrated that self-determined profiles were associated with higher ratings in the PE subject. Similar results were found by Standage et al. (2006) regarding the levels of self-determined motivation reported by students who positively predicted PE teacher qualifications. The assumption that autonomous motivation increases positive outcomes not only in the educational context (Ryan and Deci, 2020) but also in PE (Standage et al., 2006; Cid et al., 2019) is fundamental to SDT.

On the other hand, the AGT postulates that the motivational climate generated by the teacher (e.g., the keys to success or failure that define an activity) can influence positively or negatively at different levels in the classroom. In the same way, the study developed by Gutiérrez and López (2012b) found a positive and significant association between the task-oriented learning climate promoted by the teacher and the students' grades in PE. Similar results were found by Şahin et al. (2018), showing that the task climate was determined as predictor of academic achievement among PE and sports undergraduate students. Thus, the way the teacher structures and develops his classes can generate in students a series of adaptive behaviors in the classroom, including academic performance (Sevil et al., 2017).

As previously described in the literature, academic performance has been addressed from AGT and SDT in an isolated manner in the PE context, but few studies have been carried out by integrating both frameworks or perspectives. An exception is the study developed by Sevil et al. (2017), revealing a significant and positive relationship between task-oriented climate, BPNs, self-determined motivation, and academic performance. However, the study conducted by Sevil et al. (2017) in Spanish secondary students showed that the task-oriented motivational climate (instead of the autonomous motivation) predicted academic performance in PE (35% of the explained variance). Similarly, Cerasoli et al. (2014) sought to clarify the relationships between intrinsic motivation, mastery goal orientation, and performance by using a three-wave panel study and hypotheses drawn from SDT and AGT. They reported that mastery goals mediated (explained) the relationship between intrinsic motivation and academic performance.

Despite the high correlation found in the present study between the PE grades and overall grades, autonomous motivation toward PE did not act as a significant predictor of overall academic performance. These results are not in line with previous studies in that self-determined motivation predicted academic performance in other subjects (Wentzel, 2017). A large empirically based literature has demonstrated the positive relationships of the most autonomous forms of classroom motivation with academic outcomes (Howard et al., 2017). Specifically, Taylor et al. (2014) conducted a meta-analysis highlighting the significant role of intrinsic motivation on predicting school achievement. The results may be due to the instruments used for the study, where motivation of a specific subject (PE) was analyzed, and need not be in agreement with students' overall academic motivation. The prospective to measure motivation from a more contextual point of view is proposed, assessing the possible level of prediction of the students' motivation on their specific and overall academic performance (Baños et al., 2020).

Traditionally, academic performance in PE has been associated with individual factors, but more and more studies indicate the teacher–student and student–student interactions as well as motivational processes as key factors of academic performance in PE (Sevil et al., 2017). In this sense, it is essential that the teacher favors task-oriented climates that satisfy BPNs, leading to autonomous motivation. Some authors point out that cognitive skills (intelligence, hours of study) are the most affected as determinants of academic achievement in the literature (Poropat, 2011), which could explain the low prediction rate of motivational processes on performance in PE. However, the study of motivational factors can provide a more complete perspective for the teaching–learning process to conclude successfully.

There are few studies that have jointly analyzed motivation, disciplined behaviors, and academic performance. Based on AGT, Gutiérrez and López (2012b) analyzed motivation, students' behavior, and academic achievement in a sample of 2,189 PE students. The results showed that the task-oriented climate predicted the discipline behavior, although the best predictor of academic performance was the teachers' assessment of student behavior. Complementary, Baños et al. (2018) analyzed the effect of teachers' gender on the motivational climate, disciplined behaviors, future practice intentions, and academic performance. Finally, a recent study by Cid et al. (2019) tested a SEM where PE grades were predicted by autonomous motivation and in turn by BPNs, which were also predicted by task-oriented climate. Therefore, the motivational climate in PE classes enhanced by the PE teacher has a significant impact on the BPNs satisfaction. This fact has a positive impact on how PE students regulate their behavior, as well as on how the autonomous regulation has a significant impact in PE grades (Cid et al., 2019). The teaching role is decisive in creating the best contextual conditions to generate adaptive behaviors on students and to carry out the teaching–learning process in order to culminate in a successful manner as well.

Thus, the testing of a predictive model including disciplined behaviors and academic performance as positive student outcomes of motivational processes (integrating AGT and SDT frameworks) is the main strength of this study. The results are in line with the postulates of the Hierarchical Model of Motivation (Vallerand, 2001), which emphasizes the importance of antecedents in the emergence of more self-determined motivation forms and its consequences. In addition, this study provides a more complete knowledge of the motivational processes underlying disciplined behaviors and the academic performance of PE secondary students. The main limitation of the study is the cross-sectional design, which does not allow generalizations such as the experimental designs that are proposed as prospective. It would be also appropriate to continue to dig into this research topic but in other educational stages and including other antecedents regarding the "dark side" of student motivation as ego-oriented climate, controlled motivation, amotivation, and other consequences, such as undisciplined behavior, extracurricular sports practice, or physical activity levels. Furthermore, it would be also interesting to propose a triangulation of methods, obtaining information from the teacher and external observers. To conclude, this study contributes to the knowledge of students' behavior and will help teachers to foment environments that optimize the teaching–learning process and lead students to a more autonomous motivation and its positive cognitive (PE academic performance) and behavioral (discipline) consequences.

ETHICS STATEMENT

The University Ethics Committee of the University of Extremadura reviewed and approved the research in accordance with the principles set out in the Declaration of Helsinki. Written informed consent to participate in this study was provided by the participants' legal guardian/next of kin.

AUTHOR CONTRIBUTIONS

FC and AG-A conceptualized and designed the study. FC, AG-A, LM-A, and MC recruited the subjects. MC and LM-A collected the data. FC and MC organized the database. FC and AG-A carried out the statistical analysis. FC, LM-A, MC, and AG-A wrote the first manuscript draft. FC, AG-A, and LM-A developed the final manuscript draft, contributed to English proofreading, and reviewed and edited the final version of the manuscript. All authors contributed to manuscript revision and approved the definitive manuscript.

ACKNOWLEDGMENTS

We thank the school, the teachers, and the children for their participation in this study. We also thank G. Sanz for his assistance with the English proofreading.

REFERENCES

Abós, Á, Sevil, J., Julián, J. A., Abarca-Sos, A., and García-González, L. (2017). Improving students' predisposition towards physical education by optimizing their motivational processes in an acrosport unit. *Eur. Phys. Educ. Rev.* 23, 444–460. doi: 10.1177/1356336X16654390

Abós, Á, Sevil, J., Martín-Albo, J., Julián, J. A., and García-González, L. (2018). An integrative framework to validate the Need-Supportive Teaching Style Scale (NSTSS) in secondary teachers through exploratory structural equation modeling. *Contemp. Educ. Psychol.* 52, 48–60. doi: 10.1016/j.cedpsych.2018.01.001

Adie, J. W., Duda, J. L., and Ntoumanis, N. (2012). Perceived coach-autonomy support, basic need satisfaction and the well- and ill-being of elite youth soccer players: a longitudinal investigation. *Psychol. Sport Exerc.* 13, 51–59. doi: 10.1016/j.psychsport.2011.07.008

Aelterman, N., Vansteenkiste, M., Van Keer, H., De Meyer, J., Van den Berghe, L., and Haerens, L. (2013). Development and evaluation of a training on need-supportive teaching in physical education: Qualitative and quantitative findings. *Teach. Teach. Educ.* 29, 64–75. doi: 10.1016/j.tate.2012.09.001

Aelterman, N., Vansteenkiste, M., Van Keer, H., Van den Berghe, L., De Meyer, J., and Haerens, L. (2012). Students' objectively measured physical activity levels and engagement as a function of between-class and between-student differences in motivation toward physical education. *J. Sport Exerc. Psychol.* 34, 457–480. doi: 10.1123/jsep.34.4.457

Anderson, K. P., Ritter, G. W., and Zamarro, G. (2019). Understanding a vicious cycle: the relationship between student discipline and student academic outcomes. *Educ. Res.* 48, 251–262. doi: 10.3102/0013189X19848720

Baena-Extremera, A., Gómez-López, M., Granero-Gallegos, A., Ortiz-Camacho, M., and Del, M. (2015). Predicting satisfaction in physical education from motivational climate and self-determined motivation. *J. Teach. Phys. Educ.* 34, 210–224. doi: 10.1123/jtpe.2013-0165

Baños, R., Baena-Extremera, A., Ortiz-Camacho, M., and Del, M. (2020). Prediction Model of Academic Performance and Satisfaction With School According to Some Subjects of Compulsory Secondary Education. *Psychol. Rep.* 123, 435–451. doi: 10.1177/0033294118805004

Baños, R., Ortiz-Camacho, M., del, M., Baena-Extremera, A., and Zamarripa, J. (2018). Efecto del género del docente en la importancia de la Educación Física, clima motivacional, comportamientos disruptivos, la intención de práctica futura y rendimiento académico. *Ret. Nuev. Tend. Educ. fís. Dep. Recreac.* 33, 252–257.

Barkoukis, V., Taylor, I., Chanal, J., and Ntoumanis, N. (2014). The relation between student motivation and student grades in physical education: a 3-year investigation. *Scand. J. Med. Sci. Sport.* 24, e406–e414. doi: 10.1111/sms.12174

Bechter, B. E., Dimmock, J. A., and Jackson, B. (2019). A cluster-randomized controlled trial to improve student experiences in physical education: Results of a student-centered learning intervention with high school teachers. *Psychol. Sport Exerc.* 45, 101553. doi: 10.1016/j.psychsport.2019.101553

Bortoli, L., Bertollo, M., Filho, E., di Fronso, S., and Robazza, C. (2017). Implementing the TARGET model in physical education: effects on perceived psychobiosocial and motivational states in girls. *Front. Psychol.* 8:1517. doi: 10.3389/fpsyg.2017.01517

Braithwaite, R., Spray, C., and Warburton, V. E. (2011). Motivational climate interventions in physical education: a meta-analysis. *Psychol. Sport Exerc.* 12, 628–638. doi: 10.1016/j.psychsport.2011.06.005

Cecchini, J.-A., Méndez-Giménez, A., and Sánchez-Martínez, B. (2020). Effect of a TARGET-Based intervention on students' motivational change: a study throughout an academic year in physical education. *J. Teach. Phys. Educ.* 39, 1–10. doi: 10.1123/jtpe.2018-0357

Cerasoli, C. P., Nicklin, J. M., and Ford, M. T. (2014). Intrinsic motivation and extrinsic incentives jointly predict performance: a 40-year meta-analysis. *Psychol. Bull.* 140, 980–1008. doi: 10.1037/a0035661

Cervelló, E., Jiménez, R., Moya, M., and Moreno-Murcia, J. A. (2010). Validation of the spanish language version of the learning and performance orientations in physical education classes questionnaire. *Ricyde. Rev. Int. Ciencias Dep.* 6, 242–253. doi: 10.5232/ricyde2010.02006

Cervelló, E., Ruth, J., Del Villar, F., Ramos, L., and Santos-Rosa, F. J. (2004). Goal orientations, motivational climate, equality, and discipline of Spanish physical education students. *Percept. Mot. Skills* 99, 271–283. doi: 10.2466/pms.99.1.271-283

Chatzipanteli, A., Digelidis, N., and Papaioannou, A. G. (2015). Self-regulation, motivation and teaching styles in physical education classes: an intervention study. *J. Teach. Phys. Educ.* 34, 333–344. doi: 10.1123/jtpe.2013-0024

Chik, Z., and Abdullah, A. H. (2018). Effect of motivation, learning style and discipline learn about academic achievement additional mathematics. *Int. J. Acad. Res. Bus. Soc. Sci.* 8, 772–787. doi: 10.6007/ijarbss/v8-i4/4059

Cid, L., Pires, A., Borrego, C., Duarte-Mendes, P., Teixeira, D. S., Moutão, J. M., et al. (2019). Motivational determinants of physical education grades and the intention to practice sport in the future. *PLoS One* 14:e0217218. doi: 10.1371/journal.pone.0217218

Clancy, R. B., Herring, M. P., MacIntyre, T. E., and Campbell, M. (2016). A review of competitive sport motivation research. *Psychol. Sport Exerc.* 27, 232–242. doi: 10.1016/j.psychsport.2016.09.003

Cox, A., and Williams, L. (2008). The roles of perceived teacher support, motivational climate, and psychological need satisfaction in students' physical education motivation. *J. Sport Exerc. Psychol.* 30, 222–239. doi: 10.1123/jsep.30.2.222

Duda, J. L. (2013). Introduction to the special issue on the PAPA project. *Int. J. Sport Exerc. Psychol.* 11, 307–310. doi: 10.1080/1612197X.2013.839415

Ferriz, R., González-Cutre, D., and Hagger, S. M. S. (2016). Predicting healthy and unhealthy behaviors through physical education: a self-determination theory-based longitudinal approach. *Scand. J. Med. Sci. Sport.* 26, 579–592. doi: 10.1111/sms.12470

Gil-Arias, A., Claver, F., Práxedes, A., Villar, F., and Del Harvey, S. (2020). Autonomy support, motivational climate, enjoyment and perceived competence in physical education: impact of a hybrid teaching games for understanding/sport education unit. *Eur. Phys. Educ. Rev.* 26, 36–53. doi: 10.1177/1356336X18816997

Goudas, M., Biddle, S., and Fox, K. (1994). Perceived locus of causality, goal orientations, and perceived competence in school physical education classes. *Br. J. Educ. Psychol.* 64, 453–463. doi: 10.1111/j.2044-8279.1994.tb01116.x

Granero-Gallegos, A., Baños, R., Baena-Extremera, A., and Martínez-Molina, M. (2020a). Analysis of misbehaviors and satisfaction with school in secondary education according to student gender and teaching competence. *Front. Psychol.* 11:63. doi: 10.3389/fpsyg.2020.00063

Granero-Gallegos, A., Gómez-López, M., Baena-Extremera, A., and Martínez-Molina, M. (2020b). Interaction effects of disruptive behaviour and motivation profiles with teacher competence and school satisfaction in secondary school physical education. *Int. J. Environ. Res. Public Health* 17, 1–14. doi: 10.3390/ijerph17010114

Gutiérrez, M., and López, E. (2012a). Clima motivacional, razones para la disciplina y comportamiento en educación física. *Rev. Int. Med. Ciencias Act. Física Dep.* 12, 235–251.

Gutiérrez, M., and López, E. (2012b). Motivación, comportamiento de los alumnos y rendimiento académico. *Infanc. Aprendiz.* 35, 61–72. doi: 10.1174/021037012798977421

Gutiérrez, M., López, E., and Ruiz-Pérez, L. M. (2009). Strategies to keep discipline in physical education lessons: validation of measures and analysis of agreement among teachers' and pupils' perceptions. *Rev. Mex. Psicol.* 26, 203–212.

Gutiérrez, M., Ruiz, L. M., and López, E. (2010). Perceptions of motivational climate and teachers' strategies to sustain discipline as predictors of intrinsic motivation in physical education. *Span. J. Psychol.* 13, 597–608. doi: 10.1017/S1138741600002274

Haerens, L., Kirk, D., Cardon, G., De Bourdeaudhuij, I., and Vansteenkiste, M. (2010). Motivational profiles for secondary school physical education and its relationship to the adoption of a physically active lifestyle among university students. *Eur. Phys. Educ. Rev.* 16, 117–139. doi: 10.1177/1356336X10381304

Hodge, K., and Lonsdale, C. (2011). Prosocial and antisocial behavior in sport: the role of coaching style, autonomous vs. controlled motivation, and moral disengagement. *J. Sport Exerc. Psychol.* 33, 527–547. doi: 10.1123/jsep.33.4.527

Howard, J. L., Gagné, M., and Bureau, J. S. (2017). Testing a continuum structure of self-determined motivation: a meta-analysis. *Psychol. Bull.* 143, 1346–1377. doi: 10.1037/bul0000125

Hu, L., and Bentler, P. M. (1999). Cutoff criteria for fit indexes in covariance structure analysis: conventional criteria versus new alternatives. *Struct. Equ. Model. A Multidiscip. J.* 6, 1–55. doi: 10.1080/10705519909540118

IBM Corp (2017). *IBM SPSS Statistics for Windows. 2017.* Armonk, NY: IBM Corp.

Jaakkola, T., Yli-Piipari, S., Barkoukis, V., and Liukkonen, J. (2017). Relationships among perceived motivational climate, motivational regulations, enjoyment, and PA participation among Finnish physical education students. *Int. J. Sport Exerc. Psychol.* 15, 273–290. doi: 10.1080/1612197X.2015.1100209

Jiménez, R., Moreno, B., Leyton, M., and Claver, F. (2015). Motivación y estadios de cambio para el ejercicio físico en adolescentes. *Rev. Latinoam. Psicol.* 47, 196–204. doi: 10.1016/j.rlp.2014.11.001

Kirby, S., Byra, M., Readdy, T., and Wallhead, T. (2015). Effects of spectrum teaching styles on college students' psychological needs satisfaction and self-determined motivation. *Eur. Phys. Educ. Rev.* 21, 521–540. doi: 10.1177/1356336X15585010

Kline, R. B. (2011). *Principles and Practice of Structural Equation Modeling. Third.* New York, NY: Guilford Press, doi: 10.1038/156278a0

Koka, A. (2014). The relative roles of teachers and peers on students' motivation in physical education and its relationship to self-esteem and health-related quality of life. *Int. J. Sport Psychol.* 45, 398–418. doi: 10.7352/IJSP

León, J., Núñez, J. L., and Liew, J. (2015). Self-determination and stem education: effects of autonomy, motivation, and self-regulated learning on high school math achievement. *Learn. Individ. Differ.* 43, 156–163. doi: 10.1016/j.lindif.2015.08.017

Martínez-Galindo, C., Cervelló, E., and Moreno-Murcia, J. A. (2012). Predicción de las razones del alumnado para ser disciplinado en educación física. *Rev. Latinoam. Psicol.* 44, 41–52.

McCarthy, P. J. (2011). Positive emotion in sport performance: current status and future directions. *Int. Rev. Sport Exerc. Psychol.* 4, 50–69. doi: 10.1080/1750984X.2011.560955

Moreno, B., Jiménez, R., Gil-Arias, A., Aspano, M. I., and Torrero, F. (2011). Análisis de la percepción del clima motivacional, necesidades psicológicas básicas, motivación autodeterminada y conductas de disciplina de estudiantes adolescentes en las clases de Educación Física. *Eur. J. Hum. Mov.* 26, 1–24.

Moreno-Murcia, J. A., Conte, L., Hellín, P., Hellín, G., Vera, J., and Cervelló, E. (2008a). Predicción de la motivación autodeterminada según las estrategias para mantener la disciplina y la orientación motivacional en estudiantes adolescentes de educación física. *Apunt. Psicol.* 26, 501–516.

Moreno-Murcia, J. A., Gónzalez-Cutre, D., Chillón, P., and Parra, N. (2008b). Adaptación a la educación física de la escala de las necesidades psicológicas básicas en el ejercicio. *Rev. Iberoam. Psicol. Ejerc. Deport.* 25, 295–303.

Moreno-Murcia, J. A., González-Cutre, D., and Chillón, M. (2009). Preliminary validation in Spanish of a scale designed to measure motivation in physical education classes: the Perceived Locus of Causality (PLOC) Scale. *Span. J. Psychol.* 12, 327–337. doi: 10.1017/S1138741600001724

Moreno-Murcia, J. A., Sicilia, A., Cervelló, E., Huéscar, E., and Dumitru, D. C. (2011). The relationship between goal orientations, motivational climate and selfreported discipline in physical education. *J. Sport. Sci. Med.* 10, 119–129.

Muthén, L. K., and Muthén, B. O. (2012). *Mplus User's Guide, Seventh Edition.* Los Angeles, CA: Muthén & Muthén.

Nicholls, J. G. (1984). Achievement motivation: Conceptions of ability, subjective experience, task choice, and performance. *Psychol. Rev.* 91, 328–346. doi: 10.1037/0033-295X.91.3.328

Noltemeyer, A., Palmer, K., James, A. G., and Petrasek, M. (2019). Disciplinary and achievement outcomes associated with school-wide positive behavioral interventions and supports implementation level. *School Psych. Rev.* 48, 81–87. doi: 10.17105/SPR-2017-0131.V48-1

Ntoumanis, N., and Standage, M. (2009). Motivation in physical education classes: a self-determination theory perspective. *Theory Res. Educ.* 7, 194–202. doi: 10.1177/1477878509104324

Núñez, J. L., and León, J. (2019). Determinants of classroom engagement: a prospective test based on self-determination theory. *Teach. Teach. Theory Pract.* 25, 147–159. doi: 10.1080/13540602.2018.1542297

Papaioannou, A. (1994). Development of a questionnaire to measure achievement goals in physical education. *Res. Q. Exerc. Sport* 65, 11–20. doi: 10.1080/02701367.1994.10762203

Poropat, A. E. (2011). The Eysenckian personality factors and their correlations with academic performance. *Br. J. Educ. Psychol.* 81, 41–58. doi: 10.1348/000709910X497671

Rahimi, M., and Karkami, F. H. (2015). The role of teachers' classroom discipline in their teaching effectiveness and students' language learning motivation and achievement: a path method. *Iran. J. Lang. Teach. Res.* 3, 57–82.

Revelle, W., and Zinbarg, R. E. (2009). Coefficients alpha, beta, omega, and the GLB: comments on sijtsma. *Psychometrika* 74, 145–154. doi: 10.1007/s11336-008-9102-z

Ryan, R. M., and Deci, E. L. (2017). *Self-Determination Theory: Basic Psychological Needs in Motivation, Development, and Wellness.* New York, NY: Guilford Press.

Ryan, R. M., and Deci, E. L. (2020). Intrinsic and extrinsic motivation from a self-determination theory perspective: definitions, theory, practices, and future directions. *Contemp. Educ. Psychol.* 20:101860. doi: 10.1016/j.cedpsych.2020.101860

Şahin, E., Çekin, R., and Özçelik, İ.Y. (2018). Predictors of academic achievement among physical education and sports undergraduate students. *Sports* 6:8. doi: 10.3390/sports6010008

Sánchez-Oliva, D., Leo, F. M., Amado, D., Pulido-González, J. J., and García-Calvo, T. (2015). Análisis de los perfiles motivacionales y su relación con los comportamientos adaptativos en las clases de educación física. *Rev. Latinoam. Psicol.* 47, 156–166. doi: 10.1016/j.rlp.2015.06.007

Sánchez-Oliva, D., Viladrich, C., Amado, D., González-Ponce, I., and García-Calvo, T. (2014). Prediction of positive behaviors in physical education: a self-determination theory perspective. *Rev. Psicodidáctica* 19, 387–406. doi: 10.1387/RevPsicodidact.7911

Sevil, J., Abós, Á, Aibar, A., Julián, J. A., and García-González, L. (2016). Gender and corporal expression activity in physical education: effect of an intervention on students' motivational processes. *Eur. Phys. Educ. Rev.* 22, 372–389. doi: 10.1177/1356336X15613463

Sevil, J., Aibar, A., Abos, Á, and García-González, L. (2017). El clima motivacional del docente de Educación Física: ¿Puede afectar a las calificaciones del alumnado? *Retos Nuev. Tendenc. Educ. Fís. Dep. Recreact.* 2041, 98–102.

Spray, C. (2002). Motivational climate and perceived strategies to sustain pupils' discipline in physical education. *Eur. Phys. Educ. Rev.* 8, 5–20. doi: 10.1177/1356336X020081001

Spray, C., and Wang, C. K. J. (2001). Goal orientations, self-determination and pupils' discipline in physical education. *J. Sports Sci.* 19, 903–913. doi: 10.1080/026404101317108417

Standage, M., Duda, J. L., and Ntoumanis, N. (2006). Students' motivational processes and their relationship to teacher ratings in school physical education: a self-determination theory approach. *Res. Q. Exerc. Sport* 77, 100–110. doi: 10.1080/02701367.2006.10599336

Standage, M., Gillison, F. B., Ntoumanis, N., and Treasure, D. C. (2012). Predicting students' physical activity and health-related well-being: a prospective cross-domain investigation of motivation across school physical education and exercise settings. *J. Sport Exerc. Psychol.* 34, 37–60. doi: 10.1123/jsep.34.1.37

Sternberg, R. J. (2015). Successful intelligence: a model for testing intelligence beyond IQ tests. *Eur. J. Educ. Psychol.* 8, 76–84. doi: 10.1016/j.ejeps.2015.09.004

Taylor, G., Jungert, T., Mageau, G. A., Schattke, K., Dedic, H., Rosenfield, S., et al. (2014). A self-determination theory approach to predicting school achievement over time: the unique role of intrinsic motivation. *Contemp. Educ. Psychol.* 39, 342–358. doi: 10.1016/j.cedpsych.2014.08.002

Tessier, D., Sarrazin, P., and Ntoumanis, N. (2010). The effect of an intervention to improve newly qualified teachers' interpersonal style, students motivation and psychological need satisfaction in sport-based physical education. *Contemp. Educ. Psychol.* 35, 242–253. doi: 10.1016/j.cedpsych.2010.05.005

Vallerand, R. J. (2001). "A hierarchical model of intrinsic and extrinsic motivation in sport and exercise," in *Advances in Motivation in Sport and Exercise*, ed. G. C. Roberts (Champaing, IL: Human Kinetics), 263–319.

Vallerand, R. J. (2007). "Intrinsic and extrinsic motivation in sport and physical activity," in *Handbook of Sport Psychology*, eds G. Tenenbaum and R. C. Eklund (New York, NY: John Wiley & Sons), 59–83. doi: 10.1002/9781118270011.ch3

Vallerand, R. J., and Ratelle, C. F. (2002). "Intrinsic and extrinsic motivation: a hierarchical model," in *Handbook of Self-Determination Research*, ed. R. M. Ryan (Rochester, NY: University of Rochester Press), 37–63.

Van Den Berghe, L., Cardon, G., Tallir, I., Kirk, D., and Haerens, L. (2016). Dynamics of need-supportive and need-thwarting teaching behavior: the bidirectional relationship with student engagement and disengagement in the beginning of a lesson. *Phys. Educ. Sport Pedagog.* 21, 653–670. doi: 10.1080/17408989.2015.1115008

Van Den Berghe, L., Vansteenkiste, M., Cardon, G., Kirk, D., and Haerens, L. (2014). Research on self-determination in physical education: key findings and proposals for future research. *Phys. Educ. Sport Pedagog.* 19, 97–121. doi: 10.1080/17408989.2012.732563

Vasconcellos, D., Parker, P. D., Hilland, T., Cinelli, R., Owen, K. B., Kapsal, N., et al. (2019). Self-determination theory applied to physical education: a systematic review and meta-analysis. *J. Educ. Psychol.* 21, 270–279. doi: 10.1037/edu0000420

Vera, J. A., and Moreno-Murcia, J. A. (2016). Razones intrínsecas para la disciplina en estudiantes adolescentes de educación física. *Educ. XX* 1, 317–335. doi: 10.5944/educXX1.13950

Vlachopoulos, S. P., and Michailidou, S. (2006). Development and initial validation of a measure of autonomy, competence, and relatedness in exercise: The Basic Psychological Needs in Exercise Scale. *Meas. Phys. Educ. Exerc. Sci.* 10, 179–201. doi: 10.1207/s15327841mpee1003_4

Wade, L., Lubans, D. R., Smith, J., and Duncan, M. J. (2020). The impact of exercise environments on adolescents' cognitive and psychological outcomes: a randomised controlled trial. *Psychol. Sport Exerc.* 49, 101707. doi: 10.1016/j.psychsport.2020.101707

Wallhead, T., Garn, A., and Vidoni, C. (2013). Sport Education and social goals in physical education: relationships with enjoyment, relatedness, and leisure-time physical activity. *Phys. Educ. Sport Pedagog.* 18, 427–441. doi: 10.1080/17408989.2012.690377

Wentzel, K. R. (2017). "Peer relationships, motivation, and academic performance at school," in *Handbook of Competence and Motivation: Theory and Application*, eds A. J. Elliot and C. S. Dweck (New York, NY: The Guilford Press), 586–603.

Zhang, Z., and Yuan, K. H. (2016). Robust coefficients Alpha and Omega and confidence intervals with outlying observations and missing data: methods and software. *Educ. Psychol. Meas.* 76, 387–411. doi: 10.1177/0013164415594658

Zimmerman, B. J., and Kitsantas, A. (2014). Comparing students' self-discipline and self-regulation measures and their prediction of academic achievement. *Contemp. Educ. Psychol.* 39, 145–155. doi: 10.1016/j.cedpsych.2014.03.004

15

A Single Question of Parent-Reported Physical Activity Levels Estimates Objectively Measured Physical Fitness and Body Composition in Preschool Children

Pere Palou[1], Adrià Muntaner-Mas[1,2], Jaume Cantallops[1], Pere Antoni Borràs[1], Idoia Labayen[3], David Jiménez-Pavón[4,5], Cecilia Dorado García[6,7], Diego Moliner-Urdiales[8], Manuel A. Rodríguez Pérez[9], Miguel A. Rojo-Tirado[10], Cristina Cadenas-Sanchez[2,4,5], Francisco B. Ortega[2] and Josep Vidal-Conti[1]*

[1] GICAFE "Physical Activity and Exercise Sciences Research Group", University of the Balearic Islands, Palma, Spain, [2] PROFITH "PROmoting FITness and Health Through Physical Activity" Research Group, Faculty of Sport Sciences, Department of Physical Education and Sports, University of Granada, Granada, Spain, [3] Institute for Innovation & Sustainable Development in Food Chain (IS-FOOD), Public University of Navarre, Pamplona, Spain, [4] MOVE-IT Research Group and Department of Physical Education, Faculty of Education Sciences, University of Cádiz, Cádiz, Spain, [5] Biomedical Research and Innovation Institute of Cádiz (INiBICA) Research Unit, Puerta del Mar University Hospital University of Cádiz, Cádiz, Spain, [6] Research Institute of Biomedical and Health Sciences (IUIBS), University of Las Palmas de Gran Canaria, Las Palmas de Gran Canaria, Spain, [7] Department of Physical Education, University of Las Palmas de Gran Canaria, Las Palmas de Gran Canaria, Spain, [8] LIFE Research Group, University of Jaume I, Castellón de la Plana, Spain, [9] Faculty of Education Sciences, SPORT Research Group, CERNEP Research Center, University of Almería, Almería, Spain, [10] Laboratory of Exercise Physiology Research Group (LFE Research Group), Faculty of Physical Activity and Sport Sciences-INEF, Department of Health and Human Performance, Universidad Politécnica de Madrid, Madrid, Spain

Correspondence:
Adrià Muntaner-Mas
adria.muntaner@uib.es

Physical inactivity is recognized as a determinant of low physical fitness and body composition in preschool children, which in turn, are important markers of health through the lifespan. Objective methods to assess physical activity, physical fitness and body composition in preschool children are preferable; however, they have some practical limitations in the school context. Therefore, the aim of this study was to test whether a single question regarding physical activity level of preschool children, reported by their parents, could be used as an alternative screening tool of physical fitness and body composition. The information was obtained from 10 different cities throughout Spain, gathering a total of 3179 healthy preschool children (52.8% boys and 47.2% girls) aged 3–5 years. Physical activity levels of preschool children were reported by parents using a single question with five response options (very low, low, average, high, or very high). Physical fitness and body composition were assessed with the PREFIT fitness battery. The results showed that parents' perception of their children's physical activity was positively associated with all objectively measured physical fitness components ($\beta_{range} = -0.094$ to 0.113; all $p < 0.020$); and negatively with body composition indicators as measured ($\beta_{range} = -0.113$ to -0.058; all $p < 0.001$). The results showed significant differences in all physical fitness and body composition *z*-scores across the parent-reported physical activity levels (all $p < 0.017$ and all $p < 0.001$, respectively), as well as, for the fitness index ($p < 0.001$). Our study suggests that in school settings with insufficient resources to objectively assess fitness and body composition, parents-reported physical activity level by means of a single question might provide useful information about these important health markers in preschool children.

Keywords: physical fitness, motor activity, body composition, fatness, physical activity, preschool children

INTRODUCTION

Obesity is a worldwide concern that is growing among children and adolescents (Abarca-Gómez et al., 2017), and has even begun to occur in preschool children (Cadenas-Sánchez et al., 2019a). The early onset of obesity seems to be related to the occurrence of associated complications such as metabolic and cardiovascular disorders, and the risks depend partly on the age of onset and on the duration of obesity (Umer et al., 2017; Ho et al., 2019). Particularly worrying is the data coming from the World Health Organization (WHO) whose results demonstrated that in 2014 more than 41 million of children under 5 years old were classified as overweight/obese, and this fact will continue to worsen (World Health Organization, 2016). At European level, a higher prevalence of overweight/obese preschool in the south of Europe was observed, compared to those children from the north (Cadenas-Sanchez et al., 2016b). In addition, in a European cohort of 3120 children aged 2–9 years old (1016 from 2 to 6 years old) objectively measured physical activity was found an important factor to protect against clustering of CVD risk factors in young children (Jiménez-Pavón et al., 2013). At the national level, our group found that 35% of the pre-schoolers examined presented overweight/obesity were already 1.3% morbid obese (Cadenas-Sánchez et al., 2019a). A recent study with a population-based sample of 51,505 children found that the most rapid weight gain occurs between 2 and 6 years of age being those obese at that age also obese adolescents (Geserick et al., 2018). Despite preschool years represents an opportunity for obesity surveillance it is still challenging in the WHO European Region (Jones et al., 2017).

In addition to obesity, a low physical fitness level in childhood/adolescence has been considered a marker of poor health and a risk factor for multiple health outcomes at these ages and later in life (Ortega et al., 2008b; Ruiz et al., 2009). In this context, it has been shown that higher levels of cardiorespiratory fitness during childhood are related to lower risk of becoming overweight/obese across puberty (Ortega et al., 2011). However, such information is not available in preschool children, which could be due, at least partially, to the fact that there was no information about which fitness tests should be used in preschool children. A systematic review searching for any study relating fitness in preschool age with health outcomes, found no studies in this direction (Ortega et al., 2015). Fortunately, over the last years, more evidence has been accumulated on which fitness tests are more feasible, reliable and valid to be used in preschool children, in particular the PREFIT (Assessing FITness in PREschoolers) battery, which will provide new avenues to study the role of fitness in health at these early ages and later in life (Cadenas-Sánchez et al., 2014; Ortega et al., 2015; Sanchez-Delgado et al., 2015; Cadenas-Sanchez et al., 2016a; Mora-Gonzalez et al., 2017). In this context, the PREFIT project group has recently provided for the first time the physical fitness reference standards for preschool children (Cadenas-Sánchez et al., 2019b).

Since obesity and low fitness are important markers of health through the lifespan (Ortega et al., 2018), it is of public health interest to study determinants of these two modifiable risk factors as early as possible, being preschool age a sensitive stage of life. Thus, physical inactivity is a recognized determinant of obesity and low physical fitness, and it would be interesting to explore associations of physical activity with physical fitness and body composition in preschool children. Although objective methods, such as accelerometers, to assess physical activity in young individuals are preferable (Migueles et al., 2017), they have some practical limitations and most importantly they are not feasible under certain circumstances in the school context. Alternatively, parent-reported physical activity levels of their children are an alternative method, and it is of interest to test whether a single question on parents' rated physical activity level is able for screening a set of important physical fitness and body composition markers in preschool children. If so, this method could be a very useful and economic tool to be used as a predictor of health markers in preschool, similarly to what self-reported PA of older children (10–12 years old) showed in a large epidemiological study (Jiménez-Pavón et al., 2012).

Therefore, the aim of this study is to test whether a single question regarding the physical activity of children, reported by their parents, could be used as a screening tool of objectively measured physical fitness and body composition in preschool children.

MATERIALS AND METHODS

Participants and Study Design

The present study was performed under the framework of the PREFIT project[1] (Cadenas-Sánchez et al., 2014; Ortega et al., 2015; Sanchez-Delgado et al., 2015; Cadenas-Sanchez et al., 2016a; Mora-Gonzalez et al., 2017; Labayen et al., 2018). Briefly, the aim of the project was to propose a physical fitness test battery of feasible and reliable field-based tests to assess physical fitness in children aged 3–5 years and to report reference values for a better interpretation of physical fitness assessment (Cadenas-Sánchez et al., 2019a,b).

[1] http://profith.ugr.es/prefit

After several methodological studies to define the PREFIT fitness battery (Cadenas-Sánchez et al., 2014; Ortega et al., 2015; Sanchez-Delgado et al., 2015; Cadenas-Sanchez et al., 2016a; Mora-Gonzalez et al., 2017), we set up PREFIT-Spain, aiming to measure physical fitness in a geographically distributed sample of preschool children across Spain. The project involved data collection in 10 cities from the south, center, and north of Spain, gathering a total of 3179 (*M*: 4.60; SD: 0.87) healthy preschool children (52.8% boys and 47.2% girls) aged between 3 and 5 years (Cadenas-Sanchez et al., 2016a). Parents or legal guardians were informed about the purpose of the study and written informed consent was obtained from the parents of all participants. The study protocol was performed in accordance with the ethical standards and was approved by the Review Committee for Research Involving Human Subjects at the University of Granada (n° 845).

Procedure and Measures

The PREFIT battery comprises the following tests[2]: the PREFIT 20-meters shuttle-run test (PREFIT 20 m SRT) to assess cardiorespiratory fitness, handgrip strength and standing long jump tests to assess muscular strength (upper and lower limbs, respectively), 4 × 10 m SRT to assess speed-agility and one-leg stance test to assess balance (Cadenas-Sanchez et al., 2016a); and weight, height, body mass index (BMI), waist circumference, and waist-to-height ratio to assess body composition indicators. Children were assessed individually in a school-setting by trained evaluators using the following standardized equipment and procedures. Before starting the tests, evaluators performed an example to ensure that the child understood the test correctly.

Physical Fitness Measures

Cardiorespiratory fitness was assessed using a modified version of the original 20 m shuttle run test (SRT): the PREFIT 20 m SRT (Cadenas-Sánchez et al., 2014; Mora-Gonzalez et al., 2017). Participants had to run back and forth between 2 lines 20 m apart with an audio signal. The test finished when the child failed to reach the end lines concurrent with the audio signal on two consecutive occasions or when the child stops because of exhaustion. The initial stage of the PREFIT 20 m SRT was 6.5 km h^{-1}.

The handgrip strength test measures the maximal strength of the upper limb using an analog dynamometer (TKK 5001, Grip-A, Takei, Tokyo, Japan). The test protocol is reported elsewhere (España-Romero et al., 2010). The grip spans were fixed at 4.0 cm (Sanchez-Delgado et al., 2015). The best value of the two attempts for each hand was chosen, and the average of both was registered in kilograms (kg). The standing long jump test assesses the explosive strength of the lower limbs. This test consisted of jumping as far as possible with the feet together and remaining upright. The distance was measured from the take-off line to the point where the back of the heel nearest to the take-off line lands on the ground. The better of two attempts were recorded in centimeters (cm).

The 4 × 10 m SRT was used to assess speed/agility. This test consisted of running and turning as fast as possible between two parallel lines (10 m apart). To make this test easier to understand and perform for preschool children, we did not use sponges to be exchanged when crossing the lines (4 × 10 m), as the original protocol does in older children (Ortega et al., 2008a). Instead, two evaluators were located behind each line and participants had to touch the examiner's hand and go back at maximum speed. The result was measured with a stopwatch (Tremblay, CHRO 300, Gleizé, France) to the nearest 0.1 s. The best of two attempts was recorded in seconds. A higher score indicates worse performance.

Body Composition

Weight (kg) was measured without shoes and in light clothing using an electronic scale (SECA Model 869, Hamburg, Germany). Height (cm) was measured in the Frankfort plane without shoes using a stadiometer (SECA Model 213). BMI was calculated based on weight divided by height squared. The cut-off points used to classify weight status categories were those established by World Obesity Federation (WOF)[3], formerly International Obesity Task Force (IOTF) (Cole and Lobstein, 2012) and by the WHO (de Onis et al., 2007). Waist circumference (cm) was measured at the umbilical location with a non-elastic tape (SECA Model 200) at the end of a normal expiration without the tape compressing the skin. The waist-to-height ratio was calculated as waist circumference divided by height in centimeters. All measures were taken twice and the mean of the two measurements was used for analyses. All measurements were harmonized following a strict protocol to ensure standardization.

Physical Activity

As an indirect measure of the physical activity level of the children, parents were asked to answer the following question: "Your children's physical activity level excluding school time is ...?" The response options were very low, low, average, high, or very high. The response frequency by categories of parent-reported physical activity levels is shown in **Supplementary Figure S1**. For analyses, the very low and low categories were merged due to the low response frequency of the very low category.

Confounders

Paternal and maternal educational was assessed by self-report questionnaire and can be consulted elsewhere (Merino-De Haro et al., 2018). A variable with three categories was calculated for analyses and for each parent: low (no education or primary school education), medium (secondary school education, upper-secondary school education, or technical training), and high (university education). Only, age, gender, and maternal education level were introduced as potential confounders.

Statistical Analysis

Firstly, we explored which potential confounders were more strongly correlated with the study outcomes. Maternal education was more strongly associated than paternal education with

[2]http://profith.ugr.es/recursos-prefit?lang=en

[3]http://www.worldobesity.org/

TABLE 1 | Descriptive characteristics of the study population (n = 3.179).

	All (n = 3.179)		Boys (n = 1.678)						Girls (n = 1.501)					
			3 years		4 years		5 years		3 years		4 years		5 years	
Age (years)	4.60	0.87	3.53	(0.30)	4.50	(0.28)	5.54	(0.34)	3.50	(0.31)	4.53	(0.29)	5.53	(0.32)
Height (cm)	106.93	7.51	99.90	(4.67)	106.91	(4.77)	113.93	(5.49)	98.73	(4.53)	106.01	(4.74)	112.89	(4.85)
Gender [n (%)]														
Female	1501	(47.22)							443	(47.48)	509	(47.0)	549	(47.21
Male	1678	(52.83)	490	(52.52)	574	(53.0)	614	(52.79)						
Maternal education [n (%)]														
Low	210	(7)	33	(6.98)	27	(5.06)	49	(8.69)	23	(5.45)	33	(6.92)	45	(8.70)
Medium	1382	(46.34)	202	(42.71)	262	(49.06)	272	(48.23)	185	(43.84)	212	(44.44)	249	(48.16)
High	1395	(46.76)	238	(50.32)	245	(45.88)	243	(43.09)	214	(50.71)	232	(48.64)	223	(43.13)
Physical fitness														
PREFIT 20 m SRT (laps)	20.02	11.64	12.85	(7.65)	21.19	(9.51)	28.86	(13.05)	10.86	(6.36)	18.56	(8.21)	23.96	(11.45)
Handgrip strength (kg)	7.03	2.48	5.20	(1.69)	7.17	(1.90)	9.27	(2.25)	4.66	(1.58)	6.56	(1.72)	8.37	(1.97)
Standing long jump (cm)	73.63	22.25	57.57	(17.72)	77.93	(16.91)	91.45	(17.36)	50.81	(17.12)	70.60	(16.06)	84.48	(18.10)
4 × 10 m SRT (s)	16.81	2.52	18.82	(2.33)	16.36	(1.76)	14.83	(1.40)	19.77	(2.50)	16.72	(1.59)	15.46	(1.49)
Fatness														
Weight (kg)	18.99	3.75	16.55	(2.33)	18.78	(2.95)	21.62	(4.04)	16.12	(2.16)	18.52	(2.93)	21.16	(3.59)
BMI (kg/m^2)	16.48	1.76	16.53	(1.50)	16.36	(1.63)	16.55	(2.03)	16.48	(1.33)	16.41	(1.80)	16.54	(2.01)
Waist circumference (cm)	53.16	5.02	50.88	(3.80)	52.59	(4.24)	54.95	(5.57)	51.24	(3.86)	53.29	(4.88)	55.19	(5.47)
Waist-to-height ratio	0.50	0.04	0.51	(0.03)	1.49	(0.03)	0.48	(0.04)	0.52	(0.03)	0.50	(0.04)	0.49	(0.04)

SD, standard deviation; SRT, shuttle run test; BMI, body mass index. Values are presented as mean and standard deviation.

study outcomes and, thus, it was a better predictor. Partial correlation adjusted for potential confounders were used to examine the association of parent-reported physical activity levels with physical fitness and body composition indicators.

To study the association of parent-reported physical activity levels with physical fitness (PREFIT 20 m SRT, handgrip strength test, standing long jump, 4 × 10 m SRT) and body composition outcomes (weight, BMI, waist circumference, waist-to-height ratio), we conducted linear regression analysis inserting the physical fitness and body composition outcomes as dependent variables and parent-reported physical activity levels as independent variable, adjusted for sex, age and maternal education. Additionally, physical fitness and body composition *z*-scores were created and explored using analysis of covariance (adjusted for confounders) with a Bonferroni adjustment according to parent-reported physical activity levels. Also, it was created a fitness index using the average of physical fitness z-scores divided by the number of fitness outcomes (PREFIT 20 m SRT, standing long jump, 4 × 10 m SRT), and explored with an analysis of covariance with a Bonferroni adjustment according to parent-reported physical activity levels. All analyses were performed using the Statistical Package for Social Sciences (IBM SPSS Statistics for Windows, version 21.0, Armonk, NY) and the level of significance was set at $p < 0.05$. Graphics were performed using Sigmaplot version 12.5 for Windows (Systat Software, Inc., San Jose, CA, United States).

RESULTS

Descriptive characteristics of the physical fitness and body composition indicators of the sample stratified by sex and age groups (3, 4, and 5 years) are presented in **Table 1**, as means and standard deviation. The response frequency of parent-reported physical activity levels (for the whole sample and by sex) is illustrated in **Supplementary Figure S1**.

The results show the association of parent-reported physical activity levels between physical fitness and body composition measures after adjusting for sex, age and maternal education in preschool children. Children whose parents reported to have higher physical activity levels had a higher level of physical fitness in all indicators ($\beta_{range} = -0.094$ to 0.113, and *p*-value from 0.020 to <0.001) (**Table 2**). Otherwise, it was observed a negative association between parent-reported physical activity levels and all body composition indicators after adjusting for sex, age and maternal education ($\beta_{range} = -0.058$ to -0.113, all $p < 0.001$). The results showed similar trends for physical fitness and body composition of children with different age and sex (see **Supplementary Tables S1** and **S2**, respectively).

The results show the differences in objectively measured physical fitness *z*-scores (panel A) and body composition *z*-scores (panel B) across parent-reported physical activity levels. The results showed significant differences in all physical fitness and body composition *z*-scores across the parent-reported physical activity levels (all $p < 0.017$ and all $p < 0.001$, respectively) (**Figure 1**). There were pairwise significant differences in PREFIT 20 m SRT, standing long jump and the 4 × 10 m SRT between each category of the parent-reported physical activity levels after a Bonferroni adjustment (all $p < 0.038$). There were pairwise significant differences in each category of the parent-reported physical activity levels after a Bonferroni adjustment and all body composition *z*-scores between (all $p < 0.036$). However, these pairwise significant differences were not seen between the high and very high categories in neither physical fitness *z*-scores nor body composition *z*-scores ($p_{range} = 0.059$ to 0.934 and $p_{range} = 0.128$ to.355, respectively).

The results show the differences in physical fitness index across parent-reported physical activity levels, by age (**Figure 2A**) and gender (**Figure 2B**). The results showed significant differences in the fitness index across the parent-reported physical activity levels ($p < 0.001$). There were pairwise significant differences in the fitness index between each category of parent-reported physical activity levels after a Bonferroni adjustment (all $p < 0.001$). However, these pairwise significant differences were not seen between the high and very high categories ($p = 0.102$). No interaction effect was seen for age groups ($p = 0.233$) nor gender ($p = 0.722$).

DISCUSSION

This study provides evidence supporting that a single and very simple question of physical activity reported by parents can significantly estimate the physical fitness and body composition of preschool children (aged 3–5 years). More specifically, our findings support that: (1) parent-reported physical activity levels are positively associated with objectively measured physical fitness, as measured by means of the PREFIT 20 m SRT, handgrip strength, standing long jump and the 4 × 10 m SRT in children aged 3–5 years; (2) parent-reported physical activity levels are negatively related to body composition indicators, as measured by weight, BMI, waist circumference and waist-to-height ratio in children aged 3–5 years; and (3) there

TABLE 2 | Associations of parents-reported physical activity levels with objectively measured physical fitness and body composition in preschool children ($n = 3.179$).

	β	B	CI (95%)	p
PREFIT 20 m SRT (laps)	0.113	1.714	(1.252, 2.176)	< 0.001
Handgrip strength (kg)	0.031	0.100	(0.016, 0.185)	0.020
Standing long jump (cm)	0.102	2.971	(2.174, 3.768)	< 0.001
4 × 10 m SRT (s)*	−0.094	−0.309	(-0.394, -0.224)	< 0.001
Weight (kg)	−0.058	−0.284	(-0.429, -0.139)	< 0.001
BMI (kg/m²)	−0.097	−0.223	(-0.307, -0.139)	< 0.001
Waist circumference (cm)	−0.100	−0.658	(-0.883, -0.433)	< 0.001
Waist-to-height ratio	−0.113	−0.006	(-0.008, -0.004)	< 0.001

*SRT, shuttle run test; BMI, body mass index; β, beta standardized coefficients; B, beta unstandardized coefficients; CI, confidence interval (upper, lower). Parent-reported physical activity levels were considered as a predictive variable and physical fitness outcomes (PREFIT 20 m SRT, handgrip strength test, standing long jump and 4 × 10 m SRT) and body composition outcomes (weight, BMI, waist circumference and waist-to-height ratio) were considered as dependent variables. The analyses were adjusted by age, sex, and maternal education. *Lower values indicate better performance.*

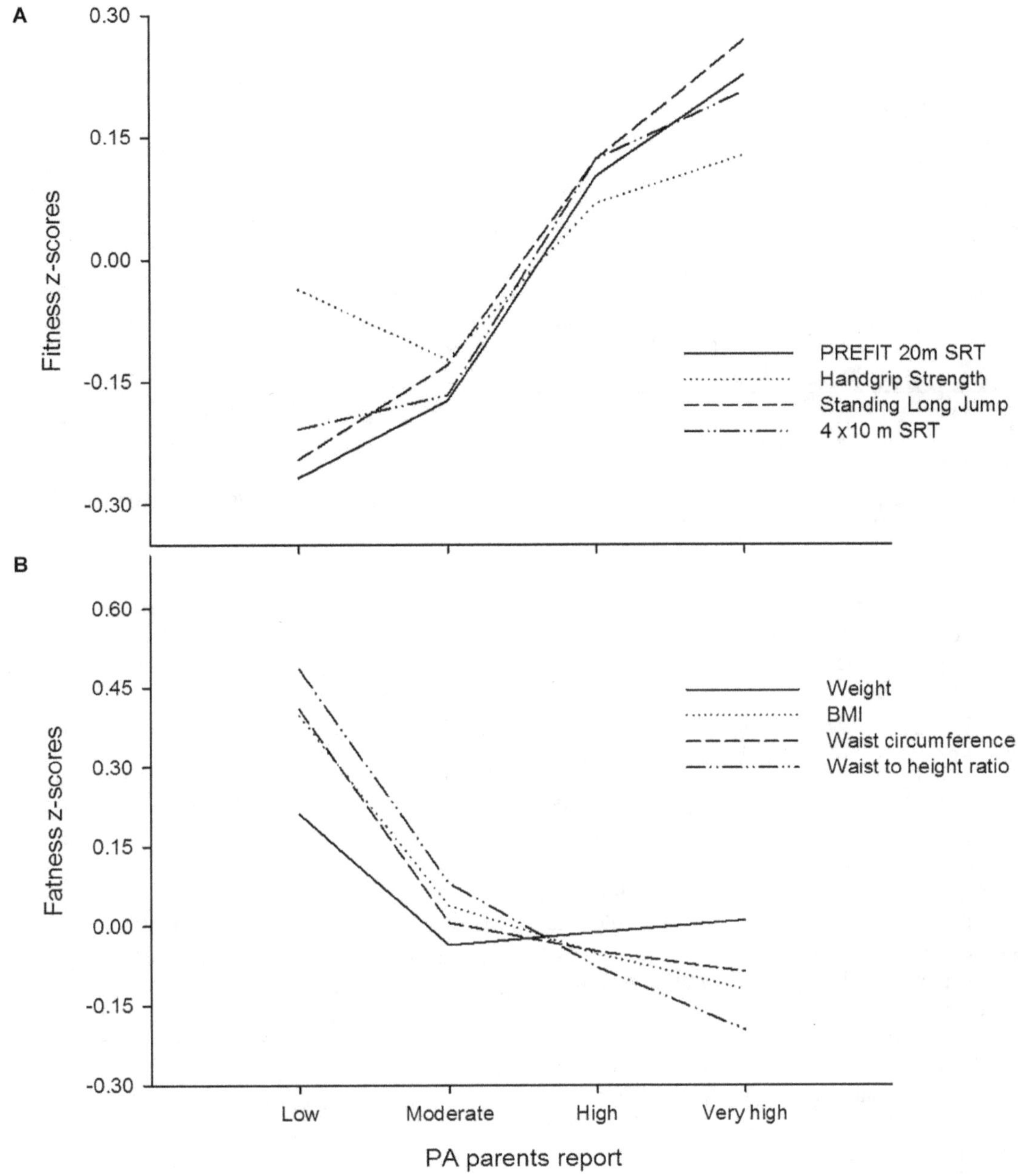

FIGURE 1 | Differences of objectively measured physical fitness *z*-scores **(A)** and body composition *z*-scores **(B)** across parents-reported physical activity levels in preschool children (*n* = 3.179). SRT, shuttle run test; BMI, body mass index; PA, physical activity. The analyses were adjusted by age, sex, and maternal education.

are pronounced differences in all physical fitness and body composition *z*-scores, as well as, in the fitness index across each category of the parent-reported physical activity levels in children aged 3–5 years.

This study shows a positive association between parent-reported physical activity levels and the PREFIT 20 m SRT. These results are in agreement with previous findings in the adult population (Emaus et al., 2010; Minder et al., 2014). For instance, Murphy et al. (1988) who found that a reported physical activity single question was associated with maximal oxygen consumption, measured by a more valid and reliable technique. Likewise, Aadahl et al. (2007) showed that reported physical activity was related to objectively measured cardiorespiratory fitness. Nevertheless, in our study inconsistent associations were seen between parent-reported physical activity levels and handgrip strength (see **Supplementary Table S1**). In fact, when analyses were undertaken by age group only was seen as an association in those older preschool children. This result does not concur with those found in other population of adults where self-reported measures of physical activity were correlated with handgrip strength (Leblanc et al., 2015). In fact, a recent systematic review has found inconsistent associations between

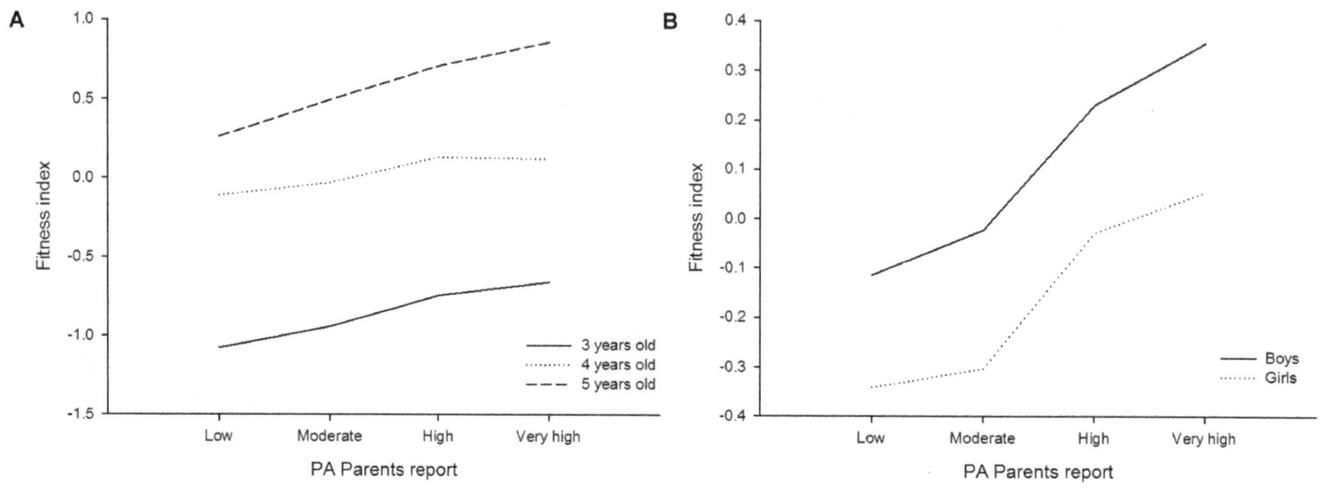

FIGURE 2 | Differences of physical fitness index across parent-reported physical activity levels, by age **(A)** and gender **(B)** in preschool children (*n* = 3.179). SRT, shuttle run test; PA, physical activity. The analyses were adjusted by age, sex, and maternal education.

muscular fitness and self-reported physical activity in children and adolescents (Smith et al., 2019). Otherwise, our data showed that parent-reported physical activity levels correlate strongly with lower body strength as measured by means of standing long jump. In this sense, it can be hypothesized that uncontrolled variables (fat-free mass, fat mass) in our sample might explain the discrepancies between the associations of parent-reported physical activity levels and the distinct components of the muscular strength (Artero et al., 2010).

A negative association between parent-reported physical activity levels and body composition indicators was found in this investigation. To our knowledge, there are no studies that analyze this association in preschool children, and that's why this study opens a new window in order to estimate childhood obesity based on physical activity information reported by parents. Recent studies have found that higher moderate-to-vigorous physical activity (MVPA) and/or vigorous physical activity of preschool children are associated with better body composition (Leppänen et al., 2016, 2017; Fang et al., 2017). In this context, a self-reported methodology to assess physical activity levels of preschool children has not been recommended (Oliver et al., 2007), however, parents might do with somewhat validity (Pate et al., 2010). Taking this evidence together, it can be suggested that parent-reported physical activity levels of preschool children might be an alternative to estimate objectively measured body composition indicators since physical activity is associated with body composition at an early age.

Our results also showed that there was a pronounced difference between children with very low/low physically active (who had worse physical fitness and body composition) and the rest of the categories with higher reported physical activity; however, the question did not discriminate so accurately between those preschool children reported by their parents as being moderate, high and very high active. This finding suggests that our question might be more useful in more extreme cases (between very low/low and high/very high active). In this context, the question proposed in this investigation could be used to perform the first screening with large samples of preschool in order to detect the most extreme cases with a marked risk of worse physical fitness and body composition. Thus, objective and direct measures could be administered only in those participants who have already been detected at higher risk. Therefore, this single question about PA levels would serve to identify children at a higher risk of low fitness and worse body composition avoiding the complications associated with direct and objectively measurement.

Limitations and Strengths

This research has several limitations. The cross-sectional nature of the study and the use of an indirect measure of physical activity levels should be considered with caution. In addition, despite all associations of parent-reported physical activity levels between physical fitness and body composition were statistically significant the standardized regression coefficients were small. Likewise, the reliability of the single question has not been yet proved, which could be another drawback. To our knowledge, this large, population-based study on preschool children is the first that covers geographically most of the regions of Spain. Also, the use of a quick and single question able to identify vital markers of physical health at such early ages should be considered as something powerful.

CONCLUSION

Our study suggests that a single question of parent-reported physical activity levels might provide meaningful information to identify children at a higher risk of important physical health markers such as physical fitness and body composition in preschool children. Therefore, a single question could be an alternative for a physical health screening at early ages, especially for epidemiological and intervention studies with insufficient resources or even in school settings where objective methods cannot be applied.

ETHICS STATEMENT

The study protocol was performed in accordance with the ethical standards and was approved by the Review Committee for Research Involving Human Subjects at the University of Granada (number 845).

AUTHOR CONTRIBUTIONS

CC-S and FBO conceptualized and designed the study. CC-S organized the database. AM-M, CC-S, FBO, and JV-C carried out the statistical analysis. PP, AM-M, JC, PB, FBO, and JV-C wrote the first draft of the manuscript. PP, AM-M, JC, PB, FBO, and JV-C wrote the sections of the manuscript. All authors contributed to the manuscript revision, read, and approved the final version of the manuscript.

Programme under the grant agreement no. 667302, the University of Granada, Plan Propio de Investigación 2016, Excellence Actions: Units of Excellence, the Unit of Excellence on Exercise and Health (UCEES), the Junta de Andalucia, Consejeria de Conocimiento, Investigación y Universidades, the EXERNET Research Network on Exercise and Health in Special Populations (DEP2005-00046/ACTI), the SAMID III Network, RETICS, funded by the PN I+D+I 2017-2021 (Spain), ISCIII-Sub-Directorate General for Research Assessment and Promotion, and the European Regional Development Fund (ERDF) (Ref. RD16/002). IL was supported by the Spanish Ministry of Economy and Competitiveness (DEP2016-78377-R), the "Fondos Estructurales de la Unión Europea (FEDER), Una manera de hacer Europa", the Public University of Navarra, Plan de Promoción de Grupos de Investigación, and the EXERNET Research Network on Exercise and Health in Special Populations (DEP2005-00046/ACTI). DJ-P was supported by a grant from the Spanish Ministry of Science and Innovation - MINECO (RYC-2014-16938), the Spanish Ministry of Economy and Competitiveness - MINECO/FEDER (DEP2016-76123-R), the Government of Andalusia, Integrated Territorial Initiative 2014–2020 for the province of Cádiz (PI-0002-2017), the European Union's ERASMUS+SPORT Programme (Grant Agreement 603121-EPP-1-2018-1-ES-SPO-SCP), and the EXERNET Research Network on Exercise and Health in Special Populations (DEP2005-00046/ACTI).

REFERENCES

Aadahl, M., Kjaer, M., Kristensen, J. H., Mollerup, B., and Jørgensen, T. (2007). Self-reported physical activity compared with maximal oxygen uptake in adults. *Eur. J. Cardiovasc. Prev. Rehabil.* 14, 422–428. doi: 10.1097/HJR.0b013e3280128d00

Abarca-Gómez, L., Abdeen, Z. A., Hamid, Z. A., Abu-Rmeileh, N. M., Acosta-Cazares, B., Acuin, C., et al. (2017). Worldwide trends in body-mass index, underweight, overweight, and obesity from 1975 to 2016: a pooled analysis of 2416 population-based measurement studies in 128·9 million children, adolescents, and adults. *Lancet* 390, 2627–2642. doi: 10.1016/S0140-6736(17)32129-3

Artero, E. G., España-Romero, V., Ortega, F. B., Jiménez-Pavón, D., Ruiz, J. R., Vicente-Rodríguez, G., et al. (2010). Health-related fitness in adolescents: underweight, and not only overweight, as an influencing factor. The AVENA study. *Scand. J. Med. Sci. Sport.* 20, 418–427. doi: 10.1111/j.1600-0838.2009.00959.x

Cadenas-Sánchez, C., Alcántara-Moral, F., Sánchez-Delgado, G., Mora-González, J., Martínez-Téllez, B., Herrador-Colmenero, M., et al. (2014). Assessment of cardiorespiratory fitness in preschool children: adaptation of the 20 metres shuttle run test. *Nutr. Hosp.* 30, 1333–1343. doi: 10.3305/nh.2014.30.6.7859

Cadenas-Sánchez, C., Intemann, T., Labayen, I., Artero, E. G., Alvarez-Bueno, C., Sanchis-Moysi, J., et al. (2019a). Prevalence of severe/morbid obesity and other weight status and anthropometric reference standards in Spanish preschool children: the PREFIT project. *Pediatr. Res.* doi: 10.1038/s41390-019-0325-8 [Epub ahead of print].

Cadenas-Sánchez, C., Intemann, T., Labayen, I., Peinado, A. B., Vidal-Conti, J., Sanchis-Moysi, J., et al. (2019b). Physical fitness reference standards for preschool children: the PREFIT project. *J. Sci. Med. Sport* 22, 430–437. doi: 10.1016/j.jsams.2018.09.227

Cadenas-Sanchez, C., Martinez-Tellez, B., Sanchez-Delgado, G., Mora-Gonzalez, J., Castro-Piñero, J., Löf, M., et al. (2016a). Assessing physical fitness in preschool children: feasibility, reliability and practical recommendations for the PREFIT battery. *J. Sci. Med. Sport* 19, 910–915. doi: 10.1016/j.jsams.2016.02.003

Cadenas-Sanchez, C., Nyström, C., Sanchez-Delgado, G., Martinez-Tellez, B., Mora-Gonzalez, J., Risinger, A. S., et al. (2016b). Prevalence of overweight/obesity and fitness level in preschool children from the north compared with the south of Europe: an exploration with two countries. *Pediatr. Obes.* 11, 403–410. doi: 10.1111/ijpo.12079

Cole, T. J., and Lobstein, T. (2012). Extended international (IOTF) body mass index cut-offs for thinness, overweight and obesity. *Pediatr. Obes.* 7, 284–294. doi: 10.1111/j.2047-6310.2012.Y00064.x

de Onis, M., Onyango, A. W., Borghi, E., Siyam, A., Nishida, C., and Siekmann, J. (2007). Development of a WHO growth reference for school-aged children and adolescents. *Bull. World Health Organ.* 85, 660–667. doi: 10.2471/blt.07.043497

Emaus, A., Degerstrøm, J., Wilsgaard, T., Hansen, B. H., Dieli-Conwright, C. M., Furberg, A.-S., et al. (2010). Does a variation in self-reported physical activity reflect variation in objectively measured physical activity, resting heart rate, and physical fitness? Results from the Tromsø study. *Scand. J. Public Health* 38, 105–118. doi: 10.1177/1403494810378919

España-Romero, V., Ortega, F. B., Vicente-Rodríguez, G., Artero, E. G., and Ruiz, J. R. (2010). Elbow position affects handgrip strength in adolescents: validity and reliability of JAMAR, DYNEx, and TKK dynamometers. *J. Strength Cond. Res.* 24, 272–277. doi: 10.1519/JSC.0b013e3181b296a5

Fang, H., Quan, M., Zhou, T., Sun, S., Zhang, J., Zhang, H., et al. (2017). Relationship between physical activity and physical fitness in preschool children: a cross-sectional study. *Biomed. Res. Int.* 2017, 1–8. doi: 10.1155/2017/9314026

Geserick, M., Vogel, M., Gausche, R., Lipek, T., Spielau, U., Keller, E., et al. (2018). Acceleration of BMI in early childhood and risk of sustained obesity. *N. Engl. J. Med.* 379, 1303–1312. doi: 10.1056/NEJMoa1803527

Ho, H. C. H., Maddaloni, E., and Buzzetti, R. (2019). Risk factors and predictive biomarkers of early cardiovascular disease in obese youth. *Diabetes. Metab. Res. Rev.* 35:e3134. doi: 10.1002/dmrr.3134

Jiménez-Pavón, D., Fernández-Alvira, J. M., te Velde, S. J., Brug, J., Bere, E., Jan, N., et al. (2012). Associations of parental education and parental physical activity (PA) with children's PA: the ENERGY cross-sectional study. *Prev. Med.* 55, 310–314. doi: 10.1016/j.ypmed.2012.07.011

Jiménez-Pavón, D., Konstabel, K., Bergman, P., Ahrens, W., Pohlabeln, H., Hadjigeorgiou, C., et al. (2013). Physical activity and clustered cardiovascular disease risk factors in young children: a cross-sectional study (the IDEFICS study). *BMC Med.* 11:172. doi: 10.1186/1741-7015-11-172

Jones, R. E., Jewell, J., Saksena, R., Ramos Salas, X., and Breda, J. (2017). Overweight and obesity in children under 5 years: surveillance opportunities and challenges for the WHO European Region. *Front. Public Health* 5:58. doi: 10.3389/fpubh.2017.00058

Labayen, G. I., Arenaza, L., Medrano, M., García, N., Cadenas-Sanchez, C., and Ortega, F. B. (2018). Associations between the adherence to the Mediterranean diet and cardiorespiratory fitness with total and central obesity in preschool children: the PREFIT project. *Eur. J. Nutr.* 57, 2975–2983. doi: 10.1007/s00394-017-1571-3

Leblanc, A., Pescatello, L. S., Taylor, B. A., Capizzi, J. A., Clarkson, P. M., Michael White, C., et al. (2015). Relationships between physical activity and muscular strength among healthy adults across the lifespan. *Springerplus* 4:557. doi: 10.1186/s40064-015-1357-0

Leppänen, M. H., Henriksson, P., Delisle Nyström, C., Henriksson, H., Ortega, F. B., Pomeroy, J., et al. (2017). Longitudinal physical activity, body composition, and physical fitness in preschoolers. *Med. Sci. Sport Exerc.* 49, 2078–2085. doi: 10.1249/MSS.0000000000001313

Leppänen, M. H., Nyström, C. D., Henriksson, P., Pomeroy, J., Ruiz, J. R., Ortega, F. B., et al. (2016). Physical activity intensity, sedentary behavior, body composition and physical fitness in 4-year-old children: results from the ministop trial. *Int. J. Obes.* 40, 1126–1133. doi: 10.1038/ijo.2016.54

Merino-De Haro, I., Mora-Gonzalez, J., Cadenas-Sanchez, C., Borras, P. A., Benito, P. J., Chiva-Bartoll, O., et al. (2018). Higher socioeconomic status is related to healthier levels of fatness and fitness already at 3 to 5 years of age: the PREFIT project. *J. Sports Sci.* 37, 1327–1337. doi: 10.1080/02640414.2018.1558509

Migueles, J. H., Cadenas-Sanchez, C., Ekelund, U., Delisle Nyström, C., Mora-Gonzalez, J., Löf, M., et al. (2017). Accelerometer data collection and processing criteria to assess physical activity and other outcomes: a systematic review and practical considerations. *Sport Med.* 47, 1821–1845. doi: 10.1007/s40279-017-0716-0

Minder, C. M., Shaya, G. E., Michos, E. D., Keenan, T. E., Blumenthal, R. S., Nasir, K., et al. (2014). Relation between self-reported physical activity level, fitness, and cardiometabolic risk. *Am. J. Cardiol.* 113, 637–643. doi: 10.1016/j.amjcard.2013.11.010

Mora-Gonzalez, J., Cadenas-Sanchez, C., Martinez-Tellez, B., Sanchez-Delgado, G., Ruiz, J. R., Léger, L., et al. (2017). Estimating VO2max in children aged 5–6 years through the preschool-adapted 20-m shuttle-run test (PREFIT). *Eur. J. Appl. Physiol.* 117, 2295–2307. doi: 10.1007/s00421-017-3717-7

Murphy, J. K., Alpert, B. S., Christman, J. V., and Willey, E. S. (1988). Physical fitness in children: a survey method based on parental report. *Am. J. Public Health* 78, 708–710. doi: 10.2105/ajph.78.6.708

Oliver, M., Schofield, G. M., and Kolt, G. S. (2007). Physical activity in preschoolers: understanding prevalence and measurement issues. *Sport Med.* 37, 1045–1070. doi: 10.2165/00007256-200737120-00004

Ortega, F. B., Artero, E. G., Ruiz, J. R., Vicente Rodriguez, G., Bergman, P., Hagströmer, M., et al. (2008a). Reliability of health-related physical fitness tests in European adolescents. The HELENA Study. *Int. J. Obes.* 32, 49–57. doi: 10.1038/ijo.2008.183

Ortega, F. B., Cadenas-Sanchez, C., Lee, D., Ruiz, J., Blair, S., and Sui, X. (2018). Fitness and fatness as health markers through the lifespan: an overview of current knowledge. *Prog. Prev. Med.* 3:e0013. doi: 10.1097/pp9.0000000000000013

Ortega, F. B., Cadenas-Sánchez, C., Sánchez-Delgado, G., Mora-González, J., Martínez-Téllez, B., Artero, E. G., et al. (2015). Systematic review and proposal of a field-based physical fitness-test battery in preschool children: the PREFIT battery. *Sport Med.* 45, 533–555. doi: 10.1007/s40279-014-0281-8

Ortega, F. B., Labayen, I., Ruiz, J. R., Kurvinen, E., Loit, H.-M., Harro, J., et al. (2011). Improvements in fitness reduce the risk of becoming overweight across puberty. *Med. Sci. Sports Exerc.* 43, 1891–1897. doi: 10.1249/MSS.0b013e3182190d71

Ortega, F. B., Ruiz, J. R., Castillo, M. J., and Sjöström, M. (2008b). Physical fitness in childhood and adolescence: a powerful marker of health. *Int. J. Obes.* 32, 1–11. doi: 10.1038/sj.ijo.0803774

Pate, R. R., O'Neill, J. R., and Mitchell, J. (2010). Measurement of physical activity in preschool children. *Med. Sci. Sports Exerc.* 42, 508–512. doi: 10.1249/MSS.0b013e3181cea116

Ruiz, J., Castro-Piñero, J., Artero, E. G., Ortega, F. B., Sjöström, M., Suni, J., et al. (2009). Predictive validity of health-related fitness in youth: a systematic review. *Br. J. Sports Med.* 43, 909–923. doi: 10.1136/bjsm.2008.056499

Sanchez-Delgado, G., Cadenas-Sanchez, C., Mora-Gonzalez, J., Martinez-Tellez, B., Chillón, P., Löf, M., et al. (2015). Assessment of handgrip strength in preschool children aged 3 to 5 years. *J. Hand Surg.* 40, 966–972. doi: 10.1177/1753193415592328

Smith, J. J., Eather, N., Weaver, R. G., Riley, N., Beets, M. W., and Lubans, D. R. (2019). Behavioral correlates of muscular fitness in children and adolescents: a systematic review. *Sport Med.* 49, 887–904. doi: 10.1007/s40279-019-01089-7

Umer, A., Kelley, G. A., Cottrell, L. E., Giacobbi, P., Innes, K. E., and Lilly, C. L. (2017). Childhood obesity and adult cardiovascular disease risk factors: a systematic review with meta-analysis. *BMC Public Health* 17:683. doi: 10.1186/s12889-017-4691-z

World Health Organization (2016). *Global Strategy on Diet, Physical Activity and Health.* Available at: https://www.who.int/dietphysicalactivity/childhood/en/ (accessed April 3, 2019).

16

A Mixed Methods Study to Examine the Influence of CLIL on Physical Education Lessons: Analysis of Social Interactions and Physical Activity Levels

Celina Salvador-García[1,2], Carlos Capella-Peris[3], Oscar Chiva-Bartoll[2] and Pedro Jesús Ruiz-Montero[4]*

[1] *Faculty of Education, International University of La Rioja, Logroño, Spain,* [2] *Department of Education and Specific Didactics, Jaume I University, Castellón de la Plana, Spain,* [3] *Department of Physical and Sports Education, University of Valencia, Valencia, Spain,* [4] *Faculty of Education and Sport Sciences, University of Granada, Melilla, Spain*

***Correspondence:**
Oscar Chiva-Bartoll
ochiva@uji.es;
ochiva@edu.uji.es

Physical Education is often selected for applying multilingual initiatives through the use of a content and language integrated learning (CLIL) approach. However, it is still unclear whether the introduction of such an approach might entail losing the essence of physical education and distorting its basic purposes. The aim of this study is to analyze the impact of CLIL on physical education lessons. Given the purpose of this study, a mixed methodological approach based on a sequential exploratory design divided into two different phases is used. We begin with initial qualitative data collection (phase I), consisting of the analysis of interviews with 12 participants (8 teachers and 4 students). Based on its analysis, two foci are identified: social relationships and physical activity. Then, informed by the results obtained, a quantitative approach is used (phase II), differentiating these two sets of data to make a more in-depth analysis of them. On the one hand, a sociometric questionnaire was applied to analyze the social relationships between CLIL students. On the other hand, a quasi-experimental design (n = 49) was implemented using accelerometry to measure moderate to vigorous physical activity (MVPA) in the physical education sessions. Regarding physical activity, the results show that levels of MVPA are higher in the experimental group (CLIL) than in the control group, a result which clarifies the divergent viewpoints of the interviewees. However, focusing on social relationships, the sociometric questionnaire results show that there were no statistically significative changes, although some signs of a slight effect on students' relationships arise depending on their gender. Therefore, more research would be necessary to further study the effect of CLIL in this regard.

Keywords: physical education, CLIL, moderate-vigorous physical activity, pedagogical approach, mixed methods, social relationships

INTRODUCTION

Currently, Physical Education has been claimed to generate different 'educationally beneficial outcomes for students, across a range of domains' (Kirk, 2013, p. 978). This may be explained by the fact that this subject is defined by the two words that form its name (Kirk, 2010). In other words, Physical Education has the potential to promote learning related to different spheres, not only the physical one, but also the social, personal and cognitive (Dyson et al., 2004; McEvoy et al., 2017). However, there are various historical and philosophical accounts outlining the journey Physical Education has taken throughout its history, and even today there may be different viewpoints on its current understanding. As an example, some purposes of Physical Education may be: (1) development of motor and sport-specific skills, (2) promotion of health-related fitness and active lifestyles, and (3) personal, social and moral development (Hardman, 2011).

Despite Physical Education's holistic power, there is a 'growing movement to develop and adopt classroom-based physical activity in an effort to increase physical activity within the school day' (Quarmby et al., 2019, p. 2). This tendency is related to the aforementioned first and second functions of Physical Education, and responds to the worrisome concern due to the decrease in moderate to vigorous physical activity (MVPA) in school-aged children (Hollis et al., 2017; Viciana et al., 2019). In fact, Physical Education lessons are the only opportunity to engage in physical activity for many adolescents and children (Meyer et al., 2013; Aljuhani and Sandercock, 2019). Therefore, this subject is crucial in contributing to the recommendations on daily amount of physical activity (World Health Organization, 2010; Viciana et al., 2019).

The third purpose of Physical Education stated by Hardman (2011) refers to personal, social and moral development; and it usually constitutes one of the main goals of European Physical Education programs (Opstoel et al., 2019). Indeed, Physical Education is seen as a great opportunity to develop the students' personality and socialization (Weiss, 2011; Andueza and Lavega, 2017) given its social nature and the particular context it generates. However, it is important to mention that simply participating in Physical Education lessons does not automatically lead to the development of such skills (Cryan and Martinek, 2017; Opstoel et al., 2019).

In addition to the aforementioned functions, Physical Education has increasingly been involved in the development of programs devoted to the learning of another language (Baena-Extremera et al., 2017; Lamb and King, 2019), often through the CLIL (Content and Language Integrated Learning) approach (Coral et al., 2017; Salvador-García and Chiva-Bartoll, 2017). This stems from the need to improve second-language education and bilingualism, which is an essential skill in today's society (Marsh, 2002). However, several voices claim that non-linguistic subjects, as is the case of Physical Education, are undervalued when this approach is applied (Pérez-Cañado, 2017). Furthermore, the introduction of CLIL inevitably entails a change in the development of the lessons (Coyle, 2015). Consequently, it is worrisome that Physical Education might lose its identity when introducing another language in class (Merino, 2016), because this subject should ensure that its particular purposes are achieved.

The main aim of this study is to analyze the impact of CLIL on Physical Education lessons, bearing in mind the essential functions of the subject.

MIXED METHODS

All methods of data collection have limitations. Qualitative methods can provide in-depth information whereas quantitative methods can test predictive associations. Mixed-methods studies collect and combine qualitative and quantitative data in order to build on the complementary strengths of both qualitative and quantitative methods (Creswell and Plano Clark, 2017). In this regard, a considerable amount of literature defends that mixing different types of methods can strengthen a study (Greene and Caracelli, 1997).

In order to utilize the benefits of each method, we employed a sequential exploratory design to integrate qualitative and quantitative methods (Creswell and Plano Clark, 2017). This design was conducted in two phases, with equal status given to both phases of research. The qualitative data collected in Phase 1 informed the design of the quantitative study in Phase II. Such a design was chosen because there was a need to begin with initial qualitative data collection so as to identify the focus of the possible variables to examine (Tashakkori and Teddlie, 1998). In this case, we needed to narrow the possible effects of CLIL on Physical Education in order to analyze them objectively.

Participants in the first phase of data collection were high school students and teachers who had been using the CLIL approach in Physical Education lessons. From the interviews, we identified two main themes related to the influence of CLIL on Physical Education as a subject. Finding out whether there was an effect due to CLIL on these two themes became the two branches investigated in phase II of the study. In this second phase, we used a sociometric questionnaire and accelerometry to test the predictive associations identified in the interviews. This quantitative approach allowed us to examine whether the qualitative findings were supported by objective measures. Both approaches carried equal weight in the resulting discussion. **Figure 1** shows the stages followed in the design. The following sections detail each phase, including participants, method, data analysis and findings of each.

Phase I (Qualitative Study)

Research Question

What impact will CLIL have on Physical Education lessons from the perspective of the students and teachers involved?

Participants

On the one hand, eight Spanish teachers of Physical Education with CLIL (four female and four male) composed the sample of the study. They are teachers in different high schools and they have been implementing the CLIL approach for at least 3 years.

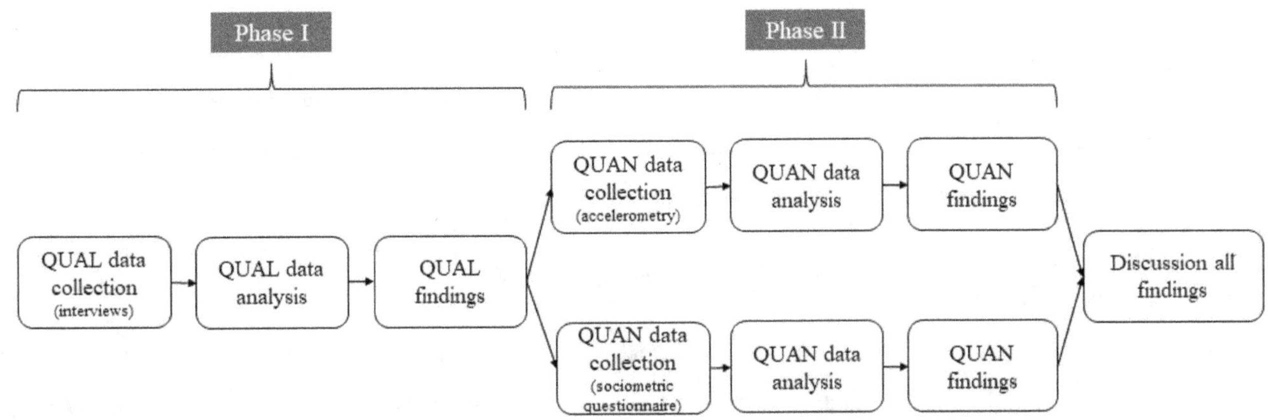

FIGURE 1 | Stages of the sequential exploratory design.

Furthermore, they all have an official certificate that enables them to carry out Physical Education lessons in English. On the other hand, four 15- to 17-year-old Spanish students were also selected. In their case, they had been doing Physical Education through CLIL for at least a term in their high school.

Intentional sampling was chosen in an attempt to achieve representativeness among both teachers and students (Patton, 2002). Therefore, regarding the teachers, we considered features such as age (25–40 n = 4; 41–60 n = 4), gender (female n = 2; male n = 6) and CLIL experience (3–5 years n = 4; 5–8 years n = 4). With respect to the students, the representative quotas of participants were based on their gender (female n = 2; male n = 2), English marks for the last academic year (high marks n = 2; low marks n = 2) and Physical Education marks for the last academic year (high marks n = 2; low marks n = 2).

All the participants had received detailed information about ethical considerations regarding informed consent and confidentiality, building on guidelines of the ethics committee of Universitat Jaume I and had thereafter agreed to participate in the study. In addition, the students' parents or guardians signed an informed consent document.

Method

All participant interviews were carried out by the same interviewer. We used a semi-structured interview format because, according to literature, this instrument allows the participants to describe detailed personal information, but the interviewer still has good control over the information received. In addition, they ensured a degree of comparability across interviews and allowed for different themes to arise (Creswell, 2012). Therefore, the use of this type of data collection was appropriate to identify the possible effects of CLIL on Physical Education, which was the main topic of the interview guide. Previous literature helped us to frame the interview questions, which were organized around the aims of Physical Education (Hardman, 2011), although other questions emerged from the dialog between interviewer and interviewees to probe for more relevant data (Mackey and Gass, 2005; DiCicco-Bloom and Crabtree, 2006). The interviews started with general questions, followed by other more specific ones to reconstruct the interviewees' subjective theories without biasing them (Flick, 2014). The structure of the interviews is presented in **Table 1**.

The initial part of the interview involves the interviewer making a brief presentation, explaining to the interviewees the following points: the confidentiality of their identity, the use of recording exclusively for research purposes, the possibility of stopping the recording at any time during the interview and the non-obligation to answer all questions. They also clarified that the interviews were anonymous, as recommended by the protocols of this technique.

The teachers' interviews were individual, whereas the students were interviewed as a group to combine individual experiences and build a collective discourse, comparing and contrasting different viewpoints and therefore avoiding any distortion of their perceptions. All the interviews were recorded with a SONY ICD-P530F recorder and they were carried out in Spanish. After the data analysis a professional translator translated them into English for publication. Pseudonyms are used to protect the interviewees' identities.

Data Analysis

Initially, the research team read all transcripts to provide a holistic review of the participants' viewpoints on the effects of CLIL on Physical Education. Next, we exported the interviews into NVivo-11 software. Later, we met to discuss initial reactions and develop potential categories related to the essential features of Physical Education. Then, the representative quotes were grouped together within these categories. Finally, a member checking process was carried out to ensure inter-rater reliability (Johnson and Christensen, 2016).

Findings

The research team identified two main categories that pointed to the effects generated by CLIL on Physical Education according to the interviewees' viewpoints. In this respect, 'social relationships' and 'physical activity' were the aspects that could be affected by the use of this innovative approach.

TABLE 1 | Structure of the interviews.

	Issues addressed			
	Teachers' interviews		Students' interviews	
Interview parts	**Issues**	**Basic interview guide**	**Issues**	**Basic interview guide**
"Ice-breaker" questions	Information on personal matters, language proficiency, work experience and educational, and training attainments.	What is your teaching experience (and using CLIL)? What is your English level? What specific training have you undergone to do CLIL?	Information on personal matters, general opinions about the subject.	• What do you think of Physical Education? • How do you feel about the subject?
General questions	Preparation of the classes.	• What is your general opinion regarding Physical Education with CLIL? • How do you prepare your CLIL lessons?	Learning in physical education The acquisition of language skills.	• Has CLIL hindered your learning of the subject? How? Why (not)? • Why was CLIL (not) helpful for language learning?
Specific questions	Class development: strengths, limitations. Differences between using and not using the CLIL approach.	• What are the advantages of using CLIL in Physical Education? • What are the disadvantages of using CLIL in Physical Education? • What are the differences in CLIL and non-CLIL Physical Education? And regarding motor and sport-specific skills/activity or movement/personal, social and moral development?	Advantages and disadvantages of the CLIL approach in physical education classes. Differences regarding classes without the CLIL approach.	• Why can CLIL be beneficial for students in Physical Education? • What are the disadvantages of using CLIL in Physical Education? • What are the differences in CLIL and non-CLIL Physical Education? And regarding motor and sport-specific skills/activity or movement/personal, social and moral development?
Conclusion question	Further observations			

Social relationships

With regard to the 'social relationships' category, the idea that CLIL entails a change was shared by all interviewees. For example, the students clearly stated that '*speaking in English in the lessons helped us to be more attentive with our classmates. If you were able to understand the instructions, you were actively involved in helping the rest of the students*' (Student 2). Consequently, students were led to increase their work as a team or '*group collaboration: since I don't understand, you explain it to me*' (Student 3).

The teachers noticed an increase in the students' helpfulness too, as is illustrated in the following quote:

> '*There is more collaboration among students, of course. I think that any handicap you (the teacher) bring to class will be a challenge for the pupils and, therefore, it will help (to enhance teamwork). In this case, it was English language, but (...) any new handicap will lead to an increase in everyone's collaboration*' (Teacher 3).

In addition, according to the teachers, this increase in students' interactions was also a consequence of the type of tasks and the methodology that CLIL entails.

> '*One of the ways of promoting language use is by doing cooperative tasks. When planning the sessions, there is a need to search for cooperative structures to boost language use. In addition, I can help because it is something mandatory at a specific moment of the lesson (...) but I believe that showing a weakness and sharing it with your classmates, being conscious of the fact that we are more similar than we had thought, being aware of our sameness... Sharing all these feelings generates an emotional atmosphere that truly promotes learning with the other*' (Teacher 4).

All in all, according to the interviewees' perceptions, the use of CLIL increases collaboration and the feeling of sameness within the group while enhancing the number of interactions between students. Therefore, CLIL might entail a change in the social atmosphere of the group.

Physical activity

Physical activity was the second category identified. However, participants reported divergent perspectives regarding this aspect. On the one hand, all students share a common discourse, which is also supported by some of the Physical Education teachers. According to their viewpoint, the implementation of CLIL does not hinder the amount of physical activity carried out in Physical Education lessons. The following quotes illustrate this idea:

> '*I have adapted the theoretical content, but the practical content has not been adapted*' (Teacher 2).

> '*The activities and the practice itself have remained the same*' (Teacher 7).

In the same vein, despite the required methodological changes due to CLIL that were not noticed by students, one of them stated that '*it is exactly the same learning in English or in Spanish. The only difference is that we use a different language*' (Student 1). In fact, none of the adolescents thought that CLIL could diminish their time engaged in physical activity.

On the other hand, some teachers were concerned with this issue and showed an opposing opinion. Specifically, they believed that the use of a different language implied more teacher talking time and a slowing of students' understanding that could also decrease the students' physical activity time. In the words of one of the teachers:

> '*Obviously, the explanations are longer. You have to explain the same thing (compared to a non-CLIL group) and you (the teacher) do not have the same knowledge, skill and speed when speaking in English*' (Teacher 3).

Also, a different teacher reported that although physical activity was still an important part of the lessons, the amount of time that students were engaged in it could be affected because it was more difficult for students to understand an activity and start it. This can be perceived in the following quote, in which the teacher mentions both aspects:

> '*I think that the sport's essence, its physical activity, was the same, it (CLIL) was not an obstacle. They may be slower to understand an activity, but once you have performed it, students worked with no difference (compared to non-CLIL students)*' (Teacher 4).

To sum up, despite the fact that all interviewees thought that students' quality of movement was the same regardless of CLIL, some teachers did worry about the amount of time that students were engaged in physical activity.

Phase II (Quantitative Study)

Hypotheses

- The social relationships measured by the sociometric questionnaire conducted by the experimental group will improve after application of the CLIL approach.
- The amount of time that students are engaged in physical activity will be less for the experimental (CLIL) group than for the control (non-CLIL) group.

Participants

Once the findings of the first phase of the study were clear and the foci of the subsequent phase of the study were established (social relationships and physical activity), the participants for the second phase were recruited. In total, the convenience sample for the quantitative study consisted of 49 13- to 14-year-old students. Participants in the accelerometry analysis were divided into the experimental group (CLIL), composed of 13 girls and 10 boys, and the control group (non-CLIL), composed of 19 girls and 7 boys. This sample presented a statistically proportional distribution in terms of the gender variable between the groups $\chi^2(N = 49) = 1.05$, $p = 0.306$. The mean age was 13.8 ($\pm$0.18). Only the experimental group participated in the sociometric questionnaire measures. They did not have prior experience in Physical Education through CLIL. We decided that the group of participants in phase II of the study would not be the same as in phase I in order to avoid their attitudes and behavior being influenced by the interviews carried out in advance. Therefore, a different group of students, without CLIL experience, was selected.

For this part of the study the principal and the Physical Education teacher agreed to participate by establishing a memorandum of understanding. The students' parents or guardians also signed an informed consent document.

Measures

To identify possible changes in the social relationships of the students in the experimental group, a sociometric questionnaire was applied at the beginning and at the end of the term. The three units included within this period were the first time that the students in the experimental group had done Physical Education through the CLIL approach. Sociometric methods are the most common form of measuring the status of individuals within groups to understand their relationships (Chelcea, 2005). The sociometric questionnaire consisted of four questions where students were asked to express sympathetic relationships in terms of their attraction or repulsion to classmates. These questions were: (a) Which classmates do you most like being with in Physical Education lessons? (b) Which classmates do you least like being with in Physical Education lessons? (c) Which classmates can help you to learn more in Physical Education lessons? (d) Which classmates can't help you to learn in Physical Education lessons? A peer nomination technique in which participants were asked to nominate peers in order of importance was used. It is imperative to note that pre-test measures were taken before the first CLIL unit started. In addition, due to the sensitive nature of the questionnaire, students were provided with a private area to individually complete them and asked not to discuss the task with their classmates.

In order to discern whether there was an effect on students' physical activity levels, the instruments selected were accelerometers (a device that measures the acceleration of a body through high-frequency recordings in order to discriminate behavioral patterns of physical activity). They are considered one of the most reliable ways of measuring levels of physical activity and were selected because they do not interfere with Physical Education sessions (Calahorro et al., 2015). In this study, the GENEActiv Original triaxial accelerometer was used. Data recruitment took place during a unit taught in January–February 2017. Both the experimental and control group had two 50-min lessons per week in the morning, in which accelerometer-based outcome measures were taken from all the students. The research design corresponds to a quasi-experimental design based on non-equivalent natural groups to make an objective analysis of physical activity levels in Physical Education lessons. The same Physical Education teacher taught both groups the same content (athletics) in an attempt to control potential 'teacher-related' confounding. Each student wore an accelerometer for the entire lesson on his/her left wrist. To control differing durations of Physical Education lessons, physical activity data were collected during the entire lesson because the English language was used with the experimental group throughout this time. The measurements were taken in six practical sessions of each group.

An experienced external observer conducted practice observations of all the lessons of both groups and completed the CLIL planning and observation checklist (Mehisto et al., 2008) to ensure this approach was properly implemented.

Data Analysis

Regarding the sociometric questionnaire, the data were analyzed to produce descriptive categorical results. The analysis of social relationships was conducted using the student peer nomination questionnaire with the experimental group (CLIL) in Spanish. After the peer nomination questionnaires were collected, frequency of positive and negative nominations was calculated for each student to determine social dynamics within the group. The mean scores of the ratings were computed for each student. Specifically, the number of nominations was divided by the number of students who took the questionnaire. This analysis let us identify the increase, maintenance or decrease in the number of positive and negative nominations.

For its part, we followed previous literature on accelerometry and we conducted the analyses unifying the moderate and vigorous categories into one variable called Moderate-Vigorous Physical Activity (MVPA). Specifically, the time spent on MVPA was calculated by applying previously calibrated and validated cut-off points for this type of population (Phillips et al., 2013). The data recorded were exported into the statistical package SPSS-24. Then, a multivariate analysis was used to analyze the effect of the group variable on MVPA time.

Findings

With reference to the sociometric questionnaire, a *t*-student analysis was conducted to determine whether there were differences between pre- and post-test measures regarding the four questions about relationships with classmates. This analysis was also performed differentiating by gender. The results do not show significant differences between the students' score pre- and post-test measures. However, **Table 2** also presents some interesting outcomes when comparing the results obtained by males and females. Regarding question (c) "Which classmates can help you to learn more in Physical Education lessons?", girls increased their scores from pre-test ($M = 0.96$, $SD = 0.113$) to post-test ($M = 0.141$, $SD = 0.183$), whereas boys decreased their scores from pre-test ($M = 0.134$, $SD = 0.226$) to post-test ($M = 0.061$, $SD = 0.182$). In fact, only one of the questions, (b), shows similar trends between boys and girls. These results suggest that the CLIL program may have different effects on students' relationships depending on their gender.

For its part, the multivariate analysis performed showed significant main effects for the group variable [Wilks' $\Lambda = 0.637$, $F(1,49) = 25.664$; $p < 0.001$; $\eta^2 = 0.363$] on students' physical activity level. In addition, partial eta square showed that the differences between the score obtained by the control group (non-CLIL) and the experimental group (CLIL) in students' physical activity levels (sedentary-light and moderate-vigorous) is 36.3%. **Table 3** presents the mean percentages of time that both groups spent at levels of sedentary-light and moderate-vigorous physical activity throughout the unit.

DISCUSSION OF QUALITATIVE AND QUANTITATIVE FINDINGS

The integrated mixed methods research strategy with a two-phase exploratory sequential design has been instrumental in improving our understanding of CLIL in the Physical Education field to examine the influence of this approach on the subject's basic purposes: (1) development of motor and sport-specific

TABLE 2 | Difference between study samples by gender and total in four sociometric questions about sympathetic relationships in terms of attraction or repulsion to classmates.

Sociometric questions	Female group (*n* = 13)				Male group (*n* = 10)				Total group (*n* = 23)			
	Pre-intervention	Post-intervention	*p*-value	Cohen's *d*	Pre-intervention	Post-intervention	*p*-value	Cohen's *d*	Pre-intervention	Post-intervention	*p*-value	Cohen's *d*
	Mean (*SD*)	Mean (*SD*)			Mean (*SD*)	Mean (*SD*)			Mean (*SD*)	Mean (*SD*)		
(a) …classmates you most like in PE…	0.117 ± 0.189	0.121 ± 0.056	0.893	−0.028*	0.131 ± 0.178	0.121 ± 0.160	0.726	0.059*	0.122 ± 0.071	0.121 ± 0.061	0.912	0.003
(b) …classmates you like least in PE…	0.118 ± 0.139	0.134 ± 0.182	0.497	−0.098	0.108 ± 0.161	0.117 ± 0.087	0.770	−0.069	0.114 ± 0.107	0.126 ± 0.145	0.470	−0.094
(c) …classmates who can help you learn in PE…	0.096 ± 0.133	0.141 ± 0.183	0.582	−0.238*	0.134 ± 0.226	0.061 ± 0.182	0.396	0.355*	0.113 ± 0.176	0.105 ± 0.149	0.895	0.049
(d) …classmates who can't help you learn in PE…	0.123 ± 0.132	0.143 ± 0.216	0.821	−0.111*	0.132 ± 0.195	0.086 ± 0.112	0.609	0.289*	0.126 ± 0.158	0.119 ± 0.175	0.900	0.041

*Opposing trends depending on gender.

TABLE 3 | ANOVA for students' physical activity level (SLPA/MVPA) by group of participants (CLIL/non-CLIL).

Physical activity level	Group	Mean (*SD*)	*F*	η^2
SLPA	Non-CLIL	72.79 (4.28)	25.664***	0.363
	CLIL	65.95 (4.95)		
MVPA	Non-CLIL	27.21 (4.28)	25.664***	0.363
	CLIL	34.04 (4.95)		

****p < 0.001. Mean refers to percentage per session. SLPA, sedentary-light physical activity; MVPA, moderate vigorous physical activity.*

skills, (2) promotion of health-related fitness and active lifestyles, and (3) personal, social and moral development (Hardman, 2011). While directly administered interviews in the first phase have been useful to narrow the study's aims, the use of a sociometric questionnaire and accelerometry in the second phase allowed us to analyze social relationships and physical activity levels objectively within Physical Education lessons.

Despite the fact that mixed approaches are increasingly being advocated as a means to better comprehend educational concepts and contexts (Johnson and Onwuegbuzie, 2004; Tolan and Deutsch, 2015), there are still limited examples of their combination in the literature. Combining qualitative and quantitative methods enhanced the validity of our findings because we could triangulate results that examine the same phenomenon across different methods, we could expand and better elaborate our findings, and we could unveil contradictory findings that resulted from the use of different methods (Greene et al., 1989; Tolan and Deutsch, 2015). Relevant findings emerged at each phase of the research process and are reported by the two foci into which phase II is divided.

Consistent with previous literature, participants described how Physical Education with CLIL provided students with more options to help one another, interact with other peers, be more attentive, increase teamwork and share similar weaknesses (Coyle et al., 2010; Coyle, 2015; Salvador-García et al., 2018; Lamb and King, 2019). These aspects are linked to the personal and social spheres of Physical Education (Dyson et al., 2004; Hardman, 2011). Their mention by the interviewees may be explained because CLIL entails a type of talking and interaction that is different from that of traditional lessons (Casal, 2016), resulting in the promotion of social skills and peer relations. On this account, CLIL programs go beyond the mere usage of the target language in content in order to include other essential lifelong skills such as social ones (Torres-Rincon and Cuesta-Medina, 2019).

The interviews illustrate that the Physical Education teachers interviewed feel the need to use collaborative activities when planning lessons through the CLIL approach. In this regard, the introduction of collaborative activities can also be useful to strengthen social dynamics within the group, enhancing prosocial behavior and empathy among students (Andueza and Lavega, 2017). In addition, this means that CLIL may entail a change in Physical Education methodology, making it more participative, inclusive and collaborative, which are ultimately some of the current trends in Physical Education because these features help to achieve a range of educationally beneficial objectives related to many different domains, such as the physical, lifestyle, affective, social and cognitive (Dyson et al., 2004; Kirk, 2010, 2013). All in all, the use of CLIL in the area of Physical Education may help align the subject with its current principles (Lamb and King, 2019).

Participants also stated that, according to their experiences, introducing CLIL contributed to the development of positive relationships between students (Casal, 2016; Bower, 2019). Similarly, a case study analyzing CLIL with Physical Education concluded that there was an improvement in social interaction and a sense of sharing among students (Christopher et al., 2012). Therefore, using CLIL could entail a change in the social dynamics of the group (Salvador-García et al., 2018). However, our quantitative findings do not totally align with the interview findings, since no significant differences were found when comparing pre- and post-test measures of the sociometric questionnaire. Despite these results, in general terms, there are some interesting outcomes when comparing the results obtained by gender. In this regard, three of the questions show opposing trends when the mean scores of males and females are compared. This might be related to the differences by gender that are often found regarding both interpersonal relations, for example, focusing on acceptance within the group (Andueza and Lavega, 2017), and CLIL (Doiz et al., 2014; Fernandez-Barrionuevo and Baena-Extremera, 2018). Therefore, it is necessary to carry out further research on this topic, because the effects on sociometric measures might need longer to appear (van der Wilt et al., 2019).

Regarding the first and second purposes of Physical Education (Hardman, 2011), that is to say, those closely linked to the physical sphere, interviewees also expressed their opinions on CLIL's possible effects and accelerometry allowed us to analyze it objectively. Contrary to the stereotypes of many critical voices who claim that physical activity levels decrease in Physical Education with CLIL (Coral et al., 2017; Martinez and Garcia, 2017), we did find evidence in both the interviews and accelerometry results that the quality of physical activity is not necessarily diminished. In addition, despite some teachers' concerns about their explanations being longer when applying CLIL (Lo and Macaro, 2015; Salvador-García and Chiva-Bartoll, 2017), the percentage of time that students were engaged in MVPA was also maintained.

We can explain such physical activity analytical results only by combining them with the findings from the qualitative study. In our case, the interviewed students were willing to help each other understand, maybe due to the high levels of motivation that are usually linked to Physical Education through CLIL (Baena-Extremera et al., 2017; Lamb and King, 2019). In addition, using CLIL may entail an increase in students' attentiveness (Zindler, 2013; Salvador-García and Chiva-Bartoll, 2017), or the use of teaching strategies that teachers employ to enhance students' understanding (Gomez and Jimenez-Silva, 2012; Salvador-García et al., 2019). In this regard, teachers who apply CLIL tend to be more concerned with the vocabulary and language structures they use to ensure effective communication (Ting, 2011; Zindler, 2013). However, this contrasts with other authors who claim that some teachers may overuse language learning materials such as flashcards and, consequently, the teacher talking time is increased while students' activity time is diminished (Coral et al., 2017). More research is needed to further investigate these aspects and better understand how Physical Education sessions are carried out when the CLIL approach is used.

CONCLUSION

Addressing the stated research objective through the application of a unique mixed method strategy with exploratory sequential design has been useful in our study, as it puts students and teachers at the center of CLIL research in the field of Physical Education and focuses on the basic features of Physical Education. One of the main purposes of Physical Education refers to personal, social and moral development (Hardman, 2011). In this regard, the interviews undertaken revealed the potential role that CLIL may play in improving social relationships between students; however, the sociometric questionnaire findings only show some very slight trends in gender-based outcomes. In any case, the interpretation of these results yields some interesting inferences leading to the conclusion that the use of a CLIL approach might change the social interactions in class for the better. Thus, CLIL might strengthen one of the main purposes of Physical Education.

Regarding the aims of Physical Education related to development of motor and sport-specific skills and promotion of health-related fitness and active lifestyles (Hardman, 2011), some participants wondered whether physical activity levels would be altered due to the application of CLIL. Despite being recurrent in their responses, the interviewees did not reach any consensus about this concern, so in the second phase of the study a measurement of MVPA through accelerometry objectively showed that MVPA was not jeopardized, with the CLIL group obtaining higher levels of MVPA than the non-CLIL group. These results represent an outstanding finding, since they certainly shed new light on one of the most widespread concerns in this field. Therefore, according to our study, the CLIL approach does not necessarily hinder the basic purposes of Physical Education, which was a concern for many scholars (Merino, 2016; Coral et al., 2017; Pérez-Cañado, 2017). In fact, it might contribute to its development.

This study has some limitations. The quantitative part of the study relies on data collected with a limited sample. Also, given the fact that the study was carried out in Spain, the findings might not be transferable to all contexts. However, these are common issues that come with educational research that attempts to uncover intervention programs (Sandoval and Bell, 2004). We are convinced, instead, that by highlighting the views of these groups of participants and sharing the quantitative measures obtained, we have contributed to knowledge on how the CLIL approach can influence Physical Education. Furthermore, it should be noted that qualitative research does not attempt to generalize knowledge in a categorical way, but rather aspires to deepen our knowledge about contextualized phenomena. It does take advantage of the results obtained to relate them to existing literature and thus increase the conceptual framework of the field (Denzin and Lincoln, 2005). It is in this way that, from an interpretative paradigm, this study helps broaden knowledge in Physical Education research (Pérez-Samaniego et al., 2011).

ETHICS STATEMENT

This studies involving human participants were reviewed and approved by Deontological Commission of the University Jaume I:UJI-PREDOC/2016/03. Written informed consent to participate in this study was provided by the participants' legal guardian/next of kin.

AUTHOR CONTRIBUTIONS

OC-B and CS-G conceived the idea presented and designed the study. CS-G and CC-P organized the database. PR-M and CC-P performed the statistical analysis. CS-G wrote the first draft of the manuscript. OC-B, CS-G, and CC-P reviewed the methodological sections of the manuscript. All authors contributed to revision of the manuscript and read and approved the submitted version.

ACKNOWLEDGMENTS

The authors would like to thank the professional services for manuscript revision and editing assistance, and especially all the teachers and students involved in the study.

REFERENCES

Aljuhani, O., and Sandercock, G. (2019). Contribution of physical education to the daily physical activity of schoolchildren in Saudi Arabia. *Int. J. Environ. Res. Public Health* 16:2397. doi: 10.3390/ijerph16132397

Andueza, J., and Lavega, P. (2017). Incidencia de los juegos cooperativos en las relaciones interpersonales. *Movimento* 23, 213–228. doi: 10.22456/1982-8918.65002

Baena-Extremera, A., Gómez-López, M., and Granero-Gallegos, A. (2017). Aprendizaje de la educación física bilingüe a partir de las metas de logro y el clima de aprendizaje. *Porta Linguarum* 28, 81–93.

Bower, K. (2019). 'Speaking French alive': learner perspectives on their motivation in content and language integrated learning in England. *Innov. Lang. Learn. Teach.* 13, 45–60. doi: 10.1080/17501229.2017.1314483

Calahorro, F., Torres-Luque, G., López-Fernández, I., Alejandro, S.-L., Garatachea, N., and Álvarez, E. (2015). Actividad física y acelerometría: orientaciones metodológicas, recomendaciones y patrones. *Nutr. Hosp.* 31, 115–128. doi: 10.3305/nh.2015.31.1.7450

Casal, S. (2016). Cooperative assessment for learning in CLIL contexts. *Estud. Sobre Educación* 31, 139–157. doi: 10.15581/004.31.139-157

Chelcea, S. (2005). *Social Psychology*. Bucharest: Economică.

Christopher, A. A., bin Dzakiria, H., and bin Mohamed, A. H. (2012). Teaching english through sports: a case study. *Asian EFL J.* 59, 20–29.

Coral, J., Urbiola, M., Sabaté, E., Bofill, J., Lleixà, T., and Vilà Baños, R. (2017). Does the teaching of physical education in a foreign language jeopardise children's physical activity time? A pilot study. *Int. J. Biling. Educ. Biling.* 1–16. doi: 10.1080/13670050.2017.1407289

Coyle, D. (2015). Strengthening integrated learning: towards a new era for pluriliteracies and intercultural learning. *Lat. Am. J.Content Lang. Integr. Learn.* 8, 84–103. doi: 10.5294/laclil.2015.8.2.2

Coyle, D., Hood, P., and Marsh, D. (2010). *CLIL Content and Language Integrated Learning*. Cambridge: Cambridge University Press.

Creswell, J. W. (2012). *Qualitative Inquiry and Research Design: Choosing Among Five Approaches*, 3rd Edn. London: SAGE Publications.

Creswell, J. W., and Plano Clark, V. L. (2017). *Designing and Conducting Mixed Methods Research*, 3rd Edn. Newbury Park, CA: SAGE Publications.

Cryan, M., and Martinek, T. (2017). Youth sport development through soccer: an evaluation of an after-school program using the TPSR model. *Phys. Educ.* 127–149. doi: 10.18666/TPE-2017-V74-I1-6901

Denzin, N. K., and Lincoln, Y. S. (2005). "Introduction: the discipline and practice of qualitative research," in *The Sage Handbook of Qualitative Research*, eds N. K. Denzin, and Y. S. Lincoln (Thousand Oaks, CA: Sage Publications), 1–32.

DiCicco-Bloom, B., and Crabtree, B. F. (2006). The qualitative research interview. *Med. Educ.* 40, 314–321. doi: 10.1111/j.1365-2929.2006.02418.x

Doiz, A., Lasagabaster, D., and Sierra, M. (2014). CLIL and motivation: the effect of individual and contextual variables. *Lang. Learn* 42, 209–224. doi: 10.1080/09571736.2014.889508

Dyson, B., Griffin, L. L., and Hastie, P. (2004). Sport education, tactical games, and cooperative learning: theoretical and pedagogical considerations. *Quest* 226–240. doi: 10.1080/00336297.2004.10491823 74,

Fernandez-Barrionuevo, E., and Baena-Extremera, A. (2018). Motivation in physical education and foreign language learning in clil teaching: gender differences and implications for future studies. *Porta Linguarum: revista internacional de didáctica de las lenguas extranjeras* 207–220.

Flick, U. (2014). *An Introduction to Qualitative Research*, 5th Edn. Thousand Oaks, CA: Sage Publications.

Gomez, C. L., and Jimenez-Silva, M. (2012). The physical educator as a language teacher for english language learners. *Strategies* 25, 14–17. doi: 10.1080/08924562.2012.10592157

Greene, J. C., and Caracelli, V. J. (eds) (1997). *Advances in Mixed-Method Evaluation: The Challenges And Benefits Of Integrating Diverse Paradigms (New Directions for Evaluation, 74).* San Francisco, CA: Jossey-Bass. 56,

Greene, J. C., Caracelli, V. J., and Graham, W. F. (1989). Toward a conceptual framework for mixed-method evaluation designs. *Educ. Eval. Policy Anal.* 255–274. doi: 10.3102/01623737011003255

Hardman, K. (2011). "Global issues in the situation of physical education in schools," in *Contemporary Issues in Physical Education*, eds K. Hardman, and K. Green (Maidenhead: Meyer and Meyer Sport), 11–29.

Hollis, J. L., Sutherland, R., Williams, A. J., Campbell, E., Nathan, N., Wolfenden, L., et al. (2017). A systematic review and meta-analysis of moderate-to-vigorous physical activity levels in secondary school physical education lessons. *Int. J. Behav. Nutr. Phys. Act.* 14:52. doi: 10.1186/s12966-017-0504-0

Johnson, R. B., and Christensen, T. L. (2016). *Educational Research. Quantitative, Qualitative and Mixed Approaches*, 6th Edn. Thousand Oaks, CA: SAGE Publications.

Johnson, R. B., and Onwuegbuzie, A. J. (2004). Mixed methods research: a research paradigm whose time has come. *Educ. Res.* 33, 14–26. doi: 10.3102/0013189X033007014

Kirk, D. (2010). *Physical Education Futures*. London: Routledge.

Kirk, D. (2013). Educational value and models-based practice in physical education. *Educ. Phil. Theor.* 45, 973–986. doi: 10.1080/00131857.2013.785352

Lamb, P., and King, G. (2019). Another platform and a changed context: student experiences of developing spontaneous speaking in French through physical education. *Eur. Phys. Educ. Rev.*

Lo, Y. Y., and Macaro, E. (2015). Getting used to content and language integrated learning: what can classroom interaction reveal? *Lang. Learn. J.* 43, 239–255. doi: 10.1080/09571736.2015.1053281

Mackey, A., and Gass, S. M. (2005). *Second Language Research: Methodology and Design*. Mahwah, NJ: Lawrence Erlbaum Associates.

Marsh, D. (2002). *CLIL/EMILE – The European Dimension: Actions, Trends and Foresight Potential*. Finland: University of Jäyvskylä.

Martinez, F. J., and Garcia, E. (2017). Influencia del bilingüismo en el tiempo de compromiso motor en educación física. *Retos* 32, 178–182.

McEvoy, E., Heikinaro-Johansson, P., and MacPhail, A. (2017). Physical education teacher educators' views regarding the purpose(s) of school physical education. *Sport Educ. Soc.* 22, 812–824. doi: 10.1080/13573322.2015.1075971

Mehisto, P., Marsh, D., and Frigols, M. J. (2008). *Uncovering CLIL: Content and Language Integrated Learning in Bilingual and Multilingual Education*. Oxford: MacMillan Education.

Merino, J. (2016). "Non-linguistic content in CLIL: is its learning diminished?," in *CLIL Experiences in Secondary and Tertiary Education: In Search of Good Practices*, eds D. Lasagabaster, and A. Doiz (Bristol: Peter Lang), 17–43.

Meyer, U., Roth, R., Zahner, L., Gerber, M., Puder, J. J., Hebestreit, H., et al. (2013). Contribution of physical education to overall physical activity. *Scand. J. Med. Sci. Sports* 23, 600–606. doi: 10.1111/j.1600-0838.2011.01425.x

Opstoel, K., Chapelle, L., Prins, F. J., De Meester, A., Haerens, L., van Tartwijk, J., et al. (2019). Personal and social development in physical education and sports: a review study. *Eur. Phys. Educ. Rev.*

Patton, M. Q. (2002). *Qualitative Research and Evaluation Methods*, 3rd Edn. London: SAGE Publications.

Pérez-Cañado, M. L. (2017). Stopping the "pendulum effect" in CLIL research: finding the balance between pollyanna and scrooge. *Appl. Ling. Rev.* 8, 79–99. doi: 10.1515/applirev-2016-2001

Pérez-Samaniego, V. M., Devís-Devís, J., Smith, B. M., and Sparkes, A. C. (2011). La investigación narrativa en la educación física y el deporte: qué es y para qué sirve. *Movimento* 17, 11–38. doi: 10.22456/1982-8918.17752

Phillips, L. R. S., Parfitt, G., and Rowlands, A. V. (2013). Calibration of the GENEA accelerometer for assessment of physical activity intensity in children. *J. Sci. Med. Sport* 16, 124–128. doi: 10.1016/j.jsams.2012.05.013

Quarmby, T., Daly-Smith, A., and Kime, N. (2019). 'You get some very archaic ideas of what teaching is ...': primary school teachers' perceptions of the barriers to physically active lessons. *Education 3-13* 47, 308–321. doi: 10.1080/03004279.2018.1437462

Salvador-García, C., Chiva-Bartoll, O., and Capella-Peris, C. (2019). Bilingual physical education: the effects of CLIL on physical activity levels. *Int. J. Biling. Educ. Biling.* 1–10. doi: 10.1080/13670050.2019.1639131

Salvador-García, C., and Chiva-Bartoll, Ò (2017). CLIL in teaching physical education: views of the teachers in the Spanish context. *J. Phys. Educ. Sport* 17, 1130–1138. doi: 10.7752/jpes.2017.03174

Salvador-García, C., Chiva-Bartoll, Ò, and Vergaz, J. J. (2018). Percepción del alumnado sobre el uso del método AICLE en educación física: estudio de caso. *Retos* 33, 138–142.

Sandoval, W. A., and Bell, P. (2004). Design-based research methods for studying learning in context: introduction. *Educ. Psychol.* 39, 199–201. doi: 10.1207/s15326985ep3904_1

Tashakkori, A., and Teddlie, C. (1998). *Mixed Methodology: Combining Qualitative and Quantitative Approaches: Applied Social Research Methods Series*, Vol. 46. Thousand Oaks, CA: Sage Publications.

Ting, Y. L. T. (2011). CLIL . not only not immersion but also more than the sum of its parts. *ELT J.* 65, 314–317. doi: 10.1093/elt/ccr026

Tolan, P. H., and Deutsch, N. L. (2015). "Mixed methods in developmental science," in *Handbook of Child Psychology and Developmental Science: Theory and Method*, eds W. F. Overton, P. C. M. Molenaar, and R. M. Lerner (Hoboken, NJ: John Wiley and Sons Inc), 713–757. doi: 10.1002/9781118963418.childpsy119

Torres-Rincon, J. C., and Cuesta-Medina, L. M. (2019). Situated practice in CLIL: voices from colombian teachers. *GIST Educ. Learn. Res. J.* 18, 109–141. doi: 10.26817/16925777.456

van der Wilt, F., van der Veen, C., van Kruistum, C., and van Oers, B. (2019). Why do children become rejected by their peers? a review of studies into the relationship between oral communicative competence and sociometric status in childhood. *Educ. Psychol. Rev.* 31, 699–724. doi: 10.1007/s10648-019-09479-z

Viciana, J., Mayorga-Vega, D., and Parra-Saldías, M. (2019). Adolescents' physical activity levels on physical education and non-physical education days according to gender, age, and weight status. *Eur. Phys. Educ. Rev.* 25, 143–155. doi: 10.1177/1356336X17706683

Weiss, M. R. (2011). Teach the children well: a holistic approach to developing psychosocial and behavioral competencies through physical education. *Quest* 63, 55–65. doi: 10.1080/00336297.2011.10483663

World Health Organization, (2010). *Global Recommendation on Physical Activity for Health*. Geneva: World Health Organization.

Zindler, K. (2013). *Content and Language Integrated Learning (CLIL) and PE in England: An Exploratory Study*. Doctoral Dissertation, University of Sheffield, Sheffield.

17

Basic Psychological Needs and Sports Satisfaction among Brazilian Athletes and Coaches: The Mediating Role of the Dyadic Relationship

Andressa Ribeiro Contreira[1], José Roberto Andrade do Nascimento Junior[2], Nayara Malheiros Caruzzo[1,3], Luciane Cristina Arantes da Costa[1], Patrícia Aparecida Gaion[1], Sandro Victor Alves Melo[1,4] and Lenamar Fiorese[1]*

[1] Grupo de Estudos de Psicologia do Esporte e Desempenho Humano, Physical Education Department, Universidade Estadual de Maringá, Maringá, Brazil, [2] Grupo de Estudos em Psicologia do Esporte e do Exercício, Physical Education Department, Universidade Federal do Vale do São Francisco, Petrolina, Brazil, [3] Duke Global Health Institute, Duke University, Durham, NC, United States, [4] Health and Sports Science Center, Universidade Federal do Acre, Rio Branco, Brazil

***Correspondence:**
Andressa Ribeiro Contreira
andressacontreira@gmail.com

Even though sport satisfaction has proved an important element for youngsters to keep practicing sports, little is known on the sport satisfaction of coaches. Moreover, the coach-athlete relationship is acknowledged as a key element for sport success, but whether its importance is the same for coaches and athletes is yet to be investigated. Our study analyzed the mediating role of the coach-athlete relationship in associating the satisfaction of basic psychological needs and sport satisfaction of Brazilian coaches and athletes. 364 coaches and athletes participated in the study representing 182 dyads from different sports according to the following instruments: Basic Needs Satisfaction Sport Scale (BNSSS), Coach-Athlete Relationship Questionnaire, athlete and coach versions (CART-Q), and the Athletic Satisfaction Questionnaire (ASQ). Data analysis followed a Structural Equation Modeling (SEM) with a significance level of $p < 0.05$, generating results in which the mediating model for coaches was not adequately fit, while the direct model, without mediation, was adequately fit and explained 48% of sport satisfaction variance. For athletes, the mediating model has shown adequate fit and explained 81% of the sport satisfaction variance, leading us to conclude that the quality of the coach-athlete relationship can be considered a determining factor for the satisfaction of young Brazilian athletes' basic psychological needs as well as sport satisfaction, but proved not as relevant to their coaches.

Keywords: interpersonal relationships, satisfaction, motivation, sport, psychological need

INTRODUCTION

Studies in the high-performance sport context have intensively focused on factors to contribute to the well-being of athletes considering that the environment favors tense situations and emotional alterations (Balaguer et al., 2012). In this context, the Theory of Self-determination (TAD) points out to the satisfaction of basic psychological needs (autonomy, competence, and relationships) as key factors to achieve well-being by encompassing universally essential elements to the integrity of human development (Deci and Ryan, 2012). Recent studies have indicated that when feeling independent to control emotions and truly connected to a social environment through the support of their coaches, athletes are more likely to reach self-determined motivation and consequently feel satisfied with their sports (Deci et al., 2013; Reynoulds and Mcdonough, 2015; Gurrola et al., 2016).

Such evidence is supported by the micro theory of Basic Psychological Needs (Deci and Ryan, 2012), which states that social environments conducted by significant persons (such as teachers, coaches, parents) favor the satisfaction of athletes' basic needs for providing them with psychological experiences that positively affect their motivation and performance (Balaguer et al., 2012; Deci et al., 2013; González et al., 2015). In contrast, poorly adapted environments can frustrate the need of youngsters and consequently lower their participation in sports and sense of personal fulfilment, in addition to generate both emotional and physical fatigue (Bartholomew et al., 2011; Gurrola et al., 2016).

Recent studies have pointed out that athletes' satisfaction with team structural and procedural aspects, such as group environment and sport experiences, is associated with the optimization of both cognitive and emotional performance (Riemer and Chelladurai, 1998; Jowett and Poczwardowski, 2007; Lee et al., 2017; Ntomali et al., 2017; Rocchi and Pelletier, 2018). Additionally, athletes' satisfaction favors the development of group cohesion (García-Calvo et al., 2014; Kim and Cruz, 2016), intrinsic motivation (Mageau and Vallerand, 2003; Cranmer and Sollitto, 2015), establishment of effective communication (Sullivan and Gee, 2007; Kao and Tsai, 2016), and well-being (Kim and Cruz, 2016; Jowett et al., 2017).

In this perspective, we highlight the relevance of sport satisfaction to the well-being and performance of athletes, which has been explained according to variables such as leadership styles (Kao and Tsai, 2016; Kim and Cruz, 2016; Ntomali et al., 2017), social support (Cranmer and Sollitto, 2015), and motivational environment (Bekiari and Syrmpas, 2015). The behavior of sport leaders has proved a determinant role in athletes' satisfaction (Kao and Tsai, 2016) and social support is important when transmitting information from coaches for contributing to the emotional support of athletes (Cranmer and Sollitto, 2015). In addition, a motivational environment acts as catalyst for athletes' motivation regarding their engagement in sports and consequently their satisfaction with sport experiences (Bekiari and Syrmpas, 2015).

In an effort to understand how motivation and sport satisfaction relate to positive experiences and the optimization of athletes' performance (Vallerand, 2000; Kao and Tsai, 2016; Lee et al., 2017), our study bases on the TAD to investigate natural or intrinsic human tendencies to behave in an efficient, healthy manner. The TAD remains one of the most commonly used theoretical approaches and approaches the reasons leading an individual to initiate, remain or quit their activities (Ryan and Deci, 2017). The micro theory of Basic Psychological Needs predicts universally essential elements for human development, motivation, integrity, and general well-being emerging upon the satisfaction of basic psychological needs regarding autonomy, competence, and personal relationships (Ryan and Deci, 2017).

Specifically, autonomy corresponds to the individual's ability to feel in control of their actions and decisions. Competence refers to the need of an individual to feel efficient enough to reach their desired results. Personal relationships are based on an innate capacity of individuals to perceive themselves truly connected to a social environment (Deci and Ryan, 2012; Reynoulds and Mcdonough, 2015). Researches indicate that athletes who see themselves as able to manage their actions within the sport context feel physically and psychologically able to performe their functions and feel accepted in their teams, in addition to being more likely to feel intrinsically motivated, thus facilitating the perception of sport satisfaction (Deci et al., 2013; Bekiari and Syrmpas, 2015; Reynoulds and Mcdonough, 2015; Gurrola et al., 2016; Monteiro et al., 2018; Vieira et al., 2018).

However, despite the important impact that motivation can have on athletes' satisfaction (Mageau and Vallerand, 2003; Bekiari and Syrmpas, 2015; Lee et al., 2017), most studies have focused on athletes (Cranmer and Sollitto, 2015; Kao and Tsai, 2016; Kim and Cruz, 2016; Ntomali et al., 2017) rather than the perspective of sport coaches (Lorimer, 2009; Lorimer and Jowett, 2009; Kim and Cruz, 2016). It is known that even more important than the isolate perception of athletes or coaches, their combined views, characterized as dyads, can provide more efficient and thorough information on sport experiences (Lorimer and Jowett, 2009; Jowett, 2017).

The quality of the coach-athlete relationship is considered a central axis in the sport context defined as a combination of inter-relations involving thoughts, feelings, and behaviors of coaches and athletes (Jowett and Poczwardowski, 2007; Jowett, 2017). Such relationship has been studied from the integrated model 3+1Cs (Jowett and Poczwardowski, 2007) incorporating affective (closeness), cognitive (commitment), and behavior (complementarity) components of the dyad, in addition to the degree to which athletes' and coaches' perceptions interconnect (co-orientation) (Rhind and Jowett, 2012).

Studies have reported that close dyadic relationships based on respect, affection, and commitment benefit the development of athlete excellence contributing to the personal growth of both athletes and coaches (Cheuczuk et al., 2016; Davis et al., 2018; Avci et al., 2018). In contrast, dyads characterized by distance and absence of commitment imply interpersonal conflicts, exhaustion, dissatisfaction, and lack of interest inside and outside the sport context (Jowett and Lavalee, 2007; Antonini et al., 2011; Li et al., 2015; Jowett and Shanmugam, 2016; Davis et al., 2018).

Our study considers the importance of motivational aspects for athletes' satisfaction and the impact of social psychology in the sport context (Jowett and Poczwardowski, 2007) and seeks to improve the scientific knowledge discussing the implications in the dyadic relationships to promote positive psychological aspects for coaches and young Brazilian athletes taking into account affective, cognitive, and behavior aspects, representing the gap investigated in our study *per se*. The fostering of harmonious sport environments generates potential literature evidence regarding athletes' development (Jowett, 2017;

Ryan and Deci, 2017); however, it is yet to be clarified whether such development is also applicable to coaches (Lorimer, 2009; Lorimer and Jowett, 2009; Kao and Tsai, 2016).

Thus, the analysis of positive psychological variables in the perspective of the main social actors in the sport context (coach and athlete) enables a larger view on the personal and interpersonal factors that focus on their well-being and performance beyond the perspective of isolated influences from coaches' behavior. Considering these remarks, our goal was to investigate the mediating impact of the coach-athlete relationship on the association between basic psychological needs and athletes' satisfaction of coaches and young Brazilian athletes.

Hypothesis

Our first hypothesis involves a positive association between sport motivation, characterized by the satisfaction of basic psychological needs, and sport satisfaction for both coaches and athletes considering that autonomous and competent individuals who also feel connected to their peers are more likely to feel satisfied (González et al., 2015). Our second hypothesis considers that coach-athlete relationship will increase the impact of motivation over sport satisfaction since positive coach-athlete relationships may improve these individuals' physical and psychological well-being providing them with better performance and satisfaction with the sport (Jowett and Shanmugam, 2016).

MATERIALS AND METHODS

Participants

Aiming at representing the dyadic relationships, we calculated the sample size by considering the limiting number of coaches participating in the competition, which was performed for finite samples with a 95-confidence level and a five-percent confidence interval (Richardson et al., 2012). We included a total of 540 coaches to insure the participation of at least 159 dyads (n = 159 coaches; n = 159 athletes). Inclusion criteria as follows: (1) having qualified for the national stage of the main youth sporting event in Brazil, the Youth School Games; (2) a coach-athlete relationship of over 3 months (Hampson and Jowett, 2014; Sagar and Jowett, 2015; Nicholls and Perry, 2016). We selected the athletes intentionally after sampling the coaches. Based on the inclusion criteria for the coaches – team and individual sport types – coaches were requested to indicate an athlete who met criterion 3 (a 3-month old relationship) to constitute the dyad.

A total of 189 dyads participated in the study (378 subjects), however, seven pairs were excluded for having answered the questionnaires incorrectly, which generated a final total of 364 individuals representing 182 dyads. The average age in the samples was 40.47 ± 9.7 years old for coaches and 16.24 ± 0.81 years old for athletes. The individuals represented all five regions of Brazil and 13 different sports: volleyball (n = 30; 16.5%), judo (n = 30; 16.5%), basketball (n = 29; 15.9%), handball (n = 23; 12.6%), track and field (n = 22; 12.1%), futsal (n = 12; 6.6%), swimming (n = 12; 6.6%), Olympic wrestling (n = 7; 3.8%), table tennis (n = 5; 2.7%), chess (n = 5; 2.7%), cycling (n = 3; 1.6%), rhythmic gymnastics (n = 3; 1.6%), and beach volleyball (n = 1; 0.5%).

Measures

We used the Brazilian version of the Basic Needs Satisfaction in Sport Scale (Nascimento Junior et al., 2018), originally developed by Ng et al. (2011), to investigate the satisfaction of basic psychological needs of coaches and athletes. Differently from the original scale (which has five dimensions: competence, choice, internal perceived locus of causality, volition, and relatedness), the Brazilian scale is constituted of only one general dimension of autonomy. It was pointed out as a necessary change during the various phases of the instrument adaptation to the Portuguese language, such as at the content analysis phase and factor structure analysis (EFA and CFA). In the EFA, the authors tested different models in order to find the best fit since the content analysis revealed inconsistencies. Thus, the instrument is composed of 12 items distributed in three dimensions: competence (item 6 "I feel that I am good at my sport"), autonomy (item 1 "In my sport, I fell that I am pursuing my personal goals") and relatedness (item 4 "There are people in my sport who care about me"), which is available for reader consultation (Nascimento Junior et al., 2018). Answers are given in a 7-point Likert scale ranging from 1– "Not true at all" to 7– "Very true." Scale Confirmatory Factor Analysis (CFA) presented acceptable fit for athletes [$X^2(51)$ = 82.137; p = 0.004; X^2/df = 1.611; CFI = 0.94; GFI = 0.93; TLI = 0.93; RMSEA = 0.06; P(rmsea < 0.05) = 0.268]. We submitted the scale to a process of content validation in order to adjust its items for coaches, which generated acceptable Content Validity Coefficient (CVC = 0.91). CFA analysis for coaches also revealed acceptable fit [$X^2(51)$ = 104.208; p = 0.001; X^2/df = 2.043; CFI = 0.93; GFI = 0.92; TLI = 0.90; RMSEA = 0.07; P(rmsea < 0.05) = 0.023].

To measure coaches' and athletes' direct perspective of their social relationships, we adopted the Portuguese version of the Coach-Athlete Relationship Questionnaire (Vieira et al., 2015 athlete version – $\alpha > 0.70$; Contreira et al., 2019 coach version – $\alpha = 0.86$). The scale was originally developed by Jowett and Ntoumanis (2004) and comprises 11 items assessing the following three dimensions: closeness (item 3 "I like my coach/athlete"), commitment (item 2 "I am committed to my coach/athlete"), and complementarity (item 10 "In my training with my coach/athlete, I am willing to do my best") Items answered in a seven-point Likert scale ranging from 1-"Strongly disagree" to 7-"Strongly agree." CFA revealed instrument's acceptable fit for athletes [$X^2(39)$ = 93.926; p = 0.001; X^2/df = 2.408; CFI = 0.90; GFI = 0.92; TLI = 0.87; RMSEA = 0.08; P(rmsea < 0.05) = 0.04] and coaches [$X^2(37)$ = 76.284; p = 0.001; X^2/df = 2.062; CFI = 0.90; GFI = 0.94; TLI = 0.88; RMSEA = 0.07; P(rmsea < 0.05) = 0.04].

We used the version of the (Borrego et al., 2010) Athlete Satisfaction Questionnaire (Riemer and Chelladurai, 1998) validated for the Portuguese language. This instrument assesses the level of athletes' satisfaction with their sport experiences and is composed of 53 statements answered in a Likert scale ranging from 1-"Not at all satisfied" to 7-"Extremely satisfied," encompassing a 15-level scale of satisfaction. In this study, we used a shorter 11-item version that assesses only the following three dimensions: training and instruction (item 7 "The training that I receive/give from/to my coach/athlete regarding technique and tactics of my position"), individual performance (item 1 "The level on which my performance goals were reached during the season"), and personal treatment (item 11 "How my coach/athlete supports me"), regarded as directly relevant for the coach-athlete relationship study (Jowett and Don Carolis, 2003; Jowett, 2008; Lorimer, 2009; Lorimer and Jowett, 2009). This same short version of the questionnaire had been used in a previous research involving coaches and athletes (Jowett, 2008; Lorimer, 2009; Jowett and Nezlek, 2011). The scale CFA showed acceptable fit for athletes [$X^2(41) = 69.852$; $p = 0.003$; $X^2/df = 1.704$; CFI = 0.95; GFI = 0.94; TLI = 0.93; RMSEA = 0.06; $P(\text{rmsea} < 0.05) = 0.198$]. With the help of a specialists committee, a version of the instrument was adapted for coaches and generated a satisfactory content validity (CVC > 0.80). Coach-version CFA also revealed acceptable fit indices [$X^2(32) = 98.184$; $p = 0.001$; $X^2/\text{df} = 3.068$; CFI = 0.92; GFI = 0.90; TLI = 0.90; RMSEA = 0.09; $P(\text{rmsea} < 0.05) = 0.001$].

Procedure

This study was approved by the Ethics Committee of a Brazilian university under statement number 1.324.411/2015. All participants and legal representatives had read and signed an Informed Consent Term. Data gathering occurred during the Youth School Games, regarded as the most important competition for athletes at this age group in the country. We collected the data at the locations where the competitions were being held as well as in individuals' accommodations according to their availability. The individuals answered the questions in group, but filling the questionnaire individually, averaging 20 min per person. Data collection with athletes and coaches occurred throughout the competition held in November 2015.

Data Analysis

Preliminary Analysis

We performed an exploratory data analysis with descriptive statistics as mean (x), standard deviation (sd). We compared the BPN satisfaction, athletics satisfaction and CAR between athletes and coaches through an independent student *t*-test ($p < 0.05$). All analyses were performed using Amos 22.0.

Main Analysis

Our main goal was to verify whether CAR mediated the relationship between BPN satisfaction (independent variable) and athlete's satisfaction (dependent variable) using a Structural Equation Modeling (SEM) on software Amos 22.0, following the two-step model building approach recommend by Anderson and Gerbing (1988). The first step involves testing the measurement model through a Confirmatory Factor Analysis (CFA), while in the second step the hypothesized structural model is tested.

The internal consistency of the measurement model (Step 1) was assessed by composite reliability (CR) (Hair et al., 2005), while average variance extracted (AVE) were estimated to assess convergent validity (Fornell and Larcker, 1981). A CR equal or higher than 0.7 and an AVE equal or higher than 0.5 are considered reliable and valid constructs (Fornell and Larcker, 1981). Discriminant validity was established whenever AVE for each construct exceeded the squared correlations between the construct in question and any other construct (Fornell and Larcker, 1981).

Before the main analysis, we verified the data for normality, missing values, and outliers for all study variables following the procedure outlined by Tabachnick and Fidell (2013). Examination of skewness and kurtosis for all variables indicated univariate normality based on the cut-off values of skewness < 3.0 and kurtosis < 10.0 (Kline, 2016). Analysis of Mardia's multivariate coefficient (Athletes = 38.62; Coaches = 52.35) indicated that the data distribution derived from multivariate normality, which justified the use of the Bollen-Stine bootstrap procedure to obtain a corrected Chi-squared value (Athletes – $p = 0.194$; Coaches – $p = 0.005$) of the estimated coefficients for the Maximum Likelihood Estimator (Bollen and Stine, 1993). After excluding seven pairs (coaches and athletes), no missing data was identified. We verified the occurrence of outliers using the Square Mahalanobis distance (D^2) since the absence of such cases is a prerequisite for this analysis.

We used several fit indices to assess the model fit according to Hu and Bentler (1999) recommendations: chi square ($\chi 2$), Normalized Chi-Square ($\chi 2/\text{df}$), Comparative Fit Index (CFI), Tucker-Lewis Index (TLI), Root Mean Square Error of Approximation (RMSEA), and its associated ninety-percent Confidence Interval (CI). CFI and TLI values close to or above 0.95, RMSEA values close to or below 0.08, and the lower end of 90% CI of the RMSEA containing the value of 0.05 represent an excellent fit to the data for the hypothesized model (Hu and Bentler, 1999). Furthermore, we used these indices for both Step 1 and Step 2. Fit quality for the structural model (Step 2) was also assessed through its factor loadings (FL) and items individual reliability (Marôco, 2010). Based on Kline's recommendation (2016), the reference for path interpretation included small effect below 0.20; medium effect between 0.20 and 0.49; and large effect above 0.50 ($p < 0.05$).

Mediation Analysis

In order to test the theoretical model proposed for the study, the mediation effects were verified by the indirect effects (Williams and MacKinnon, 2008). Bias-corrected bootstrapped point estimates for the indirect effects of the independent variable on the dependent variable were estimated, considering 95% confidence intervals. Significant indirect effects were considered (at alfa = 0.05) if its 95% confidence intervals does not include zero. Bias corrected and accelerated intervals supported by a 1000 samples bootstrapping were used to make inferences. Bootstrapping procedures have been recommended Williams and MacKinnon (2008) as more efficient and powerful detecting indirect effects in smaller samples.

RESULTS

Descriptive Results

The brazilian coach and athlete sociodemographic profile are shown in **Table 1**. Most of the coaches were male (82.4%),

TABLE 1 | Sociodemographic profile of Brazilian coaches and athletes (n = 182 dyads).

Variables	*F*	(%)
Gender		
Coaches		
Male	150	82.4
Female	32	17.6
Athletes		
Male	88	48.4
Female	94	51.6
Type of Sport		
Individual	87	47.8
Teams	95	52.2
Coach-athlete dyads		
<1 year	07	3.8
1–5 years	114	62.6
>5 years	51	28.0
Years experience		
Coaches		
<5 years	08	4.4
5 a 10 years	36	19.8
>10 years	135	74.2
Athletes		
<1 year	02	1.1
1 a 5 years	87	48.1
>5 years	84	46.4
Region of Brazil		
South	23	12.6
Southeast	25	13.7
West center	28	15.4
Northeast	62	34.1
North	43	23.6

Source: the authors.

TABLE 2 | Coach-athlete relationship, basic psychological needs and sport satisfaction comparison between coaches and athletes (n = 182 dyads).

Variables	Coaches *X* (SD)	Athletes *X* (SD)	*P*
CAR			
Closeness	6.54 (0.84)	6.69 (0.56)	**0.03***
Commitment	6.24 (0.81)	6.16 (0.84)	0.54
Complementarity	6.54 (0.61)	6.52 (0.58)	0.08
BPN			
Competence	6.17 (0.76)	5.97 (0.80)	**0.01***
Autonomy	6.52 (0.63)	6.66 (0.55)	**0.01***
Relatedness	5.84 (0.95)	6.30 (0.82)	**0.01***
ST			
Training-instruction	6.18 (0.74)	6.41 (0.77)	**0.01***
Individual performance	5.88 (0.77)	5.81 (0.83)	0.58
Personal treatment	6.31 (0.67)	6.47 (0.63)	**0.01***

*Independent sample t-test (*p < 0.05). CAR (Coach-athlete relationship); BPN (basic psychological needs); ST (sport satisfaction). Source: the authors. The values in bold correspond to the significance level of the comparisons made. These values showed statistically significant differences between the groups.*

whereas most of athletes were female (51.6%). Over half of coach-athletes dyades (62.6%) had one to 5 years of relationship. The majority of coaches has more than 10 years in the field (74.2%), while most athlete showed 1–5 years experience (48.1%).

Table 2 shows the descriptive data for the main variables in the study. Athletes and coaches had different perceptions only for closeness, with athletes (6.69 ± 0.56) perceiving higher levels than coaches (6.54 ± 0.84) (p = 0.03). Regarding the basic needs =, we found that coaches (6.17 ± 0.76) felt more competent than athletes (5.97 ± 0.80) ($p < 0.01$), while athletes presented higher autonomy (6.66 ± 0.55) and relatedness (6.30 ± 0.82) than coaches (6.52 ± 0.63 and 5.84 ± 0.95, respectively) ($p < 0.01$). Athletes have also shown higher levels of satisfaction with training and instruction (6.41 ± 0.77) and personal treatment (6.47 ± 0.63) than coaches (6.18 ± 0.74 and 6.31 ± 0.67, respectively) ($p < 0.01$).

Table 3 shows the correlations between basic needs satisfaction, coach-athlete relationship and sport satisfaction. Coach data are displayed in the upper triangle and correlation values for athletes in the lower triangle. Significant correlations were obtained for most variables for coaches, while athletes presented correlations among all variables ($p < 0.05$). The strongest correlation between different constructs for coaches occurred between BPN's competence and ST's training and instruction (r = 0.57) as well as between CAR complementarity and ST personal treatment (r = 0.52).

Measurement Model (Step 1)

Initially, we tested a three-factor measurement model through CFA (SEM Step 1) by assessing the relationship of the items analyzed with their respective latent factors. Acceptable fit indices were obtained for both coaches [$X^2(24)$ = 55.17; p = 0.001; X^2/df = 2.51; CFI = 0.94; GFI = 0.94; TLI = 0.90; NFI = 0.90; RMSEA = 0.08; P(rmsea < 0.05) = 0.014] and athletes [$X^2(24)$ = 47.35; p = 0.003; X^2/df = 1.97; CFI = 0.94; GFI = 0.95; TLI = 0.91; NFI = 0.90; RMSEA = 0.07; P(rmsea < 0.05) = 0.103]. Moreover, local adjustment and the internal reliability of items also proved adequate, since all paths had significant FL > 0.50. In this sense, the latent model was confirmed and enabled for SEM Step 2. In order to assess the convergent validity, AVE was computed. The AVE values were as follows for athletes and coaches, respectively,: BPN = 0.45/0.53; CAR = 0.47/0.50; and ST = 0.53/0.51. Only two variables showed AVE lower the cut-off, however, these values were very close to 0.50. We observed that the BPN revealed to be discriminant to the others (AVE > SC) for both athletes and coaches. CAR and ST revealed to be discriminant to the others (AVE > SC) just for coaches, while, for athletes, CAR and ST showed higher SC (0.76) than their AVE. This result can be related to the association between these variables, which assess similar constructs (Jowett and Don Carolis, 2003; Jowett, 2008; Lorimer, 2009). The composite reliability values were as follows for athletes and coaches: BPN = 0.65/0.78; CAR = 0.71/0.74; and ST = 0.78/0.75.

Structural Equation Modeling (Step 2)

Direct Effect

Firstly, we tested a model with direct paths between BPN and ST (**Figure 1**), which had adequate fit (**Table 4**) with

TABLE 3 | Correlation matrix for study variables.

Variables	CAR			BPN			Athletic satisfaction		
	1	2	3	4	5	6	7	8	9
1. Closeness	–	0.49*	0.42*	0.21*	0.12	0.15*	0.24*	0.43*	0.47*
2. Commitment	0.43*	–	0.53*	0.30*	0.37*	0.22*	0.43*	0.40*	0.53*
3. Complementarity	0.55*	0.55*	–	0.43*	0.41*	0.34*	0.40*	0.36*	0.35*
4. Competence	0.19*	0.27*	0.30*	–	0.52*	0.43*	0.57*	0.31*	0.33*
5. Autonomy	0.27*	0.34*	0.33*	0.40*	–	0.32*	0.42*	0.39*	0.46*
6. Relatedness	0.23*	0.32*	0.29*	0.17*	0.25*	–	0.28*	0.17*	0.31*
7. Training-instruction	0.42*	0.42*	0.46*	0.25*	0.25*	0.32*	–	0.63*	0.51*
8. Individual performance	0.24*	0.36*	0.29*	0.35*	0.28*	0.22*	0.48*	–	0.52
9. Personal treatment	0.45*	0.50*	0.52*	0.36*	0.30*	0.25*	0.55*	0.43*	–

**Pearson correlations, significant values for $p < 0.05$. Upper triangle (Correlation coefficients for coaches) – Lower triangle (Correlation coefficients for athletes). CART (1. Closeness; 2.Commitment; 3. Complementarity); BPN (4. Competence; 5. Autonomy; 6. Relatedness); ST (7. Training-instruction; 8. Individual performance; 9. Personal treatment). CAR: coach-athlete relationship subscales; BPN: Basic Psychological needs subscale. Source: the authors. Bold values correspond to statistically significant correlations between variables.*

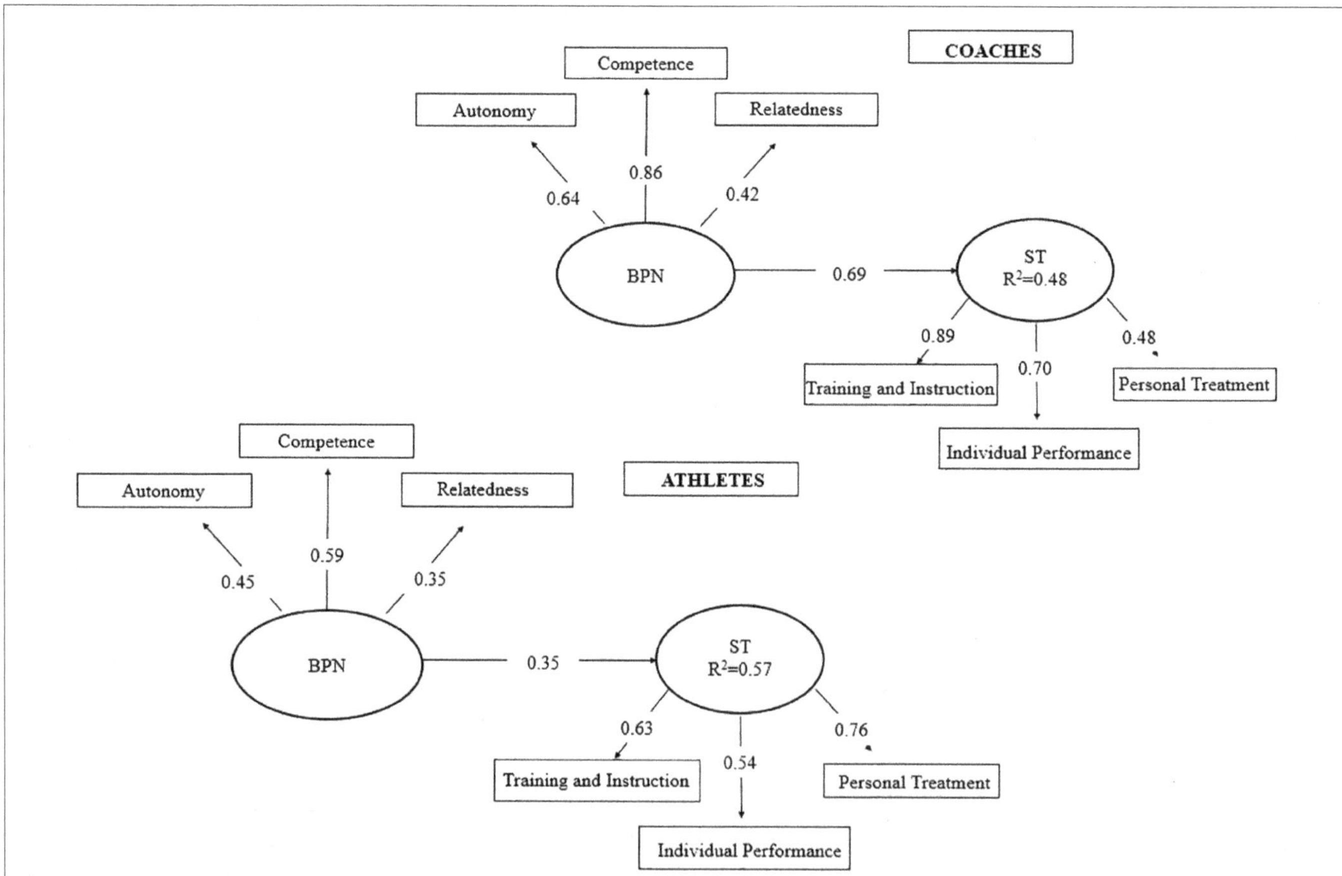

FIGURE 1 | Structural equation model of BPN impact over coaches and athletes satisfaction (n = 182 dyads).

BPN explaining 48% and 57% of ST variance for coaches and athletes, respectively.

Indirect Effect

We tested a second model including CAR as a mediating variable over the BPN effect on satisfaction. The model for coaches did not show adequate fit (**Table 4**), still, model paths and shared variance indicated the CAR mediating role (**Figure 2**). Meanwhile, the model for athletes presented acceptable fit (**Table 4**) and evidenced a significant mild-strength mediating positive effect of CAR suggesting the importance of young athletes attributing it to the relationship with their coaches (**Figure 2**).

By analyzing Bootstrapped parameter estimates for coaches (**Table 5**), we found that their satisfaction (ST) had a 54%

TABLE 4 | Fit indices comparison with and without mediation for coaches and athletes' structural equation model (n = 182).

Models	B/Sχ^2	χ^2/df	RMSEA [95% C.I.]	CFI	TLI
Coaches					
No mediation	23.34	2.92	0.10 [0.09–0.12]	0.95	0.90
CAR mediation	90.17	3.76	0.12 [0.10–0.13]	0.87	0.81
Athletes					
No mediation	14.37	2.05	0.08 [0.06–0.08]	0.95	0.90
CAR mediation	34.97	1.52	0.05 [0.04–0.06]	0.97	0.95

B/SX² = Bollen-stine Chi-Square; df = Degrees of freedom; X²/df = Normalized chi-square; RMSEA = Root mean square error of approximation; TLI = Tucker-lewis index; CFI = Comparative fitness index. Source: the authors.

explained variance from BPN + CAR and CAR shared 47% of its variance with BPN. A strong positive effect occurred from BPN to ST (β = 0.56; $p < 0.05$) as well as a mild positive effect from CAR to ST (β = 0.22; $p < 0.05$). The impact of BPN over ST increased when mediated by the independent indirect CAR effect (β = 0.15) (total effect β = 0.71).

When analyzing the mediating Bootstrapped parameter estimates for athletes (**Table 5**), we observe that 81% of the variance in their satisfaction levels (ST) could be predicted by BPN + CAR and CAR was explained in 49% by the BPN. The direct path between BPN and ST had a weak positive effect (β = 0.17; $p < 0.05$) and a strong positive effect emerged from CAR to ST (β = 0.77; $p < 0.05$). CAR mediation revealed an independent and high indirect effect (β = 0.54) in the association ($p < 0.05$) (total effect β = 0.71).

DISCUSSION

Our aim was to examine the mediating role of coach-athlete relationship in the association between basic needs satisfaction and sport satisfaction of Brazilian coaches and athletes. Our

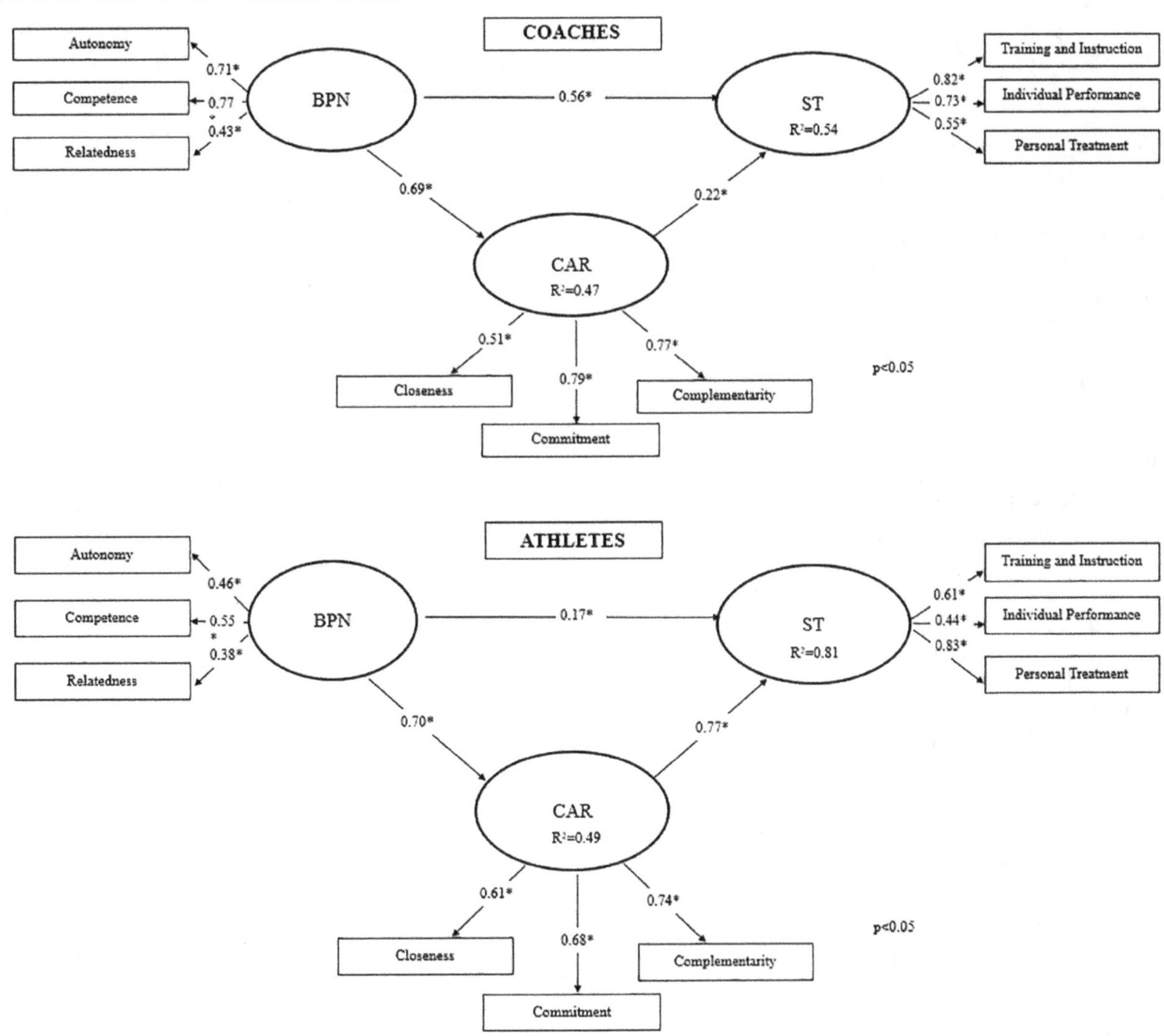

FIGURE 2 | Structural equation modeling of the CAR mediating role over the BPN impact on coaches and athletes satisfaction (n = 182 dyads).

TABLE 5 | Standardized direct and indirect effects for the structural model (M2) for coaches and athletes (n = 182 dyads).

Parameter			Effect	95% CI
Coaches				
Direct effects				
BPN	→	CAR	0.69	0.46–0.85
	→	ST	0.56	0.29–0.89
CAR	→	ST	0.22	0.08–0.48
Indirect effect of BPN via				
CAR	→	ST	0.15	0.04–0.29
Total effect			0.71	
Athletes				
Direct effects				
BPN	→	CAR	0.70	0.40–0.93
	→	ST	0.17	0.02–0.89
CAR	→	ST	0.77	0.33–1.46
Indirect effect of BPN via				
CAR	→	ST	0.54	0.31–0.76
Total effect			0.71	

*CI – Confidence interval; CAR (coach-athlete relationship); BPN (basic psychological needs); ST (sport satisfaction). *p < 0.05. Source: the authors.*

Hypothesis 1 was confirmed: BPN had a positive impact over both coaches (48%) and athletes (57%) satisfaction with slightly more relevant impact for athletes. In contrast, our Hypothesis 2 was only partially supported since such mediating model presented acceptable fit exclusively for athletes. In this model, variance of athletes' satisfaction was predicted in 81%. Although adequate fit indices were not reached, the model for coaches offered evidence regarding the role coach-athlete relationship in coach satisfaction.

Effects of Basic Psychological Needs on Athletes' Satisfaction

According to the literature, the impact of basic needs satisfaction over sport satisfaction revealed in the results confirm the predictions (**Figure 1**). According to the SDT, basic needs of autonomy, competence and relatedness are universal elements essential for human development, its integrity, and general well-being (Deci and Ryan, 2012) mainly due to their contribution to intrinsic motivation (Costa et al., 2016). A more autonomous motivation is known to be related to higher levels of satisfaction with performance, as found in a longitudinal study by Blecharz et al. (2015) involving professional Polish athletes. The study found a model explaining 57% of performance satisfaction variance and highlighted the significant indirect effect of intrinsic motivation mediating the association between self-efficacy and performance satisfaction for those athletes.

Another study approached collegiate athletes and found that those who receive support from had higher levels of satisfaction regarding their sports (Hoffmann and Loughead, 2016). Such evidence strengthen our findings by showing that when athletes feel engaged and connected to their social environment, they are more likely to present higher levels of satisfaction with their sport, which reveals how interpersonal relationships stablished in sport practices are intervening factors for athletic satisfaction.

Regarding the BPN impact over satisfaction of Brazilian coaches (**Figure 1**), our findings contribute to current knowledge on the subject with important advances considering that the field of sport psychology is yet to be further explored since most studies have focused only on athletes' satisfaction (Lorimer, 2009; Kim and Cruz, 2016). Our results revealed that coaches' BPN explained 48% of their sport satisfaction, similarly to the findings of Jowett (2008) when studying the impact of intrinsic and extrinsic motivation of coaches on their satisfaction. The author found positive effects from motivation to satisfaction upon the presence of self-determined intrinsic motivation. Rocchi and Pelletier (2018) found that coaches whose training contexts enable the satisfaction of their basic psychological needs tend to have an autonomous regulation of motivation as well as an interpersonal support attitude. In contrast, the frustration of such needs contributes to the controlled regulation of motivation and the absence of interpersonal support.

According to SDT, it is possible to state that coaches who have their basic needs met, especially regarding competence (**Table 1**), tend to reach greater satisfaction in their sport practice. Such positive evaluation of processes and outcomes regarding their experience can be explained by the SDT mini-theory of Cognitive Evaluation, which addresses the effects of social contexts on intrinsic motivation since contextual events have control aspects that influence competence perception (Lorimer, 2009; Ryan and Deci, 2017). Therefore, we understand that sport represents a social context in which a coach needs to feel capable of performing their tasks and responsibilities when coaching athletes and teams including effort and involvement in activities.

The Mediating Role of the Coach-Athlete Relationship in Sport Motivation and Satisfaction

Our mediating model indicated that the study on coach-athlete relationship led to a higher degree of explained variance for sport satisfaction suggesting that it is important for athletes to establish a good relationship with their coaches in order to feel satisfied with the sport (**Figure 2**). Our results emphasize the relevance of a positive relationship between coaches and young athletes, especially regarding their perception of closeness (affective component), as well as the dimensions of training and instruction, and personal treatment (**Table 1**). A study by Cranmer and Sollitto (2015) supports our findings by demonstrating that social support from coaches predicted better satisfaction of college athletes with their sport experiences. Coaches are considered vital for the entire process of involvement in a sport for allowing athletes to reach their maximum potential (Kim and Cruz, 2016; Ramazanoğlu, 2018) and having the potential to shape athletes' experiences in their sport context (Cranmer and Sollitto, 2015). Jowett et al. (2017) add that athletes who share a good-quality relationship with their coaches experience high levels of satisfaction of their basic needs, which establishes a positive prediction of self-determined motivation and well-being.

Considering our participants' age group, our findings are supported by evidences in the literature that show how young athletes need experienced and well-qualified coaches who offer support and orientation to help them overcome challenges and adversities in their sport (Jackson et al., 2010). In this context, the strong mediation of CAR in athletic satisfaction agrees with SDT's assumptions, which understands human behavior in interaction with the environment and how motivation will be influenced by athletes' social contexts in which a positive participation of social agents, such as teachers, colleagues, family, and coaches, can make individuals more self-determined (Ryan and Deci, 2017).

Model 3+1C's model corroborates such aspects and reveals that the relationship quality intensifies individual feelings of happiness and satisfaction upon affection reciprocity along with cognitive and behavioral aspects between coaches and athletes (Jowett and Shanmugam, 2016). Jowett and Nezlek (2011) add that close relationships of British coaches and athletes benefit satisfaction, especially for aspects of formation, training and instruction, and personal treatment, similarly to our findings.

Despite not having reached adequate fit, the mediating model for coaches presented significant paths between latent variables (**Figure 2**) indicating a potential of CAR to mediate the BPN association with coaches' satisfaction, which is regarded as deriving from a positive affective condition based on the processes and outcomes of sport experiences (Lorimer, 2009; Kim and Cruz, 2016). Thus, we consider that even though important, CAR did not prove a determining factor for these Brazilian coaches to feel satisfied with their experience of coaching young athletes.

According to our findings, Lorimer (2009) found a model in which CAR predicted 32% of British coaches' satisfaction, but with a major proportion of unexplained variance resulting from the multifaceted nature of CAR, which also varies according to specific goals and professionalism. According to Jowett (2008), complex extrinsic factors will dictate coaches' satisfaction beyond their relationships with athletes alone, such as monetary rewards, contracts, need for recognition, competition level, organizational pressure, and the technical level of the team.

Other aspects intervening in the association between CAR and coaches' satisfaction may result from the fact that some coaches base their sport experiences almost exclusively on training and instruction aspects, dedicating little time to social relationships (Lorimer, 2009). In this perspective, there is growing evidence in the literature highlighting the importance of developing positive interpersonal environments between coaches and athletes (Jowett and Poczwardowski, 2007; Jowett, 2017), which might reflect on harmonious relationships, satisfaction, psychological well-being, and improved performance for both sides. Therefore, we emphasized the need to foster social interactions between coaches and their young athletes.

CONCLUSION AND LIMITATIONS

Our study revealed that young athletes and coaches' sport satisfaction is strongly influenced by the satisfaction of their basic psychological needs. For athletes, such relationship is much stronger when mediated by the coach-athlete relationship. Our findings contribute to coaches, sport psychologists, and other professionals involved with youth sports regarding their understanding on the importance of social relationships to motivate and provide young athletes with satisfaction; in addition, it is important to promote closeness, commitment along with training and instruction. It is important for coaches to include psychological aspects and social relationships in their training and competition atmospheres to overcome mere technical and tactical aspects. In this sense, it is important for athletes to feel motivated to persist in their sport that they also feel close to their coaches in an affective relationship involving respect and trust.

Even though our study provides empirical evidence on the importance of CAR as mediator in the relationships between the BPN and the satisfaction of coaches and young Brazilian athletes, it is important to point out some limitations. Among such limitations, we highlight language adequacy in the ASQ and BNSSS for coaches since these scales originally assessed sport satisfaction and BPN satisfaction in the perspective of athletes. Aiming at verifying the validity of such adequacy, the instruments were assessed by Ph.D. professors in Sport Psychology regarding the clarity of language and practical relevance to be later applied to a reduced sample of coaches before being used in the total sample of the research. Still, the CFA indicated acceptable indices of the factorial structure of the instruments adapted to coaches. We also highlight that despite such limitation, the adequacy (adaptation) of scales allows to advance in the scientific knowledge on satisfaction and the BPN for coaches, which becomes restrict due to the lack of instruments for this population. Finally, the transversal format of study enabled significant predictions on the relationships among the variables, but did not allow causal relations whereas a longitudinal would enable more robust inferences. In this context, further studies are suggested to use a longitudinal design to monitor the variables since the perceptions of the coaches and athletes modify throughout the sport season, or even during training and competitions. We also highlight that some variables, such as personality traits, competitive level, and significant achievements by coaches, may influence the CAR mediator effect. Furthermore, our study limits to verify associations focusing on a positive perspective and does not investigate the need frustration as a negative affective condition determined by a complex evaluation of the structures, processes, and results related to sports experience influencing the CAR. Considering the importance of analyzing these variables, we suggest that further studies should include such investigation.

ETHICS STATEMENT

This study was carried out in accordance with the recommendations of Standing Committee on Ethics in Research with Humans, from the State University of Maringa with written informed consent from all subjects. All subjects gave written informed consent in accordance with the Declaration of Helsinki. The protocol was approved by the Standing Committee on Ethics in Research with Humans, under opinion 1.324.411/2015.

AUTHOR CONTRIBUTIONS

AC, LF, and JN provided the study with design and idea. AC, NC, PG, SM, and LC recruited and acquired data from participants. JN, AC, and PG analyzed and interpreted the data. AC, LF, NC, PG, LC, SM, and JN have contributed to the manuscript drafting. All authors have contributed to the study critical review and submission approval.

ACKNOWLEDGMENTS

The authors would like to thank all the coaches and athletes who kindly contributed to this research.

REFERENCES

Anderson, J. C., and Gerbing, D. W. (1988). Structural equation modeling in practice: a review and recommended two step approach. *Psychol. Bull.* 103, 411–423. doi: 10.1037//0033-2909.103.3.411

Antonini, P. R., Sagar, S. S., Huguet, S., Paquet, Y., and Jowett, S. (2011). From teacher to friend: the evolving nature of the coach-athlete relationship. *Int. J. Sport Psychol.* 42, 1–23.

Avci, K. S., Çepikkurt, F., and Kale, E. K. (2018). Examination of the relationship between coach-athlete communication levels and perceived motivational climate for volleyball players. *Univers. J. Educ. Res.* 6, 346–353. doi: 10.13189/ujer.2018.060218

Balaguer, I., González, L., Fabra, P., Castillo, I., Mercé, J., and Duda, J. L. (2012). Coaches' interpersonal style, basic psychological needs and the well-and ill-being of young soccer players: a longitudinal analysis. *J. Sports Sci.* 30, 1619–1629. doi: 10.1080/02640414.2012.731517

Bartholomew, K. J., Ntoumanis, N., Ryan, R. M., and Thøgersen-Ntoumani, C. (2011). Psychological need thwarting in the sport context: assessing the darker side of athletic experience. *J. Sport Exerc. Psychol.* 33, 75–102. doi: 10.1123/jsep.33.1.75

Bekiari, A., and Syrmpas, I. (2015). Coaches' verbal aggressiveness and motivational climate as predictors of athletes' satisfaction. *Br. J. Educ., Soc. Behav. Sci.* 9, 318–329. doi: 10.9734/BJESBS/2015/17757

Blecharz, J., Horodyska, K., Zarychta, K., Adamiec, A., and Luszczynska, A. (2015). Intrinsic motivation predicting performance satisfaction in athletes: further psychometric evaluations of the sport motivation scale-6. *Pol. Psychol. Bull.* 46, 309–319. doi: 10.1515/ppb-2015-0037

Bollen, K. A., and Stine, R. A. (1993). "Bootstrapping goodness-of-fit criteria in structural equation modelling," in *Testing Structural Equation Models*, eds K. A. Bollen and J. S. Long (Newbury Park, CA: Sage Publications), 195–226.

Borrego, C. M. C., Leitão, J. C., Alves, J., Silva, C., and Palmi, J. (2010). Análise confirmatória do questionário de satisfação do atleta: versão portuguesa. *Psicologia* 23, 110–120. doi: 10.1590/s0102-79722010000100014

Cheuczuk, F., Ferreira, L., Flores, P. P., Vieira, L. F., Vieira, J. L. L., and Junior, N. (2016). Quality of the relationship coach-athlete and goal orientation as predictors of sport performance. *Psic Teor. e Pesq.* 32, 1–8. doi: 10.1590/0102-3772e32229

Contreira, A. R., Nascimento Junior, J. R. A., Pizzo, G. C., Sitoe, S. A., Moreira, C. R., Jowett, S., et al. (2019). Psychometric properties of the brazilian version of the coach–athlete relationship questionnaire for coaches. *Int. J. Sport Sci. Coach.* 14, 285–293. doi: 10.1177/1747954119832715

Costa, L. C. A., Both, J., Passos, P. C. B., Medeiros, A. I. A., Marôco, J., and Vieira, L. F. (2016). Validação do learning climate questionnaire (LCQ): um questionário para avaliação do clima de aprendizagem. *J. Phys. Educ.* 85, 102–108.

Cranmer, G. A., and Sollitto, M. (2015). Sport support: received social support as a predictor of athlete satisfaction. *Commun. Res. Rep.* 32, 253–264. doi: 10.1080/08824096.2015.1052900

Davis, L., Appleby, R., Davis, P., Wetherell, M., and Gustafsson, H. (2018). The role of coach-athlete relationship quality in team sport athletes' psychophysiological exhaustion: implications for physical and cognitive performance. *J. Sports Sci.* 36, 1985–1992. doi: 10.1080/02640414.2018.1429176

Deci, E. L., and Ryan, R. M. (2012). *Motivation, Personality, and Development within Embedded Social Contexts: An Overview of Self-Determination Theory. The Oxford Handbook of Human Motivation.* Oxford: Oxford University Press, 85–107.

Deci, E. L., Ryan, R. M., and Guay, F. (2013). "Self-determination theory and actualization of human potential," in *Theory Driving Research: New Wave Perspectives on Self-Processes and Human Development*, eds D. McInerney, R. Craven, H. Marsh, and F. Guay, (Charlotte, NC: Information Age Press), 109–133.

Fornell, C., and Larcker, D. F. (1981). Evaluating structural equation models with unobservable variables and measurement error. *J. Mark. Res.* 18, 39–50. doi: 10.1177/002224378101800104

García-Calvo, T., Leo, F. M., Gonzalez-Ponce, I., Sánchez-Miguel, P. A., Mouratidis, A., and Ntoumanis, N. (2014). Perceived coach-created and peer-created motivational climates and their associations with team cohesion and athlete satisfaction: evidence from a longitudinal study. *J. Sports Sci.* 32, 1738–1750. doi: 10.1080/02640414.2014.918641

González, L., Castillo, I., García-Merita, M., and Balaguer, I. (2015). Apoyo a la autonomía, satisfacción de las necesidades psicológicas y bienestar: invarianza de un modelo estructural en futbolistas y bailarines. *Rev. Psicol. Deporte* 24, 121–129. doi: 10.1016/j.ijchp.2015.11.001

Gurrola, H. B. A., Rodríguez, J. L. T., Walle, J. M. L., Marco, M. I. T., and Zamarripa, J. (2016). Estilos interepersonales del entrenador, frustración de las necesidades psicológicas básicas y el burnout: un análisis longitudinal en futbolistas. *Retos* 30, 132–137.

Hair, J. F., Black, W. C., Babin, B. J., Anderson, R. E., and Tatham, R. L. (2005). *Análise Multivariada de Dados.* Porto Alegre: Bookman.

Hampson, R., and Jowett, S. (2014). Effects of coach leadership and coach–athlete relationship on collective efficacy. *Scand. J. Med. Sci. Sports.* 24, 454–460. doi: 10.1111/j.1600-0838.2012.01527.x

Hoffmann, M. D., and Loughead, T. M. (2016). A comparison of well-peer mentored and non-peer mentored athletes' perceptions of satisfaction. *J. Sports Sci.* 34, 450–458. doi: 10.1080/02640414.2015.1057517

Hu, L., and Bentler, P. M. (1999). Cutoff criteria for fit indexes in covariance structure analysis: conventional criteria versus new alternatives. *Struct. Equ. Modeling.* 6, 1–55. doi: 10.1080/10705519909540118

Jackson, B., Grove, J. R., and Beauchamp, M. R. (2010). Relational efficacy beliefs and relationship quality within coach-athlete dyads. *J. Soc. Pers. Relatsh.* 27, 1035–1050. doi: 10.1177/0265407510378123

Jowett, S. (2008). What makes coaches tick? The impact of coaches' intrinsic and extrinsic motives on their own satisfaction and that of their athletes. *Scand J. Med. Sci. Sports* 18, 664–673. doi: 10.1111/j.1600-0838.2007.00705.x

Jowett, S. (2017). Coaching effectiveness: the coach–athlete relationship at its heart. *Curr. Opin. Psychol.* 16, 154–158. doi: 10.1016/j.copsyc.2017.05.006

Jowett, S., Adie, J. W., Bartholomew, K. J., Yang, S. X., Gustafsson, H., and Lopez-Jiménez, A. (2017). Motivational processes in the coach-athlete relationship: a multi-cultural self-determination approach. *Psychol. Sport Exerc.* 32, 143–152. doi: 10.1016/j.psychsport.2017.06.004

Jowett, S., and Don Carolis, G. (2003). "The coach-athlete relationship and perceived satisfaction in team sports," in *XIth European Congress of Sport Psychology Proceedings*, ed. R. Stelter, (Copenhagen: Det Samfundsvidenskabelige Fakultets), 83–84.

Jowett, S., and Lavalee, D. (2007). *Social Psychology in Sport.* Champaign, IL: Human Kinetics.

Jowett, S., and Nezlek, J. (2011). Relationship interdependence and satisfaction with important outcomes in coach-athelete dyads. *J. Soc. Pers. Relatsh.* 29, 287–301. doi: 10.1177/0265407511420980

Jowett, S., and Ntoumanis, N. (2004). The coach–athlete relationship questionnaire (CART-Q): development and initial validation. *Scand. J. Med. Sci. Sports* 14, 245–257. doi: 10.1111/j.1600-0838.2003.00338.x

Jowett, S., and Poczwardowski, A. (2007). "Understanding the coach-athlete relationship," in *Social Psychology in Sport*, eds S. Jowett, and D. Lavalee, (Champaign, IL: Human Kinetics).

Jowett, S., and Shanmugam, V. (2016). "Relational coaching in sport: its psychological underpinnings and practical effectiveness," in *Routledge International Handbook of Sport Psychology*, eds R. Schinke, K. R. Mcgannon, and B. Smith, (Abingdon: Routledge).

Kao, S. F., and Tsai, C. Y. (2016). Transformational leadership and athlete satisfaction: the mediating role of coaching competency. *J. Appl. Sport Psychol.* 28, 469–482. doi: 10.1080/10413200.2016.1187685

Kim, H. D., and Cruz, A. B. (2016). The influence of coaches' leadership styles on athletes' satisfaction and team cohesion: a meta-analytic approach. *J. Sports Sci. Coach.* 11, 900–909. doi: 10.1177/1747954116676117

Kline, R. B. (2016). *Principles and Practice of Structural Equation Modeling.* New York: The Guilford Press.

Lee, K., Kang, S., and Kim, I. (2017). Relationships among stress, burnout, athletic identity, and athlete satisfaction in students at Korea's physical education high schools: validating differences between pathways according to ego resilience. *Psychol. Rep.* 120, 585–608. doi: 10.1177/0033294117698465

Li, B., Dittmore, S. W., and Park, J. (2015). Exploring different perceptions of coach-athlete relationship: the case of chinese olympians. *Int. J. Sports Sci. Coach.* 9, 59–76.

Lorimer, R. (2009). Coaches' satisfaction with their athletic partnerships. *Int J Sports Sci Coach.* 3, 55–64.

Lorimer, R., and Jowett, S. (2009). Empathic accuracy, meta-perspective, and satisfaction in the coach-athlete relationship. *J. Appl. Sport Psychol.* 21, 201–212. doi: 10.1080/10413200902777289

Mageau, G. A., and Vallerand, R. J. (2003). The coach-athlete relationship: a motivational model. *J. Sports Sci.* 21, 883–904. doi: 10.1080/0264041031000140374

Marôco, J. (2010). *Análise de Equações Estruturais: Fundamentos Teóricos, Softwares e Aplicações.* Lisboa: AR Publisher Editora.

Monteiro, D., Travassos, B., Teixeira, D. S., Mendes, P. D., Machado, S., Moutão, J., et al. (2018). Perceived effort in football athletes: the role of achievement goal theory and self-determination theory. *Front. Psychol.* 9:1575. doi: 10.3389/fpsyg.2018.01575

Nascimento Junior, J. R. A., Vissoci, J. R. N., and Vieira, L. F. (2018). Propriedades psicométricas da versão brasileira da escala de satisfação das necessidades básicas no esporte (BNSSS). *Psic. Teor. e Pesq.* 34:e3456. doi: 10.1590/0102.3772e3456

Ng, J. Y. Y., Lonsdale, C., and Hodge, K. (2011). The basic needs satisfaction in sport scale (BNSSS): instrument development and initial validity evidence. *J. Sport Exerc. Psychol.* 12, 257–264. doi: 10.1016/j.psychsport.2010.10.006

Nicholls, A. R., and Perry, J. L. (2016). Perceptions of coach–athlete relationship are more important to coaches than athletes in predicting dyadic coping and stress appraisals: an actor–partner independence mediation model. *Front. Psychol.* 7:447. doi: 10.3389/fpsyg.2016.00447

Ntomali, S., Psychountaki, M., Kyprianou, M., and Chairopoulou, C. (2017). Congruence between preferred and perceived coach leadership behavior and athlete satisfaction: the paradigm in synchronized swimming. *Glob. J. Hum. Soc. Sci. Res.* 17, 40-47.

Ramazanoğlu, F. (2018). Investigation of relationship between coach and athlete in terms of different variables. *Univers. J. Educ. Res.* 6, 1431–1436. doi: 10.13189/ujer.2018.060703

Reynoulds, A. J., and Mcdonough, M. H. (2015). Moderated and mediated effects of coach autonomy support, coach involvement, and psychological need satisfaction on motivation in youth soccer. *Sport Psychol.* 29, 51–61. doi: 10.1123/tsp.2014-0023

Rhind, D. J., and Jowett, S. (2012). Development of the coach-athlete relationship maintenance questionnaire (CARM-Q). *Int. J. Sports Sci. Coach.* 7, 121–137. doi: 10.1260/1747-9541.7.1.121

Richardson, R. J., Peres, J. A. S., and Wanderley, J. C. V. (2012). *Pesquisa Social: Métodos e Técnicas*, 3ª Edn, São Paulo: Atlas.

Riemer, H. A., and Chelladurai, P. (1998). Development of the athlete satisfaction questionnaire (ASQ). *J Sport Exercise Psy* 20, 127–156. doi: 10.1123/jsep.20.2.127

Rocchi, M., and Pelletier, L. (2018). How does coaches' reported interpersonal behavior align with athletes' perceptions? Consequences for female athletes' psychological needs in sport. *Sport Exerc. Perform. Psychol.* 7, 141–154. doi: 10.1037/spy0000116

Ryan, R. M., and Deci, E. L. (2017). *Self-Determination Theory: Basic Psychological Needs in Motivation, Development, and Wellness.* New York, NY: Guilford Publications.

Sagar, S. S., and Jowett, S. (2015). Fear of failure and self-control in the context of coach-athlete relationship quality. *Int. J. Sports Sci. Coach.* 9, 3–21.

Sullivan, P. J., and Gee, C. J. (2007). The relationship between athletic satisfaction and intrateam communication. *Group Dyn.* 11, 107–116. doi: 10.1037/1089-2699.11.2.107

Tabachnick, B. G., and Fidell, L. S. (2013). *Using Multivariate Statistics*, 6th Edn, Boston, MA: Pearson.

Vallerand, R. J. (2000). Deci and Ryan's self-determination theory: a view from the hierarchical model of intrinsic and extrinsic motivation. *Psychol. Inq.* 11, 312–318.

Vieira, L. F., Nascimento Junior, J. R. A., Pujals, C., Jowett, S., Codonhato, R., and Vissoci, J. R. N. (2015). Adaptação transcultural e propriedades psicométricas do questionário de relacionamento treinador-atleta brasileiro (CART-Q) – Versão atleta. *Rev. Bras. Cineantropom. Desempenho. Hum.* 17, 635–649. doi: 10.5007/1980-0037.2015v17n6p635

Vieira, L. F., Pizzo, G. C., Contreira, A. R., Lazier-Leão, T. R., Moreira, C. R., Rigoni, P. A. G., et al. (2018). Associação entre motivação e coesão de grupo no futebol profissional: o relacionamento treinador-atleta é um fator determinante? *Rev. Psicol. Deporte* 27, 51–57.

Williams, J., and MacKinnon, D. P. (2008). Resampling and distribution of the product methods for testing indirect effects in complex models. *Struct. Equ. Modeling* 15, 23–51. doi: 10.1080/10705510701758166

18

Relationship between the Practice of Physical Activity and Physical Fitness in Physical Education Students: The Integrated Regulation as a Mediating Variable

Gemma María Gea-García[1,2†], Noelia González-Gálvez[1,2†], Alejandro Espeso-García[1,2], Pablo J. Marcos-Pardo[1,2], Francisco Tomás González-Fernández[3] and Luis Manuel Martínez-Aranda[1,4]*

[1] Faculty of Sports, San Antonio Catholic University (UCAM), Murcia, Spain, [2] Health, Physical Activity, Fitness and Motor Control Performance Research Group (GISAFFCOM), San Antonio Catholic University (UCAM), Murcia, Spain, [3] Department of Physical Activity and Sport Sciences, CESAG, Comillas Pontifical University, Madrid, Spain, [4] Neuroscience of Human Movement Research Group, San Antonio Catholic University (UCAM), Murcia, Spain

***Correspondence:**
Gemma María Gea-García
gmgea@ucam.edu

† These authors have contributed equally to this work

The practice of physical activity (PA) contributes to the prevention of chronic diseases such as obesity, metabolic syndrome or cardiovascular diseases, being also directly related to the individual's physical fitness. Therefore, it is necessary to measure and monitoring the levels of PA in childhood and adolescence, since it may be useful to describe their current health status and the association with physical fitness, as well as to reveal putative consequences in the future. Within the educational field, it has been shown that physical education (PE) classes are a favorable context for the creation of healthy physical-sports habits and self-determined motivation could be a key for explaining the level of PA practice. For this reason, the purpose of this research was to study the mediating role of integrated regulation (IR) on the relationship between PA and physical fitness in children and adolescents. A total of 325 students between 11 and 14 years old participated in the study. The level of PA was estimated through the specific *Physical Activity Questionnaire for Children* (PAQ-C), while motivation and IR were measured by using the *Perceived Locus of Causality scale* (PLOC-2). In addition, physical fitness was measured through the *Eurofit fitness battery of tests*, composed of three body composition measures and seven tests of different physical capacities. The physical fitness score showed no differences when genders were compared. After regression analysis, the resulting models revealed a good adjustment and correlation between PA practice and physical fitness ($\beta = 0.173$; $p < 0.001$), being established through the macro *Process* that this relationship is partially conditioned by the IR ($\beta = 0.122$; $p = 0.03$). ROC curve analysis estimated the score of 5.88 as a cut-off point to discriminate between levels of IR for students, classified as physically active or not (AUC = 0.67; $p < 0.001$). The conclusions from these main and other complementary analyses reporting complete mediations, suggest that the IR could be decisive in predicting and explaining the relationship between the practice of PA and physical fitness at these ages, highlighting its importance for a greater adherence to the practice.

Keywords: physical activity, physical fitness, integrated regulation, IPAQ, PLOC-2, schoolchildren

INTRODUCTION

Physical activity (PA) can be defined as any body movement produced by the action of skeletal muscles that causes an increase in energy expenditure (Rauner et al., 2013; Voss et al., 2017; Chacón-Cuberos et al., 2018a). Its practice is considered a key factor in the development, promotion and maintenance of healthier lifestyle habits at any age (Møller et al., 2009; Dumith et al., 2011; Chacón-Cuberos et al., 2018a; Castro-Sánchez et al., 2019; Zurita-Ortega et al., 2019). The physiological and psychological benefits of PA have been widely studied, highlighting the physiological ones, through the prevention and treatment of various chronic diseases such as obesity, cardiovascular disease, and metabolic syndrome (Cole et al., 2000; Webber et al., 2008; Møller et al., 2009; Ahn et al., 2011; Welk et al., 2011; Benítez-Porres et al., 2016a,b; Fang et al., 2017; Chacón-Cuberos et al., 2018a; Zurita-Ortega et al., 2019). Despite these benefits, the current scientific literature seems to have found sufficient evidence to affirm that there is a decreasing trend in PA practice worldwide (Adams, 2006; Webber et al., 2008; Owen et al., 2009; Dumith et al., 2011; Wang et al., 2016; Fang et al., 2017; Palou et al., 2019; Sierra-Díaz et al., 2019). More specifically, the World Health Organization (WHO) has identified such physical inactivity as a major global problem and has ranked it as the fourth largest risk factor for mortality worldwide (Dumith et al., 2011; Wang et al., 2016; Sierra-Díaz et al., 2019). This physical inactivity is the cause of the increase and prevalence of higher levels of obesity and overweight in the population, with sectors being particularly affected in the last decade, identified as children and adolescents (Adams, 2006; Ness et al., 2007; Webber et al., 2008; Dumith et al., 2011; Henriksson et al., 2016; Wang et al., 2016; Fang et al., 2017; Chacón-Cuberos et al., 2018b; Palou et al., 2019; Sierra-Díaz et al., 2019). In this line, the current data show worrying statistics, since a high percentage of this population are below the minimum PA practice levels pre-established by the WHO. This institution recommends at least 60 min per day of moderate physical activity (MPA) and vigorous physical activity (VPA) for the maintenance of adequate levels in order to provide health benefits at these ages (Riddoch et al., 2007; Nader et al., 2008; Webber et al., 2008; Steele et al., 2009; Dumith et al., 2011; Ekelund et al., 2011; Griffiths et al., 2013; Benítez-Porres et al., 2016a; Fang et al., 2017; Onetti-Onetti et al., 2019; Riso et al., 2019). Furthermore, scientific research in recent years has supported a focused reduction in these levels of PA practice at early ages, highlighting the fact that, as in primary education, there is a decreasing tendency for PA practice levels year by year, with an increasing inactivity trend continuing through adolescence and even adulthood (Nader et al., 2008). These tendencies put the situation in the spotlight due to the implications on the current and future health of the population (Webber et al., 2008; Collings et al., 2013; Henriksson et al., 2016; Fang et al., 2017). Therefore, the study and monitoring of PA practice levels in childhood and adolescence should be a priority, since their maintenance at these ages is considered a strong predictor of adequate PA practice levels in adult life (Møller et al., 2009; Riddoch et al., 2009; Rauner et al., 2013; Henriksson et al., 2016; Chacón-Cuberos et al., 2018b; Sierra-Díaz et al., 2019).

As a complement to the concern and importance of PA practice, current research focuses on combined studies with fitness levels (PF) (Ruiz et al., 2011; Rauner et al., 2013; Henriksson et al., 2016; Schutte et al., 2016; Wang et al., 2016; Palou et al., 2019; Riso et al., 2019; Tomkinson et al., 2019; López-Gil et al., 2020), and also including other variables such as obesity (Ness et al., 2007; Steele et al., 2009; Ekelund et al., 2011; Collings et al., 2013; Rauner et al., 2013; Benítez-Porres et al., 2016b; Henriksson et al., 2016; Fang et al., 2017; Palou et al., 2019), eating habits (Agostinis-Sobrinho et al., 2018; Ramírez-Vélez et al., 2018; López-Gil et al., 2020), physical self-concept or body image (Fernández-Bustos et al., 2019; Onetti-Onetti et al., 2019), and the motivational climate (Chacón-Cuberos et al., 2018a,b, 2019; Castro-Sánchez et al., 2019; Zurita-Ortega et al., 2019), among others.

Physical fitness is defined as the set of attributes that are achieved or possessed in relation to the ability to perform PA (Pate, 1988; López-Gil et al., 2020) or exercise with a certain skill influencing the sports performance (Schutte et al., 2016). It is considered an essential prerequisite for both, the development of daily activities without fatigue and the participation and performance of activities in free-time and leisure (Cvejic et al., 2013; Rauner et al., 2013; Schutte et al., 2016). The PF components within the health area, are cardio-respiratory, muscular and motor fitness, flexibility and body composition (Rauner et al., 2013; Kolimechkov, 2017; López-Gil et al., 2020).

Physical fitness along with PA play a key role in the health status, with the study of their interaction being a major research topic (Dollman et al., 2005; Ardoy et al., 2011; Rauner et al., 2013; Henriksson et al., 2016; Wang et al., 2016; Palou et al., 2019; Riso et al., 2019; López-Gil et al., 2020). However, this interaction can result in two different situations. For instance, a greater or lesser participation or PA practice is observed as a consequence of PF levels or the capacity to perform PA and exercise. In other words, a high level of PF could lead to a positive impulse that would generate a higher level of participation and practice of PA (Dollman et al., 2005; Schutte et al., 2016). On the other hand, scientific evidence also points out the level of PA practice as a predictor of the PF level (Dumith et al., 2011; Rauner et al., 2013;

Fang et al., 2017; Palou et al., 2019), being its relationship similar to the one described above. Given higher levels of PA practice, an increase in PF levels is expected. Conversely, lower levels of PF will also be observed in situations where the levels of PA practice are low. Despite the fact that the directionality of the relationship between PF and PA does not seem to be completely clear, PA appears to be significantly conditioned by the levels of PF present in schoolchildren at this age, with aspects such as aerobic and motor fitness playing a predominant role. Therefore, low PA could be an underlying cause of the observed decrease in PF in schoolchildren (Barnett et al., 2009; Aggio et al., 2012; Fang et al., 2017). In any case, the combined association and study of PA and PF is considered a determining factor for both, follow-up and the improvement of health at all ages, especially in the children and adolescent population (Ardoy et al., 2011; Rauner et al., 2013; Henriksson et al., 2016; Fang et al., 2017; Palou et al., 2019; Riso et al., 2019).

Moreover, the habits acquired at this age will be often reproduced in adulthood, and these factors could influence and explain the acquisition of occasional healthy life-style (Chacón-Cuberos et al., 2018b; Fernández-Bustos et al., 2019; Sierra-Díaz et al., 2019). Consequently, it is necessary to gain insight studying not only the level and relationship between PA and PF, but also the reasons why the balance leans in one direction or another toward the acquisition of whether active and healthy or harmful and inactive physical sports habits. Considering that at these ages most of the day is spent in the classrooms (Ahn et al., 2011), the educational centres become the ideal location where to investigate, with the physical education (PE) playing a preponderant role (Ahn et al., 2011; Trigueros et al., 2017; Chacón-Cuberos et al., 2019; Fernández-Bustos et al., 2019) as a consequence of the environment and contents developed within this subject (Sierra-Díaz et al., 2019). PE classes are an ideal context for the creation of adherence and healthy living habits promotion associated with PA practice beyond the classroom itself (Moreno et al., 2008, 2009; Ahn et al., 2011; Dudley et al., 2011; Gillison et al., 2013; Sierra-Díaz et al., 2019). However, in order to be sure of the impact and influence of the PA, it is necessary to consider its study under the perspective of the Self-Determination Theory (SDT) (Deci and Ryan, 1985; Chacón-Cuberos et al., 2018a,b; Sierra-Díaz et al., 2019; Zurita-Ortega et al., 2019). The SDT allows to explain the reasons leading an individual to start, continue or abandon the practice of PA within the study context (Deci and Ryan, 1985; Ryan and Deci, 2000; Dudley et al., 2011; Gillison et al., 2013). The SDT is regulated by the differentiation of three types of motivation depending on the self-determination degree: intrinsic motivation (IM), extrinsic motivation (EM), and de-motivation (DE) (Deci and Ryan, 1985; Ryan and Deci, 2000; Gillison et al., 2013; Sierra-Díaz et al., 2019). IM justifies the participation and performance of activities by personal and inherent issues as a result of the enjoyment, novelty, or satisfaction involved in performing PA itself within the PE classroom. IM is the most self-determined motivation. The EM is based on the premise that external or environmental factors exist as conditioning elements in the students' behavior and participation at this age within PE classes. Four types can be differentiated: integrated, identified, introjected, and external regulation, from highest to lowest self-determination level, respectively. Each of them is identified with different reasons and/or incentives to perform PA within the PE classroom. For integrated regulation (IR), the manifestation of a behavior would allow the integration of PA practice as another routine within those considered as mandatory for the school's daily life (Ferriz et al., 2015; Trigueros et al., 2017). This type of regulation is identified with the last previous step of recognizing the personal value that PA practice would have in this case, and is the most self-determined within EM (Deci and Ryan, 1985; Ryan and Deci, 2000; Gillison et al., 2013). On the other hand, within the educational field for PE, the most self-determined expressions of motivation are associated with greater PA practice outside the classroom, with the scientific literature pointing directly to IR as the most determining motivation when explaining the involvement or not of schoolchildren in extracurricular PA (Wilson et al., 2006; Ferriz et al., 2015; Trigueros et al., 2017).

Finally, DE is identified as the absence of any type of interest toward the realization of physical-sporting activity at these ages, within the context of the educational environment for the PE (Ryan and Deci, 2000; Moreno et al., 2009; Dudley et al., 2011; Gillison et al., 2013; Sierra-Díaz et al., 2019). Thanks to this precept, it is possible to identify the causes originating some preferential behaviors toward the practice of PE at these ages, as well as the possible influence and relationship on the active and healthy life habits acquired for this population outside the classroom (Deci and Ryan, 1985; Moreno et al., 2008, 2009; Dudley et al., 2011; Gillison et al., 2013; Castro-Sánchez et al., 2019; Sierra-Díaz et al., 2019; Zurita-Ortega et al., 2019).

In spite of the relationships that may exist between PA, PF and motivation, few studies have analyzed these factors simultaneously outside of the university educational context. Therefore, the main objectives of this study were to analyze: (a) the relationship between the level of PA practice and the level of physical fitness in PE students, and (b) the mediating role of IR on the relationship between PA and physical fitness in schoolchildren.

MATERIALS AND METHODS

Design and Participants

A descriptive and cross-sectional study design with non-probability-based sampling was used. The sample was selected using a sampling for convenience. A total of 325 healthy schoolchildren aged between 11 and 14 years old from five primary schools in the Region of Murcia (Spain) participated in the study. A balanced percentage distribution by gender was provided with a sample composed by male [n = 164 (50.5%)] and female [n = 161 (49.5%)] students. Age and anthropometric characteristics data, including BMI classification (Cole et al., 2000) are shown in **Table 1**.

Sample Size

The calculations to establish the sample size were performed using G*Power 3.1.9.4 software. The significance level was set at $\alpha = 0.05$. Accordingly, the sample size (power analysis) revealed

TABLE 1 | Sample descriptive data according to the gender.

	Total (n = 325) M ± SD	Boys (n = 164; % = 50.46) M ± SD	Girls (n = 161; % = 49.54) M ± SD	p	d
Age (years)	12.39 ± 1.03	12.51 ± 1.02	12.27 ± 1.03	0.063	0.112
Height (cm)	1.50 ± 0.08	1.49 ± 0.08	1.50 ± 0.08	0.131	−0.149
3rd percentile [%(n)]	16 (52)	32 (19.6)	20 (12.4)		
15th percentile [%(n)]	26.7 (87)	48 (29.4)	38 (23.6)		
Median [%(n)]	50 (162)	72 (43.6)	91 (56.5)		
85th percentile [%(n)]	6.1 (20)	10 (6.1)	10 (6.2)		
97th percentile [%(n)]	1.2 (4)	2 (1.2)	2 (1.2)		
Weight (Kg)	45.19 ± 14.27	43.56 ± 13.29	46.86 ± 15.06	0.021*	−0.168
Span (m)	1.51 ± 0.10	1.51 ± 0.10	1.52 ± 0.10	0.298	−0.116
BMI (kg/m^2)	19.92 ± 4.82	19.39 ± 4.43	20.45 ± 5.15	0.068	−0.117
Normal weight [%(n)]	71.69 (233)	73.17 (120)	70.19 (113)		
Over weight [%(n)]	18.77 (61)	18.29 (30)	19.25 (31)		
Obese [%(n)]	9.54 (31)	8.54 (14)	10.56 (17)		
Physical fitness					
CRF (mL/kg/min)	39.98 ± 5.38	40.94 ± 5.65	39.00 ± 4.92	<0.001**	0.232
Handgrip strength (kg)†	19.65 ± 19.24	20.24 ± 26.58	19.04 ± 5.43	0.113	−0.102
Relative Handgrip strength (kg/mass kg)†	0.43 ± 0.11	0.43 ± 0.11	0.42 ± 0.11	0.234	0.133
Standing Broad Jump (m)	1.28 ± 0.24	1.34 ± .24	1.23 ± 0.22	<0.001**	0.492
Standing Broad Jump (cm)	128.25 ± 23.69	133.85 ± 23.80	122.55 ± 22.11	<0.001**	0.492
Sit-ups (n total)	19.54 ± 5.55	20.20 ± 5.54	18.88 ± 5.51	0.032*	0.239
Shuttle run 5 × 10 m (s)	16.30 ± 1.64	15.92 ± 1.66	16.69 ± 1.52	<0.001**	−0.305
Sit and reach (cm)	14.89 ± 10.70	11.55 ± 9.70	18.28 ± 10.63	<0.001**	−0.350
PFGS	0.00 ± 2.35	−0.062 ± 2.37	0.063 ± 2.34	0.631	−0.053
Physical activity total score	2.97 ± 0.73	3.03 ± 0.77	2.91 ± 0.68	0.119	0.182
Integrated regulation	5.90 ± 1.11	5.90 ± 1.17	5.91 ± 1.06	0.756	0.019

*kg, kilograms; cm, centimeters; m, meters; BMI, body mass index; mL, milliliters; min, minute; CRF, cardiorespiratory fitness; PFGS, physical fitness global score; †, mean handgrip right and left; n, number; s, seconds; p = significance level; d = effect size (d Cohen); n, number; % percentage; **p < 0.01; *p < 0.05.*

that 306 participants would obtain a 95% power to significantly detect a correlation of $r = 0.30$ in the population (Østerås et al., 2017). In order to prevent possible dropouts or elimination of recorded data by detection of abnormal response, we decided to recruit a higher number of participants.

Measurements and Materials

Physical Activity and Perceived Locus of Causality

In order to provide an estimate of the MPA to VPA levels, all students completed the international *Physical Activity Questionnaire for Children* (PAQ-C) (Crocker et al., 1997; Voss et al., 2013) validated for children aged 8–14; using the validated Spanish version by Manchola-González et al. (2017). PAQ-C is a 7-day recall composed of nine items about the frequency of physical activities at school, at home, and during leisure time (Kowalski et al., 1997). It contains nine items rated on a five-point Likert scale, where each item is rated between 1 (low PA) and 5 (high PA). Once the values were obtained for each of the items that compose the questionnaire, a final score was computed (total PA) by calculating the average value obtained in the 9 items. The PA total score allows differentiating and classifying the schoolchildren as sedentary or active according to the data obtained with the PAQ-C tool. There are several possibilities within this classification, such as the one given by Chen et al. (2008), who assigned PAQ scores ≤2 as "low activity," >2 and ≤3 as "moderate activity" and >3 as "high activity." There are also several studies that subdivide the sample into "active" and "low active/non-active" youth, such as Ogunleye et al. (2012), who divided youth into "active" and "low active" based on the median distribution of PAQ scores by age and sex. Along the same lines, Cervantes et al. (2017) differentiated between active schoolchildren when scores were above 3, and sedentary schoolchildren with scores below 3. Finally, Benítez-Porres et al. (2016a) established a ranking and differentiation between active and non-active schoolchildren based on a cut-off point of PAQ-C > 2.75. As a consequence, in this study the consideration and classification of the schoolchildren as active or non-active was established according to a mean score of 3 (Cervantes et al., 2017). The questionnaire shows an internal consistency value with a Cronbach's alpha coefficient (α) of 0.83 and a good or excellent reliability value with an inter-class correlation coefficient (ICC) of >0.73 and a 95% confidence interval.

Similarly, students performed the *Perceived Locus of Causality Scale* (PLOC-2) (Ferriz et al., 2015). Through this questionnaire, the scores obtained by the schoolchildren for the different types of motivation established by the SDT within the PE classes were recorded. The questionnaire arises as a consequence of the fusion of the Perceived Locus Causality Scale (PLOC) (Moreno et al., 2009) and the four items elaborated by Wilson et al. (2006) to measure IR. The scale is headed at the beginning by the phrase "I participate in PE classes...." It is composed of 6 factors and a total of 24 items distributed by four for each factor. The components of the scale are: IM (e.g., "because PE is fun"), IR (e.g., "because it's in line with my way of life"), identified regulation (e.g., "because I want to learn sports skills"), introjected regulation (e.g., "because I would feel bad about myself if I didn't"), external regulation (e.g., "because that's what I'm supposed to do"), and demotivation (e.g., "I really feel like I'm wasting my time in PE classes"). The instrument uses a Likert scale ranging from 1 to 7 where 1 is identified as disagreeing strongly and 7 as agreeing strongly. The reliability of the scale measured through Cronbach's alpha (α), obtained the following results by factors: $\alpha = 0.84$ (IM); $\alpha = 0.93$ (IR); $\alpha = 0.84$ (identified regulation); $\alpha = 0.69$ (introjected regulation); $\alpha = 0.69$ (for external regulation) and $\alpha = 0.82$ (demotivation). Confirmatory factor analysis showed the following adjustment rates: $\chi 2$ (235, $N = 858$) = 1147.31, $p < 0.001$, $\chi 2/gl = 4.88$, CFI = 0.92; IFI = 0.92, TLI = 0.91, RMSEA = 0.065 (IC 90% = 0.063–0.071) and SRMR = 0.065. Finally, factorial weights ranged from 0.47 to 0.90.

Physical Fitness Assessment

Several studies analyzing the PF as predictor of PA (Jaakkola et al., 2015) or the use of muscle strength field-based test to identify risk in several diseases among adolescents (Castro-Piñero et al., 2019) used a battery of PF assessment in order to obtain scientific support and strong correlations between key factors related to the health status in young population. The level of physical fitness and the different components (core strength, lower and upper body strength, agility, balance, flexibility, and endurance) were assessed using the *Eurofit Physical Fitness Test Battery* (Gulías-González et al., 2014; Purohit et al., 2016). The protocols established by the guidelines for this test battery and the American College of Sports Medicine [ACSM], 2010 were followed to guarantee the safety of the participants. In addition, to ensure the successful performance in the Test Battery, all students were informed about the protocol to perform in the experimental sessions. A usual warm-up (mostly running and dynamic stretching exercises) during 7–8 min was carried out before physical testing. The better result of two attempts per hand (*handgrip test* and *5 × 10 m shuttle run*) and three attempts for *standing broad jump* and *sit and reach test* were recorded, while only one successful attempt was allowed for the *sit-ups test* and *20 m Shuttle Run*. All tests were conducted indoors (school gym) wearing comfortable sporting attire. Jumping and running tests were carried out on wooden non-slippery floor. The recovery time between attempts was set at 2 min, except for the 5 × 10 m shuttle run test, with a complete recovery between attempts. The raw scores obtained in each physical fitness test were transformed into standardized scores (z-scores) for the entire sample. Then, an overall physical fitness general score (PFGS) was calculated. The overall PFGS score was obtained by calculating the average of the z-scores obtained in each of the PF tests (Jaakkola et al., 2015; Østerås et al., 2017; Castro-Piñero et al., 2019).

Body composition characteristics measurement

The anthropometric measurements made for the determination of weight, height and span followed the standards established by the International Society for the Advancement of Kinanthropometry (ISAK) (Esparza-Ros et al., 2019). Body weight (kg), body mass index (BMI) and % body-fat were measured without shoes using a Bioelectrical impedance analysis device (BIA) (Tanita BC-545N–Body composition monitor to measure per segment) to the nearest 0.1 kg. The Height (cm) was measured using a stadiometer (Tanita HR001 Leicester portable height rod) to the nearest 0.1 cm. The span was measured (in meters) using an anthropometric wall tape (Lufkin L1025B) and metal standoffs. The requirements and clothing for these measures were established beforehand through the information provided in the dossier given to the PE teacher, as well as in the information letter provided to parents or legal tutors and the students themselves. It was established that students should come with comfortable sportswear (short-sleeved shirt and shorts), and their height and weight must be taken barefoot. The established protocol was performed in order to ensure an adequate data collecting process during all the tests.

Cardiorespiratory fitness (CRF)

A maximum incremental field test *(20-m endurance shuttle run test)* was performed in order to estimate the maximum volume of oxygen (MOC) consumed. The test involves running between two lines separated by 20 m while following the rhythm of acoustic signals. The initial speed was set at 8.5 km/h increasing by 0.5 km/h per minute (maximum of 18.0 km/h at 20th min). Subjects were instructed to run maintaining the pace, follow the straight running line and turn properly after completing each lap. Verbal encourage was provided to ensure a full-effort test. When the subject did not reach the end line twice following the acoustic signal or stopped completely due to the fatigue, the test was finished. Léger's et al. (1988) equations were used in order to transform the states to relative MOC values (López-Gil et al., 2020).

Upper and lower body strength

Upper body muscular strength was assessed using the *handgrip strength* by a hand dynamometer with adjustable grip (TKK 5101 Grip-D, Takei®, Tokyo EH101) recording the scores in kilograms (Kg). The reported precision of the dynamometer was 0.1 kg. A short demonstration and verbal signal were provided during the test and the grip was adjusted to the hand size. The hand span was measured in both hands from the tip of the thumb to the tip of the small finger with the hand wide opened as much as possible. Therefore, the optimal grip span was selected (boys and girls) following the recommendations by España-Romero et al. (2008). The minimum time required was set at 2 s (maximum at 5 s) and two attempts per hand were allowed. The analysis was performed using the averaged best scores reached by each hand. A normalization was calculated and expressed as kg/mass kg (Ruiz et al., 2011). The *sit-up test* measures abdominal muscles function as number of sit-ups completed from lying position (knees bent at a 90°) in 30 s. The test was performed on floor mate and Casio handheld stopwatches (HS-80TW-1EF) were used for recording the time. Moreover, the *standing broad jump test* has been successfully used for measuring the lower limb explosive strength. Participants jumped horizontally from the starting line to achieve maximum distance (in cm). The test was performed three times and the best score was kept for further analysis. The test was performed in an indoor school gym in order to avoid falls caused by slipping and a classic anthropometric tape (Lufkin L1025B) of 5 m length and 3.4 cm wide was used for distance measuring.

Motor fitness and flexibility

Speed and agility were evaluated by the *5 × 10 m Shuttle test.* The participants were required to complete five repetitions of 10 m distance at the maximum possible speed between two lines placed at 5 m each other. The results were measured in seconds using Casio handheld stopwatches (HS-3V-1). Measuring tape and marker cones were used to perform the test. The best score of two attempts was used for further analysis (López-Gil et al., 2020). The *sit and reach* test was performed following specific instructions. Lower body flexibility was assessed while attempting to reach forward as far as possible keeping knees straight in a sitting position. Sit and reach box was used to record the distance reached by the hand in cm.

Procedures

Informed Consent and Previous Information

The following protocol was established to ensure similar data collection in all centres and throughout the whole process. Firstly, the schools were contacted, and a meeting with the directors was requested to inform them about the research purpose and to request their participation. After the acceptance, a meeting with the PE teachers was held. At this meeting, they were provided with all the necessary documentation and all doubts regarding the measurement protocol to be followed, instruments and tests to be carried out, were explained. In addition, the facilities and spaces available within the educational centre were visited and organized. Secondly, an adequate and similar schedule about the days and time slots was agreed. Prior to the intervention, all students and their parents or legal tutors were informed about the study characteristics as well as the possible benefits and potential risks. Subsequently, a consent form to voluntarily participate in the study was fulfilled and signed.

The study was conducted in accordance with the ethical principles of the Helsinki declaration for human research (World Medical and Association, 2013) and was approved by the institutional review board of the Catholic University San Antonio of Murcia (Code: CE031802).

Researchers visited the school in two different days (first and second phase), always at the same time of the day (10:30 am–02:30 pm), separate by at least 48 h and no more than 72 h and controlling the environmental conditions (space, temperature, and humidity). Thus, all tests were performed at the same location and time as well as with similar humidity (30–40%) and temperature (20–24°C) conditions.

Measures

Physical Activity Questionnaire for Children and PLOC-2 (approximately 30 min) were performed during the first phase (First session) by the participants. An investigator provided the questionnaires to the participants and informed them how to fill them in. In order to carry out the different questionnaires effectively, several research assistants explained the questionnaires and test protocols solving possible questions during the process. Once the questionnaires were completed, the body composition measurements and *handgrip strength test* were registered following the protocols detailed previously. In order to carry out the different tests, the participants were divided into two equal groups, making rotation (station 1: weight, height and span; and station 2: *handgrip strength test* – dynamometry). Each group was guided by a researcher who was responsible for explaining and controlling the performance of each test. The first phase was completed in 1 h.

In the second phase (second session), students performed the *5 × 10 m shuttle test, 20 m shuttle run* (first post), *the sit-and-reach test, standing broad jump* and *sit-up test* (second post). The participants kept the division in equal groups, making rotations to conduct the tests correctly. The **Figure 1** shows the complete data collection process during all the tests in both phases.

Statistical Analysis

Means (M), standard deviations (SD), percentages (%) and frequencies were calculated using descriptive statistics. Data normality and homogeneity (Kolmogorov–Smirnov and Levene tests) were conducted prior further analysis. Data variables with different units and arithmetic scales were transformed on standardized scores (Z score). Subsequently, when differences between groups were observed, an independent sample *t*-test, Mann Whitney *U* test or Pearson's chi-squared test (χ^2) were used, depending on the assumption of normality. A *post-hoc* comparison for the 2xn tables was applied (statistic contingency coefficient); including statistic value and *p*-value. The maximum expected value was 0.703; showing a small association $r < 0.3$; the *r*-value of the moderate association was between 0.3 and 0.5 and the high association $r > 0.5$. Effect size was calculated by Cohen's *d* [0.2 (small); 0.5 (medium) and >0.8 (large) effect]. In addition, multiple regression analysis was performed to determinate relationship between variables. In all cases, data independence, absence of collinearity, normality and homoscedasticity were verified. The existence of relationship between these variables was measured by Rho (ρ) of Spearman and Pearson correlation coefficients, accordingly.

In order to assess whether the association between main variables, a multiple moderated mediation analysis was performed. The mediation analysis was performed using the PROCESS macro from SPSS (SPSS Inc., Chicago, IL, United States). The resampling procedure of 10,000 bootstrap samples was used for the non-parametric sample (Preacher and Hayes, 2008), while the classical method of stepwise regression by Baron and Kenny (1986) was used for the parametric sample.

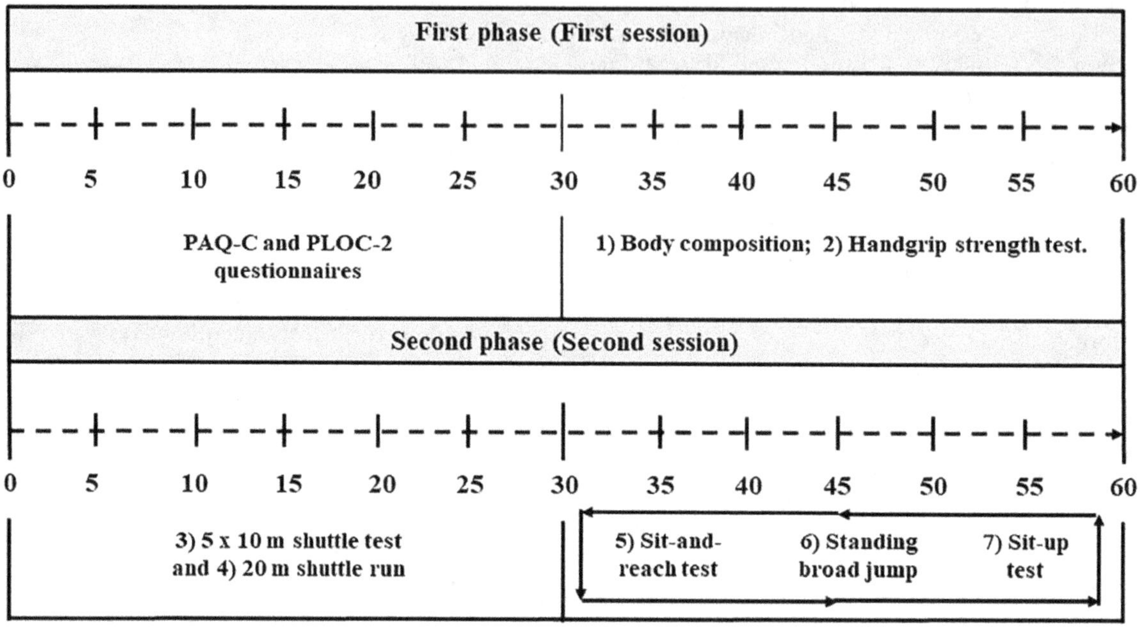

FIGURE 1 | Schematic representation of first phase (see text for full description).

Statistical significance of mediation effect was examined by test of Sobel (1982). When the *z* value was higher than 1.96 and *p* value was lower than 0.05 a mediating effect is admitted (Sobel, 1982; Preacher and Hayes, 2008).

Finally, a ROC (Receiver Operating Characteristics) curve analysis was performed to determinate the precise cut-off points of IR variable in the determination and classification of the study participants according to their classification (physically active or not). The classification accuracy for each set of cut-off points was evaluated by calculating weighted statistics, sensitivity, specificity and area under the receiver operating characteristic curve (AUC). An area of one represents a perfect rating, while an area of 0.5 represents an absence of rating accuracy. ROC-AUC values of >0.90 are considered excellent, 0.80–0.89 good, 0.70–0.79 fair, and <0.70 poor (Metz, 1978). Data analysis was performed using the software SPSS (IBM Corp., Armonk, NY, United States) for Windows, Version 24.0, as well as MedCalc 14.12.0 (Mariakerke, Belgium). The statistical significance level was set at 0.05 for all statistical comparisons.

RESULTS

The general and individual scores for each PFGS tests, as well as the PA level for both, overall level and according to gender are reported in **Table 1**. Concerning to the anthropometric characteristics, significant gender differences were only observed for the weight variable ($p = 0.021$, $d = -0.168$). Regarding the scores in the different PF tests according to gender, statistically significant differences were found for CRF ($p < 0.001$, $d = -0.232$), sit-ups ($p = 0.032$, $d = 0.239$), length jump ($p < 0.001$, $d = 0.492$), 5 × 10 m shuttle run test ($p < 0.001$, $d = -0.305$) and flexibility ($p < 0.001$, $d = -0.348$), finding higher values in girls compared to boys only for the last test.

Likewise, the anthropometric characteristics, as well as the individual scores for each PF tests according to the PA total score are shown in **Table 2**. For anthropometric characteristics, only differences in weight or BMI were obtained. In addition, we observed significant differences for the standing broad jump, sit-ups and shuttle run 5 × 10 m tests in the individual tests of the PF battery. According to the classification as sedentary or active schoolchildren, these differences were significant in the PFGS. Finally, there were also differences in the score for the IR. Specifically, the differences in individual PF tests and in the PFGS are displayed in **Figure 2**.

The different bivariate correlations according to the obtained score for the PF score index in relation to the IR and PA variables are presented in **Table 3**. Positive and statistically significant correlation was found between the PF score index and the PA level ($R = 0.174$, $p = 0.001$), the PF score index and IR ($R = 0.138$, $p = 0.003$) and between the predictor variables of PA level and IR ($R = 0.324$, $p < 0.001$).

The results (**Figure 3**) revealed that the PFGS was associated with the practice of PA ($R^2 = 0.03$, $F = 9.85$, $\beta = 0.173$, SE = 0.03, $t = 3.13$, $p = 0.001$, 95% CI = 0.035 to 0.150) and with IR ($R^2 = 0.051$, $F = 8.55$, $\beta = 0.15$, SE = 0.021, $t = 2.656$, $p < 0.008$, 95% CI = 0.014 to 0.095). In addition, the IR was associated with the practice of PA ($R^2 = 0.109$, $F = 39.13$, $\beta = 0.33$, SE = 0.081, $t = 6.25$, $p < 0.001$, 95% CI = 0.347 to 0.665).

The mediating effect of IR on the association between PA practice and PFGS was also analyzed. After including IR in the equation, the association between PA practice and PFGS remained significant, but its effect was reduced ($R^2 = 0.051$, $F = 8.55$, $\beta = 0.122$, SE = 0.128, $t = 2.11$, $p = 0.03$, 95%

TABLE 2 | Sample descriptive data according to the Physical Activity Total Score.

	Physical Activity Total Score (PAQ-C)					
	Sedentary		Active		*p*	*d*
	M	SD	M	SD		
Height (cm)	1.50	0.09	1.49	0.08	0.178	0.151
Weight (Kg)	46.56	14.62	43.39	12.88	0.043*	0.136
Span (m)	1.52	0.10	1.51	0.09	0.174	0.1000
BMI (kg/m^2)	20.31	4.74	19.36	4.55	0.048*	0.1333
Physical fitness						
CRF (mL/kg/min)	39.42	5.58	40.60	5.13	0.061	−0.121
Handgrip strength (kg)†	18.57	4.74	18.28	3.96	0.807	0.03
Relative Handgrip strength (kg/mass kg)†	0.45	4.74	0.44	3.96	0.641	0.03
Standing Long Jump (m)	1.25	0.24	1.32	0.23	0.007**	−0.301
Sit-ups (n total)	18.55	5.55	20.62	5.35	0.001**	−0.379
Shuttel run 5 × 10 m (s)	16.52	1.62	16.06	1.63	0.021*	0.149
Sit and reach (cm)	14.32	10.80	0.53	15.54	0.370	−0.059
PFGS	−0.31	2.45	0.34	2.20	0.013*	−0.280
Integrated regulation	5.59	1.23	6.27	0.82	<0.001**	0.336

*kg, kilograms; cm, centimeters; m, meters; BMI, body mass index; mL, milliliters; min, minute; CRF, cardiorespiratory fitness; PFGS, physical fitness global score; †, mean handgrip right and left; n, number; s, seconds, p = significance level; d = effect size (d Cohen); **p < 0.01; *p < 0.05.*

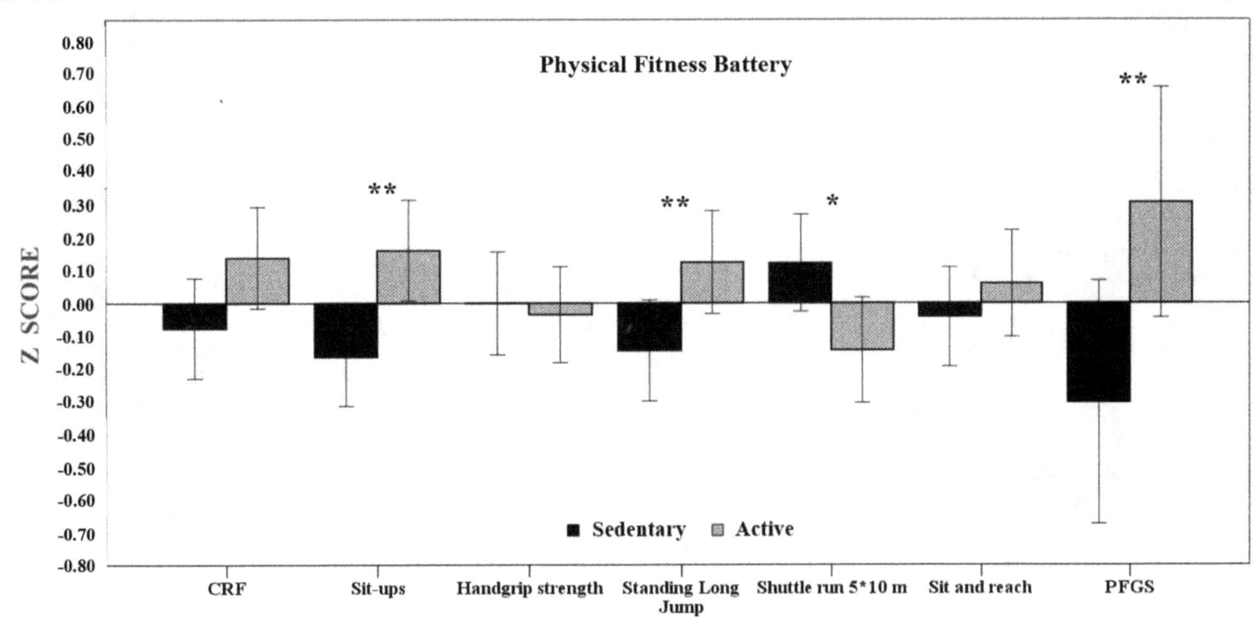

FIGURE 2 | Physical Fitness Batery [Z Scores] depending on Physical Activity Total Score. Data as shown as mean. $^{**}p < 0.01$; $^{*}p < 0.05$. Error bars indicate 95% confidence intervals.

CI = 0.004 to 0.128), suggesting that IR is a mediating variable with a partial effect. The analysis of mediation revealed both, a significant direct and indirect effect with a significant Sobel test value ($z = 2.44 \pm 0.01, p = 0.01$).

Area under the curve and the scores for the PAQ-C equivalent to the coordinates with the highest sum of sensitivity and specificity are shown in **Tables 4, 5**. The AUC of the PAQ-C score for all cases, including male and female, was significant ($p < 0.05$) and moderate discriminator was observed only for male gender (AUC > 0.7) when comparing active and non-active children, while for all case studies and female gender alone it was a weak discriminator (AUC < 0.7).

The IR score cut-off from the ROC analysis was 5.88 for the whole group and one subgroup (girls), while for boys the cut-off point was 6.37 when discriminating between active and non-active children.

TABLE 3 | Bivariate correlations between Physical Fitness Index Score and the related variables of the study.

	1	2	3
1. Physical Fitness Index Score	1		
2. Physical Activity Total Score	0.174**	1	
3. Integrated Regulation	0.138**	0.324**	1

$^{**}p < 0.01$.

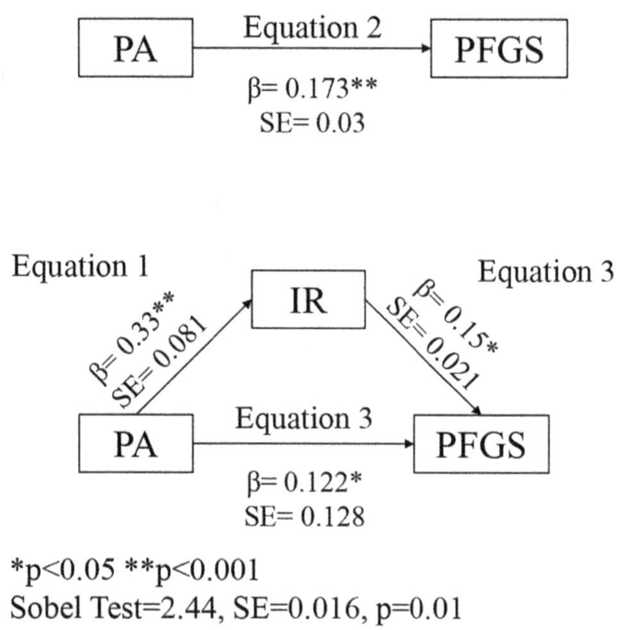

FIGURE 3 | Mediation of Physical Activity (PA) and Physical Fitness Global Score (PFGS) by Integrated Regulation (IR).

TABLE 4 | Area under the ROC curve of PAQ-C score based on integrated regulation (IR).

IR	PAQ-C score		
	Total (n = 325) Active	**Boys (n = 164) Active**	**Girls (n = 161) Active**
AUC	0.668	0.714	0.611
SE	0.030	0.041	0.045
95% CI	0.614 to 0.719	0.638 to 0.738	0.530 to 0.687
p	<0.001**	<0.001**	0.014*
Youden index	0.281	0.371	0.219

AUC, area under the curve; SE, standard error; CI, confidence interval; p, significance level; $^{**}p < 0.01$; $^{*}p < 0.05$.

Sensitivity was moderate for the different groups when considering a complete group (75.15%), or separated by gender (64.63% and 67.74% for boys and girls, respectively). However, for specificity, only one factor (boys) had a moderate-high score (75.5%), while for the whole group or girls alone showed moderate values (52.91% and 53.33%, respectively). Finally, the ability of the male gender to determine the differentiation between active or non-active was higher than the ability of the IR score for female gender and overall, as evidenced by the scores for positive and negative probability ratios on this factor compared to the others (girls alone and entire group). The same applies to positive and negative predictive values. ROC curves are shown in **Figure 4**.

DISCUSSION

In the present study we describe, compare and analyze the mediating role of IR on the relationship between the PA and PF level in school children between 11 and 14 years old. The results confirmed a positive association between PA and PF variables. In addition, the data allowed us to corroborate the IR role as a partial mediator of the established relationship between both variables. In addition, we established a cut-off point to discriminate between IR levels according to the classification (physically active or not) based on the PAQ-C scores by ROC curves analysis.

Firstly, concerning the anthropometric measures, significant differences when compared the schoolchildren gender and weight were observed (slightly higher +7.04% in girls). However, there were no significant differences in the BMI or any of the other anthropometric measures. These results are consistent with those previously reported by other studies (Jaakkola et al., 2015; Fang et al., 2017; Fernández-Bustos et al., 2019; López-Gil et al., 2020). Conversely, no significant differences were observed between genders when comparing PA levels, which is not in accordance with previous research studies where evidences of higher PA practice levels for boys were reported (Owen et al., 2009; Riddoch et al., 2009; Collings et al., 2013; Griffiths et al., 2013; Voss et al., 2017). However, several studies pointed out that such differences in the PA level could be due to significant differences in BMIs, as well as the results in measures of adiposity allowing for the identification and classification of schoolchildren with or without problems of hypertension or obesity (Riddoch et al., 2007, 2009; Owen et al., 2009; Ekelund et al., 2011; Niederer et al., 2012; Collings et al., 2013; Rauner et al., 2013; Jaakkola et al., 2015; Raistenskis et al., 2016; Wang et al., 2016; Fang et al., 2017; Fernández-Bustos et al., 2019). More precisely, those studies state that children who are obese or overweighted have a higher tendency to be physically less active (Ness et al., 2007; Rauner et al., 2013; Wang et al., 2016).

Our findings did not reveal any significant difference in the BMI by gender, which could justify the lack of differences in the PA levels in our sample. Furthermore, even if it seems evident that lower BMI levels could be associated with higher PA, the desire to lose weight in female students could be the trigger for inducing a more active behavior and, therefore, increased PA practice levels (Fernández-Bustos et al., 2019), explaining the lack of differences found in this study. The obtained scores in our research for PA practice levels are very similar to those found in previous research [e.g., PA total score = 2.97, PA score girls = 2.91, PA score boys = 3.03 in our study versus PA score total = 3.09, PA score girls = 3.11, PA score boys = 3.07 (Benítez-Porres et al., 2016b) or PA score total = 2.6 (Voss et al., 2017) or PA score girls = 2.7 and PA score boys = 2.9 (Voss et al., 2013)].

TABLE 5 | PAQ-C score cut-off points and sensitivity, specificity, likelihood ratios, and predictive values, based on integrated regulation (IR).

	Cut point	Sensitivity	95% CI	Specificity	95% CI	+LR	95% CI	−LR	95% CI	+PV	95% CI	−PV	95% CI
Total	>5.75	75.17	67.4–81.9	52.91	45.2–60.5	1.6	1.3–1.9	0.47	0.3–0.6	58	53.5–62.4	71.1	64.3–77.1
Boys	>6.25	64.63	53.3–74.9	72.5	61.4–81.9	2.35	1.6–3.5	0.49	0.4–0.7	70.7	62.0–78.1	66.7	59.2–73.4
Girls	>5.75	67.74	54.7–79.1	53.33	42.5–63.9	1.45	1.1–1.9	0.6	0.4–0.9	50	38.9–61.1	70.6	58.3–81.0

CI, confidence interval; LR, positive (+) and negative (−) likelihood ratios; PV, positive (+) and negative (−) predictive values.

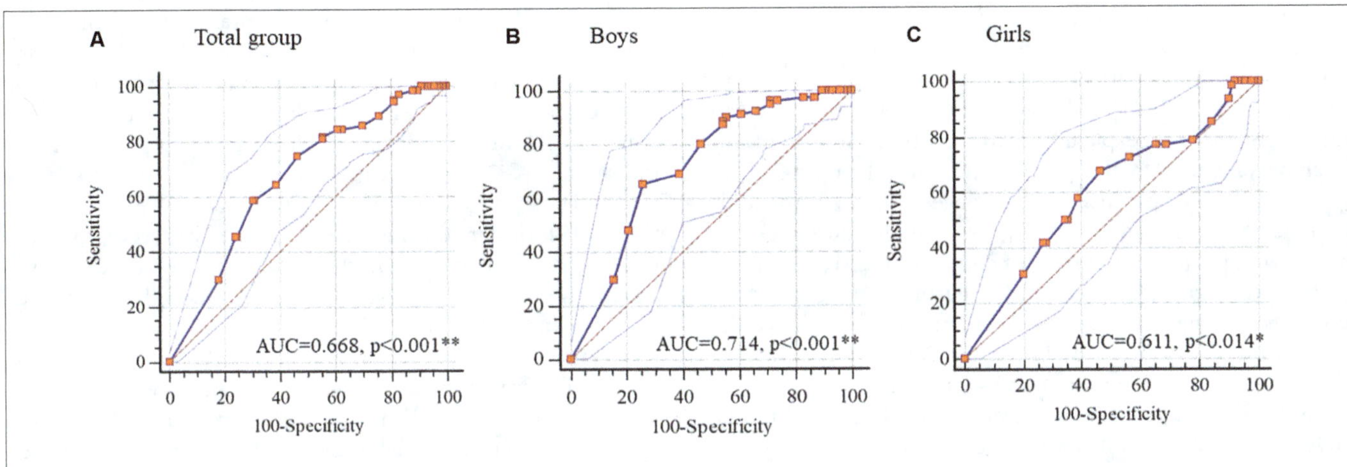

FIGURE 4 | Receiver-operator curves for the Integrated Regulation (IR) to identify PAQ-C's score of three group (**A**, Total group; **B**, Boys; and **C**, Girls). Data as shown as mean. $^{**}p < 0.01$; $^{*}p < 0.05$.

Moreover, significant differences were obtained when comparing the results for the different PF tests by gender. Specifically, boys achieved higher scores on the CRF, standing broad jump, sit-ups and 5 × 10 m shuttle run tests, while girls scored better on the sit and reach test. Although our findings are consistent to other studies (Schutte et al., 2016; Fang et al., 2017; Castro-Piñero et al., 2019; Lang et al., 2019). The interpretation of the score results should be carefully considered due to the lack of significant differences in the PA levels. Several scientific evidences highlighted an association between both factors, when higher PA practice levels are registered, an increase in PF levels is expected (Dollman et al., 2005; Dumith et al., 2011; Rauner et al., 2013; Schutte et al., 2016; Palou et al., 2019; Riso et al., 2019). The most plausible explanation for these differences by gender may be due to aspects of evolutive growth, which would allow boys to perform physical tests in a different way (Fang et al., 2017). Nevertheless, when the PFGS is considered, the gender difference was not observed, suggesting that our findings are in line with those found in the literature mentioned above. Concerning the individual results, the CRF test scores for both genders showed similarities with those identified as healthy indexes (35 and 42 ml /kg /m for girls and boys, respectively) in other studies (Lang et al., 2019). The results of the scores for lower and upper body muscle strength (mean scores) are similar to those obtained by Castro-Piñero et al. (2019) and by Segura-Jiménez et al. (2016), but there were no significant differences by gender in terms of upper limb strength levels, probably due to the different tools or the measurement period during the academic year used in each study. For PF, cardiorespiratory and muscular fitness are an important health marker associated with the risk of metabolic syndrome (Webber et al., 2008; Møller et al., 2009; Ahn et al., 2011; Welk et al., 2011; Rauner et al., 2013; Benítez-Porres et al., 2016a,b; Fang et al., 2017; Chacón-Cuberos et al., 2018b; Castro-Piñero et al., 2019; Lang et al., 2019; Zurita-Ortega et al., 2019) and, therefore, both measures and results are relevant for our research.

Taking into account the relationship between PA and PF, our results reveal both, a positive association between both factors and significant differences in the scores for the individual PF tests and the PFGS according to the classification and identification of the schoolchildren as physically active or not. Specifically, our results support the evidence that at any age, being physically active is synonymous of less difficulty and effort in facing physical tasks (Jaakkola et al., 2015). This could explain the increase in PF performance for physically active schoolchildren at both, at general and individual level (Rauner et al., 2013). Contrarily, lower levels of PF were observed in inverse situations (classification of schoolchildren as sedentary) (Dollman et al., 2005; Dumith et al., 2011; Rauner et al., 2013; Schutte et al., 2016; Wang et al., 2016; Palou et al., 2019; Riso et al., 2019). Regarding the FP test data at an individual level, there is a slightly positive trend identified with a better CRF score for physically active school children. But conversely to the results of previous studies, no statistically significant differences were observed (Ardoy et al., 2011; Cvejic et al., 2013; Rauner et al., 2013; Segura-Jiménez et al., 2016; Fang et al., 2017; Kolimechkov, 2017; Castro-Piñero et al., 2019).

The differing results could be explained by the fact that is that practice intensity has not been considered in the current study when measuring PA levels. In addition, there is some controversy about using a self-reported questionnaire to measure and assess PA because it is considered an indirect and subjective measure at these ages that may lead to an overestimation of PA practice levels (Palou et al., 2019; Riso et al., 2019). There are several investigations supporting the reliability and validity of this PAQ-C instrument for collecting this information (Biddle et al., 2011; Benítez-Porres et al., 2016a; Wang et al., 2016; Voss et al., 2017; Hidding et al., 2018), and in addition, the Spanish adaptation obtained a high test-retest reliability (ICC = 0.96) and a Cronbach's Alpha coefficient of $\alpha = 0.76$, which allows us to state a satisfactory internal consistency (Benítez-Porres et al., 2016b). Riddoch et al. (2009) made two very important findings that could explain the discrepancies found in this research compared to the previous scientific literature. Thus, the reality of PA practice at these ages differs from adults or adolescents. A high percentage of schoolchildren do not comply with the minimum recommendations for MPA and VPA practice preestablished by the WHO. Furthermore, PA is rarely performed during prolonged periods and intensities providing a good cardiorespiratory condition, since their normal activity rhythms are mostly characterized by short periods of activity.

On the other hand, schoolchildren classified with a physically active profile obtained higher scores for FP tests related to agility (Shuttle run 5 × 10 m), abdominal strength-resistance (abdominals), lower body strength (Standing Broad Jump) and flexibility (Sit and reach), obtaining an overall index (PFGS). These data show clear significant differences depending on whether they are identified as physically active or not.

In summary, our research findings are in line with scientific evidence showing differences in PF level according to PA levels (Dollman et al., 2005; Ardoy et al., 2011; Dumith et al., 2011; Cvejic et al., 2013; Rauner et al., 2013; Schutte et al., 2016; Segura-Jiménez et al., 2016; Wang et al., 2016; Fang et al., 2017; Kolimechkov, 2017; Castro-Piñero et al., 2019; Palou et al., 2019; Riso et al., 2019). The differences observed between the PFGS score in this investigation and other studies could be due to the lack of unification (aspects to be considered in the PF assessment) since each study measures different tests and/or particular aspects (in some studies only aerobic fitness, muscle strength or both are measured). Ardoy et al. (2011) highlights the promotion of other PF components along with those mentioned above, such as flexibility and agility, since they are directly involved in improving PF. Finally, the significant differences found when comparing active and non-active school children for weight and BMI reinforce our findings and statements regarding the relationship between all these elements (Ness et al., 2007; Collings et al., 2013; Rauner et al., 2013; Henriksson et al., 2016; Palou et al., 2019).

At these ages, children spend a considerable amount of time in educational institutions (Ahn et al., 2011), where the PE subject could play an important role in generating and promoting healthy lifestyles beyond the classroom itself (Moreno et al., 2008, 2009; Ahn et al., 2011; Dudley et al., 2011; Gillison et al., 2013; Fernández-Bustos et al., 2019; Sierra-Díaz et al., 2019). Through the SDT it is possible to explain the impact and influence that PE has on schoolchildren. Accordingly, our results showed significant differences in the IR score when classifying the schoolchildren as physically active or not. Moreover, when the influence of IR on the relationship between PA and PF was tested, the IR partially mediated that relationship.

Integrated regulation is the first level within the ME, which is based on the premise that external or environmental factors exist as conditioning factors to explain behavior and participation at these ages in any activity (Ryan and Deci, 2000; Moreno et al., 2009; Dudley et al., 2011; Gillison et al., 2013; Sierra-Díaz et al., 2019). Within the classroom context, one of the main purposes for the PE teacher is to achieve a better knowledge and awareness among students about the benefits of the PA practice and adequate PF levels have for their current and future health (Moreno et al., 2008, 2009; Dudley et al., 2011; Gillison et al., 2013; Chacón-Cuberos et al., 2018b; Castro-Sánchez et al., 2019; Fernández-Bustos et al., 2019; Sierra-Díaz et al., 2019). In our research, the differences between physically active and non-active schoolchildren could be related to the identification and internalization of the benefits of the PA practice for health improvement.

Additionally, the higher the student's PF, the higher their motor skills are likely to be, which will provide feedback on this pattern of active and healthy behavior, due to the optimal experience in the motor learning and technical skills acquired at PE lessons (Sierra-Díaz et al., 2019). Moreover, if we compare physically active and non-active students, the first ones will be able to overcome the challenges with less difficulty and effort together with higher guarantees of success. This is a consequence of a higher PF level (Dollman et al., 2005; Dumith et al., 2011; Rauner et al., 2013; Schutte et al., 2016; Wang et al., 2016; Palou et al., 2019; Riso et al., 2019), which will give them greater enjoyment and satisfaction in practice (Dudley et al., 2011; Gillison et al., 2013; Chacón-Cuberos et al., 2019; Sierra-Díaz et al., 2019).

The major finding of this study was that IR could be used to discriminate between physically active or non-active schoolchildren both, on an overall assessment and differentiating by gender. The established cut-off points were 5.88 (total group and female subgroup alone) and 6.37 for boys. As far as we know, this is the first study defining these cut-off points based on IR. The AUC value (general group and girls) is close to 0.70, which could invalidate the results of the diagnostic test at the clinical level, given the potential repercussions of an erroneous classification related to the presence or absence of disease. However, both tests presented acceptable levels of specificity for such discrimination and classification (Metz, 1978). Additionally, the PLOC-2 measuring instrument that allows IR recording is not a clinical diagnostic test, and also, comparatively low or similar AUC values are continuously published within this context (Benítez-Porres et al., 2016a; Voss et al., 2017). Therefore, our results could be considered as suitable as a test for differentiating levels of IR according to this classification for schoolchildren.

Finally, even though the PAQ-C questionnaire has demonstrated its validity for recording PA levels (Biddle et al., 2011; Benítez-Porres et al., 2016a; Wang et al., 2016; Voss et al., 2017; Hidding et al., 2018), the results could be influenced by the measurement instrument, being a possible limitation of this study. For this reason, it would be interesting to support the results already obtained by using better measuring instruments for a direct quantification of the PA levels. Further research is needed in order to corroborate the main findings.

CONCLUSION

To our knowledge, this is the first study that considers the mediating role of IR on the levels of PA and PF practice in school children. The findings of this novel study provide new information about the role of IR in PE classes as a supporting factor for the acquisition of not only healthy and active habits at these ages, but also for the improvement of PF levels. In addition, our findings establish a difference in the IR scores obtained by the schoolchildren according to their classification as physically active or not active, allowing us to establish cut-off points by ROC analysis. This analysis differentiates both the group of schoolchildren at a general level and by gender when classifying them according to the levels of PA practice. These cut-off points could be a useful and inexpensive way to assess the school population, in order to implement intervention strategies, especially in terms of structuring the content to be taught in the classroom. The aim is to improve motivation toward the teaching-learning process and, thus, increase the levels of PA and, consequently, improve the levels of PF.

ETHICS STATEMENT

The studies involving human participants were reviewed and approved by the University Ethics Committee of the Catholic University of Murcia (UCAM) reviewed and approved the research in accordance with the principles set out in the Declaration of Helsinki (Code: CE031802). Written informed consent to participate in this study was provided by the participants' legal guardian/next of kin. Written, informed consent was obtained from the individuals' legal guardian/next of kin for the publication of any potentially identifiable images or data included in this article.

AUTHOR CONTRIBUTIONS

GG-G and NG-G conceptualized and designed the study and carried out the statistical analysis. FG-F, LM-A, and PM-P recruited the subjects. GG-G, NG-G, and AE-G collected the data. AE-G and FG-F organized the database. GG-G, NG-G, AE-G, PM-P, FG-F, and LM-A wrote the first manuscript draft. GG-G and LM-A developed the final manuscript draft, the English proofreading, and reviewed and edited the final version of the manuscript. All authors contributed to the manuscript revision and approved the definitive manuscript.

ACKNOWLEDGMENTS

The authors thank the school, the teachers, and the children for their participation in this study. The authors also thank G. Sanz for his assistance with the English proofreading.

REFERENCES

Adams, J. (2006). Trends in physical activity and inactivity amongst US 14–18 year olds by gender, school grade and race, 1993–2003: evidence from the youth risk behavior survey. *BMC Publ. Health* 6:57. doi: 10.1186/1471-2458-6-57

Aggio, D., Ogunleye, A. A., Voss, C., and Sandercock, G. R. H. (2012). Temporal relationships between screen-time and physical activity with cardiorespiratory fitness in english schoolchildren: a 2-year longitudinal study. *Prev. Med.* 55, 37–39. doi: 10.1016/j.ypmed.2012.04.012

Agostinis-Sobrinho, C., Santos, R., Rosário, R., Moreira, C., Lopes, L., Mota, J., et al. (2018). Optimal adherence to a mediterranean diet may not overcome the deleterious effects of low physical fitness on cardiovascular disease risk in adolescents: a cross-sectional pooled analysis. *Nutrients* 10:815. doi: 10.3390/nu10070815

Ahn, S., Alicia, L., and Fedewa, A. L. (2011). A meta-analysis of the relationship between children's physical activity and mental health. *J. Pediatr. Psychol.* 36, 385–397. doi: 10.1093/jpepsy/jsq107

American College of Sports Medicine [ACSM] (2010). *ACSM's Guidelines for Exercise Testing and Prescription*, 9th Edn. London: Lippincott Williams & Wilkins.

Ardoy, D. N., Fernández-Rodríguez, J. M., Ruiz, J. R., Chillón, P., España-Romero, V., Castillo, M. J., et al. (2011). Improving physical fitness in adolescents through a school-based intervention: the EDUFIT study review. *Esp. Cardiol.* 64, 484–491. doi: 10.1016/j.recesp.2011.01.009

Barnett, L. M., van Beurden, E., Morgan, P. J., Brooks, L. O., and Beard, J. R. (2009). Childhood motor skill proficiency as a predictor of adolescent physical activity. *J. Adoles. Health* 44, 252–259. doi: 10.1016/j.jadohealth.2008.07.004

Baron, R. M., and Kenny, D. A. (1986). The moderator-mediator variable distinction in social psychological research: conceptual, strategic, and statistical considerations. *J. Pers. Soc. Psychol.* 51, 1173–1182. doi: 10.1037//0022-3514.51.6.1173

Benítez-Porres, J., Alvero-Cruz, J. R., Sardinha, L. B., Lopez-Fernández, I., and Carnero, E. A. (2016a). Cut-off values for classifying active children and adolescents using the physical activity questionnaire: PAQ-C and PAQ-A. *Nutr. Hosp.* 33, 1036–1044. doi: 10.20960/nh.564

Benítez-Porres, J., López-Fernández, I., Raya, J. F., Álvarez, S., Alvero-Cruz, J. R., and Álvarez, E. (2016b). Reliability and validity of the PAQ-C questionnaire to assess physical activity in children. *J. Sch. Health* 86, 677–685. doi: 10.1111/josh.12418

Biddle, S. J., Gorely, T., Pearson, N., and Bull, F. C. (2011). An assessment of self-reported physical activity instruments in young people for population surveillance: project ALPHA. *Int. J. Behav. Nutr. Phys. Act.* 8:1.

Castro-Piñero, J., Laurson, K. R., Artero, E. G., Ortega, F. B., Labayen, I., Ruperez, A. I., et al. (2019). Muscle strength field-based tests to identify European adolescents at risk of metabolic syndrome: the HELENA study. *J. Sci. Med. Sport* 22, 929–934. doi: 10.1016/j.jsams.2019.04.008

Castro-Sánchez, M., Zurita-Ortega, F., Pérez-Turpin, J. A., Cachón-Zagalaz, J., Cofre-Bolados, C., Suarez-Llorca, C., et al. (2019). Physical activity in natural environments is associated with motivational climate and the prevention of harmful habits: structural equation analysis. *Front. Psychol.* 10:1113. doi: 10.3389/fpsyg.2019.01113

Cervantes, K., Madaro, E., and Arrazola, M. (2017). Nivel de actividad física en niños de edades de 6 a 12 años en algunos colegios de Barranquilla-Colombia en el año 2014-2015. *Biociencias* 12, 17–23.

Chacón-Cuberos, R., Castro-Sánchez, M., Pérez-Turpin, J. A., Olmedo-Moreno, E. M., and Zurita-Ortega, F. (2019). Levels of physical activity are associated with the motivational climate and resilience in university students of physical education from Andalucía: an explanatory model. *Front. Psychol.* 10:1821. doi: 10.3389/fpsyg.2019.01821

Chacón-Cuberos, R., Zurita, F., Puertas, P., Knox, E., Cofré, C., Viciana, V., et al. (2018a). Relationship between healthy habits and perceived motivational climate in sport among university students: a structural equation model. *Sustainability* 10:938. doi: 10.3390/su10040938

Chacón-Cuberos, R., Zurita-Ortega, F., Olmedo-Moreno, E. M., Padial-Ruz, R., and Castro-Sánchez, M. (2018b). An exploratory model of psychosocial factors and healthy habits in university students of physical education depending on gender. *Int. J. Environ. Res. Public Health* 15:2430. doi: 10.3390/ijerph15112430

Chen, S. R., Lee, Y. J., Chiu, H. W., and Jeng, C. (2008). Impact of physical activity on heart rate variability in children with type 1 diabetes. *Child's Nerv. Syst.* 24, 741–747.

Cole, T. J., Bellizzi, M. C., Flegal, K. M., and Dietz, W. H. (2000). Establishing a standard definition for child overweight and obesity worldwide: international survey. *BJM* 320, 1240–1246.

Collings, P. J., Brage, S., Ridgway, C. L., Harvey, C. N., Godfrey, K. M., Inskip, H. M., et al. (2013). Physical activity intensity, sedentary time, and body composition in preschoolers. *Am. J. Clin. Nutr.* 97, 1020–1028. doi: 10.3945/ajcn.112.045088

Crocker, P. R., Bailey, D. A., Faulkner, R. A., Kowalski, K. C., and McGrath, R. (1997). Measuring general levels of physical activity: preliminary evidence for the physical activity questionnaire for older children. *Med. Sci. Sports Exerc.* 29, 1344–1349. doi: 10.1097/00005768-199710000-00011

Cvejic, D., Pejović, T., and Ostojić, S. (2013). Assessment of physical fitness in children and adolescents. *Phys. Educ. Sport* 11, 135–145.

Deci, E. L., and Ryan, R. M. (1985). *Intrinsic Motivation and Self-Determination in Human Behavior. Intrinsic Motivation and Self-Determination in Human Behavior.* New York, NY: Plenum.

Dollman, J., Norton, K., and Norton, L. (2005). Evidence for secular trends in children's physical activity behaviour. *Br. J. Sports Med.* 39, 892–897.

Dudley, D. A., Okely, A., Pearson, P., and Cotton, G. (2011). Effective physical education and school sport: a systematic review of physical education and school sport interventions targeting physical activity, movement skills and enjoyment of physical activity. *Eur. Phys. Educ. Rev.* 14:353. doi: 10.1177/1356336X11416734

Dumith, S. C., Gigante, D. P., Domingues, M. R., and Kohl, H. W. (2011). Physical activity change during adolescence: a systematic review and a pooled analysis. *Int. J. Epidemiol.* 40, 685–698. doi: 10.1093/ije/dyq272

Ekelund, U., Tomkinson, G., and Armstrong, N. (2011). What proportions of youth are physically active? Measurement issues, levels and recent time trends. *Br. J. Sports Med.* 45, 859–865.

España-Romero, V., Artero, E. G., Santaliestra-Pasias, A. M., Gutierrez, A., Castillo, M. J., and Ruiz, J. R. (2008). Hand span influences optimal grip span in boys and girls aged 6 to 12 years. *J. Hand Surg.* 33, 378–384. doi: 10.1016/j.jhsa.2007.11.013

Esparza-Ros, F., Vaquero-Cristóbal, R., and Marfell-Jones, M. (2019). *International Standards for Anthropometric Assessment.* Murcia: International Society for the Advancement of Kinanthropometry - ISAK.

Fang, H., Quan, M., Zhou, T., Sun, S., Zhang, J., Zhang, H., et al. (2017). Relationship between physical activity and physical fitness in preschool children: a cross-sectional study. *Biomed. Res. Int.* 2017:9314026. doi: 10.1155/2017/9314026

Fernández-Bustos, J. G., Infantes-Paniagua, A., Cuevas, R., and Contreras, O. R. (2019). Effect of physical activity on self-concept: theoretical model on the mediation of body image and physical self-concept in adolescents. *Front. Psychol.* 10:1537. doi: 10.3389/fpsyg.2019.01537

Ferriz, R., González-Cutre, D., and Sicilia, A. (2015). Revisión de la escala de Locus Percibido de Causaliad (PLOC) para la inclusion de la medida de de regulación integrada en educación física. *Rev. Psicol. Deporte* 24, 329–338.

Gillison, F. B., Standage, M., and Skevington, S. M. (2013). The effects of manipulating goal content and autonomy support climate on outcomes of a PE fitness class. *Psychol. Sport Exerc.* 14, 342–352. doi: 10.1016/j.psychsport.2012.11.011

Griffiths, L. J., Cortina-Borja, M., Sera, F., Pouliou, T., Geraci, M., Rich, C., et al. (2013). How active are our children? Findings from the Millennium Cohort Study. *BMJ Open* 3:e002893. doi: 10.1136/bmjopen-2013-002893

Gulías-González, R., Sánchez-López, M., Olivas-Bravo, Á, Solera-Martínez, M., and Martínez-Vizcaíno, V. (2014). Physical fitness in Spanish schoolchildren aged 6-12 years: reference values of the battery EUROFIT and associated cardiovascular risk. *J. Sch. Health* 84, 625–635. doi: 10.1111/josh.12192

Henriksson, P., Cadenas-Sánchez, C., Leppänen, M. H., Delisle-Nyström, C., Ortega, F. B., Pomeroy, J., et al. (2016). Associations of fat mass and fat-free mass with physical fitness in 4-year-old children: results from the MINISTOP Trial. *Nutrients* 8:473. doi: 10.3390/nu8080473

Hidding, L. M., Chinapaw, M. J. M., van Poppel, M. N. M., Mokkink, L. B., and Altenburg, T. M. (2018). An updated systematic review of childhood physical activity questionnaires. *Sports Med.* 48, 2797–2842. doi: 10.1007/s40279-018-0987-0

Jaakkola, T., Yli-Piipari, S., Huotari, P., Watt, A., and Liukkonen, J. (2015). Fundamental movement skills and physical fitness as predictors of physical activity: a 6-year follow-up study. *Scand. J. Med. Sci. Sports* 26, 74–81. doi: 10.1111/sms.12407

Kolimechkov, S. (2017). Physical fitness assessment in children and adolescents: a systematic review. *Eur. J. Phys. Educ. Sport Sci.* 3, 65–79. doi: 10.5281/zenodo.495725

Kowalski, K. C., Crocker, P. R., and Kowalski, N. P. (1997). Convergent validity of the physical activity questionnaire for adolescents. *Pediatr. Exerc. Sci.* 9, 342–352.

Lang, J. J., Tremblay, M. S., Ortega, F. B., Ruiz, J. R., and Tomkinson, G. R. (2019). Review of criterion-referenced standards for cardiorespiratory fitness: what percentage of 1 142 026 international children and youth are apparently healthy? *Br. J. Sports Med.* 53, 953–958.

Léger's, L. A., Mercier, D., Gadoury, C., and Lambert, J. (1988). The multistage 20 m shuttle run test for aerobic fitness. *J. Sports Sci.* 6, 93–101. doi: 10.1080/02640418808729800

López-Gil, J. F., Brazo-Sayavera, J., García- Hermoso, A., and Yuste, J. L. (2020). Adherence to Mediterranean Diet related with physical fitness and physical activity in schoolchildren aged 6–13. *Nutrients* 12:567. doi: 10.3390/nu12020567

Manchola-González, J., Bagur-Calafat, C., and Girabent-Farrés, M. (2017). Fiabilidad de la versión española del cuestionario de actividad física PAQ-C / Reliability Spanish Version of Questionnaire of Physical Activity PAQ-C. *Rev. Int. Med. Cienc. Activ. Fís. Deporte* 17, 139–152. doi: 10.15366/rimcafd2017.65.010

Metz, C. E. (1978). Basic principles of ROC analysis. *Semin. Nucl. Med.* 8, 283–298.

Møller, N. C., Kristensen, P. L., Wedderkopp, N., Andersen, L. B., and Froberg, K. (2009). Objectively measured habitual physical activity in 1997/1998 vs 2003/2004 in Danish children: the European Youth Heart Study. *Scand. J. Med. Sci. Sports* 19, 19–29. doi: 10.1111/j.1600-0838.2008.00774.x

Moreno, J. A., González-Cutre, D., and Chillón, M. (2009). Preliminary validation in spanish of a scale designed to measure motivation in physical education classes: the perceived locus of causality (PLOC) scale. *Spanish J. Psychol.* 12, 327–337. doi: 10.1017/S1138741600001724

Moreno, J. A., Parra, N., and González-Cutre, D. (2008). Influencia del apoyo a la autonomía, las metas sociales y la relación con los demás sobre la desmotivación en educación física. *Psicothema* 20, 636–641.

Nader, P. R., Bradley, R. H., Houts, R. M., McRitchie, S. L., and O'Brien, M. (2008). Moderate-to-Vigorous physical activity from ages 9 to 15 Years. *JAMA* 300, 295–305. doi: 10.1001/jama.300.3.295

Ness, A. R., Leary, S. D., Mattocks, C., Blair, S. N., Reilly, J. J., Wells, J., et al. (2007). Objectively measured physical activity and fat mass in a large cohort of children. *PLoS Med.* 4:e97. doi: 10.1371/journal.pmed.0040097

Niederer, I., Kriemler, S., Zahner, L., Bürgi, F., Ebenegger, V., Marques, P., et al. (2012). BMI group-related differences in physical fitness and physical activity in preschool-Age children: a cross-sectional analysis. *Res. Q. Exerc. Sport* 83, 12–19. doi: 10.1080/02701367.2012.10599820

Ogunleye, A. A., Voss, C., and Sandercock, G. R. (2012). Prevalence of high screen time in english youth: association with deprivation and physical activity. *J. Publ. Health* 34, 46–53.

Onetti-Onetti, W., Chinchilla-Minguet, J. L., Martins, F. M. L., and Castillo-Rodriguez, A. (2019). Self-Concept and physical activity: differences between high school and university students in Spain and Portugal. *Front. Psychol.* 10:1333. doi: 10.3389/fpsyg.2019.01333

Østerås, B., Sigmundsson, H., and Haga, M. (2017). Physical fitness levels do not affect stress levels in a sample of norwegian adolescents. *Front. Psychol.* 8:2176. doi: 10.3389/fpsyg.2017.02176

Owen, C. G., Nightingale, C. M., Rudnicka, A. R., Cook, D. G., Ekelund, U., and Whincup, P. H. (2009). Ethnic and gender differences in physical activity levels among 9–10-year-old children of white European, South Asian and African–Caribbean origin: the child heart health study in England (CHASE Study). *Int. J. Epidemiol.* 38, 1082–1093. doi: 10.1093/ije/dyp176

Palou, P., Muntaner-Mas, A., Cantallops, J., Borràs, P. A., Labayen, I., Jiménez-Pavón, D., et al. (2019). A single question of parent-reported physical activity levels estimates objectively measured physical fitness and body composition in preschool children: the PREFIT Project. *Front. Psychol.* 10:1585. doi: 10.3389/fpsyg.2019.01585

Pate, R. R. (1988). The evolving definition of physical fitness. *Quest* 40, 174–179.

Preacher, K. J., and Hayes, A. F. (2008). Asymptotic and resampling strategies for assessing and comparing indirect effects in multiple mediator models. *Behav. Res. Methods* 40, 879–891.

Purohit, S. P., Pradhan, B., and Nagendra, H. R. (2016). Effect of yoga on EUROFIT physical fitness parameters on adolescents dwelling in an orphan home: a randomized control study. *Vulnerable Child. Youth Stud.* 11, 33–46. doi: 10.1080/17450128.2016.1139764

Raistenskis, J., Sidlauskiene, A., Strukcinskiene, B., Uğur-Baysal, S., and Buckus, R. (2016). Physical activity and physical fitness in obese, overweight, and normal-weight children. *Turkish J. Med. Sci.* 46, 443–450. doi: 10.3906/sag-1411-119

Ramírez-Vélez, R., Correa-Bautista, J. E., Ojeda-Pardo, M. L., Sandoval-Cuellar, C., García-Hermoso, A., Carrillo, H. A., et al. (2018). Optimal adherence to a mediterranean diet and high muscular fitness are associated with a healthier cardiometabolic profile in collegiate students. *Nutrients* 10:511. doi: 10.3390/nu10040511

Rauner, A., Mess, F., and Woll, A. (2013). The relationship between physical activity, physical fitness and overweight in adolescents: a systematic review of studies published in or after 2000. *BMC Pediatr.* 13:19. doi: 10.1186/1471-2431-13-19

Riddoch, C. J., Leary, S. D., Ness, A. R., Blair, S. N., Deere, K., Mattocks, C., et al. (2009). Prospective associations between objective measures of physical activity and fat mass in 12-14 year old children: the Avon longitudinal study of parents and children (ALSPAC). *BMJ* 339:b4544. doi: 10.1136/bmj.b4544

Riddoch, C. J., Mattocks, C., Deere, K., Saunders, J., Kirkby, J., Tilling, K., et al. (2007). Objective measurement of levels and patterns of physical activity. *Arch. Dis. Child.* 92, 963–969. doi: 10.1136/adc.2006.112136

Riso, E. M., Toplaan, L., Viira, P., Vaiksaar, S., and Jürimäe, J. (2019). Physical fitness and physical activity of 6-7-year-old children according to weight status and sports participation. *PLoS One* 14:e0218901. doi: 10.1371/journal.pone.0218901

Ruiz, J. R., Castro-Piñero, J., España-Romero, V., Artero, E. G., Ortega, F. B., Cuenca, M. M., et al. (2011). Field-based fitness assessment in young people: the ALPHA health-related fitness test battery for children and adolescents. *Br. J. Sports Med.* 45, 518–524. doi: 10.1136/bjsm.2010.075341

Ryan, R. M., and Deci, E. L. (2000). Intrinsic and extrinsic motivations: classic definitions and new directions. *Contemp. Educ. Psychol.* 25, 54–67. doi: 10.1006/ceps.1999.1020

Schutte, N. M., Nederend, I., Hudziak, J. J., de Geus, E. J. C., and Bartels, M. (2016). Differences in adolescent physical fitness: a multivariate approach and meta-analysis. *Behav. Genet.* 46, 217–227. doi: 10.1007/s10519-015-9754-2

Segura-Jiménez, V., Parrilla-Moreno, F., Fernández-Santos, J. R., Esteban-Cornejo, I., Gómez-Martínez, S., Martínez-Gómez, D., et al. (2016). Physical fitness as a mediator between objectively measured physical activity and clustered metabolic syndrome in children and adolescents: the UP&DOWN study. *Nutr. Metab. Cardiovasc. Dis.* 26, 1011–1019. doi: 10.1016/j.numecd.2016.07.001

Sierra-Díaz, M. J., González-Víllora, S., Pastor-Vicedo, J. C., and López-Sánchez, G. F. (2019). Can we motivate students to practice physical activities and sports through models-based practice? A systematic review and meta-analysis of psychosocial factors related to physical education. *Front. Psychol.* 10:2115. doi: 10.3389/fpsyg.2019.02115

Sobel, M. E. (1982). Asymptotic confidence intervals for indirect effects in structural equation models. *Sociol. Methodol.* 13, 290–312.

Steele, R. M., Van Sluijs, E. M. F., Cassidy, A., Griffin, S. J., and Ekelund, U. (2009). Targeting sedentary time or moderate- and vigorous-intensity activity: independent relations with adiposity in a population-based sample of 10-y-old British children. *Am. J. Clin. Nutr.* 90, 1185–1192. doi: 10.3945/ajcn.2009.28153

Tomkinson, G. R., Lang, J. J., and Tremblay, M. S. (2019). Temporal trends in the cardiorespiratory fitness of children and adolescents representing 19 high-income and upper middle-income countries between 1981 and 2014. *Br. J. Sports Med.* 53, 478–486. doi: 10.1136/bjsports-2017-097982

Trigueros, R., Sicilia, A., Alcaráz-Ibáñez, A., and Dumitru, D. C. (2017). Adaptación y validación española de la escala revisada del locus percibido de causalidad (PLOC-R) en educación física. *Cuadernos Psicol. Deporte* 17, 25–32.

Voss, C., Dean, P. H., Gardern, R. F., Duncombe, S. L., and Harris, K. C. (2017). Validity and reliability of the physical activity questionnaire for children (PAQ-C) and adolescents (PAQ-A) in individuals with congenital heart disease. *PLoS One* 12:e0175806. doi: 10.1371/journal.pone.0175806

Voss, C., Ogunleye, A. A., and Sandercock, G. R. H. (2013). Physical activity questionnaire for children and adolescents: english norms and cut-off points. *Pediatr. Int.* 55, 498–507.

Wang, J. J., Baranowski, T., Lau, W. P., Chen, T. A., and Pitkethly, A. J. (2016). Validation of the physical activity questionnaire for older children (PAQ-C) among chinese children. *Biomed. Environ. Sci.* 29, 177–186. doi: 10.3967/bes2016.022

Webber, L. S., Catellier, D. J., Lytle, L. A., Murray, D. M., Pratt, C. A., and Young, D. R. (2008). Promoting physical activity in middle school girls: trial of activity for adolescent girls. *Am. J. Prevent. Med.* 34, 173–184. doi: 10.1016/j.amepre.2007.11.018

Welk, G. J., Laurson, K. R., Eisenmann, J. C., and Cureton, K. J. (2011). Development of youth aerobic-capacity standards using receiver operating characteristic curves. *Am. J. Prev. Med.* 41(4 Suppl. 2), S111–S116. doi: 10.1016/j.amepre.2011.07.007

Wilson, P. M., Rodgers, W. M., Loitz, C. C., and Scime, G. (2006). It's who I am really! The importance of integrated regulation in exercise contexts. *J. Appl. Biobehav. Res.* 11, 79–104. doi: 10.1111/j.1751-9861.2006.tb00021.x

World Medical, and Association (2013). World medical association declaration of Helsinki: ethical principles for medical research involving human subjects. *JAMA* 310, 2191–2194. doi: 10.1001/jama.2013

Zurita-Ortega, F., Badicu, G., Chacón-Cuberos, R., and Castro-Sánchez, M. (2019). Motivational climate and physical activity: a multigroup analysis in Romanian and Spanish university students. *Int. J. Environ. Res. Public Health* 16:2013. doi: 10.3390/ijerph16112013

19

Effect of Physical Activity on Self-Concept: Theoretical Model on the Mediation of Body Image and Physical Self-Concept in Adolescents

Juan Gregorio Fernández-Bustos[1], Álvaro Infantes-Paniagua[1], Ricardo Cuevas[2] and Onofre Ricardo Contreras[1]*

[1]Department of Didactics of Musical, Plastic and Physical Education, Faculty of Education of Albacete, University of Castilla-La Mancha, Albacete, Spain, [2]Department of Didactics of Musical, Plastic and Physical Education, Faculty of Education of Ciudad Real, University of Castilla-La Mancha, Ciudad Real, Spain

Correspondence:
Juan Gregorio Fernández-Bustos
juang.fernandez@uclm.es

Objective: The aim of this research was to study the mediation of body dissatisfaction, physical self-concept, and body mass index (BMI) on the relationship between physical activity and self-concept in adolescents.

Materials and Methods: A sample of 652 Spanish students between 12 and 17 years participated in a cross-sectional study. Physical self-concept and general self-concept were assessed with the Physical Self-Concept Questionnaire (CAF), body dissatisfaction with the Body Shape Questionnaire (BSQ), and physical activity was estimated with the International Physical Activity Questionnaire (IPAQ-SF). BMI was utilized as a measurement of body composition. Structural equation modeling was used to assess the results.

Results: The resulting models showed good fit indexes. Final model for all participants explained the 17% of the variance of body dissatisfaction, 57% of physical self-concept, and 60% of general self-concept. Physical activity had a positive and indirect effect on self-concept ($\beta = 0.29$, $p < 0.01$) and direct effects on body dissatisfaction ($\beta = -0.26$, $p < 0.01$) and physical self-concept ($\beta = 0.20$, $p < 0.01$). BMI had a direct effect on body dissatisfaction ($\beta = 0.31$, $p < 0.01$) and on physical self-concept ($\beta = -0.10$, $p < 0.01$) and an indirect effect on general self-concept ($\beta = -0.24$, $p < 0.01$). However, it was only associated with physical activity in males, playing a mediating role between physical activity and body dissatisfaction.

Conclusion: Physical activity can help individuals to achieve a positive self-concept and promote psychological well-being in adolescents through the improvement of physical perceptions and body satisfaction. The importance of BMI, body dissatisfaction, and physical self-concept on the configuration of the self-concept is also emphasized. Educational policymakers and Physical Education teachers should implement strategies to promote physical activity in the schools and provide a Quality Physical Education programs to increase physical activity during adolescence.

Keywords: physical activity, self-concept, physical self-concept, body image, structural equation model, adolescence

INTRODUCTION

Mental health has become a public health issue among youth all over the world, having reached a 20% prevalence rate within this population (World Health Organization, Department of Mental Health, Substance Abuse, World Psychiatric Association, International Association for Child, Adolescent Psychiatry, and Allied Professions, 2005; Belfer, 2008). In this line, physical activity (PA) is considered as one of the most important factors in the prevention and treatment of these kinds of issues (Ahn and Fedewa, 2011). Research has shown that PA can provide physiological and psychological benefits (Brown et al., 2013) related to mental health (Penedo and Dahn, 2005), including a reduction in depression and anxiety and an increase in executive function (Davis et al., 2011), psychological well-being (McMahon et al., 2017), body satisfaction (Campbell and Hausenblas, 2009), and self-concept (Marsh and Peart, 1988). Indeed, self-concept is especially relevant during the school ages, as it is considered to be a primary educational aim due to its general effects on mental status, psychological well-being, and human behavior (Rosenberg, 1985).

Many studies have associated the practice of PA with self-concept. Meta-analyses confirmed these positive relationships in PA program-based interventions aimed at improving self-concept (Liu et al., 2015), as well as in observational studies (Babic et al., 2014). However, some results seem contradictory; many studies proved that PA is positively related to self-concept (Sonstroem, 1997; Beasley and Garn, 2013; Sani et al., 2016), while others did not report that association (Annesi, 2006; Robinson et al., 2010) or made that relationship conditional on other mediating factors. For instance, some studies found that the positive relationship between PA and self-concept relied on the kind of sport practiced (Slutzky and Simpkins, 2009; Fernández-Bustos et al., 2010), only occurred among girls (Noordstar et al., 2016) or only among boys (Altıntaş et al., 2014), or was conditional based on body mass index (BMI) (Reddon et al., 2017).

Either way, according to the multidimensional and hierarchical conceptualization of self-concept (Shavelson et al., 1976), the possible effect of PA on the self-concept is mediated by one of its domains, the physical self-concept (Sonstroem, 1997; Slutzky and Simpkins, 2009). Under this theory's umbrella, Sonstroem and Morgan (1989), and later Sonstroem et al. (1994), proposed the exercise and self-esteem model (EXSEM) to explain how PA influenced self-esteem. According to this model, participating in physical activities increases the feelings of self-efficacy, improving the perceptions of sports competence and physical acceptance; in turn, this would foster general self-esteem. This model, besides having been empirically demonstrated by its authors, has been confirmed in other studies (McGannon and Spence, 2002; Murgui et al., 2016; Noordstar et al., 2016).

Body image (BI) is one of the most influential factors impacting psychological well-being, which determines the configuration of self-concept, particularly during adolescence (Thompson and Smolak, 2001; Fenton et al., 2010). Numerous studies focused on the idea that body satisfaction positively influences self-concept, as feeling comfortable with one's body produces overall positive feelings (Van den Berg et al., 2010; Buchanan et al., 2013; Fernández-Bustos et al., 2015). Nevertheless, body dissatisfaction levels are high during adolescence, especially among girls (Kantanista et al., 2015).

Likewise, another matter of concern for researchers has been how PA influences BI. A large amount of scientific literature has focused on proving how sports and PA are associated with an improved BI (Añez et al., 2018) or how sports and PA-based interventions can be utilized to improve BI (Martin-Ginis et al., 2014). Various meta-analyses and reviews have been carried out on this subject and, although it is accepted that the relationship between BI and PA is positive for males and females, the moderator role of sex is not clear. Even though Hausenblas and Fallon (2006) found a greater effect among women when compared with men, other reviews failed to find gender differences (Campbell and Hausenblas, 2009; Sabiston et al., 2018). Notwithstanding, McIntosh-Dalmedo et al. (2018) did not find enough evidence to suggest that sport- and exercise-based interventions could improve BI among female adolescents. Even so, the generalization of the findings has been disproportionately focused on women. Only one study precisely focused on men and boys (Bassett-Gunter et al., 2017), and its results showed that a positive BI was associated with a greater participation in PA. Although some mechanisms are likely to be shared between males and females, it is also possible that there is the existence of unique mechanisms. For example, a study conducted by Martin-Ginis et al. (2005) identified sex differences on the mechanisms underlying changes as a result of PA. Therefore, it is necessary to develop a better comprehension of the mechanisms underlying the effects of PA on BI between males and females.

Meta-analyses and reviews limit the whole understanding of the research into this subject, as these follow a unidirectional framework where PA improves BI, with a gap in the bidirectional nature of these associations. Unfortunately, there is no explicit theory or framework to guide the research on PA and BI. Consequently, some authors have tried to work upon the basis of other models. For instance, Martin-Ginis et al. (2012, 2014) tried to operationalize the EXSEM model (Sonstroem and Morgan, 1989), which was initially designed to describe the effects of PA on self-esteem in an effort to understand how PA has an impact on BI.

In spite of the major relationships that may exist between BI, self-concept, and PA, only a few studies have analyzed them concurrently. Fraguela-Vale et al. (2016) found that the practice of PA was simultaneously associated with both better perceptions of BI and a higher satisfaction with oneself. Blanco-Ornelas et al. (2017) showed that regular PA had an indirect and positive effect on personal self-concept through the subjective importance of physical fitness and appearance. However, Fernández-Bustos et al. (2016) found a relationship between PA and self-concept, but not between PA and physical appearance among female adolescents with body dissatisfaction. In addition to these studies, which are mainly correlational, stronger theories are needed to help us to understand the relationship between the practice of PA and self-concept and BI's role in these associations.

Therefore, this study aimed to determine the importance of PA in the configuration of self-concept in adolescents and the possible mediating role of BI and physical self-concept through a theoretical model. Additionally, we also studied the possible direct and indirect relationships between the different variables included in the model. To accomplish this objective, a new predictive model was designed by considering the EXSEM model (Sonstroem and Morgan, 1989) and a modification of Martin-Ginis et al. (2012), with the inclusion of BMI as a mediating variable. Alternative additional models were tested by sex to anticipate possible differences due to the uneven PA participation and body dissatisfaction (BD) between males and females. Moreover, adolescence is an essential period for the study of these constructs, as it is a sensitive stage for the self-concept and BI configuration and a consolidating period for lifelong PA habits.

MATERIALS AND METHODS

Participants

A total of 652 students (296 male and 356 female), aged between 12 and 17 years, participated in this study. They represented approximately 80% of the youth population of La Roda (Spain). These were all the students who were available during the day of the data collection and whose parents had previously signed an informed consent for participation. Eighteen cases were excluded for some errors in data completion or data tabulation. Therefore, the final sample included in the data analyses consisted of 634 participants (284 male and 350 female).

This is an appropriate sample size for avoiding inaccurate estimates of standard errors and fit indexes, according to the criterion proposed by Jackson (2003) for structural equation modeling (SEM). This author suggested that an ideal sample size should meet the ratio of 20 cases per each parameter to be estimated in the model or a less ideal ratio of 10 cases per parameter. Considering that our larger model contained 24 parameters to be estimated, the range of the ideal sample size would be between 240 and 480 participants.

Measures and Materials

General Self-Concept and Physical General Self-Concept

Two scales from the Physical Self-Concept Questionnaire (CAF) designed by Goñi et al. (2004) were utilized to assess the general physical self-concept (GPSC) and the general self-concept (GSC). This is the only physical self-concept questionnaire elaborated in Spanish without following any back-translation process. The questionnaire is completed by answering questions on a 5-point Likert scale (1 = false, 2 = usually false, 3 = sometimes true/sometimes false, 4 = usually true, 5 = true). Regarding the GPSC, students answered six items about their positive opinions and feelings (happiness, satisfaction, pride, and confidence) in the physical domain (e.g., "Physically, I am satisfied with myself"). With regard to the GSC, participants showed their overall satisfaction with their own selves and life by answering another six items (e.g., "I feel annoyed with myself"). The total questionnaire's reliability coefficient (Cronbach's alpha) for this study sample was $\alpha = 0.95$. By scale, it reached a reliability of $\alpha = 0.89$ for GPSC scale and $\alpha = 0.77$ for the GSC scale.

Body Dissatisfaction

The Body Shape Questionnaire (BSQ) by Cooper et al. (1987), adapted into the Spanish context (Raich et al., 1996), was used to assess body dissatisfaction (BD). The BSQ measures dissatisfaction of one's body, the fear of weight gain, physical appearance self-devaluation, the desire for weight loss, and the avoidance of situations in which one's physical appearance could get attention from others (e.g., "Have you been so worried about your shape that you have been feeling you ought to diet?"). The BSQ is a 34-item self-administered questionnaire with a 6-point Likert scale (i.e., 1 = never, 2 = rarely, 3 = sometimes, 4 = often, 5 = very often, 6 = always). Concern about body image was determined from the total score of this questionnaire (scores >81). For this study sample, the internal consistency was $\alpha = 0.97$.

Body Mass Index

A calibrated digital scale with a sensibility of 0.1 kg (Tanita UM-075) and a 2-meter altimeter (Holtex) were used to measure each participant's weight and height, respectively. These measurements were collected by two ISAK level 1 researchers to calculate the participants' BMI. Students were measured and weighted barefooted and wearing light clothes (no long trousers or sweaters were allowed). The body weight and height of each participant were measured twice, and the average between both was taken. To standardize the BMI values, participants were classified according to the cut-offs of the International Obesity Task Force (IOFT) (Cole and Lobstein, 2012) for their corresponding age and sex.

Physical Activity

The short form of the International Physical Activity Questionnaire (IPAQ-SF) was utilized to estimate PA levels. This self-reported measurement has shown reliability and validity within different contexts (Craig et al., 2003), including with the Spanish adolescent population (Aibar et al., 2016). For this study, only data on frequency and duration of both, moderate PA and vigorous PA, were considered. Light PA was therefore disregarded. With these data, a score of accumulative total weekly minutes of moderate and vigorous PA was calculated.

Procedure

The present study followed a cross-sectional design. Participants were recruited from the entire population of high school students in a Spanish city (La Roda). Prior to data collection, we informed the participants and their parents about the research aims, procedures, risks, and benefits of the study, and we obtained the required consent from the corresponding educational boards, high schools administrations, and parents of the students. Participation was voluntary with the parents' consent, and the anonymity of the participants and data confidentiality were guaranteed during the whole process. The study conformed to the deontological guidelines defined by the Declaration of Helsinki (Hong-Kong revision, 1989) and followed the recommendations of the Good Clinical Practice in the European Community (1 July 1991, document 111/3976/88) and the Spanish legislation on human clinical research (Royal Decree 561/1993 on clinical trials). The protocol was approved by the Ethics Committee on Human Research (University of Castilla La Mancha).

Questionnaires were administered in groups of 20–30 students in the assembly room of the high school (with a seating capacity of 350 people), which improved the concentration and privacy of the participants. Guidelines for fulfilling the questionnaires were verbally explained and were also written out before the start of the study. The proctors highlighted the need for the participants to carefully review each item and give sincere answers. To avoid social desirability in the answers, researchers insisted on the fact that the questionnaires were anonymous. The average duration of questionnaire fulfillment was 20 min, but the participants were given 25 min to complete the questionnaire. Once the questionnaires were completed, the students were led one by one to an adjoining room where they were weighted and measured by two expert researchers. During this process, the privacy and confidentiality of their data were similarly guaranteed.

Data Analysis

Structural equation modeling was used to analyze the data according to a predictive model. All statistical analyses were run using SPSS 24 and AMOS 24 for Windows.

Assumptions of linearity and multicollinearity were examined by inspecting the matrix scatter charts and the condition and variance inflation factor (VIF) indexes. These were obtained by using a regression analysis, with GSC as the dependent variable. The Durbin-Watson statistic was 1.88, so the variables were independent. All condition indexes were less than 7.34, except for BD (16.85), and the higher VIF value was 1.87; therefore, multicollinearity could be discarded. Finally, univariate kurtosis (range: −0.89 and 0.57) and skewness (range: −1.26 and 1.16) were examined. Although their values were not extreme, multivariate assumption was not strictly met. Nevertheless, Mardia's coefficient of multivariate kurtosis (14.95) was far from the cut-off of 70, so the use of maximum likelihood (ML) as a method of estimation was appropriate (Rodríguez and Ruiz, 2008). ML is robust to the non-normality, especially since the sample size is large (Iacobucci, 2010). To deal with this strict non-normality, SEM analysis was completed with a 1,000 replication bootstrap with a 95% bias-corrected confidence interval.

The proposed initial model and the subsequent ones included BMI and weekly minutes of PA as observable variables, while BD, GPSC, and GSC were considered latent variables with the items of the scales as their estimators. Concretely, the BD had the sum of the 34 items of BSQ as the only one indicator for this latent variable. Therefore, to achieve an identified initial model, the error's variance of the BSQ had to be estimated from its internal consistency coefficient and its variance by following Kline's (2011) suggestions. The initial model contained all theoretically possible paths (later explained) and, from this model, different nested models were proposed by following a trimming model process (Kline, 2011).

To test the fit of the models, chi-squared (χ^2), chi-squared by degrees of freedom ratio (χ^2/df), goodness of fit index (GFI), and root mean square error of approximation (RMSEA) were used as absolute fit indexes. Incremental or comparative fit indexes were also considered by including the Tucker-Lewis index (TLI) and the comparative fit index (CFI). Finally, regarding the parsimony-adjusted index, the Akaike's information criterion (AIC) and normed fit index (NFI) were used. A χ^2/df ratio < 3 was considered as acceptable (Iacobucci, 2010). Values >0.90 were considered as acceptable and > 0.95 as optimal for the NFI, TLI, GFI, and CFI indexes; for the RMSEA, the cut-off values were < 0.5 or < 0.6 as good and < 0.08 as acceptable (Hu and Bentler, 1999; Schumacker and Lomax, 2010).

RESULTS

Participants

The characteristics of the participants are shown in **Table 1**. They had an age range of 12–17 years, with a mean age of 14.59 (SD = 1.51). The weekly minutes of PA of the males was triple the time of PA undertaken by the females (♂ M = 281.46, SD = 203.19; ♀ M = 90.45, SD = 137.10). Both the GPSC and GSC were high among the males and significantly greater than among the females ($p < 0.001$). Similarly, the females were more concerned about their bodies than the males ($p > 0.001$), reaching a mean score of 85.14, which exceeded the cut-off value for body image concern of BSQ (>81).

TABLE 1 | Characteristics of the participants.

	Male (n = 284)		Female (n = 350)		All (n = 634)		
	M	**SD**	***M***	**SD**	***M***	**SD**	***p***
Age	14.50	1.51	14.66	1.50	14.59	1.51	0.177
BMI	22.36	3.93	21.81	3.64	22.05	3.78	0.069
PA minutes per week	281.46	203.19	90.45	137.10	176.01	194.57	0.000**
GPSC	23.88	5.26	19.67	6.49	21.56	6.32	0.000**
GSC	24.66	4.38	22.30	5.10	23.36	4.93	0.000**
BD (BSQ)	54.41	26.80	85.14	39.99	71.37	37.91	0.000**

BMI, body mass index; PA, physical activity; GPSC, general physical self-concept; GSC, general self-concept; BD, body dissatisfaction. M, mean; SD, standard deviation.
$^{*}p < 0.05$; $^{**}p < 0.01$; $^{***}p < 0.001$.

Structural Models

The initial model (model A1; **Figure 1**) starts at the integration of the following theories and models:

1. The EXSEM model (Sonstroem and Morgan, 1989), which established the GPSC as a mediator between the effects of PA on GSC.
2. The operationalization of the EXSEM, which highlights that the effect of PA on GSC is mediated by body satisfaction and physical perceptions (Martin-Ginis et al., 2012, 2014).
3. The model hypothesized by Fox and Corbin (1989), which reflects the multidimensional and hierarchical nature of physical self-concept by placing the perceptions of physical attractiveness as one of its dimensions. Considering body image as a dimension of physical self-concept (Fernández-Bustos et al., 2015), body satisfaction should be a mediator between PA and physical self-concept.
4. The BMI as an exogenous self-contained variable influencing body satisfaction.
5. The model of Mak et al. (2016) suggests that BMI is a mediator between PA and self-esteem.
6. Additionally, for the initial model, the possible direct effects of PA and BD on GSC were included.

The initial model fit could be improved (**Table 2**), as χ^2/df exceeded the established cut-off (χ^2/df = 3.21; GFI = 0.976; RMSEA = 0.059; CFI = 0.974; TLI = 0.956; NFI = 0.963; AIC = 115.48), and four paths reported nonsignificant effects. Therefore, we continued with the model trimming process. First, this study found no relationship between PA and BMI. Since in other studies (Kantanista et al., 2015; Sani et al., 2016) this relationship was also nonsignificant, it was excluded (model A2). This slightly improved the model fit, but the ratio χ^2/df continued to exceed the established threshold. After that, a third model (model A3) was tested by removing the effect of PA on GSC from model A2, which was the next most nonsignificant path. This step was supported by hypotheses holding that this effect is not direct but through the physical self-concept (Sonstroem and Morgan, 1989). This modification also slightly improved the model fit reaching an acceptable value of χ^2/df (2.968). Model A3 did not show a significant effect of BD on GSC. The nonexistence of this path would support the multidimensional, hierarchical conceptualization of self-concept, where BI would be a subdimension of GPSC and an influence through the GPSC (Fox and Corbin, 1989). Thus, another model (model A4) that excluded this effect was tested, showing an optimal fit (χ^2/df = 2.90; GFI = 0.975; RMSEA = 0.054; CFI = 0.975; TLI = 0.962; NFI = 0.962; AIC = 111.66) and significant effects for all the included paths (**Figure 2; Table 2**). After comparing the last two models, no statistical difference was apparent ($\Delta\chi^2$ = 1.395, Δdf = 1, p = 0.237), so we accepted the model A4 as the final model since it showed a better parsimony fit index (AIC = 111.666).

Standardized regression coefficients for each proposed direct path in the final model reached significance at $p < 0.001$ level. The strongest direct effects were reported for GPSC on GSC (β = 0.78), being positive, and between BD and GPSC (β = −0.64), being negative (**Table 3**). The results also showed that PA positively and directly influenced GPSC (β = 0.20, $p < 0.01$) and indirectly through BD (β = 0.17, $p < 0.01$). Similarly, PA had a direct effect on BD (β = −0.26, $p < 0.01$) and an indirect effect on GSC mediated by GPSC and BD (β = 0.29, $p < 0.01$). The BMI had a direct influence on BD (β = 0.32, $p < 0.01$) and GPSC (β = −0.10, $p < 0.01$) and an indirect effect on GPSC (β = −0.15, $p < 0.01$) and GSC (β = −0.14, $p < 0.01$). The final model explained 60% of the variance of GSC and 57% of the variance of GPSC.

Structural Models by Sex

The initial model A1 was further analyzed to test whether the relationships between PA and GSC were different between males and females. The same procedure was followed from the initial model, but the samples of male (model M1) and females (model F1) were considered separately. The initial models M1 and F1 showed modest fit indexes for both males and females (**Table 2**) and included different nonsignificant paths in each group. For this reason, the design of the subsequent models was different for each group, but in both cases, a model trimming process was used.

Regarding the male sample, the model M1 included three nonsignificant paths: PA→GSC, PA→BD, and BD→GSC.

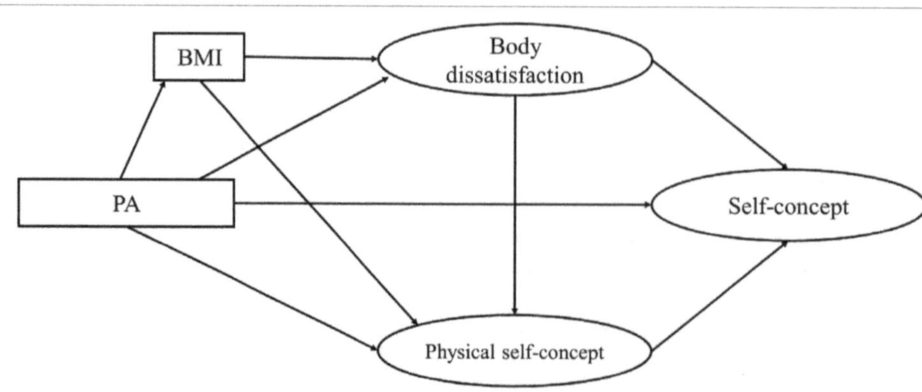

FIGURE 1 | Initial theoretical model (model A1).

TABLE 2 | Fit indexes by model and group.

Model	χ^2	*df*	χ^2/df	GFI	RMSEA	CFI	TLI	NFI	AIC
Model A1	67.487	21	3.213	0.976	0.059	0.974	0.956	0.963	115.487
Model A2	67.877	22	3.085	0.976	0.057	0.974	0.958	0.963	113.877
Model A3	68.271	23	2.968	0.975	0.055	0.975	0.960	0.963	112.271
Model A4*	69.666	24	2.902	0.975	0.054	0.974	0.962	0.962	111.666
Model M1	49.924	21	2.377	0.960	0.069	0.955	0.924	0.927	97.924
Model M2	50.063	22	2.275	0.960	0.067	0.957	0.929	0.927	96.063
Model M3*	50.980	23	2.216	0.960	0.065	0.957	0.933	0.926	94.980
Model M4	57.836	24	2.409	0.954	0.070	0.948	0.922	0.916	99.836
Model F1	40.454	21	1.926	0.974	0.051	0.980	0.966	0.960	88.454
Model F2	40.469	22	1.839	0.974	0.049	0.981	0.969	0.960	86.469
Model F3	40.566	23	1.763	0.974	0.046	0.982	0.972	0.960	84.566
Model F4*	40.936	24	1.705	0.974	0.044	0.983	0.974	0.960	82.936
Model F5	44.616	25	1.784	0.972	0.047	0.980	0.971	0.956	84.616

*A, all; M, males; F, females.*Final model.*

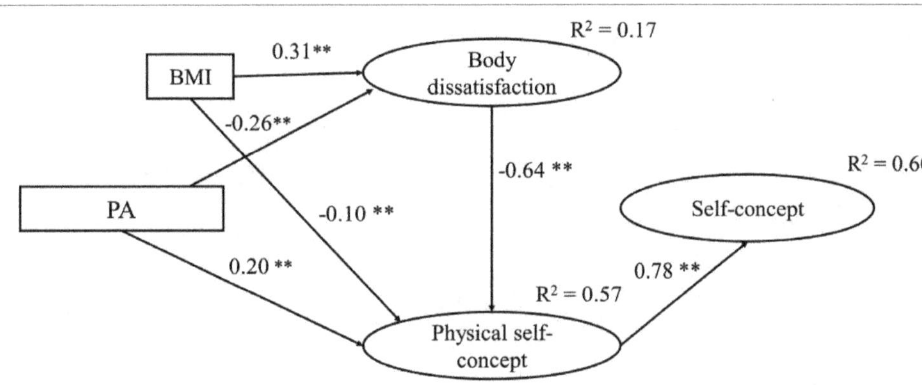

FIGURE 2 | Final theoretical model (model A4) with standardized regression coefficients (betas). $^*p < 0.05$; $^{**}p < 0.01$.

TABLE 3 | Standardized regression coefficients (direct, indirect and total effects). Final models.

	Model A4			Model M3			Model F4		
Path	D	I	T	D	I	T	D	I	T
PA→BD	−0.26**	–	−0.26**	–	−0.08**	−0.08**	−0.09	–	−0.09
PA→BMI	–	–	–	−0.20**	–	−0.20**	–	–	–
PA→GSC	–	0.29**	0.29**	–	0.17**	0.17**	–	0.21*	0.21**
PA→GPSC	0.20**	0.17**	0.37**	0.16**	0.07**	0.23**	0.21**	0.07	0.28**
BD→GSC	–	−0.50**	−0.50**	−0.28	−0.29***	−0.57**	–	−0.51**	−0.51**
BD→GPSC	−0.64**	–	−0.64**	−0.44**	–	−0.44**	−0.69**	–	−0.69**
BMI→BD	0.31**	–	0.31**	0.44**	–	0.44**	0.43**	–	0.43**
BMI→GSC	–	−0.24**	−0.24**	–	−0.36**	−0.36**	–	−0.29**	0.29**
BMI→GPSC	−0.10**	−0.20**	−0.30**	−0.17*	−0.19**	−0.36**	−0.10*	−0.29**	−0.39**
GPSC→GSC	0.78**	–	0.78**	0.65**	–	0.65**	0.74**	–	0.74**

D, direct effects; I, indirect effects; T, total effects; BMI, body mass index; PA, physical activity; GPSC, general physical self-concept; GSC, general self-concept; BD, body dissatisfaction. $^*p < 0.05$; $^{**}p < 0.01$; $^{***}p < 0.001$.

Therefore, different models were designed by following a procedure similar to the one used with the total sample. Among them, the model M3, which excluded the effects of PA on GSC and BD, showed the best fit ($\chi^2/df = 2.21$; GFI = 0.960; RMSEA = 0.065; CFI = 0.957; TLI = 0.933; NFI = 0.926; AIC = 94.98). This model also included the effect of BD on GSC, whose coefficient was close to the level of significance ($\beta = -0.28$, $p = 0.05$). Additionally, a fourth model (model M4), which excluded that effect, was tested, but it demonstrated worse fit indexes (**Table 2**). As there were no statistical differences between M2 and M3 ($\Delta\chi^2 = 0.916$, $\Delta df = 1$, $p = 0.338$), we opted for model M3 (**Figure 3**) as the final model for males because it yielded more appropriate RMSEA and AIC fit indexes.

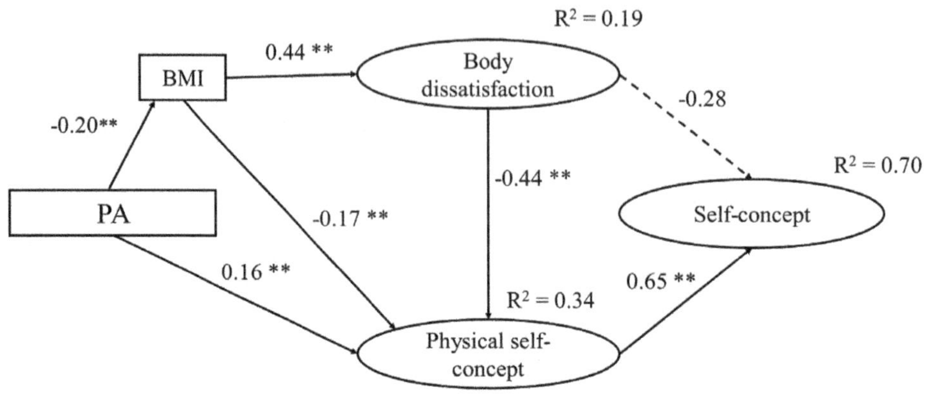

FIGURE 3 | Final model for males (model M3). $^{*}p < 0.05$; $^{**}p < 0.01$.

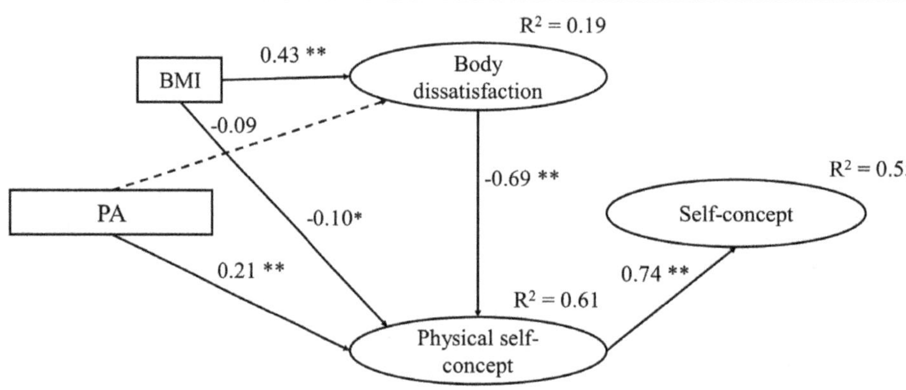

FIGURE 4 | Final model for females (model F4). $^{*}p < 0.05$; $^{**}p < 0.01$.

Concerning the female sample, four models were created in addition to model F1 by following a procedure similar to the one used with the total sample. As in model M1 for males, in model F4 for females, the effect of PA on BD was nonsignificant. Thus, we additionally tested a model F5 excluding that effect. However, the fit indexes were less acceptable than those demonstrated by the previous models (**Table 2**). Model F4 had the best fit ($\chi^2/df = 1.70$; GFI = 0.974; RMSEA = 0.044; CFI = 0.983; TLI = 0.974; NFI = 0.960; AIC = 82.93) and was not statistically different from either model F3 ($\Delta\chi^2 = 0.369$, $\Delta df = 1$, $p = 0.543$) or model F5 ($\Delta\chi^2 = 3.680$, $\Delta df = 1$, $p = 0.055$). Thus, model F4 (**Figure 4**) was selected as the final model for females. This model included the effect of PA on BD, which demonstrated a standardized coefficient very close to significance, but without reaching it ($\beta = -0.10$, $p = 0.05$).

The main differences between the final models (**Table 3**) for males (model M3) and females (model F4) were found in the direct effect of BD on GPSC (♂ $\beta = -0.44$; ♀ $\beta = -0.69$) and the indirect effect of BD on GSC (♂ $\beta = -0.29$; ♀ $\beta = -0.51$). In addition, among males, the path between PA and BMI was also considered. A negative, direct effect was found ($\beta = -0.20$, $p < 0.05$), placing BMI as a mediator between PA and BD; while among women, only a very little and direct effect of PA on BD was found ($\beta = -0.10$, $p = 0.05$). The final model for males explained 34% of the variance of GPSC and 70% of the variance of GSC, while for females, the final model explained 61 and 55%, respectively.

DISCUSSION

The aim of this study was to design a complementary and explanatory model of the relationships between PA and self-concept. For that purpose, BD, which in previous studies had been related to PA, was included in the model as a determining factor in the self-concept configuration of adolescents. GPSC was also included as a mediating variable. BMI was finally added, assuming its influence on PA, BD, and GPSC. Additionally, we aimed to know whether it was possible to yield different models distinguishing by sex. This was especially necessary as it was previously evidenced a higher physical self-concept for males (Hagger et al., 2005) and no clear moderating role of sex appears to exist in the relationship between PA and BI (Bassett-Gunter et al., 2017). This situation is evident from the different influence of the aesthetic model in men and women, which is internalized early, and especially affects females with the impetus to be thin. This makes female adolescents feel much more dissatisfaction with their bodies than their male peers (Grogan, 2006; Kantanista et al., 2015) and to have lower levels of self-esteem (Robins and Trzesniewski, 2005), as was found in the participants of the present study.

For the design of the initial model, we considered the theory about the effect of PA on self-concept and the effect of PA on BI. We started from an adaptation of EXSEM (Sonstroem and Morgan, 1989) and some aspects from the variant proposed by Martin-Ginis et al. (2012) or the role of BMI on PA and BI (Mak et al., 2016). The possible direct effects among some variables, such as PA and GSC (Sani et al., 2016), were also included. From the initial model, other different models were proposed, and those that yielded the best fit indexes and theoretically coherent were chosen as the final models. In any case, even though the most relevant theoretical aspects coincided, the final models differed between males and females.

In all cases, the important positive effect of PA on the self-concept of adolescents was confirmed, as has been seen in previous studies (Beasley and Garn, 2013; Liu et al., 2015) with no sex differences (Reddon et al., 2017). The suggested models explained more than 50% of the variance of GSC. However, the effect of PA on GSC was not direct but through one of the dimensions of self-concept, the physical self-concept (Sonstroem, 1997). Thus, in line with other studies that included the physical self-concept as a mediating variable, both the hierarchical and multidimensional conception of self-concept (Shavelson et al., 1976) and the EXSEM model are confirmed. Previous studies found a direct association of PA with self-concept but without including physical self-concept in the model (Sani et al., 2016).

Within this hierarchical model, working on GPSC, or some of its subdomains, would be easier than working on the GSC itself. The former's effect on the latter will be based on the importance that each subject confers to the physical domain (Zulaika, 2002). During adolescence, physical self-concept takes on special significance due to the importance conferred to everything that is related to the physical domain since this dimension is one of the most influential factors on the self-concept configuration in youths (Harter, 1999). In this study, that situation can be seen in the emphasized effect of GPSC on GSC in all models, being slightly more important for females.

The most well-known models explaining the physical self-concept (Fox and Corbin, 1989; Marsh et al., 1994) include physical appearance as a subdomain of physical self-concept. BI is closely related to the physical attractiveness domain, understanding the latter as one's perceptions about his/her physical appearance and his/her satisfaction and confidence with his/her self-image (Goñi et al., 2004). Therefore, BI would be a part of physical self-concept (Burns, 1990; Fernández-Bustos et al., 2015). Despite the link between BI and physical self-concept, there are only a few studies that show the relationship between them. The model presented in this study proves the large direct effect of BI on GPSC in adolescence, along with the effect on GSC, which are both very high and indirect. This supports the hierarchical and multidimensional model previously explained. In this way, many studies highlight the important relationship between BD and self-esteem in both males and females (Van den Berg et al., 2010; Fernández-Bustos et al., 2015).

Considering the lack of physical self-concept subdomains other than BI in the suggested model, PA had a positive and direct effect on GPSC, as was supported in all the previous literature, which is reinforced by the results of the meta-analysis carried out by Babic et al. (2014). Similarly, following the hierarchical model, PA indirectly influenced GPSC through its subdimension of BI, as measured by BD.

Regarding the effect of PA on BD, the three final models yielded different results. For all participants, the positive and direct effect of PA on body satisfaction was confirmed (Añez et al., 2018); this effect, however, was more relevant in females than males, which is consistent with Hausenblas and Fallon's (2006) findings. In the case of males, there was no direct effect of PA on BD, but it was mediated by BMI.

BMI was shown as a variable of especial interest in the suggested models. On the one hand, BMI proved that it plays a determining role in body satisfaction (Strauss, 2000), having a negative effect on both males and females. Indeed, high adiposity is thought to be a promoter of body dissatisfaction, as it is opposed to the aesthetic model of males and females. Therefore, the larger the deviation degree from the ideal physical shape, the greater the dissatisfaction with the resulting body (Stice and Shaw, 2002). On the other hand, BMI demonstrated negative direct and indirect effects on the perceptions of GPSC and an indirect effect on GSC. Several studies agreed that there was a relationship between obesity and lower self-esteem and worse physical perceptions (Griffiths et al., 2010; McClure et al., 2010). Altıntaş et al. (2014) considered BMI to be the best predictor of self-esteem and body satisfaction in female adolescents, being slightly less important among males. Sani et al. (2016) tried to create a model to explain the relationships between PA, BI, and self-esteem, but they only found a direct association of BMI with BI and no association with self-esteem.

Nevertheless, even though some studies associated PA with lower values of BMI (Du et al., 2013), in the present study, this was only evidenced in males, in accordance with Kantanista et al. (2015). This result can be explained in view of some evidence among females that associated a higher BMI with higher PA levels triggered by their desire to exercise to lose weight (Ingledew and Sullivan, 2002). Additionally, the possible mediating role of BMI in the relationship between PA and GSC, already hypothesized in previous studies (Reddon et al., 2017), was only supported among males, which is in line with Mak et al. (2016).

In practice, the results of this research should help to explain how the effect of PA on students' BI and self-concept is produced and to place value on the promotion of PA in educational centers. By doing that, educational policymakers will contribute to the development of not only the physical health of adolescents but also their psychological well-being at an educational stage of special difficulty, where PA tends to decrease alarmingly in comparison to early stages. These results are also relevant for Physical Education teachers to stress the importance of optimizing the time of PA during their lessons; the results can be also useful for providing a Quality Physical Education that makes students improve their physical perceptions, find pleasure in exercise, and achieve autonomous active lifestyle behaviors outside of school.

This study presents some limitations that must be taken into consideration. Among these, the assessment of a unique aspect of BI – the dissatisfaction in terms of weight loss – must be pointed out. This is particularly relevant for males, who presented an aesthetic model that tends to drive for muscularity and away from obesity. That is, BD in terms of desiring a more muscular body has been omitted, and this especially influences males. Another limitation would be the lack of more indicators of PA, in addition to the weekly minutes, as the type of activity (endurance, strength, etc.) may determine the perceptions of BI and the physical self-concept itself.

It is necessary to continue with the study of the moderating effect of sex in the relationship between PA and BI. It is also necessary to examine the potential moderators that are exclusive to male or female samples in future research and interventions. To do so, besides taking into account the differences in the configuration of the body image in both sexes, there is a need to include variables that determine the relationship between PA and BI, such as the aesthetical reasons that lead to the practice of PA or the effect of different types of physical exercises or sports on BI.

CONCLUSION

To conclude, the suggested model put emphasis on how PA is associated with a more positive self-concept during adolescence, although this effect is mediated by both physical self-concept and BI. Likewise, PA is associated with a lower BD, while BMI is shown as an important external variable in the model, whose role varied by sex. The importance of body satisfaction and physical self-concept in the configuration of GSC in adolescents is also highlighted, especially among females.

ETHICS STATEMENT

Prior to data collection, we informed the participants and their parents about the research aims, procedures, risks, and benefits of the study, and we obtained the required consent from the corresponding educational boards, high schools administrations, and parents of the students. Participation was voluntary with the parents' consent, and the anonymity of the participants and data confidentiality were guaranteed during the whole process. The study conformed to the deontological guidelines defined by the Declaration of Helsinki (Hong-Kong revision, 1989) and followed the recommendations of the Good Clinical Practice in the European Community (1 July 1991, document 111/3976/88) and the Spanish legislation on human clinical research (Royal Decree 561/1993 on clinical trials).

AUTHOR CONTRIBUTIONS

JGF-B designed the study, collected the data, wrote the article, and collaborated on the data analysis. AI-P analyzed the data and collaborated on the article wording. RC collaborated on the article wording and review. ORC designed the study and collaborated on the review of the article.

REFERENCES

Ahn, S., and Fedewa, A. L. (2011). A meta-analysis of the relationship between children's physical activity and mental health. *J. Pediatr. Psychol.* 36, 385–397. doi: 10.1093/jpepsy/jsq107

Aibar, A., García-González, L., Abarca-Sos, A., Murillo, B., and Zaragoza, J. (2016). Testing the validity of the International Physical Activity Questionnaire in early Spanish adolescents: a modified protocol for data collection. *SPORTK-Rev. Euroam. de CC Deporte* 5, 123–132. doi: 10.6018/264761

Altıntaş, A., Aşçı, F. H., Kin-İşler, A., Güven-Karahan, B., Kelecek, S., Özkan, A., et al. (2014). The role of physical activity, body mass index and maturity status in body-related perceptions and self-esteem of adolescents. *Ann. Hum. Biol.* 41, 395–402. doi: 10.3109/03014460.2013.857721

Añez, E., Fornieles-Deu, A., Fauquet-Ars, J., López-Guimerà, G., Puntí-Vidal, J., and Sánchez-Carracedo, D. (2018). Body image dissatisfaction, physical activity and screen-time in Spanish adolescents. *J. Health Psychol.* 23, 36–47. doi: 10.1177/1359105316664134

Annesi, J. J. (2006). Relations of physical self-concept and self-efficacy with frequency of voluntary physical activity in preadolescents: Implications for after-school care programming. *J. Psychosom. Res.* 61, 515–520. doi: 10.1016/j.jpsychores.2006.04.009

Babic, M. J., Morgan, P. J., Plotnikoff, R. C., Lonsdale, C., White, R. L., and Lubans, D. R. (2014). Physical activity and physical self-concept in youth: systematic review and meta-analysis. *Sports Med.* 44, 1589–1601. doi: 10.1007/s40279-014-0229-z

Bassett-Gunter, R., McEwan, D., and Kamarhie, A. (2017). Physical activity and body image among men and boys: a meta-analysis. *Body Image* 22, 114–128. doi: 10.1016/j.bodyim.2017.06.007

Beasley, E. K., and Garn, A. C. (2013). An investigation of adolescent girls' global self-concept, physical self-concept, identified regulation, and leisure-time physical activity in physical education. *J. Teach. Phys. Educ.* 32, 237–252. doi: 10.1123/jtpe.32.3.237

Belfer, M. L. (2008). Child and adolescent mental disorders: the magnitude of the problem across the globe. *J. Child Psychol. Psychiatry* 49, 226–236. doi: 10.1111/j.1469-7610.2007.01855.x

Blanco-Ornelas, L. H., Pando, B., Verónica, E., Tristán, J. L., and Mayorga-Vega, D. (2017). Actividad física, imagen corporal y autoconcepto personal en jóvenes universitarias mexicanas. *Rev. Psicol. Deporte* 26, 25–33. Available at: https://www.rpd-online.com/article/view/v26-n4-blanco-benavides-tristan-etal

Brown, H. E., Pearson, N., Braithwaite, R. E., Brown, W. J., and Biddle, S. J. (2013). Physical activity interventions and depression in children and adolescents. *Sports Med.* 43, 195–206. doi: 10.1007/s40279-012-0015-8

Buchanan, N. T., Bluestein, B. M., Nappa, A. C., Woods, K. C., and Depatie, M. M. (2013). Exploring gender differences in body image, eating pathology, and sexual harassment. *Body Image* 10, 352–360. doi: 10.1016/j.bodyim.2013.03.004

Burns, R. B. (1990). *Self-concept: Theory, measurement, development and behavior.* (Bilbao, Spain: Editorial Grupo Arrien).

Campbell, A., and Hausenblas, H. A. (2009). Effects of exercise interventions on body image: A meta-analysis. *J. Health Psychol.* 14, 780–793. doi: 10.1177/1359105309338977

Cole, T. J., and Lobstein, T. (2012). Extended international (IOTF) body mass index cut-offs for thinness, overweight and obesity. *Pediatr. Obes.* 7, 284–294. doi: 10.1111/j.2047-6310.2012.00064.x

Cooper, P. J., Taylor, M. J., Cooper, Z., and Fairbum, C. G. (1987). The development and validation of the Body Shape Questionnaire. *Int. J. Eat. Disord.* 6, 485–494. doi: 10.1002/1098-108X(198707)6:4<485::AID-EAT2260060405>3.0.CO;2-O

Craig, C. L., Marshall, A. L., Sjöström, M., Bauman, A. E., Booth, M. L., Ainsworth, B. E., et al. (2003). International physical activity questionnaire: 12-country reliability and validity. *Med. Sci. Sports Exerc.* 35, 1381–1395. doi: 10.1249/01.MSS.0000078924.61453.FB

Davis, C. L., Tomporowski, P. D., McDowell, J. E., Austin, B. P., Miller, P. H., Yanasak, N. E., et al. (2011). Exercise improves executive function and achievement and alters brain activation in overweight children: a randomized, controlled trial. *Health Psychol.* 30, 91–98. doi: 10.1037/a0021766

Du, H., Bennett, D., Li, L., Whitlock, G., Guo, Y., Collins, R., et al. (2013). Physical activity and sedentary leisure time and their associations with BMI, waist circumference, and percentage body fat in 0.5 million adults: the China Kadoorie Biobank study. *Am. J. Clin. Nutr.* 97, 487–496. doi: 10.3945/ajcn.112.046854

Fenton, C., Brooks, F., Spencer, N. H., and Morgan, A. (2010). Sustaining a positive body image in adolescence: an assets-based analysis. *Health Soc. Care Community* 18, 189–198. doi: 10.1111/j.1365-2524.2009.00888.x

Fernández-Bustos, J. G., Contreras, R. O., García, L. M., and Villora, S. G. (2010). Autoconcepto físico según la actividad físicodeportiva realizada y la motivación hacia ésta. *Rev. Lat. Am. Psicol.* 42, 251–263. doi: 10.14349/rlp.v42i2.478

Fernández-Bustos, J. G., González-Martí, I., Contreras, O., and Cuevas, R. (2015). Relación entre imagen corporal y autoconcepto físico en mujeres adolescentes. *Rev. Lat. Am. Psicol.* 47, 25–33. doi: 10.1016/S0120-05 34(15)30003-0

Fernández-Bustos, J. G., Gonzalez-Marti, I., Contreras Jordan, O. R., and Papathomas, A. (2016). Understanding the relationship between physical activity and physical self-perception in adolescent females: the role of body image. *Int. J. Sport Psychol.* 47, 373–379. doi: 10.7352/IJSP2016.47.373

Fox, K. R., and Corbin, C. B. (1989). The physical self-perception profile: development and preliminary validation. *J. Sport Exerc. Psychol.* 11, 408–433. doi: 10.1123/jsep.11.4.408

Fraguela-Vale, R., Varela Garrote, L., and Sanz Arazuri, E. (2016). Ocio deportivo, imagen corporal y satisfacción vital en jóvenes españoles. *Rev. Psicol. Deporte* 25, 33–38. Available at: https://www.rpd-online.com/article/view/v25-n4-fraguela-vale-varela-etal

Goñi, A., Ruiz de Azúa, S., and Liberal, A. (2004). El autoconcepto físico y su medida. Las propiedades psicométricas de un nuevo cuestionario. *Rev. Psicol. Deporte* 13, 195–213. Available at: https://www.rpd-online.com/article/viewFile/199/199

Griffiths, L. J., Parsons, T. J., and Hill, A. J. (2010). Self-esteem and quality of life in obese children and adolescents: a systematic review. *Int. J. Pediatr. Obes.* 5, 282–304. doi: 10.3109/17477160903473697

Grogan, S. (2006). Body image and health: contemporary perspectives. *J. Health Psychol.* 11, 523–530. doi: 10.1177/1359105306065013

Hagger, M. S., Biddle, S. J., and John Wang, C. K. (2005). Physical self-concept in adolescence: generalizability of a multidimensional, hierarchical model across gender and grade. *Educ. Psychol. Meas.* 65, 297–322. doi: 10.1177/0013164404272484

Harter, S. (1999). *The construction of the self. A developmental perspective.* (New York: The Guilford Press).

Hausenblas, H. A., and Fallon, E. A. (2006). Exercise and body image: a meta-analysis. *Psychol. Health* 21, 33–47. doi: 10.1080/14768320500105270

Hu, L. T., and Bentler, P. M. (1999). Cutoff criteria for fit indexes in covariance structure analysis: conventional criteria versus new alternatives. *Struct. Equ. Model. Multidiscip. J.* 6, 1–55. doi: 10.1080/10705519909540118

Iacobucci, D. (2010). Structural equations modeling: fit indices, sample size, and advanced topics. *J. Consum. Psychol.* 20, 90–98. doi: 10.1016/j.jcps.2009.09.003

Ingledew, D. K., and Sullivan, G. (2002). Effects of body mass and body image on exercise motives in adolescence. *Psychol. Sport Exerc.* 3, 323–338. doi: 10.1016/S1469-0292(01)00029-2

Jackson, D. L. (2003). Revisiting sample size and number of parameter estimates: some support for the N: q hypothesis. *Struct. Equ. Model.* 10, 128–141. doi: 10.1207/S15328007SEM1001_6

Kantanista, A., Osiński, W., Borowiec, J., Tomczak, M., and Król-Zielińska, M. (2015). Body image, BMI, and physical activity in girls and boys aged 14–16 years. *Body Image* 15, 40–43. doi: 10.1016/j.bodyim.2015.05.001

Kline, R. (2011). *Principles and practice of structural equation modeling.* (New York: The Guilford Press).

Liu, M., Wu, L., and Ming, Q. (2015). How does physical activity intervention improve self-esteem and self-concept in children and adolescents? Evidence from a meta-analysis. *PLoS One* 10:e0134804. doi: 10.1016/j.bodyim.2005.08.003

Mak, K. K., Cerin, E., McManus, A. M., Lai, C. M., Day, J. R., and Ho, S. Y. (2016). Mediating effects of body composition between physical activity and body esteem in Hong Kong adolescents: a structural equation modeling approach. *Eur. J. Pediatr.* 175, 31–37. doi: 10.1007/s00431-015-2586-5

Marsh, H. W., and Peart, N. D. (1988). Competitive and cooperative physical fitness training programs for girls: effects on physical fitness and multidimensional self-concepts. *J. Sport Exerc. Psychol.* 10, 390–407. doi: 10.1123/jsep.10.4.390

Marsh, H. W., Richards, G. E., Johnson, S., Roche, L., and Tremayne, P. (1994). Physical self-description questionnaire: psychometric properties and a multi trait-multi method analysis of relations to existing instruments. *J. Sport Exerc. Psychol.* 16, 270–305. doi: 10.1123/jsep.16.3.270

Martin-Ginis, K. A., Bassett-Gunter, R. L., and Conlin, C. (2012). "Body image and exercise" in *Oxford handbook of exercise psychology*. ed. E. Acevedo (Oxford, UK: Oxford University Press), 55–75.

Martin-Ginis, K. A., Eng, J. J., Arbour, K. P., Hartman, J. W., and Phillips, S. M. (2005). Mind over muscle?: sex differences in the relationship between body image change and subjective and objective physical changes following a 12-week strength-training program. *Body Image* 2, 363–372. doi: 10.1016/j.bodyim.2005.08.003

Martin-Ginis, K. A., Strong, H. A., Arent, S. M., Bray, S. R., and Bassett-Gunter, R. L. (2014). The effects of aerobic-versus strength-training on body image among young women with pre-existing body image concerns. *Body Image* 11, 219–227. doi: 10.1016/j.bodyim.2014.02.004

McClure, A. C., Tanski, S. E., Kingsbury, J., Gerrard, M., and Sargent, J. D. (2010). Characteristics associated with low self-esteem among US adolescents. *Acad. Pediatr.* 10, 238–244. doi: 10.1016/j.acap.2010.03.007

McGannon, K. R., and Spence, J. C. (2002). The effect of exercise on self-esteem: it is global or domain-specific. *Alberta Cent. Act. Living Update* 9, 1–2.

McIntosh-Dalmedo, S., Devonport, T. J., Nicholls, W., and Friesen, A. P. (2018). Examining the effects of sport and exercise interventions on body image among adolescent girls: a systematic review. *J. Sport Behav.* 41, 245–269. Available at: https://search.proquest.com/docview/2094470188?pq-origsite=gscholar

McMahon, E. M., Corcoran, P., O'Regan, G., Keeley, H., Cannon, M., Carli, V., et al. (2017). Physical activity in European adolescents and associations with anxiety, depression and well-being. *Eur. Child Adolesc. Psychiatry* 26, 111–122. doi: 10.1007/s00787-016-0875-9

Murgui, S., García, C., and García, A. (2016). Efecto de la práctica deportiva en la relación entre las habilidades motoras, el autoconcepto físico y el autoconcepto multidimensional. *Rev. Psicol. Deporte* 25, 19–25. Available at: https://www.rpd-online.com/article/view/v25-n1-murgui-garcia-garcia

Noordstar, J. J., van der Net, J., Jak, S., Helders, P. J., and Jongmans, M. J. (2016). Global self-esteem, perceived athletic competence, and physical activity in children: a longitudinal cohort study. *Psychol. Sport Exerc.* 22, 83–90. doi: 10.1016/j.psychsport.2015.06.009

Penedo, F. J., and Dahn, J. R. (2005). Exercise and well-being: a review of mental and physical health benefits associated with physical activity. *Curr. Opin. Psychiatry* 18, 189–193. doi: 10.1097/00001504-200503000-00013

Raich, R. M., Mora, M., Soler, A., Ávila, C., Clos, I., and Zapater, L. (1996). Adaptación de un instrumento de evaluación de la insatisfacción corporal. *Clín. y Salud* 7, 51–66.

Reddon, H., Meyre, D., and Cairney, J. (2017). Physical activity and global self-worth in a longitudinal study of children. *Med. Sci. Sports Exerc.* 49, 1606–1613. doi: 10.1249/MSS.0000000000001275

Robins, R. W., and Trzesniewski, K. H. (2005). Self-esteem development across the lifespan. *Curr. Dir. Psychol. Sci.* 14, 158–162. doi: 10.1111/j.0963-7214.2005.00353

Robinson, T. N., Matheson, D. M., Kraemer, H. C., Wilson, D. M., Obarzanek, E., Thompson, N. S., et al. (2010). A randomized controlled trial of culturally tailored dance and reducing screen time to prevent weight gain in low-income African American girls: Stanford GEMS. *Arch. Pediatr. Adolesc. Med.* 164, 995–1004. doi: 10.1001/archpediatrics.2010.197

Rodríguez, M. N., and Ruiz, M. A. (2008). Atenuación de la asimetría y de la curtosis de las puntuaciones observadas mediante transformaciones de variables: incidencia sobre la estructura factorial. *Psicológica* 29, 205–227. Available at: http://www.redalyc.org/articulo.oa?id=16929206

Rosenberg, M. (1985). "Self-concept and psychological well-being in adolescence" in *The development of the self.* ed. R. L. Leary (New York: Academic Press), 205–246.

Sabiston, C. M., Pila, E., Vani, M., and Thogersen-Ntoumani, C. (2018). Body image, physical activity, and sport: a scoping review. *Psychol. Sport Exerc.* 42, 48–57. doi: 10.1016/j.psychsport.2018.12.010

Sani, S. H. Z., Fathirezaie, Z., Brand, S., Pühse, U., Holsboer-Trachsler, E., Gerber, M., et al. (2016). Physical activity and self-esteem: testing direct and indirect relationships associated with psychological and physical mechanisms. *Neuropsychiatr. Dis. Treat.* 12, 2617–2625. doi: 10.2147/ndt.s116811

Schumacker, R. E., and Lomax, R. G. (2010). *A beginner's guide to structural equation modeling.* (New York, US: Routledge/Taylor & Francis Group).

Shavelson, R. J., Hubner, J. J., and Stanton, G. C. (1976). Self-concept: validation of construct interpretations. *Rev. Educ. Res.* 46, 407–441. doi: 10.2307/1170010

Slutzky, C. B., and Simpkins, S. D. (2009). The link between children's sport participation and self-esteem: exploring the mediating role of sport self-concept. *Psychol. Sport Exerc.* 10, 381–389. doi: 10.1016/j.psychsport.2008.09.006

Sonstroem, R. J. (1997). "The physical self-system: a mediator of exercise and self-esteem" in *The physical self. From motivation to well-being.* ed. K. R. Fox (Champaign: Human Kinetics), 3–26.

Sonstroem, R. J., Harlow, L. L., and Josephs, L. (1994). Exercise and self-esteem: validity of model expansion and exercise associations. *J. Sport Exerc. Psychol.* 16, 29–42. doi: 10.1123/jsep.16.1.29

Sonstroem, R. J., and Morgan, W. P. (1989). Exercise and self-esteem: rationale and model. *Med. Sci. Sports Exerc.* 21, 329–337. doi: 10.1249/00005768-198906000-00018

Stice, E., and Shaw, H. E. (2002). Role of body dissatisfaction in the onset and maintenance of eating pathology: a synthesis of research findings. *J. Psychosom. Res.* 53, 985–993. doi: 10.1016/S0022-3999(02)00488-9

Strauss, R. S. (2000). Childhood obesity and self-esteem. *Pediatrics* 105:e15. doi: 10.1542/peds.105.1.e15

Thompson, J. K., and Smolak, L. (2001). *Body image, eating disorders, and obesity in youth: Assessment, prevention, and treatment.* (Washington, DC: American Psychological Association).

Van den Berg, P. A., Mond, J., Eisenberg, M., Ackard, D., and Neumark-Sztainer, D. (2010). The link between body dissatisfaction and self-esteem in adolescents: similarities across gender, age, weight status, race/ethnicity, and socioeconomic status. *J. Adolesc. Health* 47, 290–296. doi: 10.1016/j.jadohealth.2010.02.004

World Health Organization, Department of Mental Health, Substance Abuse, World Psychiatric Association, International Association for Child, Adolescent Psychiatry, and Allied Professions (2005). *Atlas: Child and adolescent mental health resources: Global concerns, implications for the future.* (Geneva, Switzerland: World Health Organization).

Zulaika, L. (2002). Educación física y autoconcepto. Análisis relacionales y eficacia de un programa de intervención para la mejora del autoconcepto físico. *Apunts* 67:114. Available at: https://dialnet.unirioja.es/servlet/articulo?codigo=242829

20

Effects on Personal Factors Through Flipped Learning and Gamification as Combined Methodologies in Secondary Education

Adrián Segura-Robles[1]*, Arturo Fuentes-Cabrera*[2]**, María Elena Parra-González*[1] *and Jesús López-Belmonte*[2]

[1] Department of Research Methods and Diagnosis in Education, University of Granada, Granada, Spain, [2] Department of Didactics and School Organization, University of Granada, Granada, Spain

***Correspondence:**
Arturo Fuentes-Cabrera
arturofuentes@ugr.es

Purpose: This study aims to analyze the effects of a flipped and gamified program on the autonomy, competence, relation with others, satisfaction/enjoyment, intrinsic and extrinsic motivation, and boredom of students of Physical Education.

Method: The study used a control group and an experimental group to compare pretest and posttest data in both of them. Instruments used were the Basic Psychological Needs in Exercise Scale, Sport Motivation Scale, and Sport Satisfaction Instrument, all of them validated in academic literature.

Results: On one hand, data indicated that autonomy has been increased with the application of these teaching methodologies. On the other hand, students' satisfaction, enjoyment, and intrinsic motivation have improved based on the interaction with gamification and flipped learning. Finally, with all dimensions, it seems that academic performance has been improved, although not in a significative way.

Discussion/Conclusion: Results of the study provide to educational researchers valuable information for a better understanding of how flipped learning and gamification influence personal performance of Physical Education students.

Keywords: autonomy, motivation, Physical Education, flipped learning, gamification

INTRODUCTION

The intrinsic technological nature of the current era is promoting continuous changes in people's daily actions (Maldonado et al., 2019). Especially, in the field of education, technology is reaching a leading role (Area et al., 2016). This has led to the emergence of new ways of teaching and learning content from an innovative perspective, in which students assume a greater role (Li et al., 2019). Educational innovation in the new millennium has driven the emergence and constant development of training activities focused on student participation (Pereira et al., 2019). All this derives in the promulgation of the concept of active methodology as a new way of transmitting and generating a knowledge shared and elaborated by the students themselves, guided by the teacher for an optimal achievement of the objectives and consolidation of the contents (Kerrigan, 2018).

This new direction taken by the teaching practice has meant an increase in the motivation and attitude of the students (Álvarez-Rodríguez et al., 2019) due to the new opportunities and means of learning that the students have within their reach (Mat et al., 2019), bringing today's education closer to the singularities of a digital society (Nikolopoulou et al., 2019). This has encouraged not only the deployment of new ways of imparting the contents but also the appearance of new spaces and times for the instructional process (Nogueira et al., 2018), what is known as ubiquity (Cabero and Barroso, 2018).

To adapt today's education to the new demands of students developed in a time of great technological stimulation, the innovative actions of teachers, to improve the quality of training and student satisfaction, have resulted in the projection of methodological approaches. Among them are gamification and its variants such as escape room, and flipped learning, as a combination between the face-to-face and virtuality of learning moments (Parra-González et al., 2020). Specifically, in the subject of Physical Education, innovative practices are proliferating to impart the contents from a new approach in order to encourage the attitude of students on their way to effective and motivating learning (Quintero et al., 2018; Kang and Kang, 2019; Rodríguez et al., 2019; Wyant and Baek, 2019).

Gamification is one of the active methodologies that has reached a great penetration in the learning spaces of our day (Sánchez et al., 2020). This formative approach is based on the game and the transformation of formal contexts into playful learning spaces (Hanus and Fox, 2015; González et al., 2016). Despite its expansion in current teaching practice, the use of games for content delivery has been developing since the 1960s (Malone and Lepper, 1987). This game-centered approach aims to facilitate the student's effort to achieve the learning objectives and adapt to the demands, needs, and interests of the collective (Oliva, 2017; Parra-González et al., 2019). The games used have evolved over time, from the most classic of childhood to those with a large digital load that generate immersion in a virtual reality (Contreras-Espinosa, 2016). And its potential has been verified in different educational stages, positioning it as a suitable methodology for any age range (Giannakos, 2013; Dib and Adamo-Villani, 2014; Su and Cheng, 2015).

With gamification, students prepare their own knowledge structures supported by academic indicators benefited such as motivation (Pisabarro and Vivaracho, 2018; Groening and Binnewies, 2019), attitude (Lee et al., 2013; Pérez-Manzano and Almela-Baeza, 2018), interest, autonomy (Xi and Hamari, 2019), commitment (Chu and Hung, 2015), dedication (Simões et al., 2013; Wang, 2015), attraction (Area and González, 2015), collaboration (Perrotta et al., 2013), interactions between agents (teacher-students and content) (Parra-González and Segura-Robles, 2019), and problem-solving capacity (Kapp, 2012) in activities to develop.

An essential aspect of gamification is the incentive that the student receives in any progress or step that is being achieved, which has a positive impact on the psychosocial indicators, previously exposed and that are directly connected with the performance obtained by the students (Mekler et al., 2017). The recent literature on gamified practices in Physical Education reflects the potential of this teaching and learning methodology, contributing to the improvement of various academic indicators, such as motivation, involvement, and student satisfaction (Mora-González et al., 2020). The escape room is conceived as a training modality based on the gamification of the student's learning environment. This didactic approach is based on the resolution of challenges and problems raised that give rise to various instructional situations where students have to put their knowledge into practice (Agreda et al., 2019).

This methodological innovation is based on a game, challenge, or problem that students have to solve both autonomously (self-management of knowledge) and collaboratively (shared knowledge management), encouraging the participation of students in a problematic situation of a real nature or invented by the teacher (Wynn and Okie, 2017). In every escape room, students are locked in classrooms or different spaces where they have to perform different tasks, activities, challenges, tests, and riddles, among others, to obtain the "key" in a certain time that will allow them to leave the place (López-Pernas et al., 2019).

The expert literature on the state of the matter reflects that the development of training practices through escape room promotes the improvement of various academic indicators already mentioned previously by gamification. Specifically, this gamified practice improves motivation (Borrego et al., 2017), activation, participation (Sierra and Fernández Sánchez, 2019), satisfaction, attitude, and attraction of students for the learning actions to be carried out (Pérez et al., 2019) to assimilate and reinforce the contents (Eukel et al., 2017).

All these improvements produced have a direct and positive impact on student grades and, consequently, student performance (Hursen and Bass, 2019). The latter is enhanced as a result of this innovative practice of transmitting, reinforcing, and consolidating knowledge developed by the student himself in a collaborative learning experience experienced and experienced in the first person (Kinio et al., 2019).

In the field of Physical Education, these innovative practices of a gamified nature are already being carried out. Recent research reveals proposals and recommendations to efficiently perform an escape room in the classrooms to impart the contents of that subject. Also, experts in this line of study offer guidance, resources, and ideas for optimal development by teachers less experienced in the use of this training methodology (Flores, 2019; Segura and Parra, 2019).

Due to the high rate of sedentary lifestyle and obesity in the youngest population (Talarico and Janssen, 2018), it is necessary to increase the time of physical activity during the class time of the Physical Education subject. Students are in as long as possible on the move One solution to reduce the time of explanations of the contents, activities, tasks, and games to be performed is flipped learning. This innovative methodology is presented as a mix between face-to-face and digital training (Mengual et al., 2020).

This innovation of a hybrid nature implies a greater use of class time and greater activity of students because the explanations have been made prior to the face-to-face session and digitally in other contexts (Bergmann and Sams, 2012). The teacher's role is focused on generating audiovisual content so that students can view them on any mobile device with an Internet connection (López et al., 2019a). In this way, class time is devoted to deepening the didactic content and solving the students' doubts since the phase of explanation and assimilation of contents has been carried out outside the classroom (Bognar et al., 2019). This promotes an alteration and inversion of learning moments. First, the student visualizes the content at home or in any place suitable for learning and in the classroom, the assimilated in the digital environment is reinforced and implemented (Long et al., 2017).

Flipped learning is presented in impact literature as a didactic approach that has achieved relevant popularity and effectiveness at different levels, stages, and educational contexts (He et al., 2016; López et al., 2019b; Zainuddin et al., 2019). All this is reflected in various studies that demonstrate how the application of this mixed approach to learning improves motivation (Tse et al., 2019), teamwork (Kwon and Woo, 2017), attitude (Lee et al., 2018), participation and activation (Chyr et al., 2017), autonomy (González and Carrillo, 2016), commitment (Huang et al., 2018), and interactions between the agents involved and with the contents (Hwang et al., 2015). All this has a positive impact on students' grades and performance (Karabulut et al., 2018; Nortvig et al., 2018; Sola et al., 2019).

In particular, the application of flipped learning in Physical Education has shown encouraging results as reflected in the reported studies (Hinojo et al., 2018, 2020), placing this innovative approach as a methodological alternative to impart the own contents of Physical Education and, in the same way, increase intrinsic factors of the learning process such as motivation, autonomy, problem solving, the use of class time, the interaction between teacher–student, student–student, and student–content, and the deepening of content and ratings.

In short, different recent high-impact researches show the potentialities of the instructional approaches previously presented (Luong, 2019; Østerlie and Kjelaas, 2019; Quintas et al., 2020; Sargent and Casey, 2020). The novelty that this study presents concerning the existing literature focuses on the simultaneous integration of both training methodologies for the approach of contents linked to the subject of Physical Education. Despite the scientific volume that covers these teaching and learning methodologies separately in the field of education in general, the interest aroused in this work focuses on the combination of both methodological innovations in the field of physical activity and sport. Therefore, research is required to promote a change in the point of view of professionals in this educational sector, as well as the development of new training experiences adapted to the new times (Cañabate et al., 2019).

MATERIALS AND METHODS

Research Design and Data Analysis

This research has been carried out through experimental and pre-post design based on the quantitative design as indicated by experts (Hernández et al., 2014; Pérez-Escoda, 2018). This type of design has already demonstrated its effectiveness as a tool to know the effects of different tools or methodologies in the educational field (Juliá-Hurtado and Baena-Extremera, 2018; Epelde-Larrañaga et al., 2020). The objective of pre–post studies is to observe over time and to check the influence of different variables on the study population. In traditional pre–post studies, differences are only observed in one study group (Gravetter and Forzano, 2009). In order to give the results more robustness, a control group is added to the study to which no methodologies are applied. The objective is to provide the results with greater validity.

The students were divided into two groups, which we named experimental and control groups. There was a pretest and a posttest analysis in each group. The intervention on the experimental group consisted of teaching through the methodology and technique of flipped learning and escape room. In contrast, the control group follows a traditional methodology, without the use of any specific methodology.

All statistics have been carried out with the Statistical Package for the Social Sciences (SPSS) v25 program. Before carrying out the different analysis, the normality of the sample is checked, using the Kolmogorov–Smirnov test, and obtaining significant results, so that non-parametric statistics is used to perform inferential analysis. To test effect size, we use Cohen d. Effect size is a quantitative measure of the magnitude of the experimenter effect. The larger the effect size, the stronger the relationship between two variables (Harlow et al., 2016; Lenhard and Lenhard, 2016).

Participants

The participants who took part in this research were 64 students enrolled at third grade of secondary school. Other studies of a certain impact show that the size of the sample in this kind of researches does not condition the performance of these experiments (Rodríguez, 2011).

The selection of the sample was carried out through an intentional sampling due to the ease of access to the students. They are enrolled in an educational secondary school in the Autonomous City of Ceuta (Spain). This research came out as a need that one of the researchers, who also work there as a teacher, detected that something needed to be done to improve a situation.

Specifically, the students were selected from the third year of Secondary Education (n = 64; mean age = 15 years; SD = 1.62). The configuration of the two groups on which the experimentation was carried out is specified in **Table 1**.

Instruments

The instruments used to carry out this research were four scales. The first one was the Basic Psychological Needs in Exercise Scale; the version used in this research was the one validated and translated into Spanish (Moreno et al., 2008). The dimensions used and to be analyzed were autonomy, competence, and relation with others (for example, I feel like I can communicate openly with my classmates). It had a Likert-type scale from 1 (totally disagree) to 5 (totally agree).

The second scale, which was used, was Sport Motivation Scale, which was adapted to Physical Education as well (Granero-Gallegos et al., 2014), used to analyze extrinsic and intrinsic

TABLE 1 | Study groups by sex.

Groups	Boys n (%)	Girls n (%)	Total n (%)
Experimental group	17 (53.12)	15 (46.87)	32 (50)
Control group	11 (34.75)	21 (65.62)	32 (50)
Subtotal	28 (43.75)	36 (56.25)	64 (100)

motivation (for example, for the pleasure of living stimulating experiences), also with a Likert-type scale from 1 (totally disagree) to 5 (totally agree).

The third scale used was the Sport Satisfaction Instrument. The one used was the Spanish version also adapted to Physical Education (Baena-Extremera et al., 2012) to measure the satisfaction/enjoyment and boredom (for example, I usually find Physical Education in English interesting), also with a Likert-type scale from 1 (totally disagree) to 5 (totally agree). In addition, the last scale was used only at the posttest moment to measure the academic achievement. The decision about which factors were going to be analyzed was taken due to the dimensions of the questionnaire, the factors that can be influenced by the implementation of active methodologies on teaching and learning process, and both of these aspects were followed up after the scientific literature revision which was done.

Procedure

In relation to the procedure, pretests were administered to both control and experimental groups. Then, a teaching methodology based on flipped classroom and escape room was used with the experimental group. Afterward, posttests were applied on both groups to analyze the outcomes (**Figure 1**). Time between pretests and posttests was 5 weeks.

Intervention

A didactic unit consisting of eight sessions on contents related to physical condition and health was carried out to work the physical qualities such as strength, endurance, and speed. With the control group, the sessions were carried out in a traditional way. The teacher was in charge of designing the physical tasks and activities to be carried out by the student. The role assumed by the teacher in this group was purely expository and face-to-face. The teacher focused on explaining the activities of each session in the corresponding installation, always in person, and the student limited himself to carrying out the tasks without taking the lead or choosing the actions to be carried out. The training actions focused on general fitness circuits using training materials, as well as cooperative motor games. On the contrary, in the experimental group, the teacher presented audiovisual materials on a content management platform so that the students could visualize them before going to the face-to-face session. Once the students went to the class, they already had a knowledge base and information about the activities and challenges to carry out. In this group, the teacher's role is more passive. The student acquires all the prominence since he is the main agent who has to carry out each of the tests, challenges, and enigmas of the designed escape room. The tests, challenges performed by the students in the escape room had a physical component with the purpose of working on the physical qualities mentioned above. In addition, students could dress up and characterize based on the theme of the escape room. Therefore, the teacher grants the students of the experimental group autonomy and freedom to investigate, explore, and collaborate to pass all the tests and solve the final puzzle, thus including all the elements used during the experimentation.

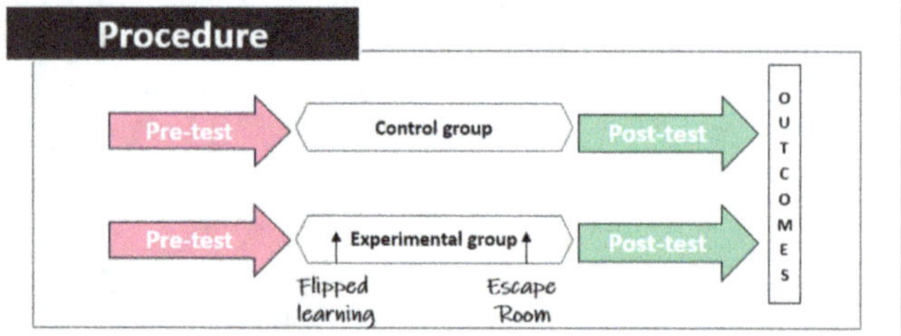

FIGURE 1 | Experimentation procedure.

RESULTS

Before carrying out the different descriptive and inferential analyses, the reliability of the instruments used through Cronbach's alpha is checked. All the results obtained show satisfactory results for each of the dimensions (Bonett and Wright, 2015).

In addition, the omega index (ω) is calculated, which, unlike the alpha coefficient, works with the factor loads, being a test less biased than the classical alpha (Salazar Vargas and Serpa Barrientos, 2017). In the same way, the results show acceptable values, between 0.70 and 0.90 (**Table 2**; Campo-Arias and Oviedo, 2008).

Table 3 shows the values obtained in the pre–post tests performed for the control group and the experimental group being similar. The highest values in the control group were obtained for competition (4.61 ± 0.13) and the lowest for extrinsic motivation (2.21 ± 0.83). Similarly, the highest values in the pretest control group were obtained for satisfaction (3.29 ± 1.02). It is in the values of the subsequent test of the experimental group that the data seem to change significantly, so that, following the main objective of the study, inferential analyses are performed on pre–post values in the control group and the experimental group to prove it.

Table 4 shows the results obtained after the analysis of the values obtained in the posttest in learning achievement dimension. This dimension is calculated using the evaluation obtained by the students at the end of classes, so it is only considered as a posttest result. Values do not show significant differences ($Z = -1.125$; $p = 0.071$). These differences, despite being unique, do not show great strength ($d = 0.11$). In this case,

TABLE 2 | Reliability and validity indices.

	Alpha (α)	Omega (ω)
Autonomy	0.87	0.89
Competence	0.90	0.88
Relation with others	0.81	0.83
Satisfaction/enjoyment	0.89	0.85
Extrinsic motivation	0.82	0.83
Intrinsic motivation	0.80	0.78
Boredom	0.84	0.81

TABLE 3 | Mean (M) and standard deviation (SD) of the results for the pretest and posttest.

	Pretest	Posttest
Traditional Learning (Control group)		
	Mean (SD)	**Mean (SD)**
Autonomy	4.09 (0.25)	4.15 (0.11)
Competence	4.10 (0.27)	4.61 (0.13)
Relation with others	3.53 (0.12)	3.49 (0.32)
Satisfaction/enjoyment	3.29 (1.02)	3.12 (0.32)
Extrinsic motivation	2.50 (0.73)	2.21 (0.83)
Intrinsic motivation	2.41 (0.51)	2.51 (0.60)
Boredom	3.31 (0.25)	3.50 (0.42)
Learning achievement		4.71 (1.91)
Gamified–Flipped Learning (Experimental group)		
	Pretest	**Posttest**
	Mean (SD)	**Mean (SD)**
Autonomy	3.99 (0.14)	4.81 (0.21)
Competence	3.82 (0.37)	4.50 (0.33)
Relation with others	4.01 (0.24)	4.91 (0.12)
Satisfaction/enjoyment	3.62 (0.71)	4.71 (0.47)
Extrinsic motivation	2.51 (0.51)	2.91 (0.61)
Intrinsic motivation	2.11 (0.42)	3.60 (0.51)
Boredom	3.20 (0.15)	1.10 (0.52)
Learning achievement		4.90 (1.01)

TABLE 4 | Mann–Whitney *U* test for learning achievement.

		Mean Rank	U	Z	p	d*
Posttest	**Traditional**	51.13	112.000	−1.125	0.071	–
	Gamified–Flipped Learning	55.12				

**The effect size of the statistical analyses was determined using Cohen's d (d_{cohen}) (Cohen, 1988).*

TABLE 5 | Wilcoxon test for dimensions in pre–post in traditional learning.

Dimensions	Groups	Mean Rank	Z	P	d
Autonomy	Pretest	40.11	1,181	0.052	–
	Posttest	42.55			
Competence	Pretest	27.17	2,224	0.055	–
	Posttest	29.09			
Relation with others	Pretest	53.35	1,347	0.261	–
	Posttest	56.19			
Satisfaction/enjoyment	Pretest	33.12	2,389	0.055	–
	Posttest	27.11			
Extrinsic motivation	Pretest	65.17	−1,288	0.071	–
	Posttest	61.35			
Intrinsic motivation	Pretest	21.13	3,436	0.002*	0.42
	Posttest	32.17			
Boredom	Pretest	38.12	−2,017	0.264*	–
	Posttest	33.94			

**Significant difference.*

TABLE 6 | Wilcoxon test for dimensions in pre–post in flipped and gamified learning.

Dimensions	Groups	Mean Rank	Z	p	d
Autonomy	Pretest	41.10	1,781	0.003*	0.22
	Posttest	53.60			
Competence	Pretest	31.07	2,224	0.060	–
	Posttest	33.10			
Relation with others	Pretest	61.32	1,047	0.002*	0.13
	Posttest	69.27			
Satisfaction/enjoyment	Pretest	23.12	2,389	0.005*	0.29
	Posttest	42.98			
Extrinsic motivation	Pretest	73.97	−2,288	0.055	–
	Posttest	60.10			
Intrinsic motivation	Pretest	21.13	2,288	0.003*	0.31
	Posttest	41.87			
Boredom	Pretest	49.01	−3,017	0.002*	0.33
	Posttest	32.10			

**Significant difference.*

flipped learning obtained a higher mean rank ($MR = 60.82$) value than traditional learning ($MR = 40.23$).

Similarly, results are analyzed in the control group (pre–post) in each of the dimensions analyzed. **Table 5** does not show significant differences between pre and post values in most dimensions. It is only Intrinsic motivation ($Z = -2{,}288$, $p = 0.55$, $d = 0.42$), in this case, effect size can be considered medium.

In **Table 6**, Wilcoxon signed-rank test shows that flipped and gamified intervention in the experimental group had a statistically significant change in five of seven dimensions analyzed. Autonomy has improved positively, obtaining results of $Z = 1{,}781$, $p = 0.03$. Although these differences are significant, they show a small effect size ($d = 0.22$). In the same way, Relation with others ($Z = 1{,}047$, $p = 0.02$, $d = 0.13$), Satisfaction/enjoyment ($Z = 2{,}389$, $p = 0.05$, $d = 0.29$), intrinsic motivation ($Z = 2{,}288$, $p = 0.03$, $d = 0.31$), and Boredom ($Z = -3{,}017$, $p = 0.02$, $d = 0.33$) show significant differences too. Effects sizes to all of them can be considered small. Only Competence ($Z = 2{,}224$, $p = 0.60$) and Extrinsic motivation ($Z = -2{,}288$, $p = 0.55$) do not show significant differences.

DISCUSSION

The present study shows the influence of techniques related to new teaching models, in learning outcomes, and in different variables related to it. Current teaching must at some time be a process of constant change in teaching practice and in the daily memory of students, with constant transformations (Maldonado et al., 2019). For this, the use of active methodologies that lead to the achievement of objectives is essential (Kerrigan, 2018), as well as the use of new ways to impart in terms of spaces and time they are related (Nogueira et al., 2018).

In this experimentation, progress in learning has been compared, referring to different variables, of two groups, which have served as control and experimental groups.

The values studied in both groups have been measured before the experiment. Subsequently, a measurement of these values has been made, obtaining interesting and specific results with the application of the new methodologies.

From the study, it can be extracted that values such as autonomy have been increased with the application of these teaching models coinciding with Parra-González et al. (2020), which is to be expected especially in the application of inverted learning as a tool for the acquisition of knowledge. In addition, social relations have been increased as a result of the implementation of new methods, as indicated by other studies (Rodríguez et al., 2019).

It should be noted that the increase in satisfaction and enjoyment that students have obtained based on the interaction with gamification and flipped learning, which corroborate the results and coincide with what has been indicated in other investigations (Area and González, 2015) and in other studies related to psychosocial factors (Mekler et al., 2017). Of course, and in accordance with what has been indicated in previous research (Pisabarro and Vivaracho, 2018), there is also an increase in the intrinsic motivation of students, which implies a better acceptance of teaching and a greater predisposition to learning, eliminating glimpses of boredom in students, which entails and connects, directly, with a better performance obtained by students, as in other cases of implementation of these methodologies (Groening and Binnewies, 2019).

However, in the experimentation, there are no significant changes in variables such as student competence, as well as in extrinsic motivation, which is not consistent with that reported by other studies and authors (Mora-González et al., 2020), without influencing the future of the student (Hinojo et al., 2020) and without having an important significance for the final result.

The prospect of this study focuses on making the scientific community aware of the potential of the combination of active methodologies, both face-to-face and digital, in the teaching and learning process in the field of Physical Education, with the purpose to raise awareness among the teaching group of the benefits reported after its application.

The main limitation of this research focuses on the nature of the sample, which is situated in a single context with certain peculiarities at a social and geographical level. This projects that the results achieved here are taken with caution as the replication of this research in other contexts may vary the findings presented here.

Therefore, as a future line of study, this study is intended to be carried out in different contexts in order to verify and consolidate the potential and advantages of this methodological combination. It can be concluded that both flipped learning for content teaching and gamification to achieve the objectives are methodologies that improve student learning, as well as multiple factors associated with the education of students in current classrooms and autonomy, relationship with others, enjoyment, intrinsic motivation, and boredom. The appearance of these teaching methods should not be renounced in a changing world that has its greatest challenge in teaching.

ETHICS STATEMENT

Ethical review and approval was not required for the study on human participants in accordance with the local legislation and institutional requirements. Written informed consent to participate in this study was provided by the participants' tutors.

AUTHOR CONTRIBUTIONS

AS-R and MP-G conceived the hypothesis of this study, analyzed the data, and performed the data interpretation of statistical analysis. AF-C and JL-B participated in data collection and wrote the manuscript with the most significant input. All authors contributed, read, and approved the final manuscript.

REFERENCES

Agreda, M., Ortiz, A., Tallón, S., and López, J. (2019). "Escape rooms: actividades gamificadas para la formación de profesionales educativos," in *Innovación y Tecnología en Contextos Educativos*, eds E. Sánchez-Rivas, J. Ruiz-Palmero, and E. Sánchez-Vega (Málaga: UMA Editorial), 399–409.

Álvarez-Rodríguez, M. D., Bellido-Márquez, M., and Atencia-Barrero, P. (2019). Enseñanza artística mediante TIC en la educación secundaria obligatoria. *Rev. Educ. Distancia* 1, 1–19. doi: 10.6018/red/59/05

Area, M., and González, C. S. (2015). De la enseñanza con libros de texto al aprendizaje en espacios online gamificados. *Educatio* 33, 1–19. doi: 10.3916/C47-2016-08

Area, M., Hernández, V., and Sosa, J. J. (2016). Models of educational integration of ICTs in the classroom. *Comunicar* 24, 79–87. doi: 10.3916/C47-2016-08

Baena-Extremera, A., Granero-Gallegos, A., Pérez-Quero, F. J., and Bracho-Amador, C. (2012). Versión española del sport satisfaction instrument (SSI) adaptado a la educación física. *Rev. Psicod.* 17, 377–395. doi: 10.1387/RevPsicodidact.4037

Bergmann, J., and Sams, A. (2012). *Flip Your Classroom: Reach Every Student in Every Class Every Day*. Oregon: International Society for Technology in Education.

Bognar, B., Sabliæ, M., and Škugor, A. (2019). "Flipped learning and online discussion in higher education teaching," in *Didactics of Smart Pedagogy*, ed. L. Daniela (Cham: Springer International Publishing), 371–392. doi: 10.1007/978-3-030-01551-0_19

Bonett, D. G., and Wright, T. A. (2015). Cronbach's alpha reliability: interval estimation, hypothesis testing, and sample size planning. *J. Organ. Behav.* 36, 3–15. doi: 10.1002/job.1960

Borrego, C., Fernández, C., Blanes, I., and Robles, S. (2017). Room escape at class: escape games activities to facilitate the motivation and learning in computer science. *J. Technol. Sci. Educ.* 7, 162–171. doi: 10.3926/jotse.247

Cabero, J., and Barroso, J. (2018). Los escenarios tecnológicos en realidad aumentada (RA): posibilidades educativas. *Aula Abierta* 47, 327–336. doi: 10.17811/rifie.47.3.2018.327-336

Cañabate, D., Tesouro, M., Puiggalí, J., and Zalagaz, M. L. (2019). Estado actual de la educación física desde el punto de vista del profesorado. Propuestas de mejora. *Retos* 35, 47–53.

Campo-Arias, A., and Oviedo, H. C. (2008). Propiedades psicométricas de una escala: la consistencia interna. *Rev. Salud Pública* 10, 831–839. doi: 10.1590/S0124-00642008000500015

Chu, H. C., and Hung, C. M. (2015). Effects of the digital game-development approach on elementary school students' learning motivation, problem solving, and learning achievement. *Int. J. Distance Educ. Technol.* 13, 87–102. doi: 10.4018/ijdet.2015010105

Chyr, W. L., Shen, P. D., Chiang, Y. C., Lin, J. B., and Tsai, C. W. (2017). Exploring the effects of online academic help-seeking and flipped learning on improving students'. *Learn. Educ. Technol. Soc.* 20, 11–23.

Cohen, J. (1988). *Statistical Power Analysis for the Behavioral Sciences.* Hillsdale, NJ: Erlbaum.

Contreras-Espinosa, R. S. (2016). Presentación. Juegos digitales y gamificación aplicados en el ámbito de la educación. *RIED* 19, 27–33. doi: 10.5944/ried.19.2.16143

Dib, H., and Adamo-Villani, N. (2014). Serious sustainability challenge game to promote teaching and learning of building sustainability. *J. Comput. Civ. Eng.* 28, 1–11. doi: 10.1061/(ASCE)CP.1943-5487.0000357

Epelde-Larrañaga, A., Oñederra Ramírez, J., and Estrada-Vidal, L. (2020). Music as a resource against bullying and cyberbullying: intervention in two centers in Spain. *Sustainability* 12:2057. doi: 10.3390/su12052057

Eukel, H. N., Frenzel, J. E., and Cernusca, D. (2017). Educational gaming for pharmacy students - design and evaluation of a diabetes-themed escape room. *Am. J. Pharm. Educ.* 81, 1–5. doi: 10.5688/ajpe8176265

Flores, G. (2019). ¿Jugamos al súper mario bros? Descripción de una experiencia gamificada en la formación del profesorado de educación física. *Retos* 36, 529–534.

Giannakos, M. N. (2013). Enjoy and learn with educational games: examining factors affecting learning performance. *Comput. Educ.* 68, 429–439. doi: 10.1016/j.compedu.2013.06.005

González, C. S., Gómez, N., Navarro, V., Cairós, M., Quirce, C., Toledo, P., et al. (2016). Learning healthy lifestyles through active videogames, motor games and the gamification of educational activities. *Comput. Hum. Behav.* 55, 529–551. doi: 10.1007/s10916-019-1293-6

González, N., and Carrillo, G. A. (2016). El aprendizaje cooperativo y la flipped classroom: una pareja ideal mediada por las TIC. *Aularia Rev. Digit. Comun.* 5, 43–48.

Granero-Gallegos, A., Baena-Extremera, A., Gómez-López, M., Sánchez-Fuentes, J. A., and Abraldes, J. A. (2014). Psychometric properties of the «sport motivation scale (SMS)» adapted to Physical Education. *J. Sports Sci. Med.* 13, 801–807.

Gravetter, F. J., and Forzano, L.-A. B. (2009). *Research Methods For The Behavioral Sciences.* Bosto, MA: Cengage Wadsworth.

Groening, C., and Binnewies, C. (2019). "Achievement unlocked!"-The impact of digital achievements as a gamification element on motivation and performance. *Comput. Hum. Behav.* 97, 151–166. doi: 10.1016/j.chb.2019.02.026

Hanus, M. D., and Fox, J. (2015). Assessing the effects of gamification in the classroom: a longitudinal study on intrinsic motivation, social comparison, satisfaction, effort, and academic performance. *Comput. Educ.* 80, 152–161. doi: 10.1016/j.compedu.2014.08.019

Harlow, L. L., Mulaik, S. A., and Steiger, J. H. (2016). *What if There Were No Significance Tests?.* Abingdon: Routledge. doi: 10.4324/9781315629049

He, W., Holton, A., Farkas, G., and Warschauer, M. (2016). The effects of flipped instruction on out-of-class study time, exam performance, and student perceptions. *Learn. Instr.* 45, 61–71. doi: 10.1016/j.learninstruc.2016.07.001

Hernández, R., Fernández, C., and Baptista, M. P. (2014). *Metodología de la Investigación.* Mexico, DF: McGrawHill.

Hinojo, F. J., López, J., Fuentes, A., Trujillo, J. M., and Pozo, S. (2020). Academic effects of the use of flipped learning in physical education. *Int. J. of Environ. Res. Public Health* 17, 1–14. doi: 10.3390/ijerph17010276

Hinojo, F. J., Mingorance, ÁC., Trujillo, J. M., Aznar, I., and Cáceres, M. P. (2018). Incidence of the flipped classroom in the physical education students' academic performance in university contexts. *Sustainability* 10, 1–13. doi: 10.3390/su10051334

Huang, B., Foon, K., and Kwan, C. (2018). Investigating the effects of gamification-enhanced flipped learning on undergraduate students' behavioral and cognitive engagement. *Interact. Learn. Environ.* 1, 1–21. doi: 10.1080/10494820.2018.1495653

Hursen, C., and Bass, C. (2019). Use of gamification applications in science education. *Int. J. Emerg. Technol. Learn.* 14, 4–23. doi: 10.3991/ijet.v14i01.8894

Hwang, G. J., Lai, C. L., and Wang, S. Y. (2015). Seamless flipped learning: a mobile technology-enhanced flipped classroom with effective learning strategies. *J. Comput. Educ.* 2, 449–473. doi: 10.1007/s40692-015-0043-0

Juliá-Hurtado, P., and Baena-Extremera, A. (2018). Mejora de la motivación y las metas sociales tras la realización de una unidad didáctica de escalada. *ESPIRAL Cuadernos del profesorado* 11, 46–51. doi: 10.25115/ecp.v11i21.1916

Kang, S., and Kang, S. (2019). The study on the application of virtual reality in adapted physical education. *Cluster Comput.* 22, 2351–2355. doi: 10.1007/s10586-018-2254-4

Kapp, K. M. (2012). The Gamification of Learning and Instruction: Game-Based Methods and Strategies for Training and Education. San Francisco: ASTD. doi: 10.1145/2207270.2211316

Karabulut, A., Jaramillo, N., and Hassall, L. (2018). Flipping to engage students: instructor perspectives on flipping large enrolment courses. *Australas. J. Educ. Technol.* 34, 123–137. doi: 10.14742/ajet.4036

Kerrigan, J. (2018). Active learning strategies for the mathematics classroom. *College Teach.* 66, 35–36. doi: 10.1080/87567555.2017.1399335

Kinio, A. E., Dufresne, L., Brandys, T., and Jetty, P. (2019). Break out of the classroom: the use of escape rooms as an alternative teaching strategy in surgical education. *J. Surgical Educ.* 76, 134–139. doi: 10.1016/j.jsurg.2018.06.030

Kwon, J., and Woo, H. (2017). The impact of flipped learning on cooperative and competitive mindsets. *Sustainability* 10, 79–94. doi: 10.3390/su10010079

Lee, J., Park, T., and Davis, R. O. (2018). What affects learner engagement in flipped learning and what predicts its outcomes? FL engagement and outcomes. *Br. J. Educ. Technol.* 0, 1–18. doi: 10.1111/bjet.12717

Lee, J. J., Ceyhan, P., Jordan-Cooley, W., and Sung, W. (2013). GREENIFY: a real-world action game for climate change education. *Simul. Gaming* 44, 349–365. doi: 10.1177/1046878112470539

Lenhard, W., and Lenhard, A. (2016). *Calculation of Effect Sizes.* Dettelbach: Psychometrica.

Li, S., Yamaguchi, S., Sukhbaatar, J., and Takada, J. (2019). The influence of teachers' professional development activities on the factors promoting ICT integration in primary schools in mongolia. *Educ. Sci.* 9, 1–18. doi: 10.3390/educsci9020078

Long, T., Cummins, J., and Waugh, M. (2017). Use of the flipped classroom instructional model in higher education: instructors' perspectives. *J. Comput. High. Educ.* 29, 179–200. doi: 10.1007/s12528-016-9119-8

López, J., Pozo, S., and Del Pino, M. J. (2019a). Projection of the flipped learning methodology in the teaching staff of cross-border contexts. *J. New Approaches Educ. Res.* 8, 184–200. doi: 10.7821/naer.2019.7.431

López, J., Pozo, S., Fuentes, A., and López, J. A. (2019b). Creación de contenidos y flipped learning: un binomio necesario para la educación del nuevo milenio. *Rev. Esp. Pedagog.* 77, 535–555. doi: 10.7453/gahmj.2015.128

López-Pernas, S., Gordillo, A., Barra, E., and Quemada, J. (2019). Examining the use of an educational escape room for teaching programming in a higher education setting. *IEEE Access* 7, 31723–31737. doi: 10.1109/ACCESS.2019.2902976

Luong, A. S. (2019). *Gamification in Physical Education: A Fun Way to Enhance Student Motivation and Physical Competence.* Dissertations Thesis, California State University, Long Beach, CA.

Maldonado, G. A., García, J., and Sampedro, B. E. (2019). El efecto de las TIC y redes sociales en estudiantes universitarios. *RIED Rev. Iberoam. Educ. Distancia* 22, 153–176. doi: 10.5944/ried.22.2.23178

Malone, T. W., and Lepper, M. R. (1987). "Making learning fun: a taxonomy of intrinsic motivations for learning," in *Aptitude, Learning and Instruction III: Conative and Affective Process Analyses*, eds R. E. Snow and M. J. Farr (Hillsdale, MI: Lawrence Erlbaum Associates), 223–253.

Mat, N. S., Abdul, A., Mat, M., Abdul, S. Z., Nun, N. F., and Hamdan, A. (2019). An evaluation of content creation for personalised learning using digital ict literacy module among aboriginal students (MLICT-OA). *Turk. Online J. Distance Educ.* 20, 41–58. doi: 10.17718/tojde.598218

Mekler, E. D., Bruhlmann, F., Tuch, A. N., and Opwis, K. (2017). Towards understanding the effects of individual gamification elements on intrinsic motivation and performance. *Comput. Hum. Behav.* 71, 525–534. doi: 10.1016/j.chb.2015.08.048

Mengual, S., López, J., Fuentes, A., and Pozo, S. (2020). Modelo estructural de factores extrínsecos influyentes en el flipped learning. *Education* 21, 75–101.

Mora-González, J., Pérez-López, I. J., Esteban-Cornejo, I., and Delgado-Fernández, M. (2020). A gamification-based intervention program that encourages physical activity improves cardiorespiratory fitness of college students:'the matrix refvolution program'. *Int. J. Environ. Res. Public Health* 17, 1–11. doi: 10.3390/ijerph17030877

Moreno, J. A., González-Cutre, D., Chillón, M., and Parra, N. (2008). Adaptación a la educación física de la escala de las necesidades psicológicas básicas en el ejercicio. *Rev. Mexicana Psicol.* 25, 295–303.

Nikolopoulou, K., Akriotou, D., and Gialamas, V. (2019). Early reading skills in english as a foreign language via ict in greece: early childhood student teachers' perceptions. *Early Child. Educ. J.* 47, 597–606. doi: 10.1007/s10643-019-00950-8

Nogueira, F., Shigueo, E., and Abdala, H. (2018). Collaborative teaching and learning strategies for communication networks. *Int. J. Eng. Educ.* 34, 527–536.

Nortvig, A. M., Petersen, A. K., and Hattesen, S. (2018). A Literature review of the factors influencing E-learning and blended learning in relation to learning outcome, student satisfaction and engagement. *Electron. J. E Learn.* 16, 46–55.

Oliva, H. A. (2017). La gamificación como estrategia metodológica en el contexto educativo universitario. *Real. Reflex.* 44, 29–47. doi: 10.5377/ryr.v44i0.3563

Østerlie, O., and Kjelaas, I. (2019). The perception of adolescents' encounter with a flipped learning intervention in norwegian physical education. *Front. Educ.* 4:114. doi: 10.3389/feduc.2019.00114

Parra-González, M. E., López, J., Segura-Robles, A., and Fuentes, A. (2020). Active and emerging methodologies for ubiquitous education: potentials of flipped learning and gamification. *Sustainability* 12, 1–11. doi: 10.3390/su120 20602

Parra-González, M. E., and Segura-Robles, A. (2019). Producción científica sobre gamificación en educación: un análisis cienciométrico. *Rev. Educ.* 5, 113–131.

Parra-González, M. E., Segura-Robles, A., Fuentes, A., and López, J. (2019). "Gamification in primary education grade. a project of gamification in tutorial action subject to increase motivation and satisfaction of the students," in *Trends and Good Practices in Research and Teaching*, eds M. León-Urrutia, E. Vázquez, N. Fair, and E. López (Barcelona: España: Octaedro), 227–241. doi: 10.36006/16184-13

Pereira, S., Fillol, J., and Moura, P. (2019). Young people learning from digital media outside of school: the informal meets the formal. *Comunicar* 27, 41–50. doi: 10.3916/C58-2019-04

Pérez, E., Gilabert, A., and Lledó, A. (2019). "Gamificación en la educación universitaria: El uso del escape room como estrategia de aprendizaje," in *Investigación e Innovación en la Enseñanza Superior. Nuevos contextos, nuevas ideas*, ed. R. Roig-Vila (Barcelona: Octaedro), 660–668.

Pérez-Escoda, A. (2018). Uso de smartphones y redes sociales en alumnos/as de Educación Primaria. *Prisma Soc.* 1, 76–91.

Pérez-Manzano, A., and Almela-Baeza, J. (2018). Gamification and transmedia for scientific promotion and for encouraging scientific careers in adolescents. *Comunicar* 26, 93–103. doi: 10.3916/C55-2018-09

Perrotta, C., Featherstone, G., Aston, H., and Houghton, E. (2013). *Game-based Learning: latest evidence and future directions. NFER Research Programme: Innovation in Education. Slough- Berkshire.* Avaliable at: https://www.nfer.ac.uk/publications/game01/game01.pdf.

Pisabarro, A. M., and Vivaracho, C. E. (2018). Gamificación en el aula: gincana de programación. *ReVisión* 11, 85–93.

Quintas, A., Bustamante, J.-C., Pradas, F., and Castellar, C. (2020). Psychological effects of gamified didactics with exergames in physical education at primary schools: results from a natural experiment. *Comput. Educ.* 152:103874. doi: 10.1016/j.compedu.2020.103874

Quintero, L. E., Jiménez, F., and Area, M. (2018). Más allá del libro de texto. La gamificación mediada con TIC como alternativa de innovación en educación física. *Retos* 34, 343–348.

Rodríguez, A. M., Romero, J. M., and Agreda, M. (2019). Impact of ICT on the teaching of physical education: a bibliometric research study. *Educ. Sport Health Phys. Act.* 3, 1–14.

Rodríguez, N. (2011). Diseños experimentales en educación. *Rev. Pedag.* 32, 147–158.

Salazar Vargas, C., and Serpa Barrientos, A. (2017). Análisis confirmatorio y coeficiente omega como propiedades psicométricas del instrumento clima laboral de sonia palma. *Rev. Investig. Psicol.* 20, 377–388. doi: 10.15381/rinvp.v20i2.14047

Sánchez, D. R., Langer, M., and Kaur, R. (2020). Gamification in the classroom: examining the impact of gamified quizzes on student learning. *Comput. Educ.* 144, 1–16. doi: 10.1016/j.compedu.2019.103666

Sargent, J., and Casey, A. (2020). Flipped learning, pedagogy and digital technology: establishing consistent practice to optimise lesson time. *Eur. Phys. Educ. Rev.* 26, 70–84. doi: 10.1177/1356336X19826603

Segura, A., and Parra, M. E. (2019). How to implement active methodologies in physical education: escape room. *ESHPA Educ. Sport Health Phys. Act.* 3, 295–306.

Sierra, M. C., and Fernández Sánchez, M. R. (2019). Gamificando el aula universitaria. Análisis de una experiencia de Escape Room en educación superior. *REXE* 18, 105–115. doi: 10.21703/rexe.20191836sierra15

Simões, J., Díaz, R., and Fernández, A. (2013). A social gamification framework for a K-6 learning platform. *Comput. Hum. Behav.* 29, 345–353. doi: 10.1016/j.chb.2012.06.007

Sola, T., Aznar, I., Romero, J. M., and Rodríguez, A. M. (2019). Eficacia del método flipped classroom en la universidad: meta-análisis de la producción científica de impacto. *REICE* 17, 25–38. doi: 10.15366/reice2019.17.1.002

Su, C. H., and Cheng, C. H. (2015). A mobile gamification learning system for improving the learning motivation and achievements: a mobile gamification learning system. *J. Comput. Assist. Learn.* 31, 268–286. doi: 10.1111/jcal.12088

Talarico, R., and Janssen, I. (2018). Compositional associations of time spent in sleep, sedentary behavior and physical activity with obesity measures in children. *Int. J. Obesity* 42, 1508–1514. doi: 10.1038/s41366-018-0053-x

Tse, W. S., Choi, L. Y. A., and Tang, W. S. (2019). Effects of video-based flipped class instruction on subject reading motivation: flipped class instruction. *Br. J. Educ. Technol.* 50, 385–398. doi: 10.1111/bjet.12569

Wang, A. I. (2015). The wear out effect of a game-based student response system. *Comput. Educ.* 82, 217–227. doi: 10.1016/j.compedu.2014.11.004

Wyant, J., and Baek, J. H. (2019). Re-thinking technology adoption in physical education. *Curric. Stud. Health Phys. Educ.* 10, 3–17. doi: 10.1080/25742981.2018.1514983

Wynn, C. T., and Okie, W. (2017). Problem-based learning and the training of secondary social studies teachers: a case study of candidate perceptions during their field experience. *Int. J. Scholarsh. Teach. Learn.* 11, 1–14. doi: 10.20429/ijsotl.2017.110216

Xi, N., and Hamari, J. (2019). Does gamification satisfy needs? A study on the relationship between gamification features and intrinsic need satisfaction. *Int. J. Inf. Manag.* 46, 210–221. doi: 10.1016/j.ijinfomgt.2018.12.002

Zainuddin, Z., Habiburrahim, H., Muluk, S., and Keumala, C. M. (2019). How do students become self-directed learners in the EFL flipped-class pedagogy? A study in higher education. *Indones. J. Appl. Linguist.* 8, 678–690. doi: 10.17509/ijal.v8i3.15270

21

Effect of Acute Physical Exercise on Executive Functions and Emotional Recognition: Analysis of Moderate to High Intensity in Young Adults

Haney Aguirre-Loaiza[1], Jaime Arenas[2], Ianelleen Arias[2], Alejandra Franco-Jímenez[3], Sergio Barbosa-Granados[4], Santiago Ramos-Bermúdez[3], Federico Ayala-Zuluaga[3,5], César Núñez[6] and Alexandre García-Mas[7]*

[1] Department of Psychology, Catholic University of Pereira, Pereira, Colombia, [2] Physical Education, University of Quindío, Armenia, Colombia, [3] Research Group Physical Activity, Cumanday, Manizales, Colombia, [4] Psychology, Cooperative University of Colombia, Pereira, Colombia, [5] Department of Physical Action, Caldas University, Manizales, Colombia, [6] Psychology Program, Universidad de Medellín, Medellín, Colombia, [7] Department of Basic Psychology, University of the Balearic Islands, Palma, Spain

***Correspondence:**
Haney Aguirre-Loaiza
haney.aguirre@ucp.edu.co

Physical exercise (PE) is associated with cognitive changes and brain function. However, it is required to clarify the effect of PE in different intensities, population groups conditions and the EF duration over different cognitive domains. Besides, no studies are known to have evaluated the contextual emotional recognition. Therefore, we studied the effect of acute PE of moderate intensities up to higher ones to the executive functions and the contextual emotional recognition. The participants were evaluated and classified in two experiments according to the IPAQ short form self-report and control measures. In both experiments, the groups were randomized, controlled, and exposed to one session of indoor cycling through intervals of high measure intensity (75–85% HRmax). Experiment 1 comprised young adults who were physically active (PA) and healthy, apparently ($n = 54$, $M_{age} = 20.7$, $SD = 2.5$). Experiment 2 involved young adults who were physically inactive (IP) and healthy, apparently ($n = 36$, $M_{age} = 21.6$, $SD = 1.8$). The duration was the only factor that varied: 45 min for PA and 30 min for PI. The executive functions were evaluated by the Stroop, TMT A/B, and verbal fluency, and the emotional recognition through a task that includes body and facial emotions in context, simultaneously. The analysis of factorial mixed ANOVA showed effects on the right choices of the indoor cycling groups in the PA, and the time response in PI. Also, other effects were observed in the controlled groups. TMT-A/B measures showed changes in the pre-test–post-test measures for both experiments. Verbal fluency performance favored the control group in both experiments. Meanwhile, the emotional recognition showed an effect of the PE in error-reduction and enhanced the scores in the right choices of body emotions. These results suggest that the EF with intensities favored cognitive processes such as inhibitory control and emotional recognition in context. We took into account the importance of high-complexity tasks design that avoid a ceiling effect. This study is the first on reporting a positive effect of PE over the emotional contextual recognition. Important clinical and educational implications are presented implications which highlight the modulatory role of EF with moderate to high intensities.

Keywords: physical exercise, cognitive neuroscience, cognitive performance, executive functions, emotional recognition, exercise psychology

INTRODUCTION

Physical exercise (PE) is an important environmental factor with positive effects on the brain and healthy behavior along different life stages (Herting et al., 2014; Hillman et al., 2014; Etnier et al., 2019), mainly when considering that less than 60% of world population does not do required PE (World Health Organization [WHO], 2018, World Health Organization [WHO], 2007). Such data, nowadays, are increasing and associated with sedentary lifestyles and low PE involvement (Guthold et al., 2018; Päivärinne et al., 2018). Thus, PE is considered a non-pharmacological strategy that has direct effects in functional and cognitive brain structures (Herting et al., 2014; Erickson et al., 2015; Prakash et al., 2015; Voss et al., 2015; Hagger, 2019). Researchers have addressed the questionings of the effect of EF on cognition from two perspectives. On the one hand, chronic effects in PE (e.g., weeks, months, and/or years). On the other hand, the immediate effect of the acute PE (e.g., one session). This study focuses on the second perspective, treating the effect of acute PE on cognitive processes and emotional recognition.

Most of the reviewed literature matches on observing positive changes of cognition after PE (Reed and Ones, 2006; Lambourne and Tomporowski, 2010; Chang et al., 2012; Donnelly et al., 2016; Ludyga et al., 2016; Sáez de Asteasu et al., 2017; Esteban-Cornejo et al., 2019; Etnier et al., 2019; Hillman et al., 2019; McSween et al., 2019). Likewise, it has been demonstrated that an acute PE brings benefits for some ways of performance on cognitive tasks after exercise. By the same token, executive functions improve after PE (Wu et al., 2019). Recent studies, however, affirm that there is not enough evidence that PE is positive for cognition or brain function and structure in child and young samples (Gunnell et al., 2018). What explains these possible contradictions is the huge methodological variety, and therefore, new investigative contributions might clarify and provide evidence of the relation of PE on cognition (Pontifex et al., 2019).

The relation between PE, cognition, brain functions, and structures seem to rest upon several factors (Chang et al., 2012, 2015; Erickson et al., 2015; Gunnell et al., 2018). For instance, duration, intensity, and PE modality, as well as the vital cycle, the type of cognitive performance and physical condition of the participant. Even the effect of PE can vary depending on the cognitive domain (Pontifex et al., 2009, 2019). These factors are relevant in questioning the relation between PE, brain and cognition. Hence, further research is required that identifies its modulating role (Labelle et al., 2013; Ludyga et al., 2016).

Addressing the related factors of PE (e.g., type, intensity, and duration), some contributions have pointed out that aerobic PE can improve cognitive performance in both young and old adults (Chang et al., 2012; Joyce et al., 2014; Tsukamoto et al., 2016). Specifically, Physiological changes have been observed by activating circuits of the prefrontal and occipital cortex in tasks that include a great cognitive effort (e.g., attention and executive control) (Chen and Chang, 2012; Basso et al., 2015). Other studies have reported that aerobic PE can enhance cognitive and neurological function (Armstrong and Welsman, 2007; Herting et al., 2014; Li et al., 2014; Reiter et al., 2015). Likewise, aerobic PE is associated with improved memory efficiency (Herting and Nagel, 2013; Voss et al., 2019) and inhibitory control performance (Pontifex et al., 2019). Even participants who were exposed to the multimodal combination (training of aerobic PE followed by cognitive training) showed improvement in cognitive performance as compared to those who only had a cognitive training (Wang et al., 2019a).

The immediate effects of PE on cognitive performance seem to be conditional on intensity of PE. Inverted U hypothesis (Gutin, 1973) supports that cognitive performance tends to have more benefits after a moderate intensity of aerobic PE (>64% Maximum heart rate – HRmax) in contrast to low ones (<50% HRmax) or high intensities (>80% HRmax). In this regard, the evidence which supports the inverted U hypothesis is wide (Pontifex et al., 2009; Hillman et al., 2014; Li et al., 2014; De Souto Barreto et al., 2016; Ludyga et al., 2016). Nonetheless, current studies inform that high intensities of PE allow to have benefits in cognitive domains as inhibitory control (Quintero et al., 2018), memory and metacognition (Zuniga et al., 2019). Further, it is important to underscore that the number of studies of PE interventions of moderate intensity is actually small compared to interventions of moderate or low intensities (Browne et al., 2017). There are even more limited studies that address the transition of moderate and high intensities.

As a matter of fact, there is no agreement on the effect of duration, type or intensity of PE on cognition and the different types of cognitive domains (Vazou et al., 2019). A line of research suggested by other authors consists of clarifying the effects of PE in people who are physically active (PA), inactive and/or sedentary. Moreover, it associates more cognitive domains (Sink et al., 2015; Tsukamoto et al., 2016; Vieira et al., 2016; Browne et al., 2017; Peruyero et al., 2017; Silva et al., 2019). Based on the above-mentioned, narrative, systematic, and meta-analytic revisions have suggested an improvement of cognitive performance after an acute session of PE (Lambourne and Tomporowski, 2010; Chang et al., 2012; Ludyga et al., 2016; Basso and Suzuki, 2017; McSween et al., 2019); yet, constructs such as emotional recognition must be studied in relation to acute PE.

In that way, understanding how environmental factors, such as PE, contribute to the performance of emotional recognition in context, and in ecological situations, is a novel area that answers to current questionings of social and cognitive neuroscience (Aviezer et al., 2008; Kumfor et al., 2018). We assumed that acute PE has positive effects on emotional recognition. Especially, whenever the aerobic exercise is combined with the demands of coordination seems that it gets more benefits on facial emotion recognition (Brand et al., 2019). In fact, the capacity of information processing, which links body movements with body-face recognition (Kumfor et al., 2018), is associated with brain regions such as motor areas, cerebellum, and fusiform gyrus (Committeri et al., 2007; Yogev-Seligmann et al., 2008), that are connected with the acute PE (Li et al., 2014; Esteban-Cornejo et al., 2019; Won et al., 2019). Recent paradigms on emotional recognition have located body information as contextual keys, taking away attention from facial recognition processing (Aviezer et al., 2008, 2012).

Based on the described evidence, that the dose-response relation in terms of intensity, duration and the type of acute PE over cognitive performance, specifically with executive functional tasks and emotional recognition, is an issue that needs to be studied. By solving the previous matter, we would contribute with knowledge about the strategy of PE, which can be a potent and promising environmental source that allows to adjust cognitive processes (executive performance to be precise) and emotional recognition. Among other scopes, it would facilitate the capacity of social human interactions in clinical and academic activities that improve the mental health of people. Thus, the main objective is to study the effect of acute PE of indoor cycling with a range of moderate and high intensity (75–85% HRmax) in regard to executive functions and emotional recognition in PA and inactive people and high apparently.

MATERIALS AND METHODS

Design and Participants

Two experiments were designed, controlled and randomized with pre-test–post-test measures, for an indoor cycling session. The process of choosing, randomizing, and selecting is shown in **Figure 1**. Initially, (n = 140) were recruited, and 90 university students were analyzed (M_{age} = 21.0, DE = 2.3). In both experiments, people were randomized by a computer-generated list through Excel (function RANDBETWEEN) from 1 to 60 in PA participants, and between 1 and 53 in physically inactive. The first experiment was carried out in young adults who were PA, and apparently healthy (n = 54). La They were randomly assigned to the experimental group and were exposed to a 45 min-session of indoor cycling, whereas the control group had no PE. The second experiment involved physically inactive young adults (n = 36) who were randomly selected for the control and experimental groups. The indoor cycling session in the second experiment lasted 30 min. The intensity of a session of PE was moderate-high ranging between 75 and 85% HRmax. The intensity ranges are: moderate between 64 and 76% HRmax, and High 76–96% HRmax (ACSM, 2018) The HRmax was calculated by Karvonen et al. (1957) 220-age (see section "Procedure").

Measure

General Characteristics

The participants answered a battery of instruments according to pre-experimental protocol (see section "Procedure"). **Table 1** provides data such as age, body mass, resting heart rate (supine position for 10 min), cognitive screening *(MoCA)*, self-report of physical activity *(IAPQ)*, and Depression *(BID)*. As expected, significative differences in the IPAQ self-report were observed ($p < 0.000$).

Measurement Screening

Cognitive screening

The MoCA: *Montreal Cognitive Assessment* measures 10 cognitive domains with satisfactory results of sensitivity and specificity, which fluctuate between 82–90% and 75–87%, respectively (Nasreddine et al., 2005). The MoCA is one of the most used instruments in clinics and research that identifies early cognitive changes. Cut-off points vary depending on educational and cultural level (O'Driscoll and Shaikh, 2017). Hence and having in mind Colombian population, one cut-off and exclusion point was assumed <24 (Pedraza et al., 2014, 2016; Gil et al., 2015).

The BDI – II: Beck Depression Inventory tests the existence or severity of depressive symptoms with 21 items. Spanish version was used (Sanz and García-Vera, 2013). The BID-II supports satisfactory psychometric evidence (Wang and Gorenstein, 2013). It was excluded such individuals whose score was >30 were excluded. The observation of depressive symptomatology can constitute a confusing factor, and thereupon, it was relevant to consider this control measure.

Physical exercise measure

The IPAQ-SF: The International Physical Activity Questionnaire – Short Form is used to facilitate a measurement and monitoring of physical activity (Craig et al., 2003), and seven questions about the last 7 days in relation to duration, minutes, hours, and days. A total measured score in METs (metabolic equivalent of task minutes per week) is recorded. The three classification levels are the following; low (e.g., walking), moderate (e.g., recreational cycling), and strong (e.g., intense aerobic activity). It is recognized as one of the most used questionnaires to determine AF level (Forsén et al., 2010; Van Poppel et al., 2010). The evidence of consistency and validity of the scores has been reported in several psychometric revisions (Sanda et al., 2017). The prior measurements are in line with the World Health Organization's global recommendations for physical activity (World Health Organization [WHO], 2007, 2010). IPAQ-SF was used with the aim of classifying active and inactive physically groups.

PARQ & You: The Physical Activity Readiness Questionnaire has been an easy-to-use tool for people between 15 and 69 years of age. The PARQ & You identifies health and cardiovascular problems from seven questions. It is usually applied to apparently healthy individuals, who have the willingness to take part in PE programs (Warburton et al., 2011). A participant's self-report which was associated with a cardiovascular problem was excluded from the study.

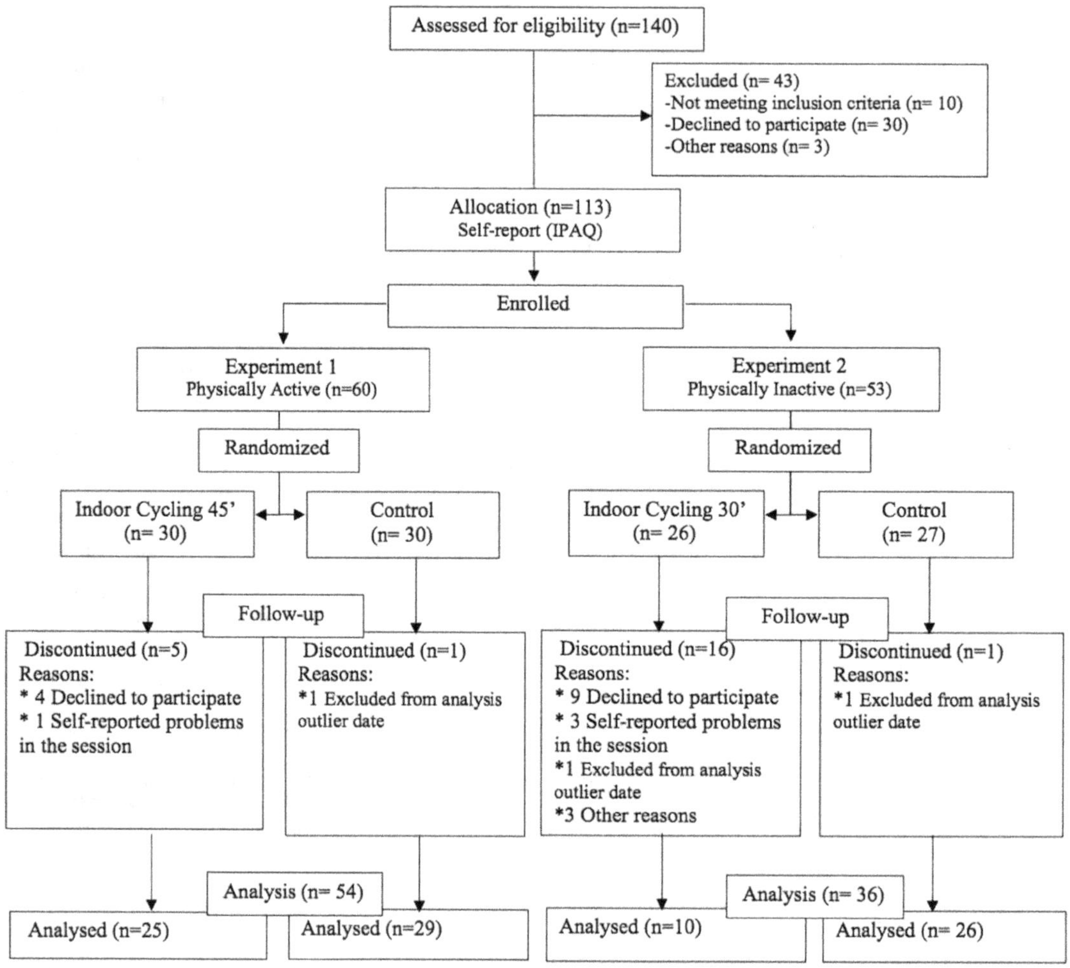

FIGURE 1 | Flow of participants throughout the study.

Task of Executive Functions

An executive functioning battery was registered, which is composed of three tasks; Stroop, TMT, and Verbal Fluency. These tasks are widely used in executive function measurement (Strauss et al., 2007). Moreover, other revisions have dealt with the PE effect on cognitive processes (Chang et al., 2012; Ludyga et al., 2016; McSween et al., 2019; Pontifex et al., 2019).

(a) Stroop: it evaluates the inhibitory control as executive process and it is associated with function in the anterior cingular cortex. An adapted version of the Stroop test version was performed in pencil and paper format by manipulating two conditions (Florez et al., 2012). In Stroop-A, the person reads written words, and as soon as it is highlighted, he/she must mention the color and avoid saying the word. In the Stroop-B, the evaluator points to the columns of words that are in color, and the individual reads what is written, but when the evaluator says the word "color," the person should mention the ink's color without naming the word. In both conditions, 84 stimuli were found. The response and the percentage of the right choices as well as answer time of the execution in both conditions was measured.

(b) The Trail Making Test (TMT) evaluates attention processes, visual scanning, mental processing, and flexibility (Reitan, 1958). It consists of two assessed parts in paper – pencil format. TMT-A deals with the sequence of ascending numbers from 1 to 25. The individuals must match the locked-numbers. The TMT-B is used for the estimation of executive functions (e.g., attention, planning, cognitive flexibility, and response inhibition). The individual has to match the aligned circles randomly by alternating between upward numbers (1–3) and the letters (A–L) (1-A-2-B, etc.). Normally, the TMT-A and the TMT-B are valid and reliable measures (Rabin et al., 2005).

(c) Verbal Fluency (Phonemic and Semantic): It evaluates the capacity to access lexicon and recover semantic information under limited conditions, and its psychometric properties are satisfactory (Borkowski et al., 1967; Strauss et al., 2007). The individual must mention as many words as he/she can, that start with the letter "S" (phonological fluency). Regarding phonological fluency, he must mention as many

TABLE 1 | Characteristics of participants.

Characteristics	Physically active (n = 54)		Physically inactive (n = 36)		t	p
	Experiment 1		Experiment 2			
	M	*SD*	*M*	*SD*		
Age (years)	20.7	2.5	21.6	1.8	−0.029	0.977
Body mass (kg)	65.5	13.8	64.3	10.6	0.325	0.746
Resting heart rate (bpm)	63.9	11.0	70.8	8.3	−1.83	0.73
Physical activity – IPAQ (METs)	6190.8	5087.1	176.8	195.6	7.07**	0.000
Depression – BDI	7.3	5.9	9.94	6.7	−1.89	0.062
Cognitive screening – MoCA	26.57	1.2	26.06	2.2	1.36	0.176

*BPM, Beat per minute; IPAQ, International physical activity questionnaire; METs, Caloric expenditure; BDI, Beck depression inventory; MoCA, Montreal cognitive assessment. **$p < 0.01$.*

words as possible in relation to a category or a common interest. We tested the "animals" category. In both tasks, 60 s were timed. Words from the same morphology or proper names were excluded. The total score is the sum of all the right words that are produced in each category.

Task Emotional Recognition

The experimental task of recognition of body-face emotions was used in context (see **Figure 2**). This paradigm was originally developed by Aviezer et al. (2008), and used in subsequent studies (Aviezer et al., 2011, 2012; Santamaría-García et al., 2019). This task consists of the representation of four basic emotions (anger, sadness, fear, and displeasure), involving body context. Each emotion is represented by the facial expression along with the body context. In the same way, the facial and corporal emotions can be either congruent or incongruent (e.g., consistent, sadness-face, and sadness-body; inconsistent, sadness-face, and anger-body). We submitted a total of 80 stimuli (Height 11.4 cm × Width 15.2 cm) which were assigned randomly in a 14" computer screen Microsoft Power Point. The task's command is "You have to select the emotional option that best describes the facial expression." Each participant had to choose the right answer from six options of basic emotions (sadness, anger, fear, disgust, happiness, and surprise). There is no time limit on task execution. The precision of correct response of the facial emotional expression was scored. The assigned scoring for the correct match of facial emotion =2 points. If the contextual influence matches the body emotion =1 point. When the person neither got the facial emotion, nor the body context right (0 points). The total score turned into a response rate (Response Accuracy = Sum of score/84 × 100).

Procedure

The volunteers participated in three stages (pre-experimental session, experimental session, and post-experimental session). To maximize transparency and replicability, the indoor Cycling program described in this manuscript follows the Consensus on Exercise Reporting Template (CERT) (Slade et al., 2016) (see **Supplementary Table S1**).

Pre-experimental Session

In the pre-experimental session, the objectives and the scope were presented. In addition to the signature of the informed consent, information about the age, weight, HR at rest, MoCA, BDI-II, IAPQ-SF, and PARQ (see **Table 1**) was collected. All of these measures were obtained in the days before the indoor cycling PE session. According to the IAPQ-SF results, the participants were classified into one of the two experiments: Experiment 1 – PA volunteers whose physical activity report was moderate and intense. Experiment 2 – physically inactive volunteers whose physical activity was in low category. The participants were instructed regarding clothing, hydration, and feeding before the PE session. The protocol of cognitive measures and emotional recognition from the pretest was executed from 45 up to 60 min before the experimental session in the fitness center. After the evaluation protocol, the instructor informed about the basic concepts, techniques and commands executed in the indoor cycling session. The instructor has a degree in Physical Education with international certification in Indoor Cycle and 10 years of experience in sports training.

Experimental Manipulation

Each experiment controlled the HR through Polar-M200, whose HR register is obtained by sensors from the wrist. The intensities of PE were moderates (64–76% HRmax), and high (76–96% HRmax) (ACSM, 2018). Data were gathered through easy connectivity between the device and the computer. The HRmax was calculated by the 220-Age formula. During the experimental session, a research assistant monitored HR behavior and the RPMs that corresponds to the training zone of each participant. The bicycles were standard and relevant to the indoor cycling aims.

Experiment 1 – Physically active group: The participants were randomly assigned to the experimental and control group (see **Figure 1**). The experimental group performed an indoor cycling session with intensities between 75 and 85% HRmax for 45 min (see **Supplementary Figure S1**). The PE protocol had three phases. Phase 1, warming up and muscle activation (10 min) 60–65% HRmax between 60 and 90 RPM (revolutions per minute). Phase 2, main work (35 min) which had six sections of 4 min with six peaks of 85% HRmax between 90

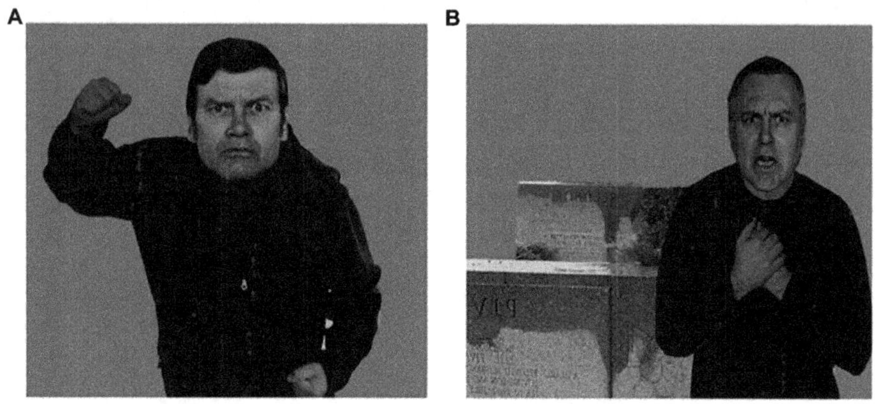

FIGURE 2 | Examples of stimuli of task face-body context. **(A)** Trial congruent face-anger and body-anger. **(B)** Trial incongruent face-anger and body-sadness. Permission obtained from Aviezer et al. (2008).

and 100 RPM, and active recovery at 75% HRmax. Phase 3, Final recovery (5 min) 60% HRmax between 50 and 70 RPM (See examples of the planimetry – additional material). The group control stayed at rest for 45 min in the facilities of the fitness center. HR measures were the following, HRrest ($M = 65.4$, $DE = 9.8$), HRmean ($M = 136.8$, $DE = 12.3$), HRmax ($M = 186.1$ $DE = 9.5$).

Experiment 2 – Sedentary group: The participants were selected randomly to the experimental and control group (see **Figure 1**). The experimental group performed an indoor cycling session of 35 min duration with intensities of 75 and 85% HRmax (see **Supplementary Figure S1**). The protocol had three phases. Phase 1, warming up and muscle activation (7 min) 65–75%HRmax between 70 and 90RPM. Phase 2, main work (17 min) with four sections of 4 min with peaks of 85%HRmax between 50 and 100RPM. Phase 3, final recovery (5 min) 75–65%HRmax between 90 and 70RPM. The control group remained at rest for 30 min after the post-test. HR measures were, HRrest ($M = 63.1$, $DE = 10.1$), HRmean ($M = 143.1$, $DE = 5.7$), HRmax ($M = 185.4$, $DE = 9.5$). In both experimental groups, the musical track was according to the RPM, intensity, intervals, and commands of the instructor (e.g., position three, sitting, etc.).

Post-experimental Session

The participants from both experiments had an individual recovery with the monitoring of resting HR. Further, each of them got hydrated during and after PE session. The post-test measure protocols were obtained after getting the resting HR.

Data Analysis

Both experiments were subjected to the following statistic procedure. The intention-to-treat principle was not carried out, therefore, per-protocol analysis was performed with those who completed the indoor cycling session (see **Figure 1**). An exploratory analysis of data was executed by calculating tendency central measures (M), of dispersion (SD) and Confidence interval (95% from the mean). *Outliers* that were observed in the box diagram and located below or above from the interquartile range *(Q3–Q1)*. In these cases, each datum was analyzed by identifying the information gathering process. To some of them, we applied Winsorizing technique, which consists of adjusting cognitive measures and emotional recognition. Three extreme cases were excluded. Each experiment analysis was executed separately in order to estimate and control the effect of every physical condition (active and inactive). Normality Kolmogorov–Smirnov assumptions were confirmed ($n > 50$) for experiment 1, PA ($p > 0.05$), and Shapiro Wilk ($n < 50$) in experiment 2, physically inactive ($p > 0.05$). The comparison of demographic, cognitive, physical activity, HR, anxiety, and depression variables were estimated with the T student test for independent samples. The contrast of the acute PE effect was performed by a Mixed Factorial ANOVA or by partially repeated measures. The dependent variables were treated separately due to the levels and conditions of analysis, which each one of these measures has (e.g., execution time, right choices). Finally, four factorial models were estimated.

(i) The first model was 4 × 2 × 2 for the stroop: four Stroop conditions (Stroop-A right choices, Stroop-A time, Stroop-B right choices, Stroop-B time) × 2 measures (pre-test–post-test) × two groups (Experimental and control).
(ii) The second model 2 × 2 × 2 analyzed TMT measures: two TMT conditions (parts A and B), × two measures (pre-test–post-test) × two groups (Experimental and Control).
(iii) The third model 2 × 2 × 2 analyzed fluency measures with verbal fluency: (phonological "S" and semantic "animals").
(iv) The fourth model 3 × 2 × 2 analyzed emotional recognition hits: three responses rate (face, body, and errors) × two measures (pre-test – post-test) × two groups (Experimental and Control).

The sphericity of each model was corrected through Greenhouse–Geisser. The meaning of interactions and principal effects were analyzed with the *post hoc* Bonferroni test. The size of the effect was estimated with Eta to the partial square.

Ethics Statement

We followed the Helsinki's declaration (WMA, 2013) and the Universal Declaration of Ethic Principles for Psychologist regulations (IUPS, 2008). The evaluation and intervention protocol was approved by the Ethics' Committee of Health Sciences Department of Universidad de Caldas (CBCS-048 Code, Record 015 of 2017) which is coherent with the rules of the Republic of Colombia (Ministerio de Salud - República de Colombia, 1993). All the participants signed the informed consent acknowledging the purposes, phases, and possible risks of the research. During the phase of experimental manipulation, there were specialized professionals for medical attention if needed.

RESULTS

Descriptive data of the PA participants (experiment 1) can be observed in **Table 2**, and for the physically inactive participants (experiment 2) in **Table 3**.

Performance Stroop Task

The Mix Anova 4 × 2 × 2 (Stroop, time, and group conditions) was not significant in the interaction, [$F(1.54,80.5) = 452$, $p = 0.588$, $\eta p^2 = 0.009$]. The stroop and time conditions (pretest and posttest) were significant [$F(1.54,80.5) = 452$, $p = 0.000$, $\eta p^2 = 0.33$]. The post-hoc analysis (See **Figure 3**) showed favorable significant differences for the indoor cycling group in the percentage of right answers of the Stroop-A condition between the pretest and the posttest ($p = 0.002$). In the same way, for the control group, significant changes were observed in the response time of the Stroop-A condition between pretest and posttest ($p = 0.009$), also the answering time of the condition of the Stroop-B, the control group was faster compared to the indoor cycling group ($p = 0.001$).

On the other hand, in the experiment 2 of the PI, the interaction conditions of the stroop, time and group was not significant [$F(1.00,57.4) = 1.44$, $p = 0.245$, $\eta p^2 = 0.041$]. The time and stroop conditions showed significant differences [$F(1.00,57.4) = 5.15$, $p = 0.004$, $\eta p^2 = 0.121$]. The post-hoc median comparison, indicated that the indoor cycling group reduced the answering time of stroop-A between the pretest and posttest ($p = 0.014$). On the other side, the control group showed better right answer percentage of stroop-B between the pretest and posttest ($p = 0.014$) (possibly due to an instrumentation effect).

Performance TMT-A/B

Task performance of TMT A/B, measures (pre-test and post-test) and the group were not significant [$F(1.00,52.0) = 0.709$, $p = 0.403$, $\eta p^2 = 0.013$]. Mean comparison indicated that the indoor-cycling group obtained a better average performance than the control group. However, these data were not significant (see **Figure 4**). The *post hoc* analysis of means Bonferroni comparison showed differences in the pre-test and post-test measures in both TMT-A/B conditions, and in both groups ($p < 0.000$, see **Figures 4A,B**).

In experiment 2, significant differences in the interaction between TMT-A/B conditions, measures, and the group were identified [$F(1.00,34.0) = 0.199$, $p = 0.658$, $\eta p^2 = 0.006$]. The interaction between the TMT-A/B conditions and the measures was significant [$F(1.00,34.0) = 6.182$, $p = 0.018$, $\eta p^2 = 0.154$] (see **Figures 4E,F**). Although the response time averages were better in the indoor-cycling than the control group, these averages were not significant in both TMT-A/B conditions ($p < 0.5$). The *post hoc* comparison identifies differences of

TABLE 2 | Descriptive dates physically active (PA) – Experiment 1.

Variable	Indoor cycling PA *n* = 25				Control PA *n* = 29			
	Pre-test		Post-test		Pre-test		Post-test	
	M	*SD*	*M*	*SD*	*M*	*SD*	*M*	*SD*
Stroop condition A								
Accuracy response (%)	95.0	4.0	97.5	2.2	97.1	3.6	97.6	2.4
Response time (seg)	80.4	14.9	73.8	11.4	78.7	24.5	69.4	20.8
Stroop condition B								
Accuracy response (%)	98.7	1.9	97.1	8.7	98.6	1.7	99.0	1.5
Response time	73.4	14.3	68.7	11.8	67.0	12.3	58.8	8.8
Trail making test								
TMT-A time (seg)	51.6	15.9	36.7	16.2	55.6	21.7	44.0	21.8
TMT-B time (seg)	91.1	43.2	66.1	22.3	90.7	30.6	77.1	27.3
Verbal fluency								
Phonemic word "S"	11.6	3.0	13.0	3.4	11.9	3.1	13.9	3.7
Semantic animal	18.6	4.5	19.6	4.3	20.8	4.5	22.0	4.2
Emotional recognition								
% Response face	42.3	12.7	44.9	14.5	44.5	11.0	46.1	12.9
% Response body	16.75	10.3	15.4	6.1	18.7	11.5	14.0	5.0
% Error	40.6	12.9	36.2	11.7	39.8	10.9	39.	10.7

TABLE 3 | Descriptive dates physically inactive (PI) – Experiment 2.

Variable	Indoor cycling PI n = 10				Control group PI n = 26			
	Pre-test		Post-test		Pre-test		Post-test	
	M	*SD*	*M*	*SD*	*M*	*SD*	*M*	*SD*
Stroop condition A								
Accuracy response (%)	95.1	4.7	98.6	1.4	94.7	7.7	97.8	2.8
Response time (seg)	81.9	19.1	68.2	17.4	70.0	14.8	66.9	12.5
Stroop condition B								
Accuracy response (%)	98.2	2.5	98.3	1.6	98.7	1.9	98.9	2.4
Response time (seg)	67.7	16.5	64.0	8.4	67.9	14.5	62.2	16.1
Trail making test								
TMT-A time (seg)	46.3	10.9	31.7	10.7	45.7	18.8	38.5	17.4
TMT-B time (seg)	85.6	44.6	73.5	36.9	98.2	47.9	88.2	37.7
Verbal fluency								
Phonemic word "S"	9.1	6.1	12.0	2.7	11.8	4.4	17.9	4.4
Semantic animal	20.6	2.9	20.8	3.0	12.1	4.0	19.2	4.8
Emotional recognition								
% Response face	48.4	9.7	52.9	14.3	41.2	13.8	41.7	15.0
% Response body	20.8	12.4	16.1	8.1	22.6	9.8	20.9	12.2
% Error	30.9	7.4	31.0	10.2	36.3	13.4	37.3	17.2

improvement in the execution of time between the pre-test and post-test measures in TMT-A/B conditions (p < 0.001, see **Figures 4E,F**).

Verbal Fluency

For experiment 1, verbal fluency conditions (greater number of words with the letter "S" and semantic category of animals), measures and the group were not significant [F(1,52) =0.057, p = 0.812, ηp^2 = 0.001]. The *post hoc* analysis indicated that the control group mentioned a greater number of the semantic animals category than the indoor-cycling group in the post-test (p < 0.042, see **Figure 4D**). The group control showed differences in the pre-test and post-test measures in relation to the "S" letter (p < 0.010, see **Figure 4C**).

Interaction between verbal fluency, time (pre-test and post-test) and group was not significant in the physically inactive participants [F(1.00,4.0) =6.182, p = 0.018, ηp^2 = 0.154]. Although the descriptive data show changes in the times, the *post hoc* analysis did not identify.

Emotional Recognition

Experiment 1 indicated that three emotional recognition conditions (% response face, body and error), measures and the group, were not significant [F(1,52) =0.553, p = 0.547, ηp^2 = 0.011] (**Figures 5A,B,F**). Measures comparison, with the *post hoc* Bonferroni showed significant differences in pre-test and post-test measures (p < 0.32) in error percentage reduction in the indoor cycling group (see, **Figure 5C**).

For experiment 2, the interaction effect between the responses of emotional recognition, measures and the group was not significant [F(1,34) =0.444, p = 0.643, ηp^2 = 0.013] (**Figures 5A,B,F**). The main effect of response percentage of emotional recognition in three conditions was significant [F(1,34) =8.816, p = 0.005, ηp^2 = 0.206]. Mean *post hoc* comparison pointed out that the indoor-cycling group had a significant reduction of the percentage of body emotion recognition in pre-test and post-test measures (p = 0.028, see **Figure 5E**). Descriptively, averages indicate that the right choices percentage of facial recognition favored the indoor cycling group (*pre-test, M* = 48.4, *DE* = 9.7; *post-test, M* = 52.9, *DE* = 14.3, see **Figure 5D**).

DISCUSSION

Our main objective was to study the effect of acute PE of indoor cycling with a moderate-high intensity range (75–85% HRmax) on executive function, and the emotional recognition in healthy people who are PA and inactive. We have outlined two experiments, each one of them for two conditions, PA (Experiment 1) and inactive (Experiment 2). Overall, we highlight two main results. First, we observed some effects of acute PE on executive functions with a specific PE tendency of indoor-cycling on physically inactive participants. Second, regarding emotional recognition, the group that was exposed to PE indoor-cycling from PA participants (Experiment 1) reduced errors significantly. Similarly, the PE indoor-cycling group from physically inactive participants had a higher percentage of right choices in facial recognition.

These findings provide evidence of the differential effect of demographic conditions (physically active and inactive), and experimental manipulations considering the type, intensity, acute PE, duration on executive functions and emotional recognition. Below, we mention main results.

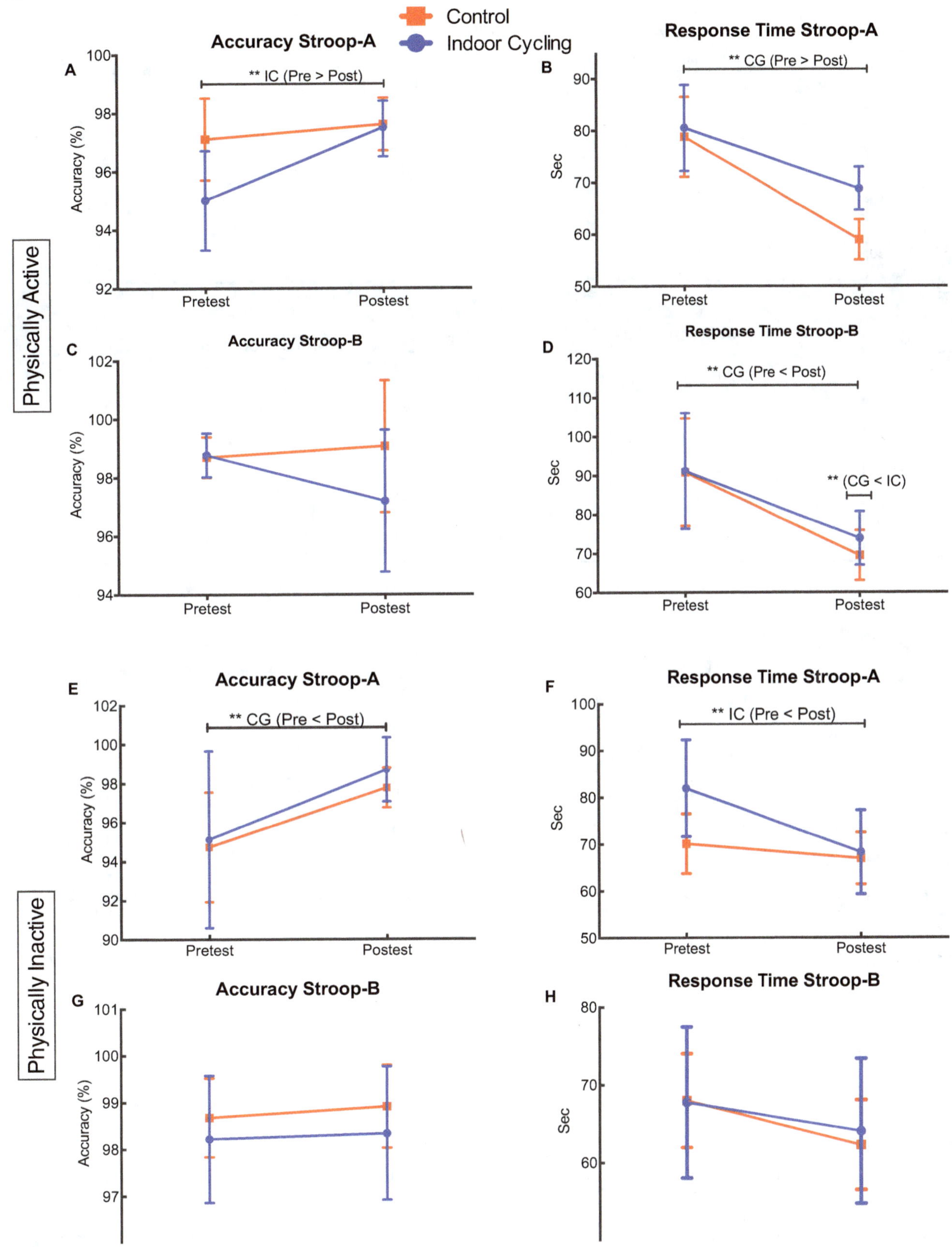

FIGURE 3 | Performance stroop task. Physically active **(A–D)** and physically inactive **(E–H)**. Means and 95% confidence interval of pre-test to post-test of stroop condition **(A,B)**. IC, indoor cycling (Experimental Group); CG, control group. ** $p < 0.01$.

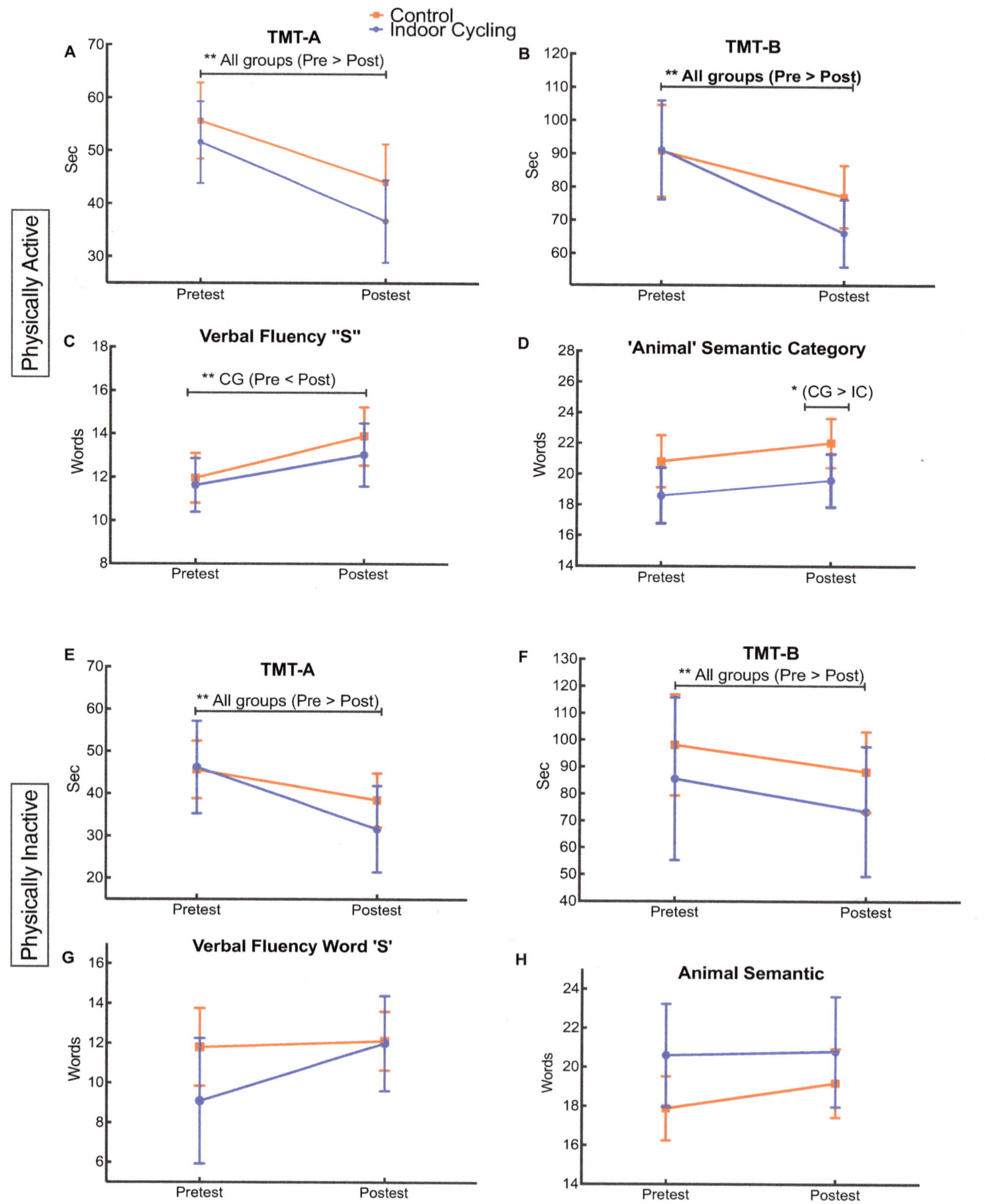

FIGURE 4 | Physically active **(A–D)** and physically inactive **(E–H)**. Means and 95% confidence interval of pre-test to post-test of TMT A/B – verbal fluency. IC, Indoor Cycling (Experimental Group); CG, control group. Physically, $^{*}p < 0.05$ and $^{**}p < 0.01$.

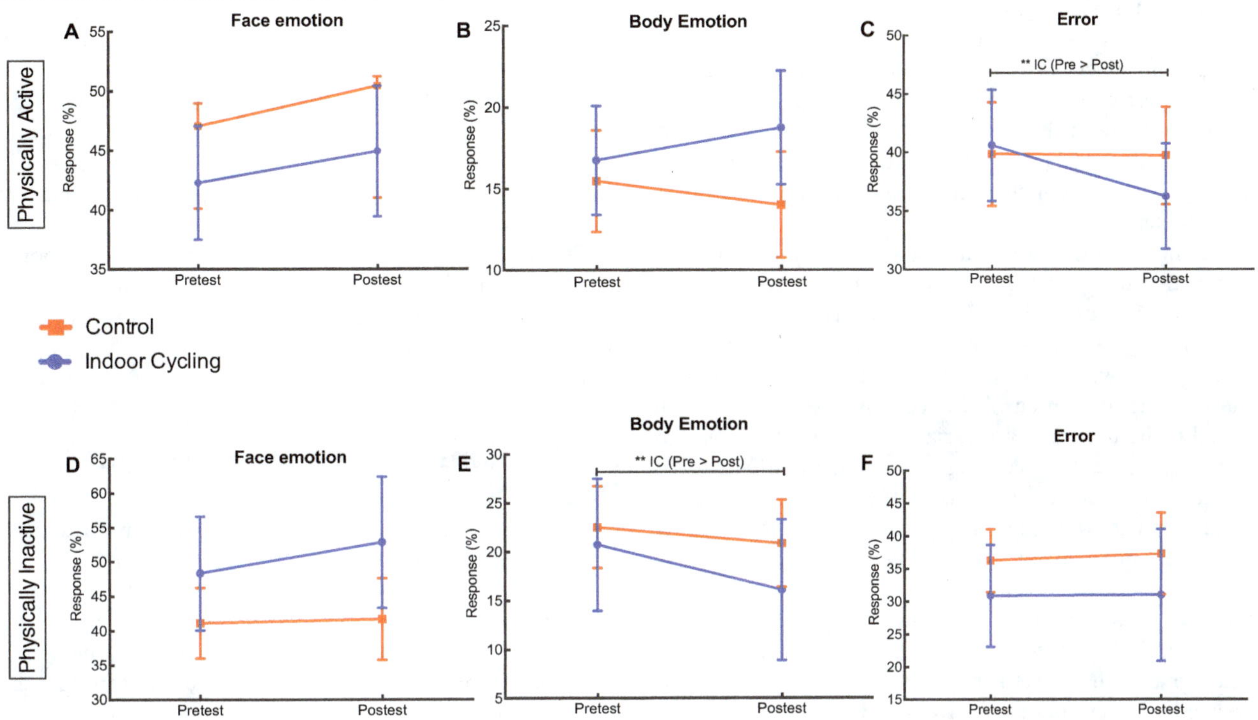

FIGURE 5 | Physically active **(A–C)** and physically inactive **(D–F)**. Means and 95% confidence interval of pre-test to post-test of emotional recognition. IC, indoor cycling (Experimental Group); CG, control group.

Executive Performance and Physical Exercise (Acute PE)

The literature that has dealt with the issues of the effect of acute PE on cognitive processes is wide (Tsukamoto et al., 2016; Akram et al., 2018; Quintero et al., 2018; Leyland et al., 2019; Wang et al., 2019b). In both experiments, we worked with a widely used battery on the executive function evaluation at clinic and research level: Stroop, TMT, and Verbal Fluency.

In this way, Experiment 1 data (PA) indicated that the group, which was subjected to PE indoor cycling, improved significantly in the Stroop-A right choices between pre and post compared to the control group. On the other hand, in the second experiment (physically inactive), the indoor cycling group improved response time in the post-test Stroop-A after the 30-min session (75–85%HRmax). Regarding the control group, Stroop-A right choices in pre-test and post-test measures and response time improved significantly compared to the indoor-cycling group.

In respect of TMT-A/B execution, significant changes enhanced for both groups, which can be explained more by a learning effect of the task than an acute differentiating effect of PE. Regarding phonological and semantic fluency, effects of PE were not observed, but the control group was significantly better. This result must be assumed with reservation on the grounds that this study only presented behavioral measures. Other types of measures and with greater precision can shed light on executive functions and semantic processing. For instance, current contributions point out that the acute PE is associated with greater neuron activation in older adults (Won et al., 2019). The neuron activation and underlying process activation of semantic memory, which is useful for the task performance of semantic processes, which constitutes a promising line of research for future studies (Szepietowska, 2019).

The prior findings are considered from three perspectives. (i) The best performance of the control group, which is PA in the performance of some executive tasks after acute PE, can be explained by a possible physical-cognitive reserve. Thus, optimum cognitive resources would be involved at execution time of the post-test task (Gajewski and Falkenstein, 2015), whereas the indoor cycling group could experiment tiredness due to moderate-high intensities of the HRmax. (ii) From a life cycle perspective, young adults tend to have a relatively stable an executive performance, different from other populations such as children and older adults. Hence, in childhood and old age greater sensibility of executive functions and toward stimuli such as the PE can be evidenced (Ludyga et al., 2016). The prior motive can explain that direct effects are not estimated. (iii) Lastly, the assumption of the hypothesis of the inverted U (Gutin, 1973) indicates that cognitive performance is diminished under high intensities of PE. Some effects of our data could provide evidence to the statement of the inverted U. Another part of our significant outcomes, however, provided evidence that transition of moderate-high intensities has also positive effects on cognitive performance.

Therefore, current studies have reported that high intensities of PE have a positive effect on executive functions in the performance of tasks such as the Stroop and attentional tasks of cancelation (Tsukamoto et al., 2016; Quintero et al., 2018). Additionally, the effect of strong acute PE may last from 30 min to 2 h after EP session (Basso et al., 2015). While it is true that the hypothesis of inverted U has a wide scientific evidence (Pontifex et al., 2009; Chang et al., 2014; De Souto Barreto et al., 2016; Ludyga et al., 2016), the discussion is still open in order to have more solid evidence.

Considering the above-mentioned, studying cognitive processes with great complexity tasks and that are coherent with the postulates of *embodied cognition* sets up a research line to explore. Specifically, simple tasks of cognitive evaluation such as the ones we implemented, and despite being widely used, have some limitations. The ceiling effect has a high rate of right choices with no variability measures, which is characteristic of a healthy neurologically population (McMorris et al., 2016; Mora-Gonzalez et al., 2019). This is a possible cause that justifies why high intensities of PE and healthy population are not sensitive to the performance of simple cognitive tasks.

Thereupon, qualification of tasks with higher complexity, which can underlie motor and cognitive processes, is an important challenge (e.g., Paradigms of Cognitive Motor Interference by using dual tasks). In such way, if the precision with tasks is evaluated, which involve all the body, similar to sport performance, those conditions can generate an intense effect of PE on cognitive processes (McMorris et al., 2016; Browne et al., 2017). In other words, associating tasks of cognitive complexity that involve the body, such as tasks that have an *embodied cognition* perspective, is a methodological and scientific challenge to be explored.

Emotional Recognition: Hypothesis of Physical Exercise as a Modulator of Social Cognition

In accordance with our revision, the studies that deal with the modulating effect of PE on emotional recognition are limited. In this sense, such issue has been addressed in our study. The found data proved that groups exposed to in one indoor-cycling sessions, from both experiments with moderate-high intensities (HRmax), had an effect on the right choices of emotional recognition in context. Thus, this finding suggests that the acute PE, apart from having cognitive benefits, which were previously mentioned, seems to have a direct effect on recognition emotional processing, and mainly, on tasks that require processing of contextual information.

Studies, which are carried out by magnetic functional resonance (fMRI), have demonstrated that body emotional posture influence in facial expression processing (Poyo-Solanas et al., 2018). Moreover, it has been suggested that the regions that are in charge of processing dynamic body movements are linked to emotional and body recognition (Kumfor et al., 2018). Using tasks of the same kind of our study, emotional recognition patterns in context in teenagers with criminal conduct have been explored (Santamaría-García et al., 2019), and with patients who suffer from frontotemporal dementia (Kumfor et al., 2018). These processes of body-face recognition are related to brain regions, as the fusiform gyrus (Committeri et al., 2007; Yogev-Seligmann et al., 2008), cingulate cortex, superior temporal gyrus, motor areas, and cerebellum. The identification of body and contextual information is very relevant for emotional recognition (De Gelder, 2006; Aviezer et al., 2012; Poyo-Solanas et al., 2018).

To sum up, our results are evidence that supports the modulator role hypothesis of PE in social cognition processes. Also, they let us put in perspective a path for new research lines, which result promising and hopeful so as to enhance the quality of life of people.

Implications, Limitation, and Future Research Directions

In agreement with the aforementioned, our results have practical implications, which are directly related to the quality of life of people. They are also pertinent for how the real world functions due to the easy access to PE in relation to its cost-benefit and non-invasiveness. The inclusion of programs of health promotion through the PE in school ages, and preventions of diseases in adulthood as a strategy to possible neurodegenerative disease emergence, hence, potential strategies of intervention at a preventive and psychoeducational level (Aguirre-Loaiza et al., 2019). Likewise, instructors and practitioners can train PA and inactive people through intervals of moderate-high intensities as part of a conditioning program as well as parallel purposes that are related with the objective of improving their cognitive processes.

On the other hand, and from a theoretical perspective, our results contribute to the increasing body of knowledge that studies modulator effect comprehension of acute PE on cognitive processes (Pontifex et al., 2019). Additionally, this study considered for the first time the immediate effect of PE in the assessment of emotional-context recognition, its huge scope and potential benefits in social human relationships. In this way, the path for future works in the line of social cognition is marked, modulating the cognitive and brain processes through PE.

This study, however, had some limitations. Firstly, physical activity measures were self-reported. The instruments use, such as the IPAQ-SF in the valoration and allocations to the experiments, was the first limitation. Therefore, more objective evaluations through aerobic conditions will allow a higher control, which is an important criterion for future studies. Secondly, our study kept isolated analysis between two experiments so as to identify a direct effect of duration and PE session intensities. Thus, it would be interesting that both sample conditions are compared (physically active and inactive) in a further analysis. Although it seems that physical condition is not a conditional requirement for temporary improvements and PE benefits (Ludyga et al., 2016). Other works, though, insist on considering physical (Labelle et al., 2013). Finally, our study worked with a single conditional capacity; there are other capacities to be studied (e.g., strength, coordination, among others). Indeed, it is possible the combination of these capacities pose an important work line yet to be studied. Likewise, manipulating a chronic PE program and linking cognitive tasks with complex paradigms is a limitation that if addressed in new proposals, it may clarify of the modulating role of PE. These results should be considered with caution due to the sample size, therefore new work is encouraged (Slade et al., 2016).

After mentioning the limitations, we deem that future studies can address: (i) research that demonstrates the role of EP with different intensities. (ii) Apart from the prior, the assessment and design of other measures of cognitive domains, which are associated to the social cognition and embodied *cognition* with greater complexity, allowing higher sensibility and specificity. For instance, dual tasks in which the body performance is linked. (iii) Effect exploration of other conditional capacities (e.g., coordination). (iv) Motor expertise exploration and analysis of the cognitive-physical reserve relation regarding the cognitive-emotional performance in context.

CONCLUSION

In summary, our findings add evidence in which the acute PE with moderate-high intensities of HRmax (75–85%) has positive effects on executive functions, and mainly, in the emotional-contextual recognition.

ETHICS STATEMENT

The research was approved by the Ethics Committee of the School of Health Sciences, Caldas University (Code CBCS-048, Acta015 from 2017). All the participants signed the informed agreement and knew the purposes of the investigation and its respective phases. The patients/participants provided their written informed consent to participate in this study.

AUTHOR CONTRIBUTIONS

HA-L, JA, IA, AF-J, SR-B, and FA-Z conceived and designed the experiments. JA, IA, SB-G, and H-AL collected data. HA-L and JA performed the statistical analysis. AF-J, CN, SB-G, HA-L, and AG-M interpreted the data. HA-L, AF-J, and SB-G wrote the original draft. HA-L, JA, IA, AF-J, SB-G, SR-B, FA-Z, CN, and AG-M reviewed, edited and drafted the manuscript, and approved the final version.

ACKNOWLEDGMENTS

We thank the participants of study, Psychology Program students, Ing. Daniela Torres of Universidad Católica de Pereira, Physical Education Program students of Universidad del Quindío, Prof. Leonardo Álzate, and Bodytech - Armenia, Colombia.

REFERENCES

ACSM, (2018). *Guidelines for Exercise Testing and Prescription*, 10th Edn. Philadelphia: Wolters Kluwer Health.

Aguirre-Loaiza, H. H., Parra, J., Bartolo, L., Cardona, M. A., and Arenas, J. A. (2019). Desempeño neuropsicológico e indicadores de frecuencia, duración y tiempo de la sesión del ejercicio físico. *Pensam. Psicol.* 17, 19–32.

Akram, M., Ghous, M., Tariq, I., Khan, H., Paracha, M., and Hussain, B. (2018). The association between physical activity with cognitive and cardiovascular deconditioning in age related decline of college students. *JPMA. J. Pakistan Med. Assoc.* 68, 1755–1758.

Armstrong, N., and Welsman, J. R. (2007). Aerobic fitness: what are we measuring? *Med. Sport Sci.* 50, 5–25. doi: 10.1159/000101073

Aviezer, H., Bentin, S., Dudarev, V., and Hassin, R. R. (2011). The Automaticity of emotional face-context integration humans are tuned to recognize facial expressions of emotion in a fast. *Hassin Trope* 11, 1406–1414. doi: 10.1037/a0023578

Aviezer, H., Hassin, R. R., Ryan, J., Grandy, C., Susskind, J., Anderson, A., et al. (2008). Angry, disgusted, or afraid? Studies on the malleability of emotion. *Psychol. Sci.* 19, 724–732. doi: 10.1111/j.1467-9280.2008.02148.x

Aviezer, H., Trope, Y., and Todorov, A. (2012). Body cues, not facial expressions, discriminate between intense positive and negative emotions. *Science* 338, 1225–1229. doi: 10.1126/science.1224313

Basso, J. C., Shang, A., Elman, M., Karmouta, R., and Suzuki, W. A. (2015). Acute exercise improves prefrontal cortex but not hippocampal function in healthy adults. *J. Int. Neuropsychol. Soc.* 21, 791–801. doi: 10.1017/S135561771500106X

Basso, J. C., and Suzuki, W. A. (2017). The effects of acute exercise on mood, cognition, neurophysiology, and neurochemical pathways: a review. *Brain Plast.* 2, 127–152. doi: 10.3233/BPL-160040

Borkowski, J., Benton, A. L., and Spreen, O. (1967). Word fluency and brain damage. *Neuropsychologia* 5, 135–140. doi: 10.1016/0028-3932(67)90015-2

Brand, S., Gerber, M., Colledge, F., Holsboer-Trachsler, E., Pühse, U., and Ludyga, S. (2019). Acute exercise and emotion recognition in young adolescents. *J. Sport Exerc. Psychol.* 41, 129–136. doi: 10.1123/jsep.2018-0160

Browne, S. E., Flynn, M. J., O'Neill, B. V., Howatson, G., Bell, P. G., and Haskell-Ramsay, C. F. (2017). Effects of acute high-intensity exercise on cognitive performance in trained individuals: a systematic review. *Progr. Brain Res.* 234, 161–187. doi: 10.1016/bs.pbr.2017.06.003

Chang, Y.-K., Chi, L., Etnier, J. L., Wang, C.-C., Chu, C.-H., and Zhou, C. (2014). Effect of acute aerobic exercise on cognitive performance: role of cardiovascular fitness. *Psychol. Sport Exerc.* 15, 464–470. doi: 10.1016/J.PSYCHSPORT.2014.04.007

Chang, Y.-K., Chu, C.-H., Wang, C.-C., Song, T.-F., and Wei, G.-X. (2015). Effect of acute exercise and cardiovascular fitness on cognitive function: an event-related cortical desynchronization study. *Psychophysiology* 52, 342–351. doi: 10.1111/psyp.12364

Chang, Y.-K., Labban, J. D., Gapin, J. I., and Etnier, J. L. (2012). The effects of acute exercise on cognitive performance: a meta-analysis. *Brain Res.* 1453, 87–101. doi: 10.1016/j.brainres.2012.02.068

Chen, P. Y., and Chang, H.-C. (2012). The coping process of patients with cancer. *Eur. J. Oncol. Nurs.* 16, 10–16. doi: 10.1016/j.ejon.2011.01.002

Committeri, G., Pitzalis, S., Galati, G., Patria, F., Pelle, G., Sabatini, U., et al. (2007). Neural bases of personal and extrapersonal neglect in humans. *Brain* 130, 431–441. doi: 10.1093/brain/awl265

Craig, C. L., Marshall, A. L., Sjöström, M., Bauman, A. E., Booth, M. L., Ainsworth, B. E., et al. (2003). International physical activity questionnaire: 12-country reliability and validity. *Med. Sc. Sports Exerci.* 35, 1381–1395. doi: 10.1249/01.MSS.0000078924.61453.FB

De Gelder, B. (2006). Towards the neurobiology of emotional body language. *Nat. Rev. Neurosci.* 7, 242–249. doi: 10.1080/10915810305084

De Souto Barreto, P., Delrieu, J., Andrieu, S., Vellas, B., and Rolland, Y. (2016). Physical activity and cognitive function in middle-aged and older adults. *Mayo Clin. Proc.* 91, 1515–1524. doi: 10.1016/j.mayocp.2016.06.032

Donnelly, J. E., Hillman, C., Castelli, D. M., Etnier, J. L., Lee, S., Tomporowski, P., et al. (2016). Physical activity, fitness, cognitive function, and academic achievement in children: a systematic review. *Med. Sci. Sports Exerc.* 48, 1197–1222. doi: 10.1249/MSS.0000000000000901.Physical

Erickson, K. I., Hillman, C., and Kramer, A. F. (2015). Physical activity, brain, and cognition. *Curr. Opin. Behav. Sci.* 4, 27–32. doi: 10.1016/j.cobeha.2015.01.005

Esteban-Cornejo, I., Rodriguez-Ayllon, M., Verdejo-Roman, J., Cadenas-Sanchez, C., Mora-Gonzalez, J., Chaddock-Heyman, L., et al. (2019). Physical fitness, white matter volume and academic performance in children: findings from the ActiveBrains and FITKids2 projects. *Front. Psychol.* 10:208. doi: 10.3389/fpsyg.2019.00208

Etnier, J. L., Drollette, E. S., and Slutsky, A. B. (2019). Physical activity and cognition: a narrative review of the evidence for older adults. *Psychol. Sport Exerci.* 42, 156–166. doi: 10.1016/J.PSYCHSPORT.2018.12.006

Florez, J. C., Ostrosky, F., and Lozano, A. (2012). *BANFE - Batería Neuorpsicológica de Funciones Ejecutivas y Lóbulos Frontales*. México DF: Manual Moderno.

Forsén, L., Loland, N. W., Vuillemin, A., Chinapaw, M. J. M., van Poppel, M. N. M., Mokkink, L. B., et al. (2010). Self-administered physical activity questionnaires for the elderly. *Sports Med.* 40, 601–623. doi: 10.2165/11531350-000000000-00000

Gajewski, P. D., and Falkenstein, M. (2015). Long-term habitual physical activity is associated with lower distractibility in a Stroop interference task in aging: behavioral and ERP evidence. *Brain Cogn.* 98, 87–101. doi: 10.1016/j.bandc.2015.06.004

Gil, L., Ruiz De Sánchez, C., Gil, F., Romero, S. J., and Pretelt Burgos, F. (2015). Validation of the montreal cognitive assessment (MoCA) in Spanish as a screening tool for mild cognitive impairment and mild dementia in patients over 65 years old in Bogotá, Colombia. *Int. J. Geriat. Psychiatry* 30, 655–662. doi: 10.1002/gps.4199

Gunnell, K. E., Poitras, V. J., LeBlanc, A., Schibli, K., Barbeau, K., Hedayati, N., et al. (2018). Physical activity and brain structure, brain function, and cognition in children and youth: a systematic review of randomized controlled trials. *Ment. Health Phys. Act.* 16, 105–127. doi: 10.1016/J.MHPA.2018.11.002

Guthold, R., Stevens, G. A., Riley, L. M., and Bull, F. C. (2018). Worldwide trends in insufficient physical activity from 2001 to 2016: a pooled analysis of 358 population-based surveys with 1.9 million participants. *Lancet. Global Health* 6, e1077–e1086. doi: 10.1016/S2214-109X(18)30357-7

Gutin, B. (1973). Exercise-induced activation and human performance: a review. *Res. Q. Am. Assoc. Health Phys. Educ. Recreat.* 44, 256–268. doi: 10.1080/10671188.1973.10615204

Hagger, M. S. (2019). Habit and physical activity: theoretical advances, practical implications, and agenda for future research. *Psychol. Sport Exerc.* 42, 118–129. doi: 10.1016/J.PSYCHSPORT.2018.12.007

Herting, M. M., Colby, J. B., Sowell, E. R., and Nagel, B. J. (2014). White matter connectivity and aerobic fitness in male adolescents. *Dev. Cogn. Neurosci.* 7, 65–75. doi: 10.1016/j.dcn.2013.11.003

Herting, M. M., and Nagel, B. J. (2013). Differences in brain activity during a verbal associative memory encoding task in high- and low-fit adolescents. *J. Cogn. Neurosci.* 25, 595–612. doi: 10.1162/jocn_a_00344

Hillman, C., Logan, N. E., and Shigeta, T. T. (2019). A review of acute physical activity effects on brain and cognition in children. *Transl. J. Am. Sport Med.* 4, 132–136.

Hillman, C., Pontifex, M. B., Castelli, D. M., Khan, N. A., Raine, L. B., Scudder, M. R., et al. (2014). Effects of the FITKids Randomized Controlled Trial on Executive Control and Brain Function. *Pediatrics* 134, e1063–e1071. doi: 10.1542/peds.2013-3219

IUPS, (2008). "Universal declaration of ethical principles for psychologists," in *Assembly of the International Union of Psychological Science*, (Palais de Chaillot: Universal Declaration).

Joyce, J., Smyth, P. J., Donnelly, A. E., and Davranche, K. (2014). The simon task and aging: does acute moderate exercise influence cognitive control? *Med. Sci. Sports Exerc.* 46, 630–639. doi: 10.1249/MSS.0b013e3182a77980

Karvonen, M., Kentala, E., and Mustala, O. (1957). The effects of training on heart rate; a longitudinal study. *Ann. Med. Exp. Biol. Fenn.* 35, 307–315.

Kumfor, F., Ibañez, A., Hutchings, R., Hazelton, J. L., Hodges, J. R., and Piguet, O. (2018). Beyond the face: how context modulates emotion processing in frontotemporal dementia subtypes. *Brain* 141, 1172–1185. doi: 10.1093/brain/awy002

Labelle, V., Bosquet, L., Mekary, S., and Bherer, L. (2013). Decline in executive control during acute bouts of exercise as a function of exercise intensity and fitness level. *Brain Cogn.* 81, 10–17. doi: 10.1016/j.bandc.2012.10.001

Lambourne, K., and Tomporowski, P. (2010). The effect of exercise-induced arousal on cognitive task performance: a meta-regression analysis. *Brain Res.* 1341, 12–24. doi: 10.1016/j.brainres.2010.03.091

Leyland, L.-A., Spencer, B., Beale, N., Jones, T., and van Reekum, C. M. (2019). The effect of cycling on cognitive function and well-being in older adults. *Plos One* 14:e0211779. doi: 10.1371/journal.pone.0211779

Li, L., Men, W. W., Chang, Y. K., Fan, M. X., Ji, L., and Wei, G. X. (2014). Acute aerobic exercise increases cortical activity during working memory: a functional MRI study in female college students. *PLoS One* 9:e99222. doi: 10.1371/journal.pone.0099222

Ludyga, S., Gerber, M., Brand, S., Holsboer-Trachsler, E., and Pühse, U. (2016). Acute effects of moderate aerobic exercise on specific aspects of executive function in different age and fitness groups: a meta-analysis. *Psychophysiology* 53, 1611–1626. doi: 10.1111/psyp.12736

McMorris, T., Turner, A., Hale, B. J., and Sproule, J. (2016). "Beyond the catecholamines hypothesis for an acute exercise–cognition interaction: a neurochemical perspective," in *Exercise-Cognition Interaction*, ed. T. McMorris, (Amsterdam: Elsevier), 65–103. doi: 10.1016/b978-0-12-800778-5.00004-9

McSween, M. P., Coombes, J. S., MacKay, C. P., Rodriguez, A. D., Erickson, K. I., Copland, D. A., et al. (2019). The immediate effects of acute aerobic exercise on cognition in healthy older adults: a systematic review. *Sports Med.* 49, 67–82. doi: 10.1007/s40279-018-01039-9

Ministerio de Salud - República de Colombia, (1993). *Resolución 8430, 1993.* Bogotá: Ministerio De Salud Resolucion §:.

Mora-Gonzalez, J., Esteban-Cornejo, I., Cadenas-Sanchez, C., Migueles, J. H., Molina-Garcia, P., Rodriguez-Ayllon, M., et al. (2019). Physical fitness, physical activity, and the executive function in children with overweight and obesity. *J. Pediatr.* 208, 50–56. doi: 10.1016/j.jpeds.2018.12.028

Nasreddine, L., Philips, A., Bedirian, V., Charbonneau, S., Whitehead, V., Collin, I., et al. (2005). The montreal cognitive assessment,MOCA:a brief screening tool for mild cognitive impairment. *Am. Geriat. Soc.* 53, 695–699. doi: 10.1029/WR017i002p00410

O'Driscoll, C., and Shaikh, M. (2017). Cross-cultural applicability of the montreal cognitive assessment (MoCA): a systematic review. *J. Alzheimer's Dis.* 58, 789–801. doi: 10.3233/JAD-161042

Päivärinne, V., Kautiainen, H., Heinonen, A., and Kiviranta, I. (2018). Relations between subdomains of physical activity, sedentary lifestyle, and quality of life in young adult men. *Scand. J. Med. Sci. Sports* 28, 1389–1396. doi: 10.1111/sms.13003

Pedraza, O. L., Salaza, A. M., Sierra, F., Soler, D., Castro, J., Castillo, P., et al. (2016). Confiabilidad, validez de criterio y discriminante del montreal cognitive assessment (MoCA) test, en un grupo de adultos de Bogotá. *Acta Méd. Colomb.* 41, 221–228.

Pedraza, O. L., Sánchez, E., Plata, S. J., Montalvo, C., Galvis, P., Chiquillo, A., et al. (2014). Puntuaciones del MoCA y el MMSE en pacientes con deterioro cognitivo leve y demencia en una clínica de memoria en Bogotá. *Acta Neurol. Colomb.* 30, 22–31.

Peruyero, F., Zapata, J., Pastor, D., and Cervelló, E. (2017). The acute effects of exercise intensity on inhibitory cognitive control in adolescents. *Front. Psychol.* 8:921. doi: 10.3389/fpsyg.2017.00921

Pontifex, M. B., Hillman, C., Fernhall, B., Thompson, K. M., and Valentini, T. A. (2009). The effect of acute aerobic and resistance exercise on working memory. *Med. Sci. Sports Exerc.* 41, 927–934. doi: 10.1249/MSS.0b013e3181907d69

Pontifex, M. B., McGowan, A. L., Chandler, M. C., Gwizdala, K. L., Parks, A. C., Fenn, K., et al. (2019). A primer on investigating the after effects of acute bouts of physical activity on cognition. *Psychol. Sport Exerc.* 40, 1–22. doi: 10.1016/j.psychsport.2018.08.015

Poyo-Solanas, M., Zhan, M., Vaessen, M., Hortensius, R., Engelen, T., and de Gelder, B. (2018). Looking at the face and seeing the whole body. Neural basis of combined face and body expressions. *Soc. Cog. Affect. Neurosci.* 13, 135–144. doi: 10.1093/scan/nsx130

Prakash, R. S., Voss, M. W., Erickson, K. I., and Kramer, A. F. (2015). Physical activity and cognitive vitality. *Annu. Rev. Psychol.* 66, 769–797. doi: 10.1146/annurev-psych-010814-015249

Quintero, A. P., Bonilla-Vargas, K. J., Correa-Bautista, J. E., Domínguez-Sanchéz, M. A., Triana-Reina, H. R., Velasco-Orjuela, G. P., et al. (2018). Acute effect of three different exercise training modalities on executive function in overweight inactive men: a secondary analysis of the BrainFit study. *Physiol. Behav.* 197, 22–28. doi: 10.1016/j.physbeh.2018.09.010

Rabin, L., Barr, W., and Burton, L. (2005). Assessment practices of clinical neuropsychologists in the United States and Canada: a survey of INS, NAN, and APA division 40 members. *Arch. Clin. Neuropsychol.* 20, 33–65. doi: 10.1016/j.acn.2004.02.005

Reed, J., and Ones, D. S. (2006). The effect of acute aerobic exercise on positive activated affect: a meta-analysis. *Psychol. Sport Exerc.* 7, 477–514. doi: 10.1016/J.PSYCHSPORT.2005.11.003

Reitan, R. M. (1958). Validity of the trail making test as an indicator of organic brain damage. *Percept. Mot. Skills* 8, 271–276. doi: 10.2466/pms.1958.8.3.271

Reiter, K., Nielson, K. A., Smith, T. J., Weiss, L. R., Alfini, A. J., and Smith, J. C. (2015). Improved cardiorespiratory fitness is associated with increased cortical thickness in mild cognitive impairment. *J. Int. Neuropsychol. Soc.* 21, 757–767. doi: 10.1017/S135561771500079X

Sáez de Asteasu, M. L., Martínez-Velilla, N., Zambom-Ferraresi, F., Casas-Herrero, Á, and Izquierdo, M. (2017). Role of physical exercise on cognitive function in healthy older adults: a systematic review of randomized clinical trials. *Ageing Res. Rev.* 37, 117–134. doi: 10.1016/J.ARR.2017.05.007

Sanda, B., Vistad, I., Haakstad, L. A. H., Berntsen, S., Sagedal, L. R., Lohne-Seiler, H., et al. (2017). Reliability and concurrent validity of the international physical activity questionnaire short form among pregnant women. *BMC Sports Sci. Med. Rehabil.* 9:7. doi: 10.1186/s13102-017-0070-4

Santamaría-García, H., Ibáñez, A., Montaño, S., García, A. M., Patiño-Saenz, M., Idarraga, C., et al. (2019). Out of context, beyond the face: neuroanatomical pathways of emotional face-body language integration in adolescent offenders. *Front. Behav.; Neurosci.* 13:1–14. doi: 10.3389/fnbeh.2019.00034

Sanz, J., and García-Vera, M. P. (2013). Rendimiento diagnóstico y estructura factorial del Inventario para la Depresión de Beck–Segunda Edición (BDI-II) en pacientes españoles con trastornos psicológicos. *Anales Psicol.* 29, 66–75. doi: 10.6018/analesps.29.1.130532

Silva, B. G. C. D., da Silva, I. C. M., Ekelund, U., Brage, S., Ong, K. K., De Lucia Rolfe, E., et al. (2019). Associations of physical activity and sedentary time with body composition in Brazilian young adults. *Sci. Rep.* 9:5444. doi: 10.1038/s41598-019-41935-2

Sink, K. M., Espeland, M. A., Castro, C. M., Church, T., Cohen, R., Dodson, J. A., et al. (2015). Effect of a 24-month physical activity intervention vs health education on cognitive outcomes in sedentary older adults. *JAMA* 314, 781–790. doi: 10.1001/jama.2015.9617

Slade, S. C., Dionne, C. E., Underwood, M., and Buchbinder, R. (2016). Consensus on exercise reporting template (CERT): explanation and elaboration statement. *Br. J. Sports Med.* 50, 1428–1437. doi: 10.1136/bjsports-2016-096651

Strauss, E., Sherman, E. M., and Spreen, O. (2007). *A Compendium of Neuropsychological Tests: Administration, Norms, and Commentary.* New York, NY: Oxford University Press.

Szepietowska, E. M. (2019). Cognitive reserve as a factor determining the level of cognitive functions in adults: a preliminary report. *Psych. Psychol. Kliniczna* 19, 32–41. doi: 10.15557/PiPK.2019.0005

Tsukamoto, H., Suga, T., Takenaka, S., Tanaka, D., Takeuchi, T., Hamaoka, T., et al. (2016). Greater impact of acute high-intensity interval exercise on post-exercise executive function compared to moderate-intensity continuous exercise. *Physiol. Behav.* 155, 224–230. doi: 10.1016/j.physbeh.2015.12.021

Van Poppel, M. N. M., Chinapaw, M. J. M., Mokkink, L. B., van Mechelen, W., and Terwee, C. B. (2010). Physical Activity Questionnaires for Adults. *Sports Med.* 40, 565–600. doi: 10.2165/11531930-000000000-00000

Vazou, S., Pesce, C., Lakes, K., and Smiley-Oyen, A. (2019). More than one road leads to Rome: a narrative review and meta-analysis of physical activity intervention effects on cognition in youth. *Int. J. Sport Exerc. Psychol.* 17, 153–178. doi: 10.1080/1612197X.2016.1223423

Vieira, R. A., Costa, E. C., Sales, M. M., Fonteles, A. I., Moraes, J. F. V. N., and Barros, J. D. F. (2016). Efeito agudo do exercício aeróbio vigoroso sobre o controle inibitório em adolescentes. *Rev. Paulista Pediat.* 34, 154–161. doi: 10.1016/J.RPPED.2015.08.004

Voss, M. W., Soto, C., Yoo, S., Sodoma, M., Vivar, C., and Van Praag, H. (2019). Exercise and hippocampal memory systems. *Trends Cogn. Sci.* 23, 318–333. doi: 10.1016/j.tics.2019.01.006

Voss, M. W., Weng, T. B., Burzynska, A. Z., Wong, C. N., Cooke, G. E., Clark, R., et al. (2015). Fitness, but not physical activity, is related to functional integrity of brain networks associated with aging. *NeuroImage* 131, 113–125. doi: 10.1016/j.neuroimage.2015.10.044

Wang, C. H., Moreau, D., Yang, C.-T., Lin, J.-T., Tsai, Y.-Y., and Tsai, C.-L. (2019a). The influence of aerobic fitness on top-down and bottom-up mechanisms of interference control. *Neuropsychology* 33, 245–255. doi: 10.1037/neu0000507

Wang, C. H., Moreau, D., Yang, C. T., Tsai, Y. Y., Lin, J. T., Liang, W. K., et al. (2019b). Aerobic exercise modulates transfer and brain signal complexity following cognitive training. *Biol. Psychol.* 144, 85–98. doi: 10.1016/j.biopsycho.2019.03.012

Wang, Y. P., and Gorenstein, C. (2013). Psychometric properties of the beck depression Inventory-II: a comprehensive review. *Rev. Bras. Psiquiat.* 35, 416–431. doi: 10.1590/1516-4446-2012-1048

Warburton, D., Jamnik, V., Bredin, S., and Gledhill, N. (2011). The physical activity readiness questionnaire for everyone (PAR-Q+) and electronic physical activity readiness medical examination (ePARmed-X+). *Health Fit. J. Can.* 4, 3–17.

WMA, (2013). *Declaracioìn de Helsinki de la AMM - Principios Eìticos Para las Investigaciones Meìdicas en Seres Humanos.* Ferney-Voltaire: World Medical Association, Inc.

Won, J., Alfini, A. J., Weiss, L. R., Michelson, C. S., Callow, D. D., Ranadive, S. M., et al. (2019). Semantic memory activation after acute exercise in healthy older adults. *J. Int. Neuropsychol. Soc.* 25, 557–568. doi: 10.1017/S1355617719000171

World Health Organization [WHO], (2007). *A Guide for Population-Based Approaches to Increasing Levels of Physical Activity: Implementation of the WHO Global Strategy On diet, Physical Activity and Health.* Geneva: WHO.

World Health Organization [WHO], (2010). *Global recommendations on physical activity for helth.* Geneva: WHO Library Cataloguing-in-Publication.

World Health Organization [WHO], (2018). *Why is physical activity important?* Available at: https://www.paho.org/hq/index.php?option=com_content&view=article&id=14459:physical-activity&Itemid=1969&lang=en (accessed on February 13, 2019).

Wu, C.-H., Karageorghis, C. I., Wang, C.-C., Chu, C.-H., Kao, S.-C., Hung, T.-M., et al. (2019). Effects of acute aerobic and resistance exercise on executive function: an ERP study. *J. Sci. Med. Sport* 22, 1367–1372. doi: 10.1016/j.jsams.2019.07.009

Yogev-Seligmann, G., Hausdorff, J. M., and Giladi, N. (2008). The role of executive function and attention in gait. *Mov. Disord.* 23, 329–342. doi: 10.1002/mds.21720

Zuniga, K. E., Mueller, M., Santana, A. R., and Kelemen, W. L. (2019). Acute aerobic exercise improves memory across intensity and fitness levels. *Memory* 27, 628–636. doi: 10.1080/09658211.2018.1546875

22

Analysis of Misbehaviors and Satisfaction with School in Secondary Education According to Student Gender and Teaching Competence

Antonio Granero-Gallegos[1,2]*, Raúl Baños*[3]**, Antonio Baena-Extremera*[4] *and Marina Martínez-Molina*[1]

[1] Faculty of Education Sciences, University of Almería, Almería, Spain, [2] Health Research Center, University of Almería, Almería, Spain, [3] Department of Physical Education and Sports Science, Autonomous University of Baja California, Ensenada, Mexico, [4] Department of Didactic of Corporal Expression, Faculty of Education Sciences, Granada, Spain

***Correspondence:**
Raúl Baños
raulfb89@gmail.com

Effective classroom management is a critical teaching skill and a key concern for educators. Disruptive behaviors disturb effective classroom management and can influence school satisfaction if the teacher does not have the competencies to control them. Two objectives were set in this work: to understand the differences that exist in school satisfaction, disruptive behaviors, and teaching competencies according to the gender of the students; and to analyze school satisfaction and disruptive student behaviors based on perceived teaching competence. A non-probabilistic and convenience sample selection process was employed, based on the subjects that we were able to access. 758 students participated (male = 45.8%) from seven public secondary schools in the Murcia Region (Spain). The age range was between 13 and 18 years (M = 15.22; DT = 1.27). A questionnaire composed of the following scales was used: *Competencies Evaluation Scale for Teachers in Physical Education, School Satisfaction* and *Disruptive Behaviors in Physical Education.* Mixed Linear Models performed with the SPSS v.23 was used for statistical analyses. The results revealed statistically significant differences based on gender and physical education teaching competencies. In conclusion, the study highlights that physical education teacher skills influence disruptive behaviors in the classroom, and that this is also related to school satisfaction. Furthermore, it highlights that boys showed higher levels of negative behaviors than girls.

Keywords: physical education, disruptive behavior, indiscipline, high school, satisfaction

INTRODUCTION

Undisciplined behaviors in the classroom are a serious problem for the teaching and learning process during adolescence (Medina and Reverte, 2019), and may have an impact on feelings regarding school satisfaction, the relationship with teachers or even on school failure (Baños et al., 2017). These types of behaviors commonly occur in the Physical Education (PE) class, producing conflictive situations between peers (students) and even with the teacher himself/herself. It is therefore advisable to solve the problem in a rapid and effective fashion (Müller et al., 2018).

Faced with these situations, the competencies of the PE teaching staff play an important role (Baños et al., 2017; Trigueros and Navarro, 2019; Granero-Gallegos et al., 2020); the way in which teachers design, organize and control their sessions can affect the students' disruptive behaviors and class outcome.

As evidenced in research by authors such as Goyette et al. (2000) and Kulinna et al. (2006), adolescents often show certain problematic behaviors in the classroom, such as idleness, disrespect, talking out of turn and/or avoiding or skipping classes, which have a negative impact on the learning environment. Even aggressive behaviors can sometimes arise in PE classes, such as bullying and peer fighting (Weiss et al., 2008). Studies looking at inappropriate behaviors in PE have demonstrated that the students' negative behavior not only affects the quality of teaching, but also interferes with peer learning (Kulinna et al., 2006; Cothran et al., 2009). Moreover, disruptive behaviors are more common at the secondary school level than in primary education classes, as evidenced by various works (e.g., Kulinna et al., 2006; Cothran and Kulinna, 2007). Adolescence, in particular, is characterized by a rebellious, non-conformist stage, a fight against authority, irresponsibility and low personal self-control. At this age, a disengagement with the school can occur, with a decreased willingness to comply with the rules and with expected behavior (Fredericks et al., 2004).

In addition, gender has been used to analyze these behaviors, both in students and in teachers. Specifically, the female gender (both teachers and students) are those who report the highest incidence of inappropriate behaviors (Kulinna et al., 2006), with females being the ones likely to receive this negativity (Cothran and Kulinna, 2007). There are several studies that have found higher levels of inappropriate behaviors among boys than among girls (Beaman et al., 2006; Kulinna et al., 2006; Cothran and Kulinna, 2007; Driessen, 2011). Boys tend to be more boisterous and disruptive with their peers (Glock and Kleen, 2017) whereas girls tend to be more proactive and less problematic (Driessen, 2011), albeit with more shy and introverted behaviors (Glock and Kleen, 2017). Furthermore, boys are often more influenced by their peers than girls are, resulting in higher levels of truancy, punishments and challenging behaviors that teachers have to face (Hadjar and Buchmann, 2016; Geven et al., 2017). Other authors (i.e., Baños et al., 2018) found that students claimed to have more aggressive behaviors during PE sessions.

Among the attributions made by the students regarding inappropriate behaviors when doing PE, the boredom they experience stands out, finding the classes monotonous, as well as expressing a certain discontent with the teacher. However, it should be noted that these are students with usually disruptive behaviors (Cothran and Kulinna, 2007). In relation to the teachers, some recent studies have linked disruptive behaviors to teacher competence as perceived by the students (Baños et al., 2019; Granero-Gallegos et al., 2019; Granero-Gallegos et al., 2020). This research related the high levels of teaching competencies with low levels of negative behavior in PE classes although the study did not cover the effect of the teaching staff's competence.

In addition, the scientific literature has stated that school satisfaction reduces student misbehavior, making it advisable to develop social and emotional skills, cognitive ability, behavioral and moral competencies, the recognition of positive behavior, belief in the future and prosocial norms (Sun, 2016). In contrast, ineffective classroom management causes disarray and interruptions produced by a few adolescents, affecting both the anxiety and stress of their peers and that of the teachers (Cothran et al., 2009).

In this way, the work of PE teachers plays a relevant part in developing good classroom behaviors. Depending on the skills that the teachers develop, they may increase or decrease negative behaviors (Rasmussen et al., 2014). Thus, teachers who have a wide repertoire of teaching styles, and who know how to adapt them to different environments and learning content, manage to improve the students' satisfaction with the school (Invernizzi et al., 2019); this is also influenced by the orientations toward learning (Agbuga et al., 2010).

Regarding the study of satisfaction, Diener's theory of subjective well-being (Diener, 2009) could be of great help. This theory consists of two dimensions, the cognitive dimension and the affective dimension. The cognitive dimension relates to the evaluative judgments of global satisfaction with life and its specific areas, while the affective dimension is identified with emotions and attachments such as fun, boredom and concern (Diener and Emmons, 1985). In this vein, Baena-Extremera and Granero-Gallegos (2015) highlight the importance of the student being satisfied and at ease in school. An adolescent who is satisfied with the school is associated with higher levels of life satisfaction (Scharenberg, 2016), with an adequate school climate managed by the teacher (Varela et al., 2018) and with better social relationships among his/her peers (Persson et al., 2016). However, a student who gets bored at school decreases the efficiency of any learning style (Ahmed et al., 2013). This is associated with higher school dropout rates (Takakura et al., 2010), and with low teacher competencies (Sun, 2016), which in turn relates to greater disruptive behavior (Baños et al., 2019).

Scientific evidence has demonstrated the impact of negative behaviors and student satisfaction on both the learning and teaching processes. However, there is not enough literature that links the skills of the PE teacher with either student satisfaction with the school or with classroom misbehavior. Therefore, this work sets out two important objectives: (1) to understand the differences that exist in terms of school satisfaction, disruptive behaviors and teaching competencies according to the gender of the students; and (2) to analyze school satisfaction and disruptive student behaviors based on perceived teaching competence. From a review of the literature, the following hypotheses are made:

(1) There will be a significant and positive correlation between school satisfaction, disruptive student behaviors and the perceived competencies of the PE teacher; however, there will be a significant and negative correlation between boredom with school, disruptive student behaviors, and the perceived competencies of the PE teacher.
(2) Boys will show more negative behaviors than girls although girls will score higher in school satisfaction and in the perception of teaching competencies.

(3) Students who perceive that PE teachers are competent will show less disruptive behavior and greater school satisfaction.

MATERIALS AND METHODS

Participants

The design of this cross-sectional study was observational and descriptive selecting a non-probabilistic convenience sample according to the people that could be accessed from public high schools located in areas of medium socioeconomic level (from Murcia and Cartagena cities). No educational center is included in the program of Teaching Compensatory, program that allocates specific, material and human resources to guarantee access, permanence and promotion in the educational system for socially disadvantaged students. A total of 758 students participated (males = 45.8%) from seven public secondary schools in the Murcia region of Spain (94% Spanish, Caucasian; 4% Arab origin; 1% East European, Caucasian; 1% South American). All students of these educational centers from 2nd, 3rd, 4th of ESO and 1st of Baccalaureate (PE is also subject compulsory) were requested to participate in this research. Incomplete answers due to errors or omissions in their responses (28) were dismissed for analysis and 34 students did not obtain parental consent to participate in this investigation. The age range was between 13 and 18 years (M = 15.22; SD = 1.27); the average age for the boys was 15.2 (SD = 1.29) and for the girls was 15.18 (SD = 1.26). The distribution in terms of course levels was as follows: 45.3% at ESO 2nd level; 20.1% at ESO 3rd level; 27.2% at ESO 4th level; and 7.5% in the 1st year of Baccalaureate. As PE is a compulsory subject for all students of the 1st year of Baccalaureate, these students were also included in this research. There were no statistically significant differences in gender × age between the included participants (p = 0.501) (see **Table 1**).

Instruments

To carry out this investigation, the next instruments have been used.

Teaching Competence

The Spanish version of the *Competencies Evaluation Scale for Teachers in Physical Education* (ETCS-PE) by Baena-Extremera et al. (2015) was used, adapted from the original *Evaluation of Teaching Competencies Scale* by Catano and Harvey (2011). It consists of eight items that measure the students' perception of teacher effectiveness. A seven-point Likert scale ranging from *low* (1, 2), *medium* (3, 4, 5), and *high* (6, 7) was used for the responses. The internal consistency indices were: Cronbach alpha (α) = 0.86; composite reliability = 0.86; Average Variance Extracted (AVE) = 0.59.

TABLE 1 | Distribution of the sample (n) according to Gender × Age (p = 0.501).

		Age			
		13 and 14 years	15 and 16 years	17 and 18 years	Total
Gender	Girl	210	164	37	411
	Boys	166	153	28	347
	Total	376	317	65	758

School Satisfaction

The Spanish version of the *Intrinsic Satisfaction Classroom Questionnaire* (ISC) by Castillo et al. (2001) was used, adapted from the original *Intrinsic Satisfaction Classroom Scale* by Nicholls et al. (1985), Nicholls (1989), and Duda and Nicholls (1992). It consists of eight items that measure the degree of school satisfaction using two subscales that measure *satisfaction/fun* (five items) and *boredom with school* (three items). For the responses, a Likert scale ranging from 1 (*totally disagree*) and 5 (*totally agree*) was used. The internal consistency indices were: *satisfaction/fun* α = 0.76, composite reliability = 0.76, AVE = 0.54; *boredom*, α = 0.70; Composite reliability = 0.72; AVE = 0.52.

Disruptive Behaviors in Physical Education

The Disruptive Conduct in Physical Education Questionnaire (CCDEF) by Granero-Gallegos and Baena-Extremera (2016) was used, which is the Spanish version of the original *Physical Education Classroom Instrument* (PECI) by Krech et al. (2010). This version consists of 17 items that measure disruptive behaviors in PE students in five subscales: (a) *Aggressive* (2 items), (b) *Low engagement or irresponsibility* (4 items), (c) *Fails to follow directions* (4 items), (d) *Distracts or disturbs others* (4 items), and (e) *Poor self-management* (3 items). A five-point Likert scale ranging from 1 (*never) to 5 (always)* was used for the responses. The internal consistency indices were: *aggressive,*α = 0.58, composite reliability = 0.81, AVE = 0.54; *low engagement or irresponsibility*, α = 0.73, composite reliability = 0.84, AVE = 0.74; *fails to follow directions*, α = 0.77, composite reliability = 0.94, AVE = 0.65; *distracts or disturbs others*, α = 0.81, composite reliability = 0.92, AVE = 0.80; *poor self-management*, α = 0.84, composite reliability = 0.96, AVE = 0.92. Given the low index achieved by Cronbach's alpha, and that the AGR subscale consists of only two items, this factor was ignored in the analyses performed.

Procedure

Permission to carry out the work was obtained from the competent bodies, be they at the secondary schools or the university. Parents and adolescents were informed about the protocol and the study's subject matter. Informed consent by both was an indispensable requirement to participate in the research. The tools measuring the different variables were administered in the classroom by the researchers themselves, without the teacher present. All participants were informed of the study objective, the voluntary and confidential nature of the responses and the data handling, as well as their rights as participants under the Helsinki Declaration (2008). This research has been approved by the Ethics Committee of the University of Murcia (REF-45-20/01/2016).

The questionnaires where completed in the classroom in about 25–30 min with the same researcher always present who expressed the possibility of consulting him about any doubts during the process, respecting the Helsinki Declaration (2008).

Data Analysis

The descriptive statistics of the items, the correlations and the internal consistency of each subscale were calculated, as well as the asymmetry and kurtosis with values close to 0 and <2.0. It is important to note that the data from this work were collected in schools so that the students could be nested based on the center, course and/or class, that is, violating the independence of observations principle. Therefore, the Mixed Linear Models analysis (MLM) were conducted, bearing in mind the individual characteristic variables of the participants and context variables. The dependent variables were the different ETCS-PE, ISC and CCDEF subscales, and the grouping or level of the school was considered a random effect, as were the student courses. The analyses were performed using the SPSS 23.0 MIXED procedure with the Restricted Maximum Likelihood Estimation Method. The Logarithm of Likelihood -2 (-2LL) (Pardo et al., 2007) was used to estimate the effects of the school and course variable on each estimated model. Different models were tested according to the different combinations of school levels and course with each of the dependent variables, including a null model. The "school" variable proved statistically significant ($p < 0.05$) in all cases, so it was estimated that the context variable "school" had an effect on each model. In addition, the intraclass correlation coefficient (ICC) was calculated for each of the compared variables. The results showed that the variance explained was greater than 6.14% in all cases, which allows us to say that a percentage of the differences between the dependent variables can be attributed to the school. The estimation method used was the restricted maximum likelihood estimation method. In light of the above, gender differences in relation to the various ETCS-PE, ISC and CCDEF subscales were calculated, in this case, the independent variable (mixed model factors) was the gender of the students. To calculate the differences according to teaching competence, the responses of this scale were categorized into three groups, low (responses 1 and 2 on the Likert scale), medium (responses 3, 4, and 5) and high (responses 6 and 7). The calculation of the differences between the three categorized groups of teaching competence in relation to satisfaction and boredom with school and disruptive behaviors was also conducted and, in this case, the independent variable (mixed model factors) was the teaching competence categorization.

Additionally, the factorial structure of each instrument was evaluated with confirmatory factor analysis (CFA) using the Maximum Likelihood method with the bootstrapping procedure, since the Mardia coefficient was high in each of the scales (16.71 in ETCS-PE; 12.51 in ISC and 292.55 in CCDEF). The different analyses were performed using the SPSS v.23 and AMOS v.22 statistical packages.

Psychometric Properties of the Instruments

Based on recommendations that discourage the use of a single overall model-fit measure (Bentler, 2007), each model was assessed using a combination of absolute and relative fit indices. The chi-squared ratio (χ^2) and the degrees of freedom (df) (χ^2/df), the comparative fit index (CFI), the Tucker-Lewis index (TLI) the incremental fit index (IFI), the root mean square error of approximation (RMSEA) with its confidence interval (CI 90%) and the Standardized Root Mean Square Residual (SRMR) were calculated. In the (χ^2/df) ratio, values < 2.0 are considered very good model fit indicators (Tabachnick and Fidell, 2007), although values < 5.0 are considered acceptable (Hu and Bentler, 1999). According to Hu and Bentler (1999), for the incremental indices (CFI, IFI, and TLI), values ≥ 0.95 are considered to indicate a good fit, although values of ≥ 0.90 are considered acceptable. These same authors consider that, for RMSEA, a value of ≤ 0.06 is considered to indicate a good fit, while for the RMSR values ≤ 0.08 are considered acceptable. As can be observed in **Table 2**, the different values for the goodness-of-fit indices of each instrument (ETCS-PE, ISC, and CCDEF) are acceptable.

RESULTS

Descriptive and Correlation Analysis

Table 3 shows that *teaching competence* presented moderately high average values, that for the ISC, the average values were higher for *bored* than for *satisfaction with school*, and that for disruptive behaviors, the average values were moderately low, oscillating between *low engagement or irresponsibility* and *poor self-management*, which presented the lowest average.

The correlations show that *teaching competence* only presented positive, moderate, and statistically significant values for *satisfaction with school*. Disruptive behaviors presented high, positive and statistically significant correlations between the same CCDEF subscales although positive correlations with more moderate values were also found between the different disruptive and *boredom with school* subscales (see **Table 3**).

Differences According to the Gender Variable

The differences were analyzed between the various subscales of teacher competence, school satisfaction and disruptive behaviors according to the gender variable. As shown in **Table 4**, the analyses indicate that there are statistically significant differences in the *boredom with school* and the four CCDEF subscales, and that, in all of them, the average values are higher for boys.

Differences According to Teaching Competence

In order to check the differences in the *satisfaction with school* and the *disruptive behaviors* subscales, according to the three *teaching competence* groups (low, medium, and high), the analysis performed indicates that the p-value associated with the comparative statistical tests of marginal averages has been calculated and corrected for multiple comparisons using SIDAK (**Table 5**).

Table 5 shows that there are statistically significant differences in all the subscales studied. In the case of satisfaction with school, the highest averages correspond to the high teaching competence

TABLE 2 | The goodness of fit index of the models.

	χ^2	df	χ^2/df	IFI	TLI	CFI	RMSEA(CI90%)	SRMR
ETCS-PE	36.04	20	1.80	0.99	0.99	0.99	0.03(0.01;0.05)	0.02
ISC	86.17	18	4.79	0.96	0.93	0.96	0.06(0.05;0.08)	0.04
CCDEF	303.09	84	3.61	0.96	0.95	0.96	0.06(0.05;0.07)	0.03

χ^2, chi-squared; df, degrees of freedom; IFI, incremental fit index; TLI, Tucker-Lewis index; CFI, comparative fit index; RMSEA, root mean square error of approximation; SRMR, standardized root mean square residual; CI, confidence interval.

TABLE 3 | Descriptives and correlations of the ECTS-PE, ISC, and CCDEF subscales.

Subscales	*M*	*SD*	1	2	3	4	5	6	7
(1) Teaching competence	5.36	1.16	–	0.19**	−0.13**	−0.19**	−0.08	−0.08	−0.09
(2) Satisfaction with school	2.80	0.97	0.23**	–	−0.40**	−0.06	0.01	−0.03	−0.03
(3) Boredom with school	3.03	1.04	−0.14**	−0.23**	–	0.30**	0.21**	0.26**	0.19**
(4) Low engagement or irresponsibility	2.00	0.90	−0.23**	0.06	0.21**	–	0.65**	0.53**	0.41**
(5) Fails to follow directions	1.65	0.94	−0.21**	0.10	0.11*	0.73**	–	0.62**	0.55**
(6) Distracts or disturbs others	1.49	0.99	−0.14*	0.08	0.20**	0.69**	0.75**	–	0.69**
(7) Poor self-management	1.42	0.83	−0.09	0.08	0.16**	0.68**	0.69**	0.83**	–

**$p < 0.05$; **$p < 0.01$; M = mean; SD = standard deviation. The upper diagonal corresponds to the girls. The lower diagonal corresponds to the boys.*

TABLE 4 | Gender differences based on the ETCS-PE, ISC, and CCDEF subscales according to the mixed regression model.

				CI95%		Statistical tests adjusted mixed model			Effect size
	Gender	**Adjusted average**	**Typical error**	**Lower**	**Higher**	***F***	**df**	***p***	***d***
Teaching competence PE	Girl	5.43	0.06	5.31	5.54	2.49	756	0.115	0.115
	Boy	5.29	0.06	5.17	5.41				
Satisfaction with school	Girl	2.80	0.04	2.71	2.89	0.00	756	0.978	0.000
	Boy	2.79	0.05	2.70	2.89				
Boredom with school	Girl	2.89	0.05	2.79	2.99	17.36	756	0.000	0.304
	Boy	3.20	0.06	3.10	3.31				
Low engagement or irresponsibility	Girl	1.88	0.04	1.80	1.97	15.86	756	0.000	0.291
	Boy	2.14	0.05	2.05	2.23				
Fails to follow directions	Girl	1.53	0.04	1.45	1.61	20.06	756	0.000	0.327
	Boy	1.80	0.04	1.71	1.89				
Distracts or disturbs others	Girl	1.37	0.04	1.29	1.44	24.45	756	0.000	0.361
	Boy	1.65	0.04	1.56	1.73				
Poor self-management	Girl	1.25	0.04	1.17	1.33	42.74	756	0.000	0.477
	Boy	1.63	0.04	1.55	1.72				

df, degrees of freedom; d, Cohen's d.

group, whereas for boredom with school and the four CCDEF subscales, the highest average values are presented by the low teaching competence group.

Regarding satisfaction with school and boredom with school, comparison tests show statistically significant differences between low and high teaching competence and between those of medium and high teaching competence, corrected using SIDAK (see **Table 5**). In the cases of disruptive behaviors, for low engagement or irresponsibility and fails to follow directions, statistically significant differences are notable between medium and high teaching competence; in the case of the Distracts or disturbs others subscale, statistically significant differences were found between high teaching competence and the other two groups, while in poor self-management, they were only found between low and high teaching competence.

DISCUSSION

This study set out two objectives: to understand the differences that exist in school satisfaction, disruptive behaviors and teaching competencies according to the gender of the students; and to analyze school satisfaction and disruptive behaviors based on teaching competence.

The results of this work relate teaching competence, satisfaction with school and inappropriate behaviors in

TABLE 5 | Differences in teaching competence (ETCS-PE) based on the ISC and CCDEF subscales according to the mixed regression model.

				CI95%		Mixed model adjusted			SIDAK[b]	Effect size
	Groups ETCS-PE[a]	Adjusted average	Typical error	Lower	Higher	F	df	p	p	d
Satisfaction with school	1	2.38	0.15	2.08	2.68				3***	0.779
	2	2.69	0.04	2.61	2.77	16.77	755	0.000	3***	0.315
	3	3.02	0.05	2.92	3.13					
Boredom with school	1	3.39	0.18	3.03	3.75				3**	0.624
	2	3.14	0.05	3.04	3.23	10.74	755	0.000	3***	0.252
	3	2.81	0.06	2.68	2.93					
Low engagement or irresponsibility	1	2.35	0.16	2.04	2.66				3**	0.764
	2	2.12	0.04	2.04	2.20	16.13	755	0.000	3***	0.309
	3	1.76	0.05	1.66	1.87					
Fails to follow directions	1	1.84	0.15	1.55	2.13					
	2	1.74	0.04	1.67	1.82	9.42	755	0.000	3***	0.236
	3	1.48	0.05	1.38	1.58					
Distracts or disturbs others	1	1.78	0.14	1.51	2.06				3*	0.456
	2	1.54	0.04	1.47	1.61	5.74	755	0.003	3*	0.184
	3	1.38	0.05	1.29	1.47					
Poor self-management	1	1.73	0.15	1.44	2.02				3*	0.421
	2	1.47	0.04	1.39	1.54	4.96	755	0.007		
	3	1.32	0.05	1.22	1.47					

**p < 0.05, **p < 0.01, ***p < 0.001; d, Cohen's d. [a]Groups: 1 = low teaching competence (n = 31), 2 = medium teaching competence (n = 459), 3 = high teaching competence (n = 268); [b]Comparison of marginal means statistical tests corrected by multiple comparisons using SIDAK. To simplify the presentation of data, only groups with statistically significant differences are displayed.*

the classroom. As in other studies (e.g., Kulinna et al., 2006; Cothran and Kulinna, 2007), the children presented higher levels of disruptive behavior. These results might be due to the boredom experienced by adolescents coming from a lack of attachment to social institutions and from disruptive behaviors at school (Feinberg et al., 2013; Granero-Gallegos et al., 2020). It is essential that students do not experience boredom in school, given that it is related to school violence, and this in turn can contribute to reduced academic performance, mental health and general well-being of the students (Huebner et al., 2014; Olweus and Breivik, 2014). In addition, boredom has been associated with high-risk behaviors such as drinking, drug use, joyriding and criminal activity (Yang and Yoh, 2005; Wegner and Flisher, 2009). Therefore, it is important that teachers work on their social skills with students and acquire sufficient competency as educators so that, amongst other things, both feel satisfied in classes (Allen et al., 2015; Trigueros and Navarro, 2019). Accordingly, this confirms Hypothesis 1.

If one looks at the mixed regression model, no significant differences were found in the teacher competence and school satisfaction variables based on gender. However, significant differences were found in the boredom with school, low engagement or irresponsibility, fails to follow directions, distracts or disturbs others and poor self-management variables, with boys presenting higher values than girls. These results are similar to those obtained in previous studies (e.g., Beaman et al., 2006; Kulinna et al., 2006; Cothran and Kulinna, 2007; Driessen, 2011), in which higher levels of disruptive behavior were also found in boys. They may be due to boys being more defiant with the teacher and more competitive with their peers, seeking to get the attention of the girls. In addition, it has been observed that males tend to engage in louder and more intentional behaviors to distract their peers in class (Glock and Kleen, 2017). Also, a possible cause for the increased level of negative behaviors has been linked to low emotional support from the teacher (Shin and Ryan, 2017). All this can be the basis for proposing more comprehensive teacher training, not only at the technical level, but also in the management of emotions, both in the initial training and in the continuous workplace training. In contrast, the girls presented more positive and less problematic behaviors, as was the case in other studies (e.g., Driessen, 2011). This may be because girls tend to demonstrate more introverted behavior, being uninvolved, shy and avoiding working as a group to give their opinion on a topic (Glock and Kleen, 2017). Therefore, this does not confirm Hypothesis 2 in its entirety.

The model analyzed based on teacher competencies found that when students perceived PE teachers as being competent, they felt more satisfied with the school, less bored and that their disruptive behavior level fell. Conversely, when students perceived their teachers as being incompetent, they became more bored and inappropriate behaviors increased. Similar results were found in the study by Baños et al. (2019), which was conducted in the same country as our work. These results suggest that the way teachers interact with their students affects classroom behavior (Ryan et al., 2015). This highlights the importance of PE teachers acquiring a great deal of skills to control and manage the sessions, creating a proactive environment among students, thus decreasing the likelihood of bad behaviors (Shin and Ryan, 2014; Fortuin et al., 2015). However, teachers reporting high levels of concern regarding how to effectively manage discipline issues in the classroom are common (Evertson and Weinstein, 2006; Tsouloupas et al., 2010) as they feel incompetent in the face of certain situations and this can be related to academic failure (Jurado-de-los-Santos and Tejada-Fernández, 2019). The inability to prevent and control student misbehavior is one of the main generators of teacher stress and anxiety, resulting in teachers burning out and increasing the likelihood of student truancy – with all the expenses that this involves for the educational system in terms of having to find substitute teachers (Tsouloupas et al., 2010; Ervasti et al., 2011). Therefore, this confirms Hypothesis 3.

PE teachers affirm that they find it more difficult to manage the boys' behavior (Jackson and Smith, 2000). These higher management issues may be due to the fact that teachers assess the temperament and educational competence of boys more negatively than those of girls (Mullola et al., 2012) and that boys more frequently show emotional opposition behaviors than girls do (McClowry et al., 2013). These differential behaviors in students and the teachers' perceptions are reflected in less intimate and more conflictive relationships between teachers and boys (Spilt et al., 2012). As a result, male students receive more reprimands (Beaman et al., 2006) than female students, making it harder to manage the boys' behavior (McClowry et al., 2013). This implies less effective classroom management with respect to males, as research has emphasized the importance of positive relationships between the teachers and the students to promote good classroom management (Marzano and Marzano, 2003). Therefore, teacher training is needed to better support trust and good management in the classroom.

CONCLUSION

The results obtained from this study identify males as having higher levels of inappropriate behaviors and the importance of students perceiving their teachers as being competent, that teachers have a command of the pedagogical content (Voss et al., 2011) and knowledge of classroom management techniques (Emmer and Stough, 2001) so that they can help reduce misbehavior in PE. Therefore, it is essential that adolescents perceive the PE teacher as competent, providing emotional support to his/her students, and that he/she continues to train in areas such as conflict resolution in the classroom, didactics and teacher pedagogy.

From this study, some recommendations can be made to bring, both to the classroom and to school. In general, the creation or strengthening of classrooms for school coexistence that improves the reflection, help, and accompaniment by other selected students can be recommended; it would be a program based on responsibility and without punishments or sanctions, and contribute to the resolution of conflicts in a positive way. By law, all educational centers must have a School Coexistence Plan, which must be implemented. More particularly, it is possible to focus on approaches that imply an enhancement of the motivation among students, especially in boys. Also, the enhancement of teaching competence in several topics (e.g., communication, work awareness, individual consideration of the student, problem-solving, social awareness, etc.), although the educational administration should supply teachers continuous training to improve social skills and capacity to solve conflicts among students.

Limitations and Strengths

The notable strengths of this work are the sample size and the theme, which can contribute to remedying one of the main problems found on a day-by-day basis in secondary schools. However, despite the novelty and interest of the topic and the results provided in this study such as the relationship between teaching competence and disruptive behaviors, as well as the implications this might have at the pedagogical and teacher-training level, certain limitations should be taken into account. The sample is composed of secondary school students from a single autonomous region and, in addition, no probabilistic sample design was carried out, so the results cannot be generalized and the method used does not allow to deeper into the disruptive causes in the classroom. Further studies should be performed in which other research designs are proposed, such as experimental studies with intervention programs to reduce disruptive behaviors in the classroom, and which consider other variables related to teacher, or mixed quantitative and qualitative research designs could be proposed, focusing on all subjects, not just PE. Some of these studies could also include private schools and public schools located in different socioeconomic level areas. On the other hand, it would also be convenient to perform longitudinal researches, with various data collections, in which the effectiveness of coexistence programs is valued.

ETHICS STATEMENT

The studies involving human participants were reviewed and approved by REF-45-20/01/2016. Written informed consent to participate in this study was provided by the participants' legal guardian/next of kin.

AUTHOR CONTRIBUTIONS

AG-G, RB, and AB-E conceived the hypothesis of this study. RB, AB-E, and MM-M participated in data collection. RB and

AG-G analyzed the data. AG-G, AB-E, and MM-M wrote the manuscript with the most significant input from AB-E. All authors contributed to data interpretation of statistical analysis and read and approved the final manuscript.

REFERENCES

Agbuga, B., Xiang, P., and McBride, R. (2010). Achievement goals and their relations to children's disruptive behaviors in an after-school physical activity program. *J. Teach. Phys. Educ.* 29, 278–294. doi: 10.1123/jtpe.29.3.278

Ahmed, W., Van der Werf, G., Kuyper, H., and Minnaert, A. (2013). Emotions, self-regulated learning, and achievement in mathematics: a growth curve analysis. *J. Educ. Psychol.* 105, 150–161. doi: 10.1037/a0030160

Allen, J. P., Hafen, C. A., Gregory, A., Mikami, A., and Pianta, R. C. (2015). Enhancing secondary school instruction and student achievement: replication and extension of the My Teaching Partner—Secondary Intervention. *J. Res. Educ. Eff.* 8, 475–489. doi: 10.1080/19345747.2015.1017680

Baena-Extremera, A., and Granero-Gallegos, A. (2015). Prediction model of satisfaction with physical education and school. *Rev. Psicodidact.* 20, 177–192. doi: 10.1387/RevPsicodidact.11268

Baena-Extremera, A., Granero-Gallegos, A., and Martínez-Molina, M. (2015). Validación española de la Escala de Evaluación de la Competencia Docente en Educación Física de secundaria [Spanish version of the Evaluation of Teaching Competencies Scale in secondary school Physical Education]. *Cuadernos de Psicología del Deporte* 15, 113–122.

Baños, R., Ortiz-Camacho, M. M., Baena-Extremera, A., and Tristán-Rodríguez, J. L. (2017). Satisfacción, motivación y rendimiento académico en estudiantes de Secundaria y Bachillerato [Satisfaction, motivation and academic performance in secondary and high school students: background, design, methodology and proposal of analysis for a research paper]. *Espiral* 10, 40–50.

Baños, R., Ortiz-Camacho, M. M., Baena-Extremera, A., and Zamarripa, J. (2018). Efecto del género del docente en la importancia de la Educación Física, clima motivacional, comportamientos disruptivos, la intención de práctica futura y rendimiento académico [Effect of teachers' gender on the importance of physical education, motivational climate, disruptive behaviours, future practice intentions, and academic performance]. *Retos* 33, 252–257.

Baños, R. F., Baena-Extremera, A., Ortiz-Camacho, M. M., Zamarripa, J., Beltrán, A., and Juvera-Portilla, J. L. (2019). Influencia de las competencias del profesorado de secundaria en los comportamientos disruptivos en el aula [Influence of the competencies of secondary teachers on disruptive behavior in the classroom]. *Espiral* 12, 3–10. doi: 10.25115/ecp.v12i24.21

Beaman, R., Wheldall, K., and Kemp, C. (2006). Differential teacher attention to boys and girls in the classroom. *Educ. Rev.* 58, 339–366. doi: 10.1080/00131910600748406

Bentler, P. M. (2007). On tests and indices for evaluating structural models. *Pers. Indiv. Differ.* 42, 825–829. doi: 10.1016/j.paid.2006.09.024

Castillo, I., Balaguer, I., and Duda, J. L. (2001). Las perspectivas de meta de los adolescentes en el contexto deportivo. *Psicothema* 14, 280–287.

Catano, V. M., and Harvey, S. (2011). Student perception of teaching effectiveness: development and validation of the Evaluation of Teaching Competencies Scale (ETCS). *Assess. Eval. High. Educ.* 36, 701–717. doi: 10.1080/02602938.2010.484879

Cothran, D. J., and Kulinna, P. H. (2007). Students' reports of misbehavior in physical education. *Res. Q. Exerc. Sport* 78, 216–224. doi: 10.1080/02701367.2007.10599419

Cothran, D. J., Kulinna, P. H., and Garrahy, D. (2009). Attributions for and consequences of student misbehavior. *Phys. Educ. Sport Pedagogy* 14, 155–167. doi: 10.1080/17408980701712148

Diener, E. (2009). "Assessing well-being: progress and opportunities," in *Assessing Well-Being. The Collected works of Ed Diener*, ed. E. Diener, (New York: Springer), 25–65. Social Indicators Research Series, 39. doi: 10.1007/978-90-481-2354-4_3

Diener, E., and Emmons, R. A. (1985). The independence of positive and negative affect. *J. Pers. Assess.* 99, 91–95.

Driessen, G. (2011). Gender differences in education: is there really a "boys' problem? *Paper presented at the Annual Meeting ECER*, Berlin

Duda, J. L., and Nicholls, J. G. (1992). Dimensions of achievement motivation in schoolwork and sport. *J. Educ. Psychol.* 84, 290–299. doi: 10.1037/0022-0663.84.3.290

Emmer, E. T., and Stough, L. M. (2001). Classroom management: a critical part of educational psychology, with implications for teacher education. *Educ. Psychol.* 36, 103–112. doi: 10.1207/S15326985EP3602_5

Ervasti, J., Kivima, M., Puusniekka, R., Luopa, P., Pentti, J., Suominen, S., et al. (2011). Students' school satisfaction as predictor of teachers' sickness absence: a prospective cohort study. *Eur. J. Public Health* 22, 215–219. doi: 10.1093/eurpub/ckr043

Evertson, C. M., and Weinstein, C. S. (2006). *Handbook of Classroom Management: Research Practice and Contemporary Issues.* Mahwah NJ: Routledge.

Feinberg, M. E., Sakuma, K. L., Hostetler, M., and McHale, S. M. (2013). Enhancing sibling relationships to prevent adolescent problem behaviors: theory, design and feasibility of Siblings Are Special. *Evlau. Program. Plann.* 36, 97–106. doi: 10.1016/j.evalprogplan.2012.08.003

Fortuin, J., van Geel, M., and Vedder, P. (2015). Peer influences on internalizing and externalizing problems among adolescents: a longitudinal social network analysis. *J. Youth Adolescence* 44, 887–897. doi: 10.1007/s10964-014-0168-x

Fredericks, J. A., Blumenfeld, P. C., and Paris, A. H. (2004). School engagement: potential of the concept, state of the evidence. *Rev. Educ. Res.* 74, 59–109. doi: 10.3102/00346543074001059

Geven, S., Jonsson, J. O., and van Tubergen, F. (2017). Gender differences in resistance to schooling: the role of dynamic peer-influence and selection processes. *J. Youth Adolescence* 46, 2421–2445. doi: 10.1007/s10964-017-0696-2

Glock, S., and Kleen, H. (2017). Gender and student misbehavior: evidence from implicit and explicit measures. *Teach. Teach. Educ.* 67, 93–103. doi: 10.1016/j.tate.2017.05.015

Goyette, R., Dore, R., and Dion, E. (2000). Pupils' misbehaviors and the reactions and causal attributions of physical education student teachers: a sequential analysis. *J. Teach. Phys. Educ.* 20, 3–14. doi: 10.1123/jtpe.20.1.3

Granero-Gallegos, A., and Baena-Extremera, A. (2016). Validación española de la version corta del Physical Education Classroom Instrument para la medición de conductas disruptivas en alumnado de secundaria [Validation of the short-form Spanish version of the Physical Education Classroom Instrument measuring secondary pupils' disruptive behaviours]. *Cuadernos de Psicología del Deporte* 16, 89–98.

Granero-Gallegos, A., Gómez-López, M., Baena-Extremera, A., and Martínez-Molina, M. (2020). Interaction effects of disruptive behaviour and motivation profiles with teacher competence and school satisfaction in secondary school physical education. *Int. J. Environ. Res. Public Health* 17:114. doi: 10.3390/ijerph17010114

Granero-Gallegos, A., Ruiz-Montero, P. J., Baena-Extremera, A., and Martínez-Molina, M. (2019). Effects of motivation, basic psychological needs, and teaching competence on disruptive behaviours in secondary school physical education students. *Int. J. Environ. Res. Public Health* 16:4828. doi: 10.3390/ijerph16234828

Hadjar, A., and Buchmann, C. (2016). "Education systems and gender inequalities in educational attainment," in *Education Systems and Inequalities: International Comparisons*, eds S. L. Christenson, A. Hadjar, and C. Gross, (Bristol: Policy Press), 159–182.

Helsinki Declaration (2008). *World Medical Association.* Available at: https://www.wma.net/what-we-do/medical-ethics/declaration-of-helsinki/doh-oct2008/

Hu, L., and Bentler, P. M. (1999). Cut-off criteria for fit indexes in covariance structure analysis: conventional criteria versus new alternatives. *Struct. Equ. Model.* 6, 1–55. doi: 10.1080/10705519909540118

Huebner, E. S., Hills, K. J., Jiang, X., Long, R. F., Kelly, R., and Lyons, M. D. (2014). "Schooling and Children's Subjective Well-Being," in *Handbook of Child Well-Being SE - 26*, eds A. Ben-Arieh, F. Casas, I. Frønes, and J. E. Korbin, (Netherlands: Springer), 797–819. doi: 10.1007/978-90-481-9063-8_26

Invernizzi, P. L., Crotti, M., Bosio, A., Cavaggioni, L., Alberti, G., and Scurati, R. (2019). Multi-teaching styles approach and active reflection: effectiveness in improving fitness level, motor competence, enjoyment, amount of physical activity, and effects on the perception of physical education lessons in primary school children. *Sustainability* 11, 405–425. doi: 10.3390/su11020405

Jackson, C., and Smith, I. D. (2000). Poles apart? An exploration of single-sex educational environments in Australia and England. *Educ. Stud.* 26, 409–422. doi: 10.1080/03055690020003610

Jurado-de-los-Santos, P., and Tejada-Fernández, J. (2019). Disrupción y fracaso escolar. Un estudio en el contexto de la Educación Secundaria Obligatoria en Cataluña [Disruption and School Failure. A Study in the Context of Secondary Compulsory Education in Catalonia]. *Estud Sobre Educ.* 36, 135–155. doi: 10.15581/004.36.135-155

Krech, P. R., Kulinna, P. H., and Cothran, D. (2010). Development of a short-form version of the Physical Education Classroom Instrument: measuring secondary pupils' disruptive behaviours. *Phys. Educ. Sport Pedagogy* 15, 209–225. doi: 10.1080/17408980903150121

Kulinna, P. H., Cothran, D., and Regualos, R. (2006). Teachers' reports of student misbehavior in physical education. *Res. Q. Exerc. Sport* 77, 32–40. doi: 10.1080/02701367.2006.10599329

Marzano, R. J., and Marzano, J. S. (2003). The key to classroom management. *Educ. Leadersh.* 61, 6–18.

McClowry, S. G., Rodriguez, E. T., Tamis-LeMonda, C. S., Spellmann, M. E., Carlson, A., and Snow, D. L. (2013). Teacher/student interactions and classroom behavior: the role of student temperament and gender. *J. Res. Child Educ.* 27, 283–301. doi: 10.1080/02568543.2013.796330

Medina, J. A., and Reverte, M. J. (2019). Incidencia de la práctica de actividad física y deportiva como reguladora de la violencia escolar. *Retos* 35, 54–60.

Müller, C. M., Hofmann, V., Begert, T., and Cillessen, A. H. (2018). Peer influence on disruptive classroom behavior depends on teachers' instructional practice. *J. Appl. Dev. Psychol.* 56, 99–108. doi: 10.1016/j.appdev.2018.04.001

Mullola, S., Ravaja, N., Lipsanen, J., Alatupa, S., Hintsanen, M., Jokela, M., et al. (2012). Gender differences in teachers' perceptions of students' temperament, educational competence, and teachability. *Br. J. Educ. Psychol.* 82, 185–206. doi: 10.1111/j.2044-8279.2010.02017.x

Nicholls, J. G. (1989). *The Competitive Ethos and Democratic Education.* Cambridge, MA: Harvard University Press.

Nicholls, J. G., Patashnick, M., and Nolen, S. B. (1985). Adolescents' theories of education. *J. Educ. Psychol.* 77, 683–692. doi: 10.1037//0022-0663.77.6.683

Olweus, D., and Breivik, K. (2014). "Plight of victims of school bullying: the opposite of well-being," in *Handbook of Child Well-Being SE* - 90, eds A. Ben-Arieh, F. Casas, I. Frønes, and J. E. Korbin, (Netherlands: Springer), 2593–2616. doi: 10.1007/978-90-481-9063-8_26

Pardo, A., Ruiz, M., and San Martín, R. (2007). Cómo ajustar e interpretar modelos multinivel con SPSS [How to fit and interpret multilevel models using SPSS]. *Psicothema* 19, 308–321.

Persson, L., Haraldsson, K., and Hagquist, C. (2016). School satisfaction and social relations: swedish school children's improvement suggestions. *Int. J. Public Health* 61, 83–90. doi: 10.1007/s00038-015-0696-5

Rasmussen, J. F., Scrabis-Fletcher, K., and Silverman, S. (2014). Relationships among tasks, time, and student practice in elementary physical education. *Phys. Educ.* 71, 114–131.

Ryan, A. M., Kuusinen, C., and Bedoya-Skoog, A. (2015). Managing peer relations: a dimension of teacher self-efficacy that varies between elementary and middle school teachers and is associated with observed classroom quality. *Contemp. Educ. Psychol.* 41, 147–156. doi: 10.1016/j.cedpsych.2015.01.002

Scharenberg, K. (2016). The interplay of social and ethnic classroom composition, tracking, and gender on students' school satisfaction. *J. Cogn. Educ. Psychol.* 15, 320–346. doi: 10.1891/1945-8959.15.2.320

Shin, H., and Ryan, A. M. (2014). Friendship networks and achievement goals: an examination of selection and influence processes and variations by gender. *J. Youth Adolescence* 43, 1453–1464. doi: 10.1007/s10964-014-0132-9

Shin, H., and Ryan, A. M. (2017). Friend influence on early adolescent disruptive behavior in the classroom: teacher emotional support matters. *Dev. Psychol.* 53, 114–126. doi: 10.1037/dev0000250

Spilt, J. L., Koomen, H. M. Y., and Jak, S. (2012). Are boys better off with male and girls with female teachers? A multilevel investigation of measurement invariance and gender match in teacher-student relationship quality. *J. Sch. Psychol.* 50, 363–378. doi: 10.1016/j.jsp.2011.12.002

Sun, R. C. (2016). Student misbehavior in Hong Kong: the predictive role of positive youth development and school satisfaction. *Appl. Res. Qual. Life* 11, 773–789. doi: 10.1007/s11482-015-9395-x

Tabachnick, B. G., and Fidell, S. A. (2007). *Using Multivariate Statistics*, 5th Edn. Boston, MA: Allyn and Bacon.

Takakura, M., Wake, N., and Kobayashi, M. (2010). The contextual effect of school satisfaction on health-risk behaviors in Japanese high school students. *J. Sch. Health* 80, 544–551. doi: 10.1111/j.1746-1561.2010.00540.x

Trigueros, R., and Navarro, N. (2019). La influencia del docente sobre la motivación, las estrategias de aprendizaje, pensamiento crítico de los estudiantes y rendimiento académico en el área de educación física. *Psychol. Soc. Educ.* 11, 137–150. doi: 10.25115/psye.v11i1.2230

Tsouloupas, C. N., Carson, R. L., Matthews, R., Grawitch, M. J., and Barber, L. K. (2010). Exploring the association between teachers' perceived student misbehaviour and emotional exhaustion: the importance of teacher efficacy beliefs and emotion regulation. *Educ. Psychol.* 30, 173–189. doi: 10.1080/01443410903494460

Varela, J. J., Zimmerman, M. A., Ryan, A. M., Stoddard, S. A., Heinze, J. E., and Alfaro, J. (2018). Life satisfaction, school satisfaction, and school violence: a mediation analysis for Chilean adolescent victims and perpetrators. *Child Indic. Res.* 11, 487–505. doi: 10.1007/s12187-016-9442-7

Voss, T., Kunter, M., and Baumert, J. (2011). Assessing teacher candidates' general pedagogical/psychological knowledge: test construction and validation. *J. Educ. Psychol.* 103, 952–969. doi: 10.1037/a0025125

Wegner, L., and Flisher, A. J. (2009). Leisure boredom and adolescent risk behaviour: a systematic literature review. *J. Child Adol. Ment. Health* 21, 1–28. doi: 10.2989/JCAMH.2009.21.1.4.806

Weiss, M. R., Smith, A. L., and Stuntz, C. P. (2008). "Moral development in sport and physical activity," in *Advances in Sport Psychology*, ed. T. S. Horn, (Champaign, IL: Human Kinetics), 187–210.

Yang, H., and Yoh, T. (2005). The relationship between free-time boredom and aggressive behavioral tendencies among college students with disabilities. *Am. J. Recreat. Ther.* 4, 11–16.

23

Mini Review of the use of the Mobile Phone and its Repercussion in the Deficit of Physical Activity

María Luisa Zagalaz-Sánchez, Javier Cachón-Zagalaz, María Sánchez-Zafra and Amador Lara-Sánchez*

Department of Musical, Plastic and Body Expression, University of Jaén, Jaén, Spain

Correspondence:
María Sánchez-Zafra
mszafra@ujaen.es

Background: Current technology has the ability to distract and evade its users, this resulting in an addiction or "escape" from the real world. The excessive use of smartphones can cause a decrease in physical activity (PA) for many people prefer to use these devices rather than do the recommended physical exercise.

Objective: The objective of this paper is to analyze the possible relation between the use of smartphones and the reduction in the practice of PA that is reflected in scientific articles.

Methods: The PRISMA statement has been followed for systematic reviews and meta-analyses in order to achieve a correct organization and integrity of the work. Our search for bibliography has been carried out in the WOS and Scopus databases, together with the research domains "Social Sciences Other Topics," "Education Educational Research," and "Sport Sciences." After applying the inclusion criteria, a total of 14 articles were obtained, these forming the base body of this research.

Results: Nine of the fourteen articles show that there is a negative relationship between the smartphone and PA practice. The age groups most studied in relation to this topic range from 13 to 18 and from 19 to 25.

Conclusion: It is our conclusion that the inappropriate use of these mobile devices is associated with low levels of motivation and practice of PA in their users. Similarly, we have emphasized the lack of scientific work dealing with this issue.

Keywords: physical activity, smartphone, addiction, sedentariness, technology

INTRODUCTION

The concern about the possible effects of Information and Communication Technologies (ICTs) is no longer new. Current studies allude to the problems caused by the excessive use of small screens, especially smartphones and, therefore, the Internet, as well as addictions to video games..., and also in relation to the dependence they create on users. Since the internet exists, problems related to its use have continuously appeared (Domínguez et al., 2012). Nowadays technology has the ability to distract and evade people from their problems, but it can also result in addictions or become an unhealthy escape from the real world (Sánchez-Zafra et al., 2019).

The speed at which technology advances makes the functionality of smartphones change continuously. Each time, they offer more applications, better camera, more power and memory.

They grant a large number of services related to leisure, such as watching television, listening to music or enjoying multiple games. In the same way, they provide current information and allow socializing with other people through social networks (Aranda et al., 2017). This makes them increasingly attractive to children, young and adults, causing certain problems and situations when there is excessive and continuous dependence on these devices (Echeburúa and de Corral, 2010; Alfaro et al., 2015; Rozgonjuk et al., 2018). Over time, smartphones users are normalizing their use, leaving aside the playful part they offer to give them a more professional and personal use. This also occurs in the educational context (Ramírez et al., 2018), where there are more than 80.000 educational Apps.

However, its problematic use can affect various factors in our daily life, causing, for instance, a lack of practice of physical activity (PA) (Sung et al., 2016; Elhai et al., 2017; Ramírez-Granizo et al., 2018). Actions such as sending messages, phoning or surfing the internet are considered sedentary and this can lead to health problems since insufficient levels of moderate and vigorous physical exercise are associated with the increase of obesity. The regular practice of pa is associated with benefits similar to those of some medical treatments. This is why it is an essential activity in our lives (Perea et al., 2015). An addictive use of smartphones is also related to a higher body mass index and a deterioration of physical health, such as loss of vision and musculoskeletal problems (Bell et al., 2014; Kim et al., 2015; Sook and Chun, 2017), in addition to loss of attention and lack of sleep, not to mention -specially among young people- the risk of using it while driving. One of the main factors associated with overuse of smartphones is age. It is the university students, along with the younger ones, who have more normalized its use in their routine (Jasso et al., 2017).

It is scientifically proven that a regular practice of PA is associated with health benefits and that a sedentary lifestyle slows them down, having negative consequences even in active people (Barkley et al., 2016). The first studies focused on the sedentary lifestyle of schoolchildren related it exclusively to the hours they spent watching television but over time it has been also applied to the rest of electronic devices with a screen (Sandercock et al., 2016). As the use of smartphones increases, the practice of PA decreases (Joshi et al., 2016) to such an extent that the fight against sedentary lifestyle and obesity necessarily includes the analysis and harm of the abusive use of smartphones. Venkatesh et al. (2017) confirm that adults addicted to these devices do less physical exercise if compared to those who are not, and Samaha and Hawi (2017) obtain the same results in a population of children. Sedentary lifestyles, motivated among other reasons by the excessive use of smartphones, are becoming one of the main concerns of society (Glynn et al., 2013).

Despite these disadvantages, the use of smartphones does not necessarily lead to sedentary actions. In fact, there are many applications in the market helping us in our practice of physical activity. Some remind users of the moment when they have to do exercise or what kind of activity they have to do that day (Patel et al., 2018). Likewise, the research by Shen et al. (2018) states that the people who practice PA most are those who most consult their smartphones for health-related issues.

Our main objective is to conduct a systematic review of scientific literature focused on the use of the smartphone and its relationship with the practice of PA in populations of different ages without diseases.

METHODOLOGY

The PRISMA statement has been followed for systematic reviews and meta-analyses (Hutton et al., 2016) in order to achieve a correct organization and integrity of the work.

Procedure and Literature Search Strategy

The literature review of the articles was carried out in November and December of 2018, paying special attention to those relating the excessive use of the smartphone with the amount of PA in the last decade.

The Web of Science (WOS) and Scopus databases have been used to search for the articles. The articles were searched using the following keywords: "mobile phone," "physical activity" and "the Boolean operator." Subsequently, the search was refined taking into account only the articles published in the research areas "Social Sciences Other Topics," "Education Educational Research," and "Sport Sciences," leaving a total of 271 documents.

Inclusion Criteria

The inclusion criteria were established: (1) articles that relate the use of smartphones to the practice of PA, (2) use that is given to mobile phones, and (3) whether the research is cross-sectional or longitudinal.

Study Selection and Data Collection Process

The first part of the search initially obtaining an amount of 1.908 articles. For the application of the first inclusion criteria, a first reading of the title and summary of the 271 selected papers was made. In a following stage, a second deeper reading was necessary to apply the rest of the inclusion criteria. After the application of these criteria, a total of 257 articles were eliminated.

Population and Scientific Literature Sample

The population of this study is set at 271 articles extracted from the WOS and Scopus databases. After applying the inclusion criteria, the study sample is refined to 14 scientific publications.

RESULTS

Evolution of the Scientific Production

Considering the selected research areas and the inclusion criteria, 271 articles related to the subject under discussion have been published in the last decade. 14 works have been selected to constitute the body of the investigation.

TABLE 1 | Basis of the study.

Authors and year	Country	Kind of investigation	Age of the Sample	Instrument*	Relation PA-smartphone
Arora et al. (2013)	United Kingdom	Cross	11–18 years old	Stadiometer Scales *Ad hoc* TUQ	Positive
Barkley and Lepp (2016)	United States	Cross	18–34 years old	GLTEQ *Ad hoc* *Ad hoc*	Negative
Beltrán-Carrillo et al. (2016)	Spain	Cross	15–16 years old	*Ad hoc*	Positive
Delfino et al. (2018)	Brazil	Cross	10–17 years old	*Ad hoc*	Negative
Haug et al. (2015)	Switzerland	Cross	15-older than 21	*Ad hoc* SAS-SV *Ad hoc*	Negative
Kim et al. (2015)	Korea	Cross	19–25 years old	SAPS Pedometer 320 Body Composition Analyzer Anthropometer	Negative
Lane et al. (2014)	Ireland	Longitudinal	9 years old	*Ad hoc*	Negative
Lepp et al. (2013)	United States	Cross	University students	SESEB *Ad hoc* *Ad hoc*	Negative
Mojica et al. (2014)	United States	Cross	11–14 years old	YRBSS *Ad hoc*	Positive
Morita et al. (2016)	Japan	Cross	12–13 years old	PA *Ad hoc*	Negative
Sevil et al. (2018)	Spain	Cross	Average age: 13 years old	*Ad hoc*	Negative
Shen et al. (2018)	Hong Kong	Cross	18-older than 65	HIE HB	Positive/Negative
Silva et al. (2017)	Portugal	Cross	13–19 years old	*Ad hoc* *Ad hoc*	Negative
Zach et al. (2016)	Israel	Longitudinal	16–18 years old	*Ad hoc* *Ad hoc*	Positive

**TUQ, technology use questionnaire; GLTEQ, godin leisure-time exercise questionnaire; SAS-SV, smartphone addiction scale short version; SAPS, smartphone addiction proneness scale; SESEB, self-efficacy survey for exercise behaviors; YRBSS, youth risk behavioral surveillance system; HIE, health information exposure; HB, health behaviors.*

Data From the Studies Selected for the Systematic Review

For the selection of the articles and their coding (**Table 1**), the following data have been taken into account: (1) authors and year of publication, (2) country where the work has been carried out, (3) type of research carried out, (4) size of the sample, (5) sample age, (6) instruments, (7) variables that have been measured, and (8) relation between PA and the use of smartphones, understanding that the latter is positive when there is an active use of these devices whereas it is negative when it is a passive or sedentary one.

The reviewed articles are spread across countries all over the world without being concentrated in any particular geographical area. The majority of the works belong to a cross sectional paradigm. With respect to the instruments, as highlighted, there is no validated universal questionnaire that measures the relation between the use of smartphones and their relationship with the practice of PA, since our approach reveals that each author has chosen a different questionnaire for their research, many of them being of own elaboration. Regarding the relationship between PA and the use of smartphones, most of the works speak of a negative, passive use, in which the time of physical exercise is considerably reduced. Others point out a positive use, focusing on applications or ways to encourage the practice of PA thanks to smartphones.

Figure 1 shows the distribution of the articles that make up the sample according to the age of the participants. Some of the studies are framed in more than one age group because they used participants of different ages. It can be seen that most of the articles focus on an age range between 13 and 18 years old (N = 8), followed by 19 to 25 years old (N = 5). The least studied ages are those under 12 (N = 2) and those above 26 (N = 2).

DISCUSSION

Most of the papers presented in the Results section share the view that there is nowadays an excessive use of smartphones among children, adolescents and adults. It is the youngest who spend

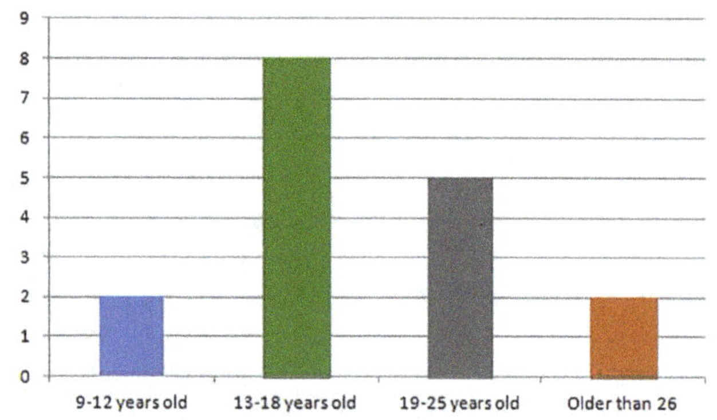

FIGURE 1 | Distribution of selected articles according to age.

more hours in front of the screens and those who have more problems and addictions (Haug et al., 2015).

In the study by Lane et al. (2014), there arises the discussion on the recommendation made by the American Academy of Pediatrics (2001) about not using smartphones for more than 2 h a day. This recommendation is not met by the sample of the articles studied, according to which children between 6 and 12 spend an average of 40 h a week talking, writing text messages, listening to music and surfing the Internet. Most of them can send text messages through the internet thanks to the data plans they have (Mojica et al., 2014). According to Sudan et al. (2016) children born in the last 20 years have been exposed to these devices since birth and, therefore, their relationship with them is different and cannot be compared with that of adults. Children are continually watching videos, playing games or talking on WhatsApp. They live attached to the smartphone.

Sevil et al. (2018) show that adolescents spend an average of 407 min a day (6.7 h) with different technological devices, smartphones being the second most used to communicate with others, for example, through WhatsApp. As with children, these adolescent users have in many cases flat data rates, which allow them to use smartphones anywhere and anytime, progressively increasing the time spent on them (De-Sola et al., 2016). Preadolescents and adolescents spend more time with smartphones, and therefore have a more sedentary behavior than younger children (Joshi et al., 2016).

Likewise, the research carried out by Lepp et al. (2013) and Barkley and Lepp (2016) show that the average number of minutes per day spent by university users is 300 and 380, respectively. Horwood and Anglim's (2018) survey showed that 54% of adults used smartphones when they should be doing other things and that 34% lost sleep hours when using them. 65% of respondents confirm that they have used smartphones for a longer time than they had originally planned. In university classes it is normal to see students using the smartphone instead of attending to the teacher. Even so, older people use less smartphones than younger ones (Barkley and Lepp, 2016).

The majority of studies imply that there are no significant differences in the use of the smartphone as far as gender is concerned, but Beltrán-Carrillo et al. (2016) state women use these devices more frequently, coinciding with other studies such as Joshi et al. (2016) or Pedrero-Pérez et al. (2018), who explain that women use instant messages and social networks more, men preferring the internet and video games.

As confirmed by most studies, the time users spend with smartphones is associated with sitting. Those who use the smartphone less spend less time sitting than those who have a more continuous use of it (Barkley and Lepp, 2016). The muscle mass of people with addiction to smartphones was much lower than that of the more moderate users. The opposite occurs with fat mass, since the more a smartphone is used, the more fat mass users have (Kim et al., 2015). Furthermore, the misuse of smartphones is associated with a greater proclivity to suffer body aches in the back, neck (today's boys are known as the generation of crouched heads), wrists, hips and knees (Silva et al., 2017).

The relation between the misuse of smartphones and the practice of PA is obvious. There are authors who speak of a negative relation, arguing that the excessive use of smartphones produces a sedentary lifestyle and inactivity, leading to a reduction in the time devoted to physical exercise. Nowadays, the majority of the population prefers to use the smartphone instead of going for a walk or doing some kind of physical exercise. The first thing young people do when they leave class and adults do when they leave work is to take the smartphone. Delfino et al. (2018) observed that users who spent more than 2 h using smartphones were physically less active than others. These researchers suggest that the practice of low intensity PA can help to reduce the time spent on these devices. Additionally, sedentary behaviors should be discouraged and foster a change from moderate physical exercises to vigorous ones (Morita et al., 2016).

The same users are aware, in many cases, that smartphones can interfere with their PA and many of them say they leave their smartphone off in order to be more active and reduce sedentary behavior (Lepp et al., 2013). On the other hand, it is found that those people who do more moderate and vigorous PA are the ones who use the smartphone most to consult health issues (Shen et al., 2018).

Conversely, smartphones can also be used to reduce sedentary levels and increase PA. It should not be forgotten that they are small devices that can be carried anywhere and used in movement (Arora et al., 2013). It is important to widespread the use of ICTs in PA classes in order to promote knowledge and increase healthy lifestyles in terms of physical exercise (Zach et al., 2016). There are a multitude of games and applications that can be used to encourage PA practice. It is important for children to know them.

Similarly, there are several studies that show that the use of messages through the smartphone aimed at enhancing the levels of PA in users is effective, since sedentary lifestyles can be reduced through reminders on the smartphone to get up when the user has been sitting for a long time, to go for a walk or do any simple exercise (McCoy et al., 2017; Dunning et al., 2018). Through virtual reality, some aspects related to PA can be improved more effectively, such as spatial orientation (Gómez-García et al., 2018).

CONCLUSION

Our analysis reveals that the number of studies that address the issue of the influence of smartphones in the practice of PA is scarce and that, in spite of having considered a whole decade in our approach, they were all published only in the last 5 years. This question has been raised globally, finding that the investigations have been carried out in different countries, inferring that it is a subject of special relevance and international significance. At the same time, we have highlighted that most of them are cross-sectional studies.

All the stages have been considered, from children to adults, and each of them shows that the inappropriate use of smartphones reduces the practice of PA, since these devices are preferred. On the other hand, some works claim that a suitable use of smartphones can foster the recommended daily exercise, for example, through applications or messages that remind and encourage the activities to be carried out.

Regarding the limitations of our study, we have only covered a decade and, consequently, this research is likely to be developed and extended to see if more articles investigating this topic have been published since the appearance of smartphones.

AUTHOR CONTRIBUTIONS

MZ-S, JC-Z, MS-Z, and AL-S contributed to the conception and design of the revision. All authors wrote some part of the manuscript and all reviewed the manuscript.

REFERENCES

Alfaro, M., Vázquez, M. E., Fierro, A., Herrero, B., Muñoz, M. F., and Rodríguez, L. (2015). Uso y riesgos de las tecnologías de la información y comunicación en adolescentes de 13-18 años. *Acta Pediátr. Esp.* 73, 126–135.

American Academy of Pediatrics (2001). Children, adolescents and television. *Pediatrics* 107, 423–426. doi: 10.1542/peds.107.2.423

Aranda, M., Fuentes, V., and García-Domingo, M. (2017). "No sin mi Smartphone": elaboración y validación de la escala de dependencia y adicción al smartphone (EDAS). *Ter. Psicol.* 35, 35–45. doi: 10.4067/s0718-48082017000100004

Arora, T., Hussain, S., Lam, K. B. H., Yao, G. L., Thomas, G. N., and Taheri, S. (2013). Exploring the complex pathways among specific types of technology, self-reported sleep duration and body mass index in UK adolescents. *Int. J. Obes.* 37, 1254–1260. doi: 10.1038/ijo.2012.209

Barkley, J. E., and Lepp, A. (2016). Mobile phone use among college students is a sedentary leisure bahavior which may interfere with exercise. *Comput. Hum. Behav.* 56, 29–33. doi: 10.1016/j.chb.2015.11.001

Barkley, J. E., Lepp, A., and Salehi-Esfahani, S. (2016). College students' mobile telephone use is positively associated withseentary behavior. *Am. J. Lifestyle Med.* 10, 437–441.

Bell, J. A., Hamer, M., Batty, G. D., Singh-Manoux, A., Sabia, S., and Kivimaki, M. (2014). Combined effect of physical activity and leisure time sitting on long-term risk of incident obesity and metabolic risk factor clustering. *Diabetologia* 57, 2048–2056. doi: 10.1007/s00125-014-3323-8

Beltrán-Carrillo, V. J., Beltrán-Carrillo, J. I., González-Cutre, D., Biddle, S. J. H., and Montero-Carretero, C. (2016). ¿Are active video games associated with less screen media or conventional physical activity? *Games Cult.* 11, 608–624.

Delfino, L., Santos, D. A., Tebar, W. R., Zanuto, E. F., Codogno, J. S., Fernandes, R. A., et al. (2018). Screen time by different devices in adolescents: association with physical inactivity domains and eating habits. *J. Sports Med. Phys. Fitn.* 58, 318–325. doi: 10.23736/S0022-4707.17.06980-8

De-Sola, J., Rodríguez, F., and Rubio, G. (2016). Cell-phone addiction: a review. *Front. Psychiatry* 7:175. doi: 10.3389/fpsyt.2016.00175

Domínguez, C., Geijo, S., Sánchez, I., Imaz, C., and Cabús, G. (2012). Revisión de los mecanismos implicados en el uso problemático de Internet. *Rev. Asoc. Esp. Neuropsiquiatr.* 32, 691–705.

Dunning, J. R., McVeigh, J. A., Goble, D., and Meiring, R. M. (2018). The effect of interrupting sedentary behavior on the cardiometabolic health of adults with sedentary occupations: a pilot study. *J. Occup. Environ. Med.* 60, 760–767. doi: 10.1097/JOM.0000000000001327

Echeburúa, E., and de Corral, P. (2010). Adicción a las nuevas tecnologías y a las redes sociales en jóvenes: un nuevo reto. *Adicciones* 22, 91–96.

Elhai, J. D., Dvorak, R. D., Levine, J. C., and Hall, B. J. (2017). Problematic smartphone use: a conceptual overview and systematic review of relations with anxiety and depression psychopathology. *J. Affect. Disord.* 207, 251–259. doi: 10.1016/j.jad.2016.08.030

Glynn, L. G., Hayes, P. S., Casey, M., Glynn, F., Alvarez-Iglesias, A., Newell, J., et al. (2013). SMART MOVE- a smartphone-based intervention to promote physical activity in primary care: study protocol for a randomized controlled trial. *Trials* 14, 1–7. doi: 10.1186/1745-6215-14-157

Gómez-García, M., Trujillo-Torres, J. M., Aznar-Díaz, I., and Cáceres-Reche, M. P. (2018). Augment reality and virtual reality for the improvement of spatial competences in Physical Education. *J. Hum. Sport Exerc.* 13, 189–198.

Haug, S., Castro, R. P., Kwon, M., Filler, A., Kowatsch, T., and Schaub, M. P. (2015). Smartphone use and smartphone addiction among young people in Switzerland. *J. Behav. Addict.* 4, 299–307. doi: 10.1556/2006.4.2015.037

Horwood, S., and Anglim, J. (2018). Personality and problematic smartphone use: a face-level analysis using the five factor model and HEXACO frameworks. *Comput. Hum. Behav.* 85, 349–359. doi: 10.1016/j.chb.2018.04.013

Hutton, B., Catalá-López, F., and Moher, D. (2016). The PRISMA statement extensión for systematic reviews incorporating network meta-analysis: PRISMA-NMA. *MedicinaClínica* 147, 31–36.

Jasso, J. L., López, F., and Díaz, R. (2017). Conducta adictiva a las redes sociales y su relación con el uso problemático del móvil. *Acta Investig. Psicol.* 7, 2832–2838. doi: 10.1016/j.aipprr.2017.11.001

Joshi, P., Cole, K., and Overton, M. (2016). Trends in sedentary behaviors among high school students: analysis of televisión and other screen-time activities. *J. Phys. Educ. Sport* 16, 1142–1145.

Kim, S. E., Kim, J. W., and Jee, Y. S. (2015). Relationship between smartphone addiction and physical activity in Chinese international students in Korea. *J. Behav. Addict.* 4, 200–205. doi: 10.1556/2006.4.2015.028

Lane, A., Harrison, M., and Murphy, N. (2014). Screen time increases risk of overweight and obesity in active and inactive 9-year-old irish children: a cross sectional analysis. *Phys. Activ. Health* 11, 985–991. doi: 10.1123/jpah.2012-0182

Lepp, A., Barkley, J. E., Sanders, G. J., Rebold, M., and Gates, P. (2013). The relationship between cell pone use, physical and sedentary activity, and cardiorespiratory fitness in a simple of U. S. college students. *Int. J. Behav. Nutr. Phys. Activ.* 10, 1–9.

McCoy, P., Leggett, S., Bhuiyan, A., Brown, D., Frye, P., and Williams, B. (2017). Text messaging: an intervention to increase physical activity among african american participants in a faith-based, competitive weight loss program. *Int. J. Environ. Res. Public Health* 14, 1–12. doi: 10.3390/ijerph14040326

Mojica, C. M., Parra-Medina, D., Yin, Z., Akopian, D., and Esparza, L. A. (2014). Assessing media access and use amog latina adolescents to inform development of a physical activity promotios intervention incorporating text messaging. *HealthPromot. Pract.* 15, 548–555. doi: 10.1177/1524839913514441

Morita, N., Nakajima, T., Okita, K., Ishihara, T., Sagawa, M., and Yamatsu, K. (2016). Relaciones entre aptitud física, obesidad, tiempo de pantalla y logros académicos en adolescentes japoneses. *Physiol. Behav.* 163, 161–166.

Patel, D. N., Nossel, C., Patricios, J., and Maboreke, J. (2018). Bright sports, physical activity investments that work: vitality active rewards-a smartphone app that incentivisesprogramme members to be physically active. *Br. J. Sports Med.* 52, 1494–1496. doi: 10.1136/bjsports-2018-099271

Pedrero-Pérez, E. J., Ruiz-Sánchez de León, J. M., Rojo-Mota, G., Llanero-Luque, M., Pedrero-Aguilar, J., Morales-Alonso, S., et al. (2018). Tecnologías de la Información y la Comunicación (TIC): uso problemático de Internet, videojuegos, teléfonos móviles, mensajería instantánea y redes sociales mediante el MULTICAGE-TIC. *Adicciones* 30, 19-32.

Perea, J. M., Aparicio, A., Mascaraque, M., and Ortega, R. M. (2015). Actividad física y sedentarismo como moduladores de la situación nutricional. *Nutr. Hospital.* 32, 20–22.

Ramírez, V., Padial, R., Torres, B., Chinchilla, J. L., and Cepero, M. (2018). Consecuencias en la competencia digital del alumnado de primaria de un programa de educación física usando la metodología ABP. *J. Sport Health Res.* 10, 361–372.

Ramírez-Granizo, I., Fernández-Revelles, A. B., Padial-Ruz, R., Espejo-Garcés, T., and García-Martínez, I. (2018). El nivel de AF y su relación con el uso problemático con los videojuegos. *Una revisiónnarrativa. J. Sport Health Res.* 10, 117–124.

Rozgonjuk, D., Kattago, M., and Täth, K. (2018). Social media use in lectures mediates the relationship between procrastination and problematic Smartphone use. *Comput. Hum. Behav.* 89, 191–198. doi: 10.1016/j.chb.2018.08.003

Samaha, M., and Hawi, N. S. (2017). Associations between screen media parenting practices and children's screen time in Lebanon. *Telemat. Inform.* 34, 351–358. doi: 10.1016/j.tele.2016.06.002

Sánchez-Zafra, M., Zurita-Ortega, F., Ramírez-Granizo, I., Puertas-Molero, P., González-Valero, G., and Ubago-Jiménez, J. L. (2019). Niveles de autoconcepto y su relación con el uso de los Videojuegos en escolares de tercer ciclo de Primaria. *J. Sport Health Res.* 11, 43–54.

Sandercock, G. R., Alibrahim, M., and Bellamy, M. (2016). Media device ownership and media use: associatons with sedentary time, physical activity and fitness in English youth. *Prevent. Med. Rep.* 4, 162–168. doi: 10.1016/j.pmedr.2016.05.013

Sevil, J., Abós, Á, Aibar, A., Sanz, M., and García-González, L. (2018). Should we reconsider sedentary screen time recommendations in adolescents? *Sport TK* 7, 75–81.

Shen, C., Wang, M. P., Wan, A., Viswanath, K., Chan, S. S. C., and Lam, T. H. (2018). Healh information exposure from information and communication technologies and its associations with health behaviors: population-based survey. *Prev. Med.* 113, 140–146. doi: 10.1016/j.ypmed.2018.05.018

Silva, A. G., Sa-Couto, P., Queirós, A., Neto, M., and Rocha, N. P. (2017). Pain, pain intensity and pain disability in high school students are differently associated with physical activity, screening hours and sleep. *BMC Musculoskelet. Disord.* 18:194. doi: 10.1186/s12891-017-1557-6

Sook, J. H., and Chun, J. S. (2017). Improving the effectiveness of smartphone addiction treatment program for adolescents: implications from focus group interviews. *Korea Instit. Health Soc. Aff.* 37, 459–494. doi: 10.15709/hswr.2017.37.3.459

Sudan, M., Olsen, J., Sigsgaard, T., and Kheifets, L. (2016). Trends in cell pone use among children in the Danish national birth cohort at ages 7 and 11 years. *J. Expo. Sci. Environ. Epidemiol.* 26, 606–612. doi: 10.1038/jes.2016.17

Sung, Y. T., Chang, K. E., and Liu, T. C. (2016). The effects on integrating mobile devices with teaching and learninng on students' learning performance: a meta-analysis and research synthesis. *Comput. Educ.* 94, 252–275. doi: 10.1016/j.compedu.2015.11.008

Venkatesh, E., Jemal, M. Y. A., and Samani, A. S. A. (2017). Smart pone usage and addiction among dental students in Saudi Arabia: a cross sectional study. *Int. J. Adolesc. Med. Health* 10, 1–6. doi: 10.1515/ijamh-2016-0133

Zach, S., Raviv, T., and Meckel, Y. (2016). Using information communication technologies (ICTs) for motivating female adolescents to exercise/run in their leisure time. *Comput. Hum. Behav.* 60, 593–601. doi: 10.1016/j.chb.2016.02.096

24

Dual Career of the U-23 Spanish Canoeing Team

Juan Gavala-González[1], Alfonso Castillo-Rodríguez[2] and José Carlos Fernández-García[3,4]*

[1] Department of Physical Education and Sports, University of Seville, Seville, Spain, [2] Department of Physical Education and Sports, University of Granada, Granada, Spain, [3] Department of Didactics of Languages, Arts and Sport, University of Malaga, Andalucía-Tech, Málaga, Spain, [4] IBIMA, Málaga, Spain

***Correspondence:**
Juan Gavala-González
jgavala@us.es

Canoeing is one of the sport disciplines that brings great success to Spain in international competitions and Olympic Games (of the 17 medals won in Rio in 2016, four were in this sport, including three gold). However, the journey to become an elite athlete coincides in time with the challenge of pursuing an academic education, which often involves making difficult choices in the training-university dichotomy. The aim of this research was to ascertain how the Spanish under-23 calm water canoeing team perceives their athletic and academic careers. The present study was carried out with the Spanish under-23 flat water canoeing team, the step prior to competition at the highest level. The study sample comprised the whole population, namely the entire national team, made up of 21 athletes (11 women and 10 men) with a mean age of 20.57 ± 2.64 years and 10.00 ± 3.49 years of experience. These athletes are usually based at La Cartuja High Performance Center (Seville) and combine their sports activity with studying toward a university degree. A double qualitative and quantitative methodology was used. For the first of these, an interview script was elaborated based on the theoretical model by Wylleman et al. (2013). Applicable consents were requested from the Spanish Royal Canoeing Federation, coaches and paddlers. Interviews were carried out with each athlete twice: at the beginning and at the end of the season/academic year, which were recorded and subsequently tabulated and analyzed. Concerning quantitative methodology, the ESTPORT dual career questionnaire validated by Sánchez-Pato et al. (2016) was used. The results show that for all the paddlers canoeing is very important. It is typically complicated for them to attend classes, and subject planning is usually based on their training schedules. In the second/last part of the course, it is stressful for these athletes to combine both activities and some drop out of school. During the course, though, they appreciate having another activity that allows them to escape from the training routine. In addition, they miss not having an academic tutor to guide and advise them. These student-athletes are aware that their sport causes them to miss out on many moments with family and friends due to training or competing. However, at present this is offset, largely because of their high level of performance, which makes it easier for them to obtain scholarships that provide economic support.

Keywords: dual career, psychological well-being, canoeing, high-education, sport

INTRODUCTION

The transition of any young person when he or she enters university is not an easy process, but when this must also be combined with training and competitions, this step becomes even more important (Tekavc et al., 2015). The dual career (DC) path undertaken by athletes involves the challenge of combining a career in sports with studies or work, a concern for most high-performance athletes (Ryba et al., 2015). In the case of student-athletes the optimal DC balance has been defined by Stambulova et al. (2015) as the combination of sport and studies that helps athletes achieve their academic and athletic goals and live a satisfying private life, maintaining their health and well-being.

It is well known that the practice of sport has been included in the strategic agenda of the European Union to promote integration among nations and cultures (European Commission, 2007). Nonetheless, when high levels of specialization and competition are achieved, the young people involved face the challenge of combining their athletic and educational preparation (Conzelmann and Nagel, 2003; Capranica and Millard-Stafford, 2011; Lobillo and Guevara, 2018), which quite often leads to their abandoning the practice of high-level sports in order to give priority to education with the aim of benefiting from future employment opportunities (Amara et al., 2004) or, conversely, to neglect academic preparation (Capranica and Millard-Stafford, 2011; Aquilina, 2013; Sohn and Hong, 2014; Guidotti et al., 2015; López de Subijana et al., 2015; Huang et al., 2016; Miro et al., 2017; Sum et al., 2017; Barriopedro et al., 2018; Krueger et al., 2018), resulting in low academic performance and limiting future and adequate inclusion in the working world (Conzelmann and Nagel, 2003; Kuettel et al., 2017; Vilanova and Puig, 2017; Barriopedro et al., 2018; López de Subijana et al., 2018).

All types of athletes are affected by the DC, regardless of social status, type of sport, location, the sex of the athlete or his or her experience (Erpič et al., 2004). According to Ryba et al. (2017), one of the main challenges faced by elite athletes between the ages of 12 and 25 is to successfully combine education and high-performance sport.

Early research (Purdy et al., 1982) indicated the negative effects of a double career on academic success. However, the most recent research suggests that talented athletes tend to perform well not only in sports, but also in the academic environment because they are highly motivated to perform well in both domains (Guidotti et al., 2015; Lupo et al., 2015; Fuchs et al., 2016; De Brandt et al., 2017; Isidori et al., 2017; Jordana et al., 2017; Kristiansen, 2017; Kuettel et al., 2017; Miro et al., 2017; Budevici-Puiu, 2018; Guirola et al., 2018; Kerstajn et al., 2018; Knight et al., 2018; Krueger et al., 2018; López de Subijana and Equiza, 2018; Ronkainen et al., 2018; Stefano and Ginevra, 2018; Tekavc and Erpic, 2018). Supporting this idea, O'Neill et al. (2013) concluded that student-athletes were determined to combine their education and sport, explaining that both dimensions strengthen their sense of identity, purpose and well-being.

Among athletes who abandoned their athletic careers due to different personal situations, a better transition and incorporation into working life was observed in those who had combined their double careers compared to those athletes who focused exclusively on their athletic careers (Aquilina, 2013; Torregrosa et al., 2015; Tshube and Feltz, 2015). Therefore, according to Stambulova and Wylleman (2015), to become long-term winners, student-athletes should first "win in the short term," i.e., adapt well to their current DC programs for possible future benefits.

The DC guarantees that the athlete will have a future outside of sports when his or her high-level career ends (Stambulova and Wylleman, 2015), although it is true that during the years in which the athlete tries to combine sport and studies, this situation causes episodes of tension and anxiety (Gustafsson et al., 2008; Aquilina, 2013; O'Neill et al., 2013; Torregrosa et al., 2015; Sorkkila et al., 2017). For this reason, in some cases, the help and support of psychologists is needed to guide the athlete to successfully continue the DC (Stambulova et al., 2009; Mateos et al., 2010). Consequently, many athletes are convinced of the importance of combining the highest level of athletic life with academic life, especially in those minority sports that do not have sufficient financial support and/or their athletic life is short (Conzelmann and Nagel, 2003; Debois et al., 2015; Gledhill and Harwood, 2015; Kuettel et al., 2017; Barriopedro et al., 2018; López de Subijana et al., 2018; Pink et al., 2018). Aware of the consequences for athletes of combining two careers, many universities and organizations at the national and state levels have created support programs (Park et al., 2013; Brown et al., 2015; López de Subijana et al., 2015; Pink et al., 2015). Also relevant are the results of Barriopedro et al. (2018), which support the holistic vision of the development of the athletic career, showing an interrelation between the academic-vocational and the athletic areas, indicating the possible role of gender in the pursuit of both careers.

We see the opposite side of this situation with some athletes who are still not aware of the reality in which they live. Everything that is not related to their athletic career is indifferent to them or they do not give it the importance they should, which causes them to miss out on opportunities that exist outside their sport (Gorley et al., 2001; Lavallee and Robinson, 2007; Stambulova et al., 2009; Kelly and Hickey, 2010; Aquilina, 2013).

All athletes have their moment and it is at that point when a conscious change is noted that their athletic career is about to end and they search for a strategy to plan for the future (Park et al., 2012). According to the study by North and Lavallee (2004), it was observed that 79% of the athletes who sensed that in a few years their athletic career would come to an end, began to plan their future for that time, showing less interest in dedicating time to training and even defending the importance of work outside the realm of sport.

However, no studies currently exist on canoeing, one of the most internationally successful sports in Spain. We therefore consider this research to be innovative as the aim of our study was to gain insight into how the Spanish under-23 flat water canoeing team members (those who are called to take over from the paddlers in the international competitions) experience the duality between their athletic and academic careers.

METHODOLOGY

Participants

The study participants comprised 21 paddlers (10 men and 11 women) with a mean age of 20.57 ± 2.64 years y 10.00 ± 3.49 years of experience from the permanent pool of the Spanish Under-23 Flat Water Canoeing Team at CEAR La Cartuja (Specialized Center for High Performance Rowing and Canoeing) in Seville. All the paddlers, in addition to competing at an international level, are enrolled in a university degree program. **Table 1** shows the characteristics of the participants. To avoid potential identification, areas of study were classified as either Sciences or Social Sciences.

Procedure

The methodology used was twofold: qualitative-quantitative. Consents were requested from the Royal Spanish Canoeing Federation, coaches and paddlers. Subsequently, individual contact was made with each athlete to arrange the date and time. In all cases, the place chosen was the facilities of CEAR La Cartuja, a space where all the athletes feel comfortable. The purpose of the study was explained to them and they were asked to consent to the use of the information, notifying them of the confidential nature and providing a brief explanation of the study. The interviews lasting between 10 and 15 min were recorded then later transcribed and analyzed-codified according to the levels of the theoretical model described. The five levels were analyzed according to two criteria, facilitators and barriers.

TABLE 1 | Characteristics of the participants.

Athlete	Sex	Age	Years of experience	Specialty	University Degree
1	Female	18	10	Kayak	Sciences
2	Female	24	12	Kayak	Social Sciences
3	Female	24	13	Kayak	Social Sciences
4	Female	19	7	Kayak	Social Sciences
5	Female	20	8	Kayak	Sciences
6	Female	18	9	Kayak	Sciences
7	Female	18	6	Kayak	Sciences
8	Female	23	7	Kayak	Social Sciences
9	Female	22	10	Kayak	Social Sciences
10	Female	27	19	Canoe	Social Sciences
11	Female	17	5	Canoe	Social Sciences
12	Male	23	14	Kayak	Social Sciences
13	Male	23	14	Kayak	Social Sciences
14	Male	19	9	Kayak	Sciences
15	Male	22	15	Kayak	Sciences
16	Male	19	5	Kayak	Social Sciences
17	Male	20	10	Kayak	Social Sciences
18	Male	19	9	Kayak	Social Sciences
19	Male	20	9	Canoe	Social Sciences
20	Male	19	9	Canoe	Social Sciences
21	Female	18	10	Kayak	Sciences

Instruments

The qualitative portion used a semi-structured interview based on the theoretical model by Wylleman et al. (2013), which is based on three main themes: (a) balancing studies and athletic career; (b) balancing economic level and athletic career and complementary studies/activity; (c) balancing psychosocial level and athletic career and complementary studies/activity. This model is a reformulation of the original holistic model by Wylleman and Lavallee (2004) which defined four stages in the athletic career: initiation, development, mastery and discontinuation. According to the holistic model of the athletic career, not only should the athletic dimension be taken into account, but also other facets involved in the development of the person such as the individual, psychosocial, academic/vocational and financial aspects. In this way, the athlete can be better understood from an overall perspective. Despite sharing elements with previous models, the differential contribution of these authors was that of presenting the athletic stages in a coordinated manner together with psychological, psychosocial and academic-vocational stages thus contributing a holistic perspective to the concept of the athlete and defining both stages and transitions for each area, adding the economic dimension in the 2013 version. In our case, the athletes studied were classified according to the above-mentioned model at the level of mastery, as they are members of the permanent Spanish Canoeing Federation team; at the psychological level at the end of adolescence/beginning of adulthood; at the psychosocial level according to their relationship with peers, family, coaches and teammates, university classmates/professors; at the academic and vocational levels as a semi-professional or professional athlete and university student and finally at the economic level with financial support from government scholarships, sponsors, and family.

The interview was therefore structured around the three basic pillars established by Wylleman et al. (2013): balancing academic career with athletic career (Athletic Level and Academic/Vocational Level blocks); balancing psychosocial level with athletic and academic careers (Psychosocial Level block); and balancing economic level with athletic and academic careers (Economic Level block). The psychological level was left out since the purpose of this research was not to assess the level of psychological maturity of the subjects.

The quantitative methodology used was the DC questionnaire called ESTPORT validated by (Sánchez-Pato et al., 2016). This questionnaire is the result of a project approved by the European Commission in 2014 entitled the "Development of an Innovative European Sport Tutorship Model for the Dual Career of Athletes" ESTPORT the aim of which was "to develop, transfer and implement an innovative EU Sport Tutorship program in different European Universities" in order to comply with the EU's DC guidelines for athletes. Therefore, due to these characteristics, this questionnaire was considered an appropriate tool and with great potential to be extrapolated to other countries.

This questionnaire was administered after the interview and completed in the presence of the interviewer. ESTPORT consists of two large blocks: the first on sociodemographic variables and the second on the DC, which in turn is divided into academic career and athletic career. The paddlers answered the questions in these blocks, which were structured into two types of answers: yes or no; or on a Likert scale ranging from very easily/totally agree, to very difficult/totally disagree, depending on the question.

Data Analysis

The statistical software packages used were *SPSS* for *Windows v.23* (*IBM SPSS Statistics*, Chicago, IL, United States) and *Microsoft Office Excel (Microsoft Corp.*, Redmond, WA, United States). To verify the normality of the variables, the *Kolmogorov–Smirnov* test was performed, and a reliability analysis was carried out using *Cronbach's alpha* statistic of the closed-ended questions on the Likert scale, regarding the perceptual dimensions of academic career, athletic career and digital competence of the athlete. Subsequently, a *t*-test was conducted with the independent variable of sex and category (semi-professional or professional). The effect size (*d*) was also calculated, which quantifies the size of the difference between the two groups (Coe and Merino, 2003). Threshold values for the effect sizes on the ANOVA test were small, 0.10; moderate, 0.25; and large, 0.40 (Cohen, 1988). The level of significance was set at $p < 0.05$.

RESULTS

This study includes both quantitative and qualitative results.

Quantitative Results

Table 2 shows the results of the reliability testing for the dimensions of academic career, athletic career and digital competence of the athlete. The dimensions evaluated show medium–high reliability values. Reliability data reported for the athletic career are scarce mainly due to the diversity in the type of response. In some cases, the responses were categorized as dichotomous values yes (1) and no (0), and in others, the answers were Likert type ranging from 1 to 5. This variety causes fluctuation in the reliability of the scale values, which suggests it would be preferable to use only one type of response. Moreover, in the academic career according to sex, reliability was lower because the perception of male athletes differs due to the type of university studies and the future professional career that they believe possible through these studies. In addition, an example of this was found in the categorization between semi-professionals and professionals, as it was observed that in the latter there were differing perceptions regarding their academic career, possibly due to the success achieved in their athletic career.

To gain insight into how student-athletes perceive their DC, it is essential to verify the variance that exists between the populations studied. **Table 3** shows the differences in perception between young men and women athletes of their academic career. There was little gender variance, with just two differences noted. The first was the distance between residence and university, with the female athletes living closer to the university than the male athletes. The second item corresponded to the importance of a better result, which the male athletes attached greater importance to than the female athletes. This lack of differences was due to the homogeneity of the sample, as they all practiced the same sport and were in a position to combine their athletic career with their university career.

The perception of the sports career of the athletes participating in the study was similar according to gender (**Table 4**). Regarding digital competence, the men used Twitter teaching support more frequently than the women ($P < 0.05$). In addition, the item of use of assignments as teaching support was marginally different ($P = 0.06$), with a higher frequency in the women.

In the athlete's perception of his or her academic career according to category (semi-professional or professional), there were once again two significant differences (**Table 5**). The first of these was regarding the time taken away from studying by their other tasks as an athlete, on which the semi-professional athletes scored 1.83/5 points, indicating that sport-related activities did not interfere with their academic work ($P < 0.05$; $d = 1.08$). The second item with the greatest variance was losing contact with their peers, on which the professional athletes had a better score (approaching disagreement), thus positively assessing their DC ($P = 0.05$; $d = 1.02$).

On the perception of athletic career and digital competency (**Table 6**) by category, no significant differences were observed, despite the fact that the effect sizes (Cohen's *d*) were large in items 72 and 73 ($d = 0.88$ y 0.84, respectively) regarding athletic career and the use of chat to support teaching ($d = 0.73$).

Qualitative Results

For a better understanding of the qualitative results, we established two blocks: circumstances that enable the athlete to maintain continuity between both careers: athletic and academic, which we call "facilitators," and by contrast, other reasons that lead the athlete to choose just one of the careers that we call "barriers."

Facilitators

Concerning the "facilitators," in the athletic realm we note that that the coaches themselves are concerned about the need and importance of the academic education of their paddlers. In fact, they view the DC as positive because this way they also think about other things, in fact E1 commented: "*It is better that they study, that they interact with other people who have nothing to do with canoeing. This way they have other things to think about... if not, if one day training goes poorly, they will be thinking about how badly they did it... if they have to think about having to go to the Faculty, etc. they forget about it sooner," "the things in the water stay in the water and have to be fixed in the water, driving themselves crazy about it only makes it worse.*"

Consistent with these words, the coaches have scheduled start times for each of the daily training sessions, although all paddlers say that coaches do not impose an obligation to attend each day's training, and even tend to modify training schedules so that their paddlers can combine going to class and training.

TABLE 2 | Reliability of the psychological variables studied.

	Cronbach's α				
	All	**Men**	**Women**	**Semi-professionals**	**Professionals**
Academic Career	0.590	0.478	0.836	0.944	0.624
Athletic Career	0.531	0.554	0.492	0.637	0.352
Digital Competence	0.871	0.711	0.714	0.723	0.661

TABLE 3 | Descriptive statistics on the perception of university student high-level athletes of their academic career.

	Item	Men (n = 10)	Women (n = 11)	T	P	d
Flexible Curriculum	Item 21	2.90 ± 0.994	3.00 ± 0.894	−0.243	0.811	0.11
Distance learning	Item 22	2.56 ± 1.014	2.91 ± 0.944	−0.806	0.431	0.36
Univ. far from home	Item 26	4.10 ± 0.994	2.55 ± 1.440	2.849	0.010	1.25
Univ. far from training	Item 27	3.90 ± 0.994	2.91 ± 1.375	1.875	0.076	0.83
Studies * training	Item 28	3.40 ± 1.506	3.27 ± 1.272	0.210	0.836	0.09
Employment * studies	Item 29	2.44 ± 1.509	2.82 ± 0.982	−0.668	0.512	0.30
Caring for family	Item 30	2.13 ± 1.246	2.09 ± 1.446	0.054	0.958	0.03
Habitual tiredness	Item 31	3.90 ± 0.994	3.82 ± 1.328	0.158	0.876	0.07
I lose course rhythm	Item 32	3.70 ± 0.949	3.82 ± 0.874	−0.297	0.770	0.13
I lose contact with peers	Item 33	3.20 ± 1.476	2.91 ± 0.944	0.544	0.593	0.23
High cost of studies	Item 34	3.78 ± 1.202	3.00 ± 1.342	1.350	0.194	0.61
University support	Item 35	4.10 ± 0.994	3.73 ± 1.348	0.715	0.484	0.31
Inflexible study schedule	Item 36	4.50 ± 0.707	3.91 ± 1.375	1.218	0.238	0.54
Inflexible training schedule	Item 37	2.50 ± 1.434	3.09 ± 1.514	−0.916	0.371	0.40
Virtual tools	Item 44	2.90 ± 1.449	3.18 ± 1.168	−0.493	0.628	0.21
Importance of studies	Item 45	4.40 ± 0.966	4.55 ± 1.214	−0.302	0.766	0.14
Time to improve grades	Item 46	3.70 ± 1.160	3.55 ± 0.820	0.355	0.726	0.15
Usefulness of studies	Item 47	4.30 ± 0.949	4.55 ± 0.934	−0.597	0.558	0.27
Satisfaction with studies	Item 48	2.30 ± 1.418	2.27 ± 0.786	0.055	0.957	0.03
Capability for high grades	Item 49	1.90 ± 1.287	2.82 ± 1.401	−1.559	0.136	0.68
Earn university degree	Item 50	4.60 ± 0.843	4.73 ± 0.467	−0.433	0.670	0.19
Importance of best result	Item 51	4.70 ± 0.675	3.73 ± 1.104	2.405	0.027	1.06
Course content	Item 52	3.50 ± 1.434	4.09 ± 1.375	−0.964	0.347	0.42
Reason for university degree	Item 53	3.30 ± 1.636	3.09 ± 1.136	0.343	0.735	0.15
Effort for qualifications	Item 54	2.50 ± 1.434	2.09 ± 1.375	0.667	0.513	0.29
Difficult assignments	Item 55	3.00 ± 1.414	3.09 ± 1.514	−0.142	0.889	0.06
Studies knowledge and skills	Item 56	4.20 ± 1.135	4.55 ± 0.934	−0.764	0.454	0.34
Importance of univ. degree	Item 57	4.20 ± 1.135	4.55 ± 0.820	−0.805	0.431	0.35
University degree * work	Item 58	4.10 ± 1.101	4.27 ± 0.905	−0.394	0.698	0.17

Univ., university.

P6 Comments: *"My coach, whenever possible, tries to help us., sometimes he lets us train later or earlier, but it's not good to train every day alone either. Besides, he doesn't force us to train, but if we push it, he reminds us that we are here thanks to a scholarship from the Federation."*

On the psychological level, all canoeists comment on how important canoeing is and has been for them, and that, today, they do not understand and would not understand their lives without this sport. At the beginning it was the social environment that stood out (P11: *"I liked most the atmosphere, my teammates, I enjoyed training at the club, I had fun"*). Whereas, today, what motivates them is to be where they are and to be able to have it all. (P2: *"I love the sensation and the appetite for more. I'm very much a perfectionist and wanted to achieve more things"*).

In relation to the psychosocial aspect, the affective part: surrounding themselves with their loved ones and their friends, this is their best time and although they have little time, and many see friends and relatives very occasionally, those days serve to "recharge batteries, escape and draw energy to continue training and their day to day" P14.

P19 comments: *"The basic pillar in all of this are friendships and your group of friends, if not, you go crazy. Family is fundamental. You need to clear your head on the weekends, get out a little bit, be with different people."*

TABLE 4 | Descriptive statistics of the perception of university student high-level athletes of their athletic career and digital competence.

Athletic career	Item	Men (n = 10)	Women (n = 11)	T	P	d
DC sports monitoring	Item 59	2.40 ± 1.265	2.36 ± 0.924	0.076	0.940	0.04
Weekly training sessions	Item 60	9.80 ± 1.135	9.55 ± 0.820	0.593	0.560	0.25
Hours of weekly training	Item 61	4.70 ± 0.483	4.36 ± 0.924	1.028	0.317	0.45
Help with studies	Item 62	3.20 ± 1.476	2.73 ± 1.272	0.788	0.440	0.34
Training and academic performance	Item 63	4.10 ± 1.287	4.45 ± 0.688	−0.798	0.435	-0.34
Coordinate studies	Item 72	1.40 ± 0.894	1.57 ± 0.976	-0.310	0.763	−0.18
Final expectations	Item 73	1.67 ± 1.211	1.20 ± 0.447	0.811	0.438	0.53
Digital competence						
Virtual campus	Item 65	3.56 ± 1.333	4.27 ± 1.348	−1.189	0.250	0.53
Forums	Item 66	2.11 ± 0.601	2.45 ± 1.635	−0.596	0.559	0.28
Assignments	Item 67	2.78 ± 1.202	3.91 ± 1.300	−2.002	0.061	0.90
Chat	Item 68	2.63 ± 1.598	2.18 ± 1.401	0.642	0.529	0.30
Skype	Item 69	1.44 ± 0.527	1.73 ± 1.348	−0.591	0.562	0.28
Facebook	Item 70	2.11 ± 1.364	2.18 ± 1.537	−0.108	0.916	0.05
Twitter	Item 71	2.33 ± 1.323	1.27 ± 0.647	2.348	0.031	1.02

DC, dual career.

TABLE 5 | Student's t-test score by academic career category.

	Item	Semi-professional (n = 6)	Professional (n = 15)	T	P	d
Flexible Curriculum	Item 21	2.50 ± 1.049	3.13 ± 0.834	−1.464	0.159	0.70
Distance learning	Item 22	2.80 ± 0.447	2.73 ± 1.100	0.130	0.898	0.08
Univ. far from home	Item 26	3.67 ± 1.033	3.13 ± 1.598	0.904	0.381	0.40
Univ. far from training	Item 27	3.50 ± 1.378	3.33 ± 1.291	0.262	0.796	0.13
Studies * training	Item 28	2.50 ± 1.643	3.67 ± 1.113	−1.896	0.073	0.83
Employment * studies	Item 29	1.83 ± 0.983	3.00 ± 1.177	−2.123	0.048	1.08
Caring for family	Item 30	1.50 ± 0.837	2.38 ± 1.446	−1.382	0.185	0.74
Habitual tiredness	Item 31	3.17 ± 1.472	4.13 ± 0.915	−1.836	0.082	0.78
I lose course rhythm	Item 32	3.83 ± 0.408	3.73 ± 1.033	0.227	0.823	0.13
I lose contact with peers	Item 33	3.83 ± 0.983	2.73 ± 1.163	2.036	0.050	1.02
High price of studies	Item 34	3.00 ± 1.225	3.47 ± 1.356	−0.681	0.505	0.36
University support	Item 35	4.00 ± 0.894	3.87 ± 1.302	0.228	0.822	0.12
Inflexible study schedule	Item 36	4.33 ± 1.033	4.13 ± 1.187	0.360	0.722	0.18
Inflexible training schedule	Item 37	2.33 ± 1.033	3.00 ± 1.604	−0.936	0.361	0.50
Virtual tools	Item 44	3.00 ± 1.549	3.07 ± 1.223	−0.105	0.918	0.05
Importance of studies	Item 45	4.17 ± 1.169	4.60 ± 1.056	−0.826	0.419	0.39
Time to improve grades	Item 46	4.00 ± 1.095	3.47 ± 0.915	1.143	0.267	0.53
Usefulness of studies	Item 47	4.50 ± 0.548	4.40 ± 1.056	0.218	0.830	0.12
Satisfaction with studies	Item 48	2.33 ± 0.816	2.27 ± 1.223	0.122	0.904	0.06
Capability for high grades	Item 49	2.33 ± 1.506	2.40 ± 1.404	−0.096	0.924	0.05
Earn university degree	Item 50	4.83 ± 0.408	4.60 ± 0.737	0.725	0.477	0.39
Importance of best result	Item 51	4.50 ± 0.548	4.07 ± 1.163	0.865	0.398	0.47
Course content	Item 52	3.67 ± 1.751	3.87 ± 1.302	−0.289	0.776	0.13
Reason for university degree	Item 53	2.67 ± 1.506	3.40 ± 1.298	−1.120	0.277	0.52
Effort for qualifications	Item 54	2.17 ± 1.169	2.33 ± 1.496	−0.243	0.810	0.12
Difficult assignments	Item 55	3.00 ± 1.095	3.07 ± 1.580	−0.094	0.926	0.05
Studies knowledge and skills	Item 56	4.50 ± 0.837	4.33 ± 1.113	0.330	0.745	0.17
Importance of univ. degree	Item 57	4.50 ± 0.837	4.33 ± 1.047	0.347	0.733	0.18
University degree * work	Item 58	4.33 ± 1.211	4.13 ± 0.915	0.413	0.684	0.19

Univ., university.

TABLE 6 | Student's *t*-test score by category of athletic career and digital competency.

Athletic career	Item	Semi-professional (n = 6)	Professional (n = 15)	T	P	d
DC sports monitoring	Item 59	2.00 ± 1.265	2.53 ± 0.990	−1.032	0.315	0.50
Weekly training sessions	Item 60	9.67 ± 1.033	9.67 ± 0.976	0.000	1.000	0.00
Hours of weekly training	Item 61	4.33 ± 1.211	4.60 ± 0.507	−0.728	0.476	0.29
Help with studies	Item 62	3.17 ± 1.329	2.87 ± 1.407	0.448	0.659	0.22
Training and academic performance	Item 63	4.00 ± 1.549	4.40 ± 0.737	−0.815	0.425	0.33
Coordinate studies	Item 72	1.00 ± 0.000	1.60 ± 0.966	−1.964	0.081	0.88
Final expectations	Item 73	1.00 ± 0.000	1.63 ± 1.061	−1.667	0.140	0.84
Digital competence						
Virtual campus	Item 65	4.40 ± 1.342	3.80 ± 1.373	0.850	0.406	0.44
Forums	Item 66	2.20 ± 1.304	2.33 ± 1.291	−0.200	0.844	0.10
Assignments	Item 67	3.80 ± 1.789	3.27 ± 1.223	0.754	0.460	0.35
Chat	Item 68	3.25 ± 1.708	2.13 ± 1.356	1.393	0.181	0.73
Skype	Item 69	1.60 ± 0.894	1.60 ± 1.121	0.000	1.000	0.00
Facebook	Item 70	2.00 ± 1.732	2.20 ± 1.373	−0.265	0.794	0.13
Twitter	Item 71	2.00 ± 1.732	1.67 ± 0.900	0.567	0.578	0.24

DC, dual career.

The academic level causes them the most distress, since attending class is very complicated as it usually coincides with training. So what they usually do is organize themselves at the beginning of the course/season. They ask their coach about the training schedules, and based on the schedule published in the faculty, they register for the courses they think they will be able to attend.

> P3: *"In September, when I arrive here, I ask the coach about the timetables and I outline the practical classes I can attend, since the theoretical ones are not compulsory, if I can attend, I go, but the other ones, I enroll because I can attend class. I try to maintain this throughout the course. although when the end of the course arrives, which coincides with the peak of the (sports) season, I spend weeks without going to the University, I'm dead!".*

In addition, peer support is essential to address this situation.

> P8: *"...Having classmates who understand your situation and support you in everything (notes, group work, exams) is priceless!! To them, I owe half my degree."*

> P10: *"My classmates know that I can't always go to class, they leave me their notes or let me know about important things the teacher has said. That way I can keep up to date. They also count on me for group work because they know that I need it so that I don't fall behind in the subject."*

Currently, the economic aspect is not an obstacle for these paddlers since most have a maintenance grant from the Federation. In addition, some meet the requirements for other grants.

> P16: *"There are scholarships to help you pay the university tuition and if you can get them it is very helpful. I also usually apply for sports scholarships based on the results. In my case, the government of my region doesn't give me anything, but there are other colleagues who receive other assistance because they are Basque or Galician...".*

> P7: *"I applied for a grant from the ministry, which I imagine they will give me. I have also just applied for the Galician high-level athlete grant and in theory they have to give me financial aid."*

Barriers

Athletic

In general, for all the paddlers on the under-23 team who combine studies and training, both commitments overlap in time. Training schedules usually coincide with class schedules, so fulfilling both obligations is impossible. The most common option is to attend only the required classes (practical) and when these overlap, change the training schedule, even if this means training alone (without teammates or coach).

> P13: *"Practically it is the day to day... mainly the practical classes usually coincide with training. I have to train here very early to arrive just in time for class or late and the truth is that it makes everything difficult for me because I arrive at class tired. it is hard to manage... at the beginning of the season, I can still... but when the peak season comes. I am just dead when I get out of the water and cannot even climb the ladder, so just imagine going to the University.'*

This academic-athletic situation affects the athlete at the psychological level with a considerable load of stress, since, as we have seen, being able to combine both activities on a daily basis is quite a complicated task.

> P15: *"Since practice is in the morning and the afternoon, I try to squeeze everything into a single session (I know I lose training quality and don't get enough rest between one and the other), but either I race against the clock or I can't manage."*

> P17: *"I finish training between 1:00 and 2:00 p.m., I get home like at 3:30p.m. I take the bike to go to the university from 4:00 to 8:00 p.m., you get home and you have to start studying because if not, you have no other time to do it."*

> P11: *"I eat in a hurry because at 3:00 pm I have to leave to go to class, which I have from 4:00 to 8:00 p.m., when I come back to*

CEAR I stay there studying, doing homework or reading a little and at about 12:00 a.m. I go to sleep."

As we can see, in the life of the under-23 paddler there is no time for anything other than training, going to class, eating and resting. In this sense, the psychosocial aspect is the most neglected, certainly not because they want to, but because of lack of time. The most surprising thing is that they accept it and as it stands today their sacrifice is compensated.

P1: *"After so much time maintaining this rhythm it's something I've internalized, but it's complicated to handle, I sacrifice many moments with friends and family. Lose many weekends, holidays, birthdays, and even evenings with friends to disconnect. You have to devote many hours to training, rest if you want to achieve something in this... and in your free time, study."*

P11: *"Friends are those who are in Galicia, I see them at Christmas or summer and that's it."*

P12: *"It's very complicated, because at the Faculty they tell me to stay for a drink, but for me, I would love to stay, but I have to train, I have to complete a training session, and maybe I could after dinner, around 9.30 at night, but the next day at 7:00 a.m. it wouldn't be realistic. so you have to be clear about what you are here for."*

Academics

The academic realm presents the most barriers, and in greater number as the course and season progresses: attendance at classes, practical work, group work, exams...to which we should add training, gatherings outside Seville and the competitions, in many cases international. Successfully combining academic and athletic life becomes impossible even with good organization and, most of the time, one of the two facets is given up due to incompatibility. In all cases, it is academic life that is abandoned because the current university system does not benefit these athletes. In fact, many of them have chosen to switch from physically attending university to distance learning because of all these issues, while others have dropped out of university completely.

P3: *"I started at the Complutense University of Madrid, when the Senior Lady's team was based at the Joaquín Blume residence in Madrid, and the following year when they told us that the training location would be changed, I decided to reconsider because the training location would be a bit volatile and I'm not going to be able to advance normally."*

P19: *"The first year I only passed one subject and last year I repeated the first year and passed a few more, I saw that it was impossible and that I was not going to be able to manage it if I wanted to continue training at a high level and I was not going to be able to pursue a career in Medicine, it is a career that you have to dedicate all your time to and be very focused, I loved it, I thought it was amazing but with this sport and the level at which I do it, for me, at least it is impossible." "The second quarter of the first year was very complicated. In the morning it was impossible to go to class. I trained every morning which is class time that you cannot change and that was the most complicated part really. Without going to class it is almost impossible to complete a career of that caliber."*

Finally, from an economic standpoint, while there are scholarships to help these athletes, very few of them benefit from an athletic scholarship since they only receive one if they have been successful in international competitions and that is usually very difficult. These athletes spend years training at the highest level but are not assured that they will have compensation that will enable them to support themselves and to achieve independence. Some of them comment that they have had to look for an apartment outside the High Performance Center, because due to poor results in the previous year, they were not granted a scholarship, even though they are still on the team. Therefore, they need economic support from their family.

P13: *"I don't receive any help or sponsorship, not from the club, or from the Asturian federation, and I don't any opportunity for a scholarship to the University because I'm not registered for the whole course, so I' m not entitled to it."*

P5: *"Canoeing in itself is not a sport that makes it easy for you on an economic level: you often have to pay for a competition yourself or if the Federation does not pay for the physiotherapist, you have to pay for the treatment yourself. Then regarding studies there are more and more scholarships, but there are no scholarships linking athletes with their studies, many scholarships are awarded for getting very good grades or for passing everything, and of course an athlete does not have the same chance as a normal student to pass everything or to get very good grades."*

These are other reasons why the paddlers admit that they cannot quit studying because they know that the day they do not get results, they will have to find another way to make a living, and without a university degree, the options are very scarce.

P9: *Who lives from canoeing in Spain? Maybe just one or two, and that's because they are civil servants, and they are able to train because they have facilities at work. I'm doing this to get to Tokyo 2020, to have the experience of an Olympic Games, not because it compensates financially."*

DISCUSSION

The purpose of the present study was to gain an understanding of the perception of life both in the athletic and the academic careers of the Spanish under-23 flat water canoeing team. The athletes showed some significant differences according to gender. The men live farther away from the university area and the sports facilities where they carry out their DC, an issue that may be related to their economic situation. Sometimes, when the problems are perceived by both populations, it is due to the university campus as well as the location where the training sessions are held frequently being located on the outskirts of the city. In addition, it is more difficult for the men to achieve a better result in their academic careers. This greater difficulty shown by the men may be associated with the constant concern that these athletes have for their future outside of sport (Stambulova and Wylleman, 2015), which translates into greater tension and anxiety (Gustafsson et al., 2008; Aquilina, 2013; O'Neill et al., 2013; Torregrosa et al., 2015; Sorkkila et al., 2017). Concluding the academic section according to gender, of note is that all the male athletes showed high scores on earning a university degree, the association between a university degree and finding work and having knowledge and skills, which indicates that they perceive excessive difficulty in achieving these goals. These concerns or difficulties demonstrate the need to incorporate tutors at universities for high-level athletes to help and support these athletes providing optimal academic guidance (Stambulova et al., 2009; Mateos et al., 2010). The perception of the sports career, however, showed no significant differences according to gender.

These athletes were classified according to their level of expertise, differentiating between professionals and semi-professionals. The former showed greater difficulty and confirmed that training time takes time away from their studies, leading to the conclusion that it is more challenging for them to combine their studies with their athletic career. In contrast, the semi-professionals claimed that training time causes a loss of contact with peers. Some studies corroborate that many athletes, especially in minority sports, are aware of the importance of combining athletic life at the highest level with academic life, mainly due to the fact that athletic careers are short (Conzelmann and Nagel, 2003; Debois et al., 2015; Gledhill and Harwood, 2015; Kuettel et al., 2017; Barriopedro et al., 2018; López de Subijana et al., 2018; Pink et al., 2018).

On a qualitative level, we have seen the shift in research on the DC since the early studies by Purdy et al. (1982) advised against it because of poor academic results, while more current studies (Guidotti et al., 2015; Lupo et al., 2015; Stambulova and Wylleman, 2015; Fuchs et al., 2016; De Brandt et al., 2017; Isidori et al., 2017; Jordana et al., 2017; Kristiansen, 2017; Kuettel et al., 2017; Miro et al., 2017; Budevici-Puiu, 2018; Guirola et al., 2018; Kerstajn et al., 2018; Knight et al., 2018; Krueger et al., 2018; Ronkainen et al., 2018; Stefano and Ginevra, 2018; Tekavc and Erpic, 2018) corroborate the desirability of a double life (academic and athletic), with which our results coincide.

Studies by Stambulova et al. (2015) suggest that the optimal balance in the DC is the combination of sport and studies, whereas Gustafsson et al. (2008), Aquilina (2013), O'Neill et al. (2013), Torregrosa et al. (2015), Ryba et al. (2017), and Sorkkila et al. (2017), warn of the complexity of successfully combining these two spheres, causing anxiety, stress and tension. This has also been verified in our study, and when these appear, the paddlers abandon their academic career, first partially (they only attend the required classes) and if their stress is very high, they drop out completely, which is consistent with the research by Purdy et al. (1982).

Concerning the economic aspect, our results agree with those of other studies such as the results by Conzelmann and Nagel (2003), Debois et al. (2015), Gledhill and Harwood (2015), Kuettel et al. (2017), Barriopedro et al. (2018), López de Subijana et al. (2018), and Pink et al. (2018) since our paddlers, despite having a maintenance grant, are aware that they must have an academic career, as no matter how successful a sporting career may be, they will never be able to earn a living from it.

This study has several limitations that must be taken into account. First, the questionnaire validated by a group of Spanish researchers in a sample of Spanish athletes appears to have discrepancies concerning the reliability and validity of the elements that comprise the sport category. Experts have proven that some of the items that refer to the knowledge of applications and use of social networks should not be considered in the athletic career category. Accordingly, we view this as a limitation and thus propose designing a new questionnaire that includes all the variables and categories in a comprehensive manner. Furthermore, it could be very interesting to consider differences in other types of sports, whether team, opponent or individual. Athletes in team sports, for example, are thought to have different perceptions of their DC, enabling variations to be found in items that can be improved or palliated due in part to a process of intervention, tutoring or mentoring, embedded within the university itself.

CONCLUSION

This is the first study to describe the perception of the DC in both professional and semi-professional under-23 canoeists. This information makes it possible to verify the difficulties currently encountered by these paddlers. According to the data extracted from the results section of the qualitative methodology, the athletes encounter specific problems that make it difficult to efficiently combine their DC. Due to the existence of these complications, we recommend the incorporation of the position of a tutor for high-level athletes into the university system to support, help and guide athletes during the times they need greater attention.

ETHICS STATEMENT

This study was performed in compliance with the 1964 Declaration of Helsinki, revised in 2013, which defines the ethical guidelines for research involving human subjects. Prior to the study, written informed consent was obtained from the participants and their legal guardians. Throughout the entire research process and afterward, the provisions of the Organic Law 15/1999 of 13 December, on the protection of personal data were applied. All the participants were treated following the ethical guidelines of respect, confidentiality and anonymity in data processing.

AUTHOR CONTRIBUTIONS

All authors listed have made a substantial, direct and intellectual contribution to the work, and approved it for publication.

ACKNOWLEDGMENTS

We would like to thank the Royal Spanish Canoeing Federation, their coaches and paddlers for the time they have dedicated to making this study a success. In particular, to María Corbera Muñoz. We would also like to thank Maria Repice for her help with the English version of this manuscript.

REFERENCES

Amara, M., Aquilina, D., and Henry, I. (2004). *Education of Elite Young Sportspersons in Europe*. Brussels: European Commission.

Aquilina, D. (2013). A study of the relationship between elite athletes' educational development and sporting performance. *Int. J. Hist. Sport* 30, 374–392. doi: 10.1080/09523367.2013.765723

Barriopedro, M., López de Subijana, C., and Muniesa, C. (2018). Insights into life after sport for spanish olympians: gender and career path perspectives. *PLoS One* 13:e0209433. doi: 10.1371/journal.pone.0209433

Brown, D. J., Fletcher, D., Henry, I., Borrie, A., Emmett, J., Buzza, A., et al. (2015). A British university case study of the transitional experiences of student-athletes. *Psychol. Sport Exerc.* 21, 78–90. doi: 10.1016/j.psychsport.2015.04.002

Budevici-Puiu, L. (2018). The importance of adopting national policy papers on dual careers in the field of sport. *Rev. Rom. Pentru Educ. Multidimens.* 10, 45–53. doi: 10.18662/rrem/16

Capranica, L., and Millard-Stafford, M. L. (2011). Youth sport specialization: how to manage competition and training? *Int. J. Sports Physiol. Perform.* 6, 572–579. doi: 10.1123/ijspp.6.4.572

Coe, R., and Merino, C. (2003). Efect size: a guide for researchers and users. *Rev. Psicol.* 21, 147–177.

Cohen, J. (1988). *Statistical Power Analysis for the Behavioral Sciences*, 2nd Edn. New Jersey, NJ: Lawrence Erlbaum Associates.

Conzelmann, A., and Nagel, S. (2003). Professional careers of the german olympic athletes. *Int. Rev. Sociol. Sport* 38, 259–280. doi: 10.1177/10126902030383001

De Brandt, K., Wylleman, P., Torregrossa, M., Defruyt, S., and Van Rossem, N. (2017). Student-athletes' perceptions of four dual career competencies. *Rev. Psicol. Del Deport.* 26, 28–33.

Debois, N., Ledon, A., and Wylleman, P. (2015). A lifespan perspective on the dual career of elite male athletes. *Psychol. Sport Exerc.* 21, 15–26. doi: 10.1016/j.psychsport.2014.07.011

European Commission (2007). *White Paper on Sport*. Brussels: Directorate-General Education and Culture.

Erpiy, S. C., Wylleman, P., and Zupančič, M. (2004). The effect of athletic and non-athletic factors on the sports career termination process. *Psychol. Sport Exerc.* 5, 45–59. doi: 10.1016/S1469-0292(02)00046-8

Fuchs, P. X., Wagner, H., Hannola, H., Niemisalo, N., Pehme, A., Puhke, R., et al. (2016). European student-athletes' perceptions on dual career outcomes and services. *Kinesiol. Slov.* 22, 31–48.

Gledhill, A., and Harwood, C. (2015). A holistic perspective on career development in UK female soccer players: a negative case analysis. *Psychol. Sport Exerc.* 21, 65–77. doi: 10.1016/j.psychsport.2015.04.003

Gorley, T., Lavallee, D., Teale, B., and Lavallee, R. M. (2001). A sampling of perceptions of potential users of the australian athlete career and education program. *Acad. Athl. J.* 15, 11–21.

Guidotti, F., Cortis, C., and Capranica, L. (2015). Dual career of european student-athletes: a systematic literature review. *Kinesiol. Slov.* 21, 5–20.

Guirola, I., Torregrosa, M., Ramis, Y., and Jaenes, J. C. (2018). Paddling upstream: facilitators and barriers to combine sport and studies. remando contracorriente: facilitadores y barreras para compaginar el deporte y los estudios. *Rev. Andaluza Med. Del Deport.* 11, 12–17. doi: 10.1016/j.ramd.2016.08.002

Gustafsson, H., Hassmén, P., Kenttä, G., and Johansson, M. (2008). A qualitative analysis of burnout in elite Swedish athletes. *Psychol. Sport Exerc.* 9, 800–816. doi: 10.1016/j.psychsport.2007.11.004

Huang, C. J., Chou, C. C., and Hung, T. M. (2016). College experiences and career barriers among semi-professional student-athletes. The influences of athletic identity and career self-efficacy. *Career Dev. Int.* 21, 571–586. doi: 10.1108/cdi-09-2015-0127

Isidori, E., Sanchez-Pato, A., and Decelis, A. (2017). "E-tutorship and dual-career of student-athletes: a pedagogical conceptualization from the results of an italian case study," in *Proceedings of the 11th International Conference on Technology, Education and Development*, eds L. G. Chova, A. L. Martinez, and I. C. Torres (Valencia: International Association of Technology, Education and Development (IATED)), 8028–8037.

Jordana, A., Torregrosa, M., Ramis, Y., and Latinjak, A. T. (2017). Elite sport retirement: a systematic review of qualitative studies. *Rev. Psicol. Del Deport.* 26, 68–74.

Kelly, P., and Hickey, C. (2010). Professional identity in the global sports entertainment industry: regulating the body, mind and soul of australian football league footballers. *J. Sociol.* 46, 27–44. doi: 10.1177/1440783309337671

Kerstajn, R., Lupo, C., Capranica, L., and Topic, M. D. (2018). Motivation towards sports and academics careers in elite winter sport Slovenian and Italian athletes: the role of internal and external factors. *Ido Mov. Cult.* 18, 29–37. doi: 10.14589/ido.18.2.4

Knight, C. J., Harwood, C. G., and Sellars, P. A. (2018). Supporting adolescent athletes' dual careers: the role of an athlete's social support network. *Psychol. Sport Exerc.* 38, 137–147. doi: 10.1016/j.psychsport.2018.06.007

Kristiansen, E. (2017). Walking the line: how young athletes balance academic studies and sport in international competition. *Sport Soc.* 20, 47–65. doi: 10.1080/17430437.2015.1124563

Krueger, H. H., Joerke, D., and Kreuz, S. (2018). Dual careers of pupils of an elite school of sports heading for university and professional careers - results of a qualitative longitudinal study. *Zeitschrift Fur Soziologie Der Erziehung Sozial.* 38, 191–208.

Kuettel, A., Boyle, E., and Schmid, J. (2017). Factors contributing to the quality of the transition out of elite sports in swiss, danish, and polish athletes. *Psychol. Sport Exerc.* 29, 27–39. doi: 10.1016/j.psychsport.2016.11.008

Lavallee, D., and Robinson, H. K. (2007). In pursuit of an identity: a qualitative exploration of retirement from women's artistic gymnastics. *Psychol. Sport Exerc.* 8, 119–141. doi: 10.1016/j.psychsport.2006.05.003

Lobillo, G., and Guevara, A. J. (2018). Desarrollo comunicacional en los clubes de fútbol españoles. Estudio de caso: Sevilla FC. *Rev. Iberoam. Ciencias la Act. Física Deport.* 7, 34–46. doi: 10.24310/riccafd.2018.v7i1.4858

López de Subijana, C., Barriopedro, M., Alberto Muniesa, C., and Galocha, J. (2018). Sport retirement among team sports: professional and amateur comparative. *Sport Tk-Rev. Euroam. Ciencias Del Deport.* 7, 41–46.

López de Subijana, C., Barriopedro, M., and Conde, E. (2015). Supporting dual career in Spain: elite athletes' barriers to study. *Psychol. Sport Exerc.* 21, 57–64. doi: 10.1016/j.psychsport.2015.04.012

López de Subijana, C., and Equiza, X. (2018). La retirada en natación: la vida fuera del agua. *Rev. Esp. Educ. Física Deport.* 421, 101–121.

Lupo, C., Guidotti, F., Goncalves, C. E., Moreira, L., Topic, M. D., Bellardini, H., et al. (2015). Motivation towards dual career of European student-athletes. *Eur. J. Sport Sci.* 15, 151–160. doi: 10.1080/17461391.2014.940557

Mateos, M., Torregrosa, M., and Cruz, J. (2010). Evaluation of a career assistance programme for elite athletes: satisfaction levels and exploration of career decision making and athletic-identity. *Kinesiol. Slov.* 14, 14–27.

Miro, S. L., Torregrosa, M., Reguela, S., Perez-Rivases, A., and Ramis, Y. (2017). Competences for planning elite sport atheltes dual career. *Rev. Psicol. Del Deport.* 26, 51–56.

North, J., and Lavallee, D. (2004). An investigation of potential users of career transition services in the United Kingdom. *Psychol. Sport Exerc.* 5, 77–84. doi: 10.1016/S1469-0292(02)00051-1

O'Neill, M., Allen, B., and Calder, A. M. (2013). Pressures to perform: an interview study of Australian high performance school-age athletes' perceptions of balancing their school and sporting lives. *Perform. Enhanc. Heal.* 2, 87–93. doi: 10.1016/j.peh.2013.06.001

Park, S., Lavallee, D., and Tod, D. (2013). "Athletes' career in the United Kingdom and the Republic of Ireland," in *Athletes' Careers Across Cultures*, eds N. Stambulova and T. Ryba (Hove: Routledge), 201–222.

Park, S., Tod, D., and Lavallee, D. (2012). Exploring the retirement from sport decision-making process based on the transtheoretical model. *Psychol. Sport Exerc.* 13, 444–453. doi: 10.1016/j.psychsport.2012.02.003

Pink, M., Saunders, J., and Stynes, J. (2015). Reconciling the maintenance of on-field success with off-field player development: a case study of a club culture within the australian football league. *Psychol. Sport Exerc.* 21, 98–108. doi: 10.1016/j.psychsport.2014.11.009

Pink, M. A., Lonie, B. E., and Saunders, J. E. (2018). The challenges of the semi-professional footballer: a case study of the management of dual career development at a Victorian football league (VFL) club. *Psychol. Sport Exerc.* 35, 160–170. doi: 10.1016/j.psychsport.2017.12.005

Purdy, D. A., Eitzen, D. S., and Hufnagel, R. (1982). Are athletes also students? The educational attainment of college athletes. *Soc. Probl.* 29, 439–448. doi: 10.2307/800032

Ronkainen, N. J., Ryba, T. V., Littlewood, M., and Selaenne, H. (2018). "School, family and then hockey!" Coaches' views on dual career in ice hockey." *Int. J. Sports Sci. Coach.* 13, 38–45. doi: 10.1177/1747954117712190

Ryba, T. V., Stambulova, N. B., Ronkainen, N. J., Bundgaard, J., and Selanne, H. (2015). Dual career pathways of transnational athletes. *Psychol. Sport Exerc.* 21, 125–134. doi: 10.1016/j.psychsport.2014.06.002

Ryba, T. V., Stambulova, N. B., Selanne, H., Aunola, K., and Nurmi, J. E. (2017). "Sport has always been first for me" but "all my free time is spent doing homework": dual career styles in late adolescence. *Psychol. Sport Exerc.* 33, 131–140. doi: 10.1016/j.psychsport.2017.08.011

Sánchez-Pato, A., Calderon, A., Arias-Estero, J. L., Garcia-Roca, J. A., Bada, J., Meroño, L., et al. (2016). Design and validation of a questionnaire about the perceptions of dual career student-athletes (ESTPORT). *Cult. Cienc. Deport.* 11, 127–147. doi: 10.12800/ccd.v11i32.713

Sohn, H., and Hong, E. A. (2014). Developing a career education guideline for korean student athletes. *Korean J. Phys. Educ.* 53, 621–633.

Sorkkila, M., Aunola, K., and Ryba, T. V. (2017). A person-oriented approach to sport and school burnout in adolescent student-athletes: the role of individual and parental expectations. *Psychol. Sport Exerc.* 28, 58–67. doi: 10.1016/j.psychsport.2016.10.004

Stambulova, N., Alfermann, D., Statler, T., and Côté, J. (2009). ISSP position stand: career development and transitions of athletes. *Int. J. Sport Exerc. Psychol.* 7, 395–412. doi: 10.1080/1612197X.2009.9671916

Stambulova, N., Engström, C., Franck, A., Linnér, L., and Lindahl, K. (2015). Searching for an optimal balance: dual career experiences of Swedish adolescent athletes. *Psychol. Sport Exerc.* 21, 4–14.

Stambulova, N. B., and Wylleman, P. (2015). Dual career development and transitions. *Psychol. Sport Exerc.* 21, 1–3. doi: 10.1016/j.psychsport.2015.05.003

Stefano, B., and Ginevra, G. (2018). The Italian approach to the dual careers of university student-athletes. *Kinesiol. Slov.* 24, 5–18.

Sum, R. K. W., Tsai, H.-H., Ha, A. S. C., Cheng, C., Wang, F., and Li, M. (2017). Social-ecological determinants of elite student athletes' dual career development in Hong Kong and Taiwan. *Sage Open* 7, 1–12. doi: 10.1177/2158244017707798

Tekavc, J., and Erpic, S. C. (2018). Dual career competences and their perceived importance in slovenian student-athletes in relation to gender. *Kinesiol. Slov.* 24, 60–69.

Tekavc, J., Wylleman, P., and Erpic, S. C. (2015). Perceptions of dual career development among elite level swimmers and basketball players. *Psychol. Sport Exerc.* 21, 27–41. doi: 10.1016/j.psychsport.2015.03.002

Torregrosa, M., Ramis, Y., Pallarés, S., Azócar, F., and Selva, C. (2015). Olympic athletes back to retirement: a qualitative longitudinal study. *Psychol. Sport Exerc.* 21, 50–56. doi: 10.1016/j.psychsport.2015.03.003

Tshube, T., and Feltz, D. L. (2015). The relationship between dual-career and post-sport career transition among elite athletes in South Africa, Botswana, Namibia and Zimbabwe. *Psychol. Sport Exerc.* 21, 109–114. doi: 10.1016/j.psychsport.2015.05.005

Vilanova, A., and Puig, N. (2017). Olympic athletes' job market entry strategies. A Typology. *Rev. Int. Sociol.* 75:e063. doi: 10.3989/ris.2017.75.2.15.98

Wylleman, P., and Lavallee, D. (2004). "A developmental perspective on transitions faced by athletes," in *Developmental Sport Psychology*, ed. M. Weiss (Morgantown, WV: Fitness Information Technology), 507–527.

Wylleman, P., Reints, A., and De Knop, P. (2013). "A developmental and holistic perspective on athletic career development," in *Foundations of Sport Management. Managing High Performance Sport*, eds P. Sotiaradou and V. De Bosscher (New York, NY: Routledge), 159–182.

Permissions

All chapters in this book were first published by Frontiers; hereby published with permission under the Creative Commons Attribution License or equivalent. Every chapter published in this book has been scrutinized by our experts. Their significance has been extensively debated. The topics covered herein carry significant findings which will fuel the growth of the discipline. They may even be implemented as practical applications or may be referred to as a beginning point for another development.

The contributors of this book come from diverse backgrounds, making this book a truly international effort. This book will bring forth new frontiers with its revolutionizing research information and detailed analysis of the nascent developments around the world.

We would like to thank all the contributing authors for lending their expertise to make the book truly unique. They have played a crucial role in the development of this book. Without their invaluable contributions this book wouldn't have been possible. They have made vital efforts to compile up to date information on the varied aspects of this subject to make this book a valuable addition to the collection of many professionals and students.

This book was conceptualized with the vision of imparting up-to-date information and advanced data in this field. To ensure the same, a matchless editorial board was set up. Every individual on the board went through rigorous rounds of assessment to prove their worth. After which they invested a large part of their time researching and compiling the most relevant data for our readers.

The editorial board has been involved in producing this book since its inception. They have spent rigorous hours researching and exploring the diverse topics which have resulted in the successful publishing of this book. They have passed on their knowledge of decades through this book. To expedite this challenging task, the publisher supported the team at every step. A small team of assistant editors was also appointed to further simplify the editing procedure and attain best results for the readers.

Apart from the editorial board, the designing team has also invested a significant amount of their time in understanding the subject and creating the most relevant covers. They scrutinized every image to scout for the most suitable representation of the subject and create an appropriate cover for the book.

The publishing team has been an ardent support to the editorial, designing and production team. Their endless efforts to recruit the best for this project, has resulted in the accomplishment of this book. They are a veteran in the field of academics and their pool of knowledge is as vast as their experience in printing. Their expertise and guidance has proved useful at every step. Their uncompromising quality standards have made this book an exceptional effort. Their encouragement from time to time has been an inspiration for everyone.

The publisher and the editorial board hope that this book will prove to be a valuable piece of knowledge for researchers, students, practitioners and scholars across the globe.

List of Contributors

Adrian A. Mosoi
Department of Psychology, Education and Teacher Training, Faculty of Psychology and Education Sciences, Transilvania University of Braşov, Braşov, Romania

Jürgen Beckmann
Department of Sport and Health Sciences, Chair of Sport Psychology, Technical University of Munich, Munich, Germany
Faculty of Health and Behavioural Sciences, School of Human Movement and Nutrition Sciences, University of Queensland, Brisbane, QLD, Australia
Department of Physical Education and Sport Sciences (PESS), University of Limerick, Limerick, Ireland

Arash Mirifar
Department of Sport and Health Sciences, Chair of Sport Psychology, Technical University of Munich, Munich, Germany

Guillaume Martinent
Laboratory of Vulnerabilities and Innovation in Sport, University of Claude Bernard Lyon 1 – University of Lyon, Lyon, France

Lorand Balint
Department of Physical Education and Special Motricity, Faculty of Physical Education and Mountain Sports, Transilvania University of Braşov, Braşov, Romania

Manuel Castro-Sánchez and Félix Zurita-Ortega
Department of Didactics of Musical, Plastic and Body Expression, Faculty of Fine Arts, University of Granada, Granada, Spain

José Antonio Pérez-Turpin
Department of Didactic General and Specific Training,
University of Alicante, Alicante, Spain

Javier Cachón-Zagalaz
Department of Didactics of Musical, Plastic and Body Expression, University of Jaén, Jaén, Spain

Cristian Cofre-Bolados
School of Physical Activity, Sports and Health Sciences,
University of Santiago-Chile, Santiago, Chile
Escuela de Ciencias del Deporte, Facultad de Salud, Universidad Santo Tomás (UST), Santiago, Chile

Concepción Suarez-Llorca
Department of Evolutionary Psychology and Didactic, University of Alicante, Alicante, Spain

Ramón Chacón-Cuberos
Departamento de Métodos de Investigación y Diagnóstico en Educación, Universidad de Granada, Granada, Spain

Pere Palou, Jaume Cantallops, Pere Antoni Borràs and Josep Vidal-Conti
GICAFE "Physical Activity and Exercise Sciences Research Group", University of the Balearic Islands, Palma, Spain

Adrià Muntaner-Mas
GICAFE "Physical Activity and Exercise Sciences Research Group", University of the Balearic Islands, Palma, Spain
PROFITH "PROmoting FITness and Health Through Physical Activity" Research Group, Faculty of Sport Sciences, Department of Physical Education and Sports, University of Granada, Granada, Spain

Idoia Labayen
Institute for Innovation & Sustainable Development in Food Chain (IS-FOOD), Public University of Navarre, Pamplona, Spain

David Jiménez-Pavón
MOVE-IT Research Group and Department of Physical Education, Faculty of Education Sciences, University of Cádiz, Cádiz, Spain
Biomedical Research and Innovation Institute of Cádiz (INiBICA) Research Unit, Puerta del Mar University Hospital University of Cádiz, Cádiz, Spain

Cecilia Dorado García
Research Institute of Biomedical and Health Sciences (IUIBS), University of Las Palmas de Gran Canaria, Las Palmas de Gran Canaria, Spain
Department of Physical Education, University of Las Palmas de Gran Canaria, Las Palmas de Gran Canaria, Spain

Diego Moliner-Urdiales
LIFE Research Group, University of Jaume I, Castellón de la Plana, Spain

Manuel A. Rodríguez Pérez
Faculty of Education Sciences, SPORT Research Group, CERNEP Research Center, University of Almería, Almería, Spain

Miguel A. Rojo-Tirado
Laboratory of Exercise Physiology Research Group (LFE Research Group), Faculty of Physical Activity and Sport Sciences-INEF, Department of Health and Human Performance, Universidad Politécnica de Madrid, Madrid, Spain

Cristina Cadenas-Sanchez
PROFITH "PROmoting FITness and Health Through Physical Activity" Research Group, Faculty of Sport Sciences, Department of Physical Education and Sports, University of Granada, Granada, Spain
MOVE-IT Research Group and Department of Physical Education, Faculty of Education Sciences, University of Cádiz, Cádiz, Spain
Biomedical Research and Innovation Institute of Cádiz (INiBICA) Research Unit, Puerta del Mar University Hospital University of Cádiz, Cádiz, Spain

Francisco B. Ortega
PROFITH "PROmoting FITness and Health Through Physical Activity" Research Group, Faculty of Sport Sciences, Department of Physical Education and Sports, University of Granada, Granada, Spain

Francisco Javier Ponseti
Department of Pedagogy, University of the Balearic Islands, Palma, Spain

Pedro L. Almeida
Departamento de Psicologia Social e Organizacional, ISPA - Instituto Universitario, Lisbon, Portugal

Joao Lameiras
Portuguese Athletics Federation, Lisbon, Portugal

Bruno Martins
GICAFE de la UIB, University of Lisbon, Lisbon, Portugal

Aurelio Olmedilla
Departamento de Personalidad, Evaluación y Tratamiento Psicológicos, University of Murcia, Murcia, Spain

Jeanette López-Walle and Orlando Reyes
Facultad de Organización Deportiva, Universidad Autónoma de Nuevo León, Nuevo León, Mexico

Alexandre Garcia-Mas
Department of Psychology, University of the Balearic Islands, Palma, Spain

Wanesa Onetti-Onetti
Faculty of Education, UNIR, International University of La Rioja, Logroño, Spain

José Luis Chinchilla-Minguet
Department of Languages, Arts and Sports, University of Málaga, Málaga, Spain

Fernando Manuel Lourenço Martins
Instituto Politécnico de Coimbra, Coimbra, Portugal
Instituto de Telecomunicações, Covilhã, Portugal

Alfonso Castillo-Rodriguez
Department of Physical Education and Sports, University of Granada, Granada, Spain

Juan Gregorio Fernández-Bustos, Álvaro Infantes-Paniagua and Onofre Ricardo Contreras
Department of Didactics of Musical, Plastic and Physical Education, Faculty of Education of Albacete, University of Castilla-La Mancha, Albacete, Spain

Ricardo Cuevas
Department of Didactics of Musical, Plastic and Physical Education, Faculty of Education of Ciudad Real, University of Castilla-La Mancha, Ciudad Real, Spain

María Luisa Zagalaz-Sánchez, María Sánchez-Zafra and Amador Lara-Sánchez
Department of Musical, Plastic and Body Expression, University of Jaén, Jaén, Spain

Antonio Granero-Gallegos
Faculty of Education Sciences, University of Almería, Almería, Spain
Health Research Center, University of Almería, Almería, Spain

Raúl Baños
Department of Physical Education and Sports Science, Autonomous University of Baja California, Ensenada, Mexico

Antonio Baena-Extremera
Department of Didactic of Corporal Expression, Faculty of Education Sciences, Granada, Spain

Marina Martínez-Molina
Faculty of Education Sciences, University of Almería, Almería, Spain

Eva María Olmedo-Moreno
Department of Research Methods and Diagnosis in Education, University of Granada, Granada, Spain

Jorge Zamarripa, René Rodríguez-Medellín and José Alberto Pérez-Garcia
Facultad de Organización Deportiva, Universidad Autónoma de Nuevo León, Nuevo León, Mexico

Fernando Otero-Saborido
Facultad de Ciencias del Deporte, Universidad Pablo de Olavide, Seville, Spain

Maritza Delgado
Facultad de Psicología, Universidad Autónoma de Nuevo León, Monterrey, Mexico

Oscar Chiva-Bartoll
Department of Education and Specific Didactics, Jaume I University, Castellón, Spain

Pedro Jesús Ruiz Montero
Department of Physical Education and Sport, Faculty of Education and Sport Sciences, University of Granada, Melilla, Spain
Faculty of Education, University of Málaga, Málaga, Spain

Carlos Capella-Peris
Department of Physical Education and Sport, University of Valencia, Valencia, Spain

Pedrona Serra
Institut Nacional d'Educació Física de Catalunya (INEFC), Universitat de Barcelona (UB), Barcelona, Spain
Department of Specific Didactics and Pedagogy, University of the Balearic Islands, Palma, Spain

Susanna Soler and Anna Vilanova
Institut Nacional d'Educació Física de Catalunya (INEFC), Universitat de Barcelona (UB), Barcelona, Spain

María José Camacho-Miñano
Department for Languages, Arts and Physical Education, Feminist Research Institute, Complutense University of Madrid, Madrid, Spain

Ana Rey-Cao
Department of Special Didactics, Universidade de Vigo, Pontevedra, Spain

David Manzano-Sánchez, Luís Conte-Marín, Manuel Gómez-López and Alfonso Valero-Valenzuela
Department of Physical Activity and Sport, Faculty of Sports Sciences, University of Murcia, Murcia, Spain

Valerii Malkin and Liudmila Rogaleva
Department of Theory of Physical Culture, Ural Federal University, Yekaterinburg, Russia

Alla Kim
Department of General and Applied Psychology, Al-Farabi Kazakh National University, Almaty, Kazakhstan

Natalya Khon
Department of Psychology, Turan University, Almaty, Kazakhstan

Andressa Ribeiro Contreira, Luciane Cristina Arantes da Costa, Patrícia Aparecida Gaion and Lenamar Fiorese
Grupo de Estudos de Psicologia do Esporte e Desempenho Humano, Physical Education Department, Universidade Estadual de Maringá, Maringá, Brazil

José Roberto Andrade do Nascimento Junior
Grupo de Estudos em Psicologia do Esporte e do Exercício, Physical Education Department, Universidade Federal do Vale do São Francisco, Petrolina, Brazil

Nayara Malheiros Caruzzo
Grupo de Estudos de Psicologia do Esporte e Desempenho Humano, Physical Education Department, Universidade Estadual de Maringá, Maringá, Brazil
Duke Global Health Institute, Duke University, Durham, NC, United States

Sandro Victor Alves Melo
Grupo de Estudos de Psicologia do Esporte e Desempenho Humano, Physical Education Department, Universidade Estadual de Maringá, Maringá, Brazil
Health and Sports Science Center, Universidade Federal do Acre, Rio Branco, Brazil

Haney Aguirre-Loaiza
Department of Psychology, Catholic University of Pereira, Pereira, Colombia

Jaime Arenas and Ianelleen Arias
Physical Education, University of Quindío, Armenia, Colombia

Alejandra Franco-Jímenez and Santiago Ramos-Bermúdez
Research Group Physical Activity, Cumanday, Manizales, Colombia

Sergio Barbosa-Granados
Psychology, Cooperative University of Colombia, Pereira, Colombia

Federico Ayala-Zuluaga
Research Group Physical Activity, Cumanday, Manizales, Colombia
Department of Physical Action, Caldas University, Manizales, Colombia

César Núñez
Psychology Program,Universidad de Medellín, Medellín, Colombia

Alexandre García-Mas
Department of Basic Psychology, University of the Balearic Islands, Palma, Spain

Celina Salvador-García
Faculty of Education, International University of La Rioja, Logroño, Spain
Department of Education and Specific Didactics, Jaume I University, Castellón de la Plana, Spain

Pedro Jesús Ruiz-Montero
Faculty of Education and Sport Sciences, University of Granada, Melilla, Spain

Ambra Gentile
Ph.D. Program in Health Promotion and Cognitive Sciences, University of Palermo, Palermo, Italy
Department of Psychology, Educational Sciences and Human Movement, University of Palermo, Palermo, Italy

Stefano Boca, Antonino Bianco and Marianna Alesi
Department of Psychology, Educational Sciences and Human Movement, University of Palermo, Palermo, Italy

Fatma Neşe Şahin and Özkan Güler
Faculty of Sports Science, Ankara University, Ankara, Turkey

Simona Pajaujiene
Department of Coaching Science, Lithuanian Sports University, Kaunas, Lithuania

Vinga Indriuniene
Department of Physical and Social Education, Lithuanian Sports University, Kaunas, Lithuania

Yolanda Demetriou and David Sturm
Department of Sport and Health Sciences, Technical University of Munich, Munich, Germany

Manuel Gómez-López
Department of Physical Activity and Sport, Faculty of Sports Sciences, University of Murcia, Murcia, Spain

Adrián Segura-Robles and María Elena Parra-González
Department of Research Methods and Diagnosis in Education, University of Granada, Granada, Spain

Arturo Fuentes-Cabrera and Jesús López-Belmonte
Department of Didactics and School Organization, University of Granada, Granada, Spain

David Hortigüela-Alcalá and Alejandra Hernando-Garijo
Faculty of Education, University of Burgos, Burgos, Spain

Sixto González-Víllora
Faculty of Education of Cuenca, University of Castilla-La Mancha, Cuenca, Spain

Juan Carlos Pastor-Vicedo
Faculty of Education of Toledo, University of Castilla-La Mancha, Toledo, Spain

Gemma María Gea-García, Noelia González-Gálvez, Alejandro Espeso-García and Pablo J. Marcos-Pardo
Faculty of Sports, San Antonio Catholic University (UCAM), Murcia, Spain
Health, Physical Activity, Fitness and Motor Control Performance Research Group (GISAFFCOM), San Antonio Catholic University (UCAM), Murcia, Spain

Francisco Tomás González-Fernández
Department of Physical Activity and Sport Sciences, CESAG, Comillas Pontifi University, Madrid, Spain

Luis Manuel Martínez-Aranda
Faculty of Sports, San Antonio Catholic University (UCAM), Murcia, Spain
Neuroscience of Human Movement Research Group, San Antonio Catholic University (UCAM), Murcia, Spain

Carlos Fernández-Espínola, Bartolomé J. Almagro, Javier A. Tamayo-Fajardo and Pedro Sáenz-López
Department of Integrated Didactics, Faculty of Education,Psychology and Sports Sciences, Universidad de Huelva, Huelva, Spain

Fernando Claver and Alexander Gil-Arias
Centre for Sport Studies, Rey Juan Carlos University, Fuenlabrada, Spain

Manuel Conejero
Faculty of Sport Science, University of Extremadura, Cáceres, Spain

Juan Gavala-González
Department of Physical Education and Sports, University of Seville, Seville, Spain

Alfonso Castillo-Rodríguez
Department of Physical Education and Sports, University of Granada, Granada, Spain

José Carlos Fernández-García
Department of Didactics of Languages, Arts and Sport, University of Malaga, Andalucía-Tech, Málaga, Spain
IBIMA, Málaga, Spain

Index

www.ingramcontent.com/pod-product-compliance
Lightning Source LLC
LaVergne TN
LVHW081030210926
848485LV00004B/987